European Fixed Income Markets

Wiley Finance Series

European Fixed Income Markets

Money, Bond, and Interest Rate Derivatives

Jonathan A. Batten
Thomas A. Fetherston
and
Peter G. Szilagyi

John Wiley & Sons, Ltd

Copyright © 2004   John Wiley & Sons Ltd, The Atrium, Southern Gate, Chichester,
West Sussex PO19 8SQ, England

Telephone   (+44) 1243 779777

Email (for orders and customer service enquiries): cs-books@wiley.co.uk
Visit our Home Page on www.wileyeurope.com or www.wiley.com

This publication is designed to provide accurate and authoritative information in regard to
the subject matter covered. It is sold on the understanding that the Publisher is not engaged
in rendering professional services. If professional advice or other expert assistance is
required, the services of a competent professional should be sought.

Other Wiley Editorial Offices

John Wiley & Sons Inc., 111 River Street, Hoboken, NJ 07030, USA

Jossey-Bass, 989 Market Street, San Francisco, CA 94103-1741, USA

Wiley-VCH Verlag GmbH, Boschstr. 12, D-69469 Weinheim, Germany

John Wiley & Sons Australia Ltd, 33 Park Road, Milton, Queensland 4064, Australia

John Wiley & Sons (Asia) Pte Ltd, 2 Clementi Loop #02-01, Jin Xing Distripark, Singapore 129809

John Wiley & Sons Canada Ltd, 22 Worcester Road, Etobicoke, Ontario, Canada M9W 1L1

Wiley also publishes its books in a variety of electronic formats. Some content that appears
in print may not be available in electronic books.

Library of Congress Cataloging-in-Publication Data

European fixed income markets : money, bond, and interest rate
derivatives / [edited by] Jonathan A. Batten, Thomas A. Fetherston,
Peter G. Szilagyi.
    p.   cm. – (Wiley finance series)
Includes bibliographical references and index.
ISBN 0-470-85053-1 (alk. paper)
1. Capital market–Europe.   2. Capital market–European Union
countries.   3. Fixed-income securities–Europe.   4. Fixed-income
securities–European Union countries.   I. Batten, Jonathan.   II. Fetherston, Thomas A.
III. Szilagyi, Peter G., 1976–   IV. Series.

HG5422 .E9844   2003
332′.041′094–dc22

                                                              2003021224

British Library Cataloguing in Publication Data

A catalogue record for this book is available from the British Library

ISBN 0-470-85053-1

Typeset in 10/12pt Times by TechBooks, New Delhi, India
Printed and bound in Great Britain by Antony Rowe Ltd, Chippenham, Wiltshire
This book is printed on acid-free paper responsibly manufactured from sustainable forestry
in which at least two trees are planted for each one used for paper production.

Anyának szeretettel, Laci és Peti

Contents

Contributors

Jan Annaert
Department of Financial Economics, Ghent University, W. Wilsonplein 5d, 900 Gent, Belgium

Jan Annaert is Associate Professor of Finance at Ghent University where he is program director of the Master program in Banking and Finance. He holds a Ph.D. from the University of Antwerp. His research, teaching and consulting focus on portfolio theory, international finance and financial risk management. Currently, he works on credit risk modelling and estimation risk issues in portfolio selection. Before joining the department of Financial Economics at Ghent University he was a senior research fellow at the Fund for Scientific Research Flanders (Belgium) and assistant professor at the Erasmus University in Rotterdam.

Caner Bakir
Department of Accounting and Finance, Monash University, Victoria 3800, Australia

Dr Caner Bakir is Assistant Lecturer in Accounting and Finance Department at Monash University, Australia. For four years, he worked as Banking Specialist in Turkey. His current research interests include financial governance, government–business relations and international political economy. His most recent article was published by *Australian Journal of Political Science*. He is a Member of Editorial Board of *International Encyclopedia of Public Policy: Governance in a Global Age* (Routledge).

Jonathan A. Batten
College of Business Administration, Seoul National University, Sillim-Dong, Kwanak-Ku, Seoul, South Korea

Jonathan Batten is Professor of Finance at Seoul National University in Korea and co-editor of the Elsevier journal "*Research in International Business and Finance*". His previous books include "Asia-Pacific Fixed Income Markets: An Analysis of the Region's Money, Bond and Interest Derivative Markets", co-edited with Thomas A. Fetherston and published by John Wiley & Sons, Singapore.

Kym Brown
Department of Accounting and Finance, Monash University, Victoria 3800, Australia

Kym Brown is based at Monash University, Melbourne, Australia. Her research interests relate to developing countries, particularly in the East Asian region. Topics of interest include macroeconomic assessments of bank efficiency, financial development and bond markets.

Charlotte Christiansen
Department of Finance, The Aarhus School of Business, 8210 Aarhus V, Denmark

Charlotte Christiansen is Associate Professor at Dept. of Finance, Aarhus School of Business and holds a PhD in finance (2001). Her main research interests are asset pricing, empirical finance, and the term structure of interest rates.

Marc J.K. De Ceuster
University of Antwerp, 2000 Antwerp, Belgium

Marc De Ceuster is Professor of Finance at the University of Antwerp and is program Director of the Master of Finance and Fiscal Sciences. Marc is also Director of Risk Management at Deloitte and Touche. He teaches and does consulting within the broad fields of financial economics, derivatives and risk management. Marc also organizes the yearly Deloitte and Touche Risk Conferences held in Antwerp. He has published in various international journals such as Journal of Empirical Research, Journal of Economic Surveys, Journal of Banking and Finance, European Financial Management.

David Edwards
Merchant Fraud & Acquiring Risk Management, National Australia Bank Limited, 9/120 Spencer Street, Melbourne, Victoria, 3000, Australia

David Edwards is an Acquiring Risk Management Analyst for the National Australia Bank in Melbourne. David graduated from Deakin University, Melbourne with a B.Com (Hons) in 2003 and has been working in banking since 2002. His other research interest areas include executive remuneration and corporate governance.

Tom Engsted
Department of Finance, The Aarhus School of Business, 8210 Aarhus V, Denmark

Tom Engsted is Professor and Head of Department at Dept. of Finance, Aarhus School of Business. Tom holds a PhD in economics (1993) from Aarhus School of Business. His main research interests are asset pricing, financial econometrics, and macroeconomics.

Thomas A. Fetherston
School of Business, University of Alabama at Birmingham, Birmingham, AL 35294, USA

Thomas Fetherston is Professor of Finance at the University of Alabama Birmingham. He is editor of the journal "*International Review of Financial Analysis*" and co-editor of "*Research in International Business and Finance*". His previous books include "Asia-Pacific Fixed Income Markets: An Analysis of the Region's Money, Bond and Interest Derivative Markets", co-edited with Jonathan A. Batten and published by John Wiley & Sons, Singapore.

Svend Jakobsen
Department of Finance, The Aarhus School of Business, 8210 Aarhus V, Denmark

Svend Jakobsen is Associate Professor at Dept. of Finance, Aarhus School of Business and holds a PhD in finance (1992). His main research interests are fixed income analysis, mortgage-backed securities, and pension funds.

Heinz R. Kubli
Aeschstrasse 2a, 8127 Forch, Switzerland

Heinz R. Kubli (1969), Dr. oec. publ., CFA, graduated in Economics and Business Administrations at the University of Zurich in 1995 and earned his doctorate in Finance in 2000. He is a partner of Fundabilis GmbH, an owner-managed asset management company, and of Sensalis GmbH, a research company specialized in quantitative research, in Zurich, Switzerland.

Cameron Makepeace
Australian and New Zealand Banking Group, Collins St., Melbourne, Victoria 3000, Australia

Cameron Makepeace is an Assistant Manager for Corporate Banking with Australia and New Zealand Banking Group Limited. Cameron graduated from Deakin University, Melbourne in 2002 with an Honours in finance.

Orazio Mastroeni
Operations Analysis Division, Directorate General Operations, European Central Bank, Frankfurt am Main, Germany

Orazio Mastroeni is a graduate in Economic Studies at the University of Rome and took his Masters Degree in International Finance in the UK. With the creation of the European Central Bank in mid-1998 he joined the Directorate General Market Operations as Senior Economist, in charge of a team working on the Eurosystem's operational framework and eligible assets. He is the Rapporteur of the Committee in charge of revising the eligibility of assets for credit operations with the European Central Bank. He participated as a speaker in a number of international conferences and has lectured at the Universities of Rome and Frankfurt. He has contributed a number of articles on the operational framework and the Eurosystem's collateral framework in financial journals and in the Monthly Bulletin of the ECB.

Albert Mentink
Fixed Income Department, AEGON Asset Management in The Hague, The Netherlands

Albert Mentink received his Master's degree in Econometrics from the University of Groningen in 1996. Currently, he works as a senior fixed income analyst at AEGON Asset Management Netherlands. He is writing his PhD on empirical analyses of the euro bond market.

Nóra Németh
Department of Budgetary Supervision, Hungarian Ministry of Employment and Labour, Budapest, Hungary

Nóra Németh has recently been appointed deputy head of the Department of Budgetary Supervision in the Hungarian Ministry of Employment and Labour. She previously earned an MSc in Business Administration and a JD in law. Nora also has held positions at Ernst & Young and the Hungarian Prime Minister's Office.

Guan-Chye Ooi
Department of Accounting and Finance, Deakin University, Melbourne 3125, Australia

Guan-Chye Ooi is a financial analyst based in Singapore. Guan-Chye graduated from Deakin University, Melbourne with a B.Com (Hons) in 2003 and has been working in the finance industry since 2002. His other interests include earnings management generally and specifically the use of derivatives to smooth earnings of the firm.

Petra Pénzes
Kopint-Datorg Economic Research, Marketing and Computing Company, Budapest, Hungary

Petra Pénzes is an economic researcher at the Kopint-Datorg Economic Research Institute in Hungary. She previously held a similar position at the Research Institute of Economics and Entrepreneurship of the Hungarian Chamber of Commerce and Industry. Petra earned an MSc in Business Administration at the Budapest University of Economic Sciences and Business Administration.

Leonid V. Philosophov
Analytic Department, Moscow Committee of Bankruptcy Affairs, Russia

Leonid Philosophov graduated in 1961 from the Moscow Institute of Physics and Technology. He has a PhD (Candidate of Sciences) dissertation, a D.Sc. degree and has been Professor of Informatics since 1992. He has worked most recently as chief of analytic department of Moscow Committee of Bankruptcy Affairs. His areas of scientific interests are bankruptcy prediction, credit risk, optimization of corporate capital structure.

Vladimir L. Philosophov
Analytic Department, Interregional Bankruptcy Service for Central Russia, Moscow, Russia

Vladimir L. Philosophov graduated in 1997 from the Moscow Aviation Institute (Economic Faculty). In 2001 he obtained his PhD (Candidate of Sciences) degree in Economics. Since 2001 he has been chief of analytic department of Interregional Bankruptcy Service for Central Russia. His areas of scientific interests are bankruptcy prediction, optimization of a firm's capital structure.

Seppo Pynnönen
Department of Mathematics and Statistics, University of Vaasa, Vaasa, Finland

Seppo Pynnönen is Professor of Statistics at the department of Mathematics and Statistics, University of Vaasa. He holds a Ph.D. in Statistics. His current research interest is in empirical finance, and he has published several refereed journal papers with his colleagues. The topics cover among others: information transmission in international stock markets, modeling bond yields, and news impact on stock returns.

Vanessa Seconnino
Department of Accounting and Finance, Deakin University, Melbourne 3125, Australia

Vanessa Seconnino completed a Bachelor of Arts/Bachelor of Commerce double degree and a Bachelor of Commerce (Honours) degree from Deakin University, Australia. On completion of studies began working for National Australia Bank in Melbourne, and is currently still working there. In addition Vanessa is undertaking further studies with the Securities Institute of Australia.

Frank S. Skinner
ISMA Centre, The University of Reading, Reading RG6 6BA, UK

Dr Frank Skinner is a Reader at the ISMA Centre located at the University of Reading, in the UK. He completed his Ph.D. in Finance at the University of Toronto and has held full time appointments in Canada and in the US. He has published in leading academic and practitioner journals *including The Journal of Banking and Finance, Journal of Fixed Income*, and the *Financial Analysts Journal*. His research is focused on debt markets and instruments, and is in demand as a consultant for such organizations as MTS, Office of Fair Trading and Watson Wyatt LLP.

László Szilágyi
Department of Economics, Budapest University of Technology and Economics, Budapest, Hungary

László Szilágyi has recently joined the Budapest University of Technology and Economics. His main areas of research include foreign direct investment directed to developing countries and China's role in the world economy. He is also a member of the College of Social Theory at the Budapest University of Economic Sciences and Public Administration.

Peter G. Szilagyi
Faculty of Economics and Business Administration, Tilburg University, Tilburg, The Netherlands

Peter Szilagyi has recently joined Tilburg University, the Netherlands. His main research interests include international capital market development and corporate finance. He holds masters degrees from the Budapest University of Economic Sciences and Public Administration and the University of Western Sydney. He has previously worked as a freelance broadcaster for the BBC World Service in the U.K. and Australia.

Carsten Tanggaard
Department of Finance, The Aarhus School of Business, 8210 Aarhus V, Denmark

Carsten Tanggaard is a Professor of Finance at the Aarhus School of Business. His published research is about financial econometrics, fixed income, market microstructure, and the term structure of interest rates.

Walter Vecchiato
Head of Risk Management, Veneto Banca, Piazza G.B. Dall'Armi 1, 31044 Montebelluna (TV) Italy

Walter Vecchiato is Head of Risk Management and Research at Veneto Banca in Montebelluna Treviso, Italy. Previously, he was Head of Credit Derivatives Analysis at Banca Intesa in Milan, Italy. He was also Professor of Applied Statistics in University of Pavia, Italy and a Visiting Researcher in Financial Econometrics at University of California at San Diego, La Jolla. He has written and published on quantitative finance and risk management techniques and been a frequent speaker for many symposiums on Finance worldwide.

Niklas Wagner
Department of Financial Management and Capital Markets, Munich University of Technology, 80333 Munich, Germany

Niklas Wagner is a lecturer in finance at Munich University of Technology, Germany. He received a Ph.D. in finance from Augsburg University and had visiting appointments at the Haas School of Business, U.C. Berkeley and at Stanford GSB. He is a former faculty member of Dresden University of Technology's Business and Economics Department. His industry background is in portfolio management with HypoVereinsbank. His research interests cover the areas of applied financial econometrics including portfolio and risk management.

Philip D. Wooldridge
Monetary and Economic Department, Bank for International Settlements, 4002 Basel, Switzerland

Philip Wooldridge is a senior economist at the Bank for International Settlements. He writes regularly about financial markets for the *BIS Quarterly Review*. Prior to joining the BIS, Philip worked at the Bank of Canada as an emerging markets analyst. He holds a master's degree in economics from the University of Toronto and is a CFA charterholder.

Martin Young
Department of Finance, Banking and Property, College of Business, Massey University, Palmerston North, New Zealand

Martin Young is currently an Associate Professor of Finance at the College of Business, Massey University, New Zealand. Prior to this he spent four years as a Senior Fellow at the Nanyang Business School, Nanyang Technological University in Singapore. As well has his academic experience, Dr Young also has wide experience working within financial markets, having been a member of the New Zealand Stock Exchange for many years. His academic publications include works in the areas of derivative usage, financial market liquidity and microstructure.

Alham Yusuf

Department of Accounting and Finance, Deakin University, Melbourne 3125, Australia

Alham Yusuf completed a Bachelor of Arts/Bachelor of Commerce double degree from Deakin University, Australia. On completion of studies Alham began working for the Victorian Public Service and is currently working at the Department of Treasury and Finance. In addition Alham is in the progress of completing a Bachelor of Commerce (Honours) degree.

Section I
Perspective on European Fixed Income and Derivative Markets

1

Introduction to the Volume

JONATHAN A. BATTEN, THOMAS A. FETHERSTON, AND PETER G. SZILAGYI

1.1 OVERVIEW

The dynamic role of capital markets (here fixed income) to efficiently channel savings funds from surplus sectors of the economy and to finance private economic ventures, which promotes economic growth and economic development, is a concept accepted and promoted by governments throughout the world. The role of fixed income markets as an efficient tool in raising finance for government projects (national and local) has been understood and appreciated for centuries (Homer and Sylla, 1996; Kindleberger, 1984). The introduction of the euro in 1999 has cast a new focus on the financial markets of the constituent countries and the critical size of the market, which comes as a result of this harmonization of macroeconomic targets. There has been a paucity of volumes with extensive coverage of the fixed income markets of European countries since the inception of the euro. The goal of this volume is to partially fill that void. The individual countrywise fixed income markets' essential characteristics and institutional details are introduced and discussed in each chapter devoted to a single country. These essential characteristics are the *sine qua non* of any viable fixed income market. A shortcoming in any of the essential characteristics threatens the viability of that fixed income market. The essential characteristics are as follows:

- A rule of law;
- A primary market where new debt issues (government and private) are systematically offered;
- Investors;
- A liquid secondary market;
- Benchmark indices;
- Independent credit-rating bodies;
- Interest rate derivative markets for risk management.

The essential characteristics do not define a successful fixed income market, but their absence will inhibit the growth and development of one. The rule of law implies that nothing more than contractual relationships will be clearly understood and enforceable through normal existing legal institutions and means. A primary market is also needed where debt offerings for the governmental and corporate bodies are publicly announced and the procedures to participate in these offerings are fair and well understood. There should be a cadre of investors, both institutional and private, who would find the instruments offered to be suitable to their portfolio interests. The existence of a liquid secondary market lowers the cost of raising money in the primary market, as it relieves the burden of having to hold a fixed income obligation to

European Fixed Income Markets: Money, Bond and Interest Rate Derivatives. Edited by J.A. Batten,
T.A. Fetherston and P.G. Szilagyi. 2004 John Wiley & Sons, Ltd. ISBN 0-470-85053-1

maturity (see Committee on the Global Financial System, 1999, 2000). Trading in the secondary market should be transparent and trading costs should be minimal. Benchmark indices (yield curves) are of utmost importance for any market for pricing and to reference individual portfolio performance. The role of independent credit-rating agencies partially relieves investors of the burden of ascertaining the ability and willingness of the borrower to repay the amount borrowed. The role and methodology followed by these independent institutions in determining their credit ratings is well understood. However, the credit rating is not a guarantee, only a guideline. Although futures and options contracts have a historical lineage centuries old, interest rate derivatives are a modern phenomenon. A very important ancillary function to raise fixed income capital and invest in the same is interest rate risk management. The interest rate derivative products first introduced in the 1970s play an integral part in interest rate risk management.

The efforts of the authors who have contributed to this volume will measurably add to the understanding of the fixed income markets of Europe. This volume is structured into two parts: a global overview section and a section focusing on the individual countries and their fixed income markets characteristics. There are 25 chapters in the volume with 30 authors, many of whom are prominent in academic and practitioner aspects of the fixed income markets field, contributing their insight to this volume.

1.1.1   European Market Data

A sense of the scope of the European fixed income markets can be captured from the data provided in Tables 1.1–1.8. The fixed income data provide intermarket comparisons for countries in the region as well as the United States. The size of the fixed income markets of Europe is presented in Table 1.1. The size of each market and the aggregate of the European developed fixed income markets are presented for the years 2000–2002. The dominant European market is the United Kingdom, whose average size and average percentage of market share for the 3 years are US$661.6 billion and 17.5%, respectively. The size of the European developed market averages US$3799.5 billion for the 3 years. The average aggregate European numbers compare well with the US market and are 42.8% of the US market size.

The emerging country markets are covered in Table 1.2. Their average aggregate size for the 3 years covered pale in comparison to the US market, which is 12.54 times as large.

The issuer classification for the developed markets is presented in Table 1.3. The data covers the period between December 2000 and December 2001. The issuing groups are governments, financial institutions, and corporate issuers. For the government category, Europe dominates the United States with a 54.8% average market share to a 28.2% average market share. For the financial institutions, the average concentration for Europe is 36.7% compared to the United States's 55.7%. For the corporate issuers, Europe lags the United States 8.5% to 16.1%. Table 1.4 breaks out European developed market country issuing data in terms of international money market instruments and notes and bonds. The notes and bonds segment of the markets dominates the money market end of the maturity range by 92.1% to 7.9%

Dimson et al.'s long term study of capital markets and their returns provides a view of European fixed income market risk-return characteristics from the turn of the twentieth century to the turn of the twenty-first century (Dimson et al., 2002). Table 1.5 provides a snapshot of market characteristics in 2000. The size of the European market is 62% of the US market, the largest debt market in the world. The average ratio of debt to gross domestic product (GDP) for Europe (94.2%) is significantly more manageable than the US measure (159%). A surprising measure is the relative importance of government debt issues for Europe (44%)

Table 1.1   International debt securities by nationality of issuer (billions US$ – all issuers)

| | Developed fixed income markets of Europe | | | | | |
| | 2000 | | 2001 | | 2002 | |
	$	% of Total Europe developed	$	% of Total Europe developed	$	% of Total Europe developed
Austria	81.0	2.6	90.3	2.5	120.7	2.6
Belgium	129.3	4.2	143.6	4.0	185.6	3.9
Denmark	23.6	0.8	25.8	0.7	28.8	0.6
Finland	38.2	1.2	39.5	1.1	50.8	1.1
France	313.7	10.2	390.1	10.9	511.3	10.8
Germany	908.7	29.5	1081.5	30.1	1462.6	30.9
Greece	27.6	0.9	30.3	0.8	49.3	1.0
Iceland	4.1	0.1	4.5	0.1	5.4	0.1
Ireland	34.7	1.1	47.7	1.3	68.7	1.5
Italy	209.4	6.8	278.4	7.8	370.2	7.8
Luxembourg	11.9	0.4	19.7	0.5	29.2	0.6
Netherlands	292.9	9.5	331.0	9.2	429.7	9.1
Norway	40.3	1.3	41.6	1.2	49.6	1.0
Portugal	34.0	1.1	47.6	1.3	67.1	1.4
Spain	156.5	5.1	182.3	5.1	246.0	5.2
Sweden	107.0	3.5	105.8	2.9	131.1	2.8
Switzerland	101.7	3.3	105.8	2.9	127.5	2.7
United Kingdom	564.4	18.3	626.7	17.4	793.7	16.8
Europe Developed	3079.0	100.0	3592.2	100.0	4727.3	100.0
United States	1736.0	48.3	2340.1	65.1	2749.3	58.2

Source: BIS, 2003.

Table 1.2   International debt securities by nationality of issuer (billions US$ – all issuers)

| | Emerging fixed income markets of Europe | | | | | |
| | 2000 | | 2001 | | 2002 | |
	$	% of Total Europe emerging	$	% of Total Europe emerging	$	% of Total Europe emerging
Croatia	107.0	63.4	105.8	62.6	131.1	64.2
Cyprus	1.3	0.8	1.8	1.1	2.0	1.0
Hungary	10.3	6.1	10.1	6.0	10.3	5.0
Poland	5.2	3.1	7.6	4.5	11.0	5.4
Russia	17.7	10.5	17.3	10.2	20.8	10.2
Slovakia	2.8	1.7	2.6	1.5	2.9	1.4
Slovenia	1.7	1.0	1.8	1.1	2.2	1.1
Turkey	22.7	13.5	21.9	13.0	23.9	11.7
Total Europe Emerging	168.7	100.0	168.9	100.0	204.2	100.0
United States	1736.0	1029.0	2340.1	1385.5	2749.3	1346.4

Source: BIS, 2003.

Table 1.3　Domestic debt securities breakdown (billions US$)

	Amounts outstanding ($)							
	All issuers		Governments		Financial institutions		Corporate issuers	
	Dec '00	Dec '01	Dec '00	Dec '01	Dec '00	Dec '01	Dec '00	Dec '01
Austria	150.8	149.7	88.2	88.2	59.4	58.5	3.2	3.0
Belgium	322.8	307.0	220.3	216.5	86.3	71.8	16.2	18.7
Czech Republic	23.4	25.7	17.9	20.5	2.8	2.6	2.7	2.7
Denmark	247.1	247.4	78.0	73.2	154.6	160.9	14.5	13.3
Finland	67.9	64.3	42.8	41.4	17.8	16.3	7.3	6.7
France	1067.8	1037.5	596.2	600.2	348.6	323.1	122.9	114.1
Germany	1713.7	1496.4	595.7	599.5	1092.9	860.4	25.1	36.5
Greece	87.0	91.5	86.8	91.2	0.2	0.3	–	–
Hungary	16.2	19.3	15.5	18.5	–	–	0.7	0.8
Ireland	31.0	28.5	21.6	17.8	100.0	100.0	9.4	10.7
Italy	1323.5	1334.9	970.3	937.5	325.9	328.3	27.3	69.1
Netherlands	342.4	351.0	164.1	158.4	131.5	141.5	46.8	51.1
Norway	58.5	59.3	26.7	25.2	28.2	29.3	3.6	4.8
Poland	32.1	44.2	32.1	44.2	–	–	–	–
Portugal	64.8	67.7	38.0	40.7	16.6	17.2	10.2	9.8
Spain	358.6	360.5	279.1	267.6	42.1	49.1	37.4	43.8
Sweden	197.1	160.3	105.2	81.4	73.2	57.5	18.7	21.4
Switzerland	157.7	153.8	53.3	53.3	75.5	72.6	29.0	25.9
Turkey	54.7	84.7	54.7	84.7	–	–	–	–
United Kingdom	896.7	920.8	426.5	411.2	285.4	288.9	184.7	220.7
Europe Developed	7213.8	7004.5	3913.0	3871.2	2741.0	2478.3	559.7	653.1
United States	14587.9	15366.6	4176.1	4271.9	8041.1	8658.2	2370.7	2436.4
% of total for the group	100.0	100.0	54.2	55.3	38.0	35.4	7.8	9.3
% of total for the US group	100.0	100.0	28.6	27.8	55.1	56.3	16.3	15.9

Source: BIS, 2003.

as opposed to the United States (53%). The aggregate European data seem to more evenly balance the importance and concentration of national government issues and issuers in the individual country chapters. In Table 1.6 the impact on fixed income returns from inflation are provided by Dimson *et al.* (2002) for the period of 1900–2000. The inflation rate for European countries is substantially higher than that of the United States. As a result, the real returns for the European fixed income instruments (government bonds and bills) are substantially lower. The US arithmetic bond and bill return for the period are 2.1% and 1%. For the European markets available, the return for bonds ranges from a high of 3.1% (Sweden and Switzerland) to a low of −0.8% (Italy). For bills, the return ranges from a high of 3% (Denmark) to a low of −2.9% (Italy), followed closely by a −2.6% return for France. The average bill return for European markets included was 0.5%. If you remove the negative outliers for the bond and bill returns, the average returns for the European bond and bill returns rise to 1.8% and 0.98%, respectively, which are close to the US measures.

Changing yields and bond prices produce interest rate risk that must be confronted and managed. Interest rate derivative securities have filled that need and provided the tools to manage interest rate risk. The existence of viable (liquid) interest derivative instruments and markets

Table 1.4 International Debt Securities Breakdown, European developed markets (billions US$)

	All issuers by country of residence							
	Money market instruments				International bonds and notes			
	Amount outstanding ($)		Net issues* ($)		Amount outstanding ($)		Net issues ($)	
	Dec '01	Dec '02	Dec '01	Dec '02	Dec '01	Dec '02	Dec '01	Dec '02
Austria	6.8	4.6	0.2	(2.5)	97.7	129.6	17.6	15.5
Belgium	13.5	15.5	3.3	0.7	40.8	58.9	10.7	9.6
Denmark	3.6	2.9	1.3	(0.9)	30.6	34.7	2.8	0.4
Finland	1.6	3.2	(0.1)	1.4	37.6	48.6	3.2	4.9
France	13.5	18.9	1.7	3.5	386.6	510.9	90.8	54.7
Germany	51.8	65.2	(26.7)	6.8	590.8	878.5	207.3	170.6
Greece	*	*	*	*	27.5	44.6	3.6	10.7
Iceland	0.9	0.8		(0.1)	3.6	4.7	0.6	0.4
Ireland	29.9	34.1	7.5	0.4	59.5	82.1	13.3	12.9
Italy	0.3		0.2	(0.3)	175.2	258.0	49.3	51.8
Luxembourg	22.1	17.5	6.4	(7.5)	79.7	107.8	27.9	14.3
Netherlands	41.9	47.3	1.7	0.8	527.5	678.2	87.4	67.1
Norway	1.7	2.0	(2.7)	0.1	39.5	47.2	5.0	4.5
Portugal	2.6	1.3	1.7	(1.5)	23.1	35.9	5.0	7.8
Spain	0.7	0.8	(0.1)	0.1	70.9	117.7	14.3	33.1
Sweden	8.7	8.8	(6.4)	(0.7)	80.6	95.6	7.9	4.8
Switzerland	1.0	1.0	(0.2)	(0.1)	14.2	17.0	(1.7)	0.4
United Kingdom	79.5	92.3	(28.2)	5.6	676.9	846.6	99.0	95.3
Europe Developed	280.1	316.2	(40.4)	5.8	2962.3	3996.6	644.0	558.8
United States	38.8	30.6	(24.1)	(11.7)	2356.5	2757.3	595.2	349.5

Source: BIS, 2003.
*Net issues of money market instruments and notes are calculated as completed issues less repayments for international bonds scheduled and early repayments from transaction data.

is necessary – these are also sufficient vehicles to provide risk management tools for risk managers. Generically, these tools (instruments) fall into a few broadly defined channels: forwards, futures, options, and swaps. They may trade on organized exchanges or over-the-counter (OTC). The data for global and European listed and OTC interest rate derivative activity for the past few years, as provided by the Bank for International Settlements (BIS, 2003), are presented in Tables 1.7 and 1.8. Table 1.7 shows that the annual average amount of listed interest rate futures contracts outstanding for Europe during the period between December 1999 and December 2002 was US$2491.3 billion. This average amount constituted 28.4% of the annual amount of listed interest rate futures contracts outstanding for all interest rate futures markets. Over the same period, the annual average amount of listed interest rate options contracts outstanding for Europe was US$2787.2 billion, which constituted 34.1% of contracts outstanding for all interest rate options markets. Rather similarly, the annual average number of listed futures contracts outstanding for Europe was 4.4 million or 26.4% of extant contracts for all interest rate futures markets. The annual average number of listed options contracts outstanding for Europe was 4 million or 37.3% of those outstanding for all interest rate futures markets. The average listed turnover share for Europe in 2001–2002 was 50.6% in futures and 32.8% in options. The importance of Europe in the OTC interest rate derivatives market can be seen

Table 1.5 European bond market values (start 2000)

	Total outstanding billions ($)	% of world	Rank in world	Bond value as % of GDP	Value of government bonds billions ($)	% of Bonds which are government
Austria	149	0.5	17	72.0	80.46	54.0
Belgium	324	1.0	9	131.0	194.40	60.0
Denmark	264	0.9	12	152.0	81.84	31.0
France	1227	4.0	5	86.0	711.66	58.0
Germany	3131	10.1	3	148.0	782.75	25.0
Greece	88	0.3	19	70.0	68.64	78.0
Ireland	32	1.0	31	34.0	23.68	74.0
Italy	1374	4.4	4	117.0	934.32	68.0
Netherlands	458	1.5	8	116.0	174.04	38.0
Spain	304	1.0	10	51.0	221.92	73.0
Sweden	188	0.6	16	79.0	94.00	50.0
Switzerland	269	0.9	11	104.0	48.42	18.0
United Kingdom	939	3.0	6	65.0	469.50	50.0
Europe	8747	29.2	2	94.2	3885.63	44.4
United States	14595	47.0	1	159.0	7735.35	53.0

Source: Dimson *et al.*, 2002.

from Table 1.8. Between June 2000 and June 2002, the average amount of euro-denominated interest rate derivatives (forwards, swaps, and options) comprised 34.4% of the annual notional values and 32% of the gross market value of extant OTC interest rate contracts.

1.2 CHAPTER OVERVIEW

Chapter 2 (Szilagyi) provides a capsule analysis of Euro area market integration. Financial integration can be expected to improve economic performance by developing the financial system through two main channels: (i) the exploitation of the scale and scope effects inherent in financial activity and (ii) increased competitive pressure on financial intermediaries. In this context, it is also reasonable to conclude that bond market integration, and development thereof, may also bring advantages in broad economic terms, as it should (i) lower the average cost of external finance; (ii) help build a more efficient capital structure and reduce maturity mismatches; (iii) provide better managing control in the corporate sector; (iv) improve the efficiency of resource allocation; (v) encourage the financing of innovation; and (vi) help distribute financial risks and potential losses more widely and possibly more efficiently.

The European Commission has now established the ambitious Financial Services Action Plan (FSAP) to create an efficient and integrated European financial market with a unified legislative framework by 2005, with measures relating to securities markets to be implemented by 2003. These efforts are consistent with the conclusion that an efficient financial sector is indeed pivotal for realizing the full-growth potential of the European Union (EU) economy. In particular, financial market integration should certainly contribute to an efficient financial sector, since many financial activities display scale economies and benefit from increased competition under Monetary Union.

The single currency environment has already brought about fundamental changes to the Euro area bond market. The euro and the implementation of the FSAP have worked toward the emergence of an integrated framework for investors and issuers alike, instigating growth

Table 1.6 European inflation, bond, and bill returns

	Inflation rates (1900–2000)			Bonds % real returns (1900–2000)			Bills % real returns (1900–2000)		
	Arithmetic mean (%)	Standard error (%)	Standard deviation (%)	Arithmetic mean (%)	Standard error (%)	Standard deviation (%)	Arithmetic mean (%)	Standard error (%)	Standard deviation (%)
Belgium	5.9	0.9	9.0	0.3	1.2	12.1	0.0	0.8	8.2
Denmark	4.3	0.6	6.5	3.3	1.2	12.5	3.0	0.6	6.4
France	8.8	1.5	14.6	0.1	1.4	14.4	−2.6	1.1	11.4
Germany	6.0	1.6	15.8	0.3	1.6	15.9	0.1	1.1	10.6
Ireland	4.7	0.7	6.8	2.4	1.3	13.3	1.4	0.6	6.0
Italy	11.7	3.6	36.6	−0.8	1.4	14.4	−2.9	1.2	12.0
Netherlands	3.1	0.5	5.0	1.5	0.9	9.4	0.8	0.5	5.2
Spain	6.4	0.7	7.2	1.9	1.2	12.0	0.6	0.6	6.1
Sweden	3.9	0.7	6.8	3.1	1.3	12.7	2.2	0.7	6.8
Switzerland	2.4	0.6	6.0	3.1	0.8	8.0	1.2	0.6	6.2
United Kingdom	4.3	0.7	6.9	2.3	1.4	14.5	1.2	0.7	6.6
Europe	5.6	1.1	11.0	1.6	1.2	12.7	0.5	0.8	7.8
United States	3.3	0.5	5.0	2.1	1.0	10.0	1.0	0.5	4.7

Source: Dimson *et al.*, 2002.

Table 1.7 Interest rate derivatives on organized exchanges

	Notional principal (billions US$)					
	Amounts outstanding				Turnover	
	Dec '99	Dec '00	Dec '01	Dec '02	2001	2002
Interest rate futures all markets	7924.8	7907.8	9265.3	9958.5	420934.2	472300.4
Interest rate futures Europe	2274.2	2201.9	2324.8	3164.2	146967.4	171353.3
% of Total due Europe	28.7	27.8	25.1	31.8	34.9	36.3
Interest rate options all markets	3755.5	4734.2	12492.8	11759.8	122765.9	154557.1
Interest rate options Europe	1300.0	1560.6	3238.4	5049.9	29512.5	42313.8
% of Total due Europe	34.6	33.0	25.9	42.9	24.0	27.4
	Contracts outstanding (number of contracts in millions)				Turnover (contracts in millions)	
Interest rate futures all markets	17.5	19.8	15.3	15.4	1057.5	1147.3
Interest rate futures Europe	3.6	4.2	4.5	5.3	538.2	578.3
% of Total due Europe	20.6	21.2	29.4	34.4	50.9	50.4
Interest rate options all markets	5.6	7.3	16.2	14.5	199.6	240.3
Interest rate options Europe	2.1	2.8	5.2	6.0	69.2	74.4
% of Total due Europe	37.5	38.4	32.1	41.4	34.7	31.0

Source: BIS, 2003.

Table 1.8   OTC interest rate derivatives (billions US$)

	Notional Amounts* ($)			Gross market value ($)		
	June '00	June '01	June '02	June '00	June '01	June '02
Total interest rate contracts	64125	67465	89995	1230	1573	2468
Forward rate agreements	6771	6537	9146	13	15	19
Interest rate swaps	47993	51407	68274	1072	1404	2214
Options	9361	9521	12575	145	154	235
Denominated in euros	22948	22405	30671	467	461	710
% of Interest derivatives in euro	35.8	33.2	34.1	38.0	29.3	28.8

Source: BIS, 2003.
*The notional amount provides a comparison of market size between related cash and derivative markets. Gross market value is the sum of the value of the contracts.

and development on a pan-European level. The integrating powers of the single currency have worked through laying the foundations for a single integrated pool of European investors, which has boosted demand in the market. Market structures are being amalgamated accordingly, which is mirrored in more closely integrated investment and trading possibilities, improved price transparency, and growing liquidity. These improvements have provided substantial benefits for both public and private borrowers, such as lower transaction costs amid a lower interest rate environment. Of course, this process is being further facilitated by the fact that banks, which have historically dominated the financial system of continental Europe, now face increasingly tough competition from the bond market. This also implies that the Euro area financial system, traditionally described as bank-based, is slowly moving toward becoming more market-based, much like that in the United States.

The chapter identifies the primary trends and developments observed in the market. Of course, these trends are not solely a result of Monetary Union, but also of various other structural factors currently affecting financial markets, such as technological, regulatory, and demographic developments, as well as the gradual implementation of the single market for financial services. On the whole, the Euro area bond market is indeed significantly larger, more diverse, and more integrated than ever before. Nonetheless, the European Central Bank (2002) warns that market participants and regulators remain unhappy with the various on-going impediments to realizing the full potential benefits of the integration process. The chief obstacles include the enduring national segmentation of the government bond market, the rather fragmented nature of trading, clearing, and settlement systems, as well as the complex patchwork of legal and regulatory requirements and nonuniform tax treatment. This suggests that the benefits so far accrued from the integration process are just a fraction of those that may be eventually realized.

Chapter 3 (Szilagyi, Fetherston, and Batten) ties the course of bond market development in emerging Europe to the level of economic and financial development in different countries in the region. The chapter examines and compares the three major forms of debt financing in the emerging European economies over the period since the mid-1990s. To facilitate cross-country comparisons, the study groups the region's economies into three groups based on their level of development. The advanced economies group includes those functioning market economies that are practically ready to meet the highly competitive pressures within the EU. This group is marked by the high quality investment grade credit ratings for these countries. The frontrunners of this group are the Czech Republic, Estonia, Hungary, Poland, and Slovenia, as well as the non-excommunist countries of Cyprus and Malta. These countries are all in the process of graduating from the emerging market class. Slovakia and even more pronouncedly Croatia (the only country out of this lot not joining the EU in 2004), Latvia, and Lithuania somewhat lag behind these front-runners. The less-advanced economies group includes the less developed and more unpredictable economies of emerging Europe, as signaled by their subinvestment-grade credit ratings. The authors classify Bulgaria, Romania, Turkey, and Russia as exemplary of this group. The prolonged crisis economies group includes the most unpredictable economies of the region, including the Balkan states of Albania, Bosnia and Herzegovina, Macedonia, Serbia and Montenegro, as well as the former Soviet republics of Belarus, Moldova, and the Ukraine.

The main source of foreign funding for emerging Europe continues to be international bank borrowing. The variation patterns of foreign lending to the region largely mirror the differences in economic and financial development among the three study groups. The region's advanced economies tend to borrow most actively, while lending to the region's less advanced economies, troubled by financial and economic setbacks over the years, has been much more erratic. It must be emphasized that the tendencies in lending to emerging Europe reflect a reassessment of the creditworthiness of many economies in the region.

While foreign bank lending to emerging Europe's stronger transition economies has been growing consistently since the early 1990s, a notable trend from the middle of the decade has been the gradual return of these economies to the international capital markets. On the whole, the development of domestic bond markets in different emerging European countries has of course taken very different courses, and is at very different stages. The markets in some of the more advanced reformer countries have rapidly evolved as a preferred source of financing, and now represent a more important source of funding than the external markets. Other countries have fallen behind, since for long they failed to provide the necessary environment for the development of their local markets. Most of the region's markets are overwhelmingly dominated by sovereign issues: few nongovernment or quasigovernment issuers have tapped these markets, since they have little or no issuance history and they lack the marketability of a sovereign issue.

Chapter 4 (Young) provides an overview of interest rate derivative evolution in Europe. The oldest official derivative market in Europe is the London International Financial Futures and Options Exchange (LIFFE), which – now as part of the Euronext Group – remains one of the premier derivatives markets in Europe, particularly for the trading of short term interest rate derivatives. LIFFE began its operations in 1982, focusing on providing products to help in the management of interest rate and currency risk. The major product lines of LIFFE remain the short term interest rate and government bond contracts that were its original strength, although one of the first futures contracts developed by LIFFE was the British government debt contract based on the long term US Treasury contracts.

Interestingly, it was the technology boom of the late nineties that gave LIFFE its biggest challenge and arguably its biggest success. The shift to electronic trading came in stages, gathering momentum through 1998 and 1999. It was driven by three major realizations. First, business could shift between market places almost instantaneously in an electronic environment. Second, the technology advances in screen-based trading platforms in the latter part of the nineties was quite dramatic. The idea that open outcry was the fairest and most efficient way of executing business was shown to be an outdated one. Finally, there was the issue of cost. Efficient screen trading was proving to be the much cheaper alternative for many reasons.

EUREX is only one serious competitor to LIFFE in the area of bond and short term interest rate futures and options trading in Europe. This German–Swiss joint venture came about through the merger of the DTB Deutsche Terminbörse, the German Options and Futures Exchange, and SOFFEX, the Swiss Options and Financial Futures Exchange, in 1998. Today it trades a wide range of bond and money market derivative products. Access to the market is available in a number of major cities, including Chicago, New York, London, and Tokyo.

EURONEXT was born through the merger of Amsterdam Exchanges (AEX), Brussels Exchanges (BXS), and Paris Bourse, and was later joined by the Lisbon and Oporto Exchange (BVLP). This merger encompassed both the cash and derivative markets. A common clearing and settlement system was put in place called Clearnet®, and Euroclear® became the settlement agency and custody platform. The thinking that had driven the decision to merge was the emergence of the single currency, and as a consequence as far the money market and bond derivatives were concerned there would be fewer products but potentially a much larger market for these products, particularly if the euro became a true competitor to the US dollar as was a real possibility.

LIFFE became Euronext.Liffe in the year 2002 and firmly established itself as one of only two major players, together with EUREX, in the bond and short term interest rate futures and options market within Europe. There is not much after EUREX and Euronext.Liffe. The only market that shows any significant volume in the trading of such products currently is Sweden's Stockholmsbörsen. Some trading in interest rate derivative products also takes place, or has taken place recently, on the Spanish Exchanges (MEFF), the Italian interest rate derivative exchange (MIF), the ADEX market in Athens, Hungary's BSE derivatives market, and the Romanian Commodities Exchange.

It is highly unlikely that the smaller European derivative markets will develop interest rate derivative products in the foreseeable future. There is certainly scope within some of the new EU entrants for the development, or further development of derivative markets, but this development will almost certainly focus on equity-based products as we have seen in other European exchanges. In a number of cases derivative market development will be more effective within a grouping of countries. NOREX, the alliance of the Danish, Swedish, Norwegian, and Icelandic exchanges may be a good model for some closely linked European countries to follow. Most of the Eastern European countries are looking to the west, and derivative market development will be based on its appropriateness within the framework of the EU model. It is possible that the European countries with closer links to Russia, and without the Euro option, may develop some interest rate derivative markets of their own as their economies develop more into free-market ones, but this is unlikely to happen quickly.

Chapter 5 (Wooldridge) introduces us to benchmark yield curves. In global fixed income markets, government bonds have long been used as benchmark instruments. The benchmark status of the government yield curve derives from a number of features that, when taken together, make government securities unique in financial markets. Benchmark interest rates, however, need not be synonymous with government yields; in principle, even corporate bonds could serve as benchmark instruments.

European fixed income markets were the first to move away from the use of government yield curves as benchmarks. Starting in the early 1990s, European investors and issuers, especially banks, increasingly referenced interest rate swaps. Banks are among the largest investors in European debt securities markets, and consequently their preferences shape the structure of European fixed income markets to a greater extent than in the US dollar market or other major markets. End investors with investment portfolios in multiple currencies and large borrowers with funding programs in multiple currencies also gradually switched over to talking in terms of yield spreads relative to swaps rather than government paper. Justifiably so, because swap curves offered a reasonably simple way to compare returns or borrowing costs in different markets, and the comparability across markets was of particular concern because of the fragmented nature of European fixed income markets prior to the introduction of the euro. A series of traumatic market events in the late 1990s, most notably the near-collapse of Long Term Capital Management in September 1998, squeezes in German bund futures contracts, and actual as well as prospective declines in the supply of European government debt prior to the most recent economic downturn, further strengthened the incentive to switch to nongovernment instruments as positioning and hedging vehicles.

The cumulative effect of the above-mentioned changes has nonetheless been insufficient to displace government securities as the preeminent benchmark in European fixed income markets. It is notable, however, that while Monetary Union created the second largest government securities market in the world, the Euro government securities market is more fragmented than its Japanese or US counterparts. Twelve different issuers participate in the Euro government securities market, and differences in issuers' credit ratings, settlement systems, tax regimes, and market conventions remain obstacles to complete integration. As a result, differences in yields on Euro area government debt have persisted even since the introduction of the euro, which has complicated the use of government securities to estimate a benchmark yield curve. The German government securities market has benefited the most from improvements in liquidity brought about by the euro, yet it appears that the Euro area benchmark yield curve continues to consist of a basket of bonds rather than a single instrument

Aside from swaps, other nongovernment yield curves also have the potential to become viable benchmark yield curves, although none has yet become as widely referenced in the euro market as government or swaps curves. An index of yields on similarly rated corporate bonds is a possible candidate for eventual elevation to benchmark status. Furthermore, many asset managers benchmark their performance against an index. Averages of yields on collateralized obligations could also be used to construct benchmark yield curves. Yield curves based on covered bonds or Pfandbriefe, or debt instruments issued by government-sponsored enterprises (GSEs) and supranational institutions are also rather promising.

Chapter 6 (Mastroeni) provides a discourse on the Pfandbrief market. In Europe it is common to refer to "covered bonds" or "mortgage bonds" when referring to different types of bonds backed by mortgage assets, public sector loans, or other types of assets such as mortgage-backed securities. The "cover" is achieved through a process of "securitization," which is in essence a method of converting a credit claim or a pool of claims into negotiable securities. This process can typically be achieved either "off-balance sheet" (this is the type of securitization most often referred to as "asset-backed"), or "on-balance sheet" (in recent times referred to as "Pfandbrief-style") or even through "synthetic securitization" – a technique that has developed in more recent times.

Off-balance sheet securitization implies the sale by a bank of a portfolio of assets to an entity (typically a so-called special purpose vehicle, separate from the issuer), which finances the acquisition of the assets by issuing debt instruments (e.g., bonds or commercial paper [CP]) or shares. In contrast, on-balance sheet securitization consists of the issuance of securities backed by securities that remain on the balance sheet of the issuer. The typical example of this type of securitization is provided by the German Pfandbrief, where assets are ring-fenced on the balance sheet of so-called "hypothekenbanken" subject to a specific legal regime. The bank then issues bonds, which provide the holders with priority right to the ring-fenced assets, in the event of a default of the issuer. The holder, therefore, benefits from a double protection: the solvency of the issuer and the solvency of the debtors of the original assets. It is interesting to note that the development of covered bonds of the Pfandbrief type has been around for more than 200 years in Europe. On the other hand, issuance of asset-backed securities (ABS) bonds is a relatively recent phenomenon, and has been brought about by innovation in the financial sector.

Having described the main differences between ABS and Pfandbrief-style products, the rest of the chapter concentrates in particular on Pfandbrief products. European Pfandbrief products are typically issued by specialized credit institutions with a narrowly defined scope of business activities and subject to special banking supervision. The best known legislation regulating this segment of the market is the German Pfandbrief legislation, which has always had national relevance and has thus kept covered bond markets segmented. Given the success of Pfandbriefe, other countries (Belgium, Finland, Ireland, Italy, Sweden, and the United Kingdom) have also taken legal steps to participate in the genre. In all the countries, the new laws aim at guaranteeing the quality of covered bond instruments with a view to reproduce the popularity and the attractiveness encountered with investors by the German Pfandbrief, also at the international level. The Pfandbrief has been assigned a capital risk weighting of 10% compared to the 20% weighting normally required for other bank bonds.

The German Pfandbrief market is the largest individual bond market in Europe in terms of outstanding amount. There are basically two types of Pfandbriefe: public Pfandbriefe (issued in order to fund loans to, or guaranteed by the sovereign government, the states, the municipalities, and other authorized public sector entities) and Mortgage Pfandbriefe (issued to finance first rate residential and commercial mortgages within Germany, other EU Member States, a European Economic Area Member State, or Switzerland).

1.2.1 Country Study Chapters

Chapter 7 on Austria (Seconnino and Yusuf) provides insight on the financial development taken by Austria over the past two decades. The evolutionary path follows a shift away from banks to insurance companies and domestic, mutual, and pension funds. The Austrian capital market has traditionally been small and inefficient in comparison to other Euro countries. As a result, the government has taken sweeping measures to improve the capital market and bring it up to West European standards. Austria's membership of the EU will only enable the country to prosper. Thus, Austria will be able to capitalize on the success of the euro to become a major international financial player. Recent developments have ensured that Austria is introducing ongoing improvements in international standards and best practices. Austria's financial market regulatory framework, and specifically the banking legislation, has been evolving as a result of the expansion and internationalization of the financial market.

Austria's excellent sovereign rating from both Moody's Investor Services and Standard & Poor's recognizes Austria's stable political system, high levels of economic wealth and diversity, and flexible market institutions. This reflects the country's positive economic fundamentals, social and political stability, a tradition of fiscal prudence, and a favorable public sector debt profile.

In the bond market, tax reforms have been implemented to encourage investor participation. In 1986, the government abolished the coupon tax on new issues because of the resulting outflow into foreign bonds, which effectively increased domestic investments. The market has doubled in size since 1990 and is considerably larger than the domestic equity market, yet it continues to rank among the smaller European markets in terms of its size (€169.1 billion outstanding at the end of 2001), representing a share of less than 1% of the overall world bond market. In terms of its relative importance, as measured as a percentage of GDP, the market ranks among the medium-sized markets (80% of GDP).

Types of bonds in the Austrian bond market include government bonds, federal Treasury certificates, Treasury notes, interest rate and government strips, corporate bonds, banking bonds, and convertible bonds. Government bonds, which comprise the single largest segment of the market, are issued through an auction procedure. Austrian bonds are bearer bonds. The bonds are also in bullet form, where early redemption or redemption in installments is not foreseen. The fixed-rate bonds pay an annual coupon. The majority of government bond trading is conducted OTC through the interbank market structure or directly between institutional investors. Österreichische Kontrollbank AG and various Austrian banks regularly compute a number of Austrian bond market indices, which serve as benchmarks. These include a performance index for market portfolios of government bonds, an index for all issuers as well as a mortgage and municipality bond indices.

Chapter 8 on Belgium (Annaert and De Ceuster) shows that the Belgian bond market is almost uniquely driven by the activity of the (federal) government. The corporate bond market is underdeveloped, since those Belgian companies that want to issue debt securities almost unanimously tap the international capital market. During the 1990s, public debt management was modernized to create attractive and liquid primary and secondary markets. The market itself is relatively large due to the high level of government debt. In 1993, the gross public debt reached a peak level of 137.9% of GDP, although the debt ratio has declined year after year since then, encouraged by the EU's Stability and Growth Pact, and reached 106.1% at the end of 2002.

Government securities, which include linear bonds (OLOs), Treasury certificates, and Treasury bills, are issued only in dematerialized form since the financial markets reform of 1991. As such, they are represented by an account registration with an account keeper approved by the Minister of Finance (or occasionally by an entry into the Ledger of the Public Debt held by the Treasury Administration). Every investor is listed with his/her account keeper depending on his/her tax status under Belgian law. Those investors that are exempt from personal income tax, e.g. nonresidents, hold an X account (eXempt account) and receive the gross income on their securities. Other investors hold an N-account (Non-exempt) and are subject to withholding taxes.

A body of primary dealers was established to enhance the placement of Belgian government securities, to ensure liquidity in the secondary market, and to promote Belgian sovereign debt. As such, primary dealers have to actively participate on a regular basis in the auctions. Besides the primary dealers, the government also attracted a number of other international market players to act as recognized dealers. The recognized dealers share the same obligations on the secondary market as the primary dealers but they are not obliged to participate in primary market activities.

Although OLOs are quoted on Euronext Brussels (mainly to allow private investors to trade), linear bonds are essentially targeted at professional investors. Consequently, the principal secondary markets are the regulated and the nonregulated off-exchange OTC markets. The Securities Regulation Fund (Rentenfonds, Fond des Rentes) is an independent public institution that draws up market regulations for all transactions on the regulated off-exchange market. It also publishes daily reference prices and volumes for all issues listed on the regulated off-exchange market. The Belgian Banking and Finance Commission is responsible for second-line supervision. As such, it controls whether the Security Regulation Fund carries out its duties as market authority. Repurchase agreements (or alternatively sell/buyback), futures and option contracts, securities swaps, and security loans are all available in the Belgium interest rate market.

Chapter 9 on the Czech Republic (Ooi and Batten) briefly looks at impact of the reform measures undertaken to move the new Czech Republic along after the collapse of communism in 1989 and later the breakup of Czechoslovakia in 1993. Prices and foreign trade were liberalized at a very early stage. The new Czech currency, Koruna became fully convertible for most business purposes (current account and capital account transactions) in 1995. In the early 1990s, most of the state-owned industries were privatized: by 1996, the state had privatized over 90% of the 1800 target companies with a total book value of nearly US$10 billion.

The bond market started to develop rapidly after 1993, when inflation dropped below 10% and the economic and political situation became more stabilized. The Czech bond market now ranks among the most developed bond markets in Central and Eastern Europe in term of foreign investor access, liquidity, and other characteristics. The market is largely dominated by government bonds, which include Treasury bills as well as medium and long term government bonds.

Corporate bonds and bank bonds comprise a relatively large segment, 13.3% and 12.4% of the market, respectively. Mortgage bonds have now also appeared in the marketplace, although along with municipal bonds these instruments continue to comprise a very small proportion of the market. These latter bonds are usually issued by cities including Brno, Plzen, Kladno, Pardubice, and Caslav to finance maintenance and development expenditures. The Czech derivatives market was established only recently; however, it has moved forward and now trades interest rate instruments such as interest swaps, interest futures, and interest options.

Chapter 10 on the Danish bond market (Christiansen, Engsted, Jakobsen, and Tanggaard) decomposes the market into government bonds, mortgage-backed bonds, corporate bonds, and fixed income derivatives. Mortgage-backed securities account for almost two thirds of the market, and the government bonds account for most of the remaining one third.

Because of the positive net cash balance of the central government's account, the nominal amount of foreign and domestic debt securities issued by the Danish central government has been steadily decreasing since 1996. Government securities are issued by the Ministry of Finance, but the issuing strategy is planned in close cooperation with the Danish Central Bank, which is in charge of the management of all central government debt (bills, notes, and bonds). The current strategy of the Danish Central Bank is to issue domestic bonds almost exclusively in the 2-, 5-, and 10-year maturity segment to build up large liquid series that are attractive to foreign investors. This strategy is supported by interest rate swaps for day-to-day risk management, while older bond series are redeemed from the market through buyback and switch operations. There is no primary dealer function in the market as such, although certain members of the Copenhagen Stock Exchange are allowed to buy new issues directly from the central bank.

Corporate bonds are hardly of any significance in financing the corporate sector. Danish corporations tend to finance their operations by bank loans and by mortgage credits. Exchange-traded corporate bonds have only existed over the past few decades. The limited trade in corporate bonds takes place at the Copenhagen Stock Exchange. The market for fixed income derivatives is also limited in size and since 2001 has been restricted to the OTC market.

The market for mortgage-backed bonds has a long history. In fact, the first mortgage bank was set up in 1797 to finance the reconstruction of the city of Copenhagen after a devastating fire. The Danish mortgage bond market is among the largest mortgage bond markets in Europe, second only to the German "Pfandbriefe" market. In fact, more than 90% of gross residential mortgage loans in Denmark are funded through the mortgage bond market. These bonds are issued by specialized mortgage credit institutions.

The secondary market for Danish bonds is organized by the Copenhagen Stock Exchange. It is essentially a multiple dealer market supported by Saxess, the joint trading system of the NOREX alliance of exchanges.

Chapter 11 (Christiansen, Engsted, Jakobsen, and Tanggaard) investigates the term structure of interest rates in Denmark over the period 1993–2002, using monthly observations on zero-coupon rates with maturities ranging from 3 months to 10 years. In particular, the Expectations Hypothesis of the Term Structure (EHTS) is tested using cointegration techniques and regressions and vector-autoregressions involving changes in interest rates and yield spreads, and yield spreads' ability to predict future interest rates over various horizons will be examined.

The term structure of interest rates is important for various reasons. First, it is related to the notion of "informational efficiency" of the bond and money markets: Are there profitable arbitrage possibilities to be exploited in these markets? Second, the relation between short- and long-interest rates is important for the transmission mechanism of monetary policy: The monetary authorities control the short rate, and only if there is a stable relation between short and long rates will the authorities also be able to control long rates and thereby influence real economic activity. Third, the spread between long and short rates may contain useful information about future interest rates, inflation, and real economic activity. For example, the monetary authorities and policymakers may be able to use the yield spread as an indicator of the inflationary pressures in the economy. Finally, the term structure of interest rates is important for mortgage financing: if the slope of the yield curve is on average positive, real estate owners may find it optimal to finance their houses using short term bonds instead of long term bonds. A number of earlier studies have analyzed the Danish term structure during the 1970s, 1980s, and the beginning of the 1990s, but research using recent data has been quite limited. The goal of the chapter is to fill this information gap.

The interest rate data used in this chapter are monthly observations from 1993 to 2002 on zero-coupon bond yields from the Danish bond market taken from the Danish financial database "Børsdatabasen," which is located at the Aarhus School of Business. The starting point of the sample was chosen to be October 1993, because in the period from the summer of 1992 to the summer of 1993 the European Monetary System (EMS) currency crisis implied a huge pressure on the Danish currency. The results presented suggest that since the EMS currency crisis in 1992–1993, the Danish term structure of interest rates has been more or less segmented into two groups. The first group contains interest rates at the short end of the market (maturities up to 1 or 2 years), where rates are closely related (cointegrated), and where yield spreads are unbiased and significant predictors of future short rates and unbiased (though insignificant) predictors of future long rates. In fact, at the short end of the maturity spectrum the EHTS with constant term premia cannot be rejected. The second group contains long term interest rates (maturities of 2 years and more), and for this group, by contrast, the EHTS is strongly rejected: long rates are not highly correlated with short rates or with other long rates, and long–short spreads do not signal future changes in neither short nor long rates.

A direct implication of these findings is that the Danish policymakers and monetary authorities may find it quite difficult to control long term interest rates by manipulating short term rates with the purpose of influencing real economic activity. Traditionally, this has been one of the standard goals of monetary policy, but as explained in the previous chapter, in recent years the main goal of the Danish monetary authorities has been to support the Danish currency, and concerns about economic growth and unemployment have not been a part of Danish monetary policy. These results lend direct support to continuing abstracting from these issues in the conduct of monetary policy.

The four Nordic countries (Finland, Iceland, Norway, and Sweden) are covered in Chapter 12 (Pynnönen). In each of these countries the bond markets have developed on their own phase. In Sweden and particularly in Finland, government bonds make up the dominating share of the total value of the bonds, about 50% in the former and about 70% in the latter. In Iceland and Norway, the private sector has become the dominating one, particularly in recent years. The largest bond market is in Sweden with an outstanding nominal value of about US$280 billion. In Finland and Norway the market size is about US$100 billion. The Icelandic market is a small one with an outstanding value of about US$12 billion. The size of the Finnish and particularly the Swedish market has been decreasing in the last 5 years, mainly due to a reduction in government debt in these countries. The level of public debt has also declined in Norway, but there and in Iceland in particular, the market has continued to grow as a result of the expansion of the private sector.

Another notable feature of the Nordic markets is the high share of foreign debt in some of the countries. In Finland and Sweden nearly 40% of government debt is foreign-based, whereas, for example, in Norway virtually all government debt is issued domestically. On the other hand, the private sector in Norway has been increasingly borrowing internationally. An obvious reason for this increase has been the large gap between Norwegian and EU or US interest rates, which has continued to prevail.

The French bond market discussed in Chapter 13 (Edwards and Makepeace) is the third largest public debt market in the EU. The French market is also very highly regarded worldwide as a benchmark reference for private sector issuance.

The market for government bonds consists of three main euro-denominated securities: short term Treasury bills known as BTFs, medium term notes known as BTANs, and long term bonds known as OATs. The issuance of government bonds in the primary market is mostly done through American auctions. The secondary market for French government bonds sees BTFs, BTANs, and OATs traded on a daily basis at a level higher than most other euro instruments. The market is, therefore, one of the most liquid in the Euro area, which compliments the explicit policy of the French government to develop the primary and secondary bond markets so that they can serve the government's borrowing requirements and aid the further development of financial markets in France.

The French derivative markets are an offspring of financial sector reforms aimed at modernizing France's financial sector. Two derivative exchanges were created for trading futures and options – Matif and Monep. Matif began operations in 1986 with the launch of its first product, the notional futures contract, and in 1988 merged with France's commodities exchange. Today it specializes in interest rate and commodity derivatives.

In Chapter 14 on Germany (Wagner) it is pointed out that bonds in Germany have traditionally played an important role in household savings on the one hand and in government debt and bank financing on the other. The German bond market is the third largest in the world and the largest in Europe. Although the German bond market is the largest in Europe, there are a few dominant features, which have characterized the German financial system over the last 50 years: The German system was, and still is, essentially bank-based, which implies that most corporations are largely dependent on bank financing. This is in sharp contrast with some other EU Member States, most notably the United Kingdom, where the financial system is market-based. The German bond market is a long term market, where 80% of debt securities are issued with an original maturity of over 4 years. Issues of short term paper such as money market and Commercial Paper (CP) have increased in recent years and now account for roughly 5%

of overall issuance. In terms of the volume of funds allocated from savers to borrowers in Germany, the bond market ranks second behind the banking sector. There have been changes in the legal system aimed at the preparation of an improved institutional setting and to support the modernization of the financial system; such efforts are vital with respect to international competition between financial centers within Europe. These regulatory changes and recent developments as well as ongoing internationalization of the markets have all forced competition in the German financial system. However, while stock exchange and derivatives markets have experienced growth, the development of debt markets, and the nongovernment segment of these in particular, continues to lag behind.

The single largest segment of the German bond market is comprised of bonds issued by commercial banks and other monetary financial institutions. As noted earlier, the Pfandbrief market is discussed in detail in Chapter 6. At the end of 2000, approximately one third of the overall outstanding German debt securities were government bonds making up a €800 billion market. Issues of corporate bonds are negligible.

Federal debt financing is based on issues of securitized debt, where different security types serve the needs of different investors such as saving needs by private households or investment by institutional investors. The market for 10-year Bunds represents the most liquid segment of the European bond market and provides a benchmark for the pricing of long-maturity bonds throughout Europe. Auctions take place via the underwriting fixed-price-reoffer method. German bond market indices are the Deutscher Rentenindex REX and the REX-performance index (REXP), both introduced in 1991. The REX is based on a theoretical market-weighted portfolio of 30 government bonds with maturities ranging from 1 to 10 years and three coupon rates, respectively. A benchmark for the short term market is the Bund future, now given as the Euro Bund future.

Secondary trading in German government bonds takes place on organized exchanges as well as OTC, the latter traditionally accounting for substantial amounts of trading. The largest regulated secondary floor market for German bonds is the Frankfurt Stock Exchange. Recently, MTS Germany, a division of EuroMTS, emerged as the electronic wholesale trading platform for German government bonds and now accounts for the bulk of trading in these securities. Bank bonds are still mostly traded OTC with the exception of Jumbo Pfandbriefe, which are mostly traded via the newly introduced electronic trading platform EuroCredit MTS. Within the EUREX platform, there is a very active derivatives market for German government bonds. Bond derivatives such as the well-known Bund future are now mostly traded via EUREX. In December 2000, the Euro Bund future accounted for 30% of all contracts traded on EUREX. With the inclusion of bonds on the trading platform in late 2000, it became possible to trade bonds and futures simultaneously in a unified trading platform, which eases arbitrage and hedging strategies.

In Chapter 15 on Greece (Fetherston) evidence of a relatively small but flourishing bond market exists since administered interest rates were replaced by regular auctions of government paper. The Finance Ministry no longer relies on sales of short term Treasury bills to retail investors to finance the public debt. Meanwhile, the debt profile has steadily lengthened with the launch of bonds carrying 10-, 15-, and 20-year maturities. These issues are reopened at intervals to create depth on the secondary market. The 10-year bond remains the most popular benchmark, but once the 20-year bond becomes established through secondary trading, Greece will launch a 30-year bond. Access to the primary market is restricted to a group of primary dealers from Greek and foreign banks. Banks outside Greece will soon have direct access to the electronic trading system – speeding transactions and deepening market liquidity. There are no private placements of government paper, while commissions on bond issues have been abolished.

With steady improvement in Greece's fiscal balance, securitization of government cash flows and an active privatization program, Greece's public finances have shown improvement in recent years. Nevertheless, reflecting the government's objectives of reducing exchange risk, establishing a liquid domestic market in government bonds, and extending the maturity of central government debt, the government bond market has continued to grow. These trends are expected to continue over the medium term, resulting in the gradual increase in size and liquidity of the domestic government bond market.

The debt issues of the government totally dominate the Greek fixed income arena and the movement to the euro has only increased the Governments domination. The corporate market is significantly smaller than the government market and is illiquid, although the movement to the euro is expected to boost corporate issuance. There is practically no secondary market for trading corporate bonds.

Chapter 16 on Hungary (Németh and Szilágyi) provides an overview of one of the largest and most mature bond markets in Central and Eastern Europe. Hungary's government bond market has expanded rapidly due to the budget's funding needs, the establishment of a national institutional investor base through the 1997 pension reform and the great deal of interest international investors have been taking in the market. An ongoing concern, however, is "the painful nonexistence" of a corporate bond market, as relatively high and variable inflation throughout the last decade has not been favorable for developing fixed income markets; the privatized banking system has been very successful in competing for corporate clients; transnational companies have access to foreign resources; and there remain structural problems owing to the size of the market. These points are so convincing that some experts even argue "it is not obvious that there is a need for a domestic-currency-denominated corporate bond market as the country marches into the EMU." In contrast to the corporate bond market, Pfandbrief-style mortgage bonds have been rapidly gaining ground and are likely to remain a competitive investment and financing vehicle with the internationalization of the Hungarian market over the next few years.

In the government bond market, a primary dealer system was established in January 1996 for the purpose of providing more secure basis for the financing of budget deficit, reducing financing costs through market mechanisms, and facilitating the expansion and transparency of the secondary market for government securities. Secondary market trading of government securities may take place on the Budapest Stock Exchange (BSE) or on the OTC market, the latter one mostly through primary dealers or the branch offices of the Treasury.

Chapter 17 on Italy (Vecchiato) provides perspective on the current state of the Italian bond market, including Europe's largest government bond market. Of course, Italy's bond market is dominated by government issues and other bonds issued by some government enterprises (such as Italian Railways). The market involves several participants: the Department of the Treasury as the issuer, the Bank of Italy, the securities regulator CONSOB, the organizer of the regulated electronic secondary market MTS Company as well as primary dealers or so-called specialists in Italian government bonds. Government debt securities include Treasury bills, zero-coupon bonds, floating-rate Treasury certificates and fixed-rate Treasury bonds.

The need to provide market participants with appropriate risk-hedging tools gave rise in 1992 to a market for government bond futures (MIF) and options (MTO). Despite a fast start, both these markets were outpaced by other more important markets especially LIFFE (for short term instruments) and, more recently, EUREX (for long term instruments).

Chapter 18 on the Netherlands (Mentink) introduces us to the change brought by the introduction of the euro on the shape of the Dutch bond market. The market is dominated by government issues, although the amount of corporate bonds issued by Dutch companies increased after the euro introduction. From a Euro area perspective, the Dutch central government is a medium-sized issuer of debt in terms of total amount of debt outstanding.

One area of common ground for issuers and investors is the Amsterdam Stock Exchange (AEX), which has now merged with exchanges in Brussels, Lisbon, and Paris into Euronext, where Dutch government bonds, corporate bonds issued by both domestic and foreign companies, and other types of bonds are all listed. Small and irregular bond trades dominate Euronext Amsterdam, suggesting that retail investors are the main participants in this part of the bond market. In contrast, large institutional investors mainly trade OTC with large investment banks, with government bonds mostly traded via an electronic trading platform that is managed by MTS Amsterdam.

Chapter 19 (Szilagyi) covers the Polish bond market, the largest and one of the most developed in all of Central and Eastern Europe. The dominant segments of the Polish debt market are the Treasury bond and Treasury bill markets, which add up to more than nine tenths of the total outstanding amount. Such disproportions are largely due to the fact that the reestablishment of the bond market itself was initially related to facilitating the management of public debt and macroeconomic stabilization in the early 1990s. It is regrettable, however, that the recent market growth has not been underpinned by adequate qualitative changes. The main defects of the market remain infrastructural and cost-related. Chief among these is the absence of a liquid secondary market, whose establishment is hindered by most domestic debt issues being privately placed because of cost efficiency and less stringent regulatory requirements. The consequent lack of market transparency is demonstrated by the continuingly weak correlation between issuer creditworthiness and risk premia. Foreign investors nonetheless show increasing interest in the market, which is because the market – similarly to the Hungarian and Czech markets – has now become part of the yield convergence play witnessed in the EU before the introduction of the euro.

Trading in publicly issued bonds may take place on the Warsaw Stock Exchange (WSE), the wholesale platform Electronic Treasury Securities Market (ETSM) and the Polish Financial Exchange. Nonetheless, well over 95% of trading in bonds, including exchange-listed bonds, takes place in the nonregulated OTC market, where the main participants are both domestic and foreign banks. This concentration of trading is dictated by higher transaction costs in the regulated markets, associated with the compulsory use of intermediaries, and the possibility in the nonregulated market to conclude transactions using the 1-day transaction settlement procedure, the so-called uncleared transactions, which are partially cleared by the National Depository for Securities (securities), and partially by the transaction participants (liquid funds). The WSE launched its derivatives market in 1998. It trades a number of financial futures contracts, including stock index futures and US dollar and euro exchange rate futures contracts. Interest rate futures have not yet been introduced. Polish Financial Exchange (PFE) offers electronic brokerage services for futures transactions as well as executes spot market trading operations on Treasury bills and bonds, and repo and reverse repo transactions. ETSM is a wholesale electronic trading platform for bulk transactions.

Chapter 20 on Portugal (Szilagyi) asserts that the Portuguese ratio of government debt to GDP is relatively low compared with other markets within the Euro area, which explains the small size of the Portuguese bond market. The convergence of interest rates to the Euro area level and the elimination of currency risk have enhanced the market's international integration, in particular with the European markets. Government debt issued in the single currency has pulled in welcome nonresident investors attracted by the rapidly narrowing but still favorably high spreads of Portuguese paper over comparable German or French issues. Meanwhile, the Public Debt Management Institute (IGCP) has completely revamped its debt management operations in line with EU requirements, which has helped Portugal face-up to increased competition as a government bond player on a pan-European level. The market has enjoyed additional recognition with the inclusion of Portuguese public debt in all major world bond indices. Regrettably, the market's nongovernment segment has failed to go through such transformation. The domestic funds that once sustained the market have now diversified into other Euro area markets which offer better trade-off between risk, liquidity, and pricing and are not subject to Portugal's 20% withholding tax. Domestic bond issuance by Portuguese corporations has promptly eclipsed since the introduction of the euro in 1999, with corporate treasuries resorting to the more liquid mainstream markets in Europe, or issuing CP and rolling them over.

It is notable that since the start of EMU, 75–80% of new Portuguese government issues have been placed through foreign primary dealers each year. It is estimated that more than two thirds of tradable Portuguese government debt is now held by nonresidents, chiefly EMU-based investors, which is one of the highest percentages in the EU. However, in the nongovernment market nonresident holdings are considerably lower, reflecting the pull of more liquid Euro markets for big institutional investors as well as the deterring effect of the withholding tax levied.

In the secondary market for government bonds, more than 70% of the turnover also involves nonresidents. Trades are by and large concentrated to the wholesale Special Public Debt Market or MEDIP, and are modest in the nonregulated OTC market as well as the other regulated markets, operated by the exchange Euronext Lisbon. A growing number of government bonds (OTs) are available for transaction and are actively traded in the pan-European platform EuroMTS, where most benchmarks of eight EU members are traded, attracting large European investors into the market. In the derivatives market, also managed by Euronext, the development of new products is still ongoing. Euronext Lisbon also provides OTC services, including a newly designed repo registration system, which was widened to include securities lending in 1999.

Chapter 21 (Philosophov and Philosophov) provides an overview of the Russian bond market. The foundations of the market were laid shortly after the disintegration of Soviet Union, when in 1993 the government promulgated a decree on the issuance of Treasury bills to attract noninflationary sources to cover its budget deficit. The market took off gradually, but the financial crisis of 1997–1998 led to a temporary shutdown. The market has since been revived, although in terms of volume it has not yet reached its pre-1998 level owing to significant budget surpluses in consecutive years.

The most important government debt instruments include Central Bank of Russia bills (OBR), Treasury bills (GKO), Treasury notes (OFZ), Ministry of Finance bonds, and federal savings bonds (OGSZ). Subfederal and municipal bonds are also issued, although few have passed listing procedures and are traded in the main trading centers, the Russian Trading System (RTS), the Moscow Interbank Currency Exchange (MICEX) and the St. Petersburg Currency Exchange (SPCE). Treasuries as well as municipal and regional securities are placed through auctions. The Central Bank has established a number of trading rules for primary dealers in the Treasury market, and a similar system is now evolving in the municipal debt market.

The most important exchange for the fixed income investor is the Moscow Interbank Currency Exchange (MICEX). The MICEX enables placement and secondary market trading of Treasury securities as well as various regional, municipal, and corporate bonds. There are 1500 remote terminals connected to the central trading depository system at the exchange and over 300 various financial institutions participate in trading.

Western rating agencies currently rate Russian Federation foreign currency obligations and some municipal issuers. The domestic agency, Skate Investor Services, rates local currency obligations issued by municipal and regional issuers.

Chapter 22 on Spain (Pénzes) shows that the Spanish bond market has been rather slow to develop into a fully fledged market, which relates to the fact that Spain's financial system is essentially bank-based and therefore most corporations are largely dependent on bank financing. Since the late 1990s, regulatory changes have greatly encouraged competition in Spain's financial sector and fostered market evolution. However, while stock exchange and derivatives markets have experienced considerable growth, the development of debt markets, and the nongovernment segment of these in particular, continues to lag behind.

The Spanish government bond market is nonetheless one of the most important in Europe, which largely owes to its sheer size. The breakdown of debt by type of security has changed substantially in recent years, reflecting continuing efforts on the part of policymakers to extend the maturity composition of government debt in response to declining interest rates and to replace nonmarketable securities with marketable ones. The other major market segment in Spain is that of Cédulas Hipotecarias or Pfandbrief-style mortgage bonds. The immense popularity of these instruments owes to their liquidity and extremely high credit quality, mostly surpassing that of Spanish government bonds.

The single largest secondary market for Spanish bonds is the unregulated OTC market, whereby trading takes place over the telephone. Trading also occurs in three regulated markets: the Book-Entry Market for public debt, where trading is primarily decentralized but two electronic trading platforms, INFOMEDAS and EuroMTS are also at hand; the AIAF market for corporate debt; and one of the four regional stock exchanges which together comprise a single stock exchange company. The only futures contract available on Spanish public debt is written on a notional 10-year government bond and is available through MEFF, the futures and options market.

Chapter 23 on Switzerland (Kubli) provides a perspective on the Swiss bond market. The market includes federal bonds, corporate and local government bonds, Swiss and foreign convertible and "cum warrants" bonds, Swiss Exchange (SWX) Eurobonds, and foreign currency bonds. The Swiss repo market, bank debentures, and interest rate futures on federal bonds traded at EUREX are further instruments, which are highly interrelated to the bond market. In recent years the issuance of domestic bonds has somewhat declined both in terms of volume and number of issues, the latter also because of the ongoing mergers among the large issuers worldwide. It is notable that as in several countries in the EU, Swiss municipalities have completely stopped issuing bonds of their own, as they now fund themselves commonly through the issuing center of Swiss communities or that of Swiss regional banks. The main investors in Swiss bonds are private investors with Swiss bank accounts followed by institutional investors such as Swiss pension funds and insurance companies, investment funds, and some foreign institutional investors, especially from the EU.

Since the secondary market in Swiss bonds is fully automated at the SWX, there is hardly any interdealer brokerage necessary. There are no official rating agencies head-quartered in Switzerland. However, either Moody's or Standard & Poor's rate about 45% of the foreign debtors. Additionally, banks like UBS, CS Group, and Cantonalbank of Zurich produce credit research reports, providing investors with credit ratings for different Swiss franc issuers. The fully automated trading on the SWX platform for bond trading has the benefit of full transparency and benefits from low transaction costs. Around 63 benchmark bond indices and subindices are published on a regular basis in the market.

Chapter 24 (Bakir and Brown) discusses the Turkish bond market. Turkey first sold government securities through periodic auctions in 1985. Government bonds and Treasury bills began trading on the Istanbul Stock Exchange (ISE) in 1991, and repo/reverse repo transactions began in 1993. The remainder of the decade was a period of rapid development; however, the onset of the recent financial crisis brought the market to a standstill.

The Central Bank of the Republic of Turkey, along with the Treasury, is involved in Turkish debt management. Government debt is predominantly purchased by domestic banks, while the main investors in corporate bonds are investment management funds and individuals; foreign investors have lost all interest in the market for the time being. The issuers of corporate bonds are generally banks, leasing companies, and manufacturing companies. There is no withholding tax on primary market security issues, but secondary market transactions are hit with a Banking and Insurance Transaction tax, which obstructs liquidity in the market.

A primary dealership mechanism has operated in Turkey since May 2000 with the aim of increasing market liquidity. The ISE aims to supply an efficient and transparent secondary market, but conducts only about a quarter of transactions, with the remainder conducted OTC. The ISE is moving to implement a fully computerized trading system, which should increase trading volumes. Some indices are also reported by the ISE for securities with up to 6 months maturity. Clearing and settlement services are provided through Takasbank.

Chapter 25 on the United Kingdom (Skinner) introduces us to the very origins of the UK bond market, a £1.2 million loan of 1694 used to finance a war with France. Over the centuries the bond market has grown in size and complexity as out of fashion securities, such as undated gilts remain outstanding and more modern securities are issued. Today the UK bond market includes gilts or UK sovereign bonds, domestic corporate, foreign corporate, and Euro corporate bonds and ranks as the fourth largest debt market in the world. The largest segment is Euro corporate bond market, partly because London is the center of the Eurobond market and partly because the vast majority of domestic corporations prefer to issue Eurobonds rather than domestic bonds. The second largest is domestic government, which is virtually all central government debt because of the United Kingdom's unitary governmental structure and attractive central government financing that is made available to municipalities. The foreign corporate or bulldog and the domestic corporate bond markets are much smaller representing approximately 10% of the overall sterling bond market.

The London Stock Exchange (LSE) is the only domestic exchange for stocks and bonds in the UK, while the Euronext.Liffe (discussed in detail in Chapter 4) specializes in derivative contracts, including a wide range of bond futures and options contracts. Even though many UK bonds, including all coupon bearing gilts and all gilt strips are listed on the LSE, most trades occur OTC. However, the LSE publishes an official closing price on the daily official list for all bonds listed on the LSE. Electronic trading is widely used and there are a number of electronic settlement systems, most notably CRESTco, which recently merged with Euroclear.

REFERENCES

Committee on the Global Financial System (1999). *How Should We Design Deep and Liquid Markets? The Case of Government Securities*. Basel: BIS.

Committee on the Global Financial System (2000). *Market Liquidity: Research Findings and Selected Policy Implications*. Basel: BIS.

Dimson, E., P. Marsh, and M. Staunton (2002). *Triumph of the Optimists*. Princeton, NJ: Princeton University Press.

European Central Bank (ECB) (2002). *Report on Financial Structures*. Frankfurt: ECB.

Homer, S. and R. Sylla (1996). *A History of Interest Rates*. New Brunswick, NJ: Rutgers University Press.

Kindleberger, C.P. (1984). *A Financial History of Western Europe*. London: George Allen and Unwin.

The Euro Area Bond Market: Integration and Development Under Monetary Union

PETER G. SZILAGYI

2.1 INTRODUCTION

In its publication of 1990 "One Market, One Money" the European Commission (EC) presented its assessment of the economic gains likely to be obtained from the euro in the future member states of Economic and Monetary Union (EMU). Three broad classes of benefits were identified: firstly, the disappearance of exchange rate variability and the reduction of transaction costs in intra-European cross-border transactions should increase microeconomic efficiency; secondly, the more stable macroeconomic environment and the focus on fiscal rectitude and price stability should lead to a growth-oriented macroeconomic environment; and finally, the creation of a large homogeneous financial area should make the Euro area more resilient to external shocks and lead to a currency that could challenge the worldwide status of the US dollar.

Perée and Steinherr (2001) correctly point out that as obvious as it was that the euro would also bring fundamental change to the Euro area's monetary organization, it is extraordinary that the original EC analysis completely disregards the potential efficiency gains to be made in the area's financial organization. But the introduction of the euro is a milestone in the financial integration process in Europe, since the creation of economy and scale and scope and the intensification of capital market competition in the Euro area act as a catalyst to financial efficiency.

Still, the European Union (EU) has come to realize that the success of the EMU also depends on the development of a better financial architecture with special attention given to a full-fledged integrated bond market. Accordingly, it has established the ambitious Financial Services Action Plan (FSAP) to create an efficient and integrated European financial market with a unified legislative framework by 2005, including an integrated securities market by 2003. These efforts are consistent with the conclusion of Levine (1997; 2002) and Thiel (2001) that an efficient financial sector is pivotal for realizing the full growth potential of an economy, which was also emphasized by the EC at the Barcelona EU summit in March 2002.

In the context of financial integration, the integration of the Euro area bond market must be given special attention. The financial systems of the European continent are traditionally bank-based, and the recent literature has often cited the recent superior growth outcomes of the US economy as evidence to the supremacy of more market-based systems. And, even though no indisputable evidence has so far been provided in the bank-based versus market-based debate (see Demigrüc-Kunt and Maksimovic, 2002), it is undeniable that the development of the bond market may yield substantial benefits in bank-based economies as well. In this respect, the European integration process is of particular significance, since the unification

European Fixed Income Markets: Money, Bond and Interest Rate Derivatives. Edited by J.A. Batten,
T.A. Fetherston and P.G. Szilagyi. © 2004 John Wiley & Sons, Ltd. ISBN 0-470-85053-1

of the continent's less developed bond markets with the more developed ones may result in positive spillover effects, which may be instrumental to realizing the EU's key strategic goal set at the Lisbon summit in March 2000 to become "the most competitive and dynamic knowledge-based economy in the world" by 2010.

The single currency environment has indeed brought about fundamental change to the Euro area bond market. The euro and the implementation of the FSAP have worked toward the emergence of an integrated framework for investors and issuers alike, instigating growth and development on a pan-European level in each segment of the market. The integrating powers of the single currency have worked through laying the foundations for a single integrated pool of European investors, which has boosted demand in the market. Market structures are being amalgamated accordingly, which is mirrored in more closely integrated investment and trading possibilities, lower transaction costs, improved price transparency, and growing liquidity. Of course, this process is being further facilitated by the fact that banks, which have historically dominated the financial system of continental Europe, now face increasingly tough competition from the financial market as Europe's traditionally underdeveloped corporate bond sector is making a promising takeoff. This also implies that the Euro area financial system, traditionally described as bank-based, is slowly moving toward becoming more market-based, much like that in the United States.

On the whole, the Euro area bond market is indeed significantly larger and more integrated than ever before. Nonetheless, there remain various ongoing impediments to realizing the full potential benefits of integration and creating a truly unified market. The chief obstacles include the enduring national segmentation of the government bond market, the fragmented nature of trading, clearing, and settlement systems, as well as the complex patchwork of legal and regulatory requirements and nonuniform tax treatment. It must also be noted that the recent market evolution is not solely a result of Monetary Union, but also of various other structural factors currently affecting financial markets, such as technological, regulatory, and demographic developments.

In this chapter, the primary trends and developments observed in the market are identified. The paper is set out as follows: In the next section the theoretical underpinnings of financial integration are outlined, and an overview of the recent financial literature is provided. This is followed by a review of recent trends in the Euro area bond market, including an overview of trends observed in the government and nongovernment bond markets as well as developments in the market infrastructure. Then recent proposals and initiatives for the reduction of market fragmentation are addressed. The final section gives some concluding remarks.

2.2 THEORETICAL UNDERPINNINGS OF FINANCIAL INTEGRATION

The priority assigned by the EU economic reform agenda to financial integration reflects an expectation of significant economic benefits from a single European financial system (EC, 2001). The economic aspects of financial integration are not straightforward, however, since the transmission channels from financial integration to changes in economic performance remain open to debate on both the theoretical and empirical levels. On the whole, it is nonetheless reasonable to conclude that financial development is positively related to economic growth. Specifically, financial integration can be expected to enhance the development of the Euro area financial system, which, in turn, will result in improved economic performance. It is also clear, on the other hand, that financial integration creates economic challenges as well as opportunities. One of these challenges relates to systemic stability, all the more so because evidence suggests that the financial globalization of recent decades has coincided with a higher frequency of international financial crises. Therefore, a major concern in the EU context is that the arrangements for regulation and supervision should be adequate to guarantee stability in a substantially more integrated financial system.

2.2.1 The Finance–Growth Linkage

Theoretical analysis stresses various channels through which an efficient financial system may influence the two fundamental sources of economic growth: capital accumulation and technical progress. The EC (2001) notes that not only does financial system efficiency maximize the opportunities for capital formation, but is also essential for embedding technical advances in the capital stock, thus allowing countries to convert technical development into higher rates of economic growth. This argument has been supported by a growing body of empirical analyses, including Merton and Bodie (1995), Levine (1997), and Levine and Zervos (1998). Levine found that there is even evidence that the level of financial development is a good predictor for future rates of economic growth, capital accumulation, and technical progress.

The design of the financial system has only recently come to be regarded as a determinant of economic growth, since growth theory has traditionally focused on the role of the interest rate as the main financial determinant. This broadening in focus has been associated with increased interest in the existence of information asymmetries within the financial system, whereby it has been found that the financial system's efficient functioning helps reduce the transaction costs that stem from such information asymmetries. Clearly, the more efficiently the financial system can intermediate savings, the more savings are available to support productive investment. In addition, according to the EC (2001) the financial system can also improve investment performance in that (i) it allows for the diversification of risk, which may induce investors to undertake riskier projects and specialized investments; (ii) it allows for an enhanced evaluation and selection of investment projects, thus possibly raising the profitability of investment; and (iii) it allows a larger proportion of savings to be invested in longer term projects, which are typically more productive than shorter term projects.

The above argument minimizes the importance of the debate on the comparative merits of bank- versus market-based financial systems. The bank-based view highlights the positive role for banks in the financial system (Allen and Gale, 2000; Benston and Smith, 1976; Diamond, 1984) and stresses the shortcomings of market-based systems (Bhide, 1993; Boot and Thakor, 1997). In contrast, the market-based view highlights the growth-enhancing role of well-functioning markets (Dinc, 2000; Holmstrom and Tirole, 1993) and stresses problems with banks (Rajan, 1992; Wenger and Kaserer, 1998). The debate between these two competing theories is relegated to the shadows by the financial services view articulated by Merton and Bodie (1995) and Levine (1997, 2002), who conclude that a financial system, irrespective of whether it is bank-based or market-based, can serve as a catalyst to growth in the real sector. A special case of this view is the law and finance view (La Porta et al., 1998), which highlights the role of the legal system in creating a financial sector that promotes growth. As Levine (2002) justly points out, these alternative theories coincide with the outstanding success of the predominately bank-based systems of Germany and Japan over the last 40 years, and the alternate more market-based systems evident in the United States and the United Kingdom. Notwithstanding the success of bank-based systems, however, it is clear that development of viable capital markets, including bond markets, is highly justified in any given financial system.

2.2.2   Financial Integration and Financial Development

Financial integration can be expected to improve economic performance through enhancing the development of the financial system. The EC (2001) points out that it is likely to develop the financial system through two main channels: the exploitation of the scale and scope effects inherent in financial activity and increased competitive pressure on financial intermediaries.

Much of the benefit from the financial integration stems from the increase in the number of actual and potential counterparts for financial transactions. An increase in the breadth and depth of financial markets should allow for a reduction in transaction costs and translate into lower cost of capital for borrowers and higher returns for investors. By expanding the pool of liquidity, financial integration also provides greater scope for diversification and makes possible more efficient risk pricing.

Financial integration also improves the efficiency of intermediation by intensifying the competition among financial intermediaries. Competition eliminates quasirents to intermediaries, maximizes the transmission of savings into investment, and encourages financial innovation. Integration will also likely enhance the competition for funds among borrowers, with spillover effects on management efficiency, innovative capacity, accountability, and transparency. In this way, integration can be expected to spur technical progress, structural change, and may even make the business environment more conducive to growth.

Whatever the benefits of financial integration, however, it may also have important implications for financial stability. The EC (2001) finds that in the Euro area, integration may serve to enhance as well as to reduce stability, as it has implications for the likely causes, nature, and the consequences of any future financial crises. This is of particular significance today, when several of the more recent financial crises, such as the Asian crisis of 1997 and the Russian crisis of 1998, have showed that globalization has increased the scope for cross-border spillovers. The EC specifically states that while the euro has eliminated the possibility of exchange rate collapses within the Euro area, the Euro exchange rate has been far from stable *vis-à-vis* other key currencies, and so exchange rate risk as a potential cause of banking crises is not entirely eliminated. Cross-border activities by financial institutions and international economic and financial linkages in general can also lead to contagion to the domestic financial system. In particular, while integration in principle offers financial institutions increased diversification opportunities, cross-border activities may lead to important foreign currency exposures in the sector, as increased competition may induce institutions to accept a higher risk exposure. And, while financial integration may change the nature of risks to the financial system, it simultaneously makes the job of bank supervisors, which continue to operate at the national level, even more difficult. In this regard, the internationalization of the banking system poses particular challenges and further underlines the explicit need to develop the Euro area bond market to help prevent potential future crises.

2.2.3   Importance and Benefits of an Integrated Bond Market

Given that empirical research has only recently begun on the broader relationship between financial integration and economic growth, it is not surprising that very little is known about the impact of bond market integration on economic performance. It is nonetheless reasonable to conclude that bond market financing brings advantages in broad economic terms. Takagi (2002) argues that developed bond markets should lower the average cost of external finance by exposing the bank to competition, help build a more efficient capital structure by managing agency costs, provide better managing control in the corporation since capital markets exert discipline on management, improve the efficiency of resource allocation by providing price signals for investment decisions, and encourage the financing of innovation. Schinasi and Smith (1998) add that effective securities markets are capable of pricing financial risks at least as well as banks, while distributing financial risks and potential losses more widely, if not also more efficiently. Sharma (2001) points out that developed bond markets should reduce maturity mismatches, occurring as a result of corporations undertaking short term loans to finance longer term projects, thus reducing interest rate exposure. And, Hakansson (1999) argues that a richness of available securities tends to enhance economic welfare and "the market forces at work on the wide array of bond prices" are likely to have a spillover effect on the health of the banking system as well.

From the point of view of both investors and issuers, as discussed by the EC (2002a), bond financing can combine some of the features of equity markets and bank loans. For investors, a bond represents an asset whose yield typically exceeds the bank deposit rate and whose value, unlike the dividend on equity, is largely independent of the issuer's financial performance. Moreover, holding a bond implies a very different risk pattern to that associated with holding equity, since it is exposed to only two risks: inflation and issuer default. The latter risk is also asymmetric, as there is a high probability that the issuer pays back and a small probability of total loss if the issuer fails. These specific features of bonds make them an attractive vehicle for longer term investment for pension funds, insurance companies, and other financial intermediaries.

For issuers, bonds provide an alternative access to financing, particularly of large investment projects that may exceed the lending capacity of an individual bank. In this sense, the issuance of bonds is an alternative to using syndicated loans, but one where the issuer is less dependent on the lending policies of the banks and has more direct access to investors, which may reduce intermediation costs. On the other end, bond issuance is also an alternative to equity financing, where the main differences not only relate to ownership rights but also to claims on income and assets, maturity, and fiscal treatment.

So, what makes a bond market efficient in delivering these benefits to investors, issuers, and the economy as a whole? The EC (2002a) argues that apart from more general considerations such as fiscal neutrality and legal certainty, the efficient functioning of a bond market requires (i) size, (ii) breadth (number of issuers), and (iii) depth (size of issues). These three features combine to provide market liquidity, which determines the ease and costs of trading a bond and so allows the bond market to fulfill the various functions outlined above. In this context, the introduction of the euro was of particular significance in the Euro area, as it offered the potential to aggregate the various national bond markets into a larger and more liquid pan-European market.

2.3 BOND MARKET DEVELOPMENT UNDER MONETARY UNION

Prior to the introduction of the euro, some Euro area member states had effective and, in some parts of the yield curve, deep and liquid bond markets. These markets, as the International Monetary Fund [IMF] (2001) points out, played important parts in facilitating effective private finance, either in – albeit small – private national securities markets or in private national banking and asset (pension) management. The launch of the single currency was nonetheless heralded as an exceptional opportunity for the development of bond markets in Europe. Market participants had immense expectations, including the following: (i) the euro would bring together a vast pool of capital that once had been fragmented into disparate currencies; (ii) it would create one large market for borrowers to tap; (iii) the issuance of cross-border securities would become simpler and less risky, while transaction costs would be substantially reduced; and (iv) uniform monetary policy would foster depth, breadth, and liquidity in financial markets, resulting in more efficient patterns of investment and lowering the cost of capital (Holder *et al.*, 2001).

In line with these high expectations, the Euro area bond market has indeed managed to firmly establish itself as the second largest in the world after the US market. The single currency environment and the implementation of the EU's ambitious FSAP aimed at creating an efficient and integrated European financial market with a unified legislative framework, have benefited investors and issuers alike, instigating growth and development on a pan-European level. The integrating powers of the euro have laid the foundations for a single pool of European investors by encouraging them to adopt a more pan-European strategy and increasing their holdings of foreign assets, while also diversifying into new asset classes. Increased demand has shaped market supply accordingly, as reflected in the recent changes in issuance activity in the Euro area.

2.3.1   Changes in Investor Behavior

The main driving force behind market development has been the increasingly intense and diverse investor appetite for Euro area debt under Monetary Union. This is not surprising given that the single currency environment has indisputably benefited both resident and nonresident investors. Nonresidents have profited from enhanced cost efficiency through simpler currency risk hedging and the creation of economy of scale. The range of benefits has been most clear-cut for resident investors, however, as argued by London Economics (2002) in their report to ECOFIN, the council of the EU's economic and finance ministers. These benefits include

- lower transaction costs, which allow investors to rebalance their portfolios more effectively;
- wider possibilities for risk diversification, which help increase the risk-adjusted rate of return of a given portfolio;
- increased price transparency, which reduces the perceived risk of asset holdings; and
- financial innovation stemming from intense competition, which may create more highly tailored and attractive financial products.

Institutional investors have promptly begun to extract these benefits through adjusting their portfolio management practices. Accordingly, two major trends have been observed in portfolio management practices: (i) that of geographical diversification, whereby investors have been diversifying from their perspective national markets into other EMU markets and (ii) that of diversification into new asset classes, namely nongovernment bonds and structured instruments.

While home-biased investors continue to stick mainly to investing in their own national markets, the single currency environment has indeed spurred cross-border investor diversification within the Euro area. London Economics (2002) reports that data available on bond subscriptions shows a wide investor base for large, liquid Euro issues by governments, agencies, or well-known corporate borrowers. For less-known or small-small issues, which were formerly sold only nationally or even regionally, the investor base has also become more diversified. The introduction of the euro has supported this process in two ways: it removed currency risk as well as certain legal barriers associated with investing in foreign currency. Such legal barriers were typically related to currency-matching requirements imposed on pension funds and insurance companies, but were in effect eliminated overnight with the disappearance of national currencies.

It nonetheless has to be said that the breakdown of investor home bias has been nowhere near as swift in the Euro area as formerly anticipated. As Santillan *et al.* (2000) point out, this is because for resident investors the benefits of diversifying into other Euro markets remain rather narrow. Indeed, administrative costs, such as those entailed when acquiring country-specific technical and legal information, are often prohibitive. On the other hand, yields to be potentially earned are generally low and homogeneous, given that all Euro area governments now enjoy very high credit ratings. With the elimination of foreign exchange risk, currency-driven investment strategies are now also impracticable within the Euro area, taking further interest out of the market. These conditions are pushing demand into the higher yielding alternative markets of the immediate EU candidates such as Poland, Hungary, and the Czech Republic, which are now also part of the same yield convergence play that was observed in the Euro area itself in the years preceding Monetary Union.

It is this homogeneity of the government bond market that has prompted portfolio managers to increasingly diversify into new, higher yielding asset classes. The investment criterion of "country creditworthiness" has now been abandoned under Monetary Union, and so investors now focus on the characteristics of individual borrowers rather than their nationality. The combined effect of these factors has boosted the already buoyant attitude of institutional investors, generating great demand for nongovernment debt instruments, discussed later in this chapter. This process has been strengthened by the fact that an increasing share of investors now gain expertise in credit risk evaluation, which appears to be dissolving the concerns investors may have had in the past with investing in nongovernment debt.

These changes in investor behavior became immediately evident in many aspects of issuance activity in the Euro area bond market. The most important of these effects were a stronger trend in overall issuing activity, a growing share of private relative to public issuance, and an increase in activity by foreign issuers (see Figure 2.1). These trends, discussed in the following two sections, may have recently slowed due to declining growth in the world economy, but they nonetheless designate a long term direction for market development in the Euro area.

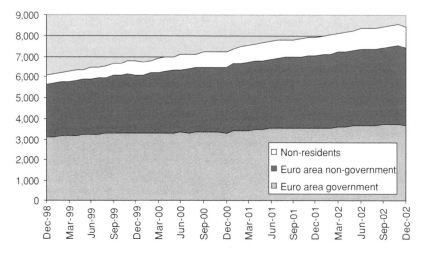

Figure 2.1 Euro-denominated debt securities by residency and sector of issuer (outstanding amount, euro billions).
Source: ECB Monthly Bulletin, March 2003. Copyright © European Central Bank, Frankfurt am Main, Germany. Reproduced with permission.

2.3.2   Trends in the Government Bond Market

The government bond market has traditionally been the dominant segment of the Euro area bond market. The removal of the captive investor base most governments enjoyed prior to Monetary Union has brought about a much more competitive environment in the marketplace, since national treasuries have had no choice but to improve the attractiveness of their securities. Competition has been greatly intensified by the recent limited growth in terms of market size, owing to the budgetary constraints imposed on member states in the Stability and Growth Pact. To that extent, the market has now come to be compared to the US municipal bond market in that it has 12 debt issuers that compete by offering either stable credit and deep liquidity or a slight interest premium (Zwick, 2002).

While comparisons can indeed be drawn between the US municipal bond market and the Euro area government bond market, there can be no question that the latter is much more highly integrated (see Dunne *et al.*, 2002). Under Monetary Union, there has been considerable convergence among countries in the structure and maturities of government debt. The share of foreign-currency debt has fallen to negligible levels, largely due to the redenomination into euros of debt formerly denominated in the national currencies. Privately placed loans have disappeared, and there is an almost complete reliance on marketable instruments. Secondary markets have become deeper and more efficient, owing to each country striving to achieve liquid benchmark-size issues.

Notwithstanding these undisputed improvements, there remain impediments to market integration and, most crucially, the full fungibility of debt issues that cannot be overlooked. The IMF (2001) lists three main sources of fragmentation. Firstly, integration has not yet gone so far as to give identical yields on different countries' securities of the same characteristics, even though credit risks are highly similar across the major countries, as evident in their credit ratings and their relatively tight intercountry spreads. This segmentation of credit risk is a matter of international law: Article 103 of the EU Treaty – the so-called "no bailout" clause – states that each EU member is responsible for its own debt and prohibits member states from being liable for other member states. Secondly, national competition, rather than coordination and cooperation, among individual member states to capture market shares and thereby achieve their debt as the Euro area benchmark preserves the fragmentation of liquidity along national lines, and as a result no uniform Euro area benchmark yield curve has been able to emerge, preventing the capturing of some of the potential gains of full integration. Finally, there also remain various structural discrepancies. For example, the euro has not brought unification of tax structures, accounting rules, settlement systems, market conventions, or issuing procedures.

2.3.2.1   Trends in Market Size

The market for the euro-denominated securities of Euro area governments, with an outstanding amount of €3689 billion in January 2003, is comparable in size to the US Treasury market. Figure 2.1 showed that the growth of market supply fell significantly in the years preceding Monetary Union, and market activity remained moderate until 2001 relative to rates recorded even in 1996. This is not unlike the situation in the United States where continual budgetary surpluses in the 1990s substantially reduced the Federal Government's funding needs. In the Euro area, this fiscal discipline is no longer an autonomous matter, but is governed by the Stability and Growth Pact contained within the Maastricht Treaty. The Pact states that EMU members must endeavor to achieve balanced budgets in the medium term, although

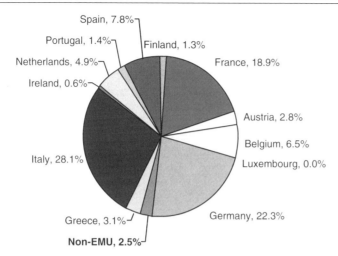

Figure 2.2 Breakdown of the euro-denominated government debt securities market (as of January 2003). *Source*: European Central Bank. Copyright © European Central Bank, Frankfurt am Main, Germany. Reproduced with permission.

deficits of up to 3% of gross domestic products are permissible during economic downswings. Accordingly, member states, such as Italy and Belgium, previously running large budget deficits financed by domestic debt issues had to duly curb their spending.

Until 2001, these self-imposed budgetary restrictions were generally complied with, assisted by cyclical factors as well as exceptional budget revenues. However, conformity has not been fully unqualified in recent years, or rather it has been interpreted with some flexibility by various member states, most notably Germany, France, and Portugal. While half of the countries posted surpluses in 2001, almost all reported deficits in 2002, with the average deficit ratio hitting 2.2% in the Euro area. The impact of these imbalances has been certainly felt in the market as the growth of issuance has begun to rise again.

A breakdown of the Euro government debt market is provided in Figure 2.2. The figure shows that the market is broadly dominated by the major Euro area borrowers. Reflecting both the relative sizes of the economy and the level of indebtedness of each government, the six largest national government debt segments are, in this order, those of Italy, Germany, France, Spain, Belgium, and the Netherlands, with these six issuers together representing 89% of the market. The market segment for securities issued by non-EMU members is dominated by those EU states that opted out of Monetary Union, i.e., the United Kingdom, Sweden, and Denmark. A growing number of emerging market governments have also appeared on the market, although issuance by Latin American sovereigns, which previously dominated this niche of the market, has suffered a serious setback since Argentina's debt default.

2.3.2.2 *Trends in Yield Development*

Although to a varying extent, Monetary Union has brought down borrowing costs for Euro area governments. The irrevocable fixing of currency parities eliminated the currency-related premia charged by resident investors, which in turn tightened intercountry spreads to historically low levels. It was widely believed that these spreads would further tighten due to the expectation

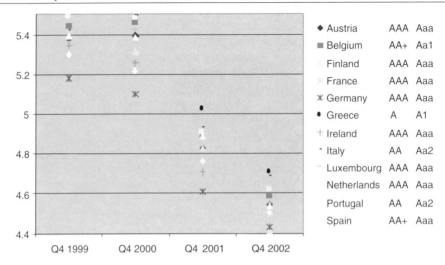

Figure 2.3 Yield spreads across Euro area sovereign debt issuers (average 10-year benchmark; percent). Standard & Poor's and Moody's long term local currency credit ratings (as of 25 March 2003). Greece joined the Euro area in 2001. No data quoted for Luxembourg in 2001 and 2002. Data in European Commission, *Quarterly Notes on the Euro-Denominated Bond Markets*, various issues.
Source: Bloomberg; Thomson Financial Datastream; Standard and Poor's; Moody's Investor Service ⓒ European Communities, 1995–2003. Reproduced with permission.

that the spread components reflecting credit and liquidity risk would also shrink. Perceived differences in credit risk were expected to lessen due to the strengthening in the fiscal positions of member states as a result of the Stability and Growth Pact. Liquidity concerns were played down due to expectations that issuers would boost issue sizes by permanently concentrating issuance on a limited number of benchmark issues.

These expectations have only partly been met. Yields have indeed converged substantially, especially when compared with the yield differentials of up to 200 basis points recorded even in 1997. However, there still remain significant intercountry spreads in the Euro area, as apparent in Figure 2.3. Blanco (2001) even showed that yield spreads over German bonds (so-called Bunds), at the time the lowest yielding securities in the Euro area, had actually widened between 1999 and 2001. Blanco concluded that investors are not yet entirely impartial to credit risk and liquidity when pricing two bonds from two different Euro area countries, for reasons that reflect a still incomplete integration. This conclusion continues to hold despite the fact that spreads have narrowed significantly since then.

As mentioned earlier, this incomplete integration in the market is largely because member states continue to primarily compete, rather than cooperate. As specifically pointed out by the EC (2002c), noncredit risk factors such as liquidity premiums could be significantly reduced by addressing residual fragmentation in a cooperative manner. Of course, credit risk differentials would remain to the extent that member states had different budgetary positions.

2.3.2.3   Changes in Issuance Strategies

In the face of stiff competition under Monetary Union, the governments of member states have been pushing hard to improve the attractiveness of their securities. Their primary aim has been to increase the liquidity of their instruments, which has provided a major impetus for restructuring and innovation in the market. Measures have included the increasing of issue sizes, the overhaul of issuance procedures, and the creation of official debt management agencies. Several initiatives (discussed later on) have also been taken to improve the market structure, including the promotion of electronic trading platforms and derivatives exchanges as well as the establishment of official repo windows and/or treasury reopening facilities.

Increase in Issue Size

Euro area governments began their search for liquidity amid the universal reduction in funding needs of the late 1990s, which prevented them from simply increasing their issuance to increase market depth. As a result, they had to consolidate their issuance. Large issuers continued to issue bonds across the maturity spectrum to maintain a comprehensive and liquid yield curve, but they issued larger volumes at fewer maturities. Under increasing competitive pressure, this practice has been broadly upheld. The determination and success of policymakers is clearly shown by the emergence of individual bond issues comparable to US Treasury benchmarks: benchmark government bonds of Germany, France, and Italy now exceed €20 billion, while Spanish issues exceeds €16 billion.

   Smaller issuers with limited borrowing requirements have been unable to match these issue sizes. They have nonetheless taken steps to improve the liquidity of their securities by concentrating issuance activity on a smaller number of benchmark instruments. To reduce the number of bonds and consolidate them into larger issues, these issuers have regularly applied buyback and bond-switching techniques, some of which have now been adopted by all Euro area member states with the notable exception of Germany. A substantial benefit of this strategy is that those issues that reach the minimum volume of €5 billion become eligible for trading in EuroMTS, a wholesale electronic trading platform that now accounts for up to half of all bond transactions in the European market. Ireland provides one of the most striking examples of these efforts: In 1999, it exchanged nearly all of its government bonds quoted on the stock exchange for new benchmarks of 3-, 5-, 10-, and 16-year maturity.

   In some cases, in order to make up for the reduced flexibility of their national markets, governments have also resorted to issuing euro-denominated Euro commercial paper and Euro medium term notes, usually placed in international offshore centers, chiefly London. The advantages these offshore centers provide over some of the domestic markets are notable, including a deep and wide market as well as lower documentation costs. Countries that have made use of these programs include Portugal, Ireland, Belgium, and Italy, as well as the non-Euro area members of Denmark and Sweden.

Changes of Issuance Procedures

Some of the recent changes in issuance procedures again tend to reflect the particular challenges imposed on individual issuers by competition under Monetary Union. Smaller countries have aimed to compensate for the loss of their captive domestic investor base by launching underwritten, syndicated bond issues instead of full-fledged auctions. These issuers, including Austria, Finland, Greece, and Portugal, have more than made up for the additional costs of syndication through the tighter pricing that resulted by improved liquidity. Even a larger issuer, Belgium has now adopted syndication to front-load new lines, even though it uses regular auctions to increase their outstanding amount subsequently.

As part of the search for liquidity, individual countries have also generally become much more transparent in their issuing policies. Member states now preannounce issue calendars and hold regular reopenings of outstanding lines. In Germany, for example, as a complement to the quarterly issuance calendar, a preview of issuance, redemption, and interest payments for the whole calendar year is also published. Primary dealer groups have also been expanded and internationalized through the inclusion of nonresident banks, chiefly from other member states (with the sole exception of Germany, which of course does not have a primary dealer system).

Aside from competing to increase the liquidity of their respective securities, member states have made some efforts to coordinate their procedures with a view to achieving positive externalities; although as has been noted, these efforts have been largely insufficient. Changes include the harmonization of market conventions, such as the computation of yields and the introduction of a single trading calendar (Trans-European Automated Real-Time Gross Settlement Express Transfer System – TARGET), which however is still not exclusively applied. More increased coordination could apply technical aspects of issuance only and include common issuance calendars, identical coupons and maturity dates and a common primary dealership system, where membership, terms of remuneration and identical quote size, bid/ask spreads, common real-time clearing, and settlement system would be standardized. So far, only unilateral measures of this type have been taken, such as the recent issuance of a 10-year bond by Austria with conditions identical to those of the German Bund of the same maturity.

Finally, one must not overlook the huge impact technological progress has had on issuance procedures in recent years. Belgium, Finland, France, and Portugal now resort to fully electronic tender systems. In the same vein, several issuers, including Finland, Italy, Portugal, and Spain have undertaken "e-placements." Technological innovation has also improved the funding policy communications of issuers, increasing market transparency and predictability. The various means of communication distributed over the internet include the preannounced auction calendars, annual reports, and periodical bulletins.

2.3.2.4 Institutional Structure of Public Debt Management

To respond more effectively to the new competitive environment, some governments have also overhauled the institutional structure of their public debt management. As part of their efforts, they have tended to set up partly market-oriented debt management agencies, which now provide an unambiguous framework for decision-making, responsibility allocation, and supervision. France Trésor was hence awarded the status of debt agency with direct accountability to the Director of the Treasury and more active management capabilities. Germany also outsourced its debt management operations to the German Federal Republic Finance Agency.

Galati and Tsatsaronis (2001) note that there appears to be little chance for the establishment of a multilateral agency that would issue debt on behalf of all EMU members. A proposal suggesting just that was met with considerable skepticism in 1999, since such a scheme would imply some form of collective responsibility for national debts, a notion that runs contrary to aforementioned Article 103 of the EU Treaty. Again, cooperating in a less formal way through fully coordinating issuance could go some way toward achieving the benefits such a multilateral agency would provide.

2.3.3 Trends in the Nongovernment Bond Market

One of the more prominent effects of the advent of the euro, coupled with the financial and technological innovation of recent years, has been a shift in the issuance of bonds from public to private borrowers in the Euro area. This trend was interrupted in 2002 due to more difficult market access conditions for nongovernment issuers as well as increased government financing needs. Nonetheless, nongovernment debt now comprises about half of total bond issuance in the Euro area, average maturities have lengthened, and issue sizes have increased with tranches above €1 billion now being commonplace. The reduction in issuance is also likely to be only a temporary, cyclical phenomenon, since it is reasonable to expect that as the economy recovers, liquidity requirements increase and confidence in the private sector will be rebuilt (London Economics, 2002).

On the whole, the market nonetheless remains relatively underdeveloped compared to that in the United States. This is largely because in continental Europe the custom of bond financing by nongovernment borrowers is nowhere near as deeply rooted in the financial system as it is in the United States. The most notable deficiency of the market remains its limited scope for holding noninvestment grade "high-yield" or "junk" bonds. As in other nongovernment bond markets in general, trading frequency is low and trading costs are high, with the notable exception of a limited number of benchmark issues and the highly liquid Pfandbriefe. This relegates nongovernment instruments to being traded over-the-counter rather than in exchanges, keeping price transparency low in the market.

2.3.3.1   Trends in Market Size

The recent explosive growth of the nongovernment bond market is perhaps the best example of how the euro is acting as a catalyst of change. The prospect of accessing a pan-European capital market through a single bond issue, thus reducing funding costs without generating currency risk, has attracted resident and nonresident issuers alike. And while nonresidents have been more measured in their response, resident borrowers have increased their net issuance severalfold compared with levels previously recorded in the legacy currencies. According to the European Central Bank (ECB) securities database, the outstanding amount of euro-denominated nonsovereign bond markets was €4742 billion at the end of 2002, which compares with €3851.8 billion in 2000 and just €2882.8 billion in 1998.

The single currency environment is not the only factor to have provided a major impetus to market activity. Until recently, also helping was the fact that the relative supply of government securities was on the decline, which boosted investor demand for nongovernment debt. The increase in demand was universal for all securities, including not only familiar corporate and financial bonds, as well as Pfandbriefe, but also high-yield junk bonds and, to an increasing extent, structured products such as asset-backed securities (ABS). Initially, investor attitude was particularly upbeat because growth took off amid the benign economic climate of the late 1990s. The first wave of bonds issued in the single currency was greeted positively by any standard, as judged by investor reception and favorable pricing, which gave the nascent euro-denominated market a momentum that carried it to a new higher level.

2.3.3.2   Types of Instruments

While analyses of the nongovernment bond market often concentrate on the nonfinancial corporate segment, it is useful to recall that the largest segment in the nongovernment bond market is in fact the segment of financial bonds, i.e., bonds issued by financial institutions. The domination of these instruments is fairly homogeneous across all countries of the Euro area despite a moderate decline in their market share, confirming the importance of bank finance in continental Europe. Specific characteristics of financial issuance are a high share (40–50% of

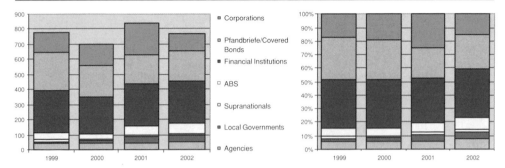

Figure 2.4 Issuance in the euro-denominated nongovernment bond market (in euro billions).
Source: Commission Services. In: European Commission (2002), *Quarterly Notes on the Euro-Denominated Bond Markets* 47. © European Communities, 1995–2003. Reproduced with permission.

total issuance) of floating-rate bonds and small- or medium-sized issues. The relative stability of these instruments is reflected in their high average credit quality.

Many innovations in the nongovernment market segment are also attributed to financial institutions. Such an innovation is the Europe-wide apparition of Pfandbrief-style mortgage bonds, such as Obligations Foncieres in France and Cédulas Hipotecarias in Spain. The attention Pfandbriefe have attracted in the European context has been motivated by several factors – not only are they proven instruments with very high credit ratings, but also the only nongovernment debt securities that can offer liquidity similar to that of government bonds. Surprisingly though, issuance in Pfandbriefe has slowed since 1999, which implies a break with the dynamic growth trend observed in this segment in the 1990s (see Figure 2.4).

A segment that is still relatively new to the Euro area is asset-backed securities. These are securities backed by assets other than mortgages, such as accounts receivable, auto loans, or home equity loans, and are an attractive alternative funding source especially for financial institutions and corporations. The ABS segment has shown impressive growth since the mid-1990s: new issuance amounted to only €8 billion even in 1995 but reached as much as €60 billion in 2001. Like Pfandbriefe, ABS are typically long term instruments with extremely high credit ratings but with floating-rate coupons.

The market for corporate bonds has expanded substantially in recent years. Since 1985, the number of rated corporate bond issuers has grown at a 25% annualized rate as disintermediation, securitization, and an original-issue speculative-grade bond market have developed in Europe. Issuance was recently boosted by those corporations that actively participated in the global wave of merger and acquisitions and hence were in great need of a flexible and inexpensive means of financing. The strategic investments undertaken in the telecommunications sector, underscoring in particular the aggressive competition for third generation mobile network licenses in some member states, also generated a healthy supply of bonds. Notably, not only was the market able to absorb the recent massive issues of telecommunications operators, but it also overcame the subsequent sudden downgrading of telecommunications issuers' credit ratings without encountering any major difficulties. Although issuance by these companies has now fallen sharply, other sectors such as utilities and transportation have in part made up for the loss of activity in this segment. Overall, however, issuance of corporate bonds was subdued in 2002, reflecting the fact that this segment has on average the lowest credit ratings and so is relatively vulnerable to the deterioration of economic conditions.

In terms of the quality of corporate bonds, there still remains a sizeable difference between the Euro area and the United States. Most notably, EC data shows that despite strong growth over the past decade, speculative-grade (lower than BBB) issuers still account for less than 10% of Euro area issues, compared with more than 40% in the United States. This is in large part because while in the United States even speculative-grade small- to medium-sized businesses get themselves rated, a similar rating culture has not yet taken root in Europe. As it is now becoming more common for European companies to have themselves assessed by a rating agency, it is likely that the share of investment grade issues will decline in the next few years, despite the fact that convincing companies that have long relied on bank loans and other short term financing to issue junk bonds remains a challenge. That said, accounting scandals and the downgrading of established companies have left their mark on investors' risk appetite, but as institutional and attitudinal barriers are overcome, investor demand for junk bonds should altogether continue to grow. An example is the fact that currently many institutions that invest public funds must still obtain permission from regulators to buy high-yield bonds, which obviously restrains demand. Also, many European investment firms lack adequate corporate credit research capabilities, having spent decades focusing mainly on sovereign risk, which discourages investment on their part in the high-yield segment.

Finally, the Euro area market has another three segments that have attracted fairly little attention recently. While supranational bonds had traditionally enjoyed a privileged position prior to Monetary Union owing to their high credit ratings and generally large volumes, they seem to have lost some ground because of strong competition. The AAA-rated European Investment Bank has remained a particularly strong issuer, seeking to create a liquid yield curve of benchmark bonds of up to €5 billion each as an alternative to European government debt in selected maturities. The segment of agency bonds, which are subject to those conditions applicable to government bonds, has shown moderate increase, with Freddie Mac, Kreditanstalt für Wiederaufbrau (KfW), and Bank Nederlandse Gemeenten launching important programs recently. The segment that has experienced the most spectacular growth is that of local bonds, largely owing to a trend of political decentralization across the Euro area, which also involves the transfer of budgetary policies toward local authorities. However, the issuance of these instruments – like that of government bonds – is expected to remain at reasonable levels, since local authorities are as much obliged to adhere to the financial criteria set out in the Stability and Growth Pact as are central governments.

2.3.3.3 Place of Issuance

It appears that Euro area borrowers often prefer issuing euro-denominated bonds offshore. This stems from the fact that the concept of a pan-European domestic bond market does not yet exist; therefore, issuers that try to reach the widest investor base possible tend to resort to the issuance of Eurobonds. This assumption, it appears, is more relevant for corporate bonds than for financial bonds, because for the issuance of the latter domestic regulations, such as the existence of a legal framework for the issuance of Pfandbriefe, remain crucial.

The undisputed offshore center for euro-denominated issuance is London, with the city attracting more than half of all issues. As a location, Luxembourg has also become increasingly popular in recent years, and is now one of the preferred locations for not only the custody of offshore corporate bonds but also German domestic issues. This underlines that the market is no longer merely a juxtaposition of national markets but, from this specific point of view, an integrated market. Again, the same is less true for bonds issued by financial institutions.

2.3.3.4   Nonresident Issuers

Although resident borrowers continue to dominate issuance in the Euro area, nonresidents have been increasingly active in the integrated market at the end of 2002. Nonresidents accounted for more than 12% of the total outstanding amount, or €1051 billion, of euro-denominated debt, which compares with just 7% at the time the euro was introduced. As has been noted earlier, €93 billion of this amount has been issued by non-EMU sovereigns, yet it is the buoyant issuance activity by nonsovereigns that deserves most attention. The fact that nonsovereign issuance has gained such momentum largely reflects the emergence of the euro as the second most important currency for international bond issuance behind the US dollar. US issuers have been particularly active in the market – despite the risk stemming from the volatility of the euro – not only because the agency Freddie Mac launched a benchmark issue in 2000 but also because of the regular issuance by US corporations.

The issuance patterns of nonresident issuers differ quite markedly from those of resident borrowers. One natural difference is that financial bonds do not dominate nonresident issuance to the same extent. In part, this difference reflects the relatively higher weight of nonbank finance against bank finance outside continental Europe, chiefly in the United States and the United Kingdom. Standard asset-liability management by banks also explains why issuance in euro by foreign banks should be relatively less pronounced than issuance by domestic banks.

2.3.4   Developments in Market Structure

Policies of the EU aimed at integrating European financial markets predate the introduction of the euro. Therefore, within such an institutional setting the introduction of the single currency may have been less of an institutional breakthrough. The euro, supported by enhancements in information technology, has nonetheless accelerated the process of harmonization and consolidation of national securities markets. This is reshaping the entire landscape of the trading, clearing and settlement industries, and supporting repo and derivatives markets in the Euro area. This is of course pivotal to ensuring the creation of a single market and increasing the efficiency of the financial sector. All the more so, because the liberalization of capital movements, the innovation and standardization of financial products as well as the international location of market participants have increased the volume of cross-border activities, with investors requiring an increasingly broad range of highly efficient and cost-effective trading and posttrading services.

Nonetheless, integration has not yet gone so far as to disentangle the fragmentation of market infrastructures along national lines. Unified platforms for debt trading such as EuroMTS and BrokerTec have proliferated, but a unified secondary market for trading is long way off, which fragments Euro liquidity in national markets. Moreover, while the unsecured Euro area money market is supported by the smoothly functioning TARGET payments system, securities and repo markets continue to rely on a fragmented network of national and cross-border securities settlement systems (SSS) and a patchwork of legal and regulatory requirements. Market rules and practices as well as nonuniform tax treatment further complicate transactions and hedging cross-market.

2.3.4.1   Integration in the Money Market

A critical first step in bond market development is the creation of a well-functioning money market. Money market instruments facilitate cash and risk management as well as position financing for both corporations and, more importantly, for banks, brokers, dealers, and institutional investors. The money market prices liquidity, which is a benchmark for pricing any fixed income instrument, and assists the development of markets for forward as well as spot interest rates. Forward rate liquidity is essential for the arbitrage-free pricing of a host of over-the-counter (OTC) derivative instruments, including forward rate agreements and interest rate swaps, as well as exchange-traded interest rate futures and options contracts.

In the Euro area money market, the introduction of a single monetary policy has ensured substantial integration. With ECB monetary operations being conducted exclusively in the single currency, the market has functioned more or less smoothly under Monetary Union. The degree of integration nonetheless varies across the different segments. In the market for unsecured interbank deposits, integration is complete and there is virtually full convergence in very short term interest rates. The high degree of convergence in these rates reflects the full acceptance of EONIA (Euro Overnight Index Average) and EURIBOR (Euro Inter-Bank Offer Rate) as uniform price references by operators. Convergence has also been helped by the efficient distribution of liquidity across the Euro area, as reflected in the high proportion (about 60%) of cross-border transactions in the total interbank activity of the largest market participants, as reported by the ECB (2001b).

In a similar manner, the Euro area derivatives market is also highly integrated. The cross-border market for Euro interest rate swaps has expanded sharply since the introduction of the euro, and the high degree of market integration is reflected in very narrow bid/ask spreads and relatively large issue sizes. Activity in other derivatives markets has also increased, with EURIBOR-based futures contracts displacing all futures contracts in legacy currencies that existed before Monetary Union.

Regrettably, the secured money market segment, including the segment for private repo transactions, remains considerably less integrated, however. The high level of fragmentation in the repo market is particularly obstructive to bond market integration in the Euro area, since the present infrastructure is unable to support liquidity on a pan-European level. The continued fragmentation reflects difficulties in the cross-border use of collateral mainly because of national differences in market practices and regulation as well as the applicable tax and legal treatments. These national differences, reflected in segmented national-based market infrastructures, can create important practical difficulties in cross-border clearing and settlement.

2.3.4.2 Pricing Benchmarks

One feature of the Euro area market that has attracted a lot of attention is the absence of a uniform benchmark yield curve for government securities. Instead, the larger member states have been competing aggressively to become the benchmark at certain maturities of the yield curve in a bid to capitalize on the cost advantage and other potential advantages that are associated with being the benchmark. German Bunds have now emerged as the 5- and 10-year benchmarks for the Euro area, while at shorter maturities investors tend to use French price references.

The emergence of German and French as well as, to a lesser extent, Italian securities as the benchmarks in certain segments of the yield curve is natural, as these states have gathered the three main liquidity pools of the Euro area government bond market (see Figure 2.2). The reason why no uniform benchmark yield curve has thus far emerged, however, is that each of these pools is simply too modest in size relative to the overall pan-European activity. As the IMF (2001) points out, no one of these pools can fulfill all pricing, hedging, investment, collateral, and liquidity needs in the way the US treasury market has served for dollar-based transactions. It also remains to be seen whether one vehicle will become the preferred safe haven, an essential function of benchmark securities, if a pan-European liquidity and credit crisis occurs.

The financial market consequence of the fragmentation of the yield curve is that liquidity at specific maturities is reduced relative to what it would be with a unified market. The IMF (2001) points out that the effective supply of liquid benchmark bonds at, say, the 10-year maturity is not the sum of 10-year issues by all governments, because each bond is not fully fungible with those of other issuers. The effective supply at some maturities is limited enough that even at the 10-year maturity, dominated by the highly liquid German Bund of issue sizes up to €25 billion, fragmentation of liquidity has been associated with adverse market events, such as squeezes.

Perée and Steinherr (2001) demonstrate that for the pricing of nongovernment debt, the absence of a single clearly defined government benchmark reference is not necessarily a problem in a practical sense. While actual pricing and hedging for sovereign borrowers is based on German, French, or Italian government bonds, nongovernment issues are priced-off the interest rate swap rate, which provides a liquid and homogeneous reference for pricing. The depth of the swap market has been enhanced by the very growth in issuance of nongovernment bonds, and especially corporate bonds, since corporate issuers often make use of swaps to convert fixed-rate liabilities into floating-rate ones. Blanco (2001) holds that interest rate swaps may even be better instruments for pricing than are benchmark government bonds, having found that between 1999 and 2001 yields on 10-year corporate bonds showed higher correlation with swaps of corresponding maturity than with benchmark government bonds.

Of course, nongovernment alternatives, such as swaps, can indeed be used to substitute for some of the functions of liquid government benchmarks. However, the IMF (2001) argues that these alternatives are far from being perfect substitutes. In particular, market participants report that the market's fragmented legal and operational infrastructure may be significant enough that some deals in bond and repo markets – such as arbitrage, position-taking, hedging and other risk-mitigation trades – that would be executed in a more integrated system are not being done in the current system.

2.3.4.3 Secondary Market Trading

Secondary market liquidity is a key ingredient in well-functioning bond markets. Investors must feel confident that they can liquidate their holdings in reasonable time and trade without significantly affecting prices. Accordingly, trading in government bonds and Pfandbriefe is now largely concentrated on wholesale electronic trading platforms, which allow for better price transparency and collection of market data. At the same time, some concentration of liquidity toward the main markets at the expense of others has also occurred since the introduction of the euro. In this context, and also because of increased turnover in the wholesale OTC market, trading of government bonds on the quickly consolidating network of European stock exchanges has become relatively less important. Meanwhile, trading in nongovernment bonds still remains largely limited to the unorganized OTC market rather than organized exchanges. It is likely, however, that in the years ahead one will observe a similar substantial migration of trading in these instruments toward electronic systems.

Electronic OTC Trading Platforms

The bulk of bond trading in the Euro area has traditionally taken place in the wholesale OTC markets. Development has been substantial under Monetary Union, driven by increased competition among member states for secondary market liquidity and the widely recognized need to create the facilities necessary for cross-border trading. Strong competition has accelerated technological innovation, mirroring similar developments in other currency areas such as the United States. The EC (2002a) reports that an estimated 60% of Euro area trading volume is electronic, whereas 5 years ago most deals were done over the telephone.

In terms of development, several different patterns have been witnessed. One notable strategy has been the export of technology. This has been displayed by the Italian MTS Group, which has exported its successful electronic system for trading of Italian government bonds, Mercato Telematico dei Titoli di Stato (MTS), to a number of countries including Belgium, Finland, France, Germany, Ireland, the Netherlands, Portugal, Spain, and even Japan, and also set up the London-based EuroMTS.

EuroMTS can be best described as a screen-based super-wholesale interdealer exchange. It is by far the most successful example of what is the most prominent trend in the Euro area OTC market: the emergence of pan-European electronic trading platforms for debt securities, offering services ranging from simple order transmission to full fledged trade execution facilities. The exchange trades benchmark government and quasi-government bonds as well as a limited number of corporate bonds and, in its EuroCredit MTS division, Pfandbrief-style mortgage bonds. To deepen liquidity, it has established a minimum size for each bond allowed onto the system at €5 billion for government issues and €3 billion for Pfandbriefe; in the corporate segment there is a minimum outstanding size of €1 billion and a minimum credit rating of BBB/Baa2. With a combined 2002 trading volume of €1.2 trillion, EuroMTS now accounts for 30–50% of secondary bond trading in the European market despite efforts by well-heeled American competitors, such as BrokerTec, eSpeed, and Instinet, to move in on its territory.

Aside from the pan-European integration of interdealer trading, there have also been numerous initiatives on the national level in the Euro area. These aim at concentrating trading activity in a limited number of platforms, thus creating economies of scale. Such an initiative was the launch of the Spanish trading platform Senaf in 1999 and the German platform EUREX Bonds in 2000. The latter was established by EUREX Frankfurt, and several other market participants, to provide a vertically integrated market for German government and agency securities.

The diversity of the interdealer market clearly indicates that the market may well be subject to substantial consolidation in the near future. Experts argue that during the internet rush there were too many new platforms established, and on many of them the trading volume is not high enough to cover the costs. The market leader MTS Group appears to be the keenest to trigger a wave of mergers. In October 2001, the group joined the platform Coredeal and finally took it over completely. There has also been discussion from time to time with EUREX Bonds regarding a possible takeover.

Recent developments in the market of online dealer-to-customers platforms mirror those in the interdealer market. On dealer-to-customer systems, institutional investors can compare the prices provided by several intermediaries simultaneously. The two most frequently noted platforms are TradeWeb and EuroMOT. However, the MTS Group has been consistently promoting its own platform, BondVision, which was recently expanded by the purchase of another, BondClick.

Exchange Trading

In terms of bond trading, stock exchanges have now become largely overshadowed by electronic trading platforms. Nonetheless, the exchange listing of government and major nongovernment issues remains a prerequisite for guaranteeing liquidity for any given security. Listing in the London market is particularly attractive to companies as it provides access to a massive pool of investors as well as gives some tax advantages.

Similar to the wholesale OTC markets, where some consolidation is predicted, the future of some Euro area stock exchanges appears uncertain. Indeed, increased cross-border trading has put great pressure on stock exchanges to integrate their trading platforms so as to provide cost-efficient Euro area-wide mechanisms. Increased integration between stock exchanges has taken place in the form of cross-border cooperation and mergers. In September 1999, eight stock exchanges (London, Frankfurt, Paris, Milan, Madrid, Amsterdam, Brussels, and Zurich) signed an agreement to create a "virtual common market" with one electronic interface, common functionality, and supported by harmonized rule-books. Furthermore, in addition to traditional stock exchanges, several "alternative trading systems" such as new electronic communication networks offering similar functionality and services to traditional exchanges have also been introduced.

Thus far, the only pan-European stock exchange is Euronext, created in September 2000 by the merger of the exchanges in Amsterdam, Brussels, and Paris. Its unified order-driven trading platform is based on the French NSC (Nouveau Système de Cotation) trading system. Clearnet, already operating in the French market, acts as central counterparty for the clearing and netting of all trades, while Euroclear provides a unified settlement and custody platform. Euronext, which is maintaining its presence in all three cities by having subsidiaries in each of them, has adopted an expansionist strategy. Accordingly, it acquired the Lisbon Stock Exchange in 2002, which consequently changed its name to Euronext Lisbon.

Derivatives Trading

The recent wave of mergers observed in the European capital market infrastructure has fundamentally altered the institutional settings of derivatives trading as well. In 1997, the merger of the Frankfurt and Swiss derivatives exchanges created EUREX, the world's volume-wise largest futures exchange at the time. In 2002, EUREX was relegated to second position, however, with the massive merger of Euronext and the London International Financial Futures and Options Exchange (LIFFE).

With regard to trading activity, the most significant development has been in the bond futures markets. Driven by the high substitutability of existing contracts after the removal of currency risk, trading is now concentrated on the 2-, 5-, and 10-year German government bond contracts traded on the EUREX, which owes in large part to these futures contracts being used not only for managing German bond interest rate risks but also Euro interest rate risks. Indeed, the size of the German futures market is large even relative to the underlying market, and the 10-year Bund contract is established as the most actively traded futures contract in the world.

A development corresponding to the dominance of Bund contracts has been a reduction in futures trading based on French, Italian, and Spanish bonds. This has seriously damaged the liquidity of these contracts as well as taken its toll on other major derivatives exchanges in Europe. More recently, trading activity in futures traded on the Matif, the French derivatives exchange (member of the Euronext Group), has been growing, but it nonetheless remains low relative to that on the EUREX. The increase in part owes the extension of deliverability on the Matif contract to some non-French – Dutch and German – bonds by Euronext.

This latter fact and the versatile use of the Bund contract indicate that market integration has now gone so far that some Euro area government securities are becoming increasingly intersubstitutable. However, it must be noted that although there has been much discussion about the creation of a single benchmark "multideliverable" futures contract, as yet no such contract has materialized. All major exchanges, but some technical detail has always squashed plans. A major problem is the issue of delivery, which reverts to the cheapest deliverable bond. A multideliverable futures contract would mean that the bond with the lowest credit rating becomes the cheapest to deliver, and the contract becomes a *de facto* single issue futures. The various tax treatments and inconsistencies in market practices, such as the lack of standard documentation for repo markets, also obstruct the construction of such a contract.

2.3.4.4 Clearing, Custody, and Settlement Systems

Bond market integration largely hinges upon investors' ability to smoothly execute cross-border transactions within the Euro area. To complete such a transaction, investors must have access to systems in different countries and/or the interaction of different settlement systems, which is typically arranged through the use of intermediaries. As described by the Giovannini Group (2001) of market experts, set up in 1996 by ECOFIN, three main intermediaries are available: (i) a local agent, which is typically a member of the foreign central securities depository (CSD) concerned; or (ii) an international CSD or (ICSD) or (iii) a global custodian, both of which provide the international investor with a single access point to national CSDs in various countries. Less often, investors use links between their local CSD and the foreign CSD.

It is the high level of fragmentation in this framework of national infrastructures and cross-border intermediaries that is often cited as one of the main impediments to bond market integration in the Euro area. There remain across Europe a very large number of entities (including 19 CSDs in the EU) whose primary business is to play a role in clearing and settlement. In consequence, as pointed out by the Giovannini Group, the pan-European investor is required to access many national systems that provide very different types of services, have different technical requirements and market practices, and operate within different tax and legal frameworks. The associated additional cost represents a major limitation on the scope for cross-border securities trading. Although these costs are difficult to quantify, recent studies confirm that the posttrade processing costs of a cross-border intersystem transaction remain multiples times higher than for a corresponding transaction within a national market (EC, 2002b).

The providers of clearing and settlement facilities have long been fully aware of these problems, which has initiated a process of consolidation in the European clearing and settlement industry. Notably, service providers now offer a growing range of services and serve a growing number of markets, which has led to the possibility to exploit synergies by integrating the different stages of the securities business value chain. The on-going wave of mergers, creation of links, and other initiatives have also acted toward the facilitation of cross-border clearing and settlement and the substantial reduction of related costs.

Clearing Systems

Demand for clearing and netting facilities has developed rapidly in Europe as a means to reduce operational risks, enhance efficiency in the usage of capital and lower transaction costs. Market participants have a strong preference for integration in the industry because this will enable them to take full advantage of clearing facilities. Regrettably, although integration has now come a long way in the industry, more far-reaching efforts remain hampered by underlying legal discrepancies, such as different bankruptcy laws.

At this stage, two clearing houses, Clearnet and the London Clearing House (LCH) are extending their services for clearing and netting facilities to more segments of the Euro area bond and repo markets. Clearnet, created by the merger of the clearing functions of the Euronext exchanges, is the counterparty for all transactions carried out on Euronext. The competitor LCH provides centralized clearing for the MTS Group. EUREX is also developing capacities as central counterparty through EUREX Clearing, aiming at extending its services beyond German government and agency securities.

In accordance with initiatives to establish a pan-European central counterparty, Clearnet, EUREX Clearing, and LCH have repeatedly explored the possibilities of various merger combinations. Discussions on the integration of clearing activities focus on issues related to governance, jurisdiction, legal status, and types of products. At the same time, integration efforts in the clearing industry have also been visible in terms of international joint ventures. An example is the establishment of the European Securities Clearing Corporation as a pan-European clearing house, which was set up by the ICSD Euroclear and the United States Government Securities Clearing Corporation and recently joined by the LCH.

Custody and Settlement Systems

In terms of custody and settlement, different trends can be observed on the national level and on the pan-European level. On the national level, the main trend has been to consolidate local infrastructures into one local CSD, which has among others produced Iberclear and Monte Titoli, the national CSDs of Spain and Italy, respectively.

On the European level, on the other hand, the chief trend has been to establish cross-border bilateral links between SSS to facilitate cross-border transfers of securities. Via these links, a national SSS provides a single point of entry that allows its customers to hold securities issued in any other SSS and to use these securities within its own country (ECB, 2001a). This is of particular importance, as the European Central Securities Depositories Association (ECSDA, 2002) has pointed out, because the intense cross-border activity and the consequent interdependence among clearing and settlement systems have intensified the risk that a disruption in one system may spread to other markets. The total number of eligible links as assessed and approved by the ECB was 66 in March 2003, covering most member states. However, activity is concentrated on a limited number of countries and is dominated by the two ICSD, Clearstream International and Euroclear. The implementation of new models, such as those links operating on a delivery versus payment (DVP) basis – note that most links do not operate on a DVP basis – or relayed links could lead to an increased use of links in the future.

The aims and strategy of the two ICSDs confirm that the pan-European integration of settlements systems is increasing. The purpose of both organizations is to achieve a model of integration offering single access to an efficient real-time settlement process, in the form of interconnected platforms as a first step. Clearstream International was created first in January 2000 with the merger between Cedel International (ICSD, Luxembourg) and Deutsche Börse Clearing (CSD, Germany). The Euroclear Group was formed in January 2001, when Euroclear Bank (ICSD, Belgium), having already absorbed CBISSO (CSD, Ireland), merged with

Sicovam (CSD, France). Since then, the Euroclear group has also acquired CIK of Belgium and Necigef of the Netherlands as well as, most recently, CRESTCo of the United Kingdom.

2.4 PROPOSALS AND INITIATIVES FOR REDUCING MARKET FRAGMENTATION

It is perhaps reasonable to argue that existing market trends, including both economic (e.g. cross-border activities) and technological (e.g. use of the internet) trends, will continue to advance financial integration in the Euro area as well as the entire EU. In the same vein, integration in the Euro area bond market will continue just as integration is progressing globally. As much as the process of financial market integration is market-driven, however, a chief reason why the European bond market remains fragmented is that there remain regulatory, tax, and legal as well as other discrepancies that continue to hinder the establishment of a truly unified system. The Committee of the Wise Men (2001) set up by the EC and headed by Alexandre Lamfalussy listed a "plethora" of such interconnected factors and barriers, including (i) the absence of clear pan-European regulation on a large number issues, which hampers the implementation of the mutual recognition system based on harmonized minimum standards, a prerequisite for the elimination of regulatory impediments to market integration; (ii) an inefficient regulatory system; (iii) inconsistent implementation of existing rules; (iv) the fragmentation of cross-border clearing and settlement; and (v) the inadequate development of pension funds.

In the broad field of financial markets, there have been several areas of discussion and a range of concrete EU policy initiatives to resolve these matters. Among these, the EU's FSAP is of particular significance. The FSAP, adopted by the European Council in 1999, is based on a program of 42 measures to provide the basic conditions for integrated wholesale and retail financial markets within the EU, consistent with safeguarding stability. A deadline of 2005 has been set for the full implementation of the FSAP, with measures relating to securities markets to be implemented by 2003. Several of these are of particular relevance to the integration of the Euro area bond market, particularly those aimed at enhancing market liquidity, ensuring investor protection, and promoting greater competition among issuers. Examples of such measures include

- the Directive on the Cross-Border Use of Collateral, already adopted, which has created a pan-European legal framework for the use of collateral;
- the Directive on Prospectuses, aiming to create a level playing field for EU issuers and reducing costs of cross-border issuance;
- the Pension Funds Directive, which is directed at the development of funded pension schemes, an important source of additional liquidity in the market;
- the updated Investment Services Directive, which will guarantee the provision of cross-border services by investment companies; and
- the initiative on EU clearing and settlement, which will remove barriers to the finalization of individual cross-border transactions as well as competitive distortions in the market infrastructure.

The FSAP may well be regarded by the EC (2001) as the blueprint for financial integration in Europe. However, its implementation has been painfully slow, which promptly reflects the inefficiency of the EU's decision-making process. To accelerate the implementation of the FSAP and, more generally, to speed up decision-making on EU securities regulation, the Lamfalussy Committee has proposed a new four-level process that would separate political from technical decisions. If the Committee's proposals are enacted, draft directives would be implemented faster and more consistently across member countries. As has been mentioned, the Giovannini Group (2001) of market experts has provided further advice to the EC on specific aspects of financial integration, notably in the areas of government debt markets, the repo market and clearing and settlement arrangements. Industry groups such as the International Swaps and Derivatives Association have also highlighted relevant legal and documentation issues to policymakers.

It is worth highlighting though that the ECOFIN believes that there is no need at present to change the institutional structure of financial supervision in the EU, under which responsibility rests at national level. However, it is accepted that cooperation in practice, both between national supervisors themselves and between national supervisors and central banks, needs to be enhanced to respond to the continuing evolution of the European market (Bank of England, 2000). On the whole, there is altogether little doubt that the development of financial markets, and bond markets in particular, is now enjoying priority with decision makers in the EU. The Committee of the Wise Men (2001) warns, however, that there are factors other than those mentioned that are not always susceptible to be dealt with by regulatory rules or market forces that are slowing down financial market integration. These also include various political and cultural discrepancies on the European level, which will be necessary to be dealt with if the full potential of an integrated European securities market is to be captured.

2.5 CONCLUSION

So far, developments in the Euro area bond market have been promising under Monetary Union. Government debt issues continue to dominate the market; however, Europe's traditionally underdeveloped nongovernment bond sector has made a promising takeoff since the introduction of the euro, in spite of a setback in 2002 due to difficult market conditions and investors' growing risk aversion. On the whole, it is reasonable to expect that market development and integration will continue to advance in the future, owing as much to on-going financial and economic trends as to technological development and financial innovation. This process is being largely underpinned by the gradual emergence of a single pan-European investor base, which increases and consolidates demand in the market, benefiting borrowers as well as investors themselves. Then, the integration trend of the Euro area bond market has also progressed substantially in terms of market structure, which is reflected in improved and increasingly integrated trading, clearing, and settlement facilities. Supported by policymaker initiatives at national and supranational level, such as increased cooperation of supervisory bodies and regulators, and the EU's FSAP, as well as a strong market-driven trend to further consolidate the market infrastructure, the integration progress is expected to proceed even more rapidly in the future.

It nonetheless cannot be ignored that while the Euro area bond market is now significantly larger and more integrated than ever before, there remain various on-going discrepancies on a pan-European level that continue to hinder the exploitation of the full potential benefits of integration and the creation of a truly unified market. The chief obstacles include the enduring national segmentation of the government bond market; the continuingly fragmented nature of trading, clearing and settlement systems; as well as the complex patchwork of legal and regulatory requirements and nonuniform tax treatment. There are also various other factors, such as political and cultural barriers that are obstructive to integration and are not always susceptible to be dealt with by regulatory rules and market forces. While these barriers must indeed be overcome, the present situation suggests that the benefits so far accrued from the integration process in the Euro area bond market are just a fraction of those that may eventually be realized once the market becomes wholly unified.

REFERENCES

Allen, F. and D. Gale (2000). *Comparing Financial Systems.* Cambridge, MA: MIT Press.

Bank of England (2000, November). *Practical Issues Arising from the Euro.*

Benston, G.J. and C.W. Smith (1976). A Transaction Cost Approach to the Theory of Financial Intermediation. *Journal of Finance* **31**(2): 215–231.

Bhide, A. (1993). The Hidden Costs of Stock Market Liquidity. *Journal of Financial Intermediation* **34**: 1–51.

Blanco, R. (2001). Euro Area Government Securities Markets: Recent Developments and Implications for Market Functioning. In: *Market Functioning and Central Bank Policy*, BIS Paper 12 Basle: BIS, pp. 65–85.

Boot, A.W.A. and A.V. Thakor (1997). Financial System Architecture. *Review of Financial Studies* **10**: 693–733.

Committee of the Wise Men (2001). *Final Report on the Regulation of European Securities Markets.* Brussels: European Commission.

Demirgüc-Kunt, A. and V. Maksimovic (2002). Funding Growth in Bank-Based and Market-Based Financial Systems: Evidence from Firm-Level Data. *Journal of Financial Economics* **65**: 337–363.

Diamond, D.W. (1984). Financial Intermediaries and Delegated Monitoring. *Review of Economic Studies* **51**(3): 393–414.

Dinc, I.S. (2000). Bank Reputation, Bank Commitment, and the Effects of Competition in Credit Markets. *Review of Financial Studies* **13**(3): 781–812.

Dunne, P.G., M.J. Moore, and R. Portes (2002). Defining Benchmark Status: An Application Using Euro-Area Bonds. NBER Working Paper W9087. Cambridge, MA: NBER.

European Central Bank (2001a). *Payment and Securities Settlement Systems in the European Union* (Blue Book) Frankfurt: ECB.

European Central Bank (2001b). Euro Bond Market. Frankfurt: ECB.

European Central Securities Depositories Association (2002, September). Clearing and Settlement in the European Union – Main Policy Issues and Future Challenges: Comments Regarding the Communication from the Commission to the Council and the European Parliament. Milan: ECSDA.

European Commission (2001). Financial Market Integration in the EU. In: The *EU Economy 2001 Review (European Economy No. 73).* Luxembourg: Office for Official Publications of the European Commission, Ch 4, pp. 121–170.

European Commission (2002a). Bond Market Integration in the EU. In: *The European Economy: 2002 Review* (ECFIN/475/02-EN). Brussels: EC, Ch. 4, pp. 135–170.

European Commission (2002b). Clearing and Settlement in the European Union – Main Policy Issues and Future Challenges: Communication from the Commission to the Council and the European Parliament. COM(2002)257. Brussels: EC.

European Commission (2002c). Quarterly Note on the Euro-Denominated Bond Markets 43 (July–September), ECFIN/269/02-EN. Brussels: EC.

Galati, G. and K. Tsatsaronis (2001). The Impact of the Euro on Europe's Financial Markets. BIS Working Paper 100. Basle: BIS.

Giovannini Group (2001). *Cross-Border Clearing and Settlement Arrangements in the European Union.* Brussels: EC.

Hakansson, N.H. (1999). The Role of a Corporate Bond Market in an Economy and in Avoiding Crises. Working Paper. University of California, San Diego, U.S.A.

Holder, M., A.K. Sinha, and J.T. Severiens (2001). The Euro and Capital Market Integration: Are We There Yet? *Managerial Finance* **27**(9): 32–40.

Holmstrom, B. and J. Tirole (1993). Market Liquidity and Performance Monitoring. *Journal of Political Economy* **101**: 678–709.

International Monetary Fund (2001). The Changing Structure of the Major Government Securities Markets: Implications for Private Financial Markets and Key Policy Issues. In: *International Capital*

Markets – Developments, Prospects and Key Policy Issues. Washington DC: IMF, Ch. IV, pp. 81–119. IMF World Economic and Financial Surveys.

La Porta, R., F. Lopez-de-Silanes, A. Shleifer, and R.W. Vishny (1998). Law and Finance. *Journal of Political Economy* **106**: 1113–1155.

Levine, R. (1997). Financial Development and Economic Growth: Views and Agenda. *Journal of Economic Literature* **35**: 688–726.

Levine, R. (2002). Bank-Based or Market-Based Financial Systems: Which is Better? *Journal of Financial Intermediation* **11**: 398–428.

Levine, R. and S. Zervos (1998). Stock Markets, Banks and Economic Growth. *American Economic Review* **88**: 537–558.

London Economics (2002, November). Quantification of the macro-economic impact of integration of EU financial markets. London Economics in association with PricewaterhouseCoopers and Oxford Economic Forecasting, Report to the European Commission DG Internal Market.

Merton, R.C. and Z. Bodie (1995). A conceptual framework for analyzing the financial environment. In Dwight B. Crane, Kenneth A. Froot, Scott P. Mason, Andre F. Perold, Robert C. Merton, Erik R. Sirri, and Peter Tufano, eds., *The Global Financial System: A Functional Perspective*. Boston: Harvard Business School Press, pp. 3–32.

Perée, E. and A. Steinherr (2001). The Euro and Capital Markets: A New Era. *The World Economy* **24**(10), 1295–1308.

Rajan, R.G. (1992). Insiders and Outsiders: The Choice between Informed and Arms Length Debt. *Journal of Finance* **47**: 1367–1400.

Santillán, J., M. Bayle, and C. Thygesen (2000). The Impact of the Euro on Money and Bond Markets. ECB Occasional Paper 1. Frankfurt: ECB.

Sharma, K. (2001). The Underlying Constraints on Corporate Bond Market Development in Southeast Asia. *World Development* **29**(8): 1405–1419.

Schinasi, G.J. and T.R. Smith (1998). Fixed Income Markets in the United States, Europe and Japan: Some Lessons for Emerging Markets. IMF Working Paper No. 98/12. International Monetary Fund Washington, DC: IMF, pp. 1–70.

Takagi, S. (2002). Fostering Capital Markets in a Bank-Based Financial System: A Review of Conceptual Issues. *Asian Development Review* **19**(1): 67–97.

Thiel, M. (2001). Finance and Economic Growth – A Review of Theory and the Available Evidence. European Commission Economic Paper 158. Brusssels: EC.

Wenger, E. and C. Kaserer (1998). The German System of Corporate Governance: A Model Which Should Not Be Imitated. In: S.W. Black and M. Moersch, eds., *Competition and Convergence in Financial Markets: The German and Anglo-American Models*. New York: North-Holland Press, pp. 41–78.

Zwick, S. (2002). Euro Bond Market Taking Shape. *Futures* **31**(3): 70–72.

3
Perspective on the Emerging European Financial Markets

PETER G. SZILAGYI, THOMAS A. FETHERSTON, AND JONATHAN A. BATTEN

3.1 INTRODUCTION

Despite substantial improvement since the mid-1990s, the debt markets of emerging Europe are underdeveloped relative to their peers in Western Europe. This is hardly surprising given the significant gap between the two regions in terms of economic and financial market development. Even in the 13 official European Union (EU) candidates – including the 10 countries that are set to join the EU in May 2004, the capitalization of bond markets relative to gross domestic product (GDP) is less than half of that in the Euro area, while the average GDP per capita in these countries is barely more than one fifth of the Euro area level.

These figures clearly indicate – albeit to a vastly varying extent – that these markets remain little used as a source of finance in the region. Market development has often been hindered by the fact that many of the region's economies have sometimes failed to provide the necessary environment on a permanent basis, including macroeconomic stability, low inflation and sustainable growth, as well as credible long term commitment and vision by government. The limited market activity of governments has also owed to the otherwise favorably low levels of public debt, which has compromised the development of government bond markets and the related market infrastructure, a prerequisite to building viable private markets. Even today, in an international context, only the bond markets of Poland, the Czech Republic, Hungary, Turkey, and – to a lesser extent – Russia play some role in the region.

To provide a perspective on the nature and problems associated with market development, this chapter examines and compares the three major forms of debt financing in the emerging European economies[1] over the period since the mid-1990s: international bank financing,[2] and securities issuance in domestic and international bond markets. To facilitate cross-country comparisons, the study groups the region's economies into three groups on the basis of their level of development:

(i) *Advanced economies*. This group includes those functioning market economies that are ready to meet the highly competitive pressures within the EU.[3] This latter fact is also

---

[1] The Bank for International Settlements (BIS) includes the following countries in the emerging European economies category: Albania, Belarus, Bosnia and Herzegovina, Bulgaria, Croatia, Cyprus, the Czech Republic, Estonia, Gibraltar, Hungary, Latvia, Lithuania, Macedonia, Malta, Moldova, Poland, Romania, Russia, Serbia and Montenegro, the Slovak Republic, Slovenia, Turkey, and the Ukraine.

[2] *International bank lending* refers to lending by banks whose central bank reports to the BIS. This includes banks from Australia, Canada, the European Economic Area, Japan, Switzerland, Turkey, the United States, and the United Kingdom.

[3] The *Luxembourg group* of EU candidates, which included Cyprus, the Czech Republic, Estonia, Hungary, Poland, and Slovenia,

European Fixed Income Markets: Money, Bond and Interest Rate Derivatives. Edited by J.A. Batten,
T.A. Fetherston and P.G. Szilagyi. © 2004 John Wiley & Sons, Ltd. ISBN 0-470-85053-1

demonstrated by the high-quality investment grade credit ratings of these countries. The front-runners of this group are the *Czech Republic, Estonia, Hungary, Poland*, and *Slovenia* as well as the non-excommunist countries of *Cyprus* and *Malta*. These countries are all in the process of graduating from the emerging market class as defined by the likes of Standard & Poor's and Moody's. *Slovakia* and to a greater extent *Croatia, Latvia*, and *Lithuania* somewhat lag these front-runners; however, with the sole exception of Croatia these countries are also all set to enter the EU on May 1, 2004.

(ii) *Less advanced economies*. This group includes the less developed and more unpredictable economies of emerging Europe, as signaled by their subinvestment grade credit ratings. Of these, *Bulgaria* and *Romania* are expected to join the EU in 2007, an aspiration that is providing a major impetus on their part to the reform effort, yet their growth prospects remain somewhat uncertain. *Turkey* is still consolidating after its worst financial and economic slowdown since 1945 and is now officially an EU candidate but has been refused accession negotiations until at least 2005. *Russia* is fast emerging from the recent financial crisis and consequently has seen its credit rating improve rapidly.

(iii) *Prolonged crisis economies*. This group includes the most unpredictable prolonged crisis economies of *Albania, Bosnia and Herzegovina, Macedonia, Serbia and Montenegro* as well as the CIS[4] states of *Belarus, Moldova*, and the *Ukraine*. Some of these economies have delivered consecutive years of significant growth; however, the long term perception of their poor investment climate continues to deter investors from this part of Europe. With the exception of the Ukraine, none of these countries are rated by international credit rating agencies, which indicates their lack of financial development.

3.2 FINANCIAL STRUCTURES IN EMERGING EUROPE

Transition economies are characterized by the underdevelopment not only of their debt markets but also of their financial systems as a whole. This should not come as a surprise given the fact that only a decade and a half ago these economies faced the enormous challenge of creating from scratch a functioning financial sector. Under central planning, financial intermediation in these countries was handled by a monobank system, relegated to being little more than "a bookkeeping mechanism for tabulating the authorities' decisions about the resources to be allocated to different enterprises and sectors" (de Larosiére, 2001). There was consequently no need for prudential and supervisory regulations, and securities markets were completely absent, since there were no marketable securities available.

This also explains why the financial systems of even the most developed of the transition economies have less depth and breadth than do the systems of Cyprus, Malta, and to a lesser extent Turkey, which are all market economies at comparable levels of development (where development is measured by GDP per capita). Most EU candidate transition economies have now completed, or advanced to a substantial degree, the restructuring and privatization of

---

started membership negotiations in March 1998. They were followed by the *Helsinki group* of candidates (Bulgaria, Latvia, Lithuania, Malta, Romania, and Slovakia) in February 2000. With the exception of Bulgaria and Romania, all of these candidates signed the Treaty of Accession on April 16, 2003, and are set to join the EU on May 1, 2004; Bulgaria and Romania are expected to follow suit in 2007 or 2008. Croatia has not yet been named as an official candidate, reflecting the country's complicated domestic and international political developments following its 1991 independence from Yugoslavia, but is now predicted to enter the EU alongside Bulgaria and Romania. Turkey, accepted as a candidate in December 1999 but refused membership negotiations by the EU ever since, is quite unlikely to enter the EU during this decade.

[4] The Commonwealth of Independent States (CIS), is an alliance of 12 of the 15 former Republics of the Soviet Union, including the European states of Belarus, Moldova, Russia and the Ukraine. The three nonmembers are the Baltic states of Estonia, Latvia, and Lithuania.

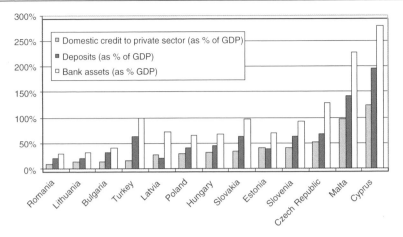

Figure 3.1   Bank Intermediation in European Union Candidates in 2001.
Source: European Commission (2002). Update of the Report on Macroeconomic and Financial Sector Stability Developments in Candidate Countries. EC Enlargement Paper 11. © European Communities, 1995–2003. Reproduced with permission.

their banking sectors. However, even in their case this has proved to be a relatively slow and painful process that has been delayed by excessive fluctuations of macroeconomic variables and has sometimes come at the cost of financial sector crises, involving portfolio restructuring and bank recapitalization with sizeable fiscal costs. The European Commission (EC) (2002) points out that even in these economies, the banking sectors still do not yet properly fulfill their financial intermediation role and, thus, do not yet fully realize their potential for supporting economic growth and macroeconomic stability. In contrast, Cyprus and Malta in particular have relatively well-developed banking sectors that provide the backbone of their otherwise bank-based financial systems. Turkey is now a somewhat different case, however, since insufficient supervision and substantial political intervention have led to the accumulation of major structural weaknesses in its financial system, which also caused the financial crisis of February 2001.

The best indicator of the extent of financial underdevelopment in transition economies is the low degree and efficiency of financial intermediation by their banking sectors. This of course varies substantially even among the EU candidates. The domestic credit to private sector relative to GDP stretched from only 10% in Romania to 54% in the Czech Republic in 2001, but again these levels are very low compared with the respective figures of Cyprus and Malta at 125% and 98%, respectively. Similarly, bank assets as a percentage of GDP in 2001 ranged from 32% in Lithuania to 129% in the Czech Republic, which compares with 279% and 226% in Cyprus and Malta, respectively, and 267% in the Euro area as a whole (Figure 3.1).

One reason behind this low level of bank intermediation is the relative aversion of banks to risk. Credit expansion has been moderate in many countries as banks pursue very conservative lending policies in the aftermath of restructuring, privatization, and the tightening of supervisory rules. Interest rate spreads between lending and deposit rates suggest inefficiencies and a lack of competition in some countries, in particular as regards the retail sector. Today, banks often continue to mobilize more savings than they are willing to place with domestic borrowers, and tend to channel the excess liquidity into foreign investments despite the high-investment needs of their local economies. Credit relationships also tend to be overwhelmingly short term as evidenced by banks' asset structure.

In light of this underdevelopment of bank intermediation, also coupled with the institutional settings of the region's financial systems as a whole, it is not surprising that the debt markets of transition economies are still in their infancy. Considerable actions have now been taken to provide impetus for bond market development – for example by way of strengthening the legislative framework, the market infrastructure, and the institutional investor base, yet in many countries even the government markets remain nascent and used predominantly for short term financing, which obstructs development in the private markets. It is notable that even in the 11 EU candidates the capitalization of government bond markets relative to GDP – as reported by the EC (2002) – is barely more than one third of that in the Euro area.

The inadequate functioning of domestic financing mechanisms forces the region's borrowers to often seek international funds. This has led to the accumulation of sizeable current account deficits and the build-up of external debt in the form of foreign loans and debt securities by various domestic entities, namely

- governments (to finance budget deficits, infrastructure projects and the like);
- local commercial banks (to invest on their own account or for on-lending to local businesses); and
- resident business (to finance capital investment).

It is only natural that this foreign exposure of these sectors is not without risks, since it exposes the economy, including public finances, to external vulnerabilities, and may exacerbate the risks associated with banks' credit exposure in their local nonfinancial sectors. A more recent testimony to these risks is the financial collapse of Turkey in February 2001, which was largely caused by the build-up of considerable foreign exchange risk exposures in the banking sector and the economy as a whole.

3.3   INTERNATIONAL BANK BORROWING

The main source of foreign funding for emerging Europe continues to be international bank borrowing. BIS data contained in Figure 3.2 show that lending to the region by BIS reporting banks amounted to US$133 billion or about 13% of the region's GDP in September 2002. Of this amount, about US$80 billion was borrowed by nonbank entities, chiefly nonfinancial corporations and to a lesser extent governments.

The figure reveals that variation in patterns of foreign lending to the region largely mirrors the differences in economic and financial development among the three study groups defined in the introduction. The region's advanced economies tend to borrow the most actively, with their outstanding bank borrowing reaching 16% of their GDP in September 2002. Of course, the level of variation is substantial within the study group itself. Non-excommunist Malta and Cyprus borrow 144% and 89% of their GDP, respectively; the reform front-runners Slovenia, the Czech Republic, and Hungary borrow 16–17%; but Latvia, Lithuania, and Poland borrow only 6–9%. The level of lending to these countries has been continuously rising since the mid-1990s, aside from a brief period in the aftermath of the Russian financial crisis of August 1998. This indicates that lender confidence in this group has been cemented by their broadly stable macroeconomic performance over this period as well as by their increasingly strong association with the EU.

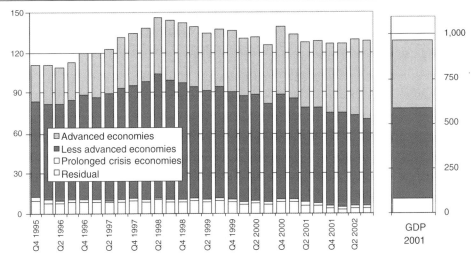

Figure 3.2   International bank lending to Emerging Europe (in billions of US dollars).
Source: Bank for International Settlements (BIS). International Banking Statistics, Table 3A, http://www.bis.org/statistics/bankstats.htm. International Monetary Fund (IMF) International Financial Statistics. Copyright © Bank for International Settlements, Basle, Switzerland. Reproduced with permission.

Foreign lending to the region's less advanced economies, troubled by financial and economic setbacks over the years, has been much more eclectic. Lending to Russia effectively collapsed in the second half of 1998 from a level of US$57 billion, and has remained low since then due to consecutive years of budget surpluses, reaching just US$28 billion (8% of GDP) in September 2002. Lending to Bulgaria and Romania (at around 6% of their GDP) was affected not only by the Russian crisis, but also by the various banking crises in the Balkans during the latter half of the 1990s. The most recent collapse of lender confidence has been suffered by Turkey, however, which saw its foreign bank borrowing fall from US$44 billion in December 2000 to just US$33 billion (or 18% of GDP) in September 2002. In light of such risk sensitivity of foreign banks, it is not surprising that lending to the third study group of prolonged crisis economies has never really picked up since the beginning of the transition process, reaching barely 3% of their GDP or US$2 billion in September 2002.

Four key points concerning international lending to the region are noteworthy. First, in the economies of the former Soviet bloc, the levels of lending to the public sector in preference to the other industry sectors have shown an increase in recent years, although the financing of public sector deficits by international bank loans is still practically irrelevant (see DePfa, 2000).

Second, a major reason for currency crises in several countries was excessive foreign borrowing without currency risk hedging to reduce the cost of capital. Although Kokoszczynski and Slawinski (1999) mentioned this point concerning the Polish corporate sector, it may also be generalized to other economies in the region. The need to dissuade domestic firms from borrowing internationally was one of the factors that prompted the evolution toward an increasingly flexible rate regime in the region's countries. Since then, it has become a major priority with governments to closely watch the financing behavior of enterprises, for example as regards their hedging policy against currency risks.

Third, prior to the debt restructuring of 1998, a feature of lending to Russia was that domestic banks increased their international borrowing by hedging themselves with short term government securities. When the Russian Treasury bill market was suspended in August 1998, domestic banks were forced to mark down the value of these securities, which caused them severe liquidity problems and paralyzed the payment system (see International Monetary Fund [IMF] 1998). Foreign creditor banks suffered large losses and reduced their holdings. Fears of bank failures led to deposit withdrawals from banks in other countries as well, including the Ukraine, Belarus, Bulgaria, and Romania. Aware of the uncertainties, individuals and companies gaining wealth from the postcommunist transition were also transferring billions of dollars abroad. These defining events largely contributed to the financial meltdown in Russia and other economies in the region.

Fourth, it must be emphasized that the tendencies in lending to emerging Europe reflect a reassessment of the creditworthiness of many economies in the region. The continuous increase in bank lending to the region's advanced economies suggests that investors are discriminating in favor of those with strong fundamentals and sustainable reform programs (IMF, 1998). The risk reassessment has, in part, been manifest as higher credit spreads on bank intermediated loans for countries with a poor investment climate and a general decline in risk tolerance among mature market investors. However, the volatile price of debt cites liquidity concerns for the entire region, and may, to a certain extent, also affect better performing economies on a short to medium term.

3.4   INTERNATIONAL DEBT ISSUES

While foreign bank lending to emerging Europe's stronger transition economies has been growing consistently since the early 1990s, a notable trend from the middle of the decade has been the gradual return of these economies to the international capital markets, which has moderated demand for international intermediation. While some countries, most notably Hungary, began issuing Eurobonds at a relatively early stage, the most dominant trend initially was the exchange of defaulted bank loans – in the form of Brady bonds – for rescheduled debt by Poland, Bulgaria, and various other countries in 1995, and later by Russia in 1997.[5] Since then, no restructured debt has been issued by these economies – Russia defaulted on its debt in 1998, but instead they have focused on issuing liquid international Eurobonds, which sometimes have been used to discreetly buy back Brady bonds in the open market.

Since then, the marked upturn in international bond issuance by the region's economies has continued, a trend that has not been broken by the recently unfavorable global economic environment and a generally heightened aversion to risk among international investors. This favorable climate is largely due to the fact that the progress toward macroeconomic stabilization, continuing structural reforms, comfortable or improving foreign currency positions, and the approaching EU membership of the region's better economies have helped reduce international investors' perception of risk in this part of the world. The region's economies have even avoided financial contagion in 2002 from Brazil and Turkey, and some of the advanced reformers have actually emerged as safe havens for investors during periods of market turbulence. According to data obtained by Thomson Financial Datastream, the yield spread of 10-year Hungarian Eurobonds to German government bonds was as low as 32 basis points (bp) in March 2003, while the spreads of Russian, Bulgarian, and Romanian Eurobonds also declined by 150–200 bp to 200–250 bp between July 2002 and March 2003. This is of course in sharp contrast with the rapid widening of the yield spreads of Turkish Eurobonds, which

---

[5] Russia's debt was not formally under the Brady plan.

were in the region of 850–870 bp at the same time, and the similarly poor investment climate of the prolonged crisis economies despite several consecutive years of economic growth.

Details of international issuance[6] in the region, as reported by the BIS, are provided in Table 3.1. Issuance in the countries not featured in the table is negligible or nonexistent. In total, emerging Europe's borrowing by way of international bond issues (US$93 billion in December 2002) remains below that of Austria and Sweden alone, and is still significantly smaller than the amount of intermediated finance provided by foreign banks to the region (US$133 billion in September 2002). Of course, international bank borrowing remains by far the more important source of foreign funding for private entities, while international bonds continue to be issued predominantly by governments. It would be expected that these markets compete with one another on efficiency criteria; therefore the small size of the private disintermediated finance market is consistent with a higher entry or cost structure, which to some extent inhibits the region's nongovernment borrowers from tapping this market as a debt alternative.

The table also reveals the extent to which the market is dominated by sovereign issues. The largest issuers in the market are Turkey (US$21 billion in December 2002), Russia (US$16 billion), Hungary (US$10 billion), and Poland and Croatia (US$5 billion each). Following the recent financial crises in Russia and Turkey, the market has now settled into being used for budget financing (although in 2002 Bulgaria also used the market for debt restructuring by swapping US$1.3 billion of Brady bonds for Eurobonds). This also explains Russia's notable lack of issuance since 2001 (due to fiscal surpluses now achieved for several consecutive years), which is expected to continue provided that oil prices do not collapse.

Historically few nongovernment or quasigovernment issuers have tapped these markets, since they have little or no issuance history, and they lack the marketability of a sovereign issue. For companies and local governments with modest borrowing needs, the cost of getting an international credit rating, hiring lawyers and investment bankers, and putting on a road show is prohibitive. The interest rate spreads of unknown or new issuers demanded by the markets have also been wider than those demanded by similarly rated Western European or US corporations in recent years, and may have discouraged borrowers (Eichengreen and Mody, 1997; Kamin and von Kleist, 1999). Those countries that have issued substantial nongovernment debt in international bonds include Poland (US$6 billion in December 2002), Russia (US$5 billion), Turkey (US$3 billion), and the Czech Republic (US$2 billion). While the bulk of these instruments is issued by banks, in some countries such as Russia, Slovakia, and Croatia the nonfinancial sector is relatively more active. For example, Russian corporations, mainly oil companies, raised US$3 billion in 2002 alone.

3.5 DOMESTIC DEBT ISSUES

The development of domestic bond markets in the various emerging European countries is at varying stages of development. The bond markets in some of the more advanced reformer countries have rapidly evolved as a preferred source of financing, and now represent a more important source of funding than do the external markets. Other countries have fallen behind since they have failed to provide the necessary environment for the development of their local markets. Key reasons include an inability (i) to maintain macroeconomic stability, low

---

[6] As defined by the BIS, international debt securities are (i) bonds issued by local residents in the domestic or international market, denominated in foreign currency or (ii) bonds issued by international issuers (corporate or other institutions such as the European Bank for Reconstruction and Development or the European Investment Bank) issuing in domestic markets, denominated in local or foreign currency.

Table 3.1   International debt securities by nationality and sector of issuer*

	Government	Financial institutions	Corporate issuers	TOTAL	Remaining maturities up to 1 year
Advanced economies					
Croatia					
1996	–	–	–	–	
1999	2.6	0.1	0	2.7	
2002	4.9	0.1	0.2	5.2	
Cyprus					
1996	0.3	0.1	0.2	0.6	0.3
1999	1.1	0.1	0.3	1.5	0.2
2002	1.3	0.7	0.1	2.1	0.1
Czech Republic					
1996	0.6	0.6	–	*1.2*	–
1999	0.6	1.5	0.2	*2.3*	0.3
2002	0.4	1.4	0.2	*2*	–
Estonia					
1996	–	–	–	–	–
1999	–	0.2	–	*0.2*	0.1
2002	0.1	0.4	0.2	*0.7*	0.2
Hungary					
1996	13.1	0.2	–	*13.3*	1.1
1999	12.1	0.4	–	*12.5*	2
2002	9.7	0.6	–	*10.3*	2.2
Latvia					
1996	–	–	–		–
1999	0.2	–	–	*0.2*	–
2002	0.4	–	–	*0.4*	–
Lithuania					
1996	0.1	–	–	*0.1*	0.1
1999	0.7	–	–	*0.7*	0.1
2002	1.5	–	–	*1.5*	0.3
Poland					
1996	0.4	0.2	–	*0.6*	–
1999	0.8	3.8	0.1	*4.7*	0.3
2002	4.9	5.8	0.3	*11*	–
Slovakia					
1996	0.3	0.1	0.2	*0.6*	–
1999	1.5	0.2	0.5	*2.2*	0.1
2002	2	0.1	0.8	*2.9*	0.9
Slovenia					
1996	0.3	–	–	*0.3*	–
1999	1.4	–	–	*1.4*	–
2002	2.2	–	–	*2.2*	–
Less advanced economies					
Bulgaria					
1996	–	0.1	–	*0.1*	–
1999	0.1	–	–	*0.1*	–
2002	1.7	–	–	*1.7*	–

(*cont.*)

Table 3.1 *(cont.)*

Romania					
1996	1	–	–	*1*	–
1999	0.7	0.1	0.2	*1*	0.1
2002	1.8	–	1	*2.8*	0.2
Russia					
1996	1	0.3	–	*1.3*	–
1999	16.8	2.1	0.4	*19.3*	0.9
2002	15.5	2.2	3.1	*20.8*	1.7
Turkey					
1996	11.7	0.6	–	*12.3*	1.6
1999	15.3	2.6	0.4	*18.3*	2.2
2002	21.4	2.1	0.4	*23.9*	3.7
Prolonged crisis economies					
Ukraine					
1996	–	–	–	–	–
1999	1.3	–	–	*1.3*	0.5
2002	0.4	–	–	*0.4*	–
Yugoslavia					
1996	–	0.1	–	*0.1*	–
1999	–	0.1	–	*0.1*	–
2002	–	0	–	*0*	–

Source: Bank for International Settlements. Securities Statistics, Tables 12A–D and 17B, http://www.bis.org/statistics/secstats.htm. Copyright © Bank for International Settlements, Basle, Switzerland. Reproduced with permission.
*Amounts outstanding in billions of US dollars at end of year.

inflation, and sustainable growth; (ii) to maintain the impetus for regulatory reform necessary for reaching an appropriate level of financial sector development; (iii) to achieve the economies of scale and scope necessary for ongoing development; and (iv) to provide a credible long term commitment and vision by government.

Poland, Hungary, and the Czech Republic are leading the way in developing their national markets. All three countries have now established a comprehensive and fairly liquid government segment, gradually increasing the issuance of longer dated bonds now that inflation has permanently declined to single-digit levels. Investor interest in these markets has been solid – international investors have relished the higher yields offered by these markets amid the low interest rates in the United States and Western Europe, and the nascent local institutional investor bases have only underpinned this demand.

As has been mentioned, while these few countries have managed to quickly develop their own markets, the same has not been the case for the region's other economies. The role of the local bond markets in the remaining countries will remain limited, mainly as a result of low levels of outstanding government securities, which is in turn a consequence of low levels of marketable debt carried over from the planned regimes and the prudent fiscal policy of the last decade. Even though fiscal deficits have been high in some countries in certain years, the average level of general government debt outstanding at end-2001 amounted to only around 37% of GDP in emerging Europe, compared with an average of 69% of GDP in the Euro area.

A comparison of domestic bond markets in emerging Europe is provided in Table 3.2. The data contained in the table are obtained from the BIS and shows the level of bonds outstanding in total and by industry sector, decomposed into public sector, financial institutions, and corporate

Table 3.2 Domestic debt securities by nationality and sector of issuer*

	Government	Financial institutions	Corporate sector	Total	Of which: remaining maturity up to a year	Total as % of GDP
Czech Republic						
1996	8.4	2.4	1.5	12.3	7.3	21
1999	20	2.6	2.4	25	18.5	46
2002	36	3.1	3.2	42.3	31.3	58
Hungary						
1996	14.8	-	0.2	15	5.2	33
1999	15.7	-	0.6	16.3	5.2	34
2002	25.3	-	0.9	26.2	9.1	41
Poland						
1996	25.7	-	-	25.7	10.2	18
1999	27.3	-	-	27.3	6.5	18
2002	50.5	-	-	50.5	10.7	28
Russia						
1996	42.6	-	-	42.6	38.9	10
1999	9.2	-	-	9.2	3.4	5
2002	6.1	-	-	6.1	2.6	2
Turkey						
1996	26.4	-	0.1	26.6	19.5	15
1999	43	-	0	43	7.1	23
2002	85.2	-	-	85.2	24.5	43

Note: Data for 2002 as of end-September.
Source: Bank for International Settlements. Securities Statistics, Tables 16A–B and 17A, http://www.bis.org/statistics/secstats.htm. Copyright © Bank for International Settements, Basle, Switzerland. Reproduced with permission.
*Amount outstanding in billions of US dollars at end of year.

sector. Because of the small domestic bond markets in the region, of the emerging countries only Turkey (US$85 billion in December 2002), Poland (US$51 billion), the Czech Republic (US$42 billion), Hungary (US$26 billion), and Russia (US$6 billion) are reported in the table. Figures reported by Merrill Lynch and the region's central banks indicate that aside from these markets the larger government bond markets include those of Slovakia (US$5 billion), Slovenia (US$3 billion), and Romania (US$2 billion).

There are a number of observations evident from the table. These markets are saturated with government instruments in terms of both outstanding balance and trading volume, and lack a significant nongovernment component. Beside its sizeable government bond market, only in the Czech Republic are corporate, municipal, and bank bonds an important category, with the outstanding debt of the private sector constituting one quarter of the market. As in the case of international issuance by the region's sovereigns, the growth of domestic government issuance largely reflects the fiscal policy of the region's economies, in that the introduction of strict limits on central bank lending has forced governments to use noninflatory debt finance to cover budget deficits.

A salient feature of the region's government bond markets, however, is that each of these markets remains relatively small. This suggests that although liquidity does not depend on size, benchmark securities are likely to be rather illiquid and infrequent in maturity. The average maturity of active instruments is also short, as a number of governments as issuers have given priority to cost minimization at the expense of increased risk exposure. This has been the case even in the mainstream Czech market, where the average maturity of domestic public sector debt remains less than 2 years, despite the fact that revenues flow from long term assets. Because finance is short term, governments are largely dependent on the liquidity situation, on the capital market, and on interest rates, while the scarcity of longer term instruments constrains the emergence of a comprehensive benchmark yield curve in these markets. The maturity structure of debt securities is nonetheless constantly improving with the trends toward issuing longer term paper, as governments are gradually expanding the yield curve at the long end – as recently seen in the flagship economies – on the basis of falling inflation and interest rates. Inflation-indexed bonds have sometimes been promoted as an alternative instrument for economies with high-inflation records, although this is not necessarily the best solution.

The development of the nongovernment segment of these markets has been hampered by a multitude of factors. Private borrowers are deterred from issuing by high entry costs, statutory restrictions, repressive regulatory processes, and a lack of government incentives. Because these instruments are rather new, each issue requires active promotion among investors. Despite offering attractive premiums to government securities, nongovernment bonds are also highly illiquid, which reduces their attractiveness to investors. There is also still a lingering potential for exchange-rate-related losses, a risk that must be borne by international investors.

Of course, the region's policymakers are aware that a major factor limiting the growth and evolution of the market is in fact the narrowness of local institutional investor bases. While the emergence of such investor bases is a function of economic development and the levels of domestic savings, for the region it is a major challenge to underpin the development of large institutional investors via contractual savings reforms. The change from a defined benefit (pay as you go) to a defined contribution (private pensions) in pension systems promises to deliver both a growth of funds and enhance professionalism in fund management (Organization for Economic Cooperation and Development (OECD), 2002). Fundamental pension reforms were first implemented in the region by Hungary, Poland, and Estonia, and have now been or are being introduced in other transition economies as well.

Overall, the data suggest that although the region's bond markets are converging toward the Western European model, most remain underdeveloped, illiquid, and structurally weak by international standards. This was greatly highlighted by the sharp drops in bond prices in response to the Russian crisis in September 1998, showing that these markets are still not deep enough to sustain substantial capital flows without strongly affecting bond prices.[7]

Infrastructural weaknesses remain a chief source of problems. In many countries, auction-based systems to sell bonds that operate on the basis of internationally accepted principles, are missing, instruments are often not standardized, and there is a general lack of transparency in the issuance process. Secondary market trading is often weak, which in part reflects the under-development of broker–dealer networks, as well as investors' preference for holding bonds to maturity due to inadequate clearing and settlement and high transaction costs. Derivatives markets for arbitrage-free bond pricing and risk transformation are also limited. Because of the lack of real-time trading information, corporate issuers frequently offer dramatically different spreads to government bonds, highlighting the difficulties of decision making under imperfect information. Only in the major markets are government bonds largely available across the yield curve, making it difficult to establish a government benchmark yield curve to use as

---

[7] As explained by DePfa Research (2000), the spread between medium term Hungarian and German government bonds (Deutsche Mark-denominated Eurobonds in the case of Hungary) rose temporarily from some 60 to over 120 bp in the wake of the Russian crisis.

the basis for pricing nongovernment debt issues. Yet another drawback of private debt is the lack of a rating system. There are mostly no local credit analysis agencies, and the culture of using ratings for risk assessment is still largely undeveloped. While some issuers have a credit assigned to them by internationally recognized rating agencies, others have no credit rating at all, and the only alternative is independent research by brokerage and banking credit analysis.

All in all, few countries exhibit well-functioning and comprehensive domestic bond markets in emerging Europe. Therefore, further policy efforts need to be undertaken that address supply and demand side impediments and further develop financial market infrastructure. Examples of supply-side strategies include providing an enabling environment conducive to financial liberalization, while ensuring investor confidence by maintaining international regulatory standards and continuing the reform of corporate governance. Demand-side strategies are more easily implementable and involve the strengthening of the role of institutional investors and mutual funds, and facilitating and building the private placement mechanism. Infrastructure improvements include competitive auctions, secondary market trading systems, and more derivatives for hedging. It is desirable to use reliable and reputable international credit rating agencies, to accelerate discussions with information vendors on the construction of benchmark yield curves, and to attempt to obtain scale and scope economies through regional settlement systems.

3.6 CONCLUSION

The debt markets of emerging Europe remain small, shallow, and illiquid relative to their peers in Western Europe, which is hardly surprising given the significant gap between the two regions in terms of economic and financial development. Even in the 13 official EU candidates – including the 10 countries that are set to join the EU in May 2004, the capitalization of bond markets relative to GDP is less than half of that in the Euro area, which clearly indicates – albeit to a vastly varying extent – that these markets remain little used as a source of finance in the region. The markets are also saturated with government instruments in terms of both outstanding balance and trading volume, and lack a significant nongovernment component. Market development has often been hindered by the fact that many of the region's economies have sometimes failed to provide the necessary environment on a permanent basis, including macroeconomic stability, low inflation and sustainable growth, as well as credible commitment by government. The limited market activity of governments has also owed to the otherwise favorably low levels of public debt, which has compromised the development of government bond markets and the related market infrastructure, a prerequisite to building viable private markets. Today, in an international context only the bond markets of Poland, the Czech Republic, Hungary, Turkey, and – to a lesser extent – Russia play some role in the region.

Of course, emerging Europe's transition economies are characterized by the underdevelopment not only of their debt markets but also of their otherwise bank-based financial systems as a whole. In light of the high-investment needs of the region, it is hardly surprising that the inadequate functioning of domestic financing mechanisms has forced the region's borrowers to often seek international funds in the form of foreign loans and debt securities. However, this and borrowers' excessive reliance on bank lending have been identified as important factors in recent financial crises in the emerging world. The underdevelopment of the region's local bond markets entails financial stability risk, higher transaction costs, a narrower financing base for the nonfinancial sector, as well as higher investment risk. The higher level of uncertainty associated with such markets could discourage capital investment or raise the cost of capital formation.

Since the development of domestic bond infrastructures is costly, it is reasonable that some of the region's economies have focused on the use of existing international infrastructure, while gradually building the necessary infrastructures domestically. Of course, the national infrastructures should be and are being constantly improved, but this is a lengthy process that requires long term vision and commitment, where policymakers recognize that the development of domestic bond markets is pivotal in ensuring that corporations have a suite of financing alternatives in the future.

REFERENCES

Batten, J. and Y.H. Kim (2001). Expanding Long-Term Financing through Bond Market Development: A Post Crisis Policy Task. In: Y.H. Kim, ed., *Government Bond Market Development in Asia*. Manila: Asian Development Bank.

Bank for International Settlements (1995–2003). *Quarterly Review: International Banking and Financial Market Developments*. Basle: BIS, Switzerland (various issues).

Bokros, L. (2001). A Perspective on Financial Sector Development in Central and Eastern Europe. In: L. Bokros, A. Fleming, and C. Votava, eds., *Financial Transition in Europe and Central Asia – Challenges in the New Decade*. Washington, DC: World Bank, pp. 13–28.

Caviglia, G., G. Krause, and C. Thimann (2002). Key Features of the Financial Sectors in EU Accession Countries. In: C. Thimann, ed., *Financial Sectors in EU Accession Countries*. Frankfurt: European Central Bank.

de Larosiére, J. (2001). Transition Economies in the Evolving Global Financial Markets. In: L. Bokros, A. Fleming, and C. Votava, eds., *Financial Transition in Europe and Central Asia – Challenges in the New Decade*. Washington, DC: World Bank, pp. 3–6.

Del Valle Borraez, C., M. Batlay, and E. Togo (1998). Overview of Fixed-Income Securities Markets in Emerging Economies. Presented at the OECD/World Bank Workshop on the Development of Fixed-income Securities Markets in Emerging Economies, Paris, December 14–16, 1998. Paris: OECD; Washington, DC: World Bank.

DePfa (2000). Public Sector Debt in the Fast Track Countries – Are the Candidates Better than the EU Members? *DePfa Research 3/2000: Public Sector Finance*. Wiesbaden: DePfa Deutsche Pfandbrief Bank.

European Central Bank (2002). *Bond Markets and Long-Term Interest Rates in European Union Accession Countries*. Frankfurt: ECB.

European Commission (2002). Update of the Report on Macroeconomic and Financial Sector Stability Developments in Candidate Countries by Directorate General for Economic and Financial Affairs. EC Enlargement Paper 11. Brussels: EC.

Eichengreen, B. and A. Mody (1997). *What Explains Changing Spreads on Emerging-Market Debt: Fundamentals or Market Sentiment*. Mimeo. Washington, DC: International Monetary Fund.

International Monetary Fund (1998). The Crisis in Emerging Economies: Interim Assessment. *World Economic Outlook*. Washington, DC: IMF, Ch. II, pp. 17–34. *World Economic and Financial Surveys Series*.

Kamin, S. and K. von Kleist (1999). *The Evolution and Determinates of Emerging Market Credit Spreads in the 1990s*. BIS Working Paper 68. Basle: BIS.

Kokoszczynski, R. and A. Slawinski (1999). *Poland's Vulnerability to Turbulence in Financial Markets. Managing Foreign Debt and Liquidity Risks*. BIS Policy Paper 8. Basle: BIS, pp. 138–146.

Köke, J. and M. Schröder (2002). *The Future of Eastern European Capital Markets*. EIB Paper 7, No. 1. Luxembourg: European Investment Bank, pp. 117–138.

Molinas, C. and G.P. Bales (2002). *Size and Structure of the World Bond Market: 2002*. New York: Merrill Lynch & Co.

Organization for Economic Cooperation and Development (2002). *Debt Management and Government Securities Markets in the 21st Century*. Paris: OECD.

Organization for Economic Cooperation and Development (2002). *OECD Public Debt Markets: Trends and Recent Structural Changes*. Paris: OECD.

Raiffeisen Zentralbank Group (2003). *Strategy East 2nd Quarter 2003*. Vienna: RZB Group.

Szilagyi, P.G., J.A. Batten, and T.A. Fetherston (2003). Disintermediation and the Development of Bond Markets in Emerging Europe. *International Journal of the Economics of Business* **10**(1): 67–82.

United Nations Economic Commission for Europe (2003). Eastern Europe and the CIS. In: *Economic Survey of Europe*, No. 1. Geneva: UNECE, Ch. 3, pp. 41–101.

4

Perspectives on European Derivative Markets

MARTIN YOUNG

4.1 INTRODUCTION AND A BRIEF HISTORY OF THE EUROPEAN DERIVATIVE MARKETS

The same forces that have been acting on all financial markets within Europe in recent years and within the European Union (EU) in particular, have been acting on the European derivative markets. Mergers and the forming of strategic alliances have been the name of the game and this consolidation process has gone hand in hand with growth in the number and nature of the derivative contracts traded in the European derivative markets.

At the beginning of the 1990s Europe had a number of derivative markets but they were, in general, newly formed. The oldest of these derivative markets was the London International Financial Futures Exchange, or LIFFE, which was founded in 1982 and started trading financial futures in the same year. The mid-to-late eighties saw the rapid introduction of a number of other European derivative markets led particularly by the Scandinavian counties. The Stockholm Options Market (SOM) was founded in 1985, followed by the Finnish Options Market (FOM) and the Danish Options and Futures Market (FUTOP) in 1987. In these later two cases the trading of financial futures started in the following year.

It was some time after the founding of LIFFE that the two major economies of Western Europe, France, and Germany began to develop their derivative markets. France began with Marche a Terme International de France (MATIF), which was founded in 1986, and in 1988 DTB Deutsche Terminbörse (DTB) came into being. Financial futures began trading in these markets in 1986 and 1990 respectively.

A number of other European countries developed derivative markets at around this time: Switzerland, the Swiss Options and Financial Futures Exchange (SOFFEX), in 1986; the Netherlands, Financiele Termijnmarkt Amsterdam NV (FTA), in 1987; Spain, Mercado Espanol de Futuros Financieros SA (MEFF), in 1989; and the Belgian Futures and Options Exchange (BELFOX), in 1990. Two futures exchanges came into existence in Italy: Mercato Italiano Futures (MIF) started operating in 1992 as an interest rate derivatives exchange; then in 1994, IDEM (Italian Derivatives Market) began operating as an equity derivatives exchange. While the nineties saw growth in the European derivative markets, the main activity of recent times has taken place since around 1998.

European Fixed Income Markets: Money, Bond and Interest Rate Derivatives. Edited by J.A. Batten,
T.A. Fetherston and P.G. Szilagyi. © 2004 John Wiley & Sons, Ltd. ISBN 0-470-85053-1

4.2   EUROPE'S MAJOR DERIVATIVE MARKETS

4.2.1   LIFFE

The oldest official derivative market in Europe is the London International Financial Futures and Options Exchange (LIFFE), and now as part of the Euronext Group it remains one of the premier derivatives market in Europe, particularly for the trading of short term interest rate derivatives.

LIFFE began its operations in 1982, focusing on providing products to help in the management of interest rate and currency risk. In fact one of the first futures contracts developed by LIFFE was the British government debt contract based on the long term US Treasury contracts pioneered by the Chicago Board of Trade in the mid-1970s. Other contracts that were introduced in that first year of operation included a 3-month Eurodollar interest rate contract, a short sterling interest rate contract, and four currency contracts on the pound, Swiss franc, yen, and deutsch mark. A Japanese government bond futures contract was introduced in 1987 and the highly successful German government Bund futures contract was introduced in 1988. By 1989, 3-month Euromark futures, 3-month European currency unit futures, and Bund options contracts had also been introduced. These were followed by 3-month Euroswiss interest rate futures and Italian government bond futures and options contracts in 1991. Changes in the financial markets over time have led to some of these products since being dropped, but the willingness of LIFFE to introduce these products showed that the exchange wished to be a dominant player in the area of financial futures.

In developing into the influential institution that it is today, mergers occurred with the London Traded Options Market (LTOM) in 1992, and with the London Commodity Exchange (LCE) in 1996. The LTOM bought with it equity options with the LCE bringing a range of commodity-based products. The major product lines of LIFFE, though, remain the short term interest rate and government bond contracts that were its original strength. Other products that followed include the Eurolira futures contact, and Bund, Euromark, and Long Gilt serial options contracts. An important development then took place in 1997 when LIFFE and the Chicago Board of Trade cross-listed products. The Chicago Board of Trade's US Treasury bond contract was launched on LIFFE and LIFFE's Bund contract was launched on the CBOT. In the same year, Bobl futures and options contacts were launched on LIFFE and LIFFE became the second largest futures and options exchange in the world.

Interestingly, it was the technology boom of the late nineties that gave LIFFE its biggest challenge and arguably its biggest success, but only after a major rethink. In July 1997, in a press release it was announced that "open outcry trading is the fairest and most efficient way of executing business in high volume futures and options contracts and so will remain LIFFE's predominant trading platform for the foreseeable future." Included in the initiatives announced at this time was the decision to retain an option for the development of a new open-outcry trading floor for the exchange at Spitalfields in London. This decision was an interesting one given the moves to screen trading that had occurred in many markets through the nineties and proved to be short-lived.

The shift to electronic trading came in stages, gathering momentum through 1998 and 1999. It was driven by three major realizations. First, business could shift between marketplaces almost instantaneously in an electronic environment. The clearest example of this for LIFFE was the shift in trading of the German government Bund contract from the trading floor at LIFFE to the screen-based trading platform at the major German derivatives exchange, the Deutsche TerminBörse. This was a great blow for LIFFE and probably the single biggest factor that drove their rethink. Second, the technology advances in screen-based trading platforms in the later part of the nineties was quite dramatic. The idea that open outcry was the fairest and most efficient way of executing business was shown to be an outdated one. Finally there was the issue of cost. Efficient screen trading was proving to be the much cheaper alternative for many reasons. In a press release in November 1998, it was stated that LIFFE had to "deliver an efficient trading platform together with the products that our customers want at a price they are prepared to pay. It is clear that nothing remotely like our current cost base is sustainable."

The major development in the move toward electronic trading began at the end of 1997. LIFFE had decided to move to electronic trading for the individual equity options using a system they were developing called LIFFE CONNECT® with a launch date of November 1998. LIFFE CONNECT® would be an order-driven trading system matching orders on the basis of time and price priority. In March of 1998, however, this development received renewed impetus when the Deutsche TerminBörse offered to implement their rather outdated DTB system at LIFFE at no charge. LIFFE quickly moved to quash this initiative and reiterated the importance of developing its own state-of-the-art trading system. Cancellation of the Spitalfields development followed shortly after. On November 30, 1998, LIFFE CONNECT® was launched for equity options and a timetable was given for the shift of other derivative products to this new system. The intention was to have all the financial futures contracts offered by LIFFE trading electronically within 8 months of this date. Long Gilt and 5-year Gilt futures came next in April 1999, followed by the index futures contracts in May. Electronic trading also began on the German, Italian, Japanese, and Euroyen bond contracts in May. This happened a month ahead of schedule. The first of LIFFE's short term interest rate contracts began trading on LIFFE CONNECT® in August 1999, and by May 2000 all financial futures and options were trading electronically.

LIFFE CONNECT® proved so successful and showed such a high level of flexibility that growth through 2000 and 2001 impressively surpassed expectations. A record 61 trillion worth of contracts were traded on LIFFE in 2000, up 21% on the previous year. For the 2001 year, the growth rate was even more impressive, up 57% to 96 trillion. In terms of number of contracts traded, these went from 131 million in 2000 to 216 million in 2001. With the financial integration that was occurring in Europe, such an impressive performance attracted suitors. In October 2001, the board of LIFFE recommended to shareholders that an offer from Euronext, which was born out of a merger between Amsterdam Exchanges, Brussels Exchanges, and the ParisBourse in September 2000, be accepted. This would enable London to become the hub for the derivatives business of Euronext. The following two quotes are taken from the Executive Summary of the submission by the London International Financial Futures and Options Exchange to the British House of Commons Treasury Committee dated January 11, 2002.

Over the last three years, LIFFE has rapidly developed a world-leading screen-based trading system, LIFFE CONNECT®, and successfully transformed itself from a floor-based, open outcry market into a wholly electronic screen-based marked, which can now be accessed directly from more cities in more countries than any other financial market in the world. Every day more business by value, over 550 billion, is entrusted to LIFFE CONNECT®, more than any other electronic exchange in the world. Furthermore the system also supports the broadest range of products of any electronic exchange worldwide, and is the only electronic system in the world capable of successfully trading highly complex short term interest rate futures and options.

The combination of Euronext and LIFFE's derivatives operations will treble the volume of business conducted through LIFFE CONNECT®. This will enable LIFFE and Euronext to respond to customer needs by providing, through a single trading platform, access to a much deeper market with a wider product range more quickly and effectively than either could otherwise have done independently.

LIFFE became Euronext.Liffe and for the year 2002 firmly established itself as one of only two major players in the bond and short term interest rate futures and options market within Europe. The other major player was EUREX, the derivatives market set up through a joint venture between Deutsche Börse AG and the Swiss Stock Exchange. On a number of contracts traded basis, EUREX traded more than double those traded by Euronext.Liffe for the first 2 months of 2003. On a value basis, however, Euronext.Liffe traded more than three times the value traded by EUREX over the same period but this was driven by the fact that Euronext.Liffe dominated the short term interest rate market while EUREX dominated the longer term interest rate market.

4.2.2 EUREX

As stated above, today there is only one serious competitor to LIFFE in the area of bond and short term interest rate futures and options trading in Europe. This competitor is EUREX. This German/Swiss joint venture came about through the merger of the DTB Deutsche Terminbörse, the German Options and Futures Exchange, and SOFFEX, the Swiss Options and Financial Futures Exchange, in 1998. DTB Deutsche Terminbörse itself came into existence in 1988 and started trading financial futures in 1990. At the time of the formation of EUREX the DTB Deutsche Terminbörse was part of the Deutsche Börse Group. SOFFEX began operations in 1986 and also started trading financial futures in 1990. During 1994 SOFFEX was integrated into the Swiss Exchange and at this time was ranked as the third largest derivatives market in Europe. In December 1996, the two derivative exchanges made the first move toward working together when a letter of intent was signed between Deutsche Börse AG and SWX Swiss Exchanges with the intent of creating a joint trading and clearing platform. This joint platform was created in September 1997.

The rationale for this move was to create a derivatives market large enough to compete effectively in the ever more integrated Europe. Integration had led to stronger competition between financial centers, and DTB Deutsche Terminbörse and SOFFEX jointly believed that this competition would become even more intense with the introduction of the Eurocurrency. By bringing these two derivative exchanges together an enhanced trading and clearing system would be developed with a multicurrency capability. Further, the larger market would have a greater range of products, higher liquidity, and lower costs. In May 1998, the combined derivate operations changed their name to EUREX and commenced trading on EUREX software. EUREX came into being as a 50/50 joint venture between the Deutsche Börse AG and the SWX Swiss Exchange. Today it trades a very internationally diverse group of products, particularly in the equity-based area, but also has a wide range of bond and money market derivative products. Access to the market is available in a number of major cities including Chicago, New York, London, and Tokyo.

Like Euronext.Liffe, EUREX also has a trans-European and greater global focus. After its formation, EUREX entered into a number of agreements with other exchanges. Within Europe, for example, a cooperation agreement was signed with the Helsinki Exchanges Group in April 1999. This cooperation agreement moved forward in August of the same year with the commencement of trading of HEX products on EUREX. More than a year earlier there had been the signing of a memorandum of understanding between Deutsche Börse AG, SWX Swiss Exchanges, and EUREX on the one hand and SBF Paris Bourse, MATIF SA, and MONEP SA on the other, to form a European alliance of exchanges. The aim was to have "one single trading system, one single clearing system, one single international network" for all derivative products and further to extend this goal to include the cash markets. The long term vision of this particular agreement was never fulfilled, however, with the French derivatives exchanges finally becoming part of the Euronext Group.

Just a month later, in March 1998, an agreement between EUREX and the Chicago Board of Trade was announced. The aim of this agreement was to create a network trading alliance between the two parties. In the first phase of the closer relationship, a common global communications network was to be set up, with the final aim being to allow access to both markets from a single screen. This aim became a reality in August 2000 and within the first month of operations over 2 million contracts were traded. By the end of 2000 there were 429 participants from 15 European countries as well as the United States trading on EUREX. Participant numbers steadied over 2001 and 2002 and by the end of 2002, EUREX had a total of 424 participants from 16 European countries, the United States, and Australia. The most number of participants were from Germany, 125; the United Kingdom, 71; the United States, 63; Switzerland, 39; France, 30; and the Netherlands, 29. In terms of market share the percentages for 2002 were as follows: Germany, 24.94%; the United Kingdom, 40.93%; the United States, 10.85%; Switzerland, 8.21%; France, 9.54%; and the Netherlands, 1.97%. The Bund future was the highest turnover product in this segment of the exchange's offerings in 2002, with 195 million contracts traded out of a total of 801.2 million for the exchange as a whole. In January 1999, EUREX had announced that it had become the world's largest derivatives market, and in terms of number of contracts traded this remains the case. Euronext.Liffe now claims to be the world's leading exchange for euro short term interest rate derivatives and equity options but EUREX remains the market leader in the bond derivative area. It would seem that the new Europe is definitely big enough for both these players in the derivatives market but there may not be sufficient room for many more serious players to join them long term.

4.2.3   Euronext Before and After the Takeover of LIFFE

On September 22, 2000, Euronext was born through the merger of Amsterdam Exchanges (AEX), Brussels Exchanges (BXS), and ParisBourse. This merger encompassed both the cash and derivative markets of all three exchanges. A common clearing and settlement system called Clearnet®, was put in place, and Euroclear® became the settlement agency and custody platform. The thinking that had driven the decision-making process at EUREX was much the same as that driving this merger. With the coming of the single currency a pan-European approach to the financial markets made the most sense. As far as the money market and bond derivatives were concerned there would be fewer products but potentially a much larger market for these products, particularly if the euro became a true competitor to the US dollar, as was a real possibility. Initially, however, the cash market was the focus of this merger, but with the later addition of LIFFE to the group the derivatives business of Euronext was consolidated into Euronext.Liffe, bringing clearly into focus the benefits of mergers in the derivative markets area.

Of the three original members of Euronext, ParisBourse had the largest derivatives operation. The derivatives side of ParisBourse operated under two separate entities: MATIF, which started trading in 1986 as an interest rate, commodities derivative market; and Le MONEP, which started operations in 1987, primarily as a stock options market. This was not the oldest derivatives operation though, as Amsterdam's derivatives markets had started up 2 years earlier. Derivatives trading started in Brussels in 1991. For the first full year of trading after the creation of the pan-European Euronext, Paris accounted for approximately 82% of Euronext's derivatives trades, with Amsterdam accounting for approximately 17% and Brussels just 1%. MATIF itself had been building alliances through the nineties as it positioned itself as a major fixed income derivatives market within Europe. In a press release in October 1996, MATIF declared its intentions in relation to developing its fixed income products during the transition to the single currency. An intention to develop relationships into North America and Asia was declared together with a strategy around which the fixed income products would be developed. This would be a three-pronged approach: "an adaptation of the existing range of products in French Francs, the creation of products in Euro covering all the maturities of the yield curve, a reduction in market access costs." Like with other exchanges the cost issue would end up focusing on open-outcry versus electronic trading.

MATIF then moved quickly to implement its strategy. In November 1996, MATIF signed an agreement with the Chicago Mercantile Exchange (CME) to allow its medium and long term interest rate contracts to be traded on the CME after trading had stopped for the day on MATIF. This was followed by a 30% cut in clearing fees in January 1997. Just days later a most significant agreement was announced between MATIF and SBF-Paris Bourse that MATIF would use the NSC electronic trading system developed by SBF-Paris Bourse for transactions outside floor trading hours. Further, the two would work together to develop a new derivatives trading system within the NSC architecture in order to reduce costs. This was the beginning of a much closer working relationship between MATIF and SBF-Paris Bourse. By mid-February another technology-driven agreement was announced, developing on from those mentioned above. MATIF and SBF-Paris Bourse signed a letter of intent with the CME and the NYMEX (New York Mercantile Exchange), whereby it was agreed that the American exchanges would adopt the NSC trading system for after-hours trading and the Paris exchanges would adopt the clearing system developed by the CME and NYMEX.

By the middle of 1997 many exchanges were actively pursuing strategic alliances, and the Deutsche Börse AG and SWX Swiss Exchanges looked to SBF-Paris Bourse as a likely long term partner. In September 1997, a joint statement from the three exchanges, MATIF and MONEP declared an intention to develop a joint market for fixed income derivatives and to also develop an integrated cash market. On the same day, SBF-Paris Bourse also announced a full takeover offer for MATIF to buy the 74% of equity that it did not already own, a proposal that was supported by MATIF's board of directors. MONEP was also to become a subsidiary of the SBF-Paris Bourse. The September announcement of the strategic alliance was followed by a further announcement in February 1998 where the same parties laid out a blueprint for the Euro alliance that would create Europe's largest derivatives market. The intention was to synchronize product development with the introduction of the euro and to have each derivative exchange operating under one trading system, one clearing system, and one international network by January 2002.

By May 1998, MATIF had completed plans to provide a full range of interest rate contracts on the euro and by early June trading in all MATIF interest rate futures went fully electronic through the NSC-VF system. The only open-outcry trading left at MATIF at this time was for their commodity futures but even this was stopped by the end of June, meaning that the entire derivative market had now changed over to electronic trading. MATIF now threw down something of a challenge to LIFFE by commencing trading in 5-year and 10-year Gilts, with 7% UK government securities as the underlying asset in July of the same year. At this time LIFFE was still struggling to accept that electronic trading was the only way forward and this move by MATIF was another factor in helping LIFFE to develop a clear vision for its trading future. The following points were made in the press release from MATIF at that time:

> The launch of the new gilt contracts on MATIF comes in response to the wish of the market participants, particularly in the UK, to benefit from the advantages of electronic trading through NSC. This offers low trading costs associated with a powerful, open-architecture system that is easy to use and provides a complete view of market depth.

Another development that happened at the same time was an alliance between MATIF, MONEP, and the two Spanish derivative exchanges, MEFF Renta Fija, which traded interest rate derivative products, and MEFF Renta Variable, which traded equity-based derivative products. The MEFF exchanges had been operating as fully electronic exchanges since they began trading in 1990. The nature of this alliance was to implement cross trading between each exchange through Euro GLOBEX®, the trading platform that was already being used jointly by MATIF and the CME. A few months later in December the Italian derivatives markets, MIF, which traded interest rate derivatives, and IDEM, which traded index futures and equity options, also signed up to join the Euro GLOBEX® alliance. A further development saw the introduction of GLOBEX® 2 in September 1998. This electronic trading system was based on the SBF-Paris Bourse's NSC system and its adoption by the CME allowed for even closer cooperation between it and MATIF. In the same month a further step was taken toward the Euro alliance when EUREX, SBF-Paris Bourse, MATIF, and MONEP signed an agreement to introduce cross-membership between EUREX, MATIF, and MONEP members. The intention was for this to be effective by the end of 1998, but the two groups were to finally go their separate ways.

Another innovation from SBF-Paris Bourse came at the end of 1998 with the introduction of Clearnet®, Europe's first clearinghouse for over-the-counter traded products. This operation was developed and run by the SBF-Paris Bourse subsidiary, Banque Centrale de Compensation. It was stated in the press release of December 10, 1998, that the launch of Clearnet® was driven by three main factors:

> 1. Because of the increasing cost of equity capital and of the growing necessity to control risks, financial institutions are even keener than before to benefit from the security guarantee that clearing houses can provide (i.e. single counterparty, clearing, market-to-market margining).
> 2. The borderline between OTC and regulated markets are becoming increasingly blurred in so far as the clearing and the guarantee of positions are concerned. On the contrary, as the recent market turmoil and uncertainty regarding counterparty credit risk demonstrates it makes sense to bring OTC and exchange-traded procedures closer so as to ensure productivity gains as well as a clearer definition of risks.
> 3. With this in mind and with the emerging Euro interest rate offering many new investment and trading opportunities, a pan-European clearing and guarantee initiative seems to be relevant with the advent of EMU.

Alliances continued to be the name of the game as 1999 got underway and in February it was announced that the CME, the two subsidiaries of SBF-Paris Bourse, MATIF SA and MONEP SA, and the Singapore International Monetary Exchange, SIMEX, were to form an electronic trading alliance named GLOBEX® Alliance. As was stated in the press release of February 8, this would be "the first major electronic trading alliance to offer trading of futures and options spanning the world's three major time zones." Members of each grouping of exchanges would have access to each other's products through compatible electronic trading systems. September of 1999 saw further expansion of GLOBEX® Alliance when both Bolsa de Mercadorias & Futures (BM&F), and Montreal Exchange joined the group. Spain's MEFF joined the alliance in June 2000. The relationship between the French derivatives markets and that of Singapore was further strengthened in December 1999 when the Paris Bourse and the Singapore Exchange's trading division signed a cross membership and cross trading agreement allowing access to both member groups to all electronically traded products in both markets.

One of the most important developments on the path to the Euronext grouping of exchanges came at the beginning of June 1999 when SBF-Paris Bourse announced a major restructuring to form one company for all its market activities. The details of this restructuring, as laid out in the June press announcement, were as follows. First, all the market operations that had come under the grouping of SBF-Paris Bourse since the beginning of 1998 were to be merged into one company called ParisBourse SBF SA. These four market operations were SBF-Paris Bourse itself, MATIF SA, MONEP SA, and the Societe du Nouveau Marche. The other major operations of SBF-Paris Bourse were the clearing-house and guarantee operations and the technology operations. The clearing-house and guarantee operations were those of the derivatives exchange operating under the name of SBF MATIF SA and Clearnet® operated by Banque Centrale de Compensation. Both clearing and guarantee operations were now to come under Banque Centrale de Compensation and trade under the name of Clearnet SBF SA. Finally the technology side of the operation was to be grouped within Euronext SBF SA, a company that was already a leader in market trading and clearing systems adopted by 15 markets globally, many of them leading markets in both equities and derivatives. The NSC trading system for derivatives, marketed by Euronext SBF SA, was also adopted by the Australian Derivatives Exchange Limited in late 1999.

On the derivatives side the year 1999 ended mixed for ParisBourse SBF SA. Derivative trading was up over 120% on the previous year overall but there had been a significant drop in trading for interest rate derivatives despite the efforts made to provide a more comprehensive grouping of products. The issue of how many fixed interest derivative markets were appropriate in the new single currency Europe was again becoming an important issue. EUREX was now well established and growing strongly in terms of fixed interest derivatives and LIFFE was making a very strong comeback. For the ParisBourse SBF SA, however, 1999 saw a 73.7% drop in interest rate futures trading from 23.3 million contracts in 1998 to just 6.1 million contracts in 1999. Trading in the 3-month EURIBOR contract, the major contract traded, fell from 5.3 million contracts in 1998 to 3 million contracts in 1999. Growth continued into 2000 but again this growth was on the equity and index options and commodity side, not on interest rate derivatives.

March 20, 2000, saw the announcement of the establishment of Euronext when the exchanges of Amsterdam, Brussels, and Paris agreed to merge to create the leading European exchange. Euronext would be incorporated as a Dutch company, Euronext NV, offering a fully integrated trading, clearing, and settlement market. Shareholders in Amsterdam Exchange, Brussels Exchange, and ParisBourse SBF SA, would exchange their shares for shares in Euronext NV, which would then become a listed public company. This would create the largest equity market and the largest equity and index options market in Europe, but would be trailing others in the fixed interest derivatives area. The technology to be used was the French NSC trading system and extending the concept of Clearnet® based on the Clearing 21® software system. The main rationale for the merger of the exchanges was to provide a market that was highly competitive in terms of cost structure and highly liquid with what would effectively be a single pan-Europe order book. It was estimated at the time that cost savings over the three exchange groupings would be approximately €50 million per year. The timeline announced was for the NSC trading system to be operational for the new integrated exchange by the first half of 2001 with full clearing implementation achieved by the second half of that year.

Euronext officially came into existence on the September 22, 2000, but the main focus of the new entity was on the equity market operation, even though each exchange's derivative market was part of the same package. Euronext Paris derivatives markets saw a solid gain in contracts traded for September 2000, even on the interest rate derivatives side, though overall interest rate derivative trading was moving ahead strongly for 2000, thanks mainly to exceptional growth in the Euro Notional Bond futures contract. For the full year fixed income derivative contracts traded rose by 606% from 1999 to 43.3 million; however, this improvement in trading activity for interest rate derivatives was short-lived and volumes went into decline again in 2001. In December 2000, Euronext announced that it was going to integrate the trading systems of its derivative markets but this initiative was finally overtaken when LIFFE joined the Euronext group.

Before this was to happen, however, Euronext was to expand further with the merger of Bolsa de Valores de Lisoa e Porto, or BVLP, into the group. BVLP was the Portuguese Exchange based in Lisbon, which itself came into existence with the merger of Lisbon Stock Exchange Association and the Porto Derivatives Exchange Association. This derivatives exchange had been operating out of Lisbon since 1996, but in terms of contracts traded was a little smaller than the Brussels derivatives exchange. Cross-trading and cross-membership agreements were also put in place with a number of exchanges. First an agreement was reached with Bourse de Luxembourg for cross-membership and cross-access. This was followed by two cross-membership and cross-trading agreements, first with the Helsinki exchanges in September 2001, and then with the Warsaw Stock Exchange in February 2002. However, in relation to derivatives trading, by far the most important development occurred in October 2001 when LIFFE recommended a full takeover by Euronext to its shareholders. This gave Euronext the opportunity to incorporate the derivatives side of its business into one clear entity. Euronext.Liffe was born comprising the derivative markets of Amsterdam, Brussels, Paris, Lisbon, and London and work began on bringing all these markets together on a single electronic trading platform, namely LIFFE CONNECT®. The timetable for this integration was early 2003 for Brussels and Paris, with Amsterdam and Lisbon to follow in 2004. On March 24, 2003, Brussels commenced trading on LIFFE CONNECT®, and then on April 14, 2003, Euronext Paris derivative products were also successfully transferred to LIFFE CONNECT®. This shift also allowed for a substantial reduction in trading fees within the now highly competitive European derivatives markets.

For the year 2002, Euronext.Liffe traded a total of 697 million futures and options contracts for an underlying value of €183 trillion, making it the world's second largest derivatives exchange. While the bulk of these contracts were individual equity and equity index products, short term interest rate products totaled 187.7 million and medium and long term interest rate products totaled 12.2 million. Breaking down the trading by region, Paris accounted for 51.2% of total trades, London for 36.4%, Amsterdam for 11.1%, and Lisbon and Brussels for 0.7% and 0.6% respectively. During 2002, LIFFE CONNECT® exceeded the 500 site barriers, of which over 60% were located outside of the United Kingdom.

4.3   AN OVERVIEW OF THE CONTRACTS TRADED ON EUREX AND EURONEXT.LIFFE

It is fair to say that Euronext.Liffe dominates the short term interest rate contracts within Europe and EUREX dominates the medium and long term segment of the market. Euronext.Liffe has moved to be a more significant player in the medium and long term segment of the market with the introduction of their Swapnote® range of products and EUREX has recently introduced a range of delta-neutral synthetic contracts also. While both markets are strong competitors, it is natural for one market to end up as the dominant one for certain products, and now that each market has found its natural strength it is likely that they will both focus more on expanding in their relative areas of competitive advantage.

4.3.1   Short Term Interest Rate Contracts

As mentioned above, this is an area in which Euronext.Liffe clearly dominates within Europe. Euronext.Liffe offered a total of 11 futures and options products as at the end of March 2003 compared with four products offered by EUREX (Table 4.1). For the year 2002, six of these products offered by Euronext.Liffe traded in excess of 1 million contracts, each with three products trading over 30 million contracts. The most popular contract was the 3-month EURIBOR interest rate futures, which traded over 100 million contracts. This was also the only actively traded short term interest rate product offered by EUREX, but trading volume was only just over half a million contracts (Table 4.2). Euronext.Liffe also offers contracts on four other major short term rates. In order of popularity these are the 3-month sterling, the 3-month Euro-Swiss franc, the 3-month Euroyen (TIBOR), and the 3-month euro (LIBOR) rate. This last contract did not trade in 2002.

Recently both exchanges have introduced a contract for 1-month EONIA (Euro Overnight Index Average) indexed futures. On December 19, 2002, Euronext.Liffe announced that it was going to launch the contract on February 4, 2003, but EUREX then moved to follow suit by launching the same product on January 21, 2003. EONIA is the effective overnight reference interest rate for the Euro averaged over a period of one calendar month. EUREX's introduction of this contract was a direct challenge to Euronext.Liffe's dominance of the short term interest rate contract market but, to date anyway, Euronext.Liffe appears to have won out. In the first month of trading Euronext.Liffe claims to have taken a 98% share of the market with 96% of open interests being held with them as at the end of February. When announcing this success, the Managing Director of sales and marketing at Euronext.Liffe

Table 4.1   Short term interest rate contracts traded on Euronext.Liffe and EUREX as at March 31, 2003

Contracts traded	Euronext.Liffe	EUREX
Futures products		
One-month EONIA indexed futures	Yes	Yes
One-month EURIBOR futures	No	Yes
Three-month EURIBOR interest rate futures	Yes	Yes
Three-month LIBOR interest rate futures	Yes	No
Three-month sterling interest rate futures	Yes	No
Three-month EuroSwiss interest rate futures	Yes	No
Three-month Euroyen (TIBOR) interest rate futures	Yes	No
Options products		
Option on 3-month EURIBOR futures	Yes	Yes
One-year mid-curve option on 3-month EURIBOR futures	Yes	No
Option on 3-month sterling futures	Yes	No
One-year mid term option on 3-month sterling futures	Yes	No
Option on 3-month Euroswiss futures	Yes	No

Source: www.eurexchange.com/products and www.liffe.com/products.

Table 4.2 Trading volumes for short term interest rate contracts traded on Euronext.Liffe and EUREX for the 2002 calendar year

Contracts traded	Euronext-Liffe	EUREX
Money market futures products		
One-month EONIA indexed futures	*	*
One-month EURIBOR futures	†	0
Three-month EURIBOR interest rate futures	105 086 163	527 815
Three-month LIBOR interest rate futures	0	†
Three-month sterling interest rate futures	34 307 727	†
Three-month EuroSwiss interest rate futures	4 976 206	†
Three-month Euroyen (TIBOR) interest rate futures	1 769	†
Money market options products		
Option on 3-month EURIBOR futures	33 643 698	0
One-year mid-curve option on 3-month EURIBOR futures	1 419 271	†
Option on 3-month sterling futures	7 364 057	†
One-year mid term option on 3-month sterling futures	346 001	†
Option on 3-month EuroSwiss futures	81 467	†

Source: EUREX Monthly Statistics December 2002 and www.liffe.com/liffedata.
†Contract not offered.
*Contract not offered until 2003.

made the following comment: "Euronext.Liffe continues as the leading provider to the European interbank market and the world's marketplace for trading Euro short term interest rate products." While EUREX is sure to continue trying to build up its market share in this segment of the market, Euronext.Liffe's dominant position here cannot be questioned at this time.

4.3.2 Medium and Long Term Interest Rate Contracts

For medium and long term interest rate products EUREX is unquestionably the market leader, though Euronext.Liffe has made some impact with the introduction of their Swapnote® product range. For Euronext.Liffe, only three products offered traded over 1 million contracts in 2002, with two of these being Euro Swapnote® products. The most actively traded product on Euronext.Liffe was the long term Gilt (sterling) futures, with 7.8 million trades taking place. EUREX, on the other hand, had six of their products trading over 1 million contracts, with three trading over 100 million contracts. Short term ($1^3/_4$–$2^1/_4$) German Federal Govt. debt (Euro-SCHATZ) futures traded 108.8 million contracts, medium term ($4^1/_2$–$5^1/_2$) German Federal Govt. debt (Euro-BOBL) futures traded 114.7 million contracts, and the long term ($8^1/_2$–$10^1/_2$) German Federal Govt. debt (Euro-BUND) futures traded 191.3 million contracts. EUREX completes its offering on the Euro yield curve with the long term (20–$30^1/_2$) German Federal Govt. debt (Euro-BUXL) futures contract but the popularity of this contract is substantially less with just over 12 500 trades in 2000. Euronext.Liffe continues to offer the Bund futures and options contracts that once traded actively on their market, but there has been virtually no trading in either product now for a number of years (Tables 4.3 and 4.4).

Both EUREX and Euronext.Liffe have introduced innovative products to this segment of the market in recent times. Euronext.Liffe has seen good success with the introduction of their Swapnote® product range, which was initially introduced on March 20, 2001. The purpose of a swap is to provide an exchange of fixed interest rates for floating interest rates and is

Table 4.3   Medium and long term interest rate contracts traded on Euronext.Liffe and EUREX as at March 31, 2003

Contracts traded	Euronext.Liffe	EUREX
Futures products		
Long term (8–13 years) Swiss Federal Govt. debt (CONF) futures	No	Yes
Short term ($1^3/_4$–$2^1/_4$) German Federal Govt. debt (Euro-SCHATZ) futures	Yes	Yes
Medium term ($4^1/_2$–$5^1/_2$) German Federal Govt. debt (Euro-BOBL) futures	No	Yes
Long term ($8^1/_2$–$10^1/_2$) German Federal Govt. debt (Euro-BUND) futures	Yes	Yes
Long term (20–$30^1/_2$) German Federal Govt. debt (Euro-BUXL) futures	No	Yes
Long term Gilt (sterling) futures	Yes	No
Long term Japanese Govt. bond futures	Yes	No
Two-year euro Swapnote®	Yes	No
Two-year US$ Swapnote®	Yes	No
Five-year euro Swapnote®	Yes	No
Five-year US$ Swapnote®	Yes	No
Ten-year euro Swapnote®	Yes	No
Ten-year US$ Swapnote®	Yes	No
Options products		
Option on short term ($1^3/_4$–$2^1/_4$) German Federal Govt. debt (Euro-SCHATZ) futures	No	Yes
Option on medium term ($4^1/_2$–$5^1/_2$) German Federal Govt. debt (Euro-BOBL) futures	No	Yes
Option on long term ($8^1/_2$–$10^1/_2$) German Federal Govt. debt (Euro-BUND) futures	Yes	Yes
Option on long term Gilt (sterling) futures	Yes	No
Option on long term Japanese Govt. bond futures	Yes	No
Delta-neutral synthetic contract between the Euro-Schatz future and option	No	Yes
Delta-neutral synthetic contract between the Euro-Bobl future and option	No	Yes
Delta-neutral synthetic contract between the Euro-Bund future and option	No	Yes
Options on 2-year euro Swapnote®	Yes	No
Options on 5-year euro Swapnote®	Yes	No
Options on 10-year euro Swapnote®	Yes	No

Source: www.eurexchange.com/products and www.liffe.com/products.

therefore a very useful product for managing interest rate risk. The Euro swap market had grown to approximately US$23 trillion by the middle of 2000 and with such high liquidity in this market it had effectively become a benchmark yield curve. Euronext.Liffe believed that by introducing these contracts they would open up the swap market to smaller players and increase the liquidity in the underlying over-the-counter market for swaps. Euronext.Liffe started by offering their Swapnote® futures product on the 2-, 5-, and 10-year euro rates and followed this up with the introduction of options on these Swapnote® products from July of the same year. The Swapnote® product range was further expanded in July 2002 with the introductions of contracts based on the US dollar swap curve. Again 2-, 5-, and 10-year futures products

Table 4.4 Trading volumes for medium and long term interest rate contracts traded on Euronext.Liffe and EUREX for the calendar year 2002

Contracts traded	Euronext.Liffe	EUREX
Futures products		
Long term (8–13 years) Swiss Federal Govt. debt (CONF) futures	*	275 392
Short term (1³/₄–2¹/₄) German Federal Govt. debt (Euro-SCHATZ) futures	228 125[†]	108 760 955
Medium term (4¹/₂–5¹/₂) German Federal Govt. debt (Euro-BOBL) futures	*	114 678 996
Long term (8¹/₂–10¹/₂) German Federal Govt. debt (Euro-BUND) futures	0	191 263 413
Long term (20–30¹/₂) German Federal Govt. debt (Euro-BUXL) futures	*	12 668
Long term Gilt (sterling) futures	7 789 011	*
Long term Japanese Govt. bond futures	37 723	*
Two-year euro Swapnote®	977 127	*
Two-year US$ Swapnote®	6 584[‡]	*
Five-year euro Swapnote®	1 437 955	*
Five-year US$ Swapnote®	13 399[‡]	*
Ten-year euro Swapnote®	1 613 672	*
Ten-year US$ Swapnote®	51 709[‡]	*
Options products		
Option on short term (1³/₄–2¹/₄) German Federal Govt. debt (Euro-SCHATZ) futures	*	8 954 263
Option on medium term (4¹/₂–5¹/₂) German Federal Govt. debt (Euro-BOBL) futures	*	4 529 387
Option on long term (8¹/₂–10¹/₂) German Federal Govt. debt (Euro-BUND) futures	0	18 125 981
Option on long term Gilt (sterling) futures	0	*
Delta-neutral synthetic contract between Euro-Schatz future and option	*	§
Delta-neutral synthetic contract between Euro-Bobl future and option	*	§
Delta-neutral synthetic contract between Euro-Bund future and option	*	§
Options on 2-year euro Swapnote®	8 816	*
Options on 5-year euro Swapnote®	5 992	*
Options on 10-year euro Swapnote®	2 730	*

Source: EUREX Monthly Statistics December 2002 and www.liffe.com/liffedata.
*Contract not offered.
[†]Contract commenced trading June 18, 2002.
[‡] Contract commenced trading July 1, 2002.
[§] Contract not offered until 2003.

were introduced, though to date these have not met with the same success achieved by their euro counterparts.

EUREX has also tried its own innovations recently with the introduction of its delta-neutral synthetic contracts. Three of these products have been introduced to date between the Euro-Schatz future and option, the Euro-Bobl future and option, and the Euro-Bund future and option. The delta value measures the sensitivity of the option price to a small instantaneous change in the value of the underlying asset. The idea behind a delta-neutral position, therefore, is to create a synthetic contract where the option position is immunized against a small instantaneous change in the price of the underlying asset by taking delta times the opposite position on the underlying asset. As these products were only introduced from the beginning of April 2003 it is too early to gauge their success. However, even if these products do not meet with the same success that the Swapnote® products have achieved, EUREX still trades nearly 37 contracts for every one of Euronext.Liffe's in this segment of the market.

4.4 EUROPE'S OTHER DERIVATIVE MARKETS

When it comes to interest rate derivative trading in Europe there is not much after EUREX and Euronext.Liffe. The only market that shows any significant volume in the trading of such products currently is Sweden's Stockholmsbörsen. Some trading in interest rate derivative products also takes place, or has taken place recently, on the Spanish Exchanges, MEFF, the Italian interest rate derivative exchange, MIF, the ADEX market in Athens, on Hungary's BSE Derivatives market and the Budapest Commodity Exchange (BCE), and on the Romanian Commodities Exchange.

The derivatives arm of Sweden's Stockholmsbörsen was originally the Stockholm options market and this derivatives market was one of Europe's oldest, having started operations in 1985. This market also started trading financial futures in the same year. This long history of derivatives trading has made the Stockholmsbörsen the major derivatives player in the Nordic region and during 2002 two significant developments occurred. First an alliance of the Nordic region exchanges, the Copenhagen Stock Exchange, Iceland Stock Exchange, Stockholmbörsen, and Oslo Børs (NOREX) progressed well and with the Oslo Exchange adopting the SAXESS share trading system all NOREX exchanges are now on the same trading system. OM, the Swedish operator of Stockholmsbörsen, also entered into a joint venture with the London Stock Exchange to start a new derivatives exchange, EDX London. This new derivatives exchange intends to begin trading in the second quarter of 2003 but has stated that it will be dealing only in equity-based derivative products. It is hoped that this move will help strengthen equity-based derivatives trading in the Nordic region.

The derivatives arm of Stockholmsbörsen trades a significant number of interest rate derivative products but stock-related products are by far the most actively traded on the exchange. Of the total contract volume of 60.9 million contracts for 2002, 55.3 million were stock related and 5.6 million were interest rate related. The most actively traded interest rate futures contract traded on Stockholmsbörsen is the STIBOR-FRA 3-month deposit contract, which had a total of 3.5 million trades for 2002. The other most actively traded contracts are the 180-day Treasury bill futures contract and the 2-, 5-, and 10-year Treasury bond futures contract. A full list of interest rate derivative contracts available on Stockholmsbörsen, together with volumes traded for 2002, is given in Table 4.5.

The official exchange in Spain for derivatives trading is MEFF, which belongs to the MEFF-AIAF-SENAF Holding de Mercados Financieros. This exchange started actively trading derivative products in 1989 and included financial derivatives from 1990. In terms of interest rate derivatives, the only actively traded product currently offered by MEFF is the Bono 10 futures product. This product was launched in 1992 and has as its underlying asset a Notional Government Bond with a 4% annual coupon. Like most of the smaller derivative markets in Europe, the main activity in financial derivatives lies with the index-based futures and options

Table 4.5   Interest rate derivative products actively traded on the Stockholmbörsen Derivatives Exchange, and number of contracts traded for the year 2002

Contract	Contracts traded
STIBOR-FRA 3-month deposit futures	3 464 781
180-Day Treasury bill futures	291 991
2-year Treasury bond futures	975 668
5-year Treasury bond futures	379 459
10-year Treasury bond futures	189 625
2-year Caisse- & Stadshypotekskassan bond futures	70 220
5-year Caisse- & Stadshypotekskassan bond futures	43 972
2-year Mortgage benchmark bond futures	85 708
5-year Mortgage benchmark bond futures	63 335
Total	5 564 759

Source: Stockholmsbörsen Report 2002.

and stock options. For the year 2002 the total trading activity on MEFF was approximately 41.4 million contracts, of which only 47 000 contracts were bond futures.

The Italian interest rate derivative exchange, Mercato Italiano Futures, or MIF, started operating in 1992 and has, over the years, traded a range of government bond and interest rate futures and options. In particular BTP futures and options have been traded together with EURIBOR futures. In 1998 this exchange came under the control of Borsa Italiana, the Italian exchange, together with IDEM, the Italian exchange for equity derivatives. As with other European derivative exchanges the equity products have dominated in recent times and IDEM is now the mainstay of derivative trading on the Borsa Italiana.

The ADEX market in Athens has been in operation since 1999 and its major growth in financial derivative products has again been in index futures and options and stock options. By the end of 2001, ADEX was ranked seventh among European derivative exchanges for contracts traded on stock index futures and eighth for stock index options. The exchange did, however, introduced a futures product on the 10-year Hellenic Republic Bond in January 2000. This product proved reasonably popular at first, with average daily volume reaching over 2000 contracts a day by May 2000. However since the beginning of 2001 the contract has effectively died and the market is now effectively a stock-based products one only.

Other derivative markets to have recently offered interest rate derivative products are the derivatives arm of the Budapest Stock Exchange, BSE, and the Budapest Commodities Exchange, BCE. The BSE again is a market that concentrates on index and equity futures but includes the following interest-rate-based products. These are 3- and 12-month discount Treasury Bills, 1- and 3-month BUBOR contract, and a 3-year Hungarian government bond contract. The BCE started operations in 1989, mainly as a grain and live stock trading operation. But in 1993 the exchange opened a financial contracts section specifically to trade currency futures. Then in 1994 an interest rate futures contract on 90-day deposits was introduced, which remained until late 1996. In September 1996 the interest rate derivative products were expanded with the introduction of a 1- and 3-month BUBOR contract. In agreement with the BSE these contracts were introduced on both exchanges on the same day. Finally the Romanian Commodities Exchange, BRM, also has a 3-month BUBOR contract that it operates together with currency contracts on the US dollar and euro.

Table 4.6   The derivative markets of European countries and those that traded interest rate derivative products recently, or are trading interest rate derivative products as at March 31, 2003

Country	Financial derivatives market	Contracts traded −2002 (million)	Interest rate derivative products
Albania	No	–	–
Austria	ÖTOB	1.3	No
Belgium	Euronext.Liffe	3.9	No
Bulgaria	No	–	–
Croatia	No	–	–
Cyprus	No	–	–
Czech Republic	Under development	–	–
Denmark	FUTOP	0.5	No
Estonia	No	–	–
Finland	HEX Derivatives	8.5	No
France	Euronext.Liffe	357.5	Yes
Germany	EUREX	801.2*	Yes
Greece	ADEX	3.7	Yes
Hungary	BSE and BCE	0.6	Yes
Iceland	No	–	–
Ireland	No	–	–
Italy	IDEM/MIF	17.3	Yes
Latvia	No	–	–
Lithuania	No	–	–
Luxembourg	No	–	–
Malta	No	–	–
Netherlands	Euronext.Liffe	77.7	No
Norway	Oslo Børs	3.0	No
Poland	Warsaw Stock Exchange	3.2	No
Portugal	Euronext.Liffe	4.0	No
Romania	BRM	N/A	Yes
Russia	MICEX	N/A	No
Slovakia	No	–	–
Slovenia	No	–	–
Spain	MEFF	41.4	Yes
Sweden	Stockholmbörsen	60.9	Yes
Switzerland	EUREX	801.2*	Yes
Turkey	No	–	–
Ukraine	No	–	–
United Kingdom	Euronext.Liffe	254.0	Yes

Source: www.eurexchange.com/products and others.
*Note contracts traded for Germany and Switzerland is the EUREX total trade.

There are a number of other derivative markets operating in Europe but none of these have ever offered interest rate derivative products or else have not done so in the recent past. Italy has its IDEM market but this currently trades only index futures and options and stock options. The same applies to Austria's ÖTOB derivatives market, Denmark's FUTOP market, which operates under the Copenhagen Stock Exchange, Finland's HEX derivatives market, and Norway's Oslo Børs. The Warsaw Stock Exchange has a derivatives arm that started operation in January 1998. This market trades index, stock, and exchange rate futures. In Russia the derivatives market, MICEX, trades index, stock, and exchange rate futures also (Table 4.6).

4.5   WHAT THE FUTURE HOLDS

When it comes to the trading of European interest rate derivative products in Europe, it is fair to say that there are now only two major players, Euronext.Liffe and EUREX, and one minor player, Stockholmbörsen. Spain's MEFF could also be considered as a very minor player. Euronext.Liffe and EUREX developed into global operators to ensure a position of power in a single currency Europe. It may well have been that LIFFE joined Euronext in order to be well positioned following an anticipated joining of the euro by the United Kingdom, though to date this has not happened. LIFFE may well have found itself out on a limb if it had not been part of a pan-European exchange with the United Kingdom in the euro. Almost all the smaller derivatives markets in Europe have grown their equity-based derivatives business only in recent years and now, even for those few markets that have continued with interest rate derivatives, find that trading in these products forms a very small percentage of their whole operation. It is perfectly reasonable to have expected this situation to develop. The smaller markets, alongside, or in conjunction with their own equity markets, are able to retain market share for the trading of equity-based derivative products that have local equities as their underlying asset. The fixed interest picture within Europe is dominated by the euro and the actions of the European Central Bank.

It is highly unlikely that the smaller European derivative markets will develop interest rate derivative products in the foreseeable future. There is certainly scope within some of the new EU entrants for the development, or further development of derivative markets, but this development will almost certainly focus on equity-based products as we have seen in other European exchanges. In a number of cases derivative market development will be more effective within a grouping of countries. NOREX may be a good model for some closely linked European countries to follow. Most of the Eastern European countries are looking to the West and derivative market development will be based on its appropriateness within the framework of the EU model. It is possible that those European countries with closer links to Russia, and without the euro option, may develop some interest rate derivative markets of their own as their economies develop more into free-market ones, but this is unlikely to happen quickly.

Will there be any viable competitors to Euronext.Liffe and EUREX in the foreseeable future? The only possibility that appears to exist at this stage would be EDX, but there would have to be a change of thinking as this is set up to be strictly an equity derivative exchange at this stage. Given Stockholmbörsen's relatively strong interest rate derivatives side, however, there may be some change of heart at a later stage. The late nineties saw alliances formed within derivative markets, with a strong specialization in interest rate derivatives that were focused on the new Europe following the introduction of the hard currency euro. This process is now largely complete apart from maybe a few more tidying-up moves. An environment in which there are two major players is normally a relatively stable one and should any other player emerge, it may well be taken out of the game relatively quickly by one or other of these major players. On the product side there is certain to be more innovations, with swap futures being a likely area for the further development of product lines. More innovations could also occur in relation to trading times and both Euronext.Liffe and EUREX will continue to try expanding their respective participant bases. Overall there is good reason to believe that the next decade will be one of consolidation for the interest rate derivative market as a whole, rather than change.

Information on the derivative markets of Europe has been obtained from the following market websites:

www.wienerborse.at
www.bxs.be
www.fondsborsen.dk
www.hex.fi
www.matif.fr
www.bourse-de-paris.fr
www.deutsche-boerse.com
www.ase.gr
www.bse.hu
www.bce.hu
www.borsaitalia.it
www.aex.nl
www.oslobors.no
www.wse.com.pl
www.bvlp.pt
www.brm.ro
www.micex.com
www.meff.es
www.stockholmborsen.se
www.swx.com
www.liffe.com
www.euronext.com
www.eurexchange.com

Information relating to LIFFE, Euronext and Euronext.Liffe, EUREX, MATIF, and Paris Bourse has been obtained from their respective press releases.

5

Benchmark Yield Curves in the Euro Market[1]

PHILIP D. WOOLDRIDGE

5.1 INTRODUCTION

The process by which prices in fixed income markets adjust to new information and move toward their equilibrium value is more efficient when market participants agree on certain instruments that can serve as references, or benchmarks, for pricing other securities. The existence of a benchmark yield curve facilitates the coordination of expectations about future short term interest rates, the extraction of information about macroeconomic prospects, assessments of the cost of funds at different borrowing horizons, and comparisons of yields across different securities. In recent decades, price discovery about future short term interest rates occurred mainly in government securities markets; the government yield curve served as the locus for positioning and hedging interest rate risks. But private sector debt instruments also have the potential to serve as benchmark yield curves. The shift toward the use of private sector yield curves as benchmarks is farthest advanced in the Euro market, where interest rate swaps are competing for benchmark status.

5.2 CHARACTERISTICS OF BENCHMARK YIELD CURVES

In global fixed income markets, government bonds have long been used as benchmark instruments. The benchmark status of the government yield curve derives from a number of features that when taken together make government securities unique in financial markets. First, central governments in most of the industrial countries are among the most creditworthy of borrowers; their securities are essentially free of the risk of default. For this reason, the government yield curve is widely regarded as the best proxy for the nominal risk-free rate. Second, owing to their large borrowing needs and long life, governments are able to offer a wider range of maturities than many other borrowers. This eases the construction of yield curves out to 30 years. Third, the large amount of government debt outstanding and the fungibility of issues facilitate trading. Therefore, government paper, especially the most recently issued ("on-the-run") securities, tends to be more liquid than nongovernment paper. Fourth, government securities, together with cash, are the most preferred form of collateral in financial markets. In particular, a number of central banks historically accepted only government securities in their open market operations and lending facilities. Finally, the existence of well-developed repo and derivatives markets for government securities enables market participants to take short and long positions that reflect their views of future interest rate movements.

---

[1] The views expressed in this chapter are those of the author and do not necessarily reflect the views of the BIS.

European Fixed Income Markets: Money, Bond and Interest Rate Derivatives. Edited by J.A. Batten, T.A. Fetherston and P.G. Szilagyi. © 2004 John Wiley & Sons, Ltd. ISBN 0-470-85053-1

Benchmark interest rates, however, need not be synonymous with government yields. In principle, even corporate bonds could serve as benchmark instruments. The usefulness of a yield curve as a benchmark for price discovery about macroeconomic prospects depends on the determinants of the term structure. Ideally, the term structure should at any given time represent the market's current expectations of future short term interest rates. In other words, no factors other than expected future spot rates should systematically affect forward interest rates. Empirical studies tend not to support the pure expectations theory of the term structure. Forward rates are affected by, in addition to expected future short term rates, time-varying term and liquidity premia, a bond's convexity, premia for a bond's deliverability into a futures contract or specialness in the repo market, and other idiosyncratic factors. In the case of bonds that contain default risk, credit risk premia and the reward investors demand for bearing risk also influence yields. Therefore, forward rates in both default-free and defaultable debt securities tend to be biased estimates of expected future spot rates. To derive market expectations, the preferred yield curve is the one in which the premia embedded in forward rates are the least influenced by idiosyncratic factors and so the most predictable (or most accurately modeled).

One of the most crucial features of a benchmark instrument is that it be liquid. A liquid market is one where participants can rapidly execute large-volume transactions with a small impact on prices (Committee on the Global Finance System [CGFS], 2000). Movements in benchmark yields should not be driven by imbalances in supply and demand but rather should exclusively reflect new information about macroeconomic fundamentals. Requirements for a deep and liquid market include a competitive market structure, where the dominant players can be challenged by new entrants; a low level of fragmentation, with a large volume of homogeneous instruments; low transactions costs, such as taxes, infrastructure costs, and compensation for liquidity provision services; a heterogeneous group of market participants, with different transaction needs, risk assessments, and investment horizons; and a sound market infrastructure, especially payment and settlement systems (CGFS, 1999c).

5.3   BENCHMARK TIPPING IN EUROPEAN BOND MARKETS

European fixed income markets were the first to move away from the use of government yield curves as benchmarks. Starting in the early 1990s, European investors and issuers, especially banks, increasingly referenced interest rate swaps. Banks and other leveraged institutions typically want to know the spread of an asset relative to their funding cost. The liabilities of most leveraged institutions are based on a short term interbank rate, such as the London Interbank Offered Rate (LIBOR) or the Euro Interbank Offered Rate (EURIBOR). Therefore, leveraged institutions prefer to benchmark asset prices against the interest rate swap curve, which embodies expectations of future LIBOR or EURIBOR. Banks are among the largest investors in European debt securities markets, and consequently their preferences shape the structure of European fixed income markets to a greater extent than in the US dollar market or other major markets. Banks were also the largest nongovernment issuers in European markets in the years before European Monetary Union. As a result, quality and liquidity conditions in the nongovernment bond market were similar to those in the swap market; most issuance by nongovernment borrowers was of high quality (AA or above) and intermediate maturity. Swap rates were thus a good proxy – and hedge – for credit products in European markets.

End investors with investment portfolios in multiple currencies and large borrowers with funding programs in multiple currencies also gradually switched over to talking in terms of yield spreads relative to swaps rather than government paper. Using government securities as benchmarks requires a detailed knowledge of government debt markets, for example, tax treatment, quote conventions, and issuance policies. Furthermore, it is sometimes difficult to identify from among the often wide range of potential alternatives the most appropriate government securities to use in constructing a benchmark yield curve. By contrast, swap curves offer a reasonably simple way to compare returns or borrowing costs in different markets. Comparability across markets was of particular concern to European issuers and investors because of the fragmented nature of European fixed income markets prior to the introduction of the euro, with more than a dozen different currencies and government yield curves traded. Therefore, Europeans embraced nongovernment benchmarks more readily than did US or Japanese market participants, with their large domestic markets.

A series of traumatic market events in the late 1990s further strengthened the incentive to switch to nongovernment instruments as positioning and hedging vehicles. The near-collapse of Long Term Capital Management in September 1998 and related events highlighted the risks inherent in the use of government bonds and associated derivatives to hedge positions in nongovernment securities – a routine strategy among dealers up until that time (CGFS, 1999b). The features that make government securities so unique may at times cause their prices to move out of synch with changes in the prices of credit products. This is especially likely to be the case during periods of financial turmoil, when losses on riskier assets often provoke a flight to quality and liquidity, which historically meant a flight to government securities. The resulting imbalance in the supply of and demand for government securities can cause the (normally stable) relationship between government and nongovernment bond yields to breakdown. Episodes of this sort had earlier forced market participants to reexamine their use of US Treasury bill rates as a proxy for private rates in the US dollar money market, eventually leading participants to reference LIBOR instead (McCauley, 2001). The events of August–October 1998, during which banks and dealers incurred losses on their short positions in government securities that more than offset any gains on their long positions in private securities, triggered a similar process in US and European bond markets.

Squeezes in German government bond futures contracts reinforced this search for alternative benchmarks. Trading in futures contracts on German government bonds soared following the establishment of EUREX, a fully electronic exchange, in 1998 (Figure 5.1). As a result of the build up of large open futures positions relative to the basket of deliverable securities, segments of the German government bond market have become vulnerable to manipulation. Indeed, there have been several attempts to corner specific futures contracts, including the Bund (10 year) contract in September 1998 and June 1999 and the Bobl (5 year) contract in March 2001 (Jeanneau and Scott, 2001). Following the squeeze in 2001, regulatory authorities introduced measures designed to deter market manipulation, such as the introduction of limits on open positions. Nevertheless, the Schatz (2 year) contract of March 2002 was again subject to a squeeze (Jeanneau and Scott, 2002). Such efforts to manipulate prices impair price discovery in futures markets by discouraging trading by other market participants and increasing the risk of idiosyncratic price movements.

The importance of idiosyncratic factors in the determination of government yields was amplified by actual and prospective declines in the supply of government debt prior to the most recent economic downturn. Supply effects were most pronounced in the US Treasury market. Reinhart and Sack (2002) decompose movements in 10-year US Treasury yields into several unobserved factors, including an idiosyncratic component to capture supply and other effects that impact only Treasury securities. They conclude that this idiosyncratic component increased noticeably in 2000, following the Treasury's implementation of a debt buyback

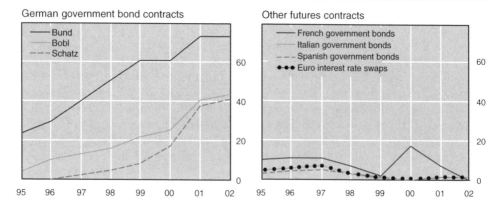

Figure 5.1   Turnover of euro interest rate futures (average daily turnover, in billions of euros). *Sources*: FOW TRADEdata; Futures Industry Association; BIS calculations. Copyright © Bank of International Settlements, Basel, Switzerland. Reproduced with permission.

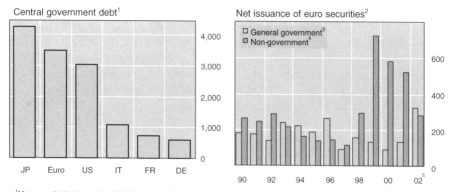

[1]Money market instruments and bonds outstanding at end-June 2002; JP = Japan; Euro = 12 euro area countries; US = United States; IT = Italy; FR = France; DE = Germany. [2]Net issuance of euro-denominated money market instruments and bonds in domestic and international markets. Domestic and international data are not fully comparable and so some securities may be counted twice. [3]Central governments, local governments and central banks. Data exclude securities issued by non-euro area governments. [4]Non-financial corporations, financial institutions, government-sponsored enterprises, supranational institutions and non-euro area governments. [5]First half of 2002 annualised.

Figure 5.2   Debt securities markets (in billions of euros). *Sources*: Dealogic Capital Data; Euroclear; International Securities Market Association; Thomson Financial Securities Data; national data; BIS calculations. Copyright © Bank for International Settlements, Basel, Switzerland. Reproduced with permission.

program. Reductions in supply had less of an impact on Euro government yields, in large part because while net issuance slowed in the late 1990s, it never actually turned negative (Figure 5.2). Nevertheless, the large revenues generated by the auction of third-generation mobile telephone licenses in Europe did contribute to a temporary increase in the scarcity premium on Euro government securities during 2000 (Blanco, 2002).

While the cumulative effect of the above-mentioned changes was not sufficient to displace government securities as the preeminent benchmark in European fixed income markets, it did set in motion a process of "benchmark tipping." Tipping refers to a situation in which the benefits of a given choice to one player depend on other players making a similar choice (Schelling,

1978). Each market participant who gives up using government securities as benchmark instruments subtracts liquidity from the government debt market and adds it to nongovernment markets. In the self-reinforcing process whereby liquid markets become more liquid, this increases the willingness of other participants to do likewise (CGFS, 2000). The replacement of 11 European currencies with a single currency in January 1999 complicated this tipping process by making obsolete many of the benchmarks in the legacy currencies and intensifying the competition for benchmark status.

5.4 GOVERNMENT SECURITIES AS BENCHMARKS

European Monetary Union created the second largest government securities market in the world. At the end of June 2002, the outstanding stock of debt securities issued by Euro area central governments totaled €3.5 trillion. By comparison, the outstanding stock of Japanese government securities equaled €4.3 trillion, and US Treasury securities €3.1 trillion (Figure 5.2). However, the Euro government securities market is more fragmented than its Japanese or US counterparts. Twelve different issuers participate in the Euro government securities market, and the single largest issuer – the Italian Treasury – accounts for less than one third of the outstanding stock of debt. Moreover, differences in issuers' credit ratings, settlement systems, tax regimes, and market conventions remain obstacles to the complete integration of the Euro government securities market (ECB, 2001a).

As a result of this continued fragmentation, differences in yields on Euro area government debt persisted even after the introduction of the euro. Indeed, immediately following European Monetary Union, individual government yield curves often looked tangled up with one another (Figure 5.3). This complicated the use of government securities to estimate a benchmark yield curve. If a yield curve truly reflects market expectations, it should be smooth; the curve should trace largely the average of expected future interest rates and not be distorted by a lack of liquidity or other market microstructure effects. This was not the case in 1999 and 2000, when the benchmark government yield curve in the Euro market was made up of more than

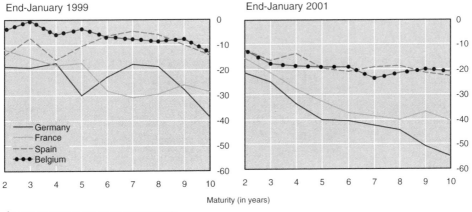

[1]Constructed from on-the-run government bonds.

Figure 5.3 Euro government yield curves[1] (spreads over euro swap rates, in basis points). *Sources*: Bloomberg; Datastream; BIS calculations. Copyright © Bank for International Settlements, Basel, Switzerland. Reproduced with permission.

one issuer: German government bonds tended to have a lower yield for short and long term maturities and French bonds for intermediate maturities.

Governments in the Euro area attempted to maintain a liquid market for their securities – and enhance the attractiveness of their securities as benchmark instruments – by modifying their debt management operations. In general, the larger are the trading supply and substitutability of a financial instrument, the higher is its liquidity (CGFS, 2000; McCauley and Remolona, 2000). With this goal in mind, Euro area governments concentrated their borrowing in fewer larger bond offerings, regularized their issuance programs, and bought back less liquid securities. Smaller governments focused their borrowing on maturities where the larger governments were less active, so as to take advantage of investor demand at different points along the yield curve. The growth of electronic cross-border trading platforms, most notably Mercato Telematico dei Titoli di Stato (MTS), also had a positive impact on the integration of government debt markets and liquidity conditions (European Central Bank [ECB], 2002). Government yield curves became smoother over time, suggesting that liquidity did improve sufficiently to allow arbitrage across maturities (Figure 5.3).

The German government securities market benefited the most from improvements in liquidity brought about by the euro. Trading in longer term exchange-traded interest rate derivatives quickly concentrated in contracts on German government bonds. Futures contracts on Spanish and Italian bonds had been actively traded in the mid-1990s but after the launch of the euro trading migrated to the German market (Figure 5.1). A revamped contract helped to boost trading in French government bond futures in 2000 and 2001. However, French futures suffered the same fate as Spanish and Italian government futures after French banks ended their program of market support (Jeanneau, 2001). Trading in German government bond futures was initially concentrated in the Bund contract but since monetary union the Bobl and Schatz contracts have also become very widely traded. The tremendous liquidity of German government futures contributed to a smoothing of the German government yield curve and by 2001 German government bonds had the lowest yields across all maturities. Despite their lower yields and improved liquidity, it remains unclear whether German government securities have fully displaced other government securities as the locus for price discovery in the Euro market. Looking at the Euro government securities to which the prices of other Euro government securities react in the cash market, Dunne *et al.* (2002) found that the benchmark yield curve continues to consist of a basket of bonds rather than a single instrument.

5.5 INTEREST RATE SWAPS COMPETE FOR BENCHMARK STATUS

Even though government securities markets appeared to gain liquidity following the launch of the euro, this was not sufficient to reverse the tipping process that had begun before monetary union. On the contrary, the fixed rate leg of interest rate swaps increasingly came to be regarded by market participants as the preeminent benchmark yield in the Euro market, against which even government securities are now often referenced.

The liquidity of euro-denominated interest rate swaps improved significantly following monetary union. According to the triennial central bank survey of foreign exchange and derivatives market activity, the average daily turnover of over-the-counter (OTC) interest rate contracts almost doubled between April 1998 and April 2001, to €231 billion (BIS, 2002). By 2001, the turnover of Euro swaps exceeded that of all interest rate products other than US Treasuries and possibly German government securities (Figure 5.4). This increase in trading activity was

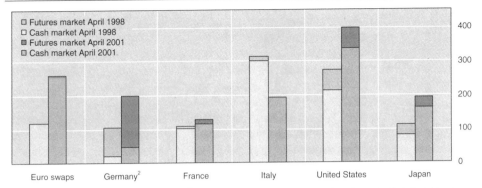

□ Futures market April 1998
□ Cash market April 1998
■ Futures market April 2001
□ Cash market April 2001

¹ Interest rate swaps and government bonds.   ²Data on cash market turnover refer only to the most actively traded bonds on Euroclear and possibly underestimate total turnover by a significant amount. Data for April 2001 refer to January 2001.

Figure 5.4 Turnover of interest rate products[1] (average daily turnover, in billions of euros). *Sources*: Euroclear; FOW TRADEdata; Futures Industry Association; national data; BIS calculations. Copyright © Bank for International Settlements, Basel, Switzerland. Reproduced with permission.

accompanied by a tightening of bid/ask spreads. The bid/ask spread declined from 2–3 basis points for 10-year Deutsche mark swaps to 1–2 basis points for Euro swaps – comparable to spreads in the German government securities market. However, the swaps market tends to be less deep than the German government securities market, with smaller quote sizes. Swaps referenced to the Euro Overnight Index Average Rate (EONIA) are now the most liquid segment of the Euro money market (ECB, 2001b). The longer term segment of the swaps market is also becoming more widely traded, although beyond 10 years liquidity conditions are often better in government securities markets.

Liquidity in the swaps market was enhanced by the rapid integration of markets in the Euro legacy currencies. Unlike the Euro government yield curve, a single Euro swap curve emerged almost overnight. Greater diversity in the range of players using interest rate swaps also helped to boost liquidity conditions. Even governments, most notably the French and German governments, have begun to use swaps to manage their risk exposures. While in the run-up to monetary union, the interdealer segment drove the growth of the Euro swaps market, since 1999 the dealer–customer segment has become increasingly important (Figure 5.5). At the end of June 2002, positions *vis-à-vis* financial customers accounted for 42% of the outstanding notional amount of Euro interest rate swaps and positions *vis-à-vis* nonfinancial customers a further 7%. Positions *vis-à-vis* other dealers accounted for the remaining 50%.

Trading in the Euro swap market was further boosted by increased hedging activity. While the nongovernment segment of the Euro debt securities market had grown at a steady but unremarkable pace for much of the 1990s, net issuance more than doubled to an annual average of €610 billion in the 3 years following monetary union (Figure 5.1). Higher issuance volumes led to more hedging activity by dealers, investors, and issuers. In the Euro market, interest rate swaps are typically the preferred vehicle to hedge cash positions in nongovernment bonds because yield movements between swaps and nongovernment bonds tend to be more closely correlated than yield movements between government bond futures and nongovernment bonds (Blanco, 2002). Hedging activity thus contributed to a 66% increase in the notional size of the Euro swap market between 1998 and 2000 (Figure 5.5). In contrast, net open interest in the exchange-traded market for Euro interest rate derivatives remained stable during this period.

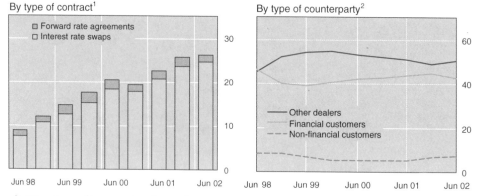

Figure 5.5 Over-the-counter interest rate derivatives (notional principal of euro-denominated derivatives).
Sources: National data; BIS calculations. Copyright © Bank for International Settlements, Basle, Switzerland. Reproduced with permission.

A benchmark yield curve constructed from the fixed rate leg of interest rate swaps has a number of advantages over a yield curve derived from bonds. First, swaps of a constant maturity are available because new swaps are traded every day. By contrast, the maturity of benchmark bonds changes as they roll down the yield curve until they are replaced or go "off the run." Second, new swaps are quoted at par and so yields are not distorted by the tax and accounting effects that impact secondary market prices for bonds trading at a discount or premium. Third, the absence of an underlying asset facilitates position-taking and unlimited supply. Short positions can be created with relative ease by taking the floating side of a swap; there is no need to borrow securities and face the risk of a squeeze. Also, since market participants can enter into as many swap contracts as they choose, idiosyncratic price movements arising from demand and supply imbalances are infrequent.

A disadvantage of swap rates is that they remain susceptible to changes in the credit quality of banks. Swaps are based on unsecured interbank deposit rates, typically EURIBOR in the Euro swaps market. Most of the banks in the EURIBOR contributor panel are rated AA, and therefore, swap rates contain a small premium for credit risk (BIS, 2001). EURIBOR, like LIBOR, is a trimmed average of rates; the highest and lowest 15% of quotes are eliminated when calculating the average. Consequently, a deterioration in the credit quality of any one bank will not distort the average rate. However, widespread financial fragility could add to uncertainty about the future path of swap rates and so deter market participants from using swaps as benchmark yields.

More significantly, the attractiveness of the interest rate swap curve as a benchmark yield curve is diminished by the structure of the market. Participants in the swaps market are exposed to the risk that a counterparty will default on its end of the agreement. Various risk mitigation techniques, including margining and collateralization, and the establishment of AAA rated derivatives subsidiaries have allayed concerns about counterparty credit risk (Remolona *et al.*, 1996). Also, swaps are usually structured such that they automatically unwind if a party's credit rating is downgraded. Nevertheless, consolidation in the financial industry has reduced the number of active swaps dealers, and so made it more difficult to diversify counterparty credit risk.

More participants might be willing to use swaps if swaps trading migrated from the OTC market to an organized exchange, where a central clearing house could act as the counterparty to all trades (McCauley, 2001). Counterparty risk is an especially important concern during periods of market volatility, and therefore, the liquidity of instruments traded on organized exchanges tends to be more robust to stress than those traded OTC (Borio, 2000; CGFS, 1999b). Steps have been taken to encourage exchange-traded activity. For example, in the early part of 2001, the London Clearing House, supported by several of the largest swaps dealers, began clearing and settling interest rate swaps. About the same time, the London International Financial Futures and Options Exchange (LIFFE) introduced 2-, 5-, and 10-year Euro swaps contracts. Trading of swap futures is still an insignificant fraction of global activity in OTC swaps or government futures (Figures 5.1 and 5.4). In the absence of a significant pickup in exchange-traded activity, swaps are likely to coexist with, rather than displace, government securities as the dominant positioning and hedging vehicles in the Euro market.

5.6 PROSPECTS FOR OTHER NONGOVERNMENT BENCHMARKS

Other nongovernment yield curves also have the potential to become viable benchmark yield curves, although none has yet become as widely referenced in the Euro market as government or swaps curves. The launch of the euro greatly expanded the universe of instruments that could be used as benchmarks and, moreover, triggered a competition among issuers to offer a highly liquid instrument that could serve as a benchmark.

An index of yields on similarly rated corporate bonds is a possible candidate for eventual elevation to benchmark status. Yield curves constructed from a population of comparable bonds are already the benchmark for pricing credit risk in the primary market (Bank for International Settlement [BIS], 2001). Furthermore, many asset managers benchmark their performance against an index. In principle, the benchmark role of fixed income indices could also extend to yield curves for pricing interest rate risk. A wide range of corporate bond indices is available, but to date none has gained broad acceptance among market participants in this latter role. Further improvements in their pricing and especially liquidity are necessary before they can become viable benchmark yield curves. To this end, some market participants have proposed the construction of a futures contract based on a basket of corporate bonds.

Debt instruments issued by government-sponsored enterprises (GSE) and supranational institutions look more promising. GSE and supranationals are often as highly rated as the governments that support them. Following the example set by government issuers, several established programs of large, regular bond offerings at key maturities. The European Investment Bank was the first, launching its Euro Area Reference Notes in early 1999. Freddie Mac of the United States followed in late 2000 and Kreditanstalt für Wiederaufbau of Germany in 2001. There are some signs that such programs are having the desired effect of concentrating liquidity. Between 1997 and 2000, there was a noticeable increase in the size and average daily turnover of nongovernment bonds that continued to trade actively in the Euro market several months after issuance (BIS, 2001). Nevertheless, the use of such bonds as benchmarks is hindered by their lower liquidity compared to swaps or government securities and the absence of well-developed repo and derivatives markets.

Averages of yields on collateralized obligations could be used to construct benchmark yield curves. In the US dollar market, interest rates in the general collateral repo market are already widely regarded as the benchmark yield curve at very short maturities (CGFS, 1999a).

The importance of repos is evidenced by their use as monetary policy instruments by many central banks. Government securities have historically been the preferred form of collateral in repo transactions. However, in principle, other instruments could substitute for government securities. In a report on the uses of collateral in wholesale financial markets, the CGFS (2001) suggests that securitization techniques could be applied to develop substitute instruments with high credit quality and liquidity. Furthermore, the steps that nongovernment issuers are taking to enhance the transparency and liquidity of their securities could make them more attractive as collateral. Improvements in risk management and market structure could also ease the use of collateral bearing higher issuer and liquidity risks. Indeed, the Eurosystem of Central Banks already accepts a very wide range of collateral in its monetary operations, including even high-quality corporate securities and nonmarketable bank loans. The primary difficulty with using repo rates as benchmarks in the Euro market is that an integrated repo market does not yet exist. National repo markets have become more closely connected since the launch of the euro, but types of collateral, prices, and liquidity conditions still differ in each market (ECB, 2001b).

Features of the broader collateralized debt market might argue in favor of using yields on covered bonds or Pfandbriefe as benchmarks. With €820 billion outstanding at the end of June 2002, the Pfandbrief market is larger than all individual European government securities markets other than Italy. Moreover, Jumbo Pfandbriefe – issues with a minimum size of €500 million – account for more than one third of all outstanding Pfandbrief issues. Even before monetary union, Jumbo Pfandbriefe had established themselves as among the most liquid instruments available in the Euro market. Liquidity is ensured by the support of at least three market makers and the setting of a maximum bid/ask spread. Nevertheless, bid/ask spreads are not as tight as for German government securities or Euro swaps. Pfandbrief-style instruments are typically structured such that the risk of default is minimal, making them a possible substitute for government securities as a risk-free asset. In particular many Jumbos are rated AAA. Maturities extend out to 15 years, facilitating the construction of a yield curve. Finally, repo and related markets for Pfandbriefe are developing (Mastroeni, 2001). A futures contract on Jumbo Pfandbriefe was introduced by EUREX in July 1998 but discontinued a few months later, during the global financial market crisis of that year.

It is not inconceivable that the process of benchmark tipping that began in the Euro market during the 1990s could eventually result in the emergence of the Pfandbrief yield curve as the preeminent benchmark yield curve. However, at the present juncture, government securities and interest rate swaps retain many advantages over other instruments as vehicles for positioning and hedging interest rate risks in the Euro market. Foremost among these advantages is their tremendous liquidity. Transactions costs for positioning and hedging with government securities and swaps are lower than the costs associated with other instruments. Government securities have unquestionably lost their status as the long-dominant benchmarks, displaced by interest rate swaps. Yet, price discovery has yet to concentrate in the swaps market and instead the swaps curve coexists with the government curve as the preeminent benchmark yield curves in the euro market.

REFERENCES

Bank for International Settlements (2001, October). The Changing Shape of Fixed Income Markets. In: *The Changing Shape of Fixed Income Markets: A Collection of Studies by Central Bank Economists*, BIS Papers No. 5. Basel: BIS, pp. 1–43.

Bank for International Settlements (2002, March). *Triennial Central Bank Survey: Foreign Exchange and Derivatives Market Activity in 2001*. Basel: BIS.

Blanco, R. (2002, August). Euro Area Government Securities Markets: Recent Developments and Implications for Market Functioning. In: *Market Functioning and Central Bank Policy*, BIS Papers No. 12. Basel: BIS, pp. 65–85.

Borio, C. (2000, November). Market Liquidity and Stress: Selected Issues and Policy Implications. *BIS Quarterly Review: International Banking and Financial Market Developments* 38–48.

Committee on the Global Financial System (1999a, March). *Implications of Repo Markets for Central Banks*. Basel: BIS.

Committee on the Global Financial System (1999b, October). *A Review of Financial Market Events in Autumn 1998*. Basel: BIS.

Committee on the Global Financial System (1999c, October). *How Should We Design Deep and Liquid Markets? The Case of Government Securities*. Basel: BIS.

Committee on the Global Financial System (2000, March). *Market Liquidity: Research Findings and Selected Policy Implications*. Basel: BIS.

Committee on the Global Financial System (2001, March). *Collateral in Wholesale Financial Markets: Recent Trends, Risk Management and Market Dynamics*. Basel: BIS.

Dunne, P., M. Moore, and R. Portes (2002, August). Defining benchmark status: an application using euro-area bonds. National Bureau of Economic Research Working Paper 9087.

European Central Bank (2001a, July). *The Euro Bond Market*. Frankfurt: ECB.

European Central Bank (2001b, July). *The Euro Money Market*. Frankfurt: ECB.

European Central Bank (2002, October). *Report on Financial Structures*. Frankfurt: ECB.

Jeanneau, S. (2001, December). Derivatives Markets. *BIS Quarterly Review: International Banking and Financial Market Developments* 29–38.

Jeanneau, S. and R. Scott (2001, June). Anatomy of a Squeeze. *BIS Quarterly Review: International Banking and Financial Market Developments* 32–33.

Jeanneau, S. and R. Scott (2002, June). Playing Cat and Mouse in Market Squeezes. *BIS Quarterly Review: International Banking and Financial Market Developments* 32–33.

Mastroeni, O. (2001, October). Pfandbrief-Style Products in Europe. In: *The Changing Shape of Fixed Income Markets: A Collection of Studies by Central Bank Economists*, BIS Papers No. 5. Basel: BIS, pp. 44–66.

McCauley, R. (2001, March). Benchmark Tipping in the Money and Bond Markets. *BIS Quarterly Review: International Banking and Financial Market Developments* 39–45.

McCauley, R. and E. Remolona (2000, November). Size and Liquidity of Government Bond Markets. *BIS Quarterly Review: International Banking and Financial Market Developments* 52–58.

Reinhart, V. and B. Sack (2002, August). The changing Information Content of Market Interest Rates. In: *Market Functioning and Central Bank Policy*, BIS Papers No. 12. Basel: BIS, pp. 340–357.

Remolona, E., W. Bassett, and I. Geoum (1996, April). Risk Management by Structured Derivative Product Companies. *Federal Reserve Bank of New York Economic Policy Review* **2**: 17–38.

Schelling, T. (1978). *Micromotives and Macrobehaviour*, New York: Norton.

6

Some Facts on Pfandbrief Products in Europe[1]

ORAZIO MASTROENI

6.1 INTRODUCTION

Debt markets in Europe have traditionally been dominated by government issuance. Heavy borrowings by a number of European central governments, as well as restrictions limiting investors to investments in their home markets and in fixed income instruments, have contributed to generating steady investment flows toward government debt markets. On the supply side, the implementation of the Maastricht Treaty in the European Union (EU) (setting the conditions for participating in the Single Currency) and the arrival of the euro in 1999 have given a substantial contribution to the integration of capital markets in the Euro area[2] and to the emergence of new trends in debt issuance in the last decade. On the demand side the introduction of the euro has created a very large pool of "domestic" investors with a common currency and has determined an increasing internationalization of euro-denominated bond markets in the Euro area.

Governments of smaller European States, such as Portugal, Finland, and Austria, that previously relied on a captive market of domestic investors, have been confronted with the additional challenge given by the removal of currency risk, which now allows investors to invest in more liquid sovereign securities issued in other Euro area States. These governments have responded to this situation with more innovative issuing techniques, such as adding commercial paper programs and medium term note issues, widening and internationalizing their dealer groups, and increasingly resorting to underwritten syndicated deals rather than auctions. This innovative trend has stopped short of governments actually issuing jointly.

However, some of the criteria imposed by the Maastricht Treaty (namely, those limiting governments to a budget deficit no greater than 3% of GDP and a GDP to national debt ratio of 60%) have been among the principal factors reducing the relative supply of government paper *vis-à-vis* other issuers (Figure 6.1). This trend, coupled with the fact that interest rates in the Euro area have reached historically low levels, has spurred investors to look for alternative investment opportunities, mainly corporate issues as well as paper from governments of those "Accession" countries that are expected to join the EU in 2004 (e.g., Poland, Hungary, and the Czech Republic). Demand from investors also migrated to more traditional bonds issued by financial institutions, in particular toward covered bonds (of which Pfandbrief-style products are the largest segment). The recent economic slowdown and the ensuing consolidation in the industrial and financial sector have caused a slowdown in the growth rate of these markets,

---

[1] The author is responsible for the opinions and for any errors included in this chapter.
[2] The Euro area comprises those countries that have adopted the Single Currency, namely, Belgium, Germany, Greece, Spain, France, Ireland, Italy, Luxembourg, Netherlands, Austria, Portugal, and Finland.

European Fixed Income Markets: Money, Bond and Interest Rate Derivatives. Edited by J.A. Batten, T.A. Fetherston and P.G. Szilagyi. © 2004 John Wiley & Sons, Ltd. ISBN 0-470-85053-1

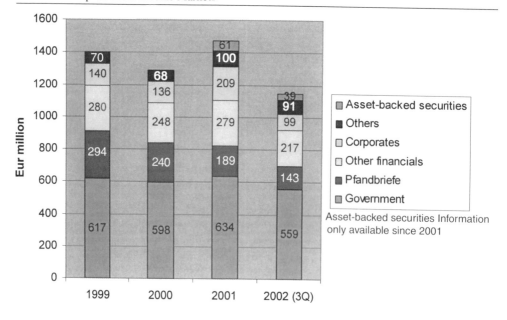

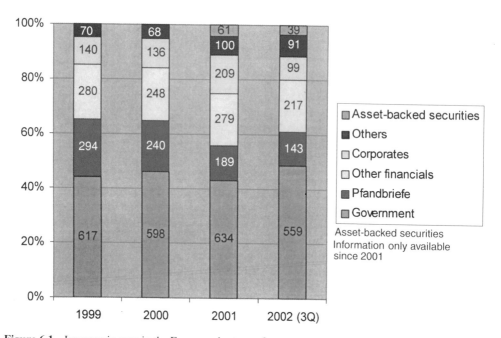

Figure 6.1 Issuance in euro in the Euro area by type of asset.
Source: European Commission. © European Communities 1995–2003. Reproduced with permission.

particularly in the corporate segment, as well as a general deterioration of the ratings both of industrial and financial names. This has increased investor's interest in fixed income assets with a perceived higher level of protection.

6.2   COVERED BONDS, PFANDBRIEF PRODUCTS, AND SECURITIZATION

In Europe it is common to refer to "covered bonds" or "mortgage bonds" when referring to different types of bonds backed by mortgage assets, public sector loans, or other types of assets such as mortgage-backed securities. Despite their long tradition, there is still no common definition. Plans for a draft EU Directive governing the issuance of securities guaranteed by a mortgage or other assets were abandoned by the European Commission following the publication in 1985 of the White Paper on the Internal Market, which put forward the principle of mutual recognition as an alternative to harmonization.[3]

The "cover" is achieved through a process of "securitization," which is in essence a method of converting a credit claim or a pool of claims into negotiable securities. This process can typically be achieved either "off-balance sheet" (this is the type of securitization most often referred to as "asset-backed") or "on-balance sheet" (in recent times referred to as "Pfandbrief-style") or even through "synthetic securitization" – a technique that has developed in more recent times.[4]

Off-balance sheet securitization implies the sale by a bank of a portfolio of assets to an entity (typically a so-called Special Purpose Vehicle, separate from the issuer), which finances the acquisition of the assets by issuing debt instruments (e.g., bonds or commercial paper) or shares. The underlying assets serve to secure the ability of the issuing entity to honor its obligations. The generic designation of asset-backed securities (ABS) derives from this direct relationship. Off-balance sheet securitization is a relatively recent development in Europe, and the amounts involved are still relatively low compared to on-balance sheet securitization; but issuance is rising steadily because of the advantages that such securities bring in terms of the possibility of mobilizing bank balance sheets.

On-balance sheet securitization consists of the issuance of securities backed by securities that remain on the balance sheet of the issuer. The typical (and probably oldest) example of this type of securitization is provided by the German Pfandbrief, where assets are ring-fenced on the balance sheet of so-called "hypothekenbanken" subject to a specific legal regime. The bank then issues bonds, which provide the holders with priority right to the ring-fenced assets, in the event of a default of the issuer. The holder, therefore, benefits from a double protection: the solvency of the issuer and the solvency of the debtors of the original assets. Table 6.1 summarizes very briefly the most important differences of the two types of assets. Pfandbrief products will be analyzed in more detail in the following sections. It is interesting to note that the development of covered bonds of the Pfandbrief type has been around for more than 100 years in Europe. On the other hand, issuance of ABS bonds is a relatively recent phenomenon and has been brought about by innovation in the financial sector.

---

[3] Nonetheless, the special character of mortgage bonds has since been captured in the 1988 Directive on the "Undertaking for Collective Investments in Transferable Securities" (UCITS). In particular, Article 22, para 4, of the Directive recognizes that the different types of mortgage bonds share certain characteristics, and therefore have to be notified by EU Member States to the European Commission.

[4] "Synthetic securitization" refers to structured transactions in which a party uses "credit derivatives" to transfer the credit risk of a specified pool of assets to third parties. The better-known and most developed type of synthetic securitization is the *credit default swap*, a bilateral financial contract aiming at buying financial protection on underlying assets or generating exposure to credit risk without actually selling or buying the related assets.

Table 6.1   Comparison between Pfandbrief products and asset-backed securities (ABS)

	Pfandbriefe	ABS
Level of standardization	Very high for Jumbos: this makes the bonds very transparent to the investors and favors liquidity in general. Relatively low for Traditional Pfandbriefe.	None: the main feature of ABS are their flexibility in relation to issuers' and investors' needs.
Nature of securities	Pfandbriefe are bank securities, where the debtor is the issuer bank. The security is guaranteed by underlying public sector or mortgage loans.	ABS are issued by special purpose vehicles based on loans that are transferred from the originator of the loans; the risk is also taken off the balance sheet of the originator.
Bankruptcy remoteness	Pfandbriefe are guaranteed by the whole amount of mortgage or public loans issued by the bank (there is a continuous turnover of the loans underlying the Pfandbrief).	ABS are guaranteed by specific pools of assets, which represent but a part of the assets of the originator bank.

Source: Peppetti and Rinaldi, 2001; ECB.

Securitization is attractive for a number of reasons. First, disposing of assets that are used as underlying assets for covered bonds allows banks to change the risk profile of their balance sheet. Second, the sale of securitized assets generates prices for assets that are difficult to value. This price availability is higher for Pfandbrief products, and lower for ABS products. Third (particularly for Pfandbrief products), these securities are more secure than uncovered bonds, as they are backed mainly by public loans or real estate (ABS are backed by income flows from other types of sources, e.g., receivables, credit card flows, even future tax flows, etc). Fourth, issuers or banks may have a wish to reduce their need for regulatory capital.[5]

Other factors that have encouraged the development of securitization (particularly for ABS products) include a regulatory climate favorable to innovation and the ability of investors to perform the complicated mathematical and risk analysis required to determine the value of ABS. Yet another important factor for the rising interest in covered bonds in recent periods has been the deterioration of banks' ratings. While the unsecured funding costs of the commercial bank sector in Europe are rising (because of weaker ratings), covered bonds have not followed suit in generating additional funding costs, as most of these assets continue to enjoy high ratings.

Having described the main differences between ABS and Pfandbrief-style products, the rest of this chapter will concentrate in particular on Pfandbrief products. European Pfandbrief products are typically issued by specialized credit institutions with a narrowly defined scope of business activities and subject to special banking supervision. The best known and oldest legislation regulating this segment of the market is the German Pfandbrief legislation. Legislation on Pfandbrief-style products has always had national relevance and has thus kept covered bond markets segmented.

It is only with the launch of the Jumbo Pfandbrief by the German mortgage banks in mid-1995 that domestic covered bonds have crossed domestic boundaries to become a better-known instrument internationally. The move of the German banks has been followed by the French,

---

[5] Banks are required by regulators to maintain capital according to the size and type of their assets on their balance sheets. Appropriate amounts of capital must be set aside by the bank to cover potential declines in asset values. Having much capital tied up on its balance sheet limits opportunities to use that capital for the purposes of generating better returns for shareholders.

Table 6.2   Characteristics of covered bond in selected European markets

	Germany	France	Spain	Luxembourg	Denmark	Sweden
Structure	Bullet	Bullet	Bullet	Bullet	Bullet	Bullet
Coupon	Fixed	Fixed	Fixed	Fixed	Fixed	Fixed
Interest days	act/act	act/act	act/act	act/act	act/act	act/act
Maturities (years)	1–15	2–15	5 and 10	2, 5, and 10	20 and 30	2–5
Market makers	€15 million	€15 million	€15 million	€15 million	€3–7 million	€2–5 million
Rating	mostly Aaa	Aaa	Aaa	mostly Aaa	Aa3 to Aa1	A1 to Aa2
Bid/offer spread	5–10 c	5–10 c	5–10 c	5–10 c	10 c	3bp
LTV	60%	60–80%	70–80%	60%	60–80%	70–75%
Cover assets	Public or mortgage	Public or mortgage	Public	Public or mortgage	Mortgage	Mortgage
Callable	No	No	No	No	Yes	No
Special supervision	German banking supervisory authority	French Bank Commission	Bank of Spain	Luxembourg Bank Commission	Danish Financial Supervisory Authority	No
Independent trustee	Yes	Yes	No	Yes	No	No
Basel risk weighting	10%	10%	10%	10%	10%	20%

Spanish, and Luxembourg regulatory authorities, which have revised and updated their existing legislations on covered bonds to enable the national financial institutions to better compete with other European financial institutions able to attract international investors investing in high-quality bonds. To mention but a few of the revisions that have taken place recently, in France the law governing *Obligations Foncières* was revised in 1999. In Luxembourg a substantial revision of the law on *Lettres de Gage* of 1993 was passed in 1997, whereas Spanish banks started to issue a maxi-version of *Cedulas Hipotecarias* as from 1999 (Table 6.2).

Given the success of Pfandbriefe and the activism of some countries in adapting their legislation, other countries also introduced or modified their legislation. In Finland, legislation on Pfandbrief was introduced in 2000, while in Ireland this occurred in 2001. In other countries (with the exception of the United Kingdom, which appears to favor more the off-balance sheet type of securitization) there are discussions to introduce or to update the legislative framework. This is the case in Sweden (where there is no special mortgage bank legislation and supervision: mortgage companies are regulated under the same general laws as other credit institutions), Belgium, and Italy. Also because of these changes, covered bond products involving mortgages and public loans are being increasingly identified with Pfandbrief products.

In all countries, the new laws aim at guaranteeing the quality of covered bond instruments with a view to reproduce the popularity and the attractiveness encountered with investors by the German Pfandbrief, also at the international level (Table 6.3). The adaptation of national laws to the German model is pursued in the light of the fact that the characterization of Pfandbrief as a quality investment product had allowed it to gain popularity at the European level compared to other high-quality nonsovereign assets. The Pfandbrief has been assigned a capital risk weighting of 10% compared to the 20% weighting normally required for other bank bonds.[6] In addition, Pfandbriefe issued in the EU and compliant with the UCITS Directive (Box 1) are not subject to certain limits on investments prescribed for institutional investors (for example, investment companies and insurance companies may buy double the amount of Pfandbriefe and

---

[6] Cfr. Art. 11 (2) of the EU Solvency Directive.

Table 6.3   Pfandbrief-style products in the EU

Austria	*Pfandbriefe*: These bonds are issued on behalf of the *Landeshypothekenbanken* by a centralized issuing institution and three separate banking groups. Loans to borrowers in the EEA and Switzerland may be used as backing collateral for these bonds. The bonds have a 10% solvency weighting. The authorities are currently working on a revision of the relevant law.
Belgium	Legislation to allow mortgage bond issuance is being prepared.
Denmark	*Realkreditobligationer*: These mortgage bonds are issued by recognized mortgage institutions, which are responsible for 90% of mortgage bond issuance. The relevant laws are currently evolving, and these bonds may come to resemble Pfandbriefe more closely. At present mortgage bonds are backed only by mortgage loan collateral and are not insulated from the bankruptcy of their issuers.
France	*Obligations Foncières*: These are backed by mortgages and public sector loans, located anywhere in the EEA. They are issued by *Societes de Credit Foncier (SCF)*, whose sole purpose is to make mortgage and public loans and refinance then through *Obligations Foncières*. SCFs are normally owned by the parent bank which acts as the servicer of the loan. Real estate collateral is marked to market. There is an effective "bankruptcy remoteness" as holders of *Obligations Foncières* rank ahead of all other creditors. SCFs are supervised by a professional auditor, who reports to the *Commission Bancaire*. There are detailed disclosure requirements on asset quality, prepayments, and interest rate sensitivity of the collateral pools. *Obligations Foncières* must be listed on at least two exchanges and have at least two ratings.
Finland	*Kiinteistovaakuudellinen joukovelkakirjalaina/ julkisyhteisova-kuudelinnen joukkovelkakirjalaina*: A new law came into effect in January 2000, closely based on the German model, which fulfils the requirements of Art. 22(4) of the UCITS Directive. Only specialized institutions are permitted to issue mortgage bonds. There are set rules for valuing mortgageable property. The loan-to-value is up to 60% of mortgageable value. There is no requirement for an independent trustee. Collateral from the EEA is acceptable. Eligible assets include public sector and mortgage loans, requiring two separate registers. There is currently a limit on substitution of collateral. Mortgage bond holders have a preferential status in any liquidation of the issuing institution.
Germany	*Pfandbriefe*: This is a general term encompassing *Hypotheken Pfandbriefe* and *Öffentliche Pfandbriefe*. The former are issued to fund loans that are secured by first ranking residential and commercial mortgages or land charges; the latter are issued to fund loans to the public sector (e.g., federal government, regional governments, municipals, and other agencies). About 80% of the outstanding amount are public Pfandbriefe, and the remaining 20% are mortgage Pfandbriefe, reflecting the difficulty involved in pooling the necessary €500 million in mortgage loans, within a short time, whereas this is far easier in the case of public sector loans. The collateral of all outstanding *Öffentliche Pfandbriefe* and *Hypotheken-Pfandbriefe* of any mortgage bank must be kept in two separate pools. Investor protection is guaranteed at two levels: through the very clear legislation defining which institutions are privileged by law to issue Pfandbriefe and through the conservative guidelines determining the quality and size of the collateral backing. The total volume of all Pfandbriefe of a mortgage bank in circulation may not exceed 60 times the amount of its own capital. Loans eligible as pool collateral must not exceed 60% of their value, regardless of the type of loan. The Federal Banking Supervisory Authority (*Bundesaufsichtamt für Kreditwesen – BAKred*) ensures that the issuers' activities comply with these regulations. They have a 10% solvency risk weighting and they qualify for Eurosystem repo operations.

Table 6.3 *(cont.)*

Ireland	A law creating *Irish Pfandbrief* was approved in 2001. These assets are modeled on the existing Pfandbrief legislation in Germany, France, and Luxembourg. Only approved "designated credit institutions" are able to issue these bonds, which are secured by mortgage loans or public loans. Assets have to be segregated in the balance sheet of the issuer. The loan-to-value ratio is be 60%. Substitution of assets must not exceed 20% of the total pool value. Holders of bonds have a priority claim over the cover assets in case of default. Assets from EEA, Canada, USA, and Switzerland are allowed, as are certain types of hedging derivatives. There are rules for asset and liability matching.
Luxembourg	*Lettres de gage*: At present three institutions have the specialized issuing license required for issuing these bonds; the first few issues are on the market. The establishing law of November 21, 1997 are closely modeled on the German precedents. The backing collateral for the *lettres de gage publiques* is public sector loans, and for *lettres de gage hypothecaires* is mortgage loans. As in Germany, there must be separate public sector and mortgage asset pools. There is a requirement for an independent trustee. A register of the collateral assets must be kept. There are requirements with regard to substitution collateral, which is limited to 20% of all collateral. There are set rules for valuing mortgage property. The loan-to-value ratio is up to 60% of mortgageable value. Collateral from all OECD countries is eligible to back *Lettres de gage*. They have a 10% solvency risk weighting and they qualify for Eurosystem repo operations.
Spain	*Cedulas hipotecarias*: They can only be backed by mortgage loans and not by public sector loans. They are collateralized by the issuing entity's entire mortgage pool rather than by a specific pool of mortgage assets. Holders of *Cedulas hipotecarias* enjoy a privileged status and have priority over mortgage book of the issuer in the event of a bankruptcy. Only the State or the issuer's employees have higher priority over the proceeds arising from liquidation in case of bankruptcy. Early amortization is not possible. Mortgage valuation is subject to conservative valuation rules (70% loan-to-value ratio) and mortgage certificates can be issued only up to 90% of an individual issuer's eligible mortgages ("overcollateralization"). The principle of matching maturities is not covered in Spanish law, which gives Spanish institutions some leeway for taking on interest rate risk arising from maturity transformation.
Sweden	Securitization of mortgage lending is only just starting. At present, the mortgage bonds differ quite materially from the Pfandbrief model, but new legislation is planned. Around 60% of mortgage loans are funded by means of mortgage bonds but these do not enjoy the preferential status of German-style Pfandbriefe. Two institutions currently dominate the issuance of mortgage bonds. The bonds do not qualify for a 10% solvency risk weighting.

Source: Fitch IBCA (2000). Reproduced by permission of Fitch, Inc.

mortgage bonds than of the other securities).[7] Finally, the Pfandbriefe and mortgage bonds that are UCITS-compliant satisfy the "financial soundness" requirement for assets to be eligible for refinancing operations with the Eurosystem and for TARGET[8] payment system purposes (Table 6.4).

---

[7] Another example of preferential treatment in Germany is that investment companies can invest up to 20% of total assets in Pfandbriefe of a single issuer, whereas the normal limit is 10%.

[8] The TARGET system (an acronym for Trans-European Automated Real-Time Gross Settlement Express Transfer) was developed by the European System of Central Banks. It consists of 15 national real-time gross settlement systems plus the ECB payment mechanism, all of which are interlinked so as to provide a uniform platform for processing cross-border payments. It is intended mainly for the settlement of monetary policy operations and large-value interbank payments, but can also handle customer payments, including smaller cross-border retail transactions.

Table 6.4   Overview of the legal status of Pfandbriefe in Europe

Country	Special law at the national level	Specific supervision	Compliant to Art 22(4) of UCITS Directive
Germany	Yes	Yes	Yes
France	Yes	Yes	Yes
Luxembourg	Yes	Yes	Yes
Spain	Yes	Yes	Yes
Austria	Yes	Yes	Yes
Finland	Yes	Yes	Yes
Sweden*	No	Yes	No
Denmark	Yes	Yes	Yes
Switzerland	Yes	Yes	Yes

Source: AGMB, 2000. Reproduced by permission of Euromoney plc.
*Special rules apply for mortgage banks.

Box 6.1 The UCITS Directive

European Union Council Directive 85/611/EEC as amended by Council Directive 88/220/EEC (the "UCITS Directive") aims at governing collective investment undertakings with a view to approximating the conditions of competition between these undertakings at the Community level, while at the same time ensuring effective and more uniform protection for unit holders, removing the restrictions on the free circulation of the units in the Community and help bring about a European Capital Market.

The Directive defines the relevant criteria that bonds must satisfy in order to be included in this EU-wide list of assets ensuring particular protection for the bondholders. This Directive tends to limit the number of potential issuers and requires that sufficient protection is in place to ensure sufficiently homogenous instruments and a sufficient degree of transparency.

In particular, Article 22(4), which is considered crucial to the essence of Pfandbriefe-style model of mortgage bond issuance, states *inter alia* that "Member States may raise the limit laid down in par. 1 (i.e. no more that 5% of assets may be invested by a UCITS in transferable assets issued by the same body) to a maximum of 25% in the case of certain bonds, when these are issued by a credit institutions which has its registered office in a member state and is subject by law to special public supervision designed to protect bond holders. In particular, sums deriving from the issue of these bonds must be invested, in conformity with the law, in assets which, during the whole period of validity of the bonds, are capable of covering claims attaching to the bonds and, which in the event of the failure of the issuer, would be used on a priority basis for the reimbursement of the principal and payment of the accrued interest."

These general criteria imply that (a) the issuer must be a credit institution domiciled in the EU; (b) the issuer country exercises special state supervision to protect bond holders, e.g., through state appointed trustees, special collateral checks or special valuation rules; (c) the sums deriving from the issue of these bonds must be placed in assets which provide sufficient cover for the liabilities deriving from the bonds for their entire duration; and (d) in the event of bankruptcy of the issuer, these assets are intended to be used to repay the capital and interest becoming due. The mortgage bank creditors have thus a preferential claim in the case of bankruptcy of the issuing institution.

6.3   THE GERMAN TRADITIONAL AND JUMBO PFANDBRIEF MARKETS

The German Pfandbrief market is the largest individual bond market in Europe in terms of outstanding amount: at June 2002 it stood at just over €1.1 trillion, bigger than the outstanding amount of any individual government in Europe (Figure 6.2).

Pfandbriefe are noncallable bonds, issued exclusively by authorized German financial institutions (private mortgage banks and public banks). The Mortgage Bank Act restricts the banks almost exclusively to funding themselves on the capital market. There are basically two types of Pfandbriefe: Public Pfandbriefe and Mortgage Pfandbriefe.[9]

Mortgage Pfandbriefe are issued to finance first-rate residential and commercial mortgages within Germany, other EU member states, an EEA member state, or Switzerland. Mortgage Pfandbriefe are collateralized by the underlying mortgage loans. The loan-to-value (LTV) of mortgages funded via Pfandbrief is limited to 60%. The volume of mortgages with an LTV of more than 60% does not qualify as collateral and must not exceed a ratio of 20% of the total outstanding amount of all mortgage loans granted by the bank. Mortgage Pfandbriefe have a maximum maturity of only 10 years.[10]

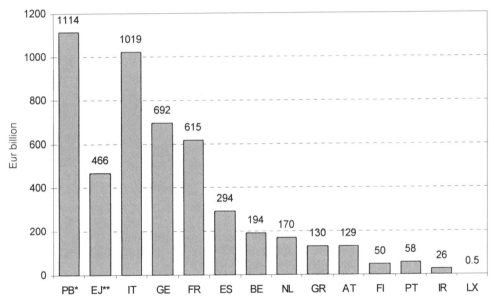

* German Pfandbriefe (Jumbo and traditional)

** German Jumbo Pfandbriefe (414 bn) and European Jumbos (obligations Foncieres, Cedulas Hipotecarias, Lettres de Gage)

Figure 6.2   Pfandbrief and government bonds outstanding in the Euro area.
Source: ECB. Copyright © European Central Bank, Frankfurt am Main, Germany. Reproduced with permission.

---

[9] A third type of Pfandbrief (Ship Mortgage) issued by ship mortgage banks plays only a minor domestic role and will not be considered in this section.

[10] This is due to the fact that according to the Mortgage Bank Act the mortgagors' right of redemption may only be suspended for a maximum of 10 years.

Public Pfandbriefe are issued to fund loans to, or guaranteed by the sovereign government, the states, the municipalities, and other authorized public sector entities in Germany and other EU or EEA member states. Bonds issued by these institutions are eligible as ordinary collateral, provided these assets do not have a risk weighting greater than 20%. Public Pfandbriefe are usually issued with a maturity of up to 10 years, but longer maturities are possible. The outstanding amount of the underlying collateral as well as its maturity and interest payments must at all times be at least as high as those for all outstanding Pfandbriefe.

The Pfandbrief issuing institutions establish and maintain separate pools of assets pledged as collateral for mortgage and public Pfandbriefe. These pools are managed dynamically, with new assets being added on an ongoing basis and existing assets being removed as loans are repaid. Nonperforming assets have to be removed immediately from the collateral pool and replaced by other eligible assets. This entire process is closely monitored by an independent trustee, which is nominated by the banking supervisory authorities. The banks themselves are supervised by the banking supervisory authorities and the Bundesbank. In the event of an issuing bank's insolvency, the outstanding Pfandbriefe and the respective collateral pools are immediately removed from the balance sheet and run as an own fund until the last Pfandbrief has matured. During this period, Pfandbrief holders have a preferential claim on the cash flow from the respective collateral assets or the proceeds from their sale. To the extent that assets in the cover pool are not sufficient to meet all claims, Pfandbriefe investors acquire a nonprivileged claim, alongside other creditors, on the institution's balance sheet assets.

6.3.1   The Jumbo Pfandbrief

The Jumbo Pfandbrief market was introduced in 1995. It was developed to deliver an increased level of standardization and enhanced liquidity characteristics to Pfandbriefe so as to attract the interest of international investors wishing to access liquid and secure instruments carrying competitive yields. The introduction of this new instrument reflected the desire of German issuers to ensure an expansion of their refinancing base and to promote the internationalization of an instrument whose issuing volumes were growing constantly. Jumbos have, among other things, the following important characteristics:

- Minimum volume of at least €500 million;
- Fixed coupon payments and bullet redemption;
- Minimum of three market makers, quoting two-way prices with a bid/offer spread of 5–10 cents for lots up to €15 million during usual trading hours;
- Repo market making for lots of €25 million with a 25 bp bid/offer spread for those Jumbos with an outstanding amount of €1.5 billion or more; and
- Listing on a German Stock Exchange.

The increase in the amount of outstanding Pfandbriefe (Figures 6.3 and 6.4) is mostly due to the increased issuance of Jumbo Pfandbriefe; at June 2002, the Jumbo Pfandbrief market reached an outstanding volume of €414 billion whereas traditional Pfandbriefe totaled €699 billion. Jumbos currently represent about 37% of all outstanding Pfandbriefe issued by German residents. Outstanding amount of Jumbos have increased ever since their inception whereas issuance of traditional Pfandbriefe has decreased steadily in absolute terms. The predominant Jumbo to be issued is the "public" Pfandbrief, which covers a share of over 90% of all Jumbos

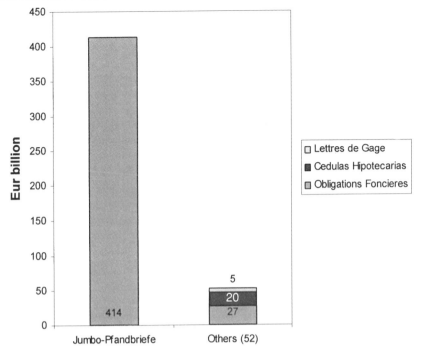

Figure 6.3 Outstanding amount of Jumbo Pfandbrief products in Europe (end of June 2002).
Source: ECB. Copyright © European Central Bank, Frankfurt am Main, Germany. Reproduced with permission.

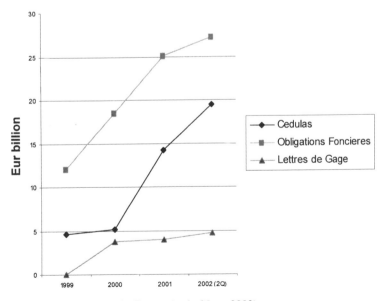

Figure 6.4 Other Jumbo products in Europe (end of June 2002).
Source: ECB. Copyright © European Central Bank, Frankfurt am Main, Germany. Reproduced with permission.

issued. This can be explained by the fact that it is easier to accumulate the cover collateral needed to achieve the minimum volume required for Jumbos by resorting to public sector loans rather than to mortgage loans. The largest Jumbos have an issue size of €5 billion. The maturity profile of Jumbos is fairly evenly distributed.

6.3.2 Issuance

When looking at issuing techniques, methods differ for traditional Pfandbriefe and Jumbo Pfandbriefe. Traditional Pfandbriefe are offered in the form of frequent issues sold in the open market. At the same time, driven by investors' demand, so-called "structured Pfandbriefe" are endowed with virtually any of the features commonly offered in international markets (such as floaters, reverse floaters, zero-coupon bonds, etc.). The size of traditional Pfandbrief issues ranges from €5 to 250 million.

In contrast, Jumbo Pfandbriefe are issued through syndicates consisting of at least three banks. For Jumbo issuance, standard international issuing and trading practices are applied. Some issuing banks have even established Euro Medium Term Note programs and Global Jumbo issuance programs to comply with international investors' demands and meeting legal requirements for purchases in primary markets by all institutional investors worldwide (Figure 6.5).

In the last few years the market has experienced changes in the pricing of Pfandbriefe. Jumbo prices are currently affected by the rating of the bonds (mostly AAA ratings – almost always higher than the rating of the issuer), the name recognition of the issuer, and the size and liquidity of the bonds. In the traditional and more illiquid Pfandbriefe market, which is by far more domestically oriented compared to the Jumbo market, such kind of price differentiation is, however, far less observable (Figures 6.6 and 6.7).

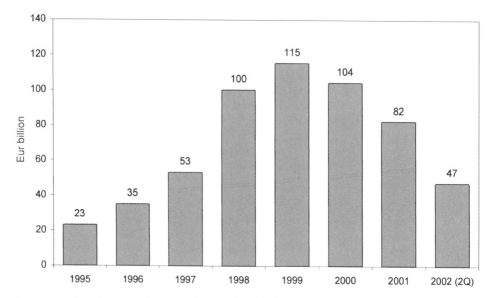

Figure 6.5 Gross issuance of German Jumbo Pfandbriefe.
Source: ECB. Copyright © European Central Bank, Frankfurt am Main, Germany. Reproduced with permission.

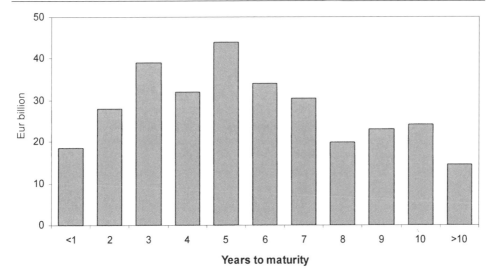

Figure 6.6 Outstanding volume of Jumbo Pfandbriefe by remaining life.
Source: ECB. Copyright © European Central Bank, Frankfurt am Main, Germany. Reproduced with permission.

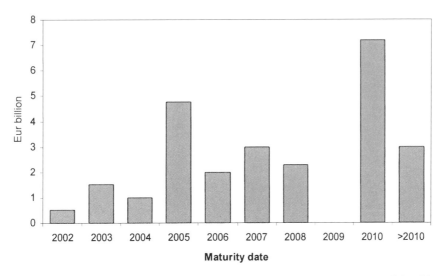

Figure 6.7 Outstanding volume of non German European Jumbo-Pfandbriefe by remaining life (end of June 2002).
Source: ECB. Copyright © European Central Bank, Frankfurt am Main, Germany. Reproduced with permission.

6.4   THE FRENCH "OBLIGATIONS FONCIÈRES"

Although the legal framework for mortgage-backed bonds has existed since 1852 in France, it is only recently that the existing laws have been updated (1999). Among the reasons that prompted the French government to review its law on mortgage-backed assets is the success achieved by German mortgage banks in issuing and marketing Pfandbriefe, which allows them to refinance themselves at competitive rates. Other reasons are the introduction of the single currency and the ensuing disappearance of currency risk, which abolished the segmentation between domestic markets and exposed domestic participants to the full force of competition.

Prior to the reform, *de facto* there was only one mortgage bank on the French market, the *Credit Foncier de France (CFF)* that was authorized to issue mortgage bonds. The reform of 1999 abolished the monopoly that CFF had enjoyed and allowed all credit and financial institutions to establish their own mortgage institutions. A very detailed definition of the role and responsibilities of mortgage banks was achieved with the reform, as was a strengthening of prudential rules and a closer control by the supervisory authorities (*Commission Bancaire*).

Central to the new structure is the "bankruptcy remoteness" of issuing vehicles in the French mortgage bond markets: issuance of *Obligations Foncières* is restricted to specific companies, *Societes de Credit Fonciers* (SCF), that have the sole purpose of acquiring and granting secured loans refinanced through *Obligations foncieres*. The holders of these bonds enjoy privileged rights ranking even above those of salaried employees and the State itself. Following the enforcement of the law, two new mortgage banks issuing *Obligations Foncières* were created in France.[11]

Although SCFs have the legal status of a bank, they are not allowed to engage in traditional banking activities and to hold equity stakes in any subsidiaries, which effectively makes these vehicles closely resemble a "special purpose vehicle" in asset-backed securitization. The bankruptcy remoteness is reinforced through their relationship with their parent company: the law requires SCFs not to be operational but to be managed by another financial institution, which is normally the parent bank. The strength of this legal framework has been recognized in the level of the ratings assigned to these bonds by international rating agencies (normally a triple A)

Issuance mechanisms are designed to enhance liquidity and transparency; the market-making schemes reflect very closely those adopted for the German Pfandbrief. Issuers and market makers agreed to set the minimum issue size to €500 million and to have all issues rated by at least 2 of the internationally recognized rating agencies. Furthermore, all *Obligations Foncières* must be assisted by a market making commitment from at least three banks, which are required to promote liquidity in the market by quoting continuous prices with bid/offer spreads of between 5 and 20 cents. Currently, only three *Obligations Foncières* qualify (in terms of issue size) to be quoted on the EuroCredit MTS.

6.5   THE SPANISH "CEDULAS HIPOTECARIAS"

The *Cedulas hipotecarias* have been around for more 130 years[12]; however, it was only after the amendment of the law governing these products in 1981 that issuance of *Cedulas* took off, and

---

[11] These are *Dexia Municipal Agency* and *Compagnie de Financement Foncier* to which all mortgages by CFF have been transferred.
[12] The *Ley del Mercao Hipotecario* was first introduced in 1869.

in 1999 the first international issue was launched in the market. As with *Obligations Foncières*, in the last few years the main reason for issuers to tap this market has been the prospect of improving their funding costs and widen the investor base, in particular to nonresident investors. *Cedulas* are considered Jumbos if they have at least €1 billion issue size; traditional issues are normally between €1 and 10 million.

Compared to the French, German, and Luxembourg products, *Cedulas* can only be backed by mortgage loans and not by public sector loans. Compared to the German Pfandbrief, their essential difference lies in the fact that they are collateralized by the issuing entity's entire mortgage pool rather than by a specific pool of mortgage assets. In line with Article 22(4) of the UCITS Directive, credit institutions wishing to enter the mortgage market have to specify this in their Statute, be authorized by the Ministry of Economic Affairs, and be subject to specific supervision by the Bank of Spain. Holders of *Cedulas hipotecarias* enjoy a privileged status and have priority over mortgage book of the issuer in the event of a bankruptcy. Only the State (if the institution owes taxes) or the issuer's employees (limited to 30 days' wage) have higher priority over the proceeds arising from liquidation in case of bankruptcy. Early amortization is not possible. Mortgage valuation is subject to conservative valuation rules (70% loan-to-value ratio) and mortgage certificates can be issued only up to 90% of an individual issuer's eligible mortgages ("overcollateralization").[13]

It is worth mentioning that *Cedulas* are the most strongly collateralized of the four instruments considered, given that they are covered by the entire pool of assets of the issuer. The principle of matching maturities is not covered in Spanish law, which gives Spanish institutions some leeway for taking on interest rate risk arising from maturity transformation. Domestic *Cedulas* are quoted on the Spanish fixed income market (AIAF), whereas the bigger international issues are marketed also outside Spain (Luxembourg, France). In December 2002 EuroCredit MTS announced that *Cedulas* qualify to be quoted on its electronic trading platform.

6.6   THE LUXEMBOURG "LETTRES DE GAGE"

The legal framework for Luxembourg's Pfandbrief was created at the end of 1997 and is, in many respects, taken from the German Mortgage Act governing German Pfandbriefe, in particular for those elements that provide the high standards of bondholder protection typical of the German Pfandbrief. This high level of protection entails that *Lettres de gage* have the same privileges, namely they have a lower risk weighting required by the Solvency Directive, they are eligible for repo operations with the ECB, and are not subject to certain limits on investments for institutional investors. However, there are some interesting differences compared to the German Pfandbrief law that have attracted the attention of issuers and investors alike. These differences enhance the flexibility of the *Lettres de gage* compared to Pfandbriefe, although they require some analysis of the potential implications for the overall risk for the instrument.[14]

---

[13] If this limit is exceeded, the issuer must offset the exceeding amount either by depositing cash or sovereign bonds with the Bank of Spain, or redeem/repurchase mortgage certificates until the limit is met, or add hew mortgages to the collateral pool. In practice, Spanish banks have issued Cedulas for much smaller amounts than the value of the eligible loan portfolio (e.g. 30%). This ratio is currently around 30–40% in the case of big issuers of *Cedulas*.

[14] Incidentally, the fact that *Lettres de gage* appear to be more flexible than German Pfandbriefe may explain why the three existing Luxembourg Pfandbrief issuers are newly founded subsidiaries of German bank groups. Currently, there are three institutions permitted to issue the Luxembourg Pfandbrief: Eurohypo Lux (a subsidiary of Deutsche Bank), Erste Europaische Pfandbrief und Kommunalkreditbank (owned by Duesseldorfer Hypothekenbank, HypothekenbankEssen and Schuupli Group, and the Pfandbrief Bank International (owned by a consortium of German banks, the biggest of which is Hypovereinsbank).

These differences are as follows:

(a) enhanced international diversification is allowed inasmuch as the underlying public loans can be from issuers in the OECD area, where 97% of public sector debt is rated AA or better (the collateral underlying the German Pfandbrief has to be located in the EEA and Switzerland).

(b) issuers are allowed to use hedging instruments (e.g. derivatives) in the cover pool (a feature present also in the French law on *Obligation Foncières*, but not in the German Pfandbrief);

(c) some additional safety clauses are included in *Lettres de gage*; the trustee of the *Lettres* must be specifically qualified (an auditor by profession) and there is a detailed regulation for the unlikely event of default, which foresees that in such a circumstance the cover pool is separated from that of the issuer and the administration taken over by the banking supervisory authority (*CSSF – Commission de Surveillance du Secteur Financier*), which implies that this Authority in practice needs to closely monitor events relating to these products. Currently no *Lettre de gage* qualifies (in terms of issue size) to be included for trading on the EuroCreditMTS. Table 6.5 summarises the main characteristics of Pfandbrief style products.

6.7   COMMON ASPECTS OF PFANDBRIEFE PRODUCTS

6.7.1   Liquidity and Market Making

Liquidity in European Pfandbrief products has significantly improved since the inception of the Jumbo market. The "Jumbo concept" has created a market segment that provides investors with a deep and transparent secondary market, which otherwise exists for only government bonds. The German Jumbo Pfandbrief market was introduced by setting minimum requirements for issue size to ensure liquidity; initially this was DEM 1 billion, which was then converted to €500 million when the euro was introduced in 1999. Nevertheless, issue sizes of €2–3 billion are not uncommon, and even issues of €5 billion have been made in the recent past. In fact, since the introduction of the electronic trading platform EuroCredit MTS (Box 2) in the year 2000, several banks have issued and reopened bonds to attain a minimum size volume of at least €3 billion, which is the minimum size for EuroCredit MTS eligibility. This trend followed expectations of electronically traded bonds outperforming traditional Pfandbriefe, thus resulting in lower funding costs in a business with very tight margins. There are currently 29 Jumbo Pfandbrief plus 3 *Obligation Foncières* issues and 1 *Cedula* traded on the EuroCredit MTS. Average aggregate daily turnover on these products is currently around €600 mln.

The average issue size of Jumbos doubled, from 0.6 billion at their inception to the current 1.5 billion in 2002. This was achieved both through the increase in the average size of new issues as well as to the "reopening" of old issues. The high liquidity is ensured also by the existence of a market-making mechanism, i.e., the commitment by at least three syndicate leaders to quote two-way prices with fixed bid/offer spreads on a continuous basis during normal trading hours.[15] Transparency is achieved by providing quotes on Reuters.

---

[15] Additional standards for Jumbo Pfandbriefe are that tappings for outstanding issues must have a minimum size of €125 million; the normal trading lot with guaranteed quotations is €15 million, with a minimum of €1 million.

Table 6.5 Comparison of the main characteristics of Jumbo Pfandbrief products in the Euro area

	Obligations Foncières	Pfandbriefe	Cedulas Hipotecarias
Issuers	Sociétés de crédit foncière (SCFs), which are credit institutions classified as finance companies by the regulator (Comité des Etablissements du Crédit et des Entreprises d'Investissement – CECEI). Any company may set up an SCF, but its parent is most likely to be a bank.	Private mortgage banks (21, be reduced to 19 in June 2002) regulated by the Mortgage Bank Law; public sector (public law) credit institutions (incl. 12 Landesbanks) regulated by the Law governing Pfandbriefe and associated debt instruments issued by public law credit institutions and two private ship mortgage banks regulated by the Ship Mortgage Bank Law	Any Spanish financial institution recognized by the Banco España (Bank of Spain).
Types of instruments generated by these issuers	OFs, which are preferential bonds (no distinction is made between those collateralized on mortgage loans and those on public sector debt), and/or other, nonpreferential instruments. The default probability on the latter would be greater than for the OFs, and the potential loss severity would be significantly higher.	Separate Mortgage PBs and Public Sector PBs, "Schiffspfandbriefe" (ships' PBs) and other, nonpreferential funding instruments, e.g. long term debt and commercial paper programs.	CHs, which are mortgage certificates, bonos hipotecarios, i.e. mortgage bonds, and other, nonpreferential banking liabilities.
Relevant laws	The 1984 Banking Law and The Savings and Protection of Financial Security Law of 25th June 1999.	The Mortgage Bank Law, the Law governing Pfandbriefe and associated debt instruments issued by Public Credit Institutions and the Ship Mortgage Bank Law. All were last amended in 1998 and are due for revision in 2002.	Mortgage Market Law 2/1981.
Supervision	Banking Commission (Commission Bancaire – CB) and the specific external auditor (contrôleur spécifique) approved by the CB. This auditor cannot also be the external auditor of the SCF's parent company.	Federal Banking Supervisory Office (FBSO) and an independent trustee (Treuhändler) appointed by the FBSO. NB: Public sector credit institutions issuing PBs are not obliged to have an FBSO appointed trustee. Because none of the banks involved are savings or cooperative banks, all are also audited by an external auditor approved by the FBSO.	Ministry of Economy & Finance through the Bank of Spain.
Permitted business activities	To acquire mortgage, specified guaranteed and public sector loans principally by issuing OFs, which are "privileged," i.e., they have preferential status in any liquidation of an SCF. SCFs are also able to originate mortgage and	Mortgage banks: noneligible mortgage lending within the EEA and the European OECD member countries and eligible mortgage lending as specified in "Collateral (eligible loans)," below, and public sector lending within	No restrictions.

(cont.)

Table 6.5 (*Cont.*)

	public sector loans. They cannot take deposits or own stakes in other companies. They may effect derivatives transactions only to the extent that the instruments involved are used for hedging. SCFs are required to employ a servicer company under contract, which must be a registered credit institution; in most cases the servicer is the parent company.	the Federal Republic of Germany and other EEA countries. Cannot take deposits. Proposed amendments to the law to allow for the inclusion of G7 countries and to specify hedging criteria. "Mixed" mortgage banks have no restrictions.	
Transfer of loans	Yes, by means of a "bordereau" (preformed document) signed by the parties to the transfer, which takes legal effect on the signing.	NA	NA
Debtor notification	As at the date of the prescribed signing of the bordereau. Transfer of title as prescribed obviates any possibility of the liquidator of a bankrupt seller deeming the transfer to be a loan not a sale.	NA	NA
Collateral (eligible loans)	First mortgage or equivalent real estate-backed loans guaranteed by an unrelated credit institution or insurance company. Any collateral backing assets for these three types of loan must be situated within the EEA. Guaranteed loans acquired by an SCF must not exceed 20% of its total assets, and the borrower must take a minimum equity stake in the property in question, depending on whether it is residential (5–10% min. equity stake) or commercial (20%). Public sector loans granted to central or federal states, regional and local authorities or public sector entities within the EEA or wholly guaranteed by such entities. Senior securitization notes issued by Fonds Communs de Crédit (FCCs) and suchlike asset-backed instruments deemed equivalent to these FCC notes by the laws of the EEA	Mortgage loan pool collateral: First mortgage loans secured on properties that may be expected to produce a safe return over a long period and must be of a type that could be adapted for third-party use. Loans secured on land, which is undeveloped, or on properties under construction are limited to the lower of 10% of total loans in the mortgage pool or twice the bank's regulatory own funds. Loans on property which do not guarantee a permanent yield, especially on pits and quarries, are excluded altogether. Backing assets for the above types of loans must be situated in the EEA or Switzerland. Loans on properties in any of these states do not recognize the preferential rights of PB holders in the event of the issuing bank's insolvency are limited to 10% of total mortgage. (This means	Only first mortgage loans (residential and commercial), excluding those "registered mortgages" that serve as collateral against bonos hipotecarios (mortgage bonds), if any. Only properties which are wholly owned by the mortgagor. All properties must be insured.

Table 6.5 (Cont.)

	countries, provided that at least 90% of the FCCs' (etc) underlying assets are of the same types as those listed above. Liquid and risk-free assets (i.e. substitution collateral). These must qualify as tier 1 "repos" for the ECB or must consist of loans or debt with a term of <1 year owed by credit institutions. Such assets must not exceed 20% of the SCF's total assets (30% with special permission from the CB). The law was changed on December 11, 2001 to incorporate lending in Switzerland, Canada, USA, and Japan. However the enforcing decree is still pending.	that only lending on properties in Austria, France and Luxembourg is restricted.) Public sector collateral pool: Loans to German federal, regional and municipal governments and public law institutions or guaranteed by one of these OR loans to such types of government in any EEA country which recognizes PB holders' preferential rights. In such countries where these rights are not recognized, such loans are limited to 10% of public sector (or outside the pool). (This means that only lending on public sector debt issued in Austria, Denmark, and France is restricted.) Substitution collateral: Substitution collateral may be included in either the mortgage or public sector pool up to 10% of its value or in both, up to 10% of their combined value. It must consist of either German Federal Republic, German Federal State (Land), EU or EEA member state or EIB issued bonds and treasury bills or guaranteed bonds, credit balances with the Bundesbank or approved credit institutions. Bonds are included in the pools at 95–100% of par value.)	
Concentration of lending by economic sector, counterparty, country, etc.	No legally imposed limits, except in regard to loan counterparties, for which the EU Directive on banks' lending concentrations is applicable.	No legally imposed limits, except for those on non German lending. Also, in the case of loan counterparties, for which the EU Directive on banks' lending concentrations is applicable.	No legally imposed limits, except in regard to loan counterparties, for which the EU Directive on banks' lending concentrations is applicable.
Real estate valuation	There should be an independent, prudent professional valuation of the real estate in question, based on its enduring properties, on both standard and local market conditions and	The "mortgageable value" is determined according to principles laid down in article 12 of the Mortgage Bank Law. It may not exceed the "prudently assessed mortgage lending	All properties collateralizing eligible mortgage loans must be valued (implicitly on a conservative basis) by

(cont.)

Table 6.5 (*Cont.*)

	on its business use and the alternative uses to which it could be put. This mortgage valuation must be expressed clearly and comprehensively in writing and must be at least equal to the market value. The valuation may simply be based on the total cost of the transaction being financed if that cost falls below certain limits. Valuations must be updated annually or triennially and must be made available to the SCF's specific external auditor.	value". In establishing this value, only the permanent characteristics of the property and only the yield, which any tenant can sustainably ensure by proper management, shall be taken into account. The value thus calculated is typically less than 90% of the market value.	surveyors approved by the Bank of Spain. Ineligible assets are not mandatory subject to this type of valuation.
Loan to value (LTV) limits for eligible loans	Real estate: The asset(s) involved must be situated in the EEA or in the French overseas territories (DOM-TOM) <60% fro grant or purchase by an SCF of a mortgage loan; <80% LTV if the SCF's portfolio is exclusively residential mortgage loans to private individuals OR if the 20% balance is financed by nonpreferential funding. (The value is set by the real estate valuation criterion defined above.) The LTV ratio can be 100% if the excess is guaranteed by a state agency. See "Collateral (eligible loans)" for law amendment.	<60% on the "mortgageable value" (see "Real estate valuation", above) of types of property listed in "Collateral (eligible loans)".	<80% LTV residential housing mortgages; <70% LTV commercial housing mortgages; In both cases the value in question is the regulatory value described in the section above.
Imposed regulatory overcollateralization	Yes. Ratio of collateralizing assets to preferential resources must be >1. Denominator of ratio is total preferential resources, including sums due in the case of preferential hedging instruments. Numerator of ratio is the sum of the following weighted assets. Guaranteed loans: 100% if guarantor's rating from Fitch, Moody's or S & P is at least AA−; 50% if guarantor is rated between A− and A+; and 0% in all other cases.	There is a specific legal requirement that the principal of and interest on assets in the collateral pools should be at least equal in value to the principal of and interest on the corresponding PBs. Also, an implicit assumption of overcollateralization underlies the Mortgage Bank Law. See "Specific legal insulation against normal bankruptcy laws".	Yes, >11%, i.e., the total amount of CHs must be <90% of the total eligible mortgage loans. If on any occasion they go over this figure, the issuer must deposit cash with the Bank of Spain equivalent to the deficiency within 10 business days. The issuer then has four months to restore the 90% ratio, either by repurchasing CHs in the

Table 6.5 (*Cont.*)

	Qualifying senior asset-backed instruments: 100% if rated at least AA−; 50% if rated between A− and A+; and 0% in all other cases. Liquid and risk-free assets: 95%. Repossessed real estate: 50%. Any other eligible assets, incl. public sector loans or bonds: 100%.		market, issuing additional qualifying mortgages or buying qualifying mortgage participations. In practice, the excess of security available to provide cover for CHs in issue in the event of liquidation is greater than 11% since security is provided by the whole mortgage portfolio, whether qualifying as collateral for CHs or not.
Fall in value of collateralized property	There is no requirement to introduce new loans into the collateral pool. The mortgage lender has no right to require more collateral from the borrower.	There is no legal requirement to introduce new loans into the mortgage collateral pool. This would be a matter for negotiation between the lending bank and the borrower; it would have no effect on the mortgage pool.	Not included in the Mortgage Market Law.
Foreign assets as collateral for loans	The asset(s) involved must be situated in the EEA. There is no limit on the proportion of non French assets, so that, theoretically at least, none need be French. See "Collateral (eligible loans)" for law amendment.	There are no restrictions on such assets based in or originating from Austria, France or Luxembourg. Otherwise, only a maximum 10% can have been originated in another EU or EEA country plus Switzerland, or a combination thereof.	Not included in the Mortgage Market Law.
Fungibility of assets and liabilities	Yes; but, the mortgage loan and public debt portfolios together constitute one integral underlying asset pool.	Yes; but although there is fungibility within the mortgage and public debt portfolios, the two are separate asset pools. There is no fungibility between one pool and the other except in the case of Federal Equalization Bonds. Theoretically, in a liquidation there could be a surfeit of collateral assets in one pool which reverts to senior debt holders, while PB holders in the other pool suffer a deficit.	Yes; security cover is provided by the whole mortgage loan portfolio, not just by those loans qualifying as collateral for CHs.

(*cont.*)

Table 6.5 (*Cont.*)

Allocation of assets to asset pools and check on required overcollateralization	An SCF must respect the overcollateralization requirement at all times. Its specific external auditor must certify that its eligible assets exceed its preferential liabilities each time it issues OFs >€500 million. The auditor must also report to the CB on these matters annually.	The independent trustee, appointed by the FBSO, checks the allocation of assets to asset pools whenever a PB is issued, and every 6 months passes a report on these allocations to the FBSO.	Allocation of assets is not applicable. Data is provided monthly by the issuer to the Bank of Spain, allowing it to check on overcollateralization.
Effect on asset pool of the establishment of specific loan loss provisions	Eligible loans specifically provided against remain eligible. The requirement for overcollateralization (see earlier section) applies.	Those loans affected are removed from the qualifying asset pool and will be replaced. The FBSO organizes a "Deckungsprüfung" (collateral check) of the mortgage and public sector pools about every 2 years. This is usually conducted by independent auditors. Also, the inbuilt tendency to overcollateralize (see "Imposed regulatory overcollateralization", above) should mean any gap is covered.	Eligible loans specifically provided against remain eligible, however, nonperforming eligible loans are excluded under Article 32(1b) of the Ministry of Finance's Reglamento Hipotecario.
Protection against mismatching	An SCF must respect the mismatch rules at all times. Each time it makes an OF issue >€500 million, its specific external auditor must check and certify the steps taken to match interest rate, maturity, and foreign exchange by hedging, etc. The specific external auditor must also check that the SCF is satisfactorily managing its interest and maturity mismatch, if any.	Interest and maturity matching are required under the Mortgage Banking Law: in particular the maturity of mortgage PBs should not materially exceed the maturity of their funding.	Taken account of in total balance sheet management.
Interest rate matching	See section above. There is, nevertheless, a risk of an interest rate mismatch arising from mortgage loan prepayments (see Risk of early prepayment of the underlying asset") below.	See section above. There is, nevertheless, some risk of an interest rate mismatch arising from mortgage loan prepayments (see "Risk of early prepayment of the underlying asset") below.	The interest rate on variable CHs must be less than or equal to the average rate on qualifying variable mortgage loans. Under Article 37(4b) of the Reglamento Hipotecario, the issuing bank must periodically provide details of these rates to the Bank of Spain.

Table 6.5 (*Cont.*)

Use of hedging instruments	The potential resultant complications in the event of the insolvency/liquidation of the SCF are considered to have been eliminated by granting preferential status to holders of OFs and swap counterparties see "Preferential claim of mortgage bond holders" below).	There could be problems in the event of the insolvency/liquidation of the bank. See "Netting agreement" and "Preferential claim of mortgage bondholders" below.
Netting agreement	SCFs may enter into normal netting agreements.	Yes; the issuing banks can enter into netting agreements. However, it is possible to set a liability attaching to one pool of assets against an asset or assets in another pool, which can upset any netting agreement, particularly in regard to hedging agreements (see "Use of hedging instruments" above).
Risk of prepayment of the underlying asset	Residential mortgage loan prepayments are permitted, but there is a penalty of up to 6 months interest or 3% of the repaid capital. Penalties (if any) on commercial mortgages are stipulated in their contracts. The SCFs can substitute liquid and risk-free assets or other eligible loans for prepaid loans, but this may not restore adequate interest cover.	Limited by the Law. Fixed-rate loans with a term of 10 years or more must run for at least 10 years before the interest rate and/or term can be renegotiated, unless prepayment is explicitly countenanced in the loan contract. If prepayment occurs within this 10-year period, then a penalty equivalent to the present value of the interest foregone is payable.
Bankruptcy remoteness	None (see next section)	Some (see next section).
Possibility of interest payment default	Some, but very low.	Some, but very low.
Possibility of principal repayment default	Some, but very low.	Some.

Source: Fitch, 2002. Reproduced by permission of Fitch, Inc.

Box 6.2 The EUROCREDIT MTS trading platform for nongovernment covered bonds

EuroMTS is a private London-based company, formed in 1999, that manages a pan-European electronic trading platform for euro-denominated benchmark government and nongovernment securities with the primary objective of enhancing the liquidity and transparency of the European bond markets. Instruments traded on this trading platform include benchmark securities from 14 government and agency issuers, namely Austria, Belgium, Finland, France, Germany, Greece, Ireland, Italy, The Netherlands, Portugal, Spain, the European Investment Bank (EIB), Freddie Mac, and Kreditanstalt fuer Wiederaufbau (KfW).

EuroCredit MTS is an electronic trading platform for high-quality covered bonds, which opened for trading on May 22, 2000. Bonds currently traded include Pfandbriefe, Obligations Foncieres, and Cédulas Hipotecarias. Additional nongovernment bond classes can be added in response to market demand. Membership of EuroCredit MTS is open to any bank. Banks that do not have formal pricing obligations on behalf of issuers in respect of covered bonds can join as Market Takers.

In order to be listed on EuroCredit MTS, nongovernment bonds must be

- collateralized with either mortgages or public sector loans, or a combination thereof.
- euro-denominated.
- in excess of €3 billion in terms of outstanding size.
- issued by an institution with total outstanding debt in excess of €10 billion in respect of the asset class of the bond in question (including that issue).
- given a triple A rating by at least one of Standard & Poor's, Fitch IBCA or Moody's.

In order for an issuer's eligible bond to be selected for the system, the issuer must be selected for quoting by at least seven existing EuroCredit MTS market makers, and must agree to inform EuroCredit MTS directly of any proposed taps to its bonds to be listed on EuroCredit MTS.

Each market maker must choose at least eight eligible bonds to quote. Eligible bonds on EuroCredit MTS, in addition to the €3 billion listing criteria, must have the commitment of at least seven market makers in order to be listed. The maximum permitted bid/offer spreads for market makers in their allocated bonds depend on the maturity buckets. The shorter bucket (1–4 years) requires maximum spreads of 6 ticks. The middle bucket (4–8 years) requires maximum spreads of 8 ticks, and the longer bucket (8–12 years) requires maximum spreads of 12 ticks. All obliged quotes are for €10 million.

Each bond is selected by at least seven different market makers, ensuring that quotes overlap and the effective best bid/offer spread is constantly tighter than the maximum permitted quoting spreads. Pfandbriefe are settled at Clearstream Banking Luxembourg and Euroclear, while Obligations Foncieres are settled at Euroclear France, on a gross delivery versus payment basis. Settlement cycle is T+3

In terms of traded volumes, in November 2002, single-sided daily volumes averaged around €630 million, with 29 Jumbo issues eligible for trading.

6.7.2 Repo Markets

The availability of the Jumbo Pfandbrief has spurred the development of connected market segments trading this product and allowing hedging strategies to market participants. The sustained turnover recorded for Pfandbriefe can be ascribed, among other things, to the existence of repo market maker arrangements on Pfandbriefe, which have contributed to an improvement of the liquidity in the Jumbo market. In fact, a liquid repo market is a necessary condition to guarantee a liquid secondary cash market, especially when it is characterized by active market making.

The first repo market making scheme, which is an extension of the market making commitment seen on cash deals on Pfandbriefe, originated in 1998 on the initiative of 17 market makers (the lead managers which typically guarantee the market making in the cash market). They are committed to quoting bid/ask prices for liquid issues with a volume of at least €1.25 billion and a 2-year residual maturity. Repo maturities range from 1 week to 1 month.[16] In terms of volume, Pfandbrief repo trading volumes presently average between €6 and 8 billion per day. This telephone market making remains the dominant form of repo trading in Jumbo covered bonds.

The second repo market making activity started in January 2001, when the Jumbo Pfandbrief was accepted (together with Freddie Mac and EIB Reference Notes) as underlying for repo trades on the electronic "Repo Trading Facility" managed by EuroCredit MTS.

Among the Jumbo covered bonds, the most active trading remains concentrated on German Jumbo Pfandbriefe (85%), "Obligations Foncières" account for another 10%, while Cedulàs hipotecarias and Luxembourg 'lettres de gage' account for the rest. Repos in specific covered bonds may also be available on request in smaller size in over-the-counter trading, with most banks active in this market. The bigger Jumbo issues are typically used for hedging purposes and trade more actively in the repo market. The average trading size is around €20 million but trades up to €150 million are possible. The ready availability of Jumbo Pfandbrief collateral makes it trade generally cheap in the repo market. Most of the trading (90%) actually takes place in the short maturities between Spot-Next until one week.

The repo market is dominated by banks (80%), mostly for market making purposes. The mortgage banks themselves actually play only a minor role in the repo market. Investment funds and insurance companies account for the other 20% by repoing out their stocks of Jumbo collateral.

In addition to the repo market, a futures contract on the Jumbo Pfandbrief started to be traded – even if only for a short time – on the EUREX futures exchange in July 1998. However, the low volumes recorded after a few months of existence led to a discontinuation of this contract.[17]

6.7.3 Market Indices

With the introduction of the euro in 1999, the Jumbo Pfandbrief was included as an asset class in a number of European bond market indices (Figure 6.8).[18] Depending on the index provider, Pfandbriefe account for between 40% and 60% of the nonsovereign segment in the

---

[16] Market makers have to quote two-way prices for up to €15 mn with a 25 bp bid/offer spread. Depfa has a special arrangement with the market makers for four of its Global Jumbo Pfandbriefe to quote a 20 bp bid/offer. Jumbos trade around EURIBOR flat if they are general collateral. There is no particular sector of the curve which is most likely to be special in the repo market. The bigger Jumbo Pfandbrief benchmark issues are typically used for hedging purposes and trade more actively in the repo market. Jumbo Pfandbriefe are mostly made available for repo borrowing by investment funds and the mortgage banks themselves.

[17] The timing of the introduction of the futures contract was probably unfortunate, as it coincided with a period of strong instability and volatility in the world financial markets in conjunction with the emerging markets crisis, which possibly hindered the development of new types of instruments because of the "flight to quality" that occurred during this period.

[18] These indices are Salomon's Euro Broad Investment-Grade bond Index, which has a 9% weighting of Pfandbriefe, Merrill Lynch's EMU Broad Market index with 7% (in addition to traditional Pfandbriefe with 12.5%), Lehman Brothers' bond index with 4% of Jumbos (and 13% in traditional pfandbriefe), and Morgan Stanley's bond index with 7% in Jumbos. The JP Morgan Aggregate Index Europe and the Bear-Stern indices also include Pfandbriefe.

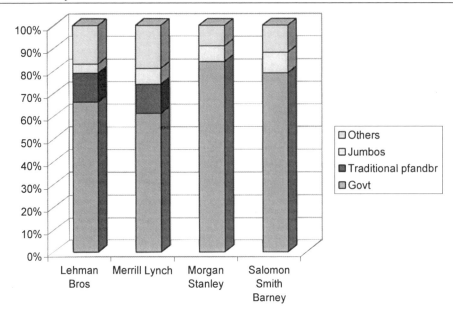

Figure 6.8   The Pfandbrief in the European bond indices.
Source: ECB. Copyright © European Central Bank, Frankfurt am Main, Germany. Reproduced with permission.

Euro area. The substantial weight in such indexes implies that the Pfandbrief is an instrument that index-tracking fixed income investors and fund managers cannot overlook. This fact has generated sizeable acquisitions by institutional investors; it is estimated that currently about 20% of Jumbo issues are held by investors outside Germany. Aside from these "World indices," the market for Jumbos is also captured by Reuters' PFANDTOP index (calculated on the basis of market makers' quotations and published daily), which covers all Jumbos issued in the EU and tracks their performance.

6.8   ASPECTS CHARACTERIZING THE "QUALITY" OF PFANDBRIEF PRODUCTS

Since Pfandbrief style products are subject to very stringent regulation as to their characteristics, they have established themselves as low-risk products. The following sections review some of the regulatory aspects relating to Pfandbrief products.

6.8.1   The "Specialist Bank" Principle

National legislators have opted for "the specialist bank" principle, which implies some restrictions on the freedom of business of the issuers of Pfandbrief and a tight provisioning to remove the risk of any such institution becoming insolvent. Mortgage bank activity is restricted to certain types of loans (for example, in Germany, public sector lending and mortgage financing). By focusing on a restricted number of business activities, which are considered to be fundamentally "safe," the specialist bank principle is meant to ensure against any insolvency of the issuers.

6.8.2   The Credit Quality of the Cover Assets

The quality of cover assets is an important criterion for the quality of the Pfandbrief. The simplest and still the dominant approach consists of establishing an exclusive list of eligible cover assets. The national legislator normally defines those assets that are eligible as cover assets. There are a number of elements characterizing the cover asset:

(a) Value of underlying assets;
(b) Treatment of risk relating to interest rate, currencies, and other risks;
(c) Geographical extension of underlying assets;
(d) Use of derivative instruments in the asset pool.

6.8.2.1   *Value of Underlying Assets*

In *mortgage lending*, first-level mortgages within the EU or the European Economic Area are acceptable as underlying assets under most European Pfandbrief laws. National situations vary considerably, with, for example, Spain only allowing domestic mortgage assets as cover for its Cedulas Hipotecarias, whereas Luxembourg, Germany, and Ireland allow OECD-wide mortgage and public sector assets to be used for its Pfandbriefe. Limits on the amounts of loans granted against real property exist in all countries and are designed to protect the Pfandbrief creditor against the potential erosion of the market value of the underlying mortgage asset. Loan-to-Value (LTV) ratios in the EU range between 60% and 80%. Besides the setting of conservative LTV ratios, careful *valuation of real property* is a critical safety element to the "covered bond" holder. The rules, which regulate the valuation of real property are mostly laid down in legal provisions by public authorities (in Germany, Denmark, France, Spain, and Portugal) but may also be found in the articles of the respective mortgage bank associations (Sweden and Finland).

In most jurisdictions, the issuers of Pfandbriefe are not only active in mortgage lending but also focus on *public sector lending*, which typically refers to credits granted to the public sector (i.e., central, regional, and local government authorities and other public bodies and institutions guaranteed by one of the aforementioned public authorities). Public sector lending may be done in the form of direct loans, loans secured by a public authority, or in the form of direct purchases of public sector bonds. While Austria confines public sector lending to the domestic market, most countries allow public sector lending within the EU or the European Economic Area or as in the case of Luxembourg within OECD countries.

Furthermore, a mortgage bank need not only purchase mortgage or public sector assets. As the example of the French mortgage bank act shows mortgage-backed securities may also be used as coverage for the issuance of "covered bond." Further, the quality of a noneligible assets may be enhanced via a *guarantee* provided by a financial institution or an insurance company.

6.8.2.2   *Risk Relating to Interest Rate, Currencies, and Other Risks*

The assets must not include excessive risk relating to interest rate, currency, or other risks. *Currency risk* hedging is prescribed by all Pfandbrief regulation, while the scope to specifically take on *interest rate risk* varies significantly between the different jurisdictions. Duration mismatches between cover assets and liabilities may drive a wedge between asset and liability value when yield curves shift. Accordingly, interest rate risks must be adequately managed and limited in size. The amount of interest rate risk that issuers of covered bonds may assume differs from country to country. Every European covered bond law with the exception of Denmark and

Switzerland allows for a limited amount of interest rate mismatch. Typically, the Pfandbrief laws require that the cash flows from the assets (principal and coupon income) will, at least, match the cash flows due on the covered bonds over the lifetime of both the cover assets and the Pfandbrief. This can also be achieved via sufficient overcollateralization or via adequate substitute collateral and does not require that the maturities match exactly.

While maturity mismatches represent a potential source of risk to the Pfandbrief creditors, they can also be a source of profit to the issuers. However, typically, issuers will not assume excessive risk in their collateral pools since this may threaten the Pfandbrief rating and erode the refinancing costs of issuers. In an industry with structurally low margins, any deterioration in funding conditions has severe repercussions. It is, therefore, more likely that issuers concentrate their "excessive" interest rate risk in the noneligible part of their business. However, while this is not a risk to the Pfandbrief creditor, it is of concern to the unsecured creditor as it might threaten the mortgage bank itself without endangering the covered asset pools. Until very recently, there have been no explicit constraints or controls on the amount of the interest rate risk that mortgage banks may hold in the noneligible part of the asset side business. Germany was the first country to introduce explicit upper limits on the amount of interest rate risk for the whole banking portfolio, i.e. eligible and noneligible business.

On the mortgage lending side, the risk from noneligible loans in excess of the LTV ratios has been limited in a number of countries conscious of the particular risk character of this type of activity. No such regulations exist for the public sector lending businesses (with the exception of recent regulatory changes in Germany). Mortgage banks may thus (and in fact, do) carry significant amounts of public sector assets on their books.

The right of the borrower to prepay a loan may also threaten the security of the bond holder by introducing the risk of a *maturity mismatch* between assets and liabilities, which may potentially erode the value of the underlying cover assets. The possibility of borrowers to prepay on their mortgage loans varies significantly between countries. While German mortgage banks are protected against prepayments through substantial prepayment penalties, Danish borrowers may prepay after a formal 2-month notification to the mortgage bank without prepayment penalty. The possibility to prepay introduces an additional element of risk into the asset-liability management process of a mortgage bank. If the borrower can prepay but the bonds issued are noncallable, as is the case in Germany and France, the right to prepay without substantial prepayment penalty is a potential risk for the mortgage bank.

6.8.2.3   Geographical Extension of Underlying Assets

The different European covered bond laws only apply within the national frontiers. As the issuers become active in cross-border lending, other legislative environments need to be taken into account. This aspect is particularly relevant in the event of bankruptcy of the mortgage bank when the creditor of covered bonds wants to enforce his priority claim on the cover assets. Different national legislation may not recognize the priority claim of the creditors on the assets, leading to conflicting claims on the cover assets. For example, the German mortgage bank act imposes a 10% limit on foreign mortgage and public sector lending activities where the priority claim of the Pfandbrief holder on the cover assets in case of default is not guaranteed.

Even within the EU, there are significant differences in legislation. Thus, the status of the creditor of "covered bonds" relative to the cover assets in case of the bankruptcy of the mortgage bank is not always clear. Under these circumstances, the 10% limit in Germany is a very important additional security element for the buyers of German Pfandbrief, which almost no other European Pfandbrief law currently offers. More importantly, legislation tends to be all the more different, the wider the geographical lending area. More specifically, the extension of the geographical lending area to Japan, the United States, and Canada (foreseen for example in the French and German legislation) makes the 10% limit even more relevant. The absence of such a limit should be considered a serious problem in the case of those countries (e.g. Luxembourg) where mortgage banks are allowed to extend mortgage and public sector loans to the OECD area without restrictions.

6.8.2.4 Use of Derivative Instruments in the Asset Pool

If the use of derivative instruments is made, it must be ensured that the asset pool does not contain any risks ensuing from the default of a derivative's counterparty. The use of derivative instruments in the European mortgage bank business has greatly increased in recent years and has raised the potential risks related to these instruments. The growing size of individual transactions, particularly since the inception of the Jumbo Pfandbrief market, has raised the amount of risk in these transactions and thus the need for appropriate hedging techniques. The increasing use of swaps or other derivative instruments as hedging tool for cover assets has raised the exposure of asset pools to the counterparty risk incurred via these transactions. There is a need for legislative action to protect the covered bond creditor against such risk. France was the first country to protect the investor from any risks emanating from derivatives in case of a default. In case of an insolvency of the mortgage bank, the derivatives linked to the asset pool will not be unwound but will be continued until all creditors of covered bonds have been satisfied. The French law provides insufficient protection, however, against the risk of a swap counterparty going bankrupt. In this case, the swap would have to be unwound and the asset pool would be exposed to a loss from the residual claims on the defaulted swap counterparty. To limit the exposure of the creditor to default by the swap counterparty, additional measures are necessary.

6.8.3 Preferential Claim and Bankruptcy Remoteness

The quality of the assets may not guarantee repayment of interest and principal to the creditor if they are not accompanied by *bankruptcy remoteness*. Similarly, the bankruptcy remoteness of the assets or the asset pool will not provide sufficient protection if the quality of the assets is not high enough. Both conditions need to be met simultaneously to provide the investor with a maximum level of security.

While most national legislations have comprised the cover assets in separate asset pools designed solely to separate the cover assets from the other nonprivileged assets, in some other countries there is no distinction between privileged and nonprivileged assets. The practical implementation of the cover principle depends on national legal frameworks.

* The simplest example of the cover principle is the "pass-through principle" where bonds are issued in parallel to loans being granted. Hence there is a perfect match between payments on the bonds and repayments on the loans. There is also a perfect match between the pools of security and the bonds being issued. In the "pass-through principle" the mortgage banks' only function is to act as intermediary between debtors and creditors. This method is adopted in Denmark, where Danish mortgage banks issue bonds in parallel to granting new loans; thus, there is a specific relationship between a bond issue and the underlying mortgages both in terms of payments and in terms of security.

- No special purpose vehicles are created, and there is *segregation* into separate asset pools in the issuing bank's books of the loans collateralizing mortgage loans and of those collateralizing public loans. This method is adopted for German Pfandbriefe. If the issuing bank goes into liquidation, the Pfandbrief holders would not suffer any untimely repayments or redemption.

- A *special purpose vehicle* is created; this is the case of Obligations Foncières in France, where a Societe de Credit Foncier (SCF), is created. This is a registered credit institution that does not originate the loans collateralising its Obligations Foncières but rather buys them from another originator, normally the parent bank setting up the SCF. In case of a default, the holders of Obligations Foncières will have a preferential claim over all the assets of the issuing SCF so that these preferential creditors will remain fully remunerated and will be paid off in a timely manner.

- The covered instrument is not secured by a separate pool of collateral, and the safety is based on the principle of *overcollateralization* of loans. This is, for example, the case for Swedish mortgage bonds or for Spanish Cedulas Hipotecarias, which can be issued by any financial institution recognized by the Bank of Spain. There are no restrictions on the activities of the issuer, which also originates the loans backing the Cedulas. In case of default, the bank's whole mortgage loan portfolio provides cover and the holders of Cedulas are granted preferential treatment (though after claims from the State and from employees have been satisfied). Although in would be very unlikely that holders of Cedulas would suffer any loss, they could suffer temporary interruption of remuneration and redemption as the liquidation procedures are carried out.

A preferential claim on the assets within the cover pool will not guarantee, in itself, that the cover pools can be considered bankruptcy remote. In the event of insolvency of the issuer of a Pfandbrief, the creditor must not only have a preferential claim on the assets in the cover pool but the asset pools may also need to be continued. If the Pfandbrief becomes due, this will entail early liquidation of the underlying assets in the cover pool. It is thus critical that the Pfandbrief do not become due in order to avoid any mismatch between the cash flows of the cover assets and the Pfandbrief. If these became due, they would become due at par. The assets, however, will not necessarily be sold at par. Thus even an inherently solvent asset pool may not be sufficient to satisfy all claims if the "covered bonds" are paid back before maturity.

While the continuation of the asset pools beyond the default of the issuer of Pfandbrief is an essential security mechanism, it is only provided in the legislation of some European "covered bond" (i.e., Germany, France, Luxembourg, Ireland, and Finland).

6.8.4 Regulatory Treatment of Covered Bonds and Preferential Investment Treatment

As previously mentioned, the basic characteristics of covered bonds can vary significantly across the different national legislation. While no common legal European standard for "covered bonds" exists or is foreseen, covered bonds enjoy preferential treatment in investment policies of investment funds and insurance companies. According to Article 22(4) of the UCITS Directive (Box 1), member States of the EU have the discretionary right to raise the limits for the holdings in the bonds of one single issuer from the standard 5% to 25% in the case of bonds which (a) *are* issued by a credit institution registered in the EU, subject by law to special public supervision designed to protect bond holders ("specialty principle"); (b) have the sums deriving from the issue of these bonds invested in conformity with the law so that for the whole maturity period, the bonds are covered ("cover principle"); and (c) in the event of a failure of the issuer, are used on a priority basis for the reimbursement of principal and payment of accrued interest.

Favorable treatment in the investment policy of insurance companies is also accorded to Pfandbrief, which fulfill the UCITS Directive. Member States are allowed to raise the limits for the investment policy of the insurance companies to 40%.

The UCITS Directive is also relevant with regards to the solvency ratios for credit institutions: the Member States can fix a risk-weighting of 10% for the bonds defined in Article 22(4) of the UCITS directive. The high security standard of covered bonds is thus not only reflected in preferential investment policies but, also, in a low risk weighting for EU credit institutions relative to other "unsecured" bonds issued by EU credit institutions, which are weighted at 20%. Currently, Belgium, Denmark, Germany, Finland, Spain, Austria, France, Luxembourg, the Netherlands, and Greece have fixed a 10% solvency ratio for the list of "covered bonds" defined under Article 22(4) of UCITS.[19]

Pfandbriefe also have a privileged role in the Eurosystem[20] monetary policy operations. The European Central Bank has recognized the high security standard of "covered bonds," specifying that bonds that fulfill Article 22(4) of the UCITS Directive are eligible as tier 1 collateral for monetary operations within the Eurosystem. Particularly German banks hold a significant amount of "covered bonds" as collateral for their liquidity transactions with the Eurosystem. Since these bonds benefit from a 10% solvency ratio, they may be cheaper to hold as collateral than government bonds for the regular liquidity transactions with the ESCB. The combination of a low solvency ratio and a recognized level of security has generated a substantial amount of buying interest from banks.

6.9   CONCLUSIONS AND PROSPECTS

After the continued growth in issuance recorded in the last 5 years, the Pfandbrief market appears to be going through a period of consolidation. In 2001 and 2002 gross issuance of Pfandbrief slowed down substantially, following a deterioration in the market conditions. The intention announced by the biggest German mortgage bank to launch the first 30-year Jumbo Pfandbriefe ever did not materialize.

On the supply side, the widening of yield spread *vis-à-vis* swap rates, together with increasingly tighter margins caused by competition, have raised the funding costs for issuers, and caused some of them to hold back from new issuance. Some more structural changes in the markets are also affecting new issuance. New lending to domestic public authorities, which provides the underlying collateral for the vast amount of Pfandbrief issued, is experiencing lower growth rates because of the ongoing fiscal consolidation in the EU. Some changes in the tax deductibility rules for housing and a weak property market have reduced the amount of mortgage loans available as underlying. The tighter margins currently characterizing issuance require banks to issue higher volumes of Pfandbriefe to ensure profitability. Enhancing profit margins requires developing lending business outside the traditional lending markets.

---

[19] It is not yet clear, if or how the risk weighting for Pfandbriefe would change under the new BASLE II proposals. Today, the Pfandbrief and other "covered bonds" are weighted 20% just as any other financial institution outside of the EU. It is likely, however, that the EU will again accord a preferential treatment for "covered bonds" under the new UCITS directive given the significant interest member states are likely to have in such a step.

[20] The Eurosystem is the group of 12 European central banks that have adopted the euro as a currency.

In this respect, the innovations included in new legislation on Pfandbriefe, which extend the geographical area for mortgage banks' lending activities to a wider area than the EEA, aim at removing some of the bottlenecks that have limited the lending business in recent periods.

Notwithstanding the progress made in individual countries, and the boost given to this asset class by the introduction of the single currency, the lack of uniformity between the different Pfandbriefe products is still perceived as being a drawback: the international investor wishing to invest in Pfandbriefe has to comb through different laws and regulations that characterize distinct European markets. Although (legislative) competition between different countries has ensured some convergence of the characteristics of covered bonds, so far there has not been any concerted action at the European level to create a common legislation specifically for covered bonds and in particular for the Pfandbrief. National laws are, therefore, expected to continue to prevail for some time to come.

Despite the disparities in the national legal frameworks and the fact that a further harmonization of these regulations appears to be unlikely, different national legislations are nonetheless converging toward similar rules to ensure the competitiveness of these assets in the different countries. The introduction of the euro has also contributed to homogenizing the markets for Pfandbriefe and many of the challenges faced by these types of instruments are the same across the countries.

The German Jumbo Pfandbrief market remains the reference covered bond market in Europe but market conditions in Germany have changed significantly over the past 2 years. The industry is merging and strategic reorientation is taking place. Poor margins and deteriorating funding conditions are expected to continue for some time. The amendment of the German mortgage bank act has opened up new business possibilities to the German mortgage banks in a number of areas, at the same time improving the security profile of the German Pfandbrief.

The abolition of state guarantees ("Gewährträgerhaftung und Anstaltslast") by 2005 are expected to bring further changes in the Pfandbrief market, which is currently characterized by the coexistence of public and private Pfandbrief issuers. Private mortgage banks will no longer be able to lend to German public banks as these lose the state guarantees and investors will no longer receive the additional public sector guarantees they currently acquire if they purchase a Landesbank Pfandbrief. The new freedoms of business beyond the European borders will offer new business opportunities for some of the more internationally oriented mortgage banks, while the domestically oriented institutions will have to focus more on domestic niche business. The German Pfandbrief is likely to keep its dominant position in the European "covered bond" market *vis-à-vis* other Pfandbrief products and little competition from alternative products such as ABS or MBS is expected.

REFERENCES

ABN-Amro (2001). Covered Bonds in Europe. *Fixed Income Research Series.*
Association of German Mortgage Banks (2002). The Pfandbrief: Facts and Figures 2002. Köln, Germany: AGMB. www.pfandbrief.org/pfandbrief/index_vdh.html.
AGMB (Association of German Mortgage Banks – Euromoney) (2000). *The Pfandbrief: A European Perspective.* Euromoney Publications.
Barclays Bank (2000, September). The Luxembourg Pfandbrief. *European Covered Bond Series.* London: Barclays Bank.
Barclays Bank (2001, February). *Asset Covered Securities: The Irish Pfandbrief. EU Covered Bond Series* 4. London: Barclays Bank
Battley, N. and P. Wedd (1997). *The European Bond markets.* New York: McGraw-Hill.

Commerzbank (2001, May). *The European Covered Bond Market.* Frankfurtm: Commerzbank securities.

Deutsche Bank (2001, November). Covered Bonds in Europe. *Global Market Research Series.* Frankfurt: Deutsche Bank.

Deutsche Bank – Euromoney (2000). *Euroland – Integrating European Capital Markets.* London: Euromoney Books.

Dresdner Bank (2001, July). *The Jumbo Pfandbrief Market.*

European Commission (2000–2002). *Quarterly Note on Euro-Denominated Bond Markets.* Various issues. http://europa.eu.int/comm/economy_finance/document/financialmarkt/financialmrkt_en.htm.

European Central Bank (2002). The Euro Money Market. Occasional Papers Series. Frankfurt: ECB. www.ecb.int.

European Central Bank (2001). The Euro Bond Market. Occasional Papers Series. Frankfurt: ECB. www.ecb.int.

European Mortgage Federation (2001). *Mortgage Banks and the Mortgage Bond in Europe.* Baden-Baden: Nomos Verlagsgeselschaft.

European Mortgage Federation (2001). *Hypostat: Mortgage and Property Markets in Europe.* Bruxelles: European Mortgage Federation.

European Mortgage Federation (2001). Mortgage Market Europe 2001. Acts of the conference held in Rome on October 29–30, 2001.

EuroMTS (2002). Various Press Releases. www.euromts-ltd.com.

Fitch IBCA (2000, May). German Pfandbriefe and Analogous Funding Instruments Elsewhere in Europe.

Hypo Vereinsbank (1999, May). Clarifications on the Collateral Pool of German Pfandbriefe. Fixed Income Series. Munchen: Hypo Vereinsbank.

Langerbein, M. and M. Schulte (2001). The European Covered Bond Family and the Luxembourg Pfandbrief. In: *Fixed Income Market Review.* Luxembourg.

Levinson, M. (1999). *Guide to Financial Markets.* The Economist Books – Profile Books.

Mastroeni, O. (2001, October). Pfandbrief-Style Products in Europe. In: *The Changing Shape of Fixed Income Markets: A Collection of Studies by Central Bank Economists.* Basel: Bank for International Settlements. BIS Papers Series. www.bis.org.

Morgan Stanley Dean Witter (1999, October). Obligations Foncières: shaping up well. Fixed Income Research Series. London.

Peppetti, A. and Rinaldi, R. (2001). I covered bond in Europa e le ipotesi di sviluppo in Italia in "Bancaria" N.6/2001. Rome: Associazione Bancaria Italiana.

Santillan, J. *et al.* (2000). The Impact of the Euro on Money and Bond Markets. Occasional Papers Series. Frankfurt: European Central Bank. www.ecb.int.

WestLB (2002, June). *Update on the German Pfandbrief Market.* Westdeutsche Landesbank, Düsseldorf. June.

WestLB (2000, December). *Bond Special on Pfandbriefe and Jumbos.* Westdeutsche Landesbank, Düsseldorf.

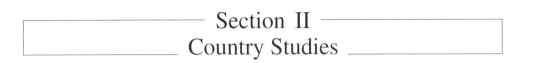

Section II
Country Studies

7

Austria

VANESSA SECONNINO AND ALHAM YUSUF

7.1 INTRODUCTION

Over the past decade, in Austria, there has been a shift from banks to insurance companies and domestic, mutual and pension funds as the repository for household savings and intermediation activities. However, even though investors have shifted their money from bank accounts, these other financial institutions are usually bank-owned entities. As a result, the scope of financial intermediation has been altered, while the overall market structure has not. Overall, Austria's financial system is small in comparison with the other European countries and suffers from the problems of bank-based systems, such as poor shareholder rights, market inefficiencies, and poor company reporting and disclosure requirements.

The Austrian capital market has traditionally been small and inefficient in comparison to other Euro countries. As a result the Austrian government has taken sweeping measures to improve the capital markets and bring it up to West European standards. Company disclosure rules have become more stringent and there have been crackdowns on money laundering. Recent amendments to financial market's legislation will ensure that share ownership becomes more attractive for Austrians and international investors. In the past few years share ownership has increased, the volume of fund assets has increased, and so have the number of companies listing on the stock exchange. The strengthening domestic market will ensure that international investment in Austria also flourishes.

The Oesterreichische Nationalbank, Austria's Central Bank, has focused its main objective on the achievement of monetary policy and price stability as well as preserving the soundness of financial markets to remain in line with expectations of the Euro zone. Austria's development levels are quite low in comparison to the rest of the European Union (EU) countries. Trading in the capital markets is quite low relative to other capital markets. Austria is a bank-based economy and intermediaries continue to dominate the capital markets. However with the integration of the EU this may change toward a fairer and more efficient capital markets, and consequently heighten the level of development across Austria.

7.2 REGULATION

Recent developments have ensured that Austria is introducing ongoing improvements in international standards and best practices. Austria's financial market regulatory framework, and specifically the banking legislation, has been evolving as a result of the expansion and internationalization of the financial market. The full liberalization of the financial markets began with the implementation of the Banking Act in 1993 (Austrian Central Bank, 2000a).

European Fixed Income Markets: Money, Bond and Interest Rate Derivatives. Edited by J.A. Batten,
T.A. Fetherston and P.G. Szilagyi. © 2004 John Wiley & Sons, Ltd. ISBN 0-470-85053-1

There are a number of participants in the regulation and management of the financial markets in Austria. The institutions that have responsibility for the regulation and efficient operations of the financial market are listed as follows:

- Austrian Central Bank (Oesterreichische Nationalbank – OeNB);
- Austrian Central Depository (Oesterreichische Kontrollbank AG – OeKB);
- Austrian Securities Authority (Bundeswertpapieraufsicht – BWA);
- Federal Ministry for Finance (Bundesministerium für Finanzen – BMF); and
- Austrian Financial Market Authority (Finanzmarktaufsicht – FMA).

The FMA has recently been established and has assumed the powers and tasked previously performed by the BWA and BMF:

7.2.1   Austrian Central Bank (Oesterreichische Nationalbank – OeNB)

The OeNB is responsible for the execution of tasks as part of the European System of Central Banks (ESCB) and the execution of tasks as the Austrian Central Bank (2001).

The OeNB's role in financial market regulation lies in the responsibility for the supervision of the banking system. It is empowered with the ability to perform on-site inspections and targeted examinations of the credit and market risk of banks. In the past, the OeNB focused on external audits and off-site analysis, with only a small percentage of banks being examined. The new focus aims to inspect all Austrian banks periodically. The on-site inspections will review the banks application of policy and procedures, with respect to risk management and internal controls. On-site examinations are also being expanded to include foreign establishments of Austrian banks. This will facilitate the identification and monitoring of the country risk exposure of Austrian banking groups.

Austria's banking sector has continued to undergo changes and consolidation. As of June 2002, Austria has 907 banks, a figure that has fallen from a total of 923 (June 2001), with a total of 4,526 branches. The banking sector is organized into seven sectors. These include:

- Joint stock banks (61)
- Savings banks (66)
- State mortgage banks (9)
- *Raiffeisen* banks (617)
- *Volksbanken* (70)
- Housing construction savings and loan associations (5)
- Special purpose banks (79)

In addition to examinations, the OeNB collects, processes, and analyzes prudential returns and money and banking statistics to ensure the stability and effective operation of the markets. The banks are required to submit quarterly reports on asset quality and provisioning, large exposures, and eventually the regular reporting of interest rate and maturity risk. The OeNB also has a role in licensing matters and formal supervisory actions as the Banking Act stipulates that it must be consulted on these matters (International Monetary Fund, 2002).

7.2.2   Austrian Central Depository (Oesterreichische Kontrollbank AG – OeKB)

The OeKb serves as the notification office for the submission of prospectuses as required by the Capital Market Act and Investment Fund Act. Accordingly, the OeKB prepares a calendar for new issues of securities and investments. The bank also examines, provides approval, and stores all submissions for the preservation of evidence to comply with requirements of formal publication regulations and the appropriate Acts.

The bank also acts as an agent for the government in administration of government bonds and is the principal paying agent for bond issues and, it executes the clearing and settlement of stock exchange transactions. It maintains the electronic trading system (Xetra).

The OeKB's main task is to function as the central depository for Austrian securities. As the central depository, the bank acts as securities custodian and is accordingly a member of the European Central Securities Depositary Association (ECSDA), which provides connections for the settlement of international securities transactions. The bank also provides up to date information for customers that hold securities deposits; it offers online services that provide customers with electronic account information, advice on positions of securities, and events such as corporate actions and cash earnings.

In addition, the OeKB serves the function of clearing and settlement of domestic and cross-border securities transactions. Other capital market services provided by OeKB include the provision of information through a database for shares, bonds, and investment funds, and essential securities data contained in the Austrian Securities Database (WDBO) (Austrian Controller Bank AG, http://www.oekb.co.at).

7.2.3   Austrian Securities Authority (Bundeswertpapieraufsicht – BWA)

The development of the Securities Act 1996 and the establishment of the BWA in 1998, an independent institution, were qualitative steps in the promotion of efficient markets. The BWA's former role was the supervision of markets, issuers, and the stock exchange. In addition to this, the BWA was responsible for the observance of codes of practice, compliance provisions with regard to the company disclosure requirements, investor protection, and the granting of licenses to securities providers.

The BWA also contributes to the prevention of international securities crimes, through the identification of cross-border insider trading and the identification of dubious investment firms. The BWA is the central point of contact for foreign securities authorities, and it is also a member of the International Organisation of Securities Commissions (IOSCO) and the Forum of European Commissions (FESCO) (Austrian Central Bank, 1998). After the creation of the FMA it is unclear what role the BWA will play in the financial market.

7.2.4   Federal Ministry of Finance (Bundesministerium für Finanzen – BMF)

The traditional responsibilities of the BMF are budget and fiscal policies as well as monetary and customs matters. The responsibilities have evolved to incorporate a number of economic control functions and additional supervisory tasks in the banking, savings banks sector, stock exchange, and insurance industries. BMF is also the authority for federal civil service matters and administrative management. On an international level, the main BMF activities are focused on Austria's financial relations with the EU.

The Treasury Banking and Insurance Supervision Department of the agency was tasked with managing financial market related issues; included within its responsibilities were the areas of:

- currency, monetary, and foreign exchange legislation;
- banking supervision (credit and financial institutions, credit cooperatives, capital investment companies, mortgage banks, building societies, etc.);

- the Vienna Stock Exchange;
- capital market supervisory authority;
- insurance supervisory authority (companies for contract insurance, life insurance, and property insurance); and
- pension funds authority (Federal Ministry of Finance, http://www.bfm.gv.at).

7.2.5 Austrian Financial Market Authority (Finanzmarktaufsicht – FMA)

On April 1, 2002, the FMA assumed its powers and responsibilities under the Financial Market Supervision Act, marking the most significant development with regard to banking supervision in recent times. All supervisory tasks and resources and the resulting rights and duties of the BMF (banking, insurance, and pension funds) and the BWA (securities supervision) were transferred to the new independent supervisory body. One motive for the creation of FMA was the lack of independence of market supervision from the government, though the OeNB was involved in the supervisory process ultimate responsibility rested with BMF (Austrian Central Bank, 2002).

The reform has established the FMA as an institution under public law, and its independence is secured by constitutional provision. The FMA is now the single statutory supervisory body directly responsible for banking, insurance and pension funds, securities, and stock exchange supervision. The FMA supervision of financial system concentrates on the core functions performed by the financial system, rather than on institutions or sectors. The focus on the supervision of financial systems overcomes supervisory institutional segmentation of the old system, and therefore, ensures an equitable Austrian financial market for all participating financial institutions.

The creation of FMA has enhanced the enforceability of supervisory measures, as the body is awarded with administrative penal power and the power to enforce its supervisory rulings. Additionally, the FMA has the power to issue ordinances and no appeal process is possible against the rulings issued by FMA (with the exception of administrative penal rulings). The objective of enhanced supervisory measures is to ensure the ability to undertake enforceable actions more quickly, and consequently to improve the efficiency of credit institution audits (Institute of International Bankers, 2002).

FMA consists of an Executive Board and a Supervisory Board. The Executive Board has two directors, who are appointed on the recommendations of the BMF and OeNB. The Directors' terms of office are 3 years on initial appointment and 5-year terms in the event of reappointment. The Executive Board of Directors responsibilities are for all FMA's operations and for the conduct of all FMA business.

The Supervisory Board consists of eight members (Chairman, Deputy Chairman, and six other members), who are appointed to serve 5-year terms of office with the potential for reappointment. The OeNB appoints the Deputy Chairman and the two other members, while the Austrian Federal Economic Chamber proposes two members. The BMF appoints the remainder of the Supervisory Board. The board oversees the management and the conduct of FMA business, and the Supervisory Board's approval is required for the development of the FMA finance plan, rules of procedure, annual accounts, and the purchase of property (Austrian Financial Market Authority, http://www.fma.co.at).

FMA is organized into four departments:

- banking supervision;
- insurance and pension fund supervision;

- securities supervision; and
- legal services and internal control.

The organization has approximately 100 staff members, largely transferred from existing re-sources of the BMF and BWA. The FMA is looking to expand its workforce by an additional 50%, with a focus on the recruitment of bank examiners and analysts. Funding for FMA relies on direct charges to regulated institutions; only 10% of its budget or €3.5 million a year is provided by the Government (International Monetary Fund, 2002).

7.2.6   Financial Market Committee

The financial market committee has been established to ensure strategic integration and co-operation among institutions with the broad responsibility for stability. The FMA, OeNB, and BMF will each appoint a member and a deputy to the committee. The committee is scheduled to convene at least quarterly in an advisory role (Austrian Central Bank, 2002).

7.3   CREDIT RATINGS

Austria has a sovereign rating from both Moody's Investor Services and Standard & Poor's. Both rating agencies provide a high rating to Austria and attribute this to a positive economic outlook. Standard & Poor's rates Austria as AAA and state that the high sovereign credit profile recognizes Austria's stable political system, high levels of economic wealth and diversity, and flexible market institutions (Austrian Federal Financing Agency, 2001b). Moody's rates Austria as Aaa and states that this reflects the country's positive economic fundamentals, social and political stability, a tradition of fiscal prudence, and a favorable public sector debt profile (Austrian Federal Financing Agency, 2001a). Both agencies also provide a credit rating for Austrian Government debt programs and the instruments employed in the programs.

7.4   TAXATION

In the past, a number of taxation regimes were imposed on market transactions, though tax reforms have been implemented to encourage investor participation. In the early 80s a coupon tax on new issues of bonds was introduced, consequently investment in foreign-denominated securities increased. In 1986, the Austrian Government abolished the coupon tax on new is-sues because of the resulting outflow into foreign bonds, which effectively increased domestic investments. Another recent reform was implemented to stimulate growth in the market: Pre-viously the Government applied a general stock exchange turnover tax, which discouraged the widespread use of securities instruments and impeded capital market development. This stock exchange turnover tax was abolished in October 2000.

Derivatives transactions are now free of turnover taxes; however, corporate earnings from trading in options are subject to income and corporation tax. Companies report their gains and losses in their routine statements of income and are taxed accordingly. Private investors' earnings from options are subject to personal income tax.

The main tax applied to investment transactions is a withholding tax, which currently stands at 25%. In 1993, the tax was introduced on interest income derived from bank deposits (savings deposits, time deposits, deposits on current account) and interest-bearing securities (mortgage bonds, bonds, convertible bonds, profit-sharing bonds). Certain exemptions are applied:

- if the interest paying agency is located abroad;
  - interest income on foreign bank deposits and interest bearing securities (such income must be declared on the recipient's income tax return in Austria and attracts the applicable income tax rate);
- if the interest-paying agency is located within Austria;
  - interest bearing securities denominated in Austrian schillings issued before 1 January 1984;
  - interest from interest-bearing securities denominated in foreign currencies issued before 1 January 1989; and
  - interest from interest-bearing securities issued by international financial institutions before 1 October 1992 (Austrian Central Bank, 2000).

7.5   AUSTRIAN STOCK EXCHANGE (WIENER BÖRSE)

In comparison to other European countries, raising money on the stock exchange plays a minor role in Austria. Despite changes to the Capital Market Act in an attempt to attract international investors, the market capitalization of the Wiener Börse is a modest 13.1% in relation to gross domestic product (GDP), which is significantly lower than most other European countries.

Since the beginning of 2002, trading on the Wiener Börse has followed an upward trend, with the Austrian Traded Index (ATX) up about 18% at the beginning of May 2002. This is in comparison to other EU markets including Germany, which have followed a downward trend. Market liquidity on the Austrian Stock Exchange, however, remains fairly low. As a result of the integration of EU countries an effect on the Austrian Stock Exchange will be felt. The Austrian stock market, which is often seen as a gateway to the emerging eastern European markets, could serve investors as a substitute for direct (and riskier) investment in Eastern Europe. This may temporarily attract additional liquidity that is presently required.

The Vienna Stock Exchange was founded in 1771, making it one of the oldest in the world. In December 1997, the former Vienna Stock Exchange and ÖTOB AG (the Austrian Futures and Options Exchange) merged to form Wiener Börse AG. It was granted a license to operate and manage the Vienna Stock Exchange.

In June 1999, the Republic of Austria sold its 50% stake in Wiener Börse AG to 30 listed companies. The new ownership structure includes major Austrian banks and listed companies. The creation of the Wiener Börse was a major step toward establishing Vienna as an independent market for Austrian, central, and eastern European securities and their corresponding derivative instruments.

The Wiener Börse is Austria's only stock exchange. In November 1999, it introduced an electronic trading system Xetra®, which enables electronic cross-border securities trading. Trading in stocks and bonds is conducted via Xetra®.

The Austrian equity market is divided into two main markets:

- Prime market contains stocks admitted to the listing on the official market or semiofficial market that also meet stringent reporting, quality, and disclosure requirements;
- Standard market contains stocks admitted to the listing on the official market or semiofficial market that fail to meet the reporting, quality, and disclosure requirements. It is divided into two sections:

○ Standard market continuous where there is a trading participant who assumes the function of a specialist and trading is continuous in conjunction with several auctions;

○ Standard market auction where the trading procedure is auction and there is not a trading participant who assumes the function of a specialist.

7.5.1 Types of Shares

There are three types of shares traded: common shares, preferred shares, and participation certificates. According to a study by FESSEL-GfK, 15% of the Austrian population owned securities in the year 2000 (13.4% in 1999; 11.7% in 1998). As of September 2002, there are a total of 91 companies listed on the Wiener Börse. There are five settlement periods at 7 a.m., 11 a.m., 1:30 p.m., 3:30 p.m., and 5 p.m. Settlement occurs daily for all types of securities. The Securities Information Clearing and Settlement System is used to clear and settle transactions of the Wiener Börse within the clearing and settlement system. Settlement is based on a T + 3 basis.

7.5.2 Indices

The following indices are traded on the Wiener Börse:

- *ATX* – The ATX documents the price dynamics of the 22 most liquid market segments of Austrian stocks, which represent about 87.5% of total stock market turnover and about 69.6% of total market capitalization. It also serves as an underlying index for futures and options contracts traded on *Wiener Börse.* The composition of shares included in the ATX is reviewed annually according to the liquidity, market capitalization, and continuous trading segment of the share.
- *ATX50 and ATX50P* – The ATX50 comprises all the listed shares of the ATX plus up to 50 of the next most attractive shares. The index is a price index (ATX50) and a performance index (ATX50P).
- *ATXMC* – The ATXMC includes second-tier shares and is defined as ATX50 minus ATX shares. It is for shares with a lower market capitalization.
- *WBI (Wiener Börse Index)* – The WBI consists of all Austrian stocks listed on the official market of *Wiener Börse,* and therefore replicates the movement of the Austrian stock market. Each individual stock is weighted according to its market capitalization (Wiener Börse, http://www.wienerborse.at).

7.6   THE AUSTRIAN BOND MARKET

There are approximately 1200 bonds in the Austrian bond market, which have been issued by about 70 organizations. The outstanding volume of this market was €178.2 billion in 2002, with new issues in 2002 of €21.5 billion. The market's biggest issuer is the Republic of Austria, which issues *Bundesanleihen* (government bonds), accounting for 56% of the market, and *Bundesobligationen* (federal debentures), accounting for 0.4% of the market. Bank debentures account for 40% of the market's total outstanding volume (this includes mortgage bonds, municipal bonds, and cash bonds). Austrian banks also issue subordinate bonds and *Ergänzungskapital-Anleihen* (supplementary capital bonds) under the Banking Act. Corporate bonds and other nongovernment and nonbank bonds account for only about 3% of the market.

Table 7.1   The specifications of Austrian government bonds

Maturities	Not more than 50 years
Currency	euro
Dealers	Participants in the Auction Procedure
Interest rate	Fixed interest rate (act./act.); payable annually in arrear
Denomination	€1.000
Form of the notes	Bearer global notes
Status of the notes	Pari passu
Negative pledge	Yes
Cross-default rating	No Standard & Poor's AAA, Moody's Aaa
Taxation	Austrian standard
Listing	At least at the Vienna Stock Exchange
Business days	TARGET
Principal paying agent	Oesterreichische Kontrollbank AG
Clearing system	Oesterreichische Kontrollbank AG
Governing law	Austrian law
Strips	Possible

Source: Austrian Federal Financing Agency, http://www.oebfa.co.at. Reproduced by permission of Austrian Federation Financing Agency.

In 1991, the government introduced regular new issue auctions (usually for a 5-year or 10-year bond), which may have stimulated this growth. In July 1997, a 30-year bond was introduced to widen the maturity range. Standard issue size has grown – from €0.14–0.29 billion per bond to €4.3–8.8 billion since the beginning of 1997.

Overall, the Austrian bond market is smaller than the country's credit markets, but considerably larger than the equity market. The Austrian bond market ranks among the smaller European markets in terms of its size and represents less than 1% of the overall world bond market. In terms of its relative importance, measured as a percentage of GDP, it ranks among the medium-sized markets (i.e. 80% of GDP). It has, however, doubled in size since 1990.

Austrian bonds are bearer fixed-rate bonds that pay an annual coupon. The bonds are also in bullet form, where early redemption or redemption in installments is not foreseen. The types of bonds in the Austrian bond market include government bonds, federal treasury certificates, Treasury notes, interest rate and government strips, corporate bonds, banking bonds, and convertible bonds. Austrian government bonds are issued through an Auction procedure. (See Table 7.1 for specifications of Austrian Government bonds.)

The establishment of the Debt Issuance Program enables the Republic of Austria to issue bonds by selling them to a group of dealers. The program enables the Republic to respond to investor demands and market situations effectively. The program was implemented on January 28, 1999, and the participants included only those involved in the Auction procedure.

7.6.1   Government Bond Trading System and Markets

7.6.1.1   Primary Market

The Government Bond Auction Process

The auction process with an "underwritten component" on Austrian government bonds was introduced in 1989. This means that roughly half the volume issued in any 1 year was underwritten by a syndicate. Prior to this date government bonds were placed within a fixed syndicate of Austrian banks.

Table 7.2   Bidders in government-bond auctions

- ABN AMRO Bank N.V.
- Bank Austria Aktiengesellschaft*
- Bank für Arbeit und Wirtschaft Aktiengesellschaft*
- BNP Paribas
- Bayerische Hypo- und Vereinsbank Aktiengesellschaft
- CDC Marchés
- Commerzbank Aktiengesellschaft
- Crédit Agricole Indosuez
- Credit Suisse First Boston (Europe) Limited
- Deutsche Bank Aktiengesellschaft
- DG Bank Deutsche Genossenschaftsbank Aktiengesellschaft
- Dresdner Bank Aktiengesellschaft
- Erste Bank der Oesterreichischen Sparkassen AG*
- Goldman Sachs International
- HSBC CCF
- ING Bank N.V.
- Morgan Stanley & Co. International Limited
- Nomura International plc
- Oberbank AG*
- Österreichische Postsparkasse AG*
- Österreichische Volksbanken-Aktiengesellschaft*
- Raiffeisenlandesbank Oberösterreich reg. Gen.m.b.H.*
- Raiffeisen Zentralbank Österreich Aktiengesellschaft*
- Salomon Brothers International Limited
- Société Générale
- UBS AG

Source: OeNB, 2002.
*Represents Austrian Banks.

Auction Calendar

The Österreichische Bundesfinanzierungsagentur announces at the end of each year the auction dates for the following year and the nominal amount of the expected annual volume to be issued. Auctions of the government bonds usually take place on a Tuesday, with intervals of 6 weeks excluding August.

Participants

Currently only two banks participate in the auctions and act as market makers. The Austrian Federal Financing Agency (Österreichische Bundesfinanzierungsagentur) specifies which banks can participate in auctions. The decision is based on several of the bank's characteristics, including a bank's capital adequacy, the number of its domestic and foreign branches, and staff size, and turnover of fixed income portfolios in euro and other relevant currencies. Table 7.2 provides a recent list of key participants in the auction process.

Maturity and Volume of the Bond

Every year the Österreichische Bundesfinanzierungsagentur announces the nominal total that can be expected to be issued during the coming year as well as an issuing calendar. One week before each auction, the Bundesfinanzierungsagentur announces the bond's maturity and target

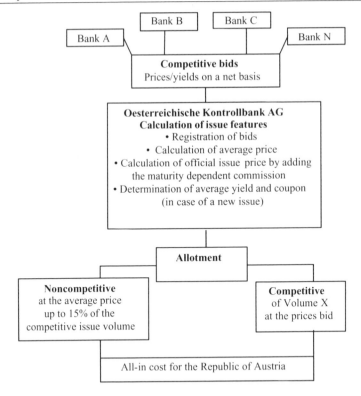

Figure 7.1   The bidding process.
Source: OeNB, 2002.

volume. Before these are announced, the participants are able to make recommendations to the government regarding the auction itself and/or terms of the bond.

The Bidding System

Figure 7.1 provides an overview of the bidding system. Each of the 26 participating banks must submit a bid for at least one 1/26th of the predicted volume of the bond. To prevent any one institution from purchasing a substantial share of the issue, the bidding system requires that an individual bank's bid cannot exceed 30% of the bond's announced volume in case of an issue amount of at least €1 billion and above.

It is required that competitive bids are submitted to *Oesterreichische Kontrollbank AG* by 11:00 a.m. on the auction day. For the issuance of Austrian government bonds both price auctions and yield auctions are foreseen, while for tap issues the bids are ranked according to price in descending order. The allotment of bonds is carried out based on the prices bid. For new issues, bids are submitted in the form of yields, as the coupon is calculated based on a weighted average of the accepted yields and an issue price as close to par as possible. The yields bids are then transformed into prices.

Noncompetitive bidding was introduced in February 2001: An additional 15% of the competitive issue amount is made available for the submission of noncompetitive bids at the average price of the accepted competitive bids. Noncompetitive bids have to be submitted by 11:00 a.m. Central European Time one business-banking day after the announcement of competitive allotments. Since May 1998 an auction procedure has been carried out through ADAS (Austrian Direct Auction System) – software developed for this purpose by *Oesterreichische Kontrollbank AG*. Since 1999, government bonds are also launched via a syndicate. Only participants in the auction procedure are eligible to act as leadmanager or co-leadmanager.

7.6.1.2   Secondary Market

The majority of the Austrian Treasury Bond trading is conducted on the over-the-counter market. This is traded through the interbank market structure or directly between institutional investors. To further increase the attractiveness of government bonds, an official strip-facility was set up in October 1996. This facility provides the possibility to trade the capital and the coupons of selected government bonds separately.

Bond-Market Indices

Oesterreichische Kontrollbank AG and various Austrian banks regularly compute a number of Austrian bond market indices.

- The Yield Index of Oesterreichische Kontrollbank AG is a daily yield to maturity, to next call, after withholding tax, etc., and other relevant key figures (e.g., duration, lifetime, etc.) for all fixed income issues (excluding *Kassenobligationen* and *Bundesobligationen*).
- The API Bond Performance Indices is a performance index for market portfolios of government bonds (API-1) and an index for all issuers (API-11, which does not include FRNs, *Kassenobligationen, Bundesobligationen*, and mortgage and municipality bonds).
- The PIA Bond Price Index is based on actual prices.
- The EFFAS Indices are gross, net, and performance indices for government bonds.
- The Goldman Sachs Austrian Government-Bond Liquid-Market Index (GS Austrian LMI) is computed daily and reflects the entirety of the Austrian government bond market and its biggest submarkets, covering the most liquid high turnover bonds.

Market Conventions

Table 7.3 provides an overview of yield conventions. The market convention is for trade plus 3 (T + 3) settlement for all domestic and international securities. The clearance and settlement of

Table 7.3   Yield Conventions

Conventions	Government bonds	Corporate bonds
Native yield	ISMA – Yield to Maturity	ISMA – Yield to Maturity
Settlement	Trade + 3B	Trade + 3B
Value	Same as settlement	Same as settlement
Ex-dividend	Same as coupon	Same as coupon
Day count	30E/360	30E/360
Holiday	Germany	Germany
Price quote	Without Accrued	Without Accrued
Rounding	3 Decimals	3 Decimals
Yield assumptions	SIA (Reg) Cash Flows	SIA (Reg) Cash Flows

Source: Austrian Central Bank, http://www.oenb.co.at.

securities takes place under the control of the Oesterreichische Kontrollbank AG (government agency).

Market Makers in Austrian Treasury Bonds

The market maker concept was first introduced into Austria in 1989. Currently there are 26 financial institutions that are labelled market makers of which 8 are Austrian and 18 are foreign. To be eligible to apply, the institutions must meet certain requirements regarding capitalization, geographical base, scope of business and human resources, and their ability to trade in Austrian and other fixed income securities. Market makers must:

- subscribe bids at auction for a minimum 1/27th of the volume announced by the Treasury.
- perform market-making functions, i.e., offer bid and ask prices for a range of Austrian debt references.
- make periodic reports to the Treasury on their debt-market activity, including trading details.

7.6.2   The Corporate Bond Market

In contrast to the large Austrian bond market, the corporate bond market is not of significance in the Austrian capital market. Only about 3% of the total bonds issued are those with corporate or nongovernment issuers. The main reasons for the small number of corporate bonds lie in the vast array of alternative debt financing in the Austrian markets, in particular cheap bank loans. For example, the cost of a bond issue is between 0.5 and 1% of the issuing volume, whereas loan expenses are only about 0.8%. In addition there is an absence of large Austrian corporations. Most Austrian businesses are only small- and medium-sized enterprises; therefore, it is unlikely that public bond issues are suitable.

The financing structure of Austrian companies is said to be the worst among European countries. Companies appear to raise capital too often through bank loans and have an equity capital rate of 28%, which is substantially lower than that of foreign companies (Germany's is 30%, France 35%, and Portugal 42%). By contrast, the debt-financing rate of Austrian companies is 65% (Italy 15%, Denmark 24%, and Portugal 48%). Consequently, securities trading in Austria is focused toward fixed income assets (especially by the Government) in preference to equities.

7.6.3   The Money Market

The introduction of the euro has led to the earlier national money markets to be integrated into a Euro area money market. The European Central Bank (ECB), including national central bank's of the Euro area member states, constitute the Eurosystem, which is the single monetary authority. The ECB conducts one single monetary policy for the whole Euro area, through euro money market operations (Euribor ACI The Financial Markets Association, 2002).

Since national currencies have ceased to exist, a major criterion for the existence of national money markets no longer applies. Liquidity smoothing no longer takes place within the interbank system of each country. This function has been transferred to the money market of the entire Euro area (Austrian Central Bank, 1998). There are a number of instruments offered in the Austrian money market; the main instruments issued are the Austrian Treasury Bill and commercial papers.

7.6.3.1 Austrian Treasury Bill (ATB)

The establishment of the ATB program provides the investor's short term products, in addition to existing debt-facilities in Austria. The program was implemented in March 1999 with a maximum amount of bills outstanding of €5 billion. It allows a period of only 2 days between launch and payment date, thus enabling the Republic to react quickly to investors' needs. The bills will be sold by auction and/or on a tap basis (Austrian Federal Financing Agency, http://www.oebfa.co.at).

The OeKB is in charge of fixing the interest rates for floating-rate Federal Treasury Bills, determining the issue price of ATB, and acts as a trustee, depository, and paying agent for coupons and redemptions of federal treasury bills issued in the money market (Austrian Controller Bank AG, 2001). The dealers participating in the market for ATB are listed as follows:

- Bank Austria Creditanstalt AG
- Bank für Arbeit und Wirtschaft AG
- Barclays Bank PLC
- Citibank International PLC
- Deutsche Bank AG, London
- Goldman Sachs International
- Lehman Brothers International (Europe)
- Raiffeisen Zentralbank Österreich AG
- UBS AG, durch Warburg Dillon Read

The specifications of the ATB are detailed as follows (Austrian Federal Financing Agency, http://www.oebfa.co.at):

Maturities	7–365 days (364 days for Sterling)
Currencies	Any currency
Interest rate	Discount, fixed, floating, index-linked, or linked to a formula
Minimum denomination	€100.000 and conventionally accepted denominations in other currencies
Form of the bills	Bearer global bills
Status of the bills	Pari passu
Cross-default	No
Rating	Standard & Poor's A-1 + , Moody's P-1
Taxation	Austrian standard
Listing	The Bills will not be listed on any stock exchange, unless otherwise agreed
Business days	Euro: TARGET and London; Other Currencies: relevant financial centre of the currency and London
Principal paying agent	Citibank N.A., London
Clearing systems	Euroclear, Cedel
Governing law	English Law

7.6.3.2 Commercial Paper

The OeKB has two commercial paper programs used to access international short term money markets. The two programs are the Euro-commercial paper (ECP) program and the US commercial paper (USCP) program; the programs specifications are detailed as follows (Austrian Controller Bank AG, http://www.oekb.co.at):

Euro Commercial Paper Program

Established	June 2000
Guarantor	Republic of Austria
Arranger	Goldman Sachs International
Dealers	Citibank International PLC, Deutsche Bank, Goldman Sachs International, J.P. Morgan Securities Ltd., and UBS Warburg
Program size	€10 billion
Currencies	Multicurrency
Maturity	Not less than 7 nor more than 365 days (364 days for STG)
Issue and paying agent	Deutsche Bank AG, London
Governing law	English Law
Issuer's lawyers	Slaughter & May
Arranger's lawyers	Clifford Chance

US Commercial Paper Program

Established	1986
Guarantor	Republic of Austria
Arranger	Goldman Sachs and Co., New York
Dealers	Goldman Sachs and Co., New York, Lehman Brothers Commercial Paper Inc., New York
Program size	US$2 billion
Maturity	Up to 270 days
Issue and paying agent	Citibank NA, New York
Governing law	New York Law
Issuer's lawyers	Shearman & Sterling

7.6.3.3 Market Performance

In 2001, the domestic money market instruments sold to or redeemed by the Republic of Austria amounted to Eurodollar 2930 million. The majority of turnover was in US dollar denominated commercial paper and certificates of deposit; a smaller number of instruments were euro denominated.

The OeKB is a leading dealer in the Austrian money market in demand and time deposits of banks. According to the OeKB through its money market operations, including ATB and commercial papers, the average daily balance outstanding in 2001 was Eurodollar 1352 million compared to Eurodollar 1946 million in 2000, Eurodollar 1565 million in 1999, and Eurodollar 1039 million in 1998 (Austrian Controller Bank, 2001). Although in recent times money market activity has been declining, the use of money market instruments in Austria has shown rapid growth since its inception (see Figure 7.2; BIS, 2002).

7.6.4 Derivatives Market

The Austrian Futures and Options Exchange (Osterreichische Termin-Optionsbörse), or as it is more commonly known, the otob derivatives market was established in 1989 by five major

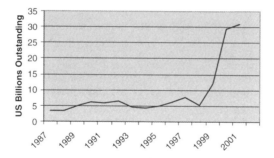

Figure 7.2   Money market instruments by country of residence (Austria).
Source: BIS, Financial Market Statistics. Copyright © Bank for International Settlements, Basle, Switzerland. Reproduced with permission.

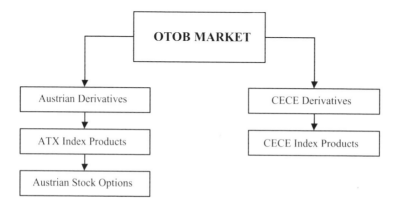

Figure 7.3   The structure of the Austrian Futures and Options Exchange (Osterreichische Termin-Optionsbörse).

Austrian banks. By the mid-1990s otob grew significantly larger with 37 Austrian banks and 1 securities dealer having ownership interests. On December 18, 1997, otob and the Vienna Stock Exchange merged to create a new company, Wiener Börse AG. This newly registered Austrian company established the first integrated Austrian stock, futures and options exchange and began the transformation of the Austrian exchange into an international finance center.

The transformation of the exchange developed segmentations of the Austrian markets. This new segmentation led to the current Osterreichische Termin-Optionsbörse structure, as shown in Figure 7.3 (Wiener Börse, 2002).

7.6.4.1   OTOB Market Products

Austrian Traded Products

The Austrian derivatives segment of the market is comprised of ATX products and Austrian stock options, which are traded in the official market. The ATX products available are ATX options and ATX futures, which are independent products.

- *Austrian Traded Index* – The ATX serves as the underlying index for futures and options contracts traded on Wiener Börse. The ATX is composed of the 22 most liquid market segments of Austrian stocks. The 22 stocks represent 87.5% of total stock market turnover and 69.6% of total market capitalization. The composition of shares included in the ATX is reviewed annually according to the liquidity, market capitalization, and continuous trading segment of the share.

- *ATX Futures and Options* – Trading futures and options on Wiener Börse takes place through a fully electronic trading system. The products available on the otob market are strictly standardized, to ensure transparent and liquid trading. The contract size, value, maturity, and exercise price of underlying stocks are predetermined. Wiener Börse AG assumes the role of counterparty to every contract to ensure that investors can liquidate their positions at anytime.

For the most traded maturities of the futures and options products, quotes are entered on a permanent basis. While for the other maturities, market-makers enter quotes upon request. The trading system ranks orders received in the trading system by time and price priority, and executes the transaction when orders are matched. At least three market participants must assume market-maker commitments under which they are obligated to place firm buy and sell orders quotes into the system for every instrument listed.

Austrian stock options provide American style call and put option contracts. Specialist participants and market makers are obliged to continuously quote buy and sell prices to assure the liquid trading of options in the market. There are currently 17 underlying stocks that are listed in the continuous trading segment.

7.6.4.2   Central and Eastern European Products

In addition to Austrian products, the otob market also provides a segment for investors to trade in CECE (Central and Eastern European Countries) derivatives, which are also traded in the official market. At least three market participants must assume market maker commitments, under which they are obligated to place firm buy and sell order quotes into the system for every instrument listed. Trading include futures and options products on the Czech Traded Index, Hungarian Traded Index, Polish Traded Index, and the Russian Traded Index.

The purpose of the indexes is to serve as an underlying for derivatives trading. The selection criterion of each component of stock is its liquidity, market capitalization, price availability, sector representation, and market interest. The CECE indexes comprises of major blue chip stocks from the four respective markets of the Central and Eastern European countries: Czech Republic, Hungary, Poland, and Russia. The indexes represent each countries most significant shares with respect to turnover and capitalization. These stocks are traded in an international environment at more than one trading place.

The index compositions are reviewed and adjusted accordingly to ensure stability in the index basket. The review is conducted by the CECE Index Family Committee, which meets on a quarterly basis. The CECE Index Management Team implements the decisions of the Committee.

In addition to the CECE indexes, Wiener Börse AG offer investors the opportunity to trade the CEX product. The CEX is comprised of four indexes, namely the CTX, HTX, PTX, and STX (Slovak Traded Index). The CEX was established as a benchmark index for the whole region and to enable flexibility for investors to trade in four different markets with one trading platform and one currency. Further flexibility is provided as all the indices are calculated in local currency, US dollars and Eurodollars.

- *Czech Traded Index (CTX)* – The main trading platform is the Prague Stock Exchange for shares and bonds. The market capitalization of shares amounted to 22.6% of GDP at the end of 2000.
- *Hungarian Traded Index (HTX)* – The Budapest Stock Exchange is the main platform of Hungary for trading of shares, bonds, and derivatives (stock futures, a future on the BUX equity index, futures on government bonds, and FX-futures for the five most important currencies).
- *Polish Traded Index (PTX)* – The Warsaw Stock Exchange is the main platform of Poland for trading of shares, bonds, some stock futures, and a future on the WIG 20, a blue-chip index. FX-futures on € and US dollar can be traded. The market capitalization of the shares amounted to 19% of GDP at the end of 2000.
- *Russian Traded Index (RTX)* – The most significant Russian exchanges are MICEX for foreign exchange, shares, and bonds, and also for derivatives trading and the Russian Trading System (RTS) as major exchange for shares. The market capitalization of shares on RTS (except Gazprom) amounted to 14.8% of GDP at the end of 2000.

In addition to these, Wiener Börse provides trading in the Russian Depositary Receipts Index (RDX). This index is based on Russian blue chips depositaries traded on the Frankfurt stock exchange. The RDX is calculated only in euro. Currently there are eight depositaries comprising the index: Gazprom DR, Lukoil DR, Mosenergo DR, Rostelecom DR, Surgutneftegaz DR, Tatneft DR, Unified Energy Systems DR, and Yukos Oil DR. These depositaries have a total market capitalization of €35 250 946 096 billion.

7.7   CONCLUSION

Austria's level of financial market development is low in comparison with other EU countries. Austria is a bank-based economy and financial intermediaries continue to dominate the capital markets. Current reforms to the Capital Market Act have attempted to increase development and efficiency of the capital market. However, there is still a long way to go. In order for development to increase in Austria there will need to be restrictions on how much cross-ownership is allowed as many powerful and wealthy banks operate in Austria and own other companies. Austria needs to take drastic steps to improve shareholders' rights. This will enhance internal financing and encourage external investment. However, with the integration of the EU this may change toward a fairer and more efficient capital markets, and consequently heighten the level of development across Austria. Austria still has many hurdles to cross, and it will be a long time until the level of development improves and trading through the capital market increases.

REFERENCES

Austrian Central Bank (1998). *The Austrian Financial Market 1998, A Survey of Austrian Capital Markets*. http://www.oenb.co.at.

Austrian Central Bank (2000a). *Experiences of the OeNB as Regards Financial Sector Reform in Austria*. http://www.cnb.cz/pdf/prag1.pdf.

Austrian Central Bank (2000b). *The Austrian Financial Market 2000, A Survey of Austrian Capital Markets*. http://www.oenb.co.at.

Austrian Central Bank (2001). *Annual Report 2001*. http://www.oenb.co.at.

Austrian Central Bank (2002). *The Austrian Banking Act and the Austrian Financial Market Authority Act, 5th edn*. http://www.oenb.co.at.

Austrian Controller Bank AG (2001). *Annual Report 2001*. http://www.oekb.co.at.

Austrian Controller Bank. AG. http://www.oekb.co.at.

Austrian Federal Financing Agency (2001a). *Moody's Investor Service 2001 Rating Report Republic of Austria*. http://www.oebfa.co.at.

Austrian Federal Financing Agency (2001b). *Standard and Poor's 2001 Rating Report Republic of Austria*. http://www.oebfa.co.at.

Austrian Federal Financing Agency. http://www.oebfa.co.at.

Austrian Financial Market Authority. http://www.fma.co.at.

Bank for International Settlements (2002, September). *Quarterly Review*. http://www.bis.org.

Euribor ACI The Financial Markets Association (2002) *The Short Term Paper Market in the Euro*. http://www.aciforex.com/images/2_acirecommendationfinal2.pdf.

Federal Ministry of Finance. http://www.bmf.gv.at.

Institute of International Bankers (2002). *Global Survey 2002, Regulatory and Market Developments*. http://www.iib.org.

International Monetary Fund (2002). *Austria: Selected Issues*. http://www.imf.org.

Wiener Börse (2002). Market Segmentation on Wiener Börse. http://www.wienerborse.at.

Wiener Börse. http://www.wienerborse.at.

8

Belgium

JAN ANNAERT AND MARC J.K. DE CEUSTER

8.1 INTRODUCTION

Since the reform of the constitution in 1993, Belgium is a federal state composed of three regions (i.e., the Flemish, the Walloon, and the Brussels-Capital region) and three communities (i.e., the Flemish, the French-speaking community, and the German-speaking community). The communities are responsible for culture, education, the use of the languages, and some matters related with the public health. The regions, on the other hand, are responsible for infrastructure, business development, environmental and economic issues, and the supervision of local authorities. The federal state has the powers to ensure monetary and political union. The Ministry of Finance organizes the financial markets and institutions.

Belgium has a very open and internationally integrated economy. The currency union it had with Luxembourg since 1921 and Luxembourg's position as an international financial center have spurred large investment flows from Belgian residents to Luxembourg banks. Typically the funds were reinvested in Belgium into public debt instruments, either directly or indirectly through the interbank market. Traditionally the savings rate among Belgian households has been very high. This resulted in an accumulation of financial assets of 308% of gross domestic product (GDP) by the end of 2000. The overall share of financial assets in foreign currency rose from 7% in 1980 to more than 20% in 1998 (Timmermans, 2000). The role of banks in attracting savings declined over the same period in favor of direct purchase of securities and mainly, investments in UCITS (collective investment undertakings) (Table 8.1).

In this chapter we first discuss the history and the structure of the Belgian Public Debt, since this explains to a large extent the structure of the Belgian bond market (Section 8.2). We show that the federal government is the primary issuer on the Belgian bond market. Therefore we first discuss government bonds in Section 8.3. Section 8.4 describes the (very small) market of corporate bonds. We do not discuss the issues on the international capital market (see Claes *et al.*, 2002, for more details on the Eurobond market). Finally, we discuss the Belgian derivatives market (Section 8.5). This chapter concludes with some references for further reading.

8.2 HISTORY AND STRUCTURE OF THE BELGIAN PUBLIC DEBT

Belgian bond markets are almost uniquely driven by the activity of the (federal) government. During the 1990s public debt management was modernized in order to create attractive and liquid primary and secondary markets. Nonfinancial sectors largely finance themselves through

European Fixed Income Markets: Money, Bond and Interest Rate Derivatives. Edited by J.A. Batten, T.A. Fetherston and P.G. Szilagyi. © 2004 John Wiley & Sons, Ltd. ISBN 0-470-85053-1

Table 8.1 Financial position by sector as % of GDP (end of 2000)

Sectors	Financial assets	Financial liabilities	Net financial position
Households	308.2	44.4	263.8
Nonfinancial corporations	215.9	315.4	−99.4
Financial Corporations	366.3	366.3	–
Government	12.1	114.3	−102.2
Total residents	902.5	840.4	62.1
Total Nonresidents	271.3	333.3	−62.1

Source: ECB, Report on Financial Structures, 2002, p. 45. Copyright © European Central Bank, Frankfurt am Main, Germany. Reproduced with permission.

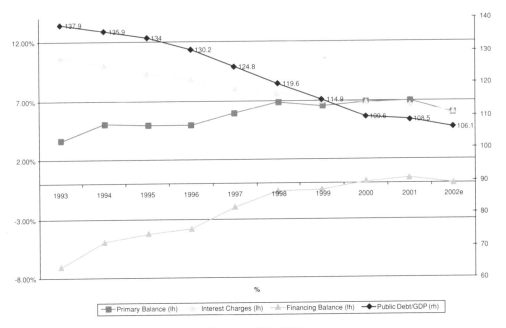

Figure 8.1 Evolution of the Belgian public debt (1993–2002).
Source: National Bank of Belgium, Annual Report, various issues.

the issuance of unlisted shares. In addition, the (family-owned) small- and medium-sized enterprises, that to a large extent dominate the Belgian economy, rely heavily on bank lending.

Nevertheless, the Belgian bond market is relatively large, owing to the high level of government debt. In 1993, the gross public debt reached a peak level of 137.9% of GDP. Since then the debt ratio has declined year after year, reaching 106.1% at the end of 2002 (see Figure 8.1). This large reduction in the relative level of government debt was encouraged by the Stability and Growth Pact, in which the EU Members committed themselves "to respect the medium-term budgetary objective of positions close to balance or in surplus set out in their stability or convergence programme ..." (Resolution of the European Council on the Stability and Growth Pact, Amsterdam, June 17, 1997). Thanks to broad political support for the restructuring of the government budget, the government aims at reaching sound budgetary positions close to balance or in surplus, even despite the recent adverse macroeconomic conditions. As can be seen in Figure 8.1, this is accomplished by targeting a significant positive primary balance (increasing from 3.60% of GDP in 1993 to 7% in 2001) and helped by the gradually decreasing interest rate level. Indeed, interest charges dropped from more than 10% of GDP in 1993 to an estimated 6.1% in 2002.

The government targets also for 2003 a balanced budget – the fourth in a row – although it should be stressed that its economic projections assume a real GDP growth rate of 2.1%. At the time of writing, the consensus forecast by The Economist Poll of forecasters was a mere 1.2%. It is therefore expected that the new federal government will have to take additional measures after the elections of May 18 to keep the balance on track.

At the end of February 2003, gross federal government debt amounted to €267.72 billion, of which 97.7% was denoted in euro. The lion share (75.7%) of it was financed by issuing linear bonds (OLOs, i.e., Obligations Linéaires – Lineaire Obligaties; see Section 8.3.1). Other financing instruments are Treasury certificates (10.8%; Section 8.3.2), traditional loans (4.4%; Section 8.3.5), state notes (3.1%; Section 8.3.4), and several *ad hoc* instruments like Treasury bills (Section 8.3.3) account for the remaining 6%. The Treasury has steadily increased the share of fixed rate debt. It currently amounts to 84.0% of total debt. Likewise, only 18.8% of total debt will mature within 12 months, indicating a relatively long average maturity of government debt. Indeed, the average maturity is about 6.1 years and the average duration of the debt in euro is 4.3 years.

8.3   GOVERNMENT BONDS

Government securities like linear bonds (OLOs; Section 8.3.1), Treasury certificates (Schatkistcertificaten – Certificats de Trésorerie; Section 3.2), and Treasury bills (Schatkistbons – Bons du Trésor; Section 3.3) are only issued in dematerialized form since the financial markets reform of 1991. As such they are represented either by an account registration with an account keeper approved by the Minister of Finance, or occasionally by an entry into the Ledger of the Public Debt held by the Treasury Administration). Every investor is listed with his account keeper, depending on his tax status under Belgian law. Those investors that are exempt from personal income tax, such as nonresidents, receive the gross income on their securities and hold an X account (exempt account). The others hold an N account (non-exempt account) and are subject to withholding taxes. The clearing of both sets of accounts is administrated by the National Bank of Belgium (NBB). Clearstream and Euroclear have access to the securities accounting system. Besides these segments oriented toward market professionals, state notes (Staatsbons – Bons d'état; Section 8.3.4) are issued within the retail segment. Traditional loans (Volksleningen – Emprunts classiques – Phillippe-loans; Section 8.3.5) that were targeted toward a mixed public of professionals and retail customers are not issued anymore but they can still be traded in the secondary market.

8.3.1   OLOs

8.3.1.1   Product Definition

OLOs are medium, long term, and very long term (up to 30 years) dematerialized bonds denominated in euro with a fixed or a (3-month EURIBOR based) floating interest rate representing a state loan. Since 1989, they are issued six times per year in successive tranches with the same characteristics (same coupon and same maturity date). As such they are perfectly fungible and form an OLO line. OLOs are reimbursable at par upon maturity. They do not contain any early redemption features. Everyone can hold linear bonds but depending on the investor's tax status they will be booked on X or N accounts.

8.3.1.2   Primary Market Organization

Procedure

Especially when opening a new line, OLOs can be issued by syndication. Since 1999 this has been the preferred way to launch a new issue in order to immediately achieve a high volume and hence liquidity. In this case, the issue price is set in consultation with the bank syndicate. Otherwise, the primary market is organized through exchange offers (against other prespecified securities of the state)[1] or, more common, monthly auctions that consist of two rounds: a competitive auction and a noncompetitive round. The Court of Audit (2001) criticized the evolution toward syndication since it gives the impression that noncompetitive issue procedures are being favored. The Treasury, however, argued that the bookbuilding process of the syndication is still based on competition whenever oversubscription takes place. The latter situation has been commonplace for the 10-year benchmark OLOs.

The competitive round.   Usually, two or three lines are auctioned. Only primary dealers and recognized dealers (see Section 8.3.1.3) are entitled to submit competitive bids at the auctions. The invitation to bid is announced on the Monday preceding the auction (D−7) via the pages of the Debt Agency on Bloomberg (BELG), Reuters (BELG/OLO or BELG/FRN), and Telerate (36365 + 36366 or 36367 + 36368). Moreover, a personal announcement message is sent to each primary dealer via the Bloomberg auction system. The day before the auction (D−1) the Treasury announces the range of the global minimum amount that will be auctioned.

On the day of the auction (D) bids must be submitted through the Bloomberg electronic auction system. Submission through fax is possible in case of technical problems. The bids are quoted in (clean) prices and the amount of the bid is expressed in thousands and as a multiple of €100 000 with a minimum of €1 million.

The auction is organized as an American tender in which all bids at higher prices than a limit price are accepted for their full amount by the Treasury. Bids submitted at the limit price are proportionally scaled down if necessary. The minimum allocated amount is still €1 million per bid and the scaled down amount is rounded to the nearest €100 000.

Both the global results of the auction and the individual results of each bidder are published only a few minutes after the cut-off time of the bidding process via the electronic Bloomberg auction system. Consecutively, they are published via the same channels (Bloomberg/Reuters/Telerate) and pages as the invitations to bid. The information disclosed guarantees transparency and consists of

− the total amount of valid bids,
− the proposed minimum and maximum prices,
− the limit price,
− the total amount allocated,

---

[1] Exchange offers can take place on voluntary basis and at a predetermined ratio against other OLOs or traditional loans that are close to maturity (<12 months). Only primary dealers and recognized dealers (see Section 8.3.1.3) are entitled to take part in exchange offers. Exchange offers are announced 4 days before the exchange (D−4). On the exchange day (D), first, the ratios are announced on the Treasury's pages. Second, the bids take place and finally, a few minutes after cut-off time, the results are published. Settlement is done through the clearing of the NBB on D+3. Currently, the Treasury uses only the exchange offer technique for exchanging its traditional loans.

– the number of successful bidders,
– the reduction percentage at the limit price,
– the weighted average price of the auction,
– the weighted average yield of the auction.

The noncompetitive round.   Primary dealers may participate in two noncompetitive sub-scriptions in order to buy OLOs at the weighted average price of the auction. Ordinary noncom-petitive subscriptions take place on the first operating TARGET (trans-European Automated Realtime Gross-settlement Express Tranfer system) day following the auction (D+1). Special noncompetitive subscriptions are organized on the second operating TARGET day following the auction (D+2).

Settlement

The primary market transactions are settled through the clearing system of the Belgian National Bank (on D+3). The amount to be paid by the bidder of fixed rate OLOs is the bid price (competitive round) or the weighted average price of the auction (noncompetitive round) plus the accrued interest. The accrued interest is calculated as a simple interest rate based on an ACT/ACT interest convention. In case of a variable rate linear bond, the same principle applies but the interest rate is calculated as a simple interest rate based on the ACT/360 convention.

Reimbursement upon Maturity

The NBB acts as the paying agent through its clearing system.

8.3.1.3   Secondary Market Organization

Market Participants

A body of *primary dealers* was established to enhance the placement of Belgian government securities, to ensure the liquidity on the secondary market, and to promote Belgian sovereign debt. As such primary dealers have to participate on a regular basis in the auctions. Moreover, they are also obliged to

– be active on the secondary market by quoting firm bid and offer prices/rates to other market participants,
– post indicative prices on their screens which are in line with the market,
– promote Belgian government securities both in Belgium and abroad,
– participate in an "interdealer broker" system for the Belgian government securities market.

In return, primary dealers exclusively can

– bear the title "primary dealer in Belgian government securities,"
– participate in the competitive auctions and the exchange transactions,
– participate in the noncompetitive rounds,
– strip and reconstitute OLOs (see later in this section).

Primary dealers are in the position of privileged counterparty regarding Treasury's debt management. Their functions, duties, and relationship to the Treasury are further described in the "code of duties" to which they subscribe.

Table 8.2 Overview of secondary markets in government bonds

	Euronext Brussels	Regulated off-exchange market	Nonregulated off-exchange market
OLOs	Yes	Yes	Yes
Stripped OLOs	No	Yes	Yes
Treasury certificates (Section 8.3.2)	No	Yes	Yes
Belgian treasury bills (Section 8.3.3)	No	No	Yes
Traditional bonds (Section 8.3.4)	Yes	No	Yes

With the introduction of the euro, an enlarged group of primary dealers was appointed to internationalize the distribution of Belgian government paper and to enhance the trading both in and outside the Euro area. For 2003 the primary dealers are ABN-AMRO Bank NV, Barclays Capital, BNP Paribas, Crédit Agricole Indosuez, Deutsche Bank AG, Dexia Bank – Dexia Banque, Fortis Bank – Fortis Banque, Goldman Sachs International, HSBC, ING BBL, JP Morgan Securities Ltd., KBC Bank NV, Morgan Stanley & Co., Schröder Salomon Smith Barney, Société Générale, and UBS Warburg.

Although 16 primary dealers are active, the primary market turns out to be heavily concentrated. The Court of Audit (2001) showed that more than half of the issues are placed by only 4 primary dealers. Admittedly, it were not necessarily the same primary dealers every year.

Besides the primary dealers, the government also attracted a number of other international market players to act as *recognized dealers*. The recognized dealers share the same obligations on the secondary market as the primary dealers, but they are not obliged to participate in primary market activities. Instead of being privileged counterparty as regards the Treasury's debt management operations they are eligible counterparty. For 2003 the recognized dealers are Caixa Geral de Depositos, Crédit Suisse First Boston, IMI San Paolo, Lehman Brothers, Nomura International PLC, and Nordea Bank.

Markets

Although OLOs are quoted on Euronext Brussels (mainly to allow private investors to trade), linear bonds are essentially targeted toward professional investors. Consequently, the principal secondary markets are the regulated and the nonregulated off-exchange markets (see Table 8.2 for a synthetic overview of all the secondary markets in Government Bonds). At the beginning of 2000, a screen-based electronic trading system (MTS Belgium) was launched by the Treasury together with the primary dealers and the Societa per il Mercato dei Titoli di Stato. MTS Belgium is a company incorporated under Belgian law and operates under supervision of the Belgian Banking and Finance Commission and the Securities Regulation Fund. MTS is a price-driven trading system in which 20 market makers (i.e. shareholding institutions and since July 2000 also nonshareholding institutions) have to quote bid and ask prices for a minimum number of hours per trading day. Minimum quantities and maximum bid/ask spreads apply. Since July 2000, non-MTS shareholding institutions can also participate as price takers in the system. At the end of 2002, seven price takers were active in MTS Belgium. The settlement of the securities listed on MTS Belgium is carried out by the NBB.

Belgian government bonds can also be traded on the pan-European trading system EuroMTS (Telematico). The Telematico platform allows for the selection of the most appropriate clearing institution, which in this case is the NBB.

OLOs coming to maturity within a year can also be subject to **buybacks** through the MTS system. The objective of these buybacks is to smoothen out the schedule of maturities and to increase the amount of the benchmark OLOs that are not offered at exchange offers. A nice side effect is that buyback prices are posted on MTS screens every day, which provides primary dealers with a virtually permanent bid price. Finally, the Treasury can also organize reverse auctions at the start of a buyback program. As with the other auctions, only primary and recognized dealers are entitled to participate and the American Tender system (multiple price system) applies.

Strips

Since 1992, Belgium has authorized the stripping of some of its linear bonds. The Belgian government designed the technique in line with the American and French systems. Under the "Separate Trading of Registered Interest and Principal of Securities" (the "STRIPS"), both capital and interest can exist as autonomous dematerialized zero bonds. In order to complete the market, it is also possible to rebundle the strips to reconstruct the original bond at any time. Stripping of an OLO can be asked by the primary as well as by the recognized dealers. Since it is a dematerialized market, they have to ask the NBB to strip or to reconstitute the bonds. Stripped securities are available only to tax-exempt investors. In order to ensure the liquidity on this market, primary dealers have to quote the most active stripped parts of the bonds on a permanent basis.

8.3.1.4 Regulatory Control

The Securities Regulation Fund (Rentenfonds, Fond des Rentes) is an independent public institution and is the first-line market authority for the regulated off-exchange market in linear bonds, split securities, and Treasury certificates. It draws up market regulation and all transactions on the regulated off-exchange market have to be reported to the Security Regulation Fund. Also the transactions on the nonregulated off-exchange market have to be reported, at least to the extent that the transaction was settled by a Belgian financial intermediary. Finally, it also publishes daily reference prices and volumes for all issues listed on the regulated off-exchange market. The Belgian Banking and Finance Commission is responsible for second-line supervision. As such it controls whether the Security Regulation Fund carries out its duties as market authority.

8.3.1.5 Market Figures

Table 8.3 reports the primary market activity over the 1999–2001 period. It can be noted that the Belgian government has been a net issuer of OLOs during the last few years. The gross issues amount €26 billion in 2001. Tenders, syndication, and exchanges are all used for substantial amounts. Within the tenders, the competitive round dominates the noncompetitive round. In 2001 (resp. 2000), the competitive round gathered €12.3 (resp. €6.9) billion whereas in the noncompetitive round only €2.8 (resp. €1.7) billion was issued. Reverse auctions and buybacks via MTS started only in 2001.

At the end of February 2003, 21 OLO lines were outstanding totaling a debt of €202.7 billion. Table 8.4 shows that all but one have a fixed coupon. Although most lines are strippable, the percentage of stripping is at maximum 17.2%. The maximum term to maturity one can at present find in the Belgian market is the OLO 31, maturing in 2028.

Table 8.3   Primary market activity of OLO*

	1999	2000	2001
Gross issues	28.3	32.1	26.0
Tender	10.7	15.1	8.6
Syndication	10.0	5.0	10.0
Exchanges	7.6	12.0	7.4
Redemptions	13.8	17.0	13.4
Reverse Auctions[†]	–	–	0.1
Bond Buy Backs (MTS)	–	–	2.2
Repayment at maturity	5.6	7.0	6.4
Exchanges	8.2	10.0	4.7
Net Issues	14.5	15.1	12.6

Source: Security Regulation Fund, Annual Reports. Reproduced from Belgian Treasury.
* Nominal values in billions of euros.
[†] Including buybacks at Euronext.

Table 8.4   Market figures (end February 2003 in euros)

Coupon	ISIN	No.	Maturity	Outstanding	Strippable	%strips
9	BE0000251570	6	28/03/03	9 233 405 955	X	10.77
7.25	BE0000265711	14	29/04/04	10 747 275 874		
7.75	BE0000275819	20	15/10/04	5 462 547 199		
6.5	BE0000273798	19	31/03/05	10 178 433 069		
4.75	BE0000294034	34	28/09/05	11 901 400 000	X	7.16
FRN	BE0000299082	39	24/04/06	2 000 000 000		
7	BE0000283896	24	15/05/06	8 465 045 674		
4.75	BE0000297060	37	28/09/06	9 610 900 000	X	0.37
6.25	BE0000286923	26	28/03/07	13 491 828 229	X	4.13
8.5	BE0000257635	9	01/10/07	8 413 164 464	X	17.16
5.75	BE0000288945	28	28/03/08	13 479 196 740	X	1.32
7.5	BE0000268749	16	29/07/08	8 682 058 029		
3.75	BE0000292012	32	28/03/09	16 463 000 000	X	1.56
5.75	BE0000295049	35	28/09/10	15 844 200 000	X	1.69
5	BE0000296054	36	28/09/11	10 546 400 000	X	0.31
5	BE0000298076	38	28/09/12	11 416 900 000	X	1.61
8	BE0000262684	12	24/12/12	8 824 896 081		
4.25	BE0000301102	41	28/09/13	5 000 000 000	X	0
8	BE0000282880	23	28/03/15	7 011 187 158	X	1.83
5.5	BE0000300096	40	28/09/17	5 669 200 000	X	2.91
5.5	BE0000291972	31	28/03/28	10 240 939 136	X	9.7
Total				202 681 977 609		

Source: www.fgov.treasury.be (as reported in April 2003). Reproduced by permission of Service Public Fédéral Finances – Trésorerie.

The activity on the secondary market can be measured in several ways. In Table 8.5 we report the average amount traded per day and the average number of daily transactions that were cleared through the NBB. It can be seen that the trade has intensified over the last years. In 2002, there were on average 553 trades a day carrying a nominal value of approximately €9.5 billion. The total amount cleared by the Belgian National Bank over 2001 was €2326 billion.

Table 8.5 Secondary market for OLO

	Average daily amount (in millions of euros)	Average daily number of transactions
1998	8272	340
1999	6831	287
2000	7738	327
2001	9201	444
2002	9435	553

Source: NBB, Statistical Bulletin, No. 2, 2003, Table 18.10.

It should be noted that these numbers include €1057 billion of the spot part of repurchase agreements and sell and buy back transactions (see Section 8.5.1). Besides this amount still €1061 billion was cleared by Euroclear. Finally, Clearstream cleared another €225 billion (Security Regulation Fund, Annual Report 2001). Through MTS Belgium, €155.9 billion was traded in 2001. EuroMTS accounted for €39.2 billion (Security Regulation Fund, Annual Report 2001).

8.3.2 Treasury Certificates

8.3.2.1 *Product Definition*

Treasury certificates are dematerialized short term zero coupon bills denominated in euro, with a maturity of maximum 1 year. The standard maturities at the time of the tender are 3, 6, and 12 months. They have been auctioned by the Treasury since 1991.

8.3.2.2 *Market Organization and Regulatory Control*

The organization of the Treasury bill market is very similar to the organization of the OLO market. Only the issue procedure differs in two respects.

1. Treasury certificates are always issued based on a competitive American tender and a noncompetitive round. No syndication or exchange transactions take place. Contrary to the OLOs where the primary and recognized dealers bid in prices (percentages of nominal value), the Treasury certificates are quoted in simple interest rates based on the ACT/360 convention.
2. Obviously, since Treasury certificates take the form of zero bonds, no stripping can take place.

8.3.2.3 *Market Figures*

The composition of the outstanding amount of Treasury certificates is very market dependent. Whereas in the beginning of the 1990s, more than 60% of the outstanding Treasury certificates had an (initial) maturity of 3 months, this market share has steadily decreased to 16% in 2003. Figure 8.2 shows that the share of the 6-month Treasury certificates is approximately equal to that of the 3-month certificates. The 12-month certificates currently dominate the market (66%). Table 8.6 gives some indication of the transactions in Treasury certificates cleared by the NBB.

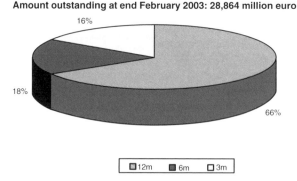

Amount outstanding at end February 2003: 28,864 million euro

Figure 8.2   Outstanding amount of Treasury certificates.
Source: www.fgov.treasury.be (as reported in April 2003). Reproduced by permission of Service Public Fédéral Finances – Trésorerie.

Table 8.6   Secondary market transactions for Treasury certificates

	Average daily amount (in millions of euros)	Average daily number of transactions
1998	1715	107
1999	1784	84
2000	1490	61
2001	1720	77
2002	1897	82

Source: NBB, Statistical Bulletin, No. 2, 2003, Table 18.10.

8.3.3   Treasury Bills

Belgian Treasury bills (BTBs) are short term dematerialized securities (usually less than 3 months) issued on tap since 1996 within an unlimited program by the Kingdom of Belgium. They can be tailored to the investor's needs and be denominated in any OECD (Organization for Economic Co-operation and Development) currency. Like Treasury certificates, Belgian Treasury bills are issued on a discount basis and are redeemed at par. BTBs are placed by a small group of dealers. In the beginning of 2003, the dealers are Fortis Bank (coarranger), Citibank (London), Deutsche Bank (London), Dexia Capital Markets, Goldman Sachs International (Arranger), KBC Bank, and UBS. The NBB is the issuing and the paying agent. The securities are held in the accounting system (X/N accounts) of the NBB. The market conditions are very similar to those of the Treasury certificates.

8.3.4   Traditional Loans

Some older government loans can still be found on the Belgian market. These include lottery bonds (an antiquity from the interbellum in which a low coupon rate was made acceptable by attaching a lottery to the bond that enabled people to gain up to €25 000) and government-backed loans issued to finance utilities. The most important segment consists of the Philippe loans (named after a former Minister of Finance Philippe Maystadt). Phillipe XVII was the last bond issued in this form. The issue was severely criticized by the industry and the Court of

Table 8.7   Amount of outstanding state notes in euros (April 2003)

Type	Number of issues	Outstanding	Percentage
5–7	27	4 445 727 478	57.7
3–5–7	13	1 646 982 933	21.4
8	14	1 611 850 000	20.9
Total		7 704 560 411	

Audit (1995–1996) since it was argued that the government mispriced the embedded interest rate options. The issue gathered a total of BEF 388.5 billion of which only BEF 15 billion was taken up by retail customers. This clearly illustrated the asymmetry in information between the retail and the professional sector.

8.3.5   State Notes

This type of bearer bonds is solely targeted at retail customers and was launched for the first time in June 1996. In doing so, the government started to compete actively with banks on the segment of the short to medium term investment horizons. Still, state notes are placed through a group of financial institutions appointed by the Minister of Finance. State notes can be registered in a public debt ledger but they are not eligible in the X/N system. State notes carry nominal values of €200, €1000, €2000, and €10 000. Table 8.7 shows that this market had €7.7 billion outstanding in April 2003.

Quarterly (March, June, September, and December) two types of state notes are issued. Systematically, a 5-year note is issued. The term to maturity of this note can be prolonged by the investor to 7 years. When the investor exercises this option, the same interest conditions apply. This 5–7 note has 27 issues outstanding in the market in April 2003 and has a market share of 57.7% of the state notes (Table 8.7). Depending on the market situation, the government can additionally choose to issue a 3–5–7 note, a 5-year note, or an 8-year note. The 3–5–7 note is a note with a maturity of 7 years. The interest rate, however, will be reset on the basis of the OLO rate after 3 and 5 years. A floor (that is higher for the 5-year revision than for the 3-year revision) applies. This 3–5–7 note has 13 outstanding issues that represent 21.4% of the market. Recently, the government preferred to issue the 8-year note (Type Didier, named after the present Minister of Finance Didier Reynders) with a fixed maturity and a fixed interest rate. In April 2003, €1.6 billion was outstanding of this type of note. In theory, also a 5-year note with an annually floating rate can be issued but up to now this option has not been chosen.

8.4   CORPORATE BONDS

The Belgian corporate bond market is not developed. If Belgian companies want to access the corporate bond market they almost unanimously choose for the international capital market. In April 2003, five Belgian bonds were listed on Euronext Brussels. Corporates are nonetheless able to issue (mainly short term) securities through the Belgian commercial paper market. Often commercial paper issues have been launched by coordination centers (i.e., special-purpose vehicles that centralize a number of management and financial services for multinational enterprises and that enjoy an advantageous tax treatment).

Table 8.8   New commercial paper programs

	1999	2000
Number of new programs	29	26
Total amount (in millions of euros)	7 240	10 362

Source: Fortis Bank, De Belgische Financiële Markten. Reproduced by permission of Fortis Bank.

Table 8.9   Secondary market transactions for commercial paper

	Average daily amount (in millions of euros)	Average daily number of transactions
1998	585	48
1999	363	50
2000	504	71
2001	508	77
2002	526	82

Source: NBB, Statistical Bulletin, No. 2, 2003, Table 18.10.

Commercial paper in Belgium can be issued under a special legislation and can take the form of Treasury bills[2] (thesauriebewijzen – billets de trésorerie) or certificates of deposit (depositocertificaten – certificats de depot). Corporates and local governments can issue Treasury bills, whereas financial companies issue certificates of deposit. Although the name of the product is different, its fundamental characteristics are the same. There is no limitation with respect to the time to maturity of commercial paper, but still most issues have a maturity shorter than 1 year. Commercial paper is always issued within the framework of a commercial paper program that is set up together with an arranger. It is placed through a dealer network on a best effort basis depending on the needs of the issuer.

Table 8.8 documents that at the end of 2000 there were 192 commercial paper programs active in the Belgian market. Six programs (one of the Belgian State and five of financial institutions) were unconstrained by a credit limit. For the programs launched in 2000, the amount of the programs varied between €25 million (WVEM) and €3000 million (NIB Capital Bank). The programs totaled a nominal value of €10 billion. The secondary market activity in commercial paper balances around €500 million per day (Table 8.9).

Securitization projects became popular at the end of the 1990s, but this market has dried up since 2000. Table 8.10 shows that especially mortgages and car loans were the favorite underlyings to be securitized. Large players were the formerly Bacob Bank (Atrium and MBS) and ING-BBL (B-Cars). Also Fortis Bank entered the market with Hypo-G and KBC Bank launched Home Loan Invest. In 2001, no securitized bonds were issued. They are listed on Euronext Brussels and hence can be traded on the secondary market.

Finally, we observe a handful of hybrid structures on the Belgian market although the number of issues outstanding (Table 8.11) make it clear that there is actually not a lot of activity going on. Since 2000, several reverse convertibles have been issued on the Belgian market as well. Their time to maturity is most often short (often 2 years) but they offer a high coupon because

---

[2] Not to be confused with the Treasury bills issued by the federal government.

Table 8.10 Securitization projects on the Belgian market (1996–2001)

Issue year	Issuer	Underlying	Nominal amount (in millions of euros)
1996	Atrium-1	Loans for social housing	188
	B-Cars 1	Car loans	372
1997	MBS-1	Mortgage loans	236
	Atrium-2	Loans for social housing	128
	B-Cars-2	Car loans	372
	Hypo-G	Mortgage loans	248
	MBS-2	Mortgage loans	372
1998	Home Loan Invest-1	Mortgage loans	372
	MBS-3	Mortgage loans	248
	Belsca	Mortgage loans	193
	MBS-4	Mortgage loans	273
	Home Loan Invest-2	Mortgage loans	496
1999	EVE	Mortgage loans	324
	B-Cars 3	Car loans	450
2000	Car Loan Invest-1	Car loans	250
2001	None	–	–

Source: Fortis Bank, De Belgische Financiële Markten, various issues. Reproduced by permission of Fortis Bank.

Table 8.11 Number of outstanding corporate bonds

	1999	2000	2001
Convertible bonds	7	6	6
Bonds with warrants	4	4	4
Straight bonds	3	3	3

of the implicit put on stocks or a stock index the investor writes. These products were very successful in the beginning of the new millennium but given the severe downward trends in the stock market their popularity decreased. The high coupon, however, still feeds people's greed. In April 2003, 24 reverse convertibles were listed on Euronext Brussels.

8.5 DERIVATIVE PRODUCTS

8.5.1 Repurchase Agreements

To guarantee the availability of securities and to enhance the performance of the secondary market in government securities, repo facilities on OLOs and Treasury certificates were created in August 2000 on the EuroMTS Repo Trading Facility. The Treasury can always deliver Treasury certificates for 1–10 business days. The maximum amount of these repurchase agreements depends on the lines and the securities underlying the transaction. Each market maker has the right to a maximum amount of €100 million for OLOs and another €100 million for Treasury certificates.

Also standard repurchase agreements between banks and/or corporates are being written on OLOs and Treasury certificates. Maturities of these contracts are mainly (very) short. The

Table 8.12   Nominal amounts of bond loans and bond swaps (in billions of euros)

	1998	1999	2000	2001
Repos	1865.1	1296.4		
Bilateral bond loans	48.5	30.7	2.2	0.0
Automatic bond loans	8.3	18.3	23.2	24.9
Bond swaps	96.8	88.0	30.0	40.0

Source: Security and Regulation Fund, Annual Reports. Reproduced from Belgian Treasury.

standard conditions of contract for the Belgian market were written down in the PSA/ISMA Global Master Repurchase Agreement and the Belgian annex thereto.

8.5.2   Futures and Option Contracts

With the introduction of the euro, the futures and options on Belgian fixed income instruments all disappeared from the market. In 1997, BXS derivatives ceased to trade BGO options (i.e., options on Belgian government bonds). In 1998, the BGB future (Belgian government bond future) and the BMB future (Belgian medium bond future) were also "delisted." The futures on the Belgian 3-month interbank rate (BIB contracts) were in 1999 converted into ERF futures (i.e., futures on 3-month EURIBOR) but in 2000 trading halted.

8.5.3   Others

As an alternative to repurchase agreements, a lot of *sell/buyback* operations are still carried out. In contrast to the repo, the buy and sell back transactions are considered to be two separate legal transactions. The commitment to buyback is not given in the spot sale contract.

Also *security loans*, whereby the lender lends securities for a charge to a borrower exist in the Belgian market. They appear in two forms: bilateral bond loans and automatic bond loans with the NBB. The latter is more expensive since the NBB offers these loans as a lender of the last resort. Hence a penalty rate is applicable. The borrower will have to provide collateral that may take the form of pledged securities. In that case, this transaction starts to resemble a securities swap.

In a *securities swap* the parties exchange securities with different characteristics for a specified period. In 1998, securities loans totaled €48 billion. The volume of the securities swaps amounted €97 million. Compared with repos, these amounts are small. In 1998, for €1865 billion repo transactions were concluded (Table 8.12).

REFERENCES

Claes, A., M.J.K. De Ceuster, and R. Polfliet (2002). Anatomy of the Eurobond market 1980–2000. *European Financial Management* **8**(3): 373–386.

Court of Audit (2001). Lineaire obligaties: instrumenten voor het beheer van de rijksschuld. Verslag van het Rekenhof aan de Kamer van Volksvertegenwoordigers.

European Central Bank (2002). *Report on Financial Structures*.

Fortis Bank, De Belgische Financiële Markten.

Security Regulation Fund, Annual Reports.

Timmermans, T. (2000). International diversification of investments in Belgium and its effects on the main Belgian securities markets. In *International Financial Markets and the Implications for Monetary and Financial Stability*, Conference Papers No. 8. Basle, Switzerland: BIS, pp. 37–56.
www.fgov.treasury.be

9

Czech Republic

GUAN-CHYE OOI AND JONATHAN A. BATTEN

9.1 INTRODUCTION

The Czech Republic was originally part of the Austro-Hungarian Empire until its collapse in 1918. Then, the Czech Republic as well as Slovakia and part of Silesia formed the newly independent state of Czechoslovakia. At that time, Czechoslovakia was considered one of the world's most economically developed countries and had a democratic, multiparty political system. Disputes between the ethnic Germans, who agitated for closer links with Germany, finally resulted in the Munich agreement in 1938, with the cession of Sudetenland to Germany.

In April 1945, the prewar President Eduard Benes and his government-in-exile returned to Prague for restoring the republic, since the Government at that time was under Soviet control. During the election of 1946, the communist party won 38% of the votes, and consequently formed a coalition government, which introduced the centrally planned economic model. Specifically, almost all aspects of economic planning and management came under the control of central government:

- The state owned most of the country's economic assets.
- Economic managers and decision-makers were restricted in their interactions with their counterparts from the west.
- Businesses were restricted to deal only with other communist countries (Bureau of European and Eurasian Affairs, 2002).

This model persisted until late 1989 when demonstrations and mass protests forced the communist party to cede power and introduce market-based mechanisms. The Czech and Slovakia portion of the government voted to dissolve the federation, and on the 1st of January 1993, the Czech Republic and Slovakia became separate nations (this peaceful transition became known as the "Velvet Revolution"). With the collapse of communism in 1989 and later the breakup of the former Czechoslovakia Federation, a number of key economic reform measures were undertaken (these are discussed hereafter).

9.1.1 Exchange Rate Policy

As a result of the devaluation on the Czechoslovakian Crown in 1990, the government introduced a new exchange rate policy to stabilize the Crown, with attempts made to prevent it from further depreciation. Finally, in January 1991, the decision was made to peg the Crown to a dollar-dominated international basket currency (see Coats *et al.*, 2003 for more details).

European Fixed Income Markets: Money, Bond and Interest Rate Derivatives. Edited by J.A. Batten,
T.A. Fetherston and P.G. Szilagyi. © 2004 John Wiley & Sons, Ltd. ISBN 0-470-85053-1

The monetary separation of the Czech and the Slovak republics followed shortly after the formal division of the Czechoslovakia Federation, with the new currency of the Czech Republic being known as "koruna" (CZK). The Czech Republic kept its exchange rate fixed until the decision was made to float the koruna in May 1997. Initially, this policy led to a substantial real appreciation of the koruna, which resulted in a deterioration of Czech industrial competitiveness and a worsening of the current account balance.

9.1.2   Privatization

In the early 1990s, most of the state-owned industries were privatized by the Czechoslovakian government (and later the Czech government) through direct sales to foreign interest, auctions, employees' ownerships, and vouchers. The voucher system was the one most commonly used. Under this approach citizens were provided with a voucher book upon payment of a fee of CZK 1000 (plus an administration fee of CZK 50). They could then use the vouchers to either buy into privatized companies directly or into a fund, which in turn would invest in newly privatized companies. Moody's Investors Service (2001) note that the first wave of voucher privatization started in 1991 and continued with a second wave until 1994. By 1996, the state had privatized over 90% of the 1800 target companies with a total book value of nearly US$10 billion. With these two waves of voucher privatization strategy, almost 10 million Czech Republic citizens (18 years and older) have participated in the privatization process.

9.1.3   Liberalization of Prices

Prices have largely been deregulated with the exception of certain sectors including energy (electricity and gas), telecommunications, postal services, passenger railway transport, residential rental, medical care, medicine, and some agricultural products.

9.1.4   Economic Reforms

The economic reform measures undertaken by the Czech Republic government have brought substantial development and ensured that the country is one of the leaders of the Central Europe's transition economies. Table 9.1 shows that there has been a significant increase in the gross domestic product (GDP) growth in the mid-1990s, which has slowed following the economic downturn in 1997 (with a negative GDP growth of 0.8%). The onset of the prolonged recession at the beginning of 1998 (which coincided with the Asian Crisis) caused GDP to further deteriorate by -1.2% and the current account deficit to widen. Growth in the GDP has subsequently improved with positive growth rate each year from 2000 to 2003 of 2.9%, 3.6%, and 3%, respectively.

The economic slowdown in the late 1990s caused many factories in the manufacturing sector to close, in turn contributing to the increase in the unemployment from 4.8% (1997) to 6.5% (1998). The unemployment problem has subsequently worsened as a result of the weakening performance of the financial sector and declining export competitiveness (owing to the appreciating koruna) and reached 8.9% in 2000. Compared with the transition in other countries, the Czech Republic has been successful in maintaining control of inflation, with inflation peaking in 1997 and then declining to just over 3% in 2002. This owes much to the practice of adherence to inflation targeting that was introduced in 1998.

Table 9.1   Key economic indicators in the Czech Republic

Economic indicators	1997	1998	1999	2000	2001	2002
GDP: volume – market prices	−0.8	−1.2	−0.4	2.9	3.6	3
GDP: deflator – market prices	8	10.7	3.1	0.9	5.7	4
Exports of goods and services: volume – national accounts basis	9.2	9.1	6.3	17.1	12	7
Imports of goods and services: volume – national accounts basis	8.1	6.5	5.4	17	13.7	7.1
Total employment	−0.6	−1.4	−2.3	−0.7	0.7	−0.4
Unemployment rate	4.8	6.5	8.8	8.9	8.2	8.6
Current account: as a percentage of GDP	−6.7	−2.5	−2.9	−5.6	−4.7	−4.7
Short term interest rate	15.9	14.3	6.9	5.4	5.2	4.3
Consumer Price Index (CPI)	8.5	10.7	2.1	3.9	4.8	3.2

Source: Organisation for Economic Co-operation and Development (OECD).

9.2   FINANCIAL MARKET REGULATION

There are three main financial regulators in the Czech Republic: the central bank (Czech National Bank), the Ministry of Finance, and the Czech Securities Commission.

9.2.1   Czech National Bank (CNB – Česká národní banka)

Initially, the central bank of Czechoslovakia was called the State Bank of Czechoslovakia. With the dissolution of Czechoslovakia in 1993, the new central bank of Czech Republic was formed. The primary objectives of the CNB are to maintain price stability and support the general economic policies of the government, leading to sustainable economic growth. More specific are (see www.cnb.cz) listed as follows:

(A) The CNB is the sole issuer and withdrawer of banknotes and coins. It organizes the printing of banknotes and the striking of coins and ensures the security of legal tender. It regularly changes the design of banknotes and coins to improve protection against counterfeiting.

(B) The CNB is authorized to issue loans to other banks at special interest rates. Besides this, it also has the right to set the rules for issuing commercial loans and administer the Czech monetary reserves and manage the Czech national debt.

(C) The CNB also performs financial operations for the government, dealing with government stock, and putting into effect its exchange rate policy.

(D) The CNB is responsible for banking supervision in the Czech Republic, it is entitled to check into bank transaction in term of their consistency with the law, issuing banking licenses, and supervises over the financial and capital marketed in the Czech Republic.

(E) The CNB provides an ambassador to the International Monetary Fund and the World Bank.

(F) The CNB is responsible for the formulation and conduct of monetary policy, and it is directed by Governors and members of the CNB board. The Governor, Vice Governors, and the members of the CNB board are appointed by the President of the Republic for renewable terms of 6 years.

The CNB can implement monetary policy through:

(A) Open market operations: Open market operations enable the CNB to determine the level of interest rates and the appropriate monetary base. When open market purchases expand the monetary base, it will increase money supply and lower short term interest rates. On the other hand, open market sales will lower the monetary base, lowering the money supply and raising short term interest rates.
(B) Changes in reserve requirements: Changes in the reserve requirements affect the money supply by causing the money supply multiplier to change. For instance, a rise in reserve requirements reduces the amount of deposit that can be supported by a given level of the monetary base and further leads to a contraction of the money supply. While a decline in reserve requirements leads to an expansion of the money supply, as more multiple deposits are created.
(C) Changes in the discount rate: The CNB sets three key interest rates – the 2-week limit repo rate, the discount rate, and the Lombard rate. The CNB's main monetary policy interest rate is the 2-week repo rate, which it uses to signal its monetary policy stance to the market, and via asset operations on the money market to influence the short end of the yield curve. However, the discount and the Lombard rates provide the floor and ceiling for short term interest rates on the money market. And hence, any change in the repo rate will also result in symmetrical changes in the discount and Lombard rates.

9.2.2 Ministry of Finance

The Ministry of Finance (MoF) is responsible for the fiscal operations and economic management of the country. Specific responsibilities include

(A) preparing the state budget;
(B) preparing the state financial account;
(C) Treasury of the Czech Republic;
(D) financial market;
(E) taxes, customs duties, and fees;
(F) financial supervision;
(G) accounting, audit, and tax consultancy;
(H) foreign exchange policy, including bills payable to and claims on foreign countries;
 (I) protection of foreign investment;
 (J) regulation of lotteries and similar games; and
(K) privatization of state property.

9.2.3 Securities Commission – Czech Securities Commission

Initially MoF was the primary supervisor over the securities market. Then on the 1st of April 1998, the Czech parliament instituted an independent and professional authority named the Czech Securities Commission (CSC), under administrative authority Act No. 15/1998 Coll. The CSC missions and objectives are as follows:

(A) Protect the investors.
(B) Ensure market transparency.
(C) Fight white-collar crime.

(D) Prepare the Czech capital market for the integration to the European Union (EU) structure.
(E) Train investors.
(F) Support companies' issue activity.

The primary roles for the Commission are summarized below (see www.csc.com.cz):

(A) The CSC acts as the state supervision on activities carried out by investment companies, securities brokers, and traders and issuers of registered securities to ensure they fulfill their disclosure duty.
(B) The CSC also provides supervision over the activities on the stock exchange, over-the-counter (OTC) market (RMS), the Securities Center, entities arranging for the settlement of trades with securities, and pension funds.
(C) CSC must ensure entities fulfill all their obligations by not using the confidential information.
(D) CSC must also ensure entities fulfill with all the obligations arising from the mandatory and voluntary take-over bids.
(E) If the CSC was suspicious of the criminal act of insider dealing, it must report it.
(F) The CSC keeps a register of regulated entities, issues the Securities Commission's Bulletin, and cooperates with other administrative bodies and institutions.

9.3 FINANCIAL MARKET PARTICIPANTS

9.3.1 Finance Sector

The Czech financial sector comprises the following groups:

(A) Commerical banks: Following the deregulation reforms introduced in the 1990s, which saw the dismantling of the state bank monopoly, Dědek (2001) notes that the number of Czech private banks increased rapidly along with foreign banks. In 2002, there were a total of 36 banks and foreign bank branches operating in Czech Republic. Of these 36 banks, 16 were controlled by foreign shareholders and 9 were branches of foreign banks, while the remaining 10 banks were controlled by local shareholders. The CNB provides the following list of licensed banks (see Table 9.2). Commercial banks raise their funds through deposits, and then use these funds for commercial purposes (e.g., loans, mortgage loans, and to buy government securities).
(B) Česká exportní banka, a.s. (Czech Export Bank) was established to facilitate the export development.
(C) Českomoravská záruční a rozvojová banka, akciová společnost (Czech-Moravian Guarantee and Development Bank) was established to provide support to small- and medium-sized businesses.
(D) Building societies have operated since 1994. There are currently six building societies that make long term housing loans. Their activities are regulated by the Act on Building Savings Banks.
(E) Mortgage banks are authorized to issue mortgage bonds and provide state-supported housing mortgage loans to the public. There are nine authorized mortgage banks.
(F) Credit unions were created under special legislation. They do not have a direct access to the money market, and hence, they can only acquire funds from deposits called shares. These institutions largely make small consumer loans to their members.

Table 9.2   A selection of securities registered on the TKD system

Issuer code	Issuers	Maturity	Volume of issue	Primary yield (%)
42607202	Česká národní banka	182	300 000	0
40111203	Česká národní banka	182	500 000	0
40111203	Česká národní banka	140	200 000	0
22103357	České MF	273	7 997	3.760 019 233
20301358	České MF	183	9 998	3.449 951 721
21110359	České MF	91	19 998	3.329 904 604
21807360	České MF	364	7 999	3.399 976 232
20905361	České MF	273	7 998	3.040 020 301
22211363	České MF	91	19 997	2.989 855 477

Source: Czech National Bank (CNB). Reproduced by permission of Czech National Bank.

9.3.2   Prague Stock Exchange

The Prague Stock Exchange (PSE) was initially established on March 23, 1871. In December 1992, the Stock Exchange Law (Stock Exchange Act 214/1992) approved the PSE to be the country's only stock exchange, and on April 6, 1993, the PSE officially started trading.

9.3.2.1   Trading System

The PSE is an electronic exchange (no trading floor) automated trading system that was established as a client/server-based open system to process the buying and selling of securities entered into the system by member firms. The PSE introduced a trading system called SPAD in May 1998, with the intention of drawing off-exchange trading volume back to the exchange. This new automated real-time trading system allows price information to be fed directly into the systems of data vendors enhancing the timeliness and transparency of information. Currently there are seven major users of the SPAD system (CESKÉ RADIOKOMUN, CESKÝ TELECOM, CEZ, ERSTE BANK, KOMERCNÍ BANKA, PHILIP MORRIS CR, and UNIPETROL); however, these firms take up the largest volume overall on the PSE. Overall, ČESKÝ TELECOM is the largest company listed with its market capitalization of CZK 85 billion (2002), followed by ČEZ and ČESKÁ SPOŘITELNA, which have market capitalization of CZK 46 billion and CZK 42 billion, respectively.

Block trading refers to trading where at least one party is an exchange member and which is registered in the exchange's trading system. These trades are prenegotiated agreements between two parties to buy and sell the securities and have been used for selling large volumes within the privatization program.

9.3.2.2   Settlement and Transfer

The Universal Securities Clearing Center (UNIVYC), formerly know as the Stock Exchange Securities Register, carries out the clearing and settlement of stock exchange transactions.

The settlement of securities trades normally consists of the simultaneous transfer of money and the delivery of securities. However, the settlement of trade may also occur without the realization of cash settlement, known as "delivery-free payment." For cash settlement, UNIVYC carries out the settlement via the clearing center of the CNB.

The settlement of stock exchange trades makes up the major share of UNIVYC's activities. Apart from that, UNIVYC also offers securities traders

- settlement of OTC trades;
- service to related to securities safe custody;
- mediation of services provided by the Securities center (SCP);
- securities lending and borrowing;
- settlement of primary issues of securities;
- administration and management of deposits for Stock Exchange Guaranty fund participants;
- seminars and training course focused on settlement issues; and
- supplementary services (such as preparation of information outputs for brokerage companies and publication of statistical information).

9.3.2.3   Markets of Securities

Securities in the PSE are traded in four different types of markets:

Main Market

The main market was officially established on September 1, 1995, and allows only the most liquid securities to be traded. The basic conditions for admission of securities to the main market are listed below:

- A minimum public issue of Kc200 million.
- A minimum of 25% of the overall issue to be issued via a public offer.
- Existence of the company for at least 3 years.

Secondary Market

The secondary market exists concurrently with the main market and also only allows highly liquid securities to trade in the exchange. The basic conditions for admission of securities to the secondary (or parallel) market are as follows:

- A minimum issued amount of Kc100 million.
- A minimum of 25% of the shares made available via a public offer.
- Existence of the company for at least 3 years.

Free Market

The free market, originally called the unlisted market, was created for issuers that did not meet the size required for main and secondary market listings but otherwise were in compliance with other listing criteria.

New Market

The general meeting of the exchange (held on September 30, 1999) approved the establishment of the new market. The main objective was to enable companies with a short history to attract finance (such as technology firms). The basic conditions for admission of securities to the new market are listed as follows:

- A minimum issued amount of Kc20 million.
- A minimum of 15% of the shares made available via a public offer.
- Existence of the company for at least 1 year.

9.4 MONEY AND FIXED INCOME INSTRUMENTS

9.4.1 Money Market

The money market instruments offered by the CNB are basically short term debt instruments (with the maturity less than 1 year). These include the following:

9.4.1.1 Treasury Bills

Treasury bills are short term debt instruments, which are issued by the government (Treasury department of the MoF) to finance the state budget deficit. Treasury bills usually have a maturity of up to 1 year (standard maturities are 13, 26, 39, and 52 weeks) and have a nominal value of CZK 1 million. These instruments have a nominal value of CZK 1 million (about US$30 000).

9.4.1.2 Czech National Bank (CNB) Bills

CNB bills are short term debt instruments (usually with a 6-month maturity) that are issued by the CNB for liquidity management purposes. These are typically repo operations transactions. A sample of CNB bills (Česká národní banka) that are registered on the TKD (short term bond trading system) are provided in Table 9.3. This list also includes some short term bonds issued by MoF (České MF). The TKD is predominantly used by the MoF to issue Treasury bills and the CNB to issue CNB bills, as well as other banks and nonbanks participants to issue short term bonds (which must be approved by the CSC). The TKD system will register all those bonds in book-entry form, and at the same time provide the settlement function for trading of these securities.

9.4.2 Bond Markets

Dvorakova (1999) notes that the bond markets in the Czech Republic only started to develop after 1993 once inflation dropped below 10%, and the economic and political situation stabilized. The Czech bond market is now ranked among the most developed bond markets in Central and Eastern Europe in term of foreign investors access, liquidity offer of instruments, and other characteristics. Market making in the bond market is dominated by foreign banks with the major firms including ABN Amro Bank, HVB Bank, Citibank a.s., Commerzbank CM, Conseq Finance, Deutsche bank, ING Bank NV, and Raiffeisenbank.

9.4.2.1 Types of Bond Instruments

Figure 9.1 provides an overview of the structure of the bond markets. During the year 2001, the total value of bonds traded on the PSE was CZK 1858.4 billion, with market capitalization increasing by 14% from the previous year. Government bonds accounted for the largest share of

Table 9.3 Licensed banks operating in the Czech Republic

Banks with mostly (more than 50%) Czech financial participation	Banks with mostly (more than 50%) foreign financial participation	Branches of foreign banks
eBanka, a.s.	Česká spořitelna, a.s.	ABN AMRO Bank NV
Plzeňská banka a.s.	Československá obchodní banka, a.s.	COMMERZBANK Aktiengesellschaft, pobočka Praha
První městská banka, a.s.	GE Capital Bank, a.s.	Deutsche Bank Aktiengesellschaft Filiale Prag, organizační složka
Union banka, a.s.	IC Banka, a.s.	ING Bank NV
Česká exportní banka, a.s.	Interbanka, akciová společnost	HSBC Bank plc – pobočka Praha
Českomoravská hypoteční banka, a.s.	J & T Banka, a.s.	Raiffeisenbank im Stiftland eG pobočka Cheb, odštěpný závod
Českomoravská záruční a rozvojová banka, akciová společnost	Komerční banka, a.s.	Sparkasse Mühlviertel – West banka a.s., pobočka České Budějovice
Českomoravská stavební spořitelna, akciová společnost	Raiffeisenbank a.s.	Všeobecná úverová banka a.s., pobočka Praha
ČS-stavební spořitelna, a.s.	Živnostenská banka, a.s.	Waldviertler Sparkasse von 1842 pobočka
HYPO stavební spořitelna a.s. Všeobecná stavební spořitelna Komerční banky, a.s.	Dresdner Bank CZ a.s. Citibank, a.s.	
	CREDIT LYONNAIS BANK PRAHA, a.s. Volksbank CZ, a.s. Raiffeisen stavební spořitelna a.s. Wüstenrot–stavební spořitelna a.s. HVB Bank Czech Republic, a.s.	

Source: Czech National Bank (CNB). Reproduced by permission of Czech National Bank.

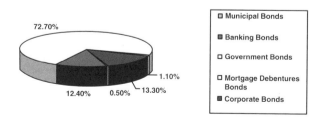

Figure 9.1 Bond structure in Czech Republic.
Source: Prague Stock Exchange (PSE). Reproduced by permission of Prague Stock Exchange.

Table 9.4   Bond trading on the Prague Stock Exchange

	Number of bonds issued						
	1995	1996	1997	1998	1999	2000	2001
Main market	20	26	33	33	30	30	28
Secondary market	0	1	2	3	3	11	14
Free market	28	53	57	62	62	53	42
Total	48	80	92	98	95	94	84
Total Value of bond trades (CZK millions)	69 764	143 264	433 236	687 598	1 024 029	958 688	1 858 380
Market Capitalization (CZK millions)	87 832	136 918	174 005	198 107	231 116	280 075	319 399

Source: Prague Stock Exchange (PSE). Reproduced by permission of Prague Stock Exchange.

the bond market with 72.7%, followed by corporate bonds 13.3%, and banking bonds 12.4%. Mortgage debentures bonds and municipal bonds accounted only for 1.1% and 0.5% of total bonds traded. These securities were traded in the main, secondary, and free markets of the PSE (see Table 9.4)

Government Bonds

The Czech Republic government has been issuing government bonds since the beginning of 1992. The basic instruments are medium term government bonds and long term government bonds. Overall these instruments account for the majority of the bonds issued in the bond market. Medium term government bonds are fixed coupon bonds with a standard maturities of 2 and 5 years. Medium term government bonds have a nominal value of CZK 10 000 (approximately US$285) and are issued in a regular issue system. The MoF issues government bonds at a nominal value of CZK 5 billion every second month of each quarter. MoF issue the 5-year maturity bond in February and August, and 2-year maturity bonds in May and November. Recently, a new long term 15-year maturity government bond was added to the issuance schedule. The government has also issued bonds with a variable coupon, called "Flood Bonds," using an inflation-linked coupon (2.5% above the lagged 1 year inflation rate based on the consumer price index). The government issued these bonds in August 1997 to help finance expenditures connected with floods in the east of the country in that year.

Czech government bonds are initially sold on the primary market through auction to a group of direct participants (selected banks and securities dealers that comply with the conditions set by MoF and the CNB). Table 9.5 lists the direct participants in the Czech bond markets.

Corporate Bonds

Corporate bonds issued in the Czech bond market account for the second largest segment, although this segment represents a modest 13.3% of total value. The most commonly issued corporate bonds on the PSE are bonds with fixed coupons and have a maturity of 7 years (such as the bonds of CESKÝ TELECOM and KOMERCNÍ BANKA). Companies may also issue convertible bonds (where the bonds convert into stock at a date determined at the time of issue)

Table 9.5   Direct participants in the Czech Bond Markets

Treasury Bills	Medium term Government Bonds
ABN AMRO BANK NV pobočka Praha	ABN AMRO Bank NV, pobočka Praha
Citibank	Citibank
Credit Lyonnais Bank Praha	Commerzbank Capital Markets (Eastern Europe)
Česká spořitelna	Conseq Finance
Českomoravská záruční a rozvojová banka	Česká spořitelna
Československá obchodní banka	Českomoravská záruční a rozvojová banka
Dresdner Bank (ČR)	Československá obchodní banka
eBanka	Deutsche Bank AG, pobočka Praha
HSBC Bank plc – pobočka Praha	HVB Bank Czech Republic
HVB Bank Czech Republic	ING Bank NV
ING Bank NV pobočka Praha	Komerční banka
Komerční banka	PPF burzovní společnost
Živnostenská banka	Raiffeisenbank

Source: Czech National Bank. Reproduced by permission of Czech National Bank.

or preference bonds (where the bonds are issued by a joint-stock company and endowed with priority right to subscribe new shares).

Mortgage Bonds

Another type of debt instrument issued is a mortgage bond. Authorized financial institutions issue mortgage bonds, where the face value of the bond is secured by mortgage claims (at least 90%). The unique feature of these bonds is that interest is exempt from income tax. The banks authorized to issue mortgage bonds are Komerční banka, a.s.; Česká spořitelna, a.s.; Českomoravská hypoteční banka, akciová společnost; HypoVereinsbank CZ a.s.; Bank Austria Creditanstalt Czech Republic a.s.; Československá obchodní banka, a.s.; Raiffeisenbank a.s.; GE Capital Bank, a.s.; and Živnostenská banka, a.s.

Municipal Bonds

Municipal bonds account for only a small proportion of the total bond issue in the bond market (less than 0.50%). These bonds are usually issued by the cities' governments (Brno, Plzen, Kladno, Pardubice, and Caslav City Government) to finance the expenditures on maintenance and development of the cities (see Dvorakova, 1999).

9.4.3   Derivatives Markets

9.4.3.1   *OTC Trading (Bank-Based)*

The derivatives markets in the Czech Republic are a relatively recent market and initially were dominated by OTC currency and interest trading of the major Czech banks. Jilek (1999) notes that the creation of the Czech derivatives market was connected with currency instruments (such as currency forwards and currency swaps). The CNB prepared the first review of the derivatives in the Czech banking sector in September 1994, and quoted the nominal value

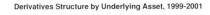

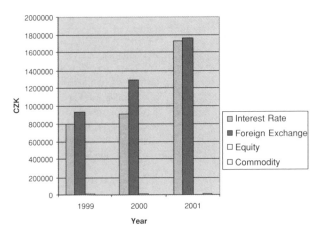

Figure 9.2   The Czech derivatives markets.
Source: Czech National Bank (CNB). Reproduced by permission of Czech National Bank.

of derivatives as CZK 31 billion (US$1.2 billion). Furthermore, these currency instruments represented more than 80% of all derivatives. Since then, the Czech derivatives market has moved forward and now trades interest rate instruments such as interest swaps, interest futures, and interest options.

Figure 9.2 records the derivatives transactions of banks from 1999 to 2001, based on the receivables from derivatives. As of 2001, the total receivables from derivatives transactions amounted to CZK 3489.3 billion, which is an increase of 58.7% from the previous year. Derivatives' trading was mostly by medium-sized banks and branches of foreign banks; trading by small banks was negligible. Trading is also concentrated in interest rate and currency products with these two groups representing 49.4% and 50.4% respectively of the total, with the balance (about 0.3%) comprising equity and commodity derivatives.

9.4.3.2   RM-System Trading

Besides the banking sector, some large corporations in the Czech Republic also deal in derivatives agreement. In 1997, the RM-System was established in cooperation with the Vienna Exchange, to enable Czech investors to trade those options and futures listed on the Vienna Exchange. The derivatives project was completed (complied with all legal, technological and security criteria) and ready to be launched on the 3rd of June 1998.

The Austrian Futures and Options Exchange (ÖTOB) gradually introduced futures and options contracts for the Hungarian Traded Index (HTX), the Czech Traded Index (CTX), Polish Traded Index (PTX), The Common Central European Index (CECE Index), and the Russian Traded Index (RTX). The CTX is not primarily intended to qualify as a benchmark for the performance of the Czech stock market. The foremost purpose of the CTX is to serve as an underlying for derivatives trading. The CTX comprises a sample of only nine Czech blue chips stocks, which represents a basket of both relatively liquid and sufficiently tradable Czech stocks.

9.4.3.3   Prague Stock Exchange (PSE) Trading

On the 2nd of August 2001, the PSE was permitted by the CSC to organize a public market for trading options and futures contracts. Trading is based on a membership principle, which includes the participation of market makers to assure sufficient liquidity in the market. All market participants can view the depth of the market via on-line connected terminals and terminals of the information agencies. Standard orders, common for these types of trades, can be inputed into the system. Order matching and subsequent contract-making follow two criteria: price and order-input time. On 17th of December 2001, the CSC granted permission for UNIVYC to settle derivatives trades.

9.5   CONCLUSION

Overall, the economy of the Czech Republic has experienced a major transformation in recent years from a centrally planned market to an open market economy where debt and equity instruments and their derivatives are now able to be traded. According to Tošovský (1997), in the 1980s, Czechoslovakia state enterprises accounted for more than 87% of national income, cooperatives accounted for 10%, and enterprises only slightly more than 2%. As a result of the reformation of centralized economy (mass privatization program, liberalization of foreign trade, liberalization of prices, etc) it has quickly shifted the Czech Republic to a market economy where these relationships have been reversed.

After the decentralization of the banking sector, the state banking monopoly was dismantled and foreign banks were allowed to participate; this lead to a rapid development for Czech's banking industry. According to Dědek (2001), the domestic banks initially were confronted by a number of problems, such as undercapitalization, shortage of long term funds necessary to support development plans, the nonexistence risk management, inexperienced staff, underdeveloped information systems, and an inefficient regulatory framework. While there has been significant and dramatic change it is worthwhile noting that the World Bank Country Study (1999) noted that there was still much more to be done: there are still inefficiencies in Czech capital market, such as weakness in the regulatory framework, fragmentation of securities markets, and lack of supervision of capital market operations. These factors continue to undermine investors' confidence in this market. However, many of these concerns are being overcome as the Czech Republic undertakes the preaccession Economic Programs for European Union Membership, which involves undertaking further policies of economic stabilization and overcoming inefficiencies in the financial markets.

REFERENCES

Bureau of European and Eurasian Affairs (2002, August). Background Note: Czech Republic. U.S. Department of State. http://www.state.gov/r/pa/ei/bgn/3237.htm/.

Coats, Warren, Douglas Laxton and David Rose (2003, March). The Czech National Bank's Forecasting and Policy Analysis System. Prague: Czech National Bank. http://www.cnb.cz/en/publikace2.php.

Czech National Bank. (2003). http://www.cnb.cz/.

Dědek, Oldřich (2001, August). Czech National Bank: Bank Consolidation in the Czech Republic. Bank for International Settlements (BIS) Paper. Basel: BIS.

Dvorakova, Anna (1999). The Bond Market in the Czech Republic. *Business and Trade* 12. http://www.mpo.cz/gc/9912/page0008.htm/ page 8.

Jilek, Josef (1999). The Czech Derivatives Market. *Czech Business and Trade* 9. http://www.mpo.cz/gc/9909/page0009.htm/ page 9.

Prague Stock Exchange (PSE): http://www.pse.cz/. (1996–2003).

RM-System: http://www.rmsystem.cz/.

Tošovský, J. (1997). Czech Republic's perspective of transition in Central and Eastern Europe. Bank for International Settlements (BIS) Review. Basel: BIS.

World Bank Country Study (1999, February). Czech Republic Capital Market Review. Washington, DC: World Bank.

Websites

BBC News. Country Profile: Czech Republic http://news.bbc.co.uk/2/hi/world/europe/country_profiles/1108489.

Country Report on Economic Policy and Trade Practices – Czech Republic (2000, March). Bureau of Economic and Business Affairs U.S. Department of State http://www.state.gov/www/issues/economic/trade_reports/1999/czechrep.html/.

Czech Republic's Ministry of Finance. http://www.mfcr.cz/.

Czech Securities Commission. http://www.sec.cz/.

Economist.com. Country Briefing: Czech Republic http://www.economist.com/countries/CzechRepublic/.

Enlargement. Czech Republic: Country Profile http://europa.eu.int/comm/enlargement/czech/index.htm.

European Stock Market Indexes Website. Czech Traded Index. http://www.ihs.ac.at/fin/finix/ctxdescrip.html.

International Monetary Fund. Report on the Observance of Standard and Codes (ROSC) Czech Republic http://www.imf.org/external/np/rosc/cze/over.htm.

Moody's Investors Services (2001, August). Global Funds Update Overview and Trends in the Czech Republic Fund Industry. *Global Credit Research,* pages 1–15.

Universal Securities Clearing Center: http://www.univyc.cz/.

10

Denmark

CHARLOTTE CHRISTIANSEN, TOM ENGSTED, SVEND JAKOBSEN,
AND CARSTEN TANGGAARD

10.1 INTRODUCTION

10.1.1 The Danish Economy

Denmark is a small open economy inhabited by 5.4 million people. In 2001 the per capita GDP was approximately Danish kroner (DKK) 250 000 (US$30 000).[1] Import and export of goods and services both amount to approximately 35% of GDP. Since 1972 Denmark has been a member of the European Community, but not a member of the European Monetary Union, i.e., Denmark still has its own currency.

The country has developed from having a large agricultural production (30% of total value added in 1900; 4% in 1997) to a service-dominated country (44% of total value added in 1900; 70% in 1997). Today industry accounts for 25% of total value added, approximately the same as in 1900.

Denmark has a relatively large public sector and a high level of government expenditures financed by taxes. Total taxes amount to approximately 50% of GDP, and for a large part of the wage earners, the marginal income tax rate is between 60% and 65%.

In the 1970s and 1980s Denmark accumulated severe foreign debt (reaching a maximum of 40% of GDP in 1984 and 1985) because of several years with current account deficits. However, since 1990 Denmark has run current account surpluses, and the foreign debt is now reduced to approximately 17% of GDP. In the 1970s and the beginning of 1980s, unemployment and inflation rates were also quite high (each reaching two-digit levels), but since then economic conditions in Denmark have – like in the rest of the industrialized world – generally become better.

Table 10.1 shows key macroeconomic figures for the Danish economy since 1997. In the years 1997–2000, the growth rate in real GDP was between 2% and 3%. In 2001, the economic growth deteriorated to slightly less than 1%. Over the same period inflation has been steadily around 2%. Unemployment has fluctuated around 4–5% and the long term interest rate around 5–6%. If we compare these figures with similar figures for the countries in the Euro area, we see that since 1998 the economic growth in Denmark has been slightly lower than the economic growth in the Euro area, whereas unemployment in Denmark has been much lower than unemployment in the Euro countries as a whole. The rate of inflation in Denmark has been more or less identical with the Euro area as a whole.

---

[1] Throughout this chapter we use the end of December 2001 exchange rate: USD 1 = DKK 8.3486. The corresponding € rate was €1 = DKK 7.4357.

European Fixed Income Markets: Money, Bond and Interest Rate Derivatives. Edited by J.A. Batten,
T.A. Fetherston and P.G. Szilagyi. © 2004 John Wiley & Sons, Ltd. ISBN 0-470-85053-1

Table 10.1   Danish and Euro area macroeconomic key figures

	Denmark (%)					Euro area (%)				
	1997	1998	1999	2000	2001	1997	1998	1999	2000	2001
Real GDP growth rate	3.0	2.5	2.3	3.0	0.9	2.4	2.9	2.7	3.4	1.6
Inflation	1.9	1.3	2.1	2.7	2.3	1.7	1.2	1.1	2.4	2.5
Unemployment	5.2	4.9	4.8	4.4	4.3	11.3	10.7	9.8	8.8	8.3
Long term interest rate	6.0	5.1	4.9	5.8	5.1	5.7	4.9	4.7	5.5	4.9

Source: Ministry of Finance.

In the last 20 years authorities in Denmark (the government and the Danish Central Bank) have pursued a wide variety of economic policies with the aim of obtaining high-economic growth, low inflation, low unemployment, trade balance surpluses, and a stable exchange rate. These initiatives include fiscal and monetary policies as well as labor market policies and more structurally oriented changes. In the next subsection a brief description of Danish monetary policy (including exchange rate policy) is given.

10.1.2   Danish Monetary Policy

The Danish monetary policy in the 1970s and the beginning of 1980s was conducted mainly with a wish to control private banks' liquidity. The Danish Central Bank defined specific upper limits for private banks' borrowing in the central bank and for banks' lending to individuals, firms, and institutions in the private and public sectors. Thus, monetary policy at that time could be characterized as control of the money supply through quantitative restrictions on private banks' lending.

In the first half of the 1980s, this system came under pressure as a consequence of the gradual liberalization of international capital movements and a new conservative government's declaration of a fixed exchange rate policy in 1983. The money supply became more or less endogenously determined, and the Danish Central Bank gradually shifted its policy toward managing the short term money market interest rate. This led to a clear reduction in the volatility of short term interest rates in Denmark.

Since 1987 private banks have had access to make day-to-day deposits in the central bank on so-called "current accounts." The central bank sets the current account interest rate ("foliorenten"), which is equivalent to the discount rate. In addition, banks may place excess liquidity on 14-day certificates of deposit ("indskudsbeviser"), which are zero-coupon bonds that yield more interest but are less liquid than current accounts. The 14-day deposit rate is also set by the central bank. Private banks may borrow from the central bank against collateral in the form of government securities, mortgage-backed bonds (MBB), or other types of bonds. The central bank's lending rate is the same as the interest rate on certificates of deposit, and therefore these loans have a maturity of 14 days. If banks need loans with more than 14-day maturity, they are referred to the interbank market where banks can borrow from each other on an uncollateralized basis. The interbank interest rate is called the "Copenhagen Interbank Offered Rate" (CIBOR) and the maturity ranges from 1 month to 1 year.

By setting the day-to-day current account interest rate and the 14-day deposit rate, the central bank controls the interest rates at the short end of the money market. In addition to this, the central bank contributes and absorbs liquidity by repurchasing and issuing certificates of deposits. These market operations are usually conducted once a week.

Up through the 1990s till today the main goal for the central bank has been to support a fixed exchange rate policy *vis-à-vis* the German mark, and since January 1999 the euro (in a referendum in 1992 and again in 2000, the Danish people voted against joining the European Monetary Union). The short term money market rate is set such that it supports a stable nominal DKK-exchange rate. A stable nominal exchange rate requires that the inflation rate in Denmark does not deviate from the inflation rate in the Euro area over longer periods of time. Thus, there is implicit inflation targeting built into the Danish monetary policy, but Denmark does not, like e.g. Sweden, formulate monetary policy in terms of explicit inflation targets. The fixed exchange rate policy is formally secured through the ERM2 exchange rate mechanism cooperation between the Danish Central Bank and the European Central Bank. The central parity rate is currently DKK 746.038 per euro 100, with a fluctuation band of $+/- 2.25\%$. If the exchange rate approaches the band, the two central banks are committed to intervene in the foreign exchange market by buying and selling Danish currency.

10.2   HISTORY AND STRUCTURE OF THE DANISH BOND MARKET

The Danish bond market is composed of government bonds, MBB, corporate bonds, and fixed income derivatives.[2] Table 10.2 shows the relative market value of some fixed income assets for 2001. MBB securities amount to almost two thirds of the total market value and the government bonds account for the remaining one third. Corporate bonds are almost insignificant.

Long term Danish government bonds go back to the nineteenth century.[3] Government bonds were issued irregularly until June 1975. To finance its operating deficit and repay its foreign debt resulting from the recession of the 1970s, the Danish state began raising capital by systematically issuing bonds (Treasury notes and Treasury bonds) and has continued this practice ever since. In 1990 Treasury bills were introduced. After the initial issue by the Danish Central Bank, the government bonds are traded on the Copenhagen Stock Exchange (CSE). By the end of 2001, the value of the outstanding government bonds was DKK 660 billion (US$79 billion), and the value has decreased slightly since 1995. Section 10.3 holds more details on Danish government bonds.

The market for MBB has a long history. In fact, the first mortgage bank was set up in 1797 to finance the reconstruction of the city of Copenhagen after a devastating fire. Since the middle of the nineteenth century the mortgage banks have played a predominant role in property financing. MBB trade as standardized financial products at the CSE. The value of the MBB was DKK 1298 billion (US$155 billion) in 2001, up from DKK 876 billion in 1995. Thus, the Danish MBB market is substantial, even by international standards. The market for Danish MBB is described in more detail in Section 10.4.

Corporate bonds are hardly of any significance in financing Danish corporations. Danish corporations tend to finance their operations by bank loans and by mortgage credits.[4] Exchange-traded corporate bonds have only existed over the past few decades. The limited trade in corporate bonds takes place at the CSE. The market for fixed income derivatives is also limited

---

[2] In this chapter we will only consider exchange-traded bonds. The remaining market is very small.

[3] More information about the Danish government bond market is available at the home page of the Danish Central Bank, www.nationalbanken.dk.

[4] The information on corporate bonds was taken from the home page of the CSE, www.xcse.dk.

Table 10.2   Market value and turnover for Danish exchange listed bonds*

Security group	Market value (DKK million)	Market value (%)	Turnover (DKK billion)	Turnover rate	Number of bond series
Treasury bonds	608 308	27.7	2390.1	3.93	45
Treasury bills	51 970	2.4	214.0	4.12	4
Standard mortgage credit[†]	1 121 575	51.1	3050.4	2.72	993
Inflation-linked mortgage credit	150 104	6.8	85.8	0.57	176
Special mortgage credit	26 045	1.2	12.7	0.49	608
Special institutions	151 183	6.9	181.1	1.20	392
Other (incl. corporate bonds)	86 370	3.9	168.2	1.95	36
Total	2 195 555	100	6102.3	2.78	2254

Source: Miscellaneous statistical information from the CSE.
*Market value and turnover statistics for Danish exchange-traded bonds as of December 31, 2001. The turnover is the total turnover in 2001.
[†] Includes callable as well as noncallable mortgage bonds. The nominal value of noncallable mortgage bonds end of 2001 amounts to DKK 160 934 million.

in size. It has only been possible to trade interest rate futures and options on the organized market in the period from 1988 to 2001. Over-the-counter (OTC) trade in fixed income derivatives has taken place since the eighties. Section 10.5 contains a description of the market for corporate bonds and interest rate derivatives.

By the end of 2001, the total value of the outstanding bond debt in Denmark added up to DKK 2351 billion (US$282 billion).[5] This figure is of course very small compared to the value of the US bond market (US$17 661 billion), but of a similar size relative to GDP; 184% for Denmark compared to 173% for the United States. In the past few years the outstanding debt has been equal to around 180% of GDP.

10.3   THE DANISH GOVERNMENT BOND MARKET[6]

10.3.1   Background

Because of the positive net cash balance of the central government's account, the nominal amount of foreign and domestic debt securities issued by the Danish central government has been steadily decreasing since 1996. At the end of 2001, the nominal value of domestic bonds issued by the Danish central government amounted to DKK 611 billion (US$73 billion) down from DKK 670 billion in 1996. The bonds are issued by the Ministry of Finance, but the issuing strategy is planned in close cooperation with the Danish Central Bank, who is in charge of the management of all central government debts.

The current strategy of the Danish Central Bank is to issue domestic bonds almost exclusively in the 2-, 5-, and 10-year maturity segment. The idea is to build up large liquid series that are attractive to foreign investors. It is expected that the large size of these on-the-run series will tend to reduce liquidity premiums and thereby lower overall borrowing costs. This strategy is supported by interest rate swaps for day-to-day risk management, while older bond series are redeemed from the market through buyback and switch operations.

---

[5] This also includes international debt.
[6] The description of the Danish government bond policy is based on Danish Central Bank (2002).

10.3.2   Types of Instruments

10.3.2.1   Treasury Bills

To account for the government's short term financing needs, the Danish Central Bank issues Treasury bills ("Skatkammerbeviser") which are zero-coupon securities with maturities up to 1 year. A new 12-month Treasury bill series is opened each quarter. Redemption dates are the first settlement day of the months of February, May, August, and November. Each month an auction is held at which the central bank sells Treasury bills. Almost all bills are bought by a few large market participants.

10.3.2.2   Government Bonds and Treasury Notes

Most government bonds are fixed-rate noncallable bullet loans with annual settlement. Danish government bond issues consist of Treasury notes ("Statsgældsbeviser") for the 2–3-year maturity segment and government bullet bonds ("Stående lån") for longer term issues. Table 10.3 shows the outstanding nominal amounts of government bond issues by October 1, 2002. By comparing to outstanding nominal amount by December 2001 the current on-the-run issues are

Table 10.3   Danish central government bond issues (October 1, 2002)

Coupon	Name	Redemption date	Price	Yield	Nominal outstanding amount (DKK million)	Change since Dec. 31, 2001
			Treasury bills		.	
0	Skatkammerbevis 2002 IV	01-11-2002	99.72	3.72	14 392	6 832
0	Skatkammerbevis 2003 I	03-02-2003	98.90	3.35	19 265	19 265
0	Skatkammerbevis 2003 II	01-05-2003	98.16	3.30	14 371	14 371
0	Skatkammerbevis 2003 III	01-08-2003	97.41	3.23	9 700	9 700
		Treasury bonds and notes				
6	Stående lån 2002	15-11-2002	100.27	3.51	28 707	−10 050
8	Stående lån 2003	15-05-2003	102.78	3.28	56 961	−3 399
5	Stående lån 2003	15-11-2003	101.87	3.26	36 689	−139
4	S 2004	15-10-2004	109.00	3.81	2 844	−
4	Statsgældsbevis 2004*	15-11-2004	101 09	3.45	37 182	37 182
7	Stående lån 2004	15-12-2004	107.24	3.51	67 101	−
5	Stående lån 2005	15-08-2005	103.68	3.62	57 511	−689
8	Stående lån 2006	15-03-2006	113.45	3.75	58 176	−7 724
7	Stående lån 2007	15-11-2007	113.74	3.98	52 069	−
4	Stående lån 2008*	15-08-2008	99.24	4.15	17 852	17 852
6	Stående lån 2009	15-11-2009	110.05	4.33	66 646	−
6	Stående lån 2011	15-11-2011	110.80	4.53	60 987	585
5	Stående lån 2013*	15-11-2013	103.14	4.63	38 045	38 045
7	Stående lån 2024	10-11-2024	126.15	5.01	25 001	−

Source: CSE.
*On-the-run issues.

easily identified as the 4% Statsgældsbevis 2004, 4% Stående lån 2008, and the 5% Stående lån 2013.

To support the liquidity of the on-the-run series the central bank engages in the so-called buyback and switch operations in which bonds in older and less liquid series are bought back from the market and immediately canceled. For 2002 this has been the case for 6% Stående lån 2002, 8% Stående lån 2003, and 8% Stående lån 2006, (cf. Table 10.3). Buyback and switch operations may be done on tap, by auction, or by announcing a period in which market participants can sell or switch older issues at fixed prices or conversion ratios. Buyback operations on short term bonds also serve to reduce the government's refinancing requirements at the final redemption date.

10.3.2.3   Other Types of Government Bonds

A small number of other government bond types exist. Historically serial bonds, i.e. bonds with equal reinstallments on principal, have been used extensively. Three serial bond series still exist with only 4% Stående lån 2004 having any significant amount outstanding. The Danish government has issued four lottery bond series with a nominal value of DKK 900 million. To complete the picture, four small perpetuals are listed on the Danish Stock Exchange – the oldest one issued in 1886. These series are mainly to the benefit of teachers in bond mathematics!

10.4   THE MARKET FOR DANISH MORTGAGE-BACKED SECURITIES[7]

10.4.1   Background

With a market value of DKK 1298 billion (US$155 billion) (96.5% of Danish GDP) and a turnover of DKK 3148 billion (US$377 billion) during 2001, the Danish mortgage bond market is among the largest mortgage bond markets in Europe, second only to the German "Pfandbriefe" market. Mortgage bonds are issued based on registered loans in real estate. More than 90% of gross residential mortgage loans in Denmark are funded through the mortgage bond market[8] (European Mortgage Federation, 2002, Table 4).

10.4.1.1   Mortgage Credit Institutions

Mortgage bonds are issued by specialized mortgage credit institutions. A number of mergers have taken place in the 200-year long history of the market, and now only eight mortgage credit institutions remain (cf. Table 10.4). Traditionally, mortgage credit institutions were formed as an association of borrowers, but in 1989 a change in the Mortgage Credit Act opened up for the formation of new institutions owned by the regular banks. Today Nykredit, BRFKredit, DLR, and LRF represent the traditional institutions. Nordea Kredit is owned by Nordea Bank, Totalkredit by an association of regional banks, and FIH by the Swedish FöreningsSparbanken. Following a merger in January 2001, the largest of the traditional mortgage credit institutions,

---

[7] Detailed descriptions of the Danish mortgage bond system are given in Association of Danish Mortgage Banks (1999) and Danske Bank Research (2001). The website of the Association of Danish Mortgage Banks, www.realkreditraadet.dk, contains a wealth of statistics and related information.

[8] Sweden has a similar high use of mortgage bonds (90%), while in Germany mortgage bonds account for 20%. Mortgage bonds are almost insignificant in the remaining European countries.

Table 10.4   Market share of Danish mortgage banks (2001)

Mortgage banks	Market share of nominal bond value (%)	Market share of gross new mortgages (%)
Realkredit Danmark	36.8	33.0
BRF Kredit	10.6	9.5
Nykredit	31.7	29.1
Totalkredit	8.6	12.2
Nordea Kredit	8.2	11.9
Others	4.0	4.2

Source: Association of Danish Mortgage Banks, Annual Report 2001. Reproduced by permission of the Association of Danish Mortgage Banks.

Realkredit Danmark is now fully owned by Danske Bank. In recent years the bank-owned institutions have gained market shares relative to the traditional institutions, probably due to the banks' extensive branch networks.

10.4.1.2   Regulation and Credit Rating

Danish mortgage credit institutions are regulated by the Financial Supervisory Authority according to the provision of the Mortgage Credit Act. All lending must be secured by centrally registered mortgages on real property. The maximum loan-to-value ratio for private property is 80%, while corporate loans have a limit of 60%. The European Union capital adequacy directives are implemented in the Mortgage Credit Act. Liable capital of a mortgage credit institution must be at least 8% of risk-weighted assets. Private mortgage loans carry a risk weight of 50%, while there is a 100% risk weight on corporate loans.

When a borrower obtains a new mortgage loan at the mortgage credit institution, the institution will fund the loan immediately through the tap-sale of the necessary amount of mortgage bonds. The borrower's revenue equals the proceeds from the sale. The *balance principle* of the Mortgage Credit Act demands a very close match between payments on loans and the type of bonds issued. Effectively this requires that the terms on the loan (e.g., fixed rate, 30-year, 6% coupon rate) correspond exactly to the terms of the mortgage bond issued. In general, all loan payments (less a 0.6% servicing fee) are passed through to the mortgage bond investors, who receive their pro-rata share of the repayments. Therefore, investors assume the full interest rate and prepayment risk. Nonpayment by the borrower will start a standard procedure, which may lead to a forced sale of the property. Any loss to the mortgage credit institution will be written down in the reserves.

The Danish mortgage bond market has been functioning for 200 years without a single default on any of the issues. The rating of the five big institutions range from Aa2 to Aaa and the conclusion from a recent report from Moody's is that "Danish mortgage bonds are very strong and very low-risk financial instruments" (Moody's, 2002).

A single caveat should be mentioned here: For 200 years the Danish mortgage loans have been issued as callable, fixed-rate loans, which protect the borrower against increasing as well as decreasing interest rates. However, for the last 5 years a large number of borrowers have turned to adjustable-rate loans, with less protection against an increase in interest rates. This change could introduce a new kind of credit risk into the Danish mortgage credit system.

10.4.2   Types of Mortgage Bonds

10.4.2.1   Callable Mortgage Credit Bonds

The majority of Danish mortgage bonds are backed by callable, fixed coupon, annuity loans. The annuity loans (also known as level pay) amortize with constant quarterly payments, which implies that interest payments decrease and principal payments increase over time. All loans backing a particular bond have the same coupon rate and amortizing principle, and different bond series are used for loans with maturities of 10, 15, 20, and 30 years, respectively. Each bond series is open for issuance in a 3-year period after which it is closed and a new range of bonds is opened. Mortgage bonds are named by the institution, the final maturity date (i.e., the date at which all mortgage loans should be fully redeemed), and the coupon rate, e.g. Nykredit 6% 2035.

The loans have a fixed rate for say 30 years, but the borrower is allowed to call (prepay) the loan at par value at any time until maturity. A drop in market rates could induce a borrower with an 8% loan to refinance using a new 6% bond. If the new bond is issued at par value, the borrower will reduce his interest payments by 2% points.

The lower the market rate relative to the coupon rate of the bond, the more the borrowers will decide to prepay their loan. This will reduce the market value of the bonds relative to a similar noncallable bond because prepayments will increase principal payments and thereby shorten the life of the bond.

The quarterly conditional prepayment rate (CPR) denotes the share of remaining borrowers, who decide to prepay their loans. Figure 10.1 shows quarterly CPR for Realkredit Danmark (RD) 7% and 8% 2029 in the period from April 1999 to October 2002. To indicate the level of

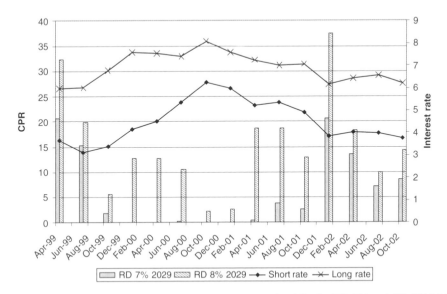

Figure 10.1   Long and short term mortgage rates together with CPR for RD 7% and 8% 2029 MBB (April 1999 to October 2002). Rates have been lagged 3 months to account for the term of notice
Source: CPR is taken from the CSE. The short rate is the 1–2 year noncallable mortgage rate. The long rate is the rate on 30-year callable mortgage bonds as defined by the Association of Danish Mortgage Banks.

interest rates the chart also shows the 1-year and the 10-year mortgage rates. It is evident that lower interest rates increase prepayments and that CPR increases with the level of the coupon rate relative to market rates.[9]

As an alternative to prepayment, borrowers are allowed to buy back bonds at the market price and redeem their loans through the delivery of the bonds to the mortgage credit institution. Buybacks are used in place of prepayment, whenever the market price of the bond is below par value. As bonds are bought at current market prices buybacks will not have any direct impact on the investors' return.

The fixed coupon-rate combined with the possibility of prepayment and buyback protects the borrower under a wide range of interest rate scenarios. Mortgage payments stay unchanged if interest rates increase and the borrower who wants to move has the option of buying back the bond at market value, thus avoiding the lock-in effects known from the US mortgage bond system. Conversely, if interest rates decrease, the prepayment option will protect the borrower against insolvency risk.

The protection of the borrower comes at the expense of investors, who therefore need to forecast future prepayment rates to price the mortgage bonds.

10.4.2.2 Noncallable Mortgage Bonds

Another type of mortgage loan is the adjustable rate mortgage loans ("Flexlån"). These loans are granted as 30-year annuity loans, but are funded through the sale of short term noncallable bullet bonds. The interest rate used in the calculation of the loan payments is equal to the yield on the bullet bonds issued. The bullet bonds are redeemed at maturity and new bullet bonds are sold at an auction held in December to fund the remaining principal on the loans. Each year loan payments are changed to reflect the yield on the newly issued bullet bond.

Since the introduction in 1996, the adjustable rate mortgage loans have gained a large market share relative to the traditional callable loans (cf. also Figure 10.3). The bond maturities range from 1 to 11 years with January 1st as the common annual payment date. Each year institutions open a new 11-year bond series. All series stay open for new issues until maturity. Short term 1–2-year bullet loans account for 65% of the adjustable rate mortgage loans, followed by 5-year bonds with 10.8% of nominal value outstanding (October 1, 2002). Some loans are funded using a mix of bullet bonds of several maturities.

The noncallable mortgage bonds, especially the 1-year bonds, are highly liquid with a yield spread of only 10–30 basis points to similar government bonds. Given the typical servicing fee of 60 basis points, this system allows even small household loans to be funded at a rate less than 100 basis points above Treasuries!

10.4.2.3 Adjustable Rate Bonds

A single mortgage credit institution, Totalkredit, grants adjustable rate bonds ("boligXlaan") funded using a 5-year bond. The bond has quarterly payments, but the coupon rate is reset twice a year based on the 6-month CIBOR plus a spread of 0.3549%. The coupon rate for the bonds are capped at 6.44%, but series with a 7.7% cap also exist. After 5 years the bonds are redeemed and new bonds are issued to cover the remaining principal.

---

[9] The similar Realkredit Danmark 6% 2029 had no prepayments during this period.

10.4.2.4   Inflation-Linked Mortgage Bonds

Different types, in fact very different types, of inflation-linked bonds are present in the Danish mortgage bond market. Mortgage loans based on inflation-linked bonds typically carry some kind of government subsidy. The market for inflation-linked bonds is dominated by the so-called IS bonds (subsidized housing), which accounts for more than 81% of nominal amount outstanding.

10.4.3   Pricing Danish MBB

The noncallable mortgage bonds are standard fixed-rate noncallable bullet loans with low credit risk and high liquidity. They are priced almost like an otherwise identical government bond.

The valuation of callable fixed-rate bonds is much more complex due to the prepayment option. Analysts at the Danish financial institutions employ a range of sophisticated models to value these bonds. Stochastic term structure models are used for modeling yield curve changes. Most analysts price MBB relative to the swap yield curve with a volatility structure determined by current swaption and cap quotes.

The prepayment behavior of borrowers is captured by an estimated prepayment function, which states CPR as a function of a number of variables. Typical explanatory variables include prepayment gain, the spread between long and short term rates, historical prepayment activity (burn-out), and the loan-size distribution. Data on cash flow profiles, borrower composition, preliminary redemptions, and actual prepayment rates are made public by the mortgage credit institutions and available through a number of data distributors.

Figure 10.2 shows the market price of a callable mortgage bond, Realkredit Danmark 9% 2026, compared to the noncallable government bond, 8% Danske Stat 2006, in the period from January 1995 to February 1999. Prices are shown as a function of the government bond's yield to maturity. During this particular 4-year period, the market witnessed a sharp decrease

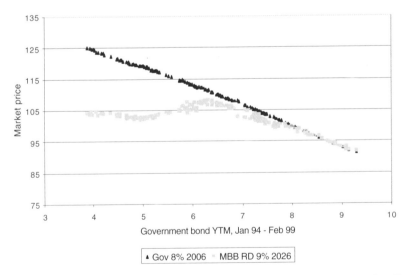

Figure 10.2   Government and mortgage bond prices as a function of the government bond's yield to maturity.
Source: CSE.

Table 10.5 Key statistics for selected "Realkredit Danmark" callable mortgage bonds

Coupon	End year	Price	No prepayment			Prepayment adjusted		
			Yield	Duration	Convexity	OAS*	OAD*	OAC*
8	2032	104.95	7.70	8.97	1.83	37	−0.50	−1.85
7	2032	102.56	6.92	9.42	1.92	49	1.30	−4.09
6	2032	99.95	6.14	9.88	2.02	43	5.61	−2.84
5	2032	95.23	5.56	10.25	2.09	16	8.39	−0.88
7	2019	104.13	6.52	6.11	0.76	65	1.32	−2.27
6	2019	102.03	5.82	6.39	0.80	59	2.93	−2.45
5	2019	98.44	5.33	6.73	0.87	37	5.60	−1.15
5	2012	101.23	4.78	3.90	0.30	34	3.31	−0.54
4	2012	98.55	4.43	3.92	0.29	9	3.78	−0.23

Source: Scanrate and Reuters Danish Mortgage Backed Securities Model, October 1, 2002. Reproduced by permission of Scanrate Financial Systems.
* OAS: option-adjusted spread; OAD: option-adjusted duration; OAC: option-adjusted convexity.

in interest rates. At high levels of interest rates, the MBB behaves like a noncallable bond. However, when interest rates fall, borrowers start to prepay. As shown in Figure 10.1 not all borrowers prepay immediately, which allows for the MBB price to rise somewhat above par. However, when rates become low the MBB price will move toward the value of a very short term bond.

Traditional bond statistics like the yield to maturity and Macauley duration provided by the CSE assume zero prepayments and will not be able to capture the risk and return characteristics of these bonds. Instead investors use more complex statistics like prepayment (option) adjusted duration (OAD), which measures the relative change in price caused by a parallel shift in the underlying yield curve. Other widely used statistics are option-adjusted spread (OAS) and option-adjusted convexity (OAC). So-called delta equivalent cash flows and factor analysis are used in the calculation of, e.g., value-at-risk. Yet, these measures are confined to small changes in the underlying rates and they do not fully reflect the complex behavior of the bond price. To account for this, more and more investors turn to Monte Carlo simulation or scenario-based forecasts of total return.

Table 10.5 shows option-adjusted risk and return statistics for some large MBB issued by Realkredit Danmark. Note that for high-coupon bonds (7–8%) with high prepayment risk, there is a large difference between the OAD and the standard Macauley duration based on scheduled cash flow, while the two duration measures converge for low-coupon rates. The 8% bond has a negative OAD, which means that an increase in interest rate *increases* the value due to the reduced prepayment risk. OAC is negative for all MBBs. One should note that the numbers (and definitions) of option adjusted statistics vary somewhat between the different models used in the Danish bond market.

10.5 OTHER FIXED INCOME INSTRUMENTS

10.5.1 Corporate Bonds

The Danish corporate bonds are traded on the CSE. Corporate bonds are issued to raise capital, but only a few companies make use of this possibility. The size of the market for corporate bonds is very small compared to the markets for other kinds of fixed income securities in Denmark, only 2%. Also the absolute size is small; by the end of 2001 the market value of the outstanding corporate bonds amounts to DKK 25 854 million (US$3097 million). Since 1994, the market value of the corporate bonds has been increasing until 1998 after which it has decreased to its present value (Statistics Denmark, www.dst.dk). The traded corporate bonds are bullet bonds. The majority of these (68%) are issued with maturities between 6 and 10 years, and around a quarter have maturities below 5 years. The bulk of the traded bonds expire in less than 5 years (CSE, www.xcse.dk).

The largest part of the corporate bonds are issued by semigovernment organizations, i.e., government-related corporations (42%) of which the Oresund Bridge Syndicate accounts for around half of it.[10] The second-largest group of bonds is composed of foreign and international loans issued in DKK (35%). The third largest group of bonds are issued by financial institutions by way of loans issued as subordinated debt (19%). Other types of corporate bonds are traded in negligible amounts. The relative market value of the three types of corporate bonds is included in parenthesis (CSE, www.xcse.dk).

10.5.2 Fixed Income Derivatives

Since September 2001 trading in fixed income derivatives has been restricted to the OTC market. The supply side consists of just a few major financial institutions. Apart from being less liquid, the Danish OTC market is organized like other OTC markets, e.g. the US OTC market. At the end of 2001 the notional amount of the outstanding OTC interest rate swaps was DKK 693 billion (US$83 billion) and the gross market value amounted to DKK 8.4 billion (US$1 billion).[11] Compared to the two previous years the size of the market has been reduced to around a quarter. This is due to the increased use of euro interest rate derivatives.

Overall, the fixed income derivatives can be divided into three categories: Swaps, plain vanilla option contracts, and exotic option contracts. The vast majority of the traded derivatives are interest rate swaps. Companies and financial institutions use interest rate swaps to hedge floating rate loans. The floating rate payments occur semiannually, whereas, the fixed-rate payments take place annually. The day count convention is also different for the floating-rate and the fixed-rate payments, actual/360 and 30/360, respectively. Swaps with maturities from 6 months to 30 years are quoted.

Plain vanilla contracts include caps, floors, and swaptions. These contracts serve the same hedging purposes as interest rate swaps. Plain vanillas as well as exotic contracts are mainly traded as embedded contracts as part of financial packages. The plain vanilla contracts have maturities up to 10 years, and the underlying swaps for the swaptions have maturities up to 25 years.

The smallest part of the fixed income derivatives market is made up of exotic contracts, including Bermudan options, digital options, CMS (constant maturity swap) floors, and average-rate caps. The exotic contracts are used to hedge the prepayment risk of mortgage-backed securities, for instance by the own investing portfolios departments of financial institutions.

---

[10] The Oresund Bridge is the bridge connecting Denmark and Sweden.

[11] The Bank for International Settlements (2002) contains the data on the size of the Danish OTC interest rate market (Statistical appendix, Table 21B).

10.6 MARKET PARTICIPANTS, REGULATION, AND TRADING

At the formal level, the CSE organizes trading in exchange listed Danish stocks, bonds, and derivatives. A summary of bond market turnover is given in Table 10.2.

The total turnover of Danish bonds in 2001 was DKK 6102 billion (US$731 billion). Treasury securities are the most traded with a turnover rate (turnover/market value) of 3.93 for bonds and 2.78 for bills. The turnover in mortgage credit bonds is also substantial, although this number changes a lot over time depending on the need for refinancing of mortgage loans.

10.6.1 Important Investors on the Danish Bond Market

Table 10.6 indicates the ownership distribution for the Danish bond market. The market is dominated by institutional and public sector investors who own more than 67%. Foreign investors account for 32% of the government bond market, but just 11% of the mortgage bond market, in total 17%. Overall, the direct holdings by households are just 7%, but they hold a relatively large share of other bonds (27%), probably due to the low coupon rates on most corporate bonds and therefore better after-tax returns.

10.6.2 The Primary Market for Danish Exchange-Traded Bonds

The Danish Central Bank uses the infrastructure of the CSE for both its secondary market offerings (tap-sale) as well as the opening auctions conducted in certain issues. The secondary market for bonds is essentially a multiple dealer market supported by the trading system Saxess.

The Saxess trading system is the joint trading system of the Norex alliance of exchanges; the exchanges in Oslo, Stockholm, and Reykjavik are also members of the group. The trading system Saxess, originally developed for equity trading, was introduced in 1999 in Copenhagen and Stockholm. The bond market in Copenhagen was moved to Saxess in the fall of 2000.

There is no primary dealer function on the Danish Treasury market. Certain members of the CSE are allowed to buy new issues directly from the central bank. The system resembles a primary dealer system, but there are no special obligations or privileges linked to the function as buyer in this market (Danish Central Bank, 2002).

Table 10.6 Ownership distribution of Danish bonds at the end of 2001

Owner category	Govt bonds (%)	Mortgage backed (%)	Other bonds (%)	Total (%)
Financial institutions	25	39	37	35
Insurance and pension	12	25	20	21
Public sector	22	7	4	11
Other trades	5	7	3	6
Households	2	7	27	7
Foreign investors	32	11	5	17
Unknown	3	3	2	3
Total nominal outstanding value (DKK billion)	628.3	1445.6	138.3	2212.2

Source: Association of Danish Mortgage Banks, Annual Report, 2001 (Table 3).

10.6.2.1   Government Bonds

The procedure for public offerings of Treasury securities is different for bills and bonds. Treasury bills are issued in a standard uniform price auction with pro-rata sharing for equal bids at the closing yield. Information on the offered issues and other conditions are published together with the announcement of the auction date, which is normally the second-last trading day of every month. Members of the CSE and counter parties in the Danish central bank's market operations are eligible to submit bids to the auction. Bidders submit their bids (quoted in yields to 2 decimals) electronically before 11:30 a.m. on the day of the auction, and the result is published at 12:00 noon on the same day. Bids are received for all Treasury bills with time to maturity 3 months or less. This electronic system is a subsystem of the Saxess.

The primary market for Treasury bonds is quite different from the typical auctions structure used in many markets (United States and Sweden, for example). There is an opening auction for new issues, but the majority of the public offerings are issued through so-called tap-sales; that is, even after the initial opening of a new Treasury bond additional offerings will be submitted to the Saxess order book. It is the stated belief of the central bank and the Ministry of Finance that the tap-sale, which is internationally unique, reduces the overall debt financing costs of the Danish government by reducing under-pricing and by allowing for a better match between financing needs and bond issuance. The opening auction for a new issue is conducted within 1–2 weeks after the announcement of the new security. The announcement message gives details about maturity, coupon, and opening day, but no volume indication is announced.

On the day of the auction the central bank announces an upper limit on the size of the day's offering. Technically, the offering is submitted as a limit sell-order to the Saxess order book. The central bank announces the exact time at which the offer will be submitted, but the limit price is not known until the time of the order submission. In the minutes and seconds before, bidders submit their bids as limit buy-orders to the Saxess order book. The order book is completely transparent with full identification of all bids with size and price. Therefore, the central bank is able to see the full demand curve, although there is a hidden-order function that can be used to hide some of the depth. Round lots are for DKK 1 million principal.

The auction is concluded by automatic order match using price and time priority. From a technical point of view this is not a genuine call auction. Rather, it is a continuous auction completed over a short time interval. This implies that the auction is a discriminatory price auction (in contrast with the auction format for Treasury bills, which is uniform).

10.6.2.2   Mortgage-Backed Bonds

The primary offering of callable mortgage bonds is conducted as tap-sales. The mortgage institution issues a loan to the debtor and funds the loan by selling bonds directly into the market. Thus, as a general rule, the primary market is completely intertwined with the secondary market, and new issues are traded exactly the same way as in the secondary market.

The same procedure is used for the initial funding of mortgage loans based on short term noncallable bonds. However, at redemption new bonds must be issued to fund the remaining principal on the loans. The two largest mortgage institutions issue new bonds in much the same way as Treasury bills (cf. Section 10.3.2.1) at an annual auction held in December. Bids are solicited from members of the CSE and posted into the electronic *issuing* system at the CSE. The auction is a uniform price auction.

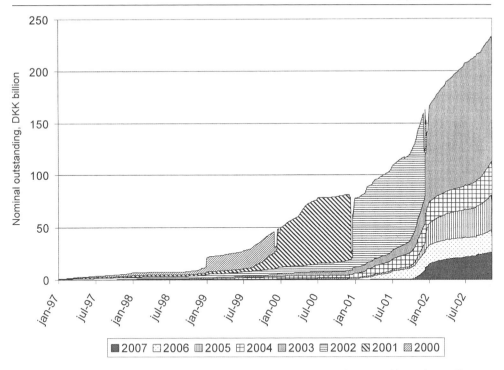

Figure 10.3 Nominal value outstanding of noncallable mortgage bonds grouped by end year (January 1997 to November 2002). The sum is taken across all mortgage credit institutions. Includes DKK denominated bonds only. Bonds maturing after 2007 are not shown (<DKK 3 billion)
Source: Scanrate Financial System based on CSE.

Figure 10.3 shows the daily time series of nominal amounts outstanding for all noncallable mortgage bonds grouped by end year. For the series "2002" ending January 1, 2002, the outstanding amount increases by new tap-sales up until December 2000, when the auction held to refinance the 2001 issue results in a sharp increase in outstanding amount. New tap-sales occur and finally, in December 2001 the loan is refinanced using the 2003 and longer term bond series.

10.6.3   The Secondary Market for Trading in Danish Bonds

The secondary market for Danish bonds is at the formal level organized as an electronic exchange by the CSE. Limit buy and sell-orders can be routed to the order book. Trades are concluded by accept match, i.e., by a member's direct accept of an order. Orders can be fully or partially accepted although order qualifications (all-or-none for example) are allowed. Orders can be partially, but not fully, hidden. In contrast to the issuing markets, the continuous market displays member identification on the screens. The accept match function in the order book facilitates the dealer market by avoiding the strict price/time priority used for equity trading.

Round lots are DKK 1 million principal value for benchmark bonds, while it is DKK 0.1 million for others. Thus, the exchange market for bonds is primarily confined to professional and institutional investors. Private investors buy bonds in the retail market organized by the banks. Most banks have electronic systems, which support online trade in bonds at prices quoted by the bank but subject to best execution regulation. Retail trades, as all other off-market trades, must be reported to and are broadcasted by the CSE to the market.

In addition to execution via the order book, traders may negotiate and conclude trades bilaterally by telephone contacts. In practice, and historically, most trading has been executed as off-exchange trade. In this respect the Danish bond market is not very different from other markets. Retail trades (formal limit DKK 3 million market value) are subject to best execution regulation. The most direct and testable condition is that trades must be executed at prices equal to or better than prices in the order book at the time of trade.

There are two market maker arrangements in the Danish bond market. One of them is organized by the Danish Securities Dealers Association ("Børsmæglerforeningen") and the other by the CSE. Both are quote-on-request arrangements in the telephone market. There is no formal market making in the electronic trading system. The CSE market maker arrangement is confined to the 10-year Treasury bond, while the arrangement by the Danish Securities Dealer Association is for a broader selection of Treasury securities.

10.6.4 Regulators of the Danish Bond Market

The Danish bond market is regulated at different levels. At the most detailed level, the CSE "market surveillance unit" monitors the trading process on the exchange, most notably trying to prevent market manipulation and insider trading. At the more general level, the Danish Financial Supervisory Authority ("Finanstilsynet") monitors solvency in financial institutions. The Financial Supervisory Authority acts according to different laws passed in the Danish parliament ("Folketinget"). The Securities Council ("Fondsrådet") issues regulation on general market quality, e.g., regulation on off-market trading in non-Danish securities and investor protection (e.g. best execution rules). The Danish Central Bank ("Danmarks Nationalbank") is responsible for the overall financial stability; that is it monitors how the macroeconomic environment affects bond markets, e.g., credit policies and leverage in the banking sector may have an effect on financial stability. Declining interest rates affect the risk of pension funds having issued rate-guaranteed liabilities.

In 1983, and as a world-first, all listed Danish bonds were converted from being physical securities to electronic book-entries at the Central Securities Center ("Værdipapircentralen"). All listed shares were converted to electronic form in 1988. The Central Securities Center undertakes the clearing and settlement of all securities traded at the CSE.

10.6.5 Market Conventions

The typical market convention for all Danish bonds (except Treasury bills) is for settlement after trade plus 3 business days. The Danish holiday calendar is used. Quotes are given as clean prices less accrued interest, which is calculated using actual/actual day basis. The yield to maturity is quoted using yearly compounding. The settlement of Treasury bills is trade day plus 2 business days.

REFERENCES

Association of Danish Mortgage Banks ("Realkreditrådet") (2001). Annual Report 2001.

Association of Danish Mortgage Banks ("Realkreditrådet"). www.realkreditraadet.dk.

Association of Danish Mortgage Banks ("Realkreditrådet") (1999). *Mortgage Financing in Denmark.*

Bank for International Settlements. (2002, June). *Quarterly Review*.

CSE ("Københavns Fondsbørs"). www.xcse.dk.

Danish Central Bank ("Nationalbanken") (2002). *Danish Government Borrowing and Debt 2001*.

Danish Central Bank ("Nationalbanken"). *www.nationalbanken.dk*.

Danske Bank Research (2001). *Danish Mortgage Bonds – A Market Description*.

European Mortgage Federation (2002). *Quarterly Figures* 31(2) pp. 1–4.

Ministry of Finance (2002, May). *Den Økonomiske Redegørelse*.

Moody's (2002). *Danish Mortgage Bonds (Realkreditobligationer): Highly Secure Financial Instruments*.

Statistics Denmark (Danmarks Statistik). www.dst.dk.

11

An Empirical Study of the Term Structure of Interest Rates in Denmark (1993–2002)

CHARLOTTE CHRISTIANSEN, TOM ENGSTED, SVEND JAKOBSEN, AND CARSTEN TANGGAARD

11.1 INTRODUCTION

In this chapter we investigate the term structure of interest rates in Denmark over the period 1993–2002 using monthly observations on zero-coupon rates, with maturities ranging from 3 months to 10 years. In particular, the Expectations Hypothesis of the Term Structure (EHTS) will be tested using cointegration techniques and regressions and vector-autoregressions involving changes in interest rates and yield spreads, and yield spread's ability to predict future interest rates over various horizons will be examined.

The term structure of interest rates is important for various reasons. First, it is related to the notion of "informational efficiency" of the bond and money markets: Are there profitable arbitrage possibilities to be exploited in these markets? Second, the relation between short- and long-interest rates is important for the transmission mechanism of monetary policy: The monetary authorities control the short rate, and only if there is a stable relation between short and long rates will the authorities also be able to control long rates and thereby influence real economic activity. Third, the spread between long and short rates may contain useful information about future interest rates, inflation, and real economic activity. For example, the monetary authorities and policy makers may be able to use the yield spread as an indicator of the inflationary pressures in the economy. Finally, the term structure of interest rates is important for mortgage financing: If the slope of the yield curve is on average positive, real estate owners may find it optimal to finance their houses using short term bonds instead of long term bonds.

A number of earlier studies have analyzed the Danish term structure during the 1970s, 1980s, and the beginning of the 1990s, but research using recent data has been quite limited. The purpose of this chapter is to fill this gap. Gerlach and Smets (1997) do not reject the EHTS for Denmark using data from 1977 to 1993. Engsted and Tanggaard (1995) and Engsted (1996) find that over the period 1976–1993 the EHTS is generally rejected, but they also find that in those periods when the Danish Central Bank has allowed interest rates to be very volatile, either through money supply targeting (as in the period up to the mid-1980s) or in specific attempts to support the Danish currency (as in the 1992–1993 EMS (European Monetary System) currency crisis), several of the implications of the EHTS are in fact borne out in the data. In particular, yield spreads predict short term interest rates in the direction implied

European Fixed Income Markets: Money, Bond and Interest Rate Derivatives. Edited by J.A. Batten,
T.A. Fetherston and P.G. Szilagyi. © 2004 John Wiley & Sons, Ltd. ISBN 0-470-85053-1

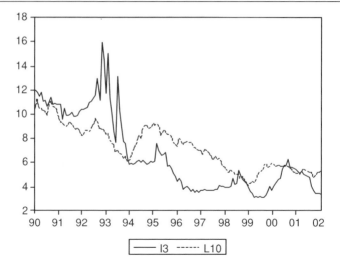

Figure 11.1   Three-month and 10-year interest rates (1990–2002).

by the hypothesis. Engsted and Nyholm (2000) document formally, using a Markov regime switching approach, that important changes in the Danish term structure have taken place during the period from 1976 to 1997.

The EMS crisis in 1992–1993 resulted in dramatic increases in short term Danish interest rates (see Figure 11.1), and this period clearly stands out as "unusual." Since October 1993 no abrupt changes in the Danish term structure seem to have taken place. The 3-month rate has fluctuated in the range from 3% to 8%, while the 10-year rate has fluctuated between 4% and 9%. In most periods the long rate has been above the short rate, i.e., on average the slope of the yield curve has been positive. In Section 11.3 we investigate in more detail the relationship between interest rates at various maturities since October 1993. We use cointegration methods to test for a one-to-one long-run relationship between short and long term interest rates, and we test the EHTS with a constant term premium using yield spread regressions and vector-autoregressions.

Our main results can be summarized as follows: Yields at the short end of the maturity spectrum are highly correlated and interest rate spreads predict future interest rates in the direction implied by the EHTS. Longer term interest rates, however, do not behave in accordance with the EHTS. Thus, the long end of the term structure seems to be segmented from the short end.

11.2   THE EHTS AND ITS TESTABLE IMPLICATIONS

The EHTS can be stated in linearized form as (c.f. Campbell and Shiller, 1991)

$$R_{n,t} = \frac{1}{k} \sum_{i=0}^{k-1} E_t R_{m,t+mi} + c(n, m), \qquad k = \frac{n}{m}, \quad n > m \qquad (1)$$

where $R_{n,t}$ and $R_{m,t}$ are n-period and m-period zero-coupon bond yields, respectively, and $c(n,m)$ is a term premium that is assumed time-invariant but maturity-dependent. E_t is the expectational operator conditional on information at time t. The long rate is set in the market as a simple average of expected future short rates plus a term premium.

The EHTS can also be formulated as an equation relating the spread between long and short rates, $S_{(n,m),t} = R_{n,t} - R_{m,t}$, to expected future changes in either short rates or long rates:

$$S_{(n,m),t} = \sum_{i=1}^{(n-m)/m} \frac{n-mi}{n} (R_{m,t+mi} - R_{m,t+m(i-1)}) + c(n,m), \tag{2}$$

$$S_{(n,m),t} = \frac{n-m}{m} (R_{n-m,t+m} - R_{n,t}) + c(n,m). \tag{3}$$

According to (2), if the term premium in constant, the spread between the n-period and m-period rate should predict a weighted average of changes in m-period rates over n periods. Similarly, according to (3) the spread should predict the m-period change in the n-period rate. Thus, loosely speaking, according to the EHTS, the interest rate spread reflects (apart from a term premium) market expectations of changes in the short rate over the life of the long bond as well as changes in the long rate of the life of the short bond.

Nominal interest rates are usually found to be highly persistent and close to nonstationary. Although it could be argued that in theory interest rates must be stationary (see Footnote 1 later), in a finite sample it will often be better to approximate interest rates as nonstationary processes. If interest rates are regarded as integrated of order one, I(1), then Equations (2) and (3) show that interest rate spreads will be stationary, I(0), if the EHTS holds. This means that interest rates of different maturity must *cointegrate* as suggested by Engle and Granger (1987), such that the term structure is driven by one common stochastic trend. In a system of $p > 2$ interest rates, stationary bivariate spreads imply that there should be $p - 1$ cointegrating vectors, and in each of these vectors the coefficients should sum to zero (see Engsted and Tanggaard, 1994a; Hall *et al.*, 1992).

In the next section these cointegration implications of the EHTS will be tested on the Danish data.[1] In addition, it will be investigated whether interest rate spreads have predictive power for future interest rate changes in accordance with (2) and (3). These equations can be tested by running the following two regressions

$$\sum_{i=1}^{(n-m)/m} \frac{n-mi}{n} (R_{m,t+mi} - R_{m,t+m(i-1)}) = a + bS_{(n,m),t} + e_{1,t+n-m} \tag{4}$$

$$\frac{n-m}{m} (R_{n-m,t+m} - R_{n,t}) = a + bS_{(n,m),t} + e_{2,t+m}. \tag{5}$$

Under the EHTS, slope coefficients b should equal unity. In addition, the estimates of a provide information on the sign and size of the time-invariant but maturity-dependent term premia.[2] Under the EHTS and rational expectations, the error terms in (4) and (5) are pure rational forecast errors uncorrelated with information at time t. Thus, $e_{1,t+n-m}$ and $e_{2,t+m}$ are uncorrelated with the regressor $S_{(n,m),t}$, such that simple OLS can be used to estimate a and b. However, because of the time overlap (when $n - m > 1$ in (4) and $m > 1$ in (5)), the error terms are serially correlated, which has to be taken into account when computing the standard errors of the estimates. $e_{1,t+n-m}$ will be MA($n - m - 1$) and $e_{2,t+m}$ will be MA($m - 1$). The GMM

---

[1] Pagan et al. (1996) and Taulbjerg (2001a) show that when interest rates are nonstationary, more general exponential affine arbitrage-free models of the term structure do not necessarily imply that yield spreads are stationary. An intriguing and subtle issue, however, is to what extent the assumption of nonstationary interest rates is consistent with the arbitrage-free framework.

[2] On US data, $b = 1$ is typically rejected. Roberds and Whitemann (1999), Taulbjerg (2001b), and Dai and Singleton (2002) investigate whether this rejection can be explained by a general class of affine arbitrage-free term structure models.

(generalized method of moments) procedures in Hansen (1982) and Newey and West (1987) are standard ways of correcting for this moving-average structure of the errors.

A major drawback of the above procedure is that when n becomes large relative to m in (4), and when m becomes large in (5), the degree of time overlap becomes large and, hence, the error terms become long moving-average processes. This has the unfortunate implication that the Hansen (1982) and Newey and West (1987) corrections become very unreliable (see, e.g. Hodrick, 1992; Richardson and Stock, 1989). In addition, the effective number of observations used in estimating (4) and (5) is substantially reduced when n and m are large. These problems are especially pronounced for Equation (4) because often one wants to investigate the relationship between a quite long interest rate, e.g. a 5- or 10-year rate, and a short term rate, e.g. a 1-month or 3-month rate. In that case the effective sample size is dramatically reduced and the order of the MA error becomes extremely high, making regression (4) more or less dubious.

Campbell and Shiller (1991) have suggested an alternative way of examining the spread's predictive power for future short-rate changes, that does not have these drawbacks. The idea is to set up a vector-autoregression (VAR) for the two variables $S_{(n,m),t}$ and $\Delta R_{m,t}$ (Δ is the first-difference operator), and then use the estimated VAR parameters to generate a forecast of the weighted average of changes in future short rates in accordance with the right-hand side of Equation (2). If this so-called "theoretical" spread shows a high degree of comovement with the actual spread, then variation in the actual spread to a large extent reflects the market's changing assessment of future short rates. The VAR-model does not contain any time-overlapping variables, and usually in empirical work a limited number of lags is required to obtain a well-specified system. Thus, in contrast to the procedure based on Equation (4), the effective sample size is not dramatically reduced when n becomes large, and Hodrick (1992) has shown that inference based on the VAR approach generally is much more reliable than inference based on (4).

The "theoretical" spread is generated as follows: Denote by Z_t the vector containing the two variables $\Delta R_{m,t}$ and $S_{(n,m),t}$, and let A be the VAR parameter matrix. A first-order VAR model for Z_t is written as $Z_t = A Z_{t-1} + u_t$.[3] By projecting the right-hand side of (2) onto Z_t, the "theoretical" spread is obtained as (see Campbell and Shiller, 1991, for details)

$$S'_{(n,m),t} = hA\left[I - \frac{m}{n}(I - A^n)(I - A^m)^{-1}\right](I - A)^{-1}Z_t, \tag{6}$$

where h is a row vector that picks out $\Delta R_{m,t}$ from the VAR, and I is the identity matrix. The degree of comovement of $S_{(n,m),t}$ and $S'_{(n,m),t}$ is usually measured by their pairwise correlation and by the ratio of their standard deviations.

11.3   EMPIRICAL RESULTS FOR DENMARK (1993–2002)

The interest rate data to be used in this section are monthly observations from 1993 to 2002 on zero-coupon bond yields from the Danish bond market. As in most other countries zero-coupon bonds exist only for maturities up to 1 year. Thus, yields for longer term bonds must be calculated using either cubic spline interpolation techniques (e.g., McCulloch, 1975; Nelson and Siegel, 1987) or nonparametric smoothing techniques (e.g., Linton et al., 2001; Tanggaard, 1997). The data in this study are from the Danish financial database "Børsdatabasen," which is located at the Aarhus School of Business. The zero-coupon yields are computed using the Tanggaard (1997) technique, and the maturities range from 3 months to 10 years.

---

[3] The extension to models with more than one lag is straightforward using the so-called *companion form*.

Table 11.1 Augmented Dickey–Fuller tests for unit roots

R_3	R_6	R_9	R_{12}	R_{24}	R_{60}	R_{120}
-1.97	-1.66	-1.72	-1.72	-1.88	-1.93	-1.36
$S_{(6,3)}$	$S_{(9,3)}$	$S_{(12,3)}$	$S_{(24,3)}$	$S_{(60,3)}$	$S_{(120,3)}$	
-3.33	-4.21	-4.24	-4.13	-3.25	-2.73	
$S_{(12,6)}$	$S_{(24,6)}$	$S_{(60,6)}$	$S_{(120,6)}$			
-3.91	-3.76	-2.77	-2.34			
$S_{(24,12)}$	$S_{(60,12)}$	$S_{(120,12)}$				
-3.41	-2.38	-2.14				
$S_{(60,24)}$	$S_{(120,24)}$					
-1.98	-1.92					
$S_{(120,60)}$						
-1.63						

Note: The ADF regressions contain a constant term and four augmentation lags. The 5% critical value is -2.89 (computed using Table 1 in MacKinnon, 1991).

The starting point of the sample is chosen to be October 1993. This is because in the period from the summer of 1992 to the summer of 1993 the EMS currency crisis implied a huge pressure on the Danish currency, which was supported by the Danish Central Bank through severe increases in the short term money market rate. This had a direct effect on the 3-month yield, which rose from 10% to 16% (see Figure 11.1). Thus, the relationship between short- and long-interest rates was dramatically disturbed during this short period. Engsted and Nyholm (2000) document formally the regime shift in the Danish term structure during the 1992–1993 period.

Table 11.1 reports tests for unit roots in individual interest rates and in spreads between interest rates of different maturities. As seen, Augmented Dickey–Fuller tests clearly indicate that interest rates are nonstationary, I(1). At the short end of the term structure (maturities up to 2 years), spreads are found to be stationary, I(0). This is in accordance with the EHTS. However, at the long end of the term structure, ADF tests cannot at a 5% level reject the hypothesis that spreads are I(1). It is noteworthy that even the spread between the 10-year yield and the 5-year yield seems to be nonstationary. These results indicate that the Danish term structure over the period 1993–2002 has been driven by not just a single common trend, but by several nonstationary or nearly nonstationary factors.

Further insight into this can be gained by analyzing all yields jointly in Johansen's multivariate vector error-correction (VECM) framework (Johansen, 1991). Denote by X_t the $(q \times 1)$ vector of yields with 3 month-, 6 month-, 9 month-, 1 year-, 2 year-, 5 year-, and 10 year-maturity, i.e. $q = 7$. The VECM for X_t can be written as

$$\Delta X_t = \mu + \Gamma_1 \Delta X_{t-1} + \cdots + \Gamma_{p-1} \Delta X_{t-p+1} + \Pi X_{t-1} + \varepsilon_t \qquad (7)$$

where Γ_i and Π are $(q \times q)$ coefficient matrices. Cointegration implies that the matrix Π has reduced rank, $r < q$. Tests for the cointegrating rank can be done using either the *maximal eigenvalue* test $\lambda_{\max}$, or the *trace* test λ_{trace}. Under cointegration, Π can be factorized as $\Pi = \alpha \beta'$, where β is the $(q \times r)$ matrix containing the r cointegrating vectors among the q variables, and α is the corresponding $(q \times r)$ matrix of factor loadings (error-correction parameters).

Table 11.2   Johansen cointegration analysis of the
seven-variable system containing the 3-month, 6-month,
9-month, 1-year, 2-year, 5-year, and 10-year interest rates

Hypothesis	Eigenvalue	λ_{max}	λ_{trace}
$r \leq 7$	0.47	60.83	183.85
$r \leq 6$	0.37	45.29	123.03
$r \leq 5$	0.28	32.09	77.73
$r \leq 4$	0.21	23.14	45.64
$r \leq 3$	0.14	14.07	22.50
$r \leq 2$	0.07	7.29	8.43
$r \leq 1$	0.01	1.14	1.14

Note: Based on a VAR model with two lags. The 10% critical values
for the λ_{max} test are 29.54 ($r \leq 7$); 25.51 ($r \leq 6$); 21.74 ($r \leq 5$);
18.03 ($r \leq 4$); 14.09 ($r \leq 3$); 10.29 ($r \leq 2$); 7.50 ($r \leq 1$). The 10%
critical values for the λ_{trace} test are 126.71 ($r \leq 7$); 97.17 ($r \leq 6$);
71.66 ($r \leq 5$); 49.92 ($r \leq 4$); 31.88 ($r \leq 3$); 17.79 ($r \leq 2$); 7.50
($r \leq 1$). The estimation is done using the "CATS in RATS" program
(Hansen and Juselius, 1995), which also supplies the critical values.

Table 11.3   Johansen cointegration analysis of the
four-variable system containing the 3-month, 6-month,
9-month, and 1-year interest rates

Hypothesis	Eigenvalue	λ_{max}	λ_{trace}
$r \leq 4$	0.31	35.30	71.91
$r \leq 3$	0.20	22.01	36.62
$r \leq 2$	0.11	11.84	14.61
$r \leq 1$	0.03	2.77	2.77

Note: Based on a VAR model with two lags. The 10% critical values
for the tests are identical to those in Table 11.2.

Maximum likelihood estimation of α and β is obtained by a series of reduced rank regressions
(see Johansen, 1991, for details).

The EHTS implies that $r = q - 1$. In addition, the cointegration space should be spanned
by the columns of the matrix

$$H = \begin{bmatrix} 1 & 1 & 1 & \cdots & 1 \\ -1 & 0 & 0 & \cdots & 0 \\ 0 & -1 & 0 & \cdots & 0 \\ \vdots & \vdots & \vdots & \cdots & \vdots \\ 0 & 0 & 0 & \cdots & -1 \end{bmatrix}$$

such that bivariate interest rate spreads are stationary. Within the Johansen approach this zero-
sum restriction on β can be tested by likelihood ratio tests using the standard χ^2 asymptotic
distribution.

Table 11.2 contains the results of the Johansen analysis. In the system of seven interest
rates, three or four significant cointegrating vectors are found, depending on whether the λ_{max}
or λ_{trace} test is used. This implies that the term structure is driven by more than one common
stochastic trend. In Tables 11.3–11.5 subsystems containing fewer interest rates are analyzed.

Table 11.4 Estimated cointegrating vectors for the four-variable system containing the 3-month, 6-month, 9-month, and 1-year interest rates

R_3	R_6	R_9	R_{12}	Constant
1.000	−0.466	−2.906	2.386	−0.093
1.000	−2.922	1.724	0.230	−0.311
1.000	1.455	−17.802	14.929	1.363

Note: The vectors have been normalized by the coefficient to the 3-month rate. The $\chi^2(3)$ test is a joint test for the hypothesis that the interest rate coefficients in each of the vectors sum to zero. $\chi^2(3)$ test: 4.65 (p value = 0.20).

Table 11.5 Johansen cointegration analysis of the three-variable system containing the 2-year, 5-year, and 10-year interest rates

Hypothesis	Eigenvalue	λ_{max}	λ_{trace}
$r \leq 3$	0.12	12.63	17.81
$r \leq 2$	0.04	4.02	5.18
$r \leq 1$	0.01	1.16	1.16

Note: Based on a VAR model with two lags. The 10% critical values for the tests are identical to those in Table 11.2.

Tables 11.3 and 11.4 report the results for a four-variable system containing yields at the short end of the maturity spectrum: 3-month, 6-month, 9-month, and 1-year yields. Table 11.5 reports results for a system containing the three longer term yields: 2-year, 5-year, and 10-year yields. Table 11.3 shows that among the four short term rates, three cointegrating vectors are found by the λ_{max} test, meaning that the four yields are driven by one common trend.[4] The three estimated cointegrating vectors are shown in Table 11.4. As seen, the EHTS restriction that the coefficients in each of the three vectors should sum to zero is close to being fulfilled, and the $\chi^2(3)$ test of the zero-sum restriction on the three vectors does not reject the hypothesis at significance levels below 20%. Thus, in full accordance with the univariate tests in Table 11.1, spreads at the short end of the term structure are found to be stationary.

For the system in Table 11.5, no cointegration is found, which means that each of the three longer term yields is driven by its own stochastic trend.

Taken together, the results in Tables 11.1–11.5 indicate that over the period 1993–2002, the Danish term structure has been segmented into yields at the short end of the maturity spectrum, where interest rates are closely tied together such that pairwise spreads are stationary in accordance with the EHTS, and yields at the long end of the maturity spectrum, where long term interest rates are unrelated not only to short term rates, but also to other long term rates. This is quite similar to what Engsted and Tanggaard (1994b) found for the earlier period 1985–1991.

Tables 11.6 reports results based on the predictive regressions (4) and (5). Because of the problems with time overlap when n becomes large, (4) will only be run for n equal to or less than 12 months (1 year) such that the maximum order of the MA error process is 8. For $n > 12$

---

[4] If we add the 2-year yield to this system, the λ_{max} test indicates the presence of two common trends (details are available upon request). Thus, Johansens cointegration analysis does not support the findings from the univariate tests in Table 11.1 that spreads between the 2-year yield and yields with less than 2 years to maturity are stationary.

Table 11.6 Estimates of a and b in Equations (4) and (5)

	$m = 3$		$m = 6$	
n	a	b	a	b
Eq. (4):				
6	−0.080 (0.047)	0.728 (0.230)		
9	−0.207 (0.092)	0.977 (0.236)		
12	−0.260 (0.150)	0.888 (0.257)	−0.191 (0.101)	0.869 (0.289)
Eq. (5):				
6	−0.159 (0.095)	0.456 (0.460)		
9	−0.461 (0.164)	0.954 (0.610)		
12	−0.527 (0.272)	0.861 (0.657)	−0.383 (0.203)	0.737 (0.577)
24	−0.763 (0.765)	0.962 (0.843)		
60	−0.189 (2.460)	−0.477 (1.460)	1.419 (3.065)	−2.294 (1.550)
120	2.729 (5.497)	−2.411 (1.923)	5.759 (6.975)	−4.469 (2.263)

Note: The numbers in parentheses are heteroscedasticity-and autocorrelation-consistent standard errors. In Equation (5), for $n \geq 60$ months, $R_{n-m,t}$ will be approximated by $R_{n,t}$.

Table 11.7 The comovement between actual and "theoretical" spreads

n	$m = 3$	$m = 6$	$m = 12$	$m = 24$	$m = 60$
6	0.870				
	0.705				
9	0.929				
	0.918				
12	0.937	0.816			
	0.869	0.871			
24	0.911	0.712	0.061		
	0.704	0.609	0.637		
60	0.867	0.475	−0.345		
	0.484	0.347	0.446		
120	0.921	0.730	0.151	0.018	0.357
	0.351	0.206	0.184	0.204	0.385

Note: Based on VAR models with four lags, and where the variables are measured in deviations from their sample means. The first number in each cell is the correlation between actual and theoretical spreads, where the latter is computed as in Equation (6). The second number in each cell is the ratio of the standard deviation of the theoretical spread to the standard deviation of the actual spread.

months, the VAR approach will be used instead to examine yield spreads predictive power for short term interest rates (c.f. Table 11.7 below). Similarly, regression (5) will only be run with m equal to or less than 6 months, such that the maximum order of the MA error process is 5.

Table 11.6 shows that interest rate spreads at the short end of the maturity spectrum have strong predictive power for future short-rate changes: the b coefficients are statistically significant, close to unity and, in fact, not significantly different from unity. Thus, the spread between the n- and the m-period rates predicts changes in the m-period rate with the direction and magnitude in accordance with the EHTS. At the short end of the maturity spectrum spreads also predict changes in n-period rates in accordance with the EHTS: b coefficients are also here close to unity, but standard errors are quite large so none of the coefficients are statistically significant. When n is increased to 5 or 10 years, the b estimates become negative. Thus, with long maturities yield spreads predict future long-rate changes in the direction opposite to that implied by the EHTS. When $b = 1$, the a values in Table 11.6 are estimates of (minus) the time-invariant but maturity-dependent term premium, $c(n,m)$. As seen, term premia are positive and rising with the maturity of the long bond, in full accordance with conventional wisdom.

Table 11.7 reports correlation coefficients and standard deviation ratios between actual yield spreads and "theoretical" yield spreads, where the latter are computed as in (6) based on VAR models for $\Delta R_{m,t}$ and $S_{(n,m),t}$. At the short end of the term structure, actual and theoretical spreads move closely together over time, indicating – in accordance with the results in Table 11.6 – that variation in the spread mainly reflects the market's changing expectations of future short rates, with time-varying term premia playing a minor role. At the long end of the term structure, however, the theoretical spread varies much less than – and is less correlated with – the actual spread, which implies that the long–short yield spread to a lesser extent reflects expectations of future short-rate changes. Here, variation in term premia are more important. Figures 11.2 and 11.3 show graphs of actual and theoretical spreads for the two systems with 1-year and 3-month rates, and 10-year and 3-month rates, respectively.[5]

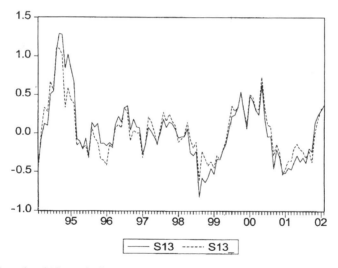

Figure 11.2   Actual and 'theoretical' spreads (demeaned), 1-year minus 3-month.

---

[5] The EHTS implies that $S_{(n,m)}$ should Granger cause ΔR_m in the VAR models, such that the sum of the $S_{(n,m)}$ coefficients in the ΔR_m equation is positive and significant. This Granger-causality implication is supported in the VAR systems when n is equal to or less than 2 years, but not in the models where $n > 2$ years (details are available upon request). This supports the conclusion that the EHTS holds at short maturities but not at long maturities.

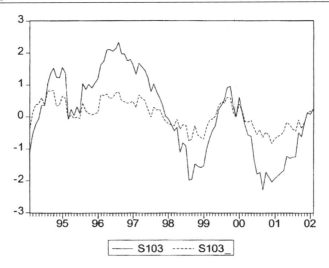

Figure 11.3   Actual and 'theoretical' spreads (demeaned), 10-year minus 3-month.

11.4   CONCLUDING REMARKS

The results in the present chapter suggest that since the EMS currency crisis in 1992–1993, the Danish term structure of interest rates has been more or less segmented into two groups. The first group contains interest rates at the short end of the market (maturities up to 1 or 2 years), where rates are closely related (cointegrated), and where yield spreads are unbiased and significant predictors of future short rates and unbiased (though insignificant) predictors of future long rates. In fact, at the short end of the maturity spectrum the EHTS with constant term premia cannot be rejected.[6] The second group contains long term interest rates (maturities of 2 years and more), and for this group, by contrast, the EHTS is strongly rejected: long rates are not highly correlated with short rates or with other long rates, and long–short spreads do not signal future changes in neither short nor long rates.

A direct implication of these findings is that the Danish policy makers and monetary authorities may find it quite difficult to control long term interest rates by manipulating short term rates with the purpose of influencing real economic activity. Traditionally this has been one of the standard goals of monetary policy, but as explained in the previous chapter, in recent years the main goal of the Danish monetary authorities has been to support the Danish currency, and concerns about economic growth and unemployment have not been a part of Danish monetary policy. Our results lend direct support to continuing abstracting from these issues in the conduct of monetary policy.

REFERENCES

Campbell, J.Y. and R.J. Shiller (1991). Yield Spreads and Interest Rate Movements: A Birds Eye View. *Review of Economic Studies* **58**: 495–514.

Dai, Q. and K.J. Singleton (2002). Expectation Puzzles, Time-Varying Risk Premia, and Affine Models of the Term Structure. *Journal of Financial Economics* **63**: 415–441.

---

[6] This stands in contrast to the results reported by Engsted and Tanggaard (1995) for the period 1985–1991: Here the EHTS was strongly rejected, also at the short end of the term structure.

Engle, R.F. and C.W.J. Granger (1987). Co-Integration and Error-Correction: Representation, Estimation, and Testing. *Econometrica* **55**: 251–276.

Engsted, T. (1996). The Predictive Power of the Money Market Term Structure. *International Journal of Forecasting* **12**: 289–295.

Engsted, T. and K. Nyholm (2000). Regime Shifts in the Danish Term Structure of Interest Rates. *Empirical Economics* **25**: 1–13.

Engsted, T. and C. Tanggaard (1994a). Cointegration and the US Term Structure. *Journal of Banking and Finance* **18**: 167–181.

Engsted, T. and C. Tanggaard (1994b). A Cointegration Analysis of Danish Zero-Coupon Bond Yields. *Applied Financial Economics* **4**: 265–278.

Engsted, T. and C. Tanggaard (1995). The Predictice Power of Yield Spreads for Future Interest Rates: Evidence from the Danish Term Structure. *Scandinavian Journal of Economics* **97**: 145–159.

Gerlach, S. and F. Smets (1997). The Term Structure of Euro-Rates: Some Evidence in Support of the Expectations Hypothesis. *Journal of International Money and Finance* **16**: 305–321.

Hall, A.D., H.M. Anderson, and C.W.J. Granger (1992). A Cointegration Analysis of Treasury Bills. *Review of Economics and Statistics* **74**: 116–126.

Hansen, L.P. (1982). Large Sample Properties of Generalized Method of Moments Estimators. *Econometrica* **50**: 1029–1054.

Hansen, H. and K. Juselius (1995). *CATS in RATS: Cointegration Analysis of Time Series.* Evanston, IL: Estima.

Hodrick. R. (1992). Dividend Yields and Expected Stock Returns: Alternative Procedures for Inference and Measurement. *Review of Financial Studies* **5**: 357–386.

Johansen, S. (1991). Estimation and Hypothesis Testing of Cointegration Vectors in Gaussian Vector Autoregressive Models. *Econometrica* **59**: 1551–1580.

Linton, O., E. Mammen, J.P. Nielsen, and C. Tanggaard (2001). Yield Curve Estimation by Kernel Smoothing Methods. *Journal of Econometrics* **105**: 185–223.

MacKinnon, J.G. (1991). Critical Values for Cointegration Tests. In: R.F. Engle and C.W.J. Granger (eds.), *Long-Run Economic Relationships.* New York: Oxford University Press.

McCulloch, J.H. (1975). The Tax-Adjusted Yield curve. *Journal of Finance* **30**: 811–830.

Nelson, C.R. and A.F. Siegel (1987). Parsimonious Modelling of Yield Curves. *Journal of Business* **60**: 473–489.

Newey, W.K. and K.D. West (1987). A Simple Positive Semi-Definite, Heteroscedasticity and Auto-correlation Consistent Covariance Matrix. *Econometrica* **55**: 703–708.

Pagan, A.R, A.D. Hall, and V. Martin (1996). Modelling the Term Structure. In: G.S. Maddala and C.R. Rao (eds.), *Handbook of Statistics*, Vol. 14. Amsterdam: Elsevier Science Publishers.

Richardson, M. and J.H. Stock (1989). Drawing Inferences from Statistics Based on Multi-Year Asset Returns. *Journal of Financial Economics* **25**: 323–348.

Roberds, W. and C.H. Whitemann (1999). Endogenous Term Premia and Anomalies in the Term Structure of Interest Rates: Explaining the Predictability Smile. *Journal of Monetary Economics* **44**: 555–580.

Tanggaard, C. (1997). Nonparametric Smoothing of Yield Curves. *Review of Quantitative Finance and Accounting* **9**: 251–267.

Taulbjerg, J. (2001a). Cointegration and Exponential Affine Models of the Term Structure. Working Paper. Aarhus, Denmark: The Aarhus School of Business.

Taulbjerg, J. (2001b). Conditional Moment Testing, Term Premia and Affine Term Structure Models. Working Paper. Aarhus, Denmark: The Aarhus School of Business.

12

Finland, Iceland, Norway, and Sweden

SEPPO PYNNÖNEN

12.1 INTRODUCTION

A key characteristic of the Nordic countries (Denmark, Finland, Iceland, Norway, and Sweden) is their extensive and active public sector (central and local government), which has formed the basis of the universal welfare state model. This model has consistently won the support of all major parties in these countries over many years. The considerable size of the respective public sectors is evident in Table 12.1, according to which only Norway's and Iceland's public sectors, measured in terms of public expenditure, are below the EU (European Union) 15 level. In Denmark, Finland, and Sweden this ratio varies from nearly 49% to 60%, which is 6–13 percentage points higher than the European average. In the United States and Japan the corresponding ratios are about 32% and 39%, which is considerably lower than the Nordic and the European standards.

In spite of the common "Nordic values" the economies have developed in an uneven manner during the last decade. The gross domestic product (GDP) per capita growth has been highest in Norway with an annual average of 3.1%. The slowest has been in Sweden with 1.8% pa. The non-EU countries, Norway and Iceland, have about 15% higher purchasing power parity (PPP) corrected GDP per capita than the other three Nordic countries. In Finland the unemployment rate remained high, close to 10%, as a consequence of the deep recession experienced by the country in the beginning of the 1990s.

Financing public expenditure is mainly covered by income and other taxes, occasionally supplemented by the sale of state-owned companies, which usually are related to basic infrastructure industry like mining, heavy engineering, and telecommunication. Taxes, however, make up the major source from 85% to close to 100% of government income. Norway is in a unique position with the substantial, mainly state-owned, petroleum industry. It has generated more than one fifth of the budgeted state income in the last few years. Norway's petroleum fund is also massive, with a market value of 44% of the country's GDP in 2002, and is estimated to grow to 54% in 2003. In order to benefit from the oil revenues in the long run the government has adopted the policy of separating the use of these revenues from other revenue payments to the State. This is accomplished by transferring the net cash flow from petroleum activities to the Government Petroleum Fund, and only the return on the Fund is spent. The government has budgeted a 4% real annual return on the Fund. Considering that the fund will soon be well above one half of Norway's GDP, the Fund provides a solid and robust basis for Norway's State budget financing.

After recovering from the early 1990s depression, all Nordic countries besides Norway have ended up with surplus in government budget policy. Thus on the income side, the share of the public sector GDP is even higher than that of expenditure, discussed above.

European Fixed Income Markets: Money, Bond and Interest Rate Derivatives. Edited by J.A. Batten, T.A. Fetherston and P.G. Szilagyi © 2004 John Wiley & Sons, Ltd. ISBN 0-470-85053-1

Table 12.1 Nordic countries' GDPs and size of public sectors* in the year 2001

Country	Population (million)	GDP (billion US$)	Public sector (% of GDP)	GDP per capita ('000 US$)	GDP per capita ('000 US$) (PPP)	GDP per capita pa growth (1990–2000)	Unemployment rate for the year 2000 (%)
Denmark	5.3	161.5	53.5	30.4	27.1	2.1	4.7
Finland	5.2	120.9	48.7	23.2	26.1	2.4	9.7
Iceland	0.3	7.7	39.6	25.7	30.1	1.8	2.3
Norway	4.5	163.7	41.9	36.4	30.2†	3.1	3.5
Sweden	8.8	209.8	58.1	23.8	25.6	1.6	5.9
EU 15	377.4	7 889.9	47.0	20.9	24.3†	n/a	8.2
US	278.1	10 143.2	31.7†	36.5	35.6†	2.2	4.0
Japan	126.8	4 141.4	38.9†	32.7	26.4	1.1	4.7

Source: Statistics Finland, Statistics Norway for the size of the public sector of Norway, European Central Bank. Reproduced by permission of Statistics Finland and Statistics Norway. Copyright © European Central Bank, Frankfurt am Main, Germany.

*Public sector consists of consumption of general government including central government, state government, local government, and social security sectors.

†Year 2000.

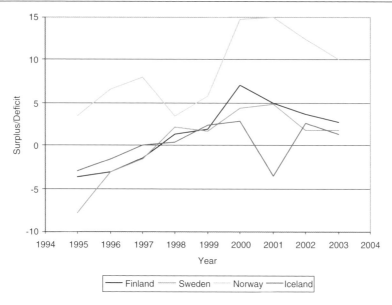

Figure 12.1   General government surpluses in Nordic countries (% of GDP).
Note: 2002 and 2003 are estimates
Source: Eurostat and ministries of finance of the countries.

Belonging to the EU regulates the member countries in a number of ways. The EU institutes a single monetary policy, but it maintains national responsibility for other economic, like fiscal, policies. The Stage Three of EMU (European Monetary Union), however, binds the national economy to a strict fiscal policy in order to maintain economic stability. As of 2003, Iceland and Norway are not direct members of the EU, but belong to the European Economic Area (EEA), which has an impact on their economic and other policies. At present, in 2003, Finland is the only Nordic country in Stage Three of the EMU. However, Sweden and Denmark have virtually also adapted their fiscal policies to these frameworks and are expected to eventually adopt the euro as their currency. Two essential aspects of the strict EU fiscal policy guidelines relate to the budget deficit and public debt. The deficit should be below 3% of the national GDP. As seen from Figure 12.1, all the four Nordic countries meet this demand. Since 1998 all these countries, except Iceland, have run a government budget surplus. Norway has the highest ratio, recording a budget surplus of 15% to GDP in recent years.

According to the other main criteria, the government debt should not exceed 60% of the national GDP. Figure 12.2 shows the percentage of government debt in the four Nordic countries with reference to Japan, the United Kingdom, and the United States. All the Nordic countries are below the 60% line, with Norway having a ratio half that of the other Nordic countries.

Against this background there is no obvious net borrowing requirement for the Nordic governments. Nevertheless, there are other reasons for governments to keep on issuing new loans. One is to payoff maturing loans while another is that the governments see an important role in setting a liquid reference rate for pricing corporate bonds.

Thus overall, the public economies of the Nordic countries are in sound financial and economic state, which is reflected in Table 12.2 by the high credit ratings declared by the major rating companies (Fitch, Moody's, and Standard & Poor's). Finland and Norway have the highest ratings for their long term debt by all rating companies. The lowest rating is for Iceland, which Standard & Poor's rate as A+ on long term foreign currency debt. Figure 12.3

Table 12.2   Credit ratings as of December 2002

	Moody's rating	Standard & Poor's	Fitch rating
Finland	Aaa/Aaa	AAA/AAA	AAA/AAA
Iceland	Aa3/Aaa	A+/AA+	AA−/AAA
Norway	Aaa/Aaa	AAA/AAA	AAA/AAA
Sweden	Aaa/Aaa	AA+/AAA	AA+/AAA
Germany	Aaa/Aaa	AAA/AAA	AAA/AAA
United Kingdom	Aaa/Aaa	AAA/AAA	AAA/AAA
United States	Aaa/Aaa	AAA/AAA	AAA/AAA
Japan	Aa1/A2	AA−/AA−	AA/AA−

Source: Ministry of Finance, Finland, Iceland National Department Management Agency.
Note: Long term foreign/domestic loans.

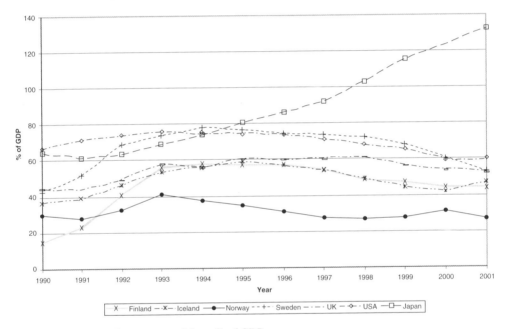

Figure 12.2   General government debt as % of GDP.
Source: BIS. Copyright © Bank for International Settlements, Basle, Switzerland. Reproduced with permission.

depicts the yield curves of the four Nordic countries together with the United Kingdom, the United States, and Japan. This figure shows that the level of interest rates is lower in the United States and Japan (across the entire term structure), while Finland and Sweden have the lowest interest rates, and Iceland and Norway have the highest, in the Nordic region.

12.2   STRUCTURE OF THE MARKETS

Although there is long and related economic and cultural history between the four Nordic countries, the bond markets have developed at their own pace in each country. Figure 12.4 gives the size of the bond markets in each country together with Germany, the United Kingdom, the

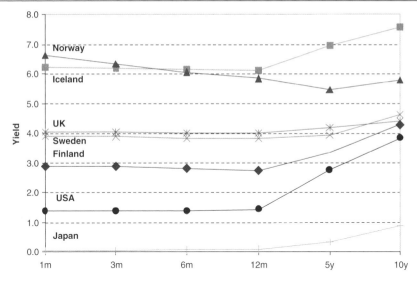

Figure 12.3 Yield curves of four Nordic countries with major markets as of December 30, 2002. Data for the graph are from National Central Banks of the countries.

United States, and Japan as reference. This figure records debt by sector (public, financial, and corporate) and by location (domestic or international).

In Sweden and particularly in Finland, government bonds make up the dominating share of the total value of the bonds: about 50% in the former, and about 70% in the latter. In Iceland and Norway the private sector has become the dominant in recent years. The largest bond market is in Sweden, with an outstanding nominal value of about US$280 billion. In Finland and Norway the size is about US$100 billion. Iceland has a small bond market with outstanding value of about US$12 billion. In Finland, and particularly in Sweden, the general trend of total debt has been decreasing during the last 5 years, mainly because of the reduction in the government debt. In Finland, public debt reached a maximum in 1996 of US$92.4 billion, which was reduced down to US$67.8 billion in 2001. In Sweden the highest was in 1996 with debt of US$225 billion. Since then it has reduced by almost one half to US$124 billion in 2001. The public debt has also been reduced in Norway. In Norway and above all in Iceland, however, the general trend of the size of the total debt has been upwards because of the expansion of the private sector. Compared with the major markets of the United Kingdom, the United States, and Japan, the trend in Nordic countries has therefore been quite different. In the major markets the total value outstanding (including private debt) has been mainly growing since 1993. In the United Kingdom the growth has been almost 150% from 1993 to 2001, in the United States 86%, and in Japan 42%.

Another notable feature of the Nordic markets is the share of foreign debt. In Finland and Sweden close to 40% of the government debt is foreign based, whereas, for example, in Norway virtually all government debt is domestic. On the other hand the private sector in Norway has markedly increased their international borrowing. In 2001 the Norwegian private international debt was US$41 billion, which was about 40% of the whole debt. In 1993 the respective figures were US$10.5 billion and 15%. An obvious reason for the increase in the last 2 years has been the large gap between Norwegian and EU or US interest rates. For example, the 3-month rate in 2001 was on average close to 5 percentage points higher in Norway than in the US rate and

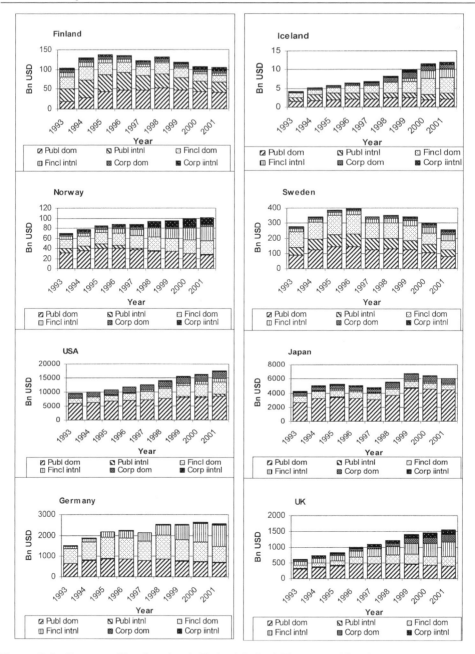

Figure 12.4   Structure of bond markets in Finland, Icaland, Norway, and Sweden.
Source: BIS. Copyright © Bank for International Settlements, Basle, Switzerland. Reproduced with permission.

close to 4 percentage points higher than the EU rate. The gap has prevailed about the same level through 2002 (cf. Figure 12.3).

12.3   FINLAND

Central government bond issues, a major part of which is targeted to institutional investors, dominate Finnish bond markets.

12.3.1   Government Bonds

In Finland, government bonds are classified into two major types: public and specialized bonds. The public bonds are intended for general subscription in public offerings, whereas the specialized bonds are issued exclusively for a specific group of buyers. The public bonds have secondary markets, and are issued in either the wholesale or retail market. Table 12.3 shows the value and the number of domestic new issues carried out by different institutes in the years 1997–2001. In terms of value, the other sectors are small compared to the size of the government issues.

Trading of government bonds occurs mainly in interbank markets. Trading was telephone based until May 8, 2002, when the Finnish State Treasury (www.statetreasury.fi) launched a new electronic trading system, MTS Finland (www.mtsfinland.com), in cooperation with MTS Belgium. The new system is believed to have markedly improved the liquidity of the Finnish government bonds: since the launch in April 2002 to November 2002 average daily volume has increased from €55 million to €275 million (*Source*: MTS News 2002). As a reference the average daily turnover on the Helsinki Stock Exchange (HEX) in 2002 was €750 million.

The growth of the Finnish bond market halted when the government succeeded in bringing its budget deficit into balance. As old debt matures, the majority is refinanced through bonds. For this and other borrowing purposes the central government uses the following channels for borrowing: Treasury bills, serial bonds, yield bonds, and short term funding.

Treasury bills have a maximum maturity of 1 year, and are zero-coupon, discount-based bearer instruments. As of November 30, 2002, about 13% (€7.2 billion) of the outstanding Finnish government debt were Treasury bills. The redemption dates of the bills vary from 1 to 364 days. The issuances are carried out according to Finnish legislation. The bills are issued in a book-entry form either through auctions held by the State Treasury or directly to banks through auctions. Investors can participate in the auctions through banks selected by the State Treasury. The value date of the bills is T+2 banking days. In the case of Treasury bills the so-called American-type (multiprice) auction practice is used. Bids having different yields can be submitted, and the State Treasury announces the highest accepted yield (in terms of nominal value), the average accepted yield, and the lowest offered yield rate along with the accepted amount and the total outstanding amount of Treasury bills after the auction.

Serial bonds are issued under several installments according to the need for financing. These bonds are the State's most important financing instruments. As of November 30, 2002, close to 70% (€37.7 billion) of the central government debt was funded using serial bonds. These bonds are fixed coupon bonds with a maturity of at least 1 year; the face value of the bond is paid in full at maturity; and the coupon is paid once a year. In order to guarantee good liquidity the bonds are issued in different maturities. The bonds are issued either in auctions arranged by the State Treasury or through bank syndicates. Investors can participate

Table 12.3 Domestic bond issues in Finland in the years 1997–2001

	1997		1998		1999		2000		2001	
	Number	Billion euros	Number	Billion euros	Number	Billion euros	Number	Billion euros	Number	Billion euros
Nonfinancial corporations	8	0.4	14	0.4	8	0.5	11	0.5	6	0.4
Financial: Banks	35	0.5	39	0.3	35	0.4	51	1.0	44	0.5
Financial: Other	33	0.7	23	0.5	11	0.2	18	0.6	8	0.2
Central government	21	9.6	15	11.1	5	4.5	3	7.4	4	7.3
Local governments	–	–	–	–	–	–	–	–	–	–
Total	97	11.2	91	12.3	59	5.6	83	9.4	62	8.4

Source: Bank of Finland (www.bof.fi). Reproduced by permission of Bank of Finland.

in auctions via approved primary dealers (as of January 2003 there were 10 primary dealers; see, www.statetreasury.fi and www.mtsfinland.com).

In the auctions of serial bonds the so-called Dutch (uniform price) method is used. The issue price is indicated to an accuracy of two decimal places such that the last number is even. Offers can be submitted at several price levels. Accepted offers are reduced to match the lowest accepted price. The State Treasury announces the issue price accepted at the auction and the corresponding yield. Additionally, the total number of offers is announced along with the number of accepted offers and the outstanding amount of serial bonds after the auction (for further details, see www.statetreasury.fi.)

Some of the serial bonds play the role of reference or benchmark bonds. In this case the issues must have adequate size, a diversified investor base, and sufficient liquidity in the secondary markets. The approved primary dealers must also have committed to maintain an active secondary market for these bonds. The benchmark status of a bond ceases when the maturity becomes less than 1 year. As of November 2002 the outstanding stock of domestic benchmark bonds was €30.5 billion. The stock of other bonds was €13.4 billion. All serial bonds are listed on HEX (www.hex.fi).

Yield bonds (face values of €1 000, €2 000, and €10 000) are the only government bonds directed to the households. They are fixed coupon bonds on which the fixed interest is paid once a year and the face value at the maturity. Maturities vary usually from 2 to 5 years. The bonds are sold in banks, post offices, and the State Treasury. They are again quoted in the HEX. As of November 2002, the outstanding stock of yield bonds was only about 1% (€0.56 billion) of the central government debt portfolio.

The Treasury can take short term funding from the financial markets to ensure the State's liquidity. The maximum length is 12 months, which can be denominated in domestic or foreign currency. Very short term funding is usually accomplished by taking so-called overnight financing from interbank markets. Amounts have been from €10 million to €200 million.

The legal basis for government borrowing is Section 82 of the Finnish Constitution Act. After the authorization of the Parliament the Council of State empowers the State Treasury to carry out borrowing activities and implement any hedging agreements. The Council, furthermore, authorizes the Ministry of Finance to issue instructions on these matters.

12.3.2 Corporate Bonds

In Finland the share of corporate bonds from the total stock of bonds has been steadily decreasing since 1993 from about 50% down to below 40% in 2001. The decreasing trend has been not only in percentage terms but also in absolute terms. For example, in 1993 the amount of financial and nonfinancial bonds outstanding was close to US$54 billion, while in 2001 the amount was about US$36 billion. Especially financial institutions have decreased their outstanding bond stock dramatically, from US$42 billion in 1993 down to US$22 billion in 2001. This trend is opposite to that prevailing elsewhere in Europe including Iceland and Norway of the Nordic countries. The major reason lies in the popularity of stock issues, particularly at the end of 1990s. Another reason is that few Finnish firms are large enough to have international credit ratings and have sufficient volume (and hence liquidity) for issuing bonds. To avoid the extra cost due to the illiquidity and lack of credit ratings, small firms find direct bank loans cheaper.

Besides ordinary bonds Finnish firms have issued convertible bonds, bonds with equity warrants and capital loan. In the last few years, the banking sector in particular has issued bonds with yield indexed to the performance of one or more of stock market indices or company

Table 12.4   Nominal value and turnover of Finnish corporate bonds in 2002

	Nominal value (million euros)	Turnover
Debentures	1576	0.2
Convertible bonds	783	12.6
Other corporate bonds	5136	1.05
Total	7495	13.9

Source: Helsinki Stock Exchange (www.hex.fi). Reproduced by permission of Helsinki Stock Exchange.

Table 12.5   Daily averages of OTC single currency interest rate derivatives net turnover of local interdealer double counting by country and counterparty in April 1998 and April 2001

	Finland		Norway		Sweden	
	April 1998	April 2001	April 1998	April 2001	April 1998	April 2001
Forward rate agreements	1779	30	2654	2591	2717	2749
Swaps	331	328	155	301	368	419
Interest rate options	8	156	7	15	483	56
Total	2118	514	2816	2907	3568	3224

Source: BIS. Triennial Central Bank Survey of Foreign Exchange and Derivatives Market Activity 2001. Copyright © Bank for International Settlements, Basle, Switzerland. Reproduced with permission.
Note: Information from Iceland was not available. Values are given in million US dollars.

stocks. In addition, debentures have also been issued by the banking sector. These and capital loans have a lower priority than other creditors in the event of a company bankrupt. Table 12.4 shows that the most traded corporate bonds in 2002 were convertible bonds with turnover of €12.6 million. Other bonds were also traded but the turnover was only €1 million. The very low liquidity of these most issued bonds indicates that they are typically held until maturity by investors.

12.3.3   Interest Rate Derivatives

Before joining the euro, forward rate agreements (FRAs) were the most important and liquid derivatives in Finland. The average daily turnover in 1998 was US$1.78 billion, which made up 84% of the daily volume of all interest rate derivatives. These markets virtually died out after the introduction of the euro, with average daily volume in 2001 being only US$30 million. Interest rate swaps are currently the most important derivatives, with average daily volume in 2001 of US$328 million, which has stayed about the same level as in 1998. Interest rate options have become the second most important fixed income derivatives, with daily average volume in 2001 of US$156 million compared to US$8 million in 1998. Overall, the total average daily volume has dropped from US$2 118 million in 1998 to US$514 in 2001, which is far below the turnover of Norway and Sweden (see Table 12.5). At the launch of the euro, trading of the Finnish fixed income and other derivatives has moved mainly from Helsinki to Eurex (www.eurex.com) in Frankfurt.

12.3.4   Regulatory Framework

The Finnish Securities Markets Act came into force in 1989. Since then it has been repeatedly amended primarily to meet EU directives. The Securities Markets Act applies to the issuance and exchange of securities as well as to public trading in securities. The Act also includes a chapter dealing with securities clearing operations. The Financial Supervision Authority (www.rahoitustarkastuskeskus.fi) monitors the operations of the securities markets. The Ministry of Finance (www.vm.fi) is primarily responsible for legislation on financial markets and for licensing. The Bank of Finland (www.bof.fi) is responsible for implementing monetary policy as defined by European Central Bank (www.ecb.int). HEX (www.hex.fi) is responsible and handles the clearing of securities trading and the business connected with the deposit and registration of securities ownership. Finland has adopted the book-entry system, wherein physical securities are replaced by entries in the book-entry accounts. No paper certificate is issued for a book entry. Paper certificates are entered into the book-entry account of the owner or assignee.

Clearing international bond transactions takes place through either Clearstream (www.clearstream.com) or Euroclear (www.euroclear.com). The securities on deposit therein are as yet not valid as collateral in the operations of the Eurosystem. The HEX and the Finnish Central Security Depository (APK, www.apk.fi) of HEX group are responsible for market supervision of the partners trading at HEX.

12.4   ICELAND

As seen from Figure 12.4 the private sector, particularly financial institutions, has an increasing role in Icelandic debt markets. In 2001 the public sector made up 30% of the total of Iceland's debt.

Indexation. Because of high inflation in the 1970s and 1980s, an important feature of the financial market in Iceland is the widespread use of indexation. Almost all long term bonds in Iceland are linked to the consumer price index (CPI), so that changes in the index immediately alter the amount of the underlying financial obligation. Short term instruments, like Treasury bills and notes, are not indexed. The longest duration for a nonindexed note is currently 6 years.

Iceland Statistics (Hagstofa Islands, www.hagstofa.is) publishes the monthly CPI. During the period between index changes, daily inflation adjustments to bond prices are made on the basis of forecasts from the Central Bank, which are published quarterly. The CPI has been used on all indexed Treasury and housing bonds and corporate bonds since April 1995. Previously, the credit terms index was used extensively. In addition, some Treasury bonds have been linked to the exchange rate of the euro against the Icelandic krona. (*Source*: Iceland Stock Exchange, Fact Book 2002, www.icex.is > English > Fact Book.)

12.4.1   Government Bonds

Icelandic *Treasury bonds* are noncallable bullet bonds with a maturity up to about 15 years. They are indexed and auctioned by the National Debt Management Agency (NDMA, www.lanasysla.is). Two benchmark issues are listed on the Iceland Stock Exchange (ICEX, www.icex.is): RIKS 05 0410 and RIKS 15 1001. As of end 2001 Treasury bonds represented 23% of the Icelandic government bond market.

Icelandic *Treasury bills* and *notes* are nonindexed zero-coupon bonds with a maturity of 0–12 months. Notes are furthermore noncallable. These are auctioned by the NDMA. All Treasury bills are listed on the ICEX, and as of December 2002 there were three notes issues listed on the ICEX.

Yields on Treasury bills are highly influenced by the 14-day repo rate, which is the main monetary instrument of the Icelandic Central Bank (www.sedlabanki.is). The Central Bank runs a tight monetary policy, which is reflected in the high yields on Treasury bills (e.g., as of December 27, 2002, the yield for a 3-month Treasury bill was 5.89%), and there was an inverted (downward sloping) yield curve of Treasury bills and Treasury notes.

12.4.2   Government-Guaranteed Bonds

Housing bonds are issued and delivered in exchange for a mortgage issued by the builder or the owner of the housing. The bonds are indexed and the coupon rate is 4.75%. The bonds also have a call-option. At present, the loan period of the housing bonds is 25 or 40 years with a single payment of outstanding amount and interest at the end of the loan period (bullet bonds). However, during the loan period, there is a quarterly drawdown of a specific number of housing bonds for redemption. The repurchase of these bonds is carried out at a public auction. A decision on repurchasing is made once the total amount of fully paid-up loans, since the last auction, has reached ISK 1500 million. The status of the total amount since the last auction is disseminated once a month.

The housing bonds are government guaranteed, and have the same rating as government bonds. The bonds are rather bond swaps than traditional mortgage bonds. The homebuyers actually apply for a mortgage bond, which is secured against the property to be bought. After that the Housing Financing Fund (www.ils.is) buys the bond and pays it by issuing to the seller a housing bond, which can be freely traded in the securities market. The homebuyers pay a fixed 5.1% on the loan. The 35 basis point gap to the 4.75% coupon rate goes to the Housing Financing Fund as the credit risk premium. The main risk is that the homebuyer will be able to refinance at a lower interest rate than the 5.1% + CPI. In the event of homebuyers paying back their loans, the Housing Financing Fund would exercise its call-option on the bonds.

Housing authority bonds are issued and sold by the Housing Financing Fund to capitalize the Fund's other loan categories. The bonds are indexed and carry a fixed interest of 2.7%. The loan period of the bonds is currently 24 or 42 years, repaid by annuity payments. These bonds are government guaranteed and have the same rating as government bonds.

12.4.3   Corporate and Municipal Bonds

A small fraction of the total Icelandic bond market consists of nongovernment guaranteed bonds. The major part of these are bank bills, other corporate bonds, and municipal bonds. Trading of these has been fairly limited. Table 12.6 shows the turnover of traded instruments at the ICEX in 2002. The total Stock Exchange turnover was ISK 1066 billion (US$13.2 billion). Equities make 30% of the turnover, the housing bonds are the next with a 28% share, and the Treasury bonds, bills, and notes make together 24% of the turnover.

12.4.4   Regulatory Framework

The legal framework in which Iceland's financial institutions operate is based on EU directives, because of Iceland's membership in the EEA. Icelandic legislation has undergone major reform

Table 12.6 Turnover of traded instruments at Iceland Stock Exchange in 2002 (million ISK)

	Turnover	Percentage
Bank bills	69 942	6.6
Housing bonds	293 471	27.5
Housing authority bonds	101 404	9.5
Treasury notes	127 986	12.0
Treasury bills	38 799	3.6
Treasury bonds	88 148	8.3
Other corporate bonds	25 576	2.4
Equities	321 333	30.1
Total	1 066 659	100.0

Source: Iceland Stock Exchange www.icex.is. Reproduced by permission of Iceland Stock Exchange.

in recent years, and regulations have been adopted in line with EU law. Up to date information on acts and regulations regarding financial markets can be found from the ICEX home page (www.icex.is), the Icelandic Parliament, Althingi (www.althingi.is), Financial Supervisory Authority (www.fme.is), and the Ministry of Commerce (www.stjr.is).

12.5 NORWAY

The private sector is playing an increasing role in the Norwegian bond markets. As indicated in Figure 12.4 the nominal value of outstanding bonds in 2001 was about US$100 billion. Since 1997, financial institutions have been the largest group with a nominal value in 2001 of US$54.4 billion. The expansion has particularly been directed to the foreign markets so that in 2001 the value of the bonds issued by the financial institutions was split approximately half between foreign and domestic markets, whereas, for example, in 1997 only 34% was foreign based. The money raised by the financial institutions from the bond markets is further lent to public and industrial companies. The industrial sector has also become increasingly active in the bond markets in recent years. For example, in 1999 only five new bonds were quoted on the Oslo Stock Exchange (OSE, www.ose.no), but in 2000 the number was 14, and 38 in 2001. The increasing trend is also clearly seen in Figure 12.4. About one half of the nominal value of the outstanding bonds is domestic based. Together with Treasury bills and certificates (including private) all are quoted and traded on the OSE.

The nominal value of outstanding Norwegian government bonds, *Treasury bonds* (excluding other public sector), was in September 30, 2002, NOK 141 billion (US$19.2 billion), which makes far less than one half of the total domestic nominal value of Norwegian bonds. The government bonds are, however, the most important instruments in Norwegian markets since they serve as benchmark bonds. From the above total amount of outstanding government bonds as of September 30, 2002, NOK 138 billion (US$18.8 billion) were benchmark bonds with maturities in steps of 2 years from 1 to 10 years.

As indicated by Table 12.7 the total turnover of government bonds in 2002 was over US$60 billion, which made up close to 80% of the total turnover of bond trading. The Treasury bills dominated the class of bills and certificates with a share of turnover of 94% of the US$23 billion total turnover of bills and certificates in 2002. Although the financial institutions make up the largest group in terms of outstanding (domestic) bonds of nominal value US$30 billion,

Table 12.7 Turnover statistics of Oslo Stock Exchange quoted fixed income securities in the year 2002

	Turnover (million US$)	Percent of sub-class total	Daily average (million US$)	Repo volume (million US$)	Daily average repo volume (million US$)	Number of transactions, daily average
Government bonds	60 437	77.9	242.7	232 577	934	99.1
Government owned enterprises	463	0.6	1.9	67	0.3	0.7
Government guaranteed	129	0.2	0.5	–	–	0.1
Local government and guaranteed	1 642	2.1	6.6	151	0.6	2.6
Bank and Insurance	9 421	12.2	37.8	489	2.0	18.7
Mortgage banks	3 296	4.3	13.2	663	2.7	6.1
Industry	1 600	2.1	6.4	8	0.0	4.3
Foreign	494	0.6	2.0	13	0.1	0.3
Loan certificates	56	0.1	0.2	–	–	0.0
Of which: Convertibles	25	0.0	0.1	–	–	0.3
Subordinated loan capital	383	0.5	1.5	–	–	2.0
Total (bonds)	77 538	77.2	311.4	233 967	940	132
Treasury bills	21 496	93.8	86.3	1 582	6.4	10.4
Mortgage banks	143	0.6	0.6	–	–	0.1
Loan certificates	1 268	5.5	5.1	–	–	1.2
Total (bills and certificates)	22 906	22.8	92.0	1 582	6.4	11.7
Total (bonds, bills, certificates)	100 444	100.0	403.4	235 549	946	144
Stocks	59 105	NA	237.4	NA	NA	8 007

Source: Oslo Stock Exchange www.ose.no. Reproduced by permission of Oslo Børs Informasjon AS.

the trading of these bonds is far less than those of government bonds. In 2002 the turnover was US$9.4 billion, which makes up 12% of the total turnover of bonds. The total daily average turnover excluding repo markets in 2002 was US$403 million compared to average daily stock market turnovers, which was US$237 million. Including the US$946 million repo daily turnover, the total trading was close to US$1.4 billion; i.e., an amount almost six times the stock market daily turnover. Virtually all of the repo trading comes from government bonds and Treasury bills. Bond turnover increased in 2002 by 42% while stock market turnover decreased almost by 22%.

On the investor side the dominant players are the professional ones. For example in 2001 pension and insurance companies owned 37.7% of the OSE quoted bonds. Banks had a 14.3% share, and foreign investors 14.4%. Government bonds are especially favored by foreigners who were the largest owner group in 2001 with a share of 37%. The role of foreign owners has generally been increasing during the last few years: in 1995 only 3.5% of the bonds were foreign owned, and in 2000 about 17%. Private investors are only a marginal owner group in Norwegian bond markets, with only a 4% share, mainly concentrated on bonds issued by the banking sector. (*Source*: www.ose.no > In English > Markets > Statistics.)

12.5.1   Trading

Trading of bonds takes place on the OSE via financial company brokers. As of December 31, 2001, about 60% of all Norwegian bonds were quoted on the OSE. Quoting on the stock exchange implies certain information responsibilities for the issuer to the exchange. In any case, virtually all big issuers make their bonds quoted at the OSE. The benchmark bonds are traded through the primary dealer system.

12.5.2   Regulatory Framework

The Norwegian Registry of Securities (VPS, Verdipapirsentralen, www.vps.no), established by law in 1985, is an electronic register for ownership of Norwegian-registered securities. VPS encompasses all Stock Exchange listed securities. It is a rights register. All investors, including foreigners, who own and/or trade in shares of companies that are registered with VPS must have their own VPS account. Foreign investors may use nominee accounts. All transactions carried out on the Exchange's trading system, or which by other means are mediated by Exchange members, are reported to the Registry for updating of the VPS accounts in question. Settlement between VPS accounts is on a gross basis, and the normal settlement cycle is T+3. Foreign investors are required to use a Norwegian registrar.

The Banking, Insurance and Securities Commission (Kredittilsynet, www.kredittilsynet.no) has the main responsibility for monitoring the Norwegian securities market. The OSE also has a supervisory role on the marketplace.

12.6   SWEDEN

12.6.1   Central Government Bonds

The total amount of Swedish public sector debt at the end of 2001 was US$124 billion. From this amount, the share of central government debt was SEK 1157 billion (US$109 billion at December 31, 2001, rate) of which SEK 613 billion (US$57.6 billion) was government bonds and SEK 251 billion (US$23.6 billion) was Treasury discount notes and bills. SEK

223 billion (US$21 billion) of the debt was in direct foreign currency, and the rest, SEK 69.5 billion (US$6.5 billion), in other debt. As of December 31, 2002, the total debt was SEK 1160 billion (US$132 billion at December 31, 2002, rate), i.e., in SEK about the same level as in the previous year, of which the outstanding stock of government bonds was SEK 659 billion (US$74.9 billion), and SEK 249 billion (US$28.3 billion) Treasury discount notes and bills. Debt in foreign currency was SEK 197 billion (US$22.4 billion).

The Swedish government bonds, the *Treasury bonds*, are issued by the Swedish state through the Swedish National Debt Office (SNDO, Riksgäldskontoret, www.rgk.se). These are bullet bonds with a fixed annual coupon payment. The lowest denomination is SEK 100 000. The maturities of the bonds are usually from 2 up to 10 years (sometimes longer maturity bonds are issued). The bonds are issued via auction through dealers (banks and securities institutions) authorized by the Debt Office. Offers in descending order are accepted until the issue amount is filled. Auction dates are published on the SNDO web page once every 6 months. Auctions of Treasury bonds are held Wednesdays, either every other week, or every 4 weeks.

Various Treasury bonds have different status. The major class are benchmark bonds with an outstanding value as of December 31, 2002, of SEK 503 billion (US$37.4 billion), from a total of SEK 659 billion (US$61.9 billion). The next largest group is *inflation-linked* (index-linked) bonds. These are interest-bearing bonds with annual payments at 3.5% or 4% of the nominal value. The holder also receives an amount above this payment depending on the change in the consumer price index over the maturity of bond. Also zero coupon bonds are issued. These bonds have maturities from 5 to 13 years, and are issued quarterly by the Debt Office's authorized banks and securities institutes. The lowest denomination is SEK 5000. As of December 31, 2002, the nominal outstanding value of these bonds was SEK 143 billion (US$13.5 billion). The rest are nonbenchmark bonds (SEK 12.9 billion) and repurchasing agreement (repo) bonds (SEK 6.7 billion).

Premium bonds are one group of Swedish state instrument issued via the SNDO. These are fixed interest bonds with annual interest payment in the form of a draw at a time in accordance with a schedule decided by the Debt Office. The maturity of this type of bond is normally from 5 to 10 years. Denomination varies from year to year, but has been mostly equal to SEK 1 000 in recent years. The bonds are issued following a decision by the SNDO, who also fixes the issue price. Some premium bond issues are carried out according to a fluctuating dividend/profit plan, where the return/yield is fixed, based on the interest rate of 180-day Swedish Treasury bill. Other premium bond issues are carried out at a fixed rate until maturity. The selling occurs through banks and financial institutions. As of December 31, 2002, the nominal outstanding value of premium bonds was SEK 40.9 billion (US$4.9 billion).

Treasury bills with a maturity of generally up to 1 year (even maturities up to 720 days have been used) are issued by the Swedish state via the SNDO. These are pure discount bonds denominated at SEK 1, 5, 10, 20, 50, and 100 million. The issuance procedure is similar to that of Treasury bonds described above. Auctions are held normally every other Wednesday. As of December 31, 2002, the nominal outstanding value of all Treasury bills was SEK 242 billion (US$22.7 billion).

In 2002 the SNDO had loans of SEK 57.1 billion from households and other small investors. Small investors can buy index-linked and premium bonds, of which the latter is more popular. For example during 2002 the SNDO collected SEK 6 billion from small investors through premium bond issues, while only SEK 229 million was collected through index-linked bond issues. In addition, SNDO offers a saving account called a National Saving Account for small investors, with interest tied to Riksbank's repo rate. At the end of 2002 small investors had SEK 14.6 billion in this account.

12.6.2   Corporate Bonds

The nominal outstanding value of financial and nonfinancial bonds at the end of 2001 was US$135 billion, or 52% of the total Swedish national debt. The nominal value of financial issuers was US$98.4 billion and nonfinancial US$36.4 billion. The amount issued by the financial sector has been steadily decreasing since 1996 when it was the major group with US$153 billion. On the other hand the amount of nonfinancial corporations has been increasing especially since 1997 when it was only US$16.9 billion. About 40% in both groups is denominated in foreign currency, and the rest is domestic. The financial sector, in particular, has been steadily increasing foreign currency bonds, which in 1993 was only 15%. Within the nonfinancial sector the fraction has stayed fairly constant. The major classes of corporate bonds are debentures, mortgage bonds, and certificates.

Debenture loans, notes, and bonds are issued by Swedish banks, credit companies, and other borrowers. These are normally fixed interest instruments with a maturity of at least 2 years. Usually these bonds are targeted to large institutional investors like insurance companies. The bonds can be traded on Stockholmsbörsen's SOX system, but because of the relatively small number of investors the liquidity of these instruments is not high.

Mortgage bonds and certificates are issued by the Swedish mortgage lending institutions, the largest of which are Statshypotekskassan (www.stadshypotekbank.se), AB Spintab (www.foreningssparbanken.se/spintab), Statensbostadfinancierings AB (www.sbab.se), SEB BoLån AB (www.seb.se), and Handelsbankens Hypotek AB. Some other companies finance their lending operations in this way, too. These are fixed income bonds with semiannual or annul interest payments. Maturity as a rule is 2 years. The bonds are traded both on OTC markets and the SOX, the Stockholm Stock Exchange (see www.stockholmsborsen.se). The liquidity of the bonds of large companies is considered to be fairly high.

12.6.3   Derivative Instruments

The Stockholm Stock Exchange is the authorized exchange and clearing organization for trading Swedish stock and fixed (interest-related) income derivatives.

Forward Rate Agreements (FRAs). International Money Market, IMM FRA, is essentially a futures contract, which has an underlying maturity of 3 months. The reference rate is 3-month STIBOR (Stockholm interbank rate). A new contract is issued every 3 months and 12 series always run simultaneously. According to the Stockholmsbörsen the liquidity of the IMM FRA market is considered to be healthy. In addition there are standardized futures contract on 2-, 5-, and 10-year government bonds, and 2- and 5-year mortgage bonds. These contracts have a life of between 3 and 6 months.

Swedish Treasury bill future VX180 is an interest rate future on a 6 month's Swedish Treasury bill. The contract size is SEK 1 million. The delivery dates are every third Wednesday in March, June, September, and December. The Swedish Treasury bills futures market is considered to be very liquid.

Besides these standardized products there are other interest-related OTC derivatives. These are formed on a customer basis according to needs. As seen in Table 12.5 the most actively traded derivative contract is the forward rate agreement, which makes up 85% of the turnover.

12.6.4   Trading

Government and mortgage bonds have been traditionally traded mostly via OTC markets with quotes disseminated by the Stockholmsbörsen. In April 2001, the electronic marketplace

Stockholmsbörsen Fixed Income (www.stockholmsborsen.se > Fixed Income) was introduced for interbank markets, as well as exchange-traded market for fixed income securities targeted primarily at private investors. As at the end of 2002 there were 1300 loans listed at Stockholmsbörsen Fixed Income.

12.6.5   Regulatory Framework

The Swedish legislation is fully harmonized with EU regulations. The principal regulatory agency the Financial Supervisory Authority oversees the activities of all financial institutions and is the licensing authority for stock brokerages. It also establishes policies for stock market operations.

12.7   NOREX ALLIANCE

In December 2000, Stockholmsbörsen, the Copenhagen Stock Exchange, the ICEX, and Oslo Børs signed a cooperation agreement with a view to creating a joint Nordic marketplace for trading in securities, called NOREX (www.norex.com). The HEX as yet is outside the alliance. The agreement provides for the four exchanges to use a common system for securities trading with effect from the first half of 2002, and to harmonize and introduce a largely identical set of rules and regulations together with a system for cross-membership between the exchanges.

The NOREX alliance will also give investors access to joint bond market using a shared trading platform. In 2002 the combined market offered about 4500 different bonds and other interest bearing securities, with daily turnover of some NOK 50 billion (US$7.2 billion). This will make NOREX the world's second largest market for trading volume in bonds and other fixed income securities, with only the London Stock Exchange generating greater trading volume.

ADDITIONAL READING

Den svenska finans marknaden (The Swedish Financial Markets) (2001). Sveriges Riksbank, 2002. www.riksbank.se > Publikationer.
Obligasjoner (2002). Publikasjoner fra Oslo Bors. www.ose.no.
Norske Finansanalytikeres Forening (2001, May). Forslag til anbefaling til konvensjoner for det norske sertifikat- og obligasjonsmarkedet. Oslo. www.finansanalytiker.no.
Suomen rahoitusmarkkinat (The Finnish Financial Markets) (2002). www.bof.fi.

Websites

Denmark
Copenhagen Stock Exchange: www.cse.dk
Finland
Helsinki Stock Exchange: www.hex.com
Iceland
Reykjavik Stock Exchange: www.icex.is
Bonds: www.bond.is
Norway
Oslo Stock Exchange: www.ose.no
Sweden
Stockholm Stock Exchange: www.stockholmsborsen.se
Nordic
www.norex.com
www.omhex.com

13

France

DAVID EDWARDS AND CAMERON MAKEPEACE

13.1 INTRODUCTION

In the two decades prior to the formation of the European Monetary Union (EMU), France's financial system underwent a transition from a state-owned bank intermediary structure to a market-based system through a focused policy of deregulation and privatization. Prior to these reforms government-owned banks held approximately 90% of deposits, and 80% of credit was provided by these banks (Dziobek *et al.*, 1999). By the year 2000, however, only five financial institutions remained in government ownership after 87 had been privatized during the 1980s and 90s (European Central Bank, 2002).

The initial transformation of the financial system began with new banking laws implemented in 1984 that saw the majority of institutions under the governance of a single set of prudential rules. With the development of the money and derivative markets, liquidity management was improved and monetary policy could be more effectively implemented. In addition to this the government privatized the state-owned banks, including BNP and Crédit Lyonnais. Further financial sector reform initiatives will be enhanced as a result of the recent alignment between the President Jacques Chirac and the government headed by Jean-Pierre Raffarin, who both sit center right. With a vast majority in the parliament and no elections scheduled for the coming years, both financial system and economic reforms have been focused on achieving long term financial system structure changes primarily through enhanced integration with other European Union (EU) countries (Deppler and Lipschitz, 2002). A key issue that needs to be addressed is a more enhanced level of disclosure. By increasing financial transparency to a level similar to traditional market-based systems such as the United States or the United Kingdom, the financial system will be able to further develop (Dziobek *et al.*, 1999).

Historically, bank credit in France has been less vital in comparison to the Euro area; however, it is still higher than in the United States. France has a well-developed money market. Comparison of the capital markets shows that France share market capitalization is higher than in the Euro area, while the bond market is rather less developed.

13.1.1 Economic Indicators

Table 13.1 demonstrates how the French economy expanded until the beginning of this decade as world trade and economies swelled. Gross Domestic Product (GDP) increased, unemployment fell, and inflation remained constant at around 1–2%. As further integration of the EU continues, the French and Euro economies are expected to prosper. Economic policy in the future is expected to focus upon tax reduction and reduced government spending, especially as

European Fixed Income Markets: Money, Bond and Interest Rate Derivatives. Edited by J.A. Batten,
T.A. Fetherston and P.G. Szilagyi. © 2004 John Wiley & Sons, Ltd. ISBN 0-470-85053-1

Table 13.1   Economic indicators

	1999	2000	2001	2002
GDP (€billion)	1354	1422	1476	1523
GDP (% change)	3.2	4.2	2.1	1.2
Unemployment (%)	10.7	9.3	8.5	8.7
Inflation (%)	0.6	1.8	1.8	1.9
Trade balance (€billion)	14.3	−4.0	2.2	8.3
Current account balance/GDP (%)	2.43	1.56	1.62	1.95
Budget balance	−1.6	−1.3	−1.4	−3.1
Public debt	66.2	65.4	65.0	66.1

Source: Banque de France, Ministry of the Economy, Finance and Industry.

pensions now impose an increasing burden given a rapidly ageing population. The benefits of earlier labor market reforms and wage moderation also give the French economy good strength (Deppler and Lipschitz, 2002).

The Raffarin cabinet is nonetheless facing a difficult period in office. Economic activity is weakening, public finances have deteriorated, unemployment is rising, and industrial unrest is mounting. Raffarin's majority in parliament should allow him to implement the much-needed pension reform, but increasing social tension could encourage Chirac to reshuffle the government, which may even lead to Raffarin being replaced as Prime Minister. Meanwhile, the deterioration in France's public finances will require the government to steer a difficult course between its domestic objectives and its external obligations. It now appears that in 2004 the budget deficit may well exceed the 3% of GDP limit set out in the Stability and Growth Pact for a third consecutive year, which should lead to Brussels taking disciplinary action. The growth forecast of less than 1% for the year 2003 is hardly more encouraging, although improving domestic and external demand should bring a modest recovery in 2004.

13.1.2   The French Bond Market

As mentioned earlier, the major reforms to France's financial system have occurred mainly in the banking sector. According to La Porta *et al.* (2002), financial systems where the government retains high ownership of banks result in the financial system growing slower and being less efficient in comparison to countries where government ownership of banks is low. Therefore, the reforms to the banking sector have been a crucial step for the long term development and expansion of France's financial system.

During the 1990s, bond market developments in France reflected the increase in market-based financing at the expense of bank financing. The recent evolution of total domestic debt emphasizes this phenomenon. Bank for International Settlements (BIS) and European Central Bank (ECB) data reveal that the size of France's domestic debt market has more than doubled since 1989, reaching €1.6 trillion in April 2003. In particular, the segment of negotiable debt instruments (titres de creance négociables) has been marked by considerable growth since its creation in 1985, as a result of a deliberate liberalization policy and the increase in the number of new and effective instruments. The liberalization of the conditions of issue in 1999 and a parallel rise in the number of foreign debt holders has also led to higher growth. The bond market is nonetheless characterized by the prominence of the general government as an issuer, although the sector's importance is decreasing slightly as the private sector becomes more significant. ECB data on the breakdown of the market is given in Table 13.2.

Table 13.2 Euro-denominated debt securities by French residents on 31 April 2003

	Short term	Long term	Total
General government	96.8	679.4	776.2
Monetary financial institutions	188.4	316.9	505.3
Nonmonetary financial institutions	0	30.4	30.4
Nonfinancial corporations	45.4	223.5	268.9
Total	330.6	1250.2	1580.8

Source: European Central Bank Securities Issues Statistics.

13.2 FINANCIAL SYSTEM REGULATION

In France, overall supervision of the financial system is the responsibility of the Minister of the Economy, Finance and Industry, who prepares the laws and approves the rules governing financial services prepared by the financial regulators. In addition, there are a number of regulatory and supervisory bodies that are responsible for regulating and monitoring the financial markets, and for overseeing financial intermediaries. The general legal framework is mainly provided by the Financial Activity Modernization Act 96-597 of July 2, 1996, which implemented in France the European Commission's Investment Services Directive 93/22.

13.2.1 Banque de France

The Banque de France has been an integral part of the European System of Central Banks (ESCB) since January 1, 1999, the date on which its new status took effect (Act of May 12, 1998). Its independence has been guaranteed by law since 1993. The Banque de France helps accomplish the tasks of and achieve the objectives assigned to the ESCB by the European Union Treaty, notably maintaining price stability. Its monetary policy powers were transferred to the ECB when the single currency took effect and, as a result, like the other central banks in the Euro area, it now implements the monetary policy decisions adopted by the Governing Council of the ECB. Acting within the framework of the ECB's orientations and instructions, the Banque de France's monetary policy council lays out "purchase conditions or the conditions on which claims or receivables are bought or sold, lent or borrowed, collateralized, or transferred by repo or reverse repo transaction, or on which interest-bearing warrants are issued, as well as the nature and scope of the guarantees accompanying loans granted by the Banque de France." As a member of the ESCB, the Banque de France supervises the money market and also monitors operation and protection of payment systems. It keeps the Treasury account and manages the physical aspects of government securities auctions on behalf of the Treasury.

13.2.2 Agency France Trésor

One of the most recent additions to the French financial system has been the establishment in 2000 of the agency France Trésor, which is charged with the responsibility of managing the French Treasury. The agency carries out the following precisely defined assignments, frequently in close collaboration with other units of the Treasury Directorate or the Ministry for the Economy, Finance and Industry:

- Projection and management of government treasury;
- Definition of government debt strategy;
- Day-to-day management of government debt;
- Risk control and management, back office;
- Macroeconomic and financial analysis;
- Business intelligence and collection and diffusion of economic information;
- International cooperation.

13.2.3 Regulatory Authorities

Under the Ministry and the Governor of the Banque de France sit three major regulators of the French financial system, whose membership includes representatives from the government and the Banque de France as well as financial professionals.

13.2.3.1 Financial Markets Council (CMF, Conseil des Marches Financiers)

In December 1997, the CMF was set up as a new supervisory authority for all markets in France, including equities, bonds, and derivatives. The 16 members of the CMF include representatives of issuers, investors, intermediaries, and their employees. The CMF lays down the compliance regulations applicable to investment service providers, market executive bodies and clearing mechanisms, securities delivery systems, and central depositories, subject to approval by the Minister. It also decides general rules governing the operation of financial activities, the rules applied to clearing houses, regulated markets, public offerings, and determines disciplinary sanctions. The powers of the CMF extend to regulated markets, but also, when necessary, to over-the-counter (OTC) transactions. It takes individual decisions in the application of these regulations.

13.2.3.2 Banking and Financial Regulations Committee (CRBF, Comité de la Réglementation Bancaire et Financière)

The CRBF sets the regulations governing credit institutions and firms providing investment services. Chaired by the Minister, the CRBF's areas of competence are (i) general rules governing the operation of the banking business; (ii) the features of transactions that financial institutions may carry out; (iii) accounting standards, management regulations, notably prudential ratios of all investment services providers other than portfolio management companies; and (iv) credit policy instruments.

13.2.3.3 Credit Institutions and Investment Firms Committee (CECEI, Comité des Établissements de Crédit et des Entreprises d'Investissement)

The CECEI is charged to make the decisions or to grant the authorizations or individual exemptions applicable to the credit institutions and investment firms, except for those specialized in portfolio management. It examines plans of French financial institutions to open branches in other EU Member States, and is also responsible for overseeing the arrival in France of lending institutions from other Member States. The Committee is chaired by the governor of the Banque de France.

13.2.4 Supervisory Authorities

13.2.4.1 Banking Commission (Commission Bancaire)

The banking commission was set up as a result of a large overhaul of the legal framework of the banking system in 1984. It replaced the former banking supervision and has been charged with the responsibility of ensuring that credit institutions and investment firms comply with all regulatory and legal provisions in force. The three major supervisory functions undertaken by the Commission are (i) the supervision of financial intermediaries, in particular the prudential supervision of credit institutions and investment firms and the supervision of investment advice companies and exchange offices; (ii) the supervision of financial information and of the markets for financial instruments; and (iii) the supervision of undertakings for collective investment.

13.2.4.2 Stock Exchange Commission (COB, Commission des Operations de Bourse)

The COB is responsible for the supervision of public offerings. The COB is empowered to issue regulations that impact on any person making public offerings and also persons involved in the trading and management of securities. The Commission is also the regulator of information that is provided to investors in the market, and is empowered to conduct investigations into potential contravention of existing regulations, individuals, and companies.

13.2.5 Regulated Fixed Income Markets

13.2.5.1 Spot Market: Euronext Paris

In September 2000, the Paris Bourse merged with the Belgian and Dutch stock exchanges and was integrated into its successor Euronext NV (a Dutch holding company). The Paris Bourse, now a subsidiary of Euronext, was accordingly renamed Euronext Paris. In 2001, Euronext also merged with the Lisbon and Oporto Stock Exchange (BVLP) and then with the London International Financial Futures and Options Exchange (LIFFE), only to become Euronext.Liffe.

Currently underway is an integration and harmonization process aimed at developing consistent trading, clearing, and settlement systems across the member markets of Euronext. As for trading, the markets now collectively use the NSC (Nouveau Système de Cotation) trading platform developed by the Paris Bourse. The NSC can handle 125 orders per second on average and up to 300 orders per second at peaks, and is now the most widely used electronic trading system in the world, bought by 18 stock exchanges. It ensures continuous trading within the following schedule:

- Preopening from 7:45 a.m. to 9:00 a.m. when the orders are entered, but without any transactions;
- Opening at 9:00 a.m. when the NSC calculates the opening price to match the largest number of bids and asks;
- Trading from 9:00 a.m. to 5:30 p.m. when the orders are executed provided there is a matching order in the central order book;
- Preclosing from 5:30 p.m. to 5:35 p.m. when the orders are entered, but not yet processed; and
- Closing at 5:35 p.m. when the closing price is calculated to match the largest number of bids and asks.

The clearing functions of Euronext were merged into a single clearing house, Clearnet SBF SA, in February 2001. Clearnet (the legal name of which is Banque Centrale de Compensation) is incorporated as a French bank that is a fully owned subsidiary of Euronext Paris. It is the central counterparty for all transactions on the Euronext exchanges. Since September 2000, Clearnet has been implementing a new integrated clearing platform called Clearing 21, which was developed in conjunction with the Chicago Mercantile Exchange (CME) and the New York Mercantile Exchange (NYMEX).

Euronext has chosen Euroclear as its preferred settlement system to provide it with integrated, straight-through processing services across all of its markets. On this account, the International Central Securities Depository (ICSD) Euroclear Bank has built a strategic partnership with Clearnet. Sicovam SA, the French Central Securities depository (CSD) became Euroclear France in January 2001 and is now a fully owned subsidiary of Euroclear Bank. Euroclear France simplified its computer system architecture in 2001 and now has a single delivery versus payment system called RGV2 (Relit Grande Vitesse). The system handles two types of transactions. The first are revocable until settled at the Banque de France, with settlement taking place several times a day. The second type of transactions are irrevocable with real-time finality of settlement. Regulated market transactions are handled as revocable transactions, and transactions with the Banque de France are irrevocable. OTC trades may be handled either way, depending on the choice of the counterparties. During the night of June 27 and June 28, 2003, Euroclear France successfully implemented the conversion from Sicovam codes to ISINs.

13.2.5.2   Derivatives Market: Matif SA

Through Euronext Paris, Euronext NV became the holding entity of the French exchange-traded derivative markets, Matif and Monep. Both Matif and Monep are regulated markets with electronic systems allowing continuous trading from 8:00 a.m. to 10:00 p.m., with a preopening session from 7:45 to 8:00 a.m., although these hours may vary from contract to contract. Matif trades futures and options on interest rates. The two bond futures contracts, on which options are also available, are

- the Euro Notional Future contract, which is based on an 8- to 10-year notional government bond constructed from a pool of French and German government securities and
- the 5-year Euro Future contract, which is based on a 3- to 5-year notional government bond constructed from a pool of French and German securities.

Monep trades futures and options on equities and equity indexes. In addition to the Matif and Monep, Euronext Paris operates derivatives markets for warrants and the newly formed weather derivatives market.

With the purchase of the LIFFE in October 2001, Euronext now operates one of the world's premier derivatives markets. In the near future, all Euronext derivative activities will be migrated to Euronext.Liffe and traded on its LIFFE CONNECT trading platform. The London market has a worldwide reputation for short term rate instruments.

13.2.6   Taxation

Resident individuals liable to income tax, interest, and redemption premiums (exempt from withholding tax) may opt for

- either a flat-rate withholding tax of 25% (including a 10% social security contribution);
- or progressive income tax, incremented by 10% social security contributions.

Nonresidents are exempt from withholding tax except on convertible bonds and similar instruments. For nonresidents located in a country bound to France by a tax treaty, proof of nonresidential status is provided by simple statement on the person's honor at each change of tax domicile. For other nonresidents domiciled in a state not bound to France by a tax treaty, proof of nonresidential status must be provided for each payment of interest.

13.3   THE FRENCH GOVERNMENT BOND MARKET

France houses the third largest public debt market in the EU after Italy and Germany, with an outstanding amount of €765.8 billion or 51% of GDP as on May 31, 2003. The market is also very highly regarded worldwide as a benchmark reference because of the regularly held auctions and fungibility, it is already the second most liquid in the world after its American equivalent. There were, in May 2003, 26 issues in the market with more than €15 billion outstanding and 37 issues with more than €10 billion. This success confirms France's joint benchmark status for sovereign debt issuance across the euro yield curve. Figure 13.1 shows the French benchmark yield curve as on March 31, 2003.

Recent French government policy has been directed to the development of both the primary and secondary markets, in part necessary to serve the government's borrowing requirements and also to assist the further development of financial markets in France. In order for this to occur, the focus of government debt management was changed to increasing levels of negotiable (tradable) debt. This practice coincided with increasing government debt levels of 25% of GDP in 1975 to 66% of GDP in 2002. The level of foreign-owned government debt also increased from 28% in 1997 to 40% in 2002, largely due to the monetary integration of the Euro area.

Another key objective identified in the French Government Debt and Treasury Management Program is the reduction of the weighted average maturity of negotiable debt. This was initiated in 2001 as by doing so, the government's debt service is expected to be reduced in the long term. The government has proposed the average debt maturity be reduced to 5 years and 4 months by the end of 2003 from the March 2003 level of 5.9 years.

13.3.1   Types of Government Debt Instruments

In 1985, the Treasury implemented a series of reforms designed to lay the foundations for the growth of a liquid, safe, and attractive government securities market. From the beginning, the

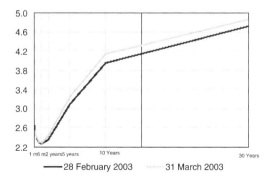

Figure 13.1   French benchmark yield curve (in percent).
Source: Banque de France, 2003.

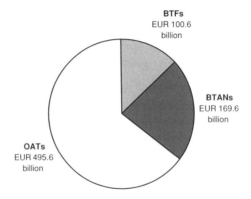

Figure 13.2   Breakdown of French government securities, 31 May 2003.
Source: Agency France Trésor.

objective was to enable the government as an issuer to borrow on optimum conditions while offering market participants standardized securities and easy and safe access to the primary and secondary markets. Accordingly, the composition of government debt was rationalized into three categories of standardized government securities: OATs, BTANs, and BTFs. These instruments, whose nominal value is €1, are distinguished by their maturity on issue. Figure 13.2 shows the breakdown of French negotiable government debt by instrument. In March 2003, the daily turnover of trading in French government securities recorded by Euroclear France came to €141.7 billion, of which €87.6 billion was in OATs and €54.1 billion in BTANs and BTFs.

13.3.1.1   Negotiable Fixed-Rate Discount Treasury Bills (BTFs, Bons du Trésor à taux fixe et à intérêts précomptés)

BTFs are short term Treasury bills with a maturity of less than 1 year. They are used to cover short term fluctuations in the government's cash position. They are auctioned every Monday at 3 p.m. as part of a quarterly calendar published in advance. Every week, one BTF with a maturity of 13 weeks is issued, and as applicable, this issue is complemented by 26- or 52-week BTFs. Certain BTFs with maturities from 4 to 7 weeks may be issued outside the calendar if needed. As of May 31, 2003 there were €100.6 billion of BTFs outstanding on the market, with a weighted average maturity of 119 days.

13.3.1.2   Negotiable Fixed-Rate Medium Term Treasury Notes with Annual Interest (BTANs, Bons du Trésor à taux fixe et à intérêts annuels)

BTANs represent medium term government debt with a maturity of either 2 or 5 years. They are auctioned on the third Thursday of each month, except April, August, and December, at 11 a.m. as part of a semiannual calendar published in advance. BTAN maturities and interest payment dates are set on the 12th of the month. As of May 31, 2003 there were €169.6 billion of BTANs outstanding on the market, with a weighted average maturity of 2.3 years.

13.3.1.3   Fungible Treasury Bonds (OATs, Obligations assimilables du Trésor)

OATs are the government's long term debt instruments with maturities ranging from 7 to 30 years. Most OATs are fixed-rate bonds redeemable on maturity, but the Treasury also issues floating-rate bonds (TEC 10 OATs pegged to an average of OAT yields with a constant maturity of 10 years) and bonds indexed to the French and Euro area inflation rate (OATi and OAT€I, respectively). OATs are auctioned on the first Thursday of each month, except April, August, and December, whereby a 10-year fixed-rate line and, depending on market conditions, other fixed or floating-rate OATs are auctioned at 11 a.m. and 3 p.m., respectively. OAT maturities and interest payment dates are set on the 25th of the month. As of May 31, 2003 there were €495.6 billion of OATs outstanding on the market, with a weighted average maturity of 8.3 years.

Every year since 1999, the Treasury reserves part of its OAT issuing program for retail investors in a bid to boost long term household savings. The so-called retail OATs (OATs particuliers) are tranches of the 10-year OAT that may be purchased by private investors at banks, post offices, tax offices, and more recently via the Internet. Apart from the special case of the period preceding the payment of the first coupon, these bonds are identical to those issued to institutional investors; they are tradable, and therefore benefit from the high liquidity of OATs in general.

13.3.1.4   Strips

The liquidity of French debt across the yield curve is fostered by the presence of a highly active strips market. In 1991, France became the first sovereign issuer to authorize stripping and has since become the benchmark for this type of product in the Euro area. Now a mature market, the French strips market compares with the OAT market itself in terms of liquidity and attracts ever-increasing interest because of the introduction of the euro and the expected increase in long term securities in view of growing pension needs. On May 31, 2003, outstanding OAT strips came to about €41.1 billion, corresponding to 9.7% of strippable OATs outstanding.

13.3.2   The Primary Dealer System

Since 1987, the French government's issuance policy has relied on a network of primary dealers (SVTs, Spécialistes en Valeurs du Trésor). The SVTs' mission is to maintain the liquidity of the primary and secondary government debt markets. As of March 2003, there are 21 SVTs in the market, 14 of which are foreign-owned banks:

- ABN-Amro Fixed Income France
- Banque Lehman Brothers SA
- BNP Paribas
- Barclays Capital France SA
- CDC Ixis Capital Markets
- Union Europeenne de CIC
- Commerzbank AG
- Crédit Agricole Indosuez
- Crédit Lyonnais
- Deutsche Bank AG
- Dresdner Kleinwort Wasserstein

- Goldman Sachs Paris Inc. & Cie
- HSBC-CFF
- JP Morgan & Cie SA
- Merrill Lynch Finance SA
- Morgan Stanley SA
- Natexis Banques Populaires
- Salomon Brothers International Ltd.
- Société Générale
- UBS Warburg France SA
- Unicredit Banca Mobiliare.

13.3.3 Auction Procedure

The principal method of issuing French government securities is the bid price system, "a la hollandaise." Bank syndication is only used in special circumstances, such as the issuance of a new type of instrument. SVTs do not have a monopoly on auctions and in trading in French government securities. Non-SVT institutions showing adequate activity in the market, as reflected in placement of French debt with end-investors and trading on the secondary market, may apply for the status of Intermediary in French government securities (IVT, Intermédiaire en Valeurs du Trésor). At present, six institutions are recognized as IVTs: two Japanese (Daiwa, Nomura), one Italian (IMI San Paolo), one Spanish (Banco Bilbao Vizcaya Argentaria), one Belgian (Banque Bruxelles Lambert), and one Swiss (Credit Suisse First Boston). These banks have no commitment on the primary market.

The auction process depends on the security type. Four business days before an auction (2 days for BTFs), the Treasury announces the lines to be auctioned and a fixed amount of BTFs, or an upper and lower limit for OATs and BTANs to be issued. Bids must be submitted to the Banque de France 10 minutes before the auction. The Treasury then determines the amount to be allocated to each line, based on the prices and volume tendered for each line auctioned. Auction results are announced within 15 minutes, thanks to the introduction of screen-based bidding and data transmission via Telesat. For all instruments, noncompetitive bids are usually taken 2 days after the competitive auction.

The Treasury may also run reverse auctions, debt exchanges, and regular repurchases. The main aim of reverse auctions is to improve the smoothness of liquidity in the secondary market by offering to retire illiquid issues. Note that no reverse auctions have been held since 1995.

13.3.4 MTS France

MTS France, the electronic trading platform for French government securities developed in partnership with Euronext Paris and MTS SpA, the Italian electronic exchange, started operations in 2000. The company is governed by a Board of Directors elected by the shareholders, which include the SVTs, MTS SpA, and Euronext Paris. Currently 23 institutions participate in the system: the 21 SVTs as market makers and 2 market takers.

All euro-denominated securities issued by the French government, with maturities ranging from 0 to 30 years are traded on MTS France. A number of euro-denominated nonsovereign securities are also listed, namely 3 CADES (Caisse d'Amortissement de la Dette Sociale) securities as well as 3 ERAP and 2 CRH (Caisse de Refinancement de l'Habitat) securities with maturities ranging from 2 to 11 years. Trading in MTS France reached €257 billion in 2002, compared with €173 billion in 2001.

Trading in MTS France is conducted via the Telematico Cash system. Trading is from 8:15 a.m. to 5:30 p.m., with a premarket open from 7:30 to 8:00 a.m. and a preliminary market from 8:00 to 8:15 a.m. Participants in the system also have access to the Telematico Repo Trading Facility (RTF), which trades buy/sell back or classic repos, depending on the instrument. The RTF is open from 8:00 a.m. to 6:30 p.m., with a postmarket open from 6:30 to 7:00 p.m. All transactions are cleared by Clearnet SBF, while settlement is conducted by Euroclear France. Market participants must subscribe to both Euroclear France and Clearnet SBF.

13.3.5   Market Conventions

The market convention is for trade plus 1 (T + 1) settlement for all government securities with the value date the same as the settlement date. The holiday calendar of the EMU gross settlement system TARGET (Trans-European Automated Real-Time Gross Settlement Express Transfer) is employed. BTF bids are quoted on a money market straight yield, whereas OATs and BTANs are quoted in price. The yield on BTFs is calculated on an actual/360-day basis; on BTANs and OATs the actual/actual basis is employed. With effect from January 4, 1999, all existing government issues were redenominated in euros.

13.4   THE FRENCH NONGOVERNMENT BOND MARKET

The size of the negotiable public debt market has given France a strong position in the nongovernment bond market. Accordingly, Paris has taken the lead in the Euro area in developing the corporate bond market in particular. According to data provided by the BIS, the French corporate bond market was worth US$200 billion at the end of 2002, compared with US$170 billion for London and US$55 billion for Frankfurt. The issuance of bonds strengthened particularly sharply, by more than twofold, between 1998 and 2001 because of the increased financing needs of corporations arising in particular from mergers and acquisitions activity. The maturity of corporate bonds may range from 3 to 15 years. With regard to short and medium term marketable instruments, nongovernment issuance is concentrated on commercial paper (CP). Table 13.2 shows that issuance by banks on the debt securities primary market accounts for around one third of total issuance, although this figure includes short term certificates of deposit. The recent surge of the market segment for bank bonds mainly reflects the success of the Pfandbrief-style Obligations Fonciéres.

Generally speaking, French banks are the main investors in the nongovernment bond market. Despite remaining small, the share of nonresident investors has gradually increased, especially with regard to commercial paper.

The following is a list of the different types of instruments available in the French nongovernment bond market.

13.4.1   Commercial Paper (Billets de Trésorerie)

These are typically short term discount instruments, although they may also be issued with fixed or floating-rate coupons. Maturities range from overnight to 180 days. With the shift to the euro, many major issuers have chosen CP as their preferred short term financing vehicle within Europe, and as a result the total value of outstanding CP reached €76 billion in March

2003, by far the largest among Euro area members. The market is one of the most open for nonresident issuers, which account for about one quarter of the market. A rapidly expanding segment of this market is that of asset-backed commercial paper (ABCP). These instruments are in effect asset securitizations refinanced on the CP market, mainly used to securitize trade receivables. ABCP constitutes more than one fifth of all outstanding CP in the French market.

13.4.2 Bonds

13.4.2.1 Bullet Bonds (Obligations Remboursables in Fine)

These are issued as standard, fixed-rate instruments with annual coupons. Bullets still remain the most popular form of bond because of their simplicity, relatively low issuance and administrative costs, and the ease to compare their yield with that of reference OATs. The market convention of repurchasing bonds on the exchange (Rachat en Bourse) permits the issuer to buy back these bonds as and whenever it chooses to, although the amount which can be repurchased each year is usually capped at issuance.

13.4.2.2 Convertible Bonds (Obligations Convertibles en Actions) and ORA Convertible Bonds (Obligations Remboursables en Actions)

These instruments are increasingly popular in the French market. Denominations are usually smaller and more irregular than for bullets. ORAs are different from traditional convertible bonds in that the bondholder automatically becomes a shareholder at redemption. Of course, they are considered to be less secure investments as a result, and therefore give higher yields. ORAs are not listed and are not allocated ISIN codes.

13.4.2.3 Floating-Rate Notes (FRNs)

These are notes with coupon payments calculated using a benchmark rate. Coupons are predetermined and quarterly. TEC 10 FRNs (Obligations a Taux Revisable et a Coupons Trimestriels References sur le CNO-TEC 10) are pegged to the TEC 10 index, taken 5 business days before the beginning of the reference period. The benchmark for Euribor FRNs (Euribor 3 Mois Revisable) is the EURIBOR (European Interbank Offer Rate) 3-month value, taken 2 business days before the beginning of the reference period. The use of EURIBOR took effect on January 1, 1999 when the Paris Interbank Offered Rate (PIBOR) ceased to be quoted.

13.4.2.4 Index-Linked Bonds (Obligations a Coupon/a Amortissement Indexe sur l'Indice)

These are notes with coupon payments, redemption price or both linked to a market index, usually the CAC40, which is the blue chip weighted index of the Premier Marché segment of Euronext Paris.

13.4.2.5 Bonds with Warrants (Obligations a Bons de Souscription d'Actions)

These instruments comprise debt contracted at a rate lower than the bond market norm. They have the added advantage of allowing the issuer to defer the dilution of their share capital.

13.4.2.6   Fungible Bonds (Obligations a Assimilation)

The majority of these issues funge on their dated date and are, therefore, treated as an increase to the outstanding amount of the original bond. These bonds are not allocated a separate ISIN code. Some of these instruments funge a year after issue on the coupon payment date and are allocated an ISIN code.

13.4.3   Pfandbrief-Style Mortgage Bonds (Obligations fonciéres)

OFs are Pfandbrief-style mortgage bonds issued in standard bullet form with 6- or 12-year maturities. Only special status financial companies known as Societes de Credit Foncier (SCF) are permitted to issue them. First introduced in October 1999, OFs were launched to rival the German Pfandbriefe, and now constitute the second largest covered bond market in Europe with outstandings of around €34 billion in February 2003.

The immense popularity of OFs owes to their extremely high credit and liquidity. Issuance mechanisms are designed to enhance liquidity and transparency; the market making schemes reflect very closely those adopted for the German Pfandbrief. Issuers and market makers agreed to set the minimum issue size to €500 million, and to have all issues rated by at least two of the internationally recognized rating agencies. Along with German Pfandbriefe and Spanish Cédulas Hipotecarias, OFs are traded on the EuroCredit MTS trading platform, part of the MTS Group, which requires a minimum outstanding volume of €3 billion. Currently, only three OFs qualify (in terms of issue size) to be quoted on EuroCreditMTS.

13.4.4   Asset-Backed Securities (ABS) Issued through Securitization Vehicles (FCC, Fonds Commun de Creances)

FCC are special purpose vehicles created for the purpose of funding outstanding debt through a cash flow obtained from a pool of receivables or financial assets that convert into cash within a certain period. Most of the operations involve the securitization of mortgages, followed by car loans and consumer credit receivables. Debt issued by FCCs is seen as attractive because of its high yield and ratings and diversity. There are currently three types of FCC bonds available: Annuity FCCs with a mortgage-like sinking fund paying interest and principal on each payment date; Average Life FCCs with similar characteristics but with undetermined maturities; and FCCs with redemption premium where interest is paid at maturity. The first French ABS were issued in 1988; the value of outstanding securitization vehicle units amounted to €15.3 billion at the end of 2001.

13.4.5   Market Conventions

The market convention is for trade plus 3 (T + 3) settlement for nongovernment debt securities with the value date the same as the settlement date. The holiday calendar of the EMU gross settlement system TARGET is employed. The yield is typically calculated on an actual/actual basis, except on EURIBOR FRNs, where the actual/360 basis is employed, and mortgage bonds, where either may be employed. With effect from January 1, 2002, all corporate bonds still in French francs were redenominated in euros.

REFERENCES

Agency France Trésor (2002). 2001/2002 Annual Report.

Agency France Trésor (2003, June). Monthly Bulletin No. 157.

Amor, J.M. (2002). *Government Bond Markets in the Euro Zone*. New York: John Wiley, pp. 123–139.

Banque de France (2002). Annual Report 2001.

Banque de France (2003, April). Banque de France Bulletin No. 112 Digest.

Deppler, M. and L. Lipschitz (2002). *France: Staff Report for the 2002 Article IV Consultation*. Washington DC: International Monetary Fund.

Dziobek, C., O. Jeanne, and A. Ubide (1999). France: Selected Issues. *IMF Staff Country Report No. 99/139*. Washington DC: International Monetary Fund.

European Central Bank (2002). *Report on Financial Structures*. Frankfurt: European Central Bank, pp. 121–140.

La Porta, R., F. Lopez-De-Silanes, and A. Shleifer (2002). Government Ownership of Banks. *Journal of Finance* **57**(1): 265–301.

14

Germany

NIKLAS WAGNER

14.1 INTRODUCTION

Bonds in Germany traditionally play an important role in household savings on the one hand and in government debt and bank financing on the other. The German bond market is the third largest in the world and the largest in Europe; the size of overall outstanding debt amounted to US$1900 billion in September 1999 (Deutsche Bundesbank [DBB], 2000). For September 2002, Bank for International Settlements (BIS, 2002a, 2002b) reported outstanding German domestic and international debt securities to total an amount that ranked the country number three worldwide, following the United States and Japan.

The size of the German bond market relates to the country's economic background and historic development. In the postwar era, Germany enjoyed a period of remarkable economic success; *Wirtschaftswunder* made Germany the third largest economy in the world, after the United States and Japan. Ingredients were external support in the form of loans via the Marshall Aid Plan, prudent fiscal and monetary policies, good relations between social partners, and the general focus on reconstructing the country after the destruction of the Second World War. An important element of the economic system was the idea of a "social" market economy, a term initially promoted by the conservatives but later backed by the leading left-wing party. The idea demanded that the economy is in fact governed by market forces, but that the government retains an important role in social welfare and in correcting market imperfections. In a broader sense it included that companies are responsible not only to their shareholders but also to other stakeholders, such as their employees, customers, suppliers, and their local communities. The concept of a social market economy contributed to harmonious labor relations. Another important element of the German economic model was the focus on bank financing, including close relations of the companies with their respective bank (*Hausbank*), which allowed a focus on long term objectives insulating business decisions from short term share-price fluctuations.

Germany has ever since played an active role within the European Union (EU), not only as a founding member but also starting with its role in the Montan-Union in the early 1950s. Still, it was not a natural way to go for Germany in leaving the deutsche mark as its successful currency of the *Wirtschaftswunder* behind. The introduction of the euro in 1999 was generally seen as an accomplishment for further economic development and integration of the EU rather than as an indication of a change in monetary policy. Hence, negotiations in the 1990s establishing the structure of the European Central Bank (ECB) led to a model consistent with Bundesbank. Also, setting up stability criteria in the Maastricht Treaty including the Stability and Growth Pact was an essential condition for the later renouncement of the country's monetary sovereignty.

European Fixed Income Markets: Money, Bond and Interest Rate Derivatives. Edited by J.A. Batten,
T.A. Fetherston and P.G. Szilagyi. © 2004 John Wiley & Sons, Ltd. ISBN 0-470-85053-1

In the meanwhile, Germany, in 2002, faced severe structural economic problems that exceeded those of other member countries. Also, doubts about the merits of the German economic model, under conditions of increasing international competition and reduced relevancy of traditional manufacturing, had risen, particularly during the second half of the 1990s. This led to increased demands for a reduction of the influence of trade unions and a deregulation of the labor market. In addition, the integration of European financial markets initiated a shift away from the reliance on long term bank financing and an increasing focus on direct financing via the capital markets. This also evoked a stronger focus of German companies on shareholder value.

The Stability and Growth Pact, which was intended to prevent the respective national governments from overspending, has now become a threat to the country itself. Germany exceeding the 3% of gross domestic product (GDP) debt threshold in 2002 was not only due to a tremendous flood catastrophe in the eastern part of the country, but also due to a weak economy and ongoing enormous public spending efforts due to its reunification. Government's annual deficit surged after reunification in 1990 when public spending efforts caused a short term booming economy together with a positive shock to interest rates, which then caused crowding-out in private investments.

The recent economic situation in Germany is characterized by high unemployment and low growth rates. Table 14.1 summarizes key economic indicators for the years 1998–2001. Between 1997 and 2001, the economy recorded an average annual growth of 1.8%, which was below average within the Euro zone (2.6%). GDP growth slowed down in 2001 and with the recent recession the forecasts remain weak. The economic recovery has stalled, and GDP growth, estimated at 0.3% in 2002, is expected to be only 0.4% in 2003 and 1.6% in 2004. Although the ECB cut its main refinancing rate by 50 basis points to 2.75% on December 5, 2002, monetary policy remains too tight from a German perspective, as the German economy is weaker than that of the Euro area as a whole, while inflation in Germany is lower, implying higher real interest rates.

Germany's trade account is stabilized by its role as the second largest exporter in the world. Exports were US$571 billion in 2001 and imports US$488 billion, resulting in a trade surplus of US$83 billion. Despite a large services deficit and a substantial outflow of current transfers, the current account recorded a surplus of US$3.8 billion (0.21% of GDP) in 2001. Table 14.1 indicates though that this was an extraordinarily good result, not achieved in the preceding

Table 14.1   Key economic indicators in Germany

	1998	1999	2000	2001
GDP per head ($ at PPP)	23 702	24 660	25 952	26 680
GDP (% real change pa)	1.96	2.05	2.86	0.57
Government consumption (% of GDP)	19.15	19.15	19.08	19.00
Budget balance (% of GDP)	−2.20	−1.55	1.18	−2.73
Consumer prices (% change pa; average)	0.91	0.58	1.94	2.48
Public debt (% of GDP)	63.21	60.88	60.81	60.26
Labor costs per hour (US$)	26.76	26.18	22.99	23.04
Recorded unemployment (%)	10.90	10.30	9.30	9.60
Current-account balance/GDP	−0.31	−0.85	−1.00	0.21
Foreign-exchange reserves (billion US$)	74	61	56	51

Source: Economist Intelligence Unit.

3 years and the outlook seems similar for the coming years. The inflation target of 2% was not achieved in 2001, but is not an issue for 2002–2004 when inflation is expected to fluctuate around 1%.

The recent economic outlook for Germany does not seem too promising and it also seems that the country's debt burden has become excessive. The central-left Social-Democratic Party, which is in government since 1998, was not yet able to stop the deterioration in public finances, although the Finance Minister strictly targets a consolidation of the public households. The objective now is to reduce expenditure and taxation in relation to GDP and to bring the deficit down to zero by 2006. With the slowing of the German economy, employment figures have remained on a high level, with new records in 2002. Forward-looking indicators have continued to decline. The general government budget deficit will therefore most probably again exceed the EU's ceiling of 3% of GDP in 2003, after already exceeding the limit in 2002. Together with fiscal consolidation, labor market reform will be at the top of the economic policy agenda, although initial measures taken so far have been disappointing.

14.2   STRUCTURE OF THE GERMAN BOND MARKET

In recent years, the national financial systems of the EU Member States have undergone an intense transformational process. In Germany, despite integration, technological innovation, and competition, the financial system did not change that dramatically over the past few decades. This is mainly because financial liberalization took place relatively early in Germany, while market orientation gradually became stronger in the 1990s.

14.2.1   Overall Situation

Although the German bond market is the largest in Europe, there are a few dominant features that have characterized the German financial system over the last 50 years: The German system was, and still is, essentially bank-based, which implies that most corporations are largely dependent on bank financing. This is in sharp contrast with some other EU Member States, most notably the United Kingdom, where the financial system is market-based. In Germany, banks, which are mostly organized as universal banks, have played and still play a central role. Households have usually held deposits with retail banks, and whenever firms needed external assets, they obtained loans from their retail bank, taking advantage of the close relationship between the bank and the firm. From about 1980 onwards, the importance of insurance corporations as alternative financial intermediaries grew. In the 1990s mutual funds became increasingly successful. For a long time, the allocation of assets via capital markets was of much less relevance, with equity financing traditionally being much less important than debt financing. Issuing securities served as the usual means of financing for banks and above all particularly for the government. The low importance of equity financing is reflected in the relatively low stock market capitalization when compared to that of other European countries.

Most household assets and liabilities are channeled via intermediaries. On the liability side, this is quite obvious since loans are the only possible source of external funds for households. In 2000 households held more than twice as many intermediated assets than shares and bonds, but the trend over the last few years has been much more toward market instruments. The behavior of corporations was different, their borrowing being mainly in the markets. This holds for both sides of the balance sheet. In a certain sense the government sector stands as an intermediary between households and firms. For the government, intermediation-oriented assets clearly outweighed market-oriented assets, but the former were very small in comparison with the other sector's financial assets as a whole. On the financing side, market orientation dominates: the government's most important source of funding has traditionally been the issuance of bonds. The German bond market is a long term market, where 80% of debt securities are issued with an original maturity of over 4 years. Issues of short term paper such as money market and commercial paper have increased during the last few years and now account for roughly 5% of overall issuance. In terms of the volume of funds allocated from savers to borrowers in Germany, the bond market ranks second behind the banking sector. At the end of 2000, €2300 billion worth of debt securities (110% of GDP) were outstanding (ECB, 2002).

14.2.2 Sectors of the Bond Market

Figure 14.1 outlines the fractions of debt issued by different domestic institutions in Germany during the years 1995–2000. Government bonds (General Government Issues, *Schuldverschreibungen der öffentlichen Hand*) are the second most important issues. Together with bonds issued by commercial banks and other monetary financial institutions (MFIs) called *Bankschuldverschreibungen*, including *Pfandbriefe*, they make up the huge bulk of the overall bond market. Issues of corporate bonds (*Industrieobligationen*) are negligible; in 1999, for example, they accounted for 0.3% of the overall volume (see DBB, 2000).

As can be seen in Figure 14.1, large growth rates in recent years were observable in MFIs' issues. In particular, the volume of *Bankschuldverschreibungen* and public *Pfandbriefe* nearly doubled between 1995 and 2000. Growth was propelled by issues of so-called

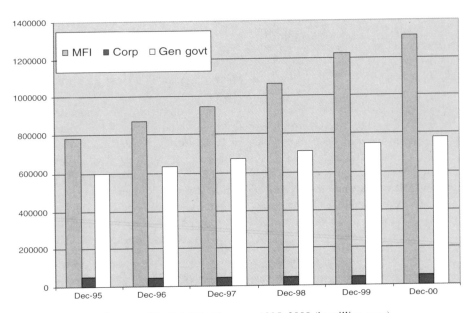

Figure 14.1 Outstanding securitized debt in Germany 1995–2000 (in million euro).
Source: Deutsche Bundesbank. Reproduced by permission of Deutsche Bundesbank.

Jumbo-Pfandbriefe, which attracted interest of foreign institutional investors; these issues are characterized by an overall issue size of at least €500 million and have a transparent and liquid secondary market.[1] The situation of the corporate bond sector is quite different. The structure of the German bond market as documented by the Figure 14.1 adds to the thesis that corporate finance via domestic issues is small and tends to be crowded-out by government and intermediated MFIs' issues.

14.2.3   Recent Capital Market Developments

Development in the capital markets during the last 10 years was accompanied by new legal regulations (*Finanzmarktförderungsgesetz*, Financial Markets Promotion Act) and changes to the existing law for the financial services industry (*Kreditwesengesetz* KWG). These changes in the legal system aimed at the preparation of an improved institutional setting and to support the modernization of the financial system; such efforts are vital with respect to international competition between financial centers within Europe. Seifert *et al.* (2000) note that Germany's position with its financial center Frankfurt is characterized by high market shares in low growth segments and vice versa. High market shares are reported in the primary equity and Eurobond markets as well as in exchange-traded derivatives (EUREX), whereas market shares in the foreign exchange markets, in equity fund management, and in over the counter (OTC) derivatives trading are rather low.

As reported by Bundesministerium der Finanzen (1999), recent regulatory changes that aim at a modernization of the German financial system include the following:

- 1990: Regulation of futures and options markets. Reduction in taxation of transactions carried out on public exchanges. Changes in mutual fund laws.
- 1994: Improvement of stockholders' rights via the introduction of an act on trading rules (*Wertpapierhandelsgesetz*) that includes rules on insider trading as well as rules on the information policy of listed corporations (*ad hoc Publizitätspflicht*).
- 1997: Changes in the *Kreditwesengesetz* KWG aimed at harmonization of legal rules concerning the providers of financial services within the EU.
- 1998: Further deregulation of capital markets and improvements in trading rules' supervision. Changes in mutual fund laws allowing for new types of funds.
- 2002: The fourth issue of the Financial Market Promotion Act aims at more flexible trading rules giving electronic trading via XETRA an enhanced legal status. For details and a critical assessment of these latest reforms, see Rudolph (2002).

Apart from these regulatory changes that aim at improving capital market structure in Germany, recent market developments indicate a gradual structural change in several directions:

- Over the past few years financial institutions including banks and insurance corporations including pension funds have become increasingly interlinked as a result of mergers and acquisitions. The process has not yet come to an end and experts expect only a few big universal financial companies to remain in the financial services industry by 2010.
- Concentration in the banking industry is due to the need for cost savings in face of falling income. This may also explain a trend toward more capital market instead of intermediated

---

[1] See Chapter 9 for a detailed description of this important segment of the European and particularly German bond market.

transactions. For example, bond financing started to play an increasingly important role for banks, given a decline in traditional deposits as customers increasingly have access to disintermediated forms of deposit such as money market funds, which were introduced in 1994.

- The new Basle Accord (BIS, 2001) is expected to have a substantial impact on Germany's commercial banks lending strategy. Since customer rating will play an increasingly important role, small- and medium-sized enterprises (SMEs) with moderate credit rating may face severe debt financing shortages, with neither bank nor capital market funds being available. This effect becomes even more severe under new records in company failures in recent years, which slowed down banks lending activities.
- A sharp increase in sales of corporate bonds in 1999 and 2000 indicates an increasing importance of the corporate bond market in Germany. Notably more than 80% of the €160 billion outstanding companies' debt securities were issued via foreign financial subsidiaries. These financial resources are then transferred back to the parent company as loans. Corporate tax advantages are likely to be the main reason for this indirect method of financing.
- In the second half of the 1990s, stock market investing and financing became more common as reflected by much increased public attention during that time. Related events that were of relevance to capital markets include the privatization of large previously state-owned businesses. The federal government consistently pursued privatization since the early 1980s, and since the mid-1990s it speeded up asset disposals. The Bavarian government also embraced privatization as far back as the early 1980s. In other states and among most municipalities until recently reluctance to divest shareholdings dominates; financial pressure led to the disposal of some assets, notably airports and utility company holdings, as with, for example, the recent sale of Frankfurt airport.
- A chance for more capital market orientation and equity financing came up with the opening of *Neuer Markt* in 1997, an exchange for relatively young German corporations. Because of the burst of the bubble in international technology stock markets in 2000 and because of the domestic issues in corporate governance, the exchange has proven unsuccessful and Deutsche Börse is going to discontinue the market by the end of 2003 while merging it into the new TECDAX sector. Hence, SMEs in general continue to depend on bank credit and still have limited, though somewhat improved, access to disintermediated forms of equity financing.
- Although mutual funds enjoyed above-average growth during the 1990s, importance is still modest by international standards. In terms of overall household assets in Germany investment funds made up 4% of all assets in 1991, where the fraction rose to 11% by the end of 2000.

These regulatory changes and recent developments as well as ongoing internationalization of the markets all have forced competition in the German financial system. However, while stock exchange and derivatives markets have experienced growth, the development of debt markets, and the nongovernment segment of these in particular, continues to lag behind. There remain numerous differences between the individual systems of financing, most notably as to whether corporations raise funds by borrowing from banks or directly through capital markets. Because banks have historically conducted the bulk of financial business, bond markets have been relatively slow to develop. Additional initiatives on the part of policymakers may allow for future progress in the bond markets where market access must be facilitated and promoted among borrowers and investors alike.

14.3   PARTICIPANTS OF THE GERMAN BOND MARKET

14.3.1   Regulators

14.3.1.1   German Central Bank (Deutsche Bundesbank)

The Deutsche Bundesbank, the central bank of the Federal Republic of Germany, is an integral part of the European System of Central Banks (ESCB). The latter comprises the ECB and the national central banks of all 15 EU Member States. In addition, the Bank is also a member of the Eurosystem, which comprises the ECB and the central banks of the 12 member states of the Economic and Monetary Union (EMU). The central bank was established in 1957 as the sole successor to the two-tier central bank system that comprised the *Bank Deutscher Länder* together with the Federal Central Banks (*Landeszentralbanken*). At the time, the Land Central Banks were legally independent bodies. Together, the institutions in the central bank system bore responsibility for the German currency from June 20, 1948, when the deutsche mark was introduced, until Deutsche Bundesbank was founded.

As a result of Bundesbank becoming part of the ESCB, the need to restructure became increasingly evident. The Bundesbank's organizational structure was changed according to the new Bundesbank Act of April 2002. However, of course, the banks primary tasks have not changed. The Bundesbank participates in the fulfillment of the ESCB's tasks with the objective of maintaining the stability of the euro. It ensures the orderly execution of domestic and foreign payments and contributes to the stability of payment and clearing systems.

The Bundesbank's executive board normally is hosted in Frankfurt. It comprises the President, the Vice President, and six other members. Its mandate is to govern and manage the Bundesbank. The Board will draw up an organizational statute to establish how responsibilities are shared out among the Board members and to determine the tasks that may be delegated to the regional offices. The members of the Board are all appointed by the President of the Federal Republic. The President, the Vice President, and two other members are nominated by the German federal government, while the other four members are nominated by the *Bundesrat* in agreement with the federal government. Bundesbank headquarters are located in Frankfurt am Main. In addition, Bundesbank maintains nine regional offices in the German federal states, namely in Stuttgart, Munich, Berlin, Hanover, Hamburg, Frankfurt am Main, Düsseldorf, Mainz, and Leipzig. These offices (formerly known as Land Central Banks) are responsible for the bank's functions in one or more of Germany's federal states. Subordinated to the regional offices are 126 branches located in the larger towns in Germany. They carry out the Bundesbank's business with the credit institutions and the public authorities in their respective areas.

Serving as a central bank, Deutsche Bundesbank is the bank of issue, the bankers' bank, the state's bank, and the guardian of the monetary reserves. Bundesbank also plays a significant role in banking supervision. Within the scope of its participation in the ESCB, it takes care of the following activities:

- Bank of issue: The ECB has the sole right to approve the issuing of banknotes within the Euro area where the ECB and the national central banks are authorized to issue banknotes. Bundesbank also puts coins into circulation, which the Federal Government may issue once the volume of coins to be issued has been approved by the ECB.
- Bankers' bank: The special status of Bundesbank as the bankers' bank is due to credit institutions being dependent on balances at the central bank in order to maintain their solvency.

They have to pay out cash to their customers and, as mentioned previously, maintain balances known as minimum reserves at the Bundesbank. Bundesbank is thus the banking system's ultimate source of refinancing. It also provides the banks with banking services for settling cashless payments.

- State's bank: Bundesbank is the principal bank of the Federal Government and, to a lesser extent, of the Länder Governments. It carries accounts for public authorities, executes payments, and assists the Federal and Länder Governments in their borrowing in the capital market. In particular, Bundesbank is responsible for Federal debt management and is the primary issuer of government debt. It is also active in market making for the various types of issued government debt.
- Guardian of the monetary reserves: As the guardian of the monetary reserves, Bundesbank holds the official monetary reserves of the Federal Republic of Germany, and invests them at interest. These reserves are mainly balances held in US dollars with banks or central banks abroad. Transactions by the national central banks with their remaining monetary reserves require the approval of the ECB from a certain volume onward, in order to maintain the uniformity of the single monetary and exchange rate policy.
- Banking supervision: As a participant in the Forum for Financial Market Supervision, Deutsche Bundesbank shares legal responsibility for the stability of the financial system. In addition, involvement of Bundesbank in the ongoing monitoring of credit and financial services institutions is now defined in the Banking Act. As a rule Bundesbank's regional offices are responsible for carrying out monitoring operations. Bundesbank's offices analyze and evaluate the reports and announcements published by the institutions. They also conduct on-site prudential audits to assess the appropriateness of the institutions' capital base and risk management procedures and evaluate the audit findings. The Federal Agency for Financial Services Supervision generally bases its prudential supervisory measures on Bundesbank's audit findings and evaluations.
- Bundesbank defines the bank's mandate as part of the ESCBas follows:

> The Deutsche Bundesbank, being the central bank of the Federal Republic of Germany, is an integral part of the ESCB. It shall participate in the performance of the ESCB's tasks with the primary objective of maintaining price stability, and shall arrange for the execution of domestic and international payments.
>
> Thus, Bundesbank, as a national central bank, implements the single monetary policy of the ESCB. In order to be able to fulfill this mandate without political pressure, Bundesbank has been granted a large degree of independence by the Parliament. It is only required to support the general economic policy of the Federal Cabinet. According to the Maastricht Treaty, neither the ECB, nor a national central bank, nor any member of their decision-making bodies may take instructions from community institutions, from any government of a member state or from any other body when exercising the powers and carrying out the tasks and duties conferred upon them.

Apart from the activities defined above, Bundesbank follows monetary policy within the scope of its participation in the ESCB, acknowledging that price stability is an essential policy task. The ECB Governing Council has defined price stability as an annual increase in the consumer price index in the Euro area of below 2%. To achieve price stability, the ECB Governing Council has also set a strategy in which the money stock occupies a position of central importance. This was inspired by the strategy previously pursued by the Bundesbank, since controlling the money stock is certainly an important condition of price stability, though it alone will not suffice. The money stock is taken into account by announcing a quantitative reference value for the growth of the broad monetary aggregate M3.

In parallel to analyzing monetary growth, the ECB Governing Council assesses the outlook for price movements and risks to price stability in the Euro area. They are assessed with the help of a wide range of economic and financial indicators. The Eurosystem publishes an aggregate version of this analysis as a macroeconomic forecast in June and December each year. However, in order for its stability policy to succeed, the ESCB must rely on the participation of public authorities and wage negotiators in the countries participating in monetary union. The ECB or, more precisely, the national central banks, which carry out monetary policy in a mostly decentralized manner, have a number of monetary policy instruments at their disposal with which they can achieve the objective of price stability by exercising influence on interest rates and liquidity:

- Open-market transactions are the core element of this set of monetary policy instruments. As they go, a distinction is made between main refinancing operations, longer term refinancing operations, fine-tuning operations, and structural operations.
- The main refinancing operations are a means of providing liquidity and are tendered weekly with a maturity of 2 weeks as reverse transactions. This instrument plays a key role since it provides most of the financial sector's liquidity.
- The provision of liquidity by means of longer term refinancing operations is also carried out using reverse transactions. However, these transactions are only tendered at 1-month intervals. These basis tenders have a maturity of 3 months.
- Fine-tuning operations are carried out on a case-by-case basis to offset unexpected fluctuations in liquidity levels.
- Structural operations can serve to adjust the structural liquidity position of the financial sector *vis-à-vis* the ESCB at regular or irregular intervals.
- The ESCB has two other instruments at its disposal: facilities that serve to provide or absorb liquidity on short notice. The interest rates on these two instruments denote the upper and lower bounds of the overnight money market rates.
- The instruments mentioned above are supplemented by the minimum reserve instrument. This means the banks have to hold balances calculated on the basis of certain liabilities at the national central banks. The balances held with the Bundesbank for this purpose are remunerated at the rate of the ESCB's main refinancing operations.

14.3.1.2   Federal Ministry of Finance

The German Federal Ministry of Finance is the issuer of Federal government debt. Under the German federal system, government debt is also issued by states (*Länder*) and communities (*Gemeinden*). Government spending and financial policy aims at the following five main objectives:

- achieving growth and employment,
- maintaining long-run financial flexibility,
- achieving fairness among social classes as well as generations, including the German Stability Program in accordance with the provisions of the Stability and Growth Pact,
- being generally understood and accepted,
- being consistent within the international economic and fiscal situation.

14.3.1.3   Federal Debt Management Agency (Bundesrepublik Deutschland – Finanzagentur GmbH)

Based on a decision of the Federal Ministry of Finance in February 2000, government debt management activities were partly withdrawn from Bundesbank and redirected to a newly established debt management agency, the *Bundesrepublik Deutschland – Finanzagentur GmbH*. The agency is a private legal entity which is fully owned by the German Federal Ministry of Finance. Its task is to cover government's borrowing requirements at the lowest possible cost, while taking financing risks into account.

The agency provides services to the Ministry of Finance and thereby supports the Federal Republic's household financing and cash management decisions. To this aim, the agency is responsible for services related to the issue of government debt, credit financing, the implementation of derivatives strategies, and money market transactions. As being authorized by the agency, Bundesbank at the moment still carries out the issue of government debt including auctions and market-making activities. Market-making in the electronic trading system EUREX, for example, has become a task of the agency itself, which is expected to assume a growing number of management activities in the future.

14.3.1.4   Federal Agency for Financial Services Supervision (Bundesanstalt für Finanzdienstleistungsaufsicht – BAFin)

The Federal Agency for Financial Services Supervision is a supervisory authority for the financial services industry in Germany. It was established following the 2002 adoption of the Law on Integrated Financial Services Supervision and now unifies the former offices for banking supervision (*Bundesaufsichtsamt für das Kreditwesen* BAKred), insurance supervision (*Bundesaufsichtsamt für das Versicherungswesen* BAV), and securities supervision (*Bundesaufsichtsamt für den Wertpapierhandel* BAWe). The BAFin is a federal institution governed by public law that belongs to the portfolio of the Federal Ministry of Finance and as such, has a legal personality. It supervises approximately 2700 banks, 800 financial services institutions, and over 700 insurance companies.

The Federal Financial Supervisory Authority BAFin is responsible for key functions of consumer protection and solvency supervision, thereby ensuring stability of the German financial system and improving its competitiveness. The BAFin has three main supervisory objectives: to safeguard the solvency of banks, financial services institutions, and insurance undertakings and to protect clients and investors. BAFin comprises three supervisory units, namely banking supervision, insurance supervision, and securities and asset-management supervision.

The main aim of the securities and asset-management supervision unit is to secure the proper functioning of the securities and derivatives markets by pursuing the objective of investor protection, market transparency, and market integrity. More precisely, objectives are given by the Securities Trading Act (*Wertpapierhandelsgesetz* WpHG) and the Securities Sales Prospectus Act (*Wertpapier-Verkaufsprospektgesetz*). They include

- preventing and taking legal action in cases of insider trading,
- monitoring compliance with reporting requirements for all securities and derivatives transactions,
- monitoring *ad hoc* disclosure requirements of listed companies,
- monitoring the disclosure requirements in case of changes in holdings of voting rights in officially listed companies,

- monitoring management practices and compliance organization of investment services firms, and
- supporting national as well as international cooperation in supervision of securities trading.

14.3.1.5   Federal Exchange Supervisory Authority (Börsenaufsicht)

The National Exchange Supervisory Authority is a Federal system of regulatory state agencies. These agencies are part of the Federal Ministry of Economics and individually oversee the local stock exchanges as well as the debt and derivatives markets. Official Trading (*Amtlicher Handel*) is regulated by the Stock Exchange Law (*Börsengesetz*) and exchange listing regulations (*Börsenzulassungsverordnung*). The Regulated Market (*Geregelter Markt*) obeys weaker rules than those in Official Trading.

The most important duties of the authority are supervision of the price formation process, investigation of violations against exchange rules and regulations, fraud prevention, and supervision of lawful conduct by exchange entities. The agency is also in charge of the supervision of trading participants admitted to exchange trading. Furthermore it participates in the field of legislation and exchange policy. The Exchange Supervisory Authority, for example in Hessia, is responsible for the legal and market supervision of the Frankfurt Stock Exchange, the *Frankfurter Wertpapierbörse*, and the derivatives exchange EUREX.

The OTC market (*Freiverkehr*) is governed by the Association of Stockbrokers (*Vereinigung der Effektenhändler*). One such association exists for each stock exchange.

14.3.2   Categories of Investors

The categories of investors in the German market may well be described by flows of funds as recorded by the ECB. These records include four sectors, namely domestic households, financial and nonfinancial corporations, and the government.

Flow of funds transactions in Germany during the 1998–2000 period showed that domestic households were able to contribute financial assets to the other sectors, whereas nonfinancial corporations and the government sector generally required external funds. The financial corporations played a more or less neutral role in line with their intermediation function. When considering the economy as a whole, net household lending was not sufficient to meet the demand of the other resident sectors for the given period. Therefore, the economy was dependent on capital inflows from abroad (ECB 2002). Hence, not only domestic financial corporations and households, but also foreign investors play a relevant role in the market.

Although subject to fluctuations on a year-to-year basis, one can give some indication of single investor group's importance and shifts in importance during recent years. By the end of 1998, about 37% of outstanding government and MFI securitized debt was held by domestic banks. Whereas their fraction remained quite stable, the share of household and domestic nonbank corporations decreased from about 39% in 1991 to 29% in 1998. This development, as well as deregulation in international capital markets, explains why foreign debt holdings heavily increased from about 16% at the end of 1991 to nearly 33% at the end of 1998. Within the domestic household and domestic nonbank investor group, holdings by private households as well as insurance companies lost importance whereas investment fund holdings gained in size (DBB, 2000).

14.3.3   Market Makers

The following is a list of primary market makers that are members of the Bund issues auction group:

- ABN AMRO Bank (Deutschland) AG
- Baden-Württembergische Bank AG
- Bankgesellschaft Berlin AG
- Barclays Bank PLC Frankfurt Branch
- Bayerische Hypo- und Vereinsbank AG
- Bayerische Landesbank
- BNP Paribas
- Bremer Landesbank Kreditanstalt Oldenburg
- Commerzbank AG
- Credit Suisse First Boston (Europe) Ltd.
- Deutsche Bank AG
- Deutsche Postbank AG
- DekaBank
- Dresdner Bank AG
- DZ BANK AG
- Goldman, Sachs & Co. oHG
- Hamburgische Landesbank
- Hesse Newman & Co. (AG & Co.) KG
- HSBC Trinkaus und Burkhardt KGaA
- ING BHF-Bank AG
- J. P. Morgan Securities Ltd.
- Landesbank Baden-Württemberg
- Landesbank Berlin
- Landesbank Hessen-Thüringen
- Landesbank Sachsen
- Lehman Brothers Bankhaus AG
- Merrill Lynch Capital Markets Bank Ltd.
- Morgan Stanley Bank AG
- Nomura Bank (Deutschland) GmbH
- Norddeutsche Landesbank
- Nordea Bank A/S
- Reuschel & Co. KG
- Salomon Brothers AG
- SANPAOLO IMI SpA
- SEB AG
- Société Générale SA
- Stadtsparkasse Köln
- The Royal Bank of Scotland
- Vereins- und Westbank AG
- UBS Warburg AG
- WestLB AG

14.3.4 Other Market Participants

Other market participants include about 250 exchange members, of which more than half are German banks. These are represented by the Association of German Banks (*Bundesverband deutscher Banken*). German banks can be grouped into three categories: private commercial banks, cooperative banks (*Volksbanken* and *Raiffeisenbanken*), and public-sector banks represented by *Landesbanken* and savings banks (*Sparkassen*). The remainder market participants are domestic and international financial institutions and brokers.

14.3.5 Rating Agencies

All government debt is currently rated. Corporate ratings tend to be at the issuer level and are not so widely recognized. Hence, most German bonds are rated by one or more of the following three agencies:

- Fitch IBCA
- Standard and Poor's
- Moody's

14.3.6 Secondary Market Trading

German government bonds are traded on organized exchanges as well as OTC, the latter traditionally accounting for substantial amounts of trading. As such, only 5% of Clearstream Banking transaction volume was traded via an exchange in January 2000 (DBB, 2000), which outlines the traditionally strong position of banks in bond trading.

The largest regulated secondary floor market for German bonds is the Frankfurt Stock Exchange. Recently, MTS Germany, a division of EuroMTS, emerged as the electronic wholesale trading platform for German government bonds and now accounts for the bulk of trading in these securities. Bank bonds are still mostly traded OTC, with the exception of *Jumbo Pfandbriefe*, which are mostly traded via the newly introduced electronic trading platform EuroCredit MTS.

14.3.6.1 Stock Exchanges: Floor Trading

There are eight official stock exchanges in Germany. Floor trading takes place in Frankfurt, Bremen, Berlin, Hannover, Hamburg, Düsseldorf, Stuttgart, and Munich. Despite this decentralized system, Frankfurt is regarded as Germany's financial center where the Frankfurt Stock Exchange (*Frankfurter Wertpapierbörse*) remains by far the largest exchange.

Trading on German exchanges is traditionally divided into the three market segments: *Amtlicher Handel* (Official Market), *Geregelter Markt* (Regulated Market), and *Freiverkehr* (Regulated Unofficial Market, OTC transactions). An issuer must have been in business for a minimum of 3 years, and is required to provide annual reports when applying for a listing on the *Amtlicher Handel*. Conditions of the issue must be disclosed in a prospectus. If the issue is accepted, then the prospectus is published in financial newspapers such as *Börsenzeitung*, *Handelsblatt*, or *Frankfurter Allgemeine Zeitung*. The *Geregelter Markt* goes back to end of the 1980s and provides a trading platform for young and smaller German domestic issues. Three years of successful trading in *Geregelter Markt* is required to qualify for listing in *Amtlicher*

Handel. The OTC sector requires a written announcement rather than a formal application in order to qualify an issue. Permission to trade is rarely refused. Although financial reports must be submitted regularly, no publication costs are incurred and no strict regulations are imposed. Detailed listing rules are given in the exchange rules for the Frankfurt Stock Exchange (*Börsenordnung für die Frankfurter Wertpapierbörse*).

In November 2002, Frankfurt Stock Exchange approved a new additional segment for the equity market called *Prime Standard Segment*. This segment addresses companies that wish to target international investors, thereby meeting high international transparency criteria. Related plans for a new segment in the bond market are not yet available.

14.3.6.2   Stock Exchanges: Electronic Trading

During the 1990s, electronic trading became increasingly important in Germany not only for trading equities, but also for trading bonds. The electronic stock exchange XETRA was originally intended for the equity market and dates back to the preceding IBIS trading system. Since its introduction on October 12, 1998, XETRA allowed for trading bonds. In the last couple of years, the spot market for government bonds has more and more changed toward electronic trading.

It is anticipated that in the future, all liquid issues – both corporate and sovereign – will be traded using an electronic trading platform. As such, after its launch in April 1999, EuroMTS is an electronic trading system that has become popular recently. It forms a European electronic trading platform for euro-denominated benchmark government and nongovernment securities. EuroMTS trading includes benchmark securities from 14 government and agency issuers, namely Austria, Belgium, Finland, France, Germany, Greece, Ireland, Italy, The Netherlands, Portugal, Spain, the European Investment Bank, Freddie Mac, and the German *Kreditanstalt für Wiederaufbau*.

Additionally to EuroMTS, EuroCredit MTS opened for trading in May 2000. EuroCredit MTS is an electronic trading platform for high-quality credit risky bonds, such as *Pfandbriefe*, where additional bond classes can be added in response to market demand. To be listed on EuroCredit MTS, nongovernment bonds must

- be euro-denominated,
- be collateralized with either mortgages or public sector loans or both,
- have an outstanding size in excess of €3 billion,
- be issued by an institution with total outstanding debt in excess of €10 billion in respect of the asset class of the bond in question (including that issue),
- have an AAA rating by at least one of the agencies, Standard & Poor's, Fitch IBCA, or Moody's.

14.3.6.3   Derivatives Exchange EUREX

As a fully electronic exchange, EUREX allows market participants decentralized and standardized access to markets within a global network. EUREX was created by Deutsche Börse AG and the Swiss Exchange in December 1996 and founded through the merger of DTB (Deutsche Terminbörse) and SOFFEX (Swiss Options and Financial Futures Exchange). Both parties agreed to develop and implement a single platform for their derivatives markets. The operational merger of the two markets was completed in September 1998.

With a posted volume of over 454 million contracts traded during the year 2000, EUREX became a leading international derivatives exchange with 432 participants from 17 different countries. Within the EUREX platform, there is a very active derivatives market for German government bonds. Bond derivatives such as the well-known Bund future are now mostly traded via EUREX. In December 2000, the Euro-Bund future accounted for 30% of all contracts traded on EUREX. With the inclusion of bonds in the trading platform in late 2000, it became possible to trade bonds and futures simultaneously in a unified trading platform that eases arbitrage and hedging strategies.

14.4   THE MARKET FOR GOVERNMENT BONDS

14.4.1   Background

As was pointed out above, the German bond market is the largest in the Euro area. At the end of 2000, approximately one third of the overall outstanding German debt securities were government bonds making up a €800 billion market nearly equaling 40% of GDP (see ECB, 2002). Federal debt financing is based on issues of securitized debt, where different security types serve the needs of different investors, such as saving needs by private households or investment by institutional investors.

Government debt is filed and managed by the German Treasury, *Bundeswertpapierverwaltung* (formerly known as *Bundesschuldenverwaltung*). The German Treasury is a federal agency and part of the German Federal Ministry of Finance. Its administrative task is to record and manage the issues of government debt. Figure 14.2 provides an overview of the fractions of securitized government debt. Various types of issued government bonds exist, where Federal bonds (Bunds), with a share of 63% in volume outstanding, and Bundesobligationen (Bobls), with a share of 19%, are dominating. These two issue types as well as

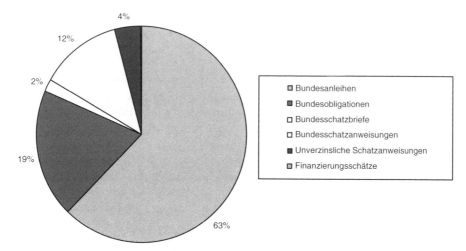

Figure 14.2   Government outstanding debt securities as of May 31, 2003 (percentage fractions out of total €712.505 million).
Note: Schuldscheindarlehen and Treuhand notes given under Kreditmarktmittel statistics are not securitized.
Source: Bundeswertpapierverwaltung (2002), www.bwpv.de – Schuldenstand.

Bundesschatzanweisungen (12% share) are exchange-traded. A small fraction of 6% of debt security issues is not exchange-traded.

Bundesbank is active in market-making for these various types of government debt. Activities include all government issues listed in *Amtlicher Handel* and traded at one of the official stock exchanges. *Bundesrepublik Deutschland – Finanzagentur GmbH* provides government bond product information via http://www.deutsche-finanzagentur.de. Details on important types of government bonds are provided in the following section.

14.4.2 Types of Instruments

(A) Unverzinsliche Schatzanweisungen (U-Schätze, Bubills, Treasury bills): Zero coupon instruments with maturities of less than 1 year, usually issued every 3 months. They are not exchange-listed.

(B) Bundesanleihen (Bunds, Federal government bonds): Fixed and floating rate bonds with maturities of 10 or 30 years, the maturity dates tending to fall on either January 4 or July 4. When interest is strippable, it is announced at issue. Floating rate notes are rarely issued; only the issue launched in September 1994 is still outstanding in 2003. The market for German 10-year Bunds represents the most liquid segment of the European bond market and provides a benchmark for the pricing of long maturity bonds throughout Europe. Implied volatility derived from options on the Euro-Bund future serves as a benchmark for assessing short term market uncertainty about future long term interest rates. The overall volume of Bunds issued was €38.0 billion in 2001 and €58.0 billion in 2000 (DBB, 2001).

(C) Bundesobligationen (Bobl, special Federal bonds): Fixed annual coupon instruments with a maturity of 5 years. An issue is usually tapped every 3 months. When a tap closes, the amount and price are announced, and a new Bobl series is issued. The overall volume of Bobls issued was €27.5 billion in 2001 as compared to €28.5 billion in 2000 (DBB, 2001).

(D) Bundesschatzanweisungen (Treasury notes): Fixed coupon notes, usually issued every 3 months by tender to the market. Issue amounts range between €5 and €7 billion. The notes are listed on all German exchanges.

(E) Bundesschatzbriefe (Federal savings bonds): Multicoupon bonds, issued at irregular intervals. They are puttable any time later than 30 days after issue where a limit is imposed on the maximal puttable amount, making them suitable for private investors. Interest on Type A is paid annually, interest on Type B deferred to maturity. The bonds are unlisted and nonnegotiable.

(F) Finanzierungsschätze (financial paper): Discounted notes tapped monthly with maturities from 1 to 2 years. The notes, which are unlisted, may not be purchased by credit institutions.

(G) Fundierungsschuldverschreibungen (funding bonds): Bonds with 3% coupons and interest payments in April and October. They were issued to underwrite German reunification, in 15 tranches, the last of which is scheduled for redemption by October 2010. The bonds are listed on the Frankfurt Stock Exchange.

(H) Treuhandobligationen/Treuhandanleihen (trust obligations/trust loans): Issued in 1993 and 1994 to finance privatization of the former German Democratic Republic's municipal-owned enterprises and properties. The trust obligations have a 10-year maturity and the trust loans a 5-year maturity. They are exchange-listed.

(I) Schuldverschreibungen des Ausgleichsfonds Währungsumstellung (Currency Conversion Equalization Fund bonds): Issued after German reunification to finance the settlement of

Table 14.2   Types of German government bond issues

Name of instrument	Maturity range	Coupon type
U-Schätze	6 months	Discounted zero coupon
Bundesanleihen (Bunds)	10 years/30 years	Fixed or floating
Bundesobligationen (Bobl)	5 years	Fixed
Bundesschatzanweisungen	2 years	3.5%–8.875% fixed coupon
Bundesschatzbriefe	Type A – 6 years Type B – 7 years	A – fixed multicoupon B – multicoupon DIP
Finanzierungsschätze	1 and 2 years	Zero
Fundierungsschuldverschreibungen	20 years (after reopening)	3% fixed
Treuhandobligationen/anleihen	5 years/10 years	Fixed
Schuldverschreibungen des Ausgleichsfonds Währungsumstellung	44 years	Floating
Schuldverschreibungen des Entschädigungsfonds	Maximum 30 years	Zero then fixed
Fonds der Deutschen Einheit	10 years/30 years	Fixed or floating

Source: Reuters. Reproduced by permission of Deutsche Bundesbank.

claims by credit institutions and foreign businesses that suffered losses from currency conversion in the former German Democratic Republic. Since August 1991, interest has been linked to the 3-month Frankfurt interbank offered rate. All the bonds are to be redeemed by July 2035. They are exchange-listed.

(J) Schuldverschreibungen des Entschädigungsfonds (indemnification fund bonds): Bonds issued in 1995 to compensate owners of property in the former German Democratic Republic that could not be reclaimed. The longest maturity is 13 years. The bonds will be redeemed over the period from January 1, 2004 to January 1, 2008. No interest is payable until January 1, 2004, when accumulated deferred interest and regular interest will become payable at a 6% coupon rate. The bonds are exchange-listed.

(K) Fonds der Deutschen Einheit (German reunification fund): Four bonds for DEM 45 billion issued to help refinance obligations of the former German Democratic Republic. They have the same conventions as Federal bonds and are traded in the same way. They are exchange-listed.

Table 14.2 lists the different types of German government bond issues with their respective maturity range and coupon type.

14.4.3   Issue Policy

In order to increase liquidity in the government bond market, the policy in issuing and trading Bunds was adapted in the period preceding the start of the EMU. The measures introduced included bond stripping, broadening the range of Federal financing instruments, and regular auctions for special types of Federal bonds.

14.4.3.1   Stripping

Bond stripping allows the creation of zero coupon bonds from issued coupon bonds. This is done via coupon-stripping: i.e., coupons are stripped and sold separately from principal.

Stripping has become popular as it, for example, allows investors to adjust income streams to their consumption needs and also allows for taxation benefits. Strips also have the immediate effect of creating benchmark yield curves, which are traded in the marketplace.

Stripping of particular series of 10- and 30-year Bunds in Germany started in mid-1997. Today, new issues of Bunds, which have coupon payments either on January 4 or July 4, are strippable. Stripping of Bunds is possible for any investment with a minimum amount of €50 000. Separation of coupons and principal is carried out by the investors' deposit agency which is either a bank or the German Treasury *Bundeswertpapierverwaltung*. The minimum nominal amount of strips is €0.01. Strips having identical maturity are pooled under one security identification number and then provide a homogeneous tradeable instrument. With stripping, "anti-stripping" is also possible; i.e., coupon bonds can be reconstructed via a zero bond and a series of coupon payments. However, in contrast to stripping, only financial corporations are allowed to carry out reconstruction. The overall volume of strip bonds amounted to €267.4 billion at the end of 2001; €2.9 billion thereof were held in stripped form (DBB, 2001).

14.4.3.2 Auction Process

There is no rigid timetable for German government bond issuance. Although Bundesbank publishes its issue calendar every 3 months, these plans are always subject to change with cancelations, substitutions, and other changes. An announcement usually appears in the market 1 week before an issue, where the conditions of single issues are publicly announced. The auction process for German government bonds (*Tenderverfahren*) is used for Bunds, partly for Bobls, as well as for *Bundesschatzanweisungen* and *Unverzinsliche Schatzanweisungen*.

The Bund issues auction group (*Bietergruppe Bundesemissionen*, which replaced the Federal Bond Consortium early in 1998) represents the institutional bidders in the auction process. Its members include those listed in Section 14.3.3. The rules of the auction process are given in detail by the Bundesbank in their *Verfahrensregeln für Tender*. The auction takes place via the underwriting fixed-price-reoffer method. It requires the issuer of the bond and every bank in the syndicate to agree on a minimum price that bidders must maintain for a given period of time. This is particularly important when individual tranches are resold. Members of the auction group are subject to a yearly ranking according to their issue volume.

A special version of the auction process has been implemented for Bobls since August 2000. In order to achieve higher emission volumes every series starts as a tap issue that has an initial maturity of 5^1/$_2$ years and a tap issue period of 6 months. After 6 months, when the series has a residual maturity of exactly 5 years, a subsequent auction is held. After another 3 months, the series will be topped-up within the scope of another auction. Shares for market-making activities will also be included in each auction to increase issue volume. At the time of the first subsequent auction, a new series will be launched as a tap issue, and this series will again have an initial maturity of 5^1/$_2$ years.

14.4.4   Market Conventions

With the exception of one floating-rate note issues, funding bonds, Federal savings bonds Type B, and financial paper, German government securities have a fixed coupon with annual coupon dates. Maturities are fixed. In general there is no provision for premature redemption

Table 14.3 Conventions in the German government bond market

Convention	Floating rate notes	Fixed rate notes
Settlement	T+3	T+3
Value date	Same as settlement	Same as settlement
Day count	Actual/actual	Actual/actual
Ex-dividend	Same as coupon	Same as coupon
Holidays	TARGET	TARGET
Calculation type	Floating rate note	Coupon

Source: Reuters. Reproduced by permission of Deutsche Bundesbank.

by the issuer by call or by drawing lots with the exception of funding bonds, bonds issued by the Currency Conversion Equalization Fund, and bonds issued by the Indemnification Fund. All German government securities are eligible for the investment of mutual funds or as life insurance cover funds. Purchases of tap issues of German government securities in the primary market, i.e. purchases not issued by auction, are free of charge to the investor where the issuers pay the placing institutions a selling commission. Table 14.3 summarizes the most important market conventions for German government debt.

14.4.5   Redenomination

Bunds, Bobls, and *Bundesschatzanweisungen* paper have been issued in euro from the start of stage three of EMU on January 1, 1999. Instruments originally denominated in deutsche mark were redenominated in euro based on the following conventions:

- Bunds, Bobls, and *Bundesschatzanweisungen* that matured after January 20, 1999, were redenominated in euro on January 1, 1999.
- Bonds have been redenominated by the investor-holding (bottom-up) method, which means that the conversion has taken place in each securities holder's individual account.
- Figures have been rounded to the nearest euro cent, applying commercial rounding rules.
- Minimum trading unit for redenominated bonds is the euro cent.
- No cash compensation has been made.
- No new ISIN codes have been introduced.
- New SICOVAM codes have been assigned to some German government bonds, including Bunds, Bobls, *Bundesschatzanweisungen*, and others.

14.4.6   Benchmarks

German bond market indices are the *Deutscher Rentenindex* REX and the REX-performance index (REXP) both introduced in 1991. The REX is based on a theoretical market-weighted portfolio of 30 government bonds with maturities ranging from 1 to 10 years and three coupon rates respectively. A benchmark for the short term market development is the Bund future, now given as the Euro-Bund future.

Bundesbank's statistics department provides interpolated zero coupon bond yields for German Bunds with maturities ranging between 1 and 10 years. Figure 14.3 plots the history of monthly yield curves during the period September 1972 to September 2002. Nominal

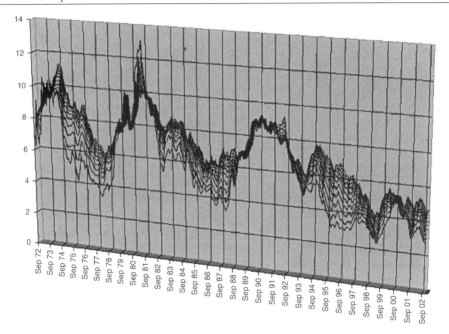

Figure 14.3 German monthly yield curves (September 1972 to September 2002).
Source: Deutsche Bundesbank. Reproduced by permission of Deutsche Bundesbank.

yields fluctuated between lower levels of around 3% for short maturities recently to levels of up to more than 12% at the beginning of the 1980s. The period after reunification in the early 1990s was characterized by an inverse term structure; i.e., short maturity bonds had higher yields than long maturity bonds. The plot also indicates that the yield curve tends to be flatter during periods of higher and increasing interest rate levels and vice versa.

14.5   CONCLUSION

Although bonds traditionally play an important role in German bank as well as government debt financing, the documentation given above illustrates substantial ongoing structural changes in the financial system. This is even more noteworthy as financial liberalization was affecting Germany as a large benchmark market for quite some time.

Several recent tendencies indicate possible lines of future development. In accordance with further structural changes and development of the country's capital markets, the financial system is expected to become less bank-based. Together with disintermediation, regulatory changes encouraged competition in the system and led to now obvious market evolution in the markets for mature equity and derivatives. The development of the markets for young equity and corporate bonds remains a challenging task for regulators in Germany. One may consider electronic bond trading as one means of enhancing the future liquidity and efficiency of the corporate bond market. A successful European secondary market platform would have the potential to increase popularity among investors and corporations alike and hence improve debt financing for large blue-chip companies as well as SMEs. The recent Jenoptik non-investment grade bond issue by Goldman Sachs and HVB may serve as an example which could mark the beginning of increased relevance of the German and the European SME high yield corporate bond market.

REFERENCES

Bank for International Settlements (2001). *The New Basle Capital Accord*. Basle: BIS.

Bank for International Settlements (2002a). *Quarterly Review: International Banking and Financial Market Developments*. Basle: BIS.

Bank for International Settlements (2002b). *Quarterly Review: Statistical Annex with International Banking Statistics*. Basle: BIS.

Bundesministerium der Finanzen (1999). *Unser Börsen- und Wertpapierwesen*. Bonn: BMF.

Bundeswertpapierverwaltung (2002). Übersicht über den Stand der Schuld der Bundesrepublik Deutschland/Umlaufende Schuld der Kreditmarktmittel, Bad Homburg. www.bwpv.de.

Deutsche Bundesbank (2000). *Der Markt für deutsche Bundeswertpapiere, 3. Auflage*. Frankfurt am Main: DBB.

Deutsche Bundesbank (2001). *Geschäftsbericht 2001*. Frankfurt am Main: DBB.

European Central Bank (2002). *Report on Financial Structures*. Frankfurt am Main: ECB, pp. 63–81 (Country Chapter on Germany).

Rudolph, B. (2002). Viertes Finanzmarktförderungsgesetz – Ist der Name Programm? *Betriebs-Berater* **57**: 1036–1041.

Seifert, W.G., A.-K. Achleitner, F. Mattern, C.C. Streit, and H.-J. Voth (2000). *European Capital Markets*. London: Macmillan.

15

Greece

THOMAS A. FETHERSTON

15.1 INTRODUCTION

Since joining the European Union (EU) in 1981, Greece has remained the poorest of EU Member States, an adverse title it has only recently begun to get around. As of January 2001 it became the twelfth member of the European Monetary Union (EMU), but its economy leaves mixed impressions: it is a market economy but the public sector continues to comprise nearly half of gross domestic product (GDP). Because of delays in economic restructuring, including the privatization of the largest state enterprises, unemployment continues to be one of the highest in the EU, while productivity and income levels are among the lowest. Tourism is one of the growth engines of the economy, but the power of the EU's financial assistance – year after year exceeding 3% of GDP – is not to be underestimated. Macroeconomic indices have improved greatly as a result of the fiscal discipline attested by Costas Simitis of the Panhellenic Socialist Movement (Pasok) who overtook as Prime Minister in 1996. But he has been rather hesitant in implementing a much-needed tax reform and slimming down the vast state bureaucracy that continues to hinder economic efficiency.

Despite the adverse international environment, Greece's economy has nonetheless maintained a remarkable momentum in recent years, resulting in an ongoing real convergence with the most developed EU Member States. In 2002, the Greek economy grew by 3.8%, barely less than that in 2001, while the GDP of the EU grew by just 1% (see Table 15.1). The robust growth rate is fueled by an increase in private consumption and investment, as a result of the increase in real disposable income and private sector funding. There is agreement that strong, domestic demand-led growth is likely to continue beyond 2003, a critical year for the EU economy.

As a result of increased economic activity, the unemployment rate also declined from 10.4% in 2001 to 9.9% in 2002, but it remains among the highest in the EU and continues to cause some social tensions. It is also noteworthy that the external sector in fact had a negative contribution of 0.2% points in GDP growth during 2002 as a result of the economy's worsening competitiveness under EMU membership (Hellenic Capital Market Commission, 2002). Greek inflation also historically exceeds the Euro area average and remains among the very highest (at the end of 2002 there was an inflation differential of 1.7% points between Greece and the Euro area). This differential is mainly due to the higher growth rates and the structural disadvantages of the Greek economy, as well as extraordinary factors such as the transition to the euro and the high sensitivity of the Greek economy to oil price fluctuations.

Under these conditions, the restrictive fiscal discipline imposed by the Simitis government is timely. Particularly so, because as in the case of Italy and Belgium, Greece's admittance into

European Fixed Income Markets: Money, Bond and Interest Rate Derivatives. Edited by J.A. Batten,
T.A. Fetherston and P.G. Szilagyi © 2004 John Wiley & Sons, Ltd. ISBN 0-470-85053-1

Table 15.1 Key economic indicators in Greece

	1999	2000	2001	2002
GDP per head (US$ at PPP)	15 840	16 450	17 490	18 340
GDP (% real growth)	3.4	4.3	4.1	3.8
Overall budget balance (% GDP)	−1.8	−1.1	−1.2	−1.1
Inflation (CPI, %, period average)	2.6	3.2	3.4	3.6
Public debt (% GDP)	104.6	102.7	99.6	106
Unemployment rate	11.9	11.1	10.4	9.9
Current account balance (% GDP)	−3.2	−4.5	−4.8	−4.7
Trade balance (% GDP)	−13.9	−16.2	−14.9	−14.3

Source: Ministry of Economy and Finance, Bank of Greece.

the EMU largely depended on the European Central Bank (ECB) overlooking the fact that the country's debt to GDP ratio continues to hover around 100%, which is in sharp contrast with the prerequisite 60% level set out in the Maastricht Treaty of 1992. The Government has now set out to reduce debt levels to 60% of GDP by the year 2010. This is to be financed through primary budget surpluses, high GDP growth rates, privatization revenues, and the revenues from the securitization of future profits of public organizations.

15.2   THE GREEK BOND MARKET

Table 15.2 indicates that the Greek bond market, at around 90% of GDP but only 1.6% of the Euro area market, is relatively small and overwhelmingly dominated by government issues. The market has historically been dominated by government securities, and somewhat contrary to expectations Monetary Union has only increased this domination. Today, the government bond market continues to grow despite a steady improvement in Greece's public finances. This growth reflects the cabinet's objectives of improving further the liquidity and efficient operation of the domestic government bond market, reducing exchange risk, and extending the maturity of central government debt (see Ministry of Economy and Finance, 2002).

These concerted efforts have also paved the way for the recent upgrading of Greek government debt in domestic currency by Moody's from A2 to A1 in November 2002, and then by Standard & Poor's from A to A+ in June 2003. Simultaneously, the yields on Greek government bonds have systematically continued to hit historically low levels. The yield of the 10-year benchmark bond fell to 4.44% by the end of 2002, which compares with 5.28% at the end of 2001. Even more crucially, the spread between 10-year Greek and German securities decreased from 38 basis points to a historical low of 23 basis points over the same period, reflecting the gradual integration of the Greek market with European ones. The shift toward low risk investments has also enhanced activity in the bond market, increasing turnover in the Electronic Secondary Treasury Bonds Market (HDAT) from €314 billion in 2001 to €566 billion in 2002. Of course, the market's stance has also been lifted by the decision of the Ministry of Economy and Finance to grant foreign financial institutions, which participate in HDAT as remote members, the primary dealer status (Bank of Greece, 2002).

On the other hand, given Greece's improving fundamentals and relatively high trend growth rate within the Euro region, it seems odd that the nongovernment bond market has not done better since the introduction of the euro. The nongovernment market remains very small, undeveloped, and highly illiquid. This is partly due to the tax system (see Section 15.3.2),

Table 15.2   The Greek bond market at the end of April 2003 (billions€)

	Short term	Long term	Total
General government	2.7	123	125.7
Financial institutions	0.4	0.1	0.5
Nonfinancial corporations	0	0.2	0.2

Source: European Central Bank Securities Issues Statistics.

which has contributed to discouraging the issue of bonds by sectors other than the central government. Over the medium term, given greater balance in the public sector and ongoing structural reforms, it is expected that the corporate bond market will reverse its recent decline and begin to expand again. Meanwhile, some activity has been observed in the asset-backed segment of the market, with the government securitizing some of its cash flows, but no private issuers have tapped this market so far.

15.3   MARKET PARTICIPANTS AND STRUCTURE

15.3.1   Regulators

15.3.1.1   Bank of Greece

The Bank of Greece was established in 1927 and began operations in May 1928. It forms part of the European System of Central Banks (ESCB), which comprises the ECB and the national central banks of all EU Member States. As of January 1, 2001, the Bank of Greece is also a member of the Eurosystem, which consists of the ECB and the central banks of Euro area Member States.

The Statute of the Bank of Greece was amended by the decisions of the general meeting of shareholders of the Bank of Greece held on December 22, 1997, and April 25, 2000, ratified by Laws 2609/98 and 2832/00 respectively, to meet the requirements of the EU Treaty. The new Statute

- explicitly states that the Bank's primary objective is to ensure price stability;
- safeguards the Bank's independence and establishes its accountability to Parliament;
- establishes a new body at the Bank of Greece, the Monetary Policy Council; and
- recognizes the Bank's legal integration into the Eurosystem as from the adoption of the single currency in Greece (January 1, 2001); in this context, the Bank of Greece contributes to the implementation of monetary policy in the Euro area, as formulated by the Governing Council of the ECB, and of exchange rate policy.

In addition to its tasks in the field of monetary and exchange rate policy, the Bank

- holds and manages the country's official foreign reserves;
- issues banknotes that have the status of legal tender;
- exercises prudential supervision of credit institutions and other financial institutions;
- promotes and oversees the smooth operation of payment and securities settlement systems;
- acts as a treasurer and fiscal agent for the government.

15.3.1.2 Hellenic Capital Market Commission

The Hellenic Capital Market Commission (HCMC) is an independent decision-making body, in the form of an independent public entity operating under the supervision of the Ministry of Economy and Finance. It is established in Athens, and the laws 148/67, 1969/91, 2166/93, 2324/95, and 2396/96 regulate its operation.

The HCMC is the body primarily responsible for ensuring the protection of investors and the compliance of market participants with capital market legislation. Its main objective is to promote the establishment of sound conditions for the operation of the capital market and to enhance public confidence both in the quality of supervision and market behavior. To achieve this objective the HCMC sets the general terms and conditions governing the organization and operation of the capital market and issues instructions on compliance procedures. All decisions on listing requirements, trading regulations, and membership obligations are established and monitored by the HCMC. Entities and organizations such as the Athens Stock Exchange, the Athens Derivatives Exchange, the Athens Derivatives Transactions Clearing House, and the Central Securities Depository are also subject to supervision by the Commission.

15.3.1.3 Government Supervisor

Such supervisor is appointed by the Ministry of Economy and Finance, and is responsible for ensuring the compliance of all trading parties with the existing rules and regulations. The Supervisor is always present during trading sessions. According to the latest developments, the responsibilities of the Government Supervisor are transferred to the HCMC.

15.3.2 Investor Taxation

All bonds and Treasury bills issued by the government or by public organizations are subject to tax, which varies according to their issue date. Greek government bonds issued prior to January 3, 1998, are subject to a tax of 7.5%, while those issued after that date are taxed at 10%. The tax on government bonds is withheld upon expiry of the coupons or upon expiry of the bonds themselves. The tax on Treasury bills is paid in advance upon purchase of the issue, unless they are renewed, in which case it is paid upon expiry. Bonds issued by banks or insurance companies are subject to a tax rate of 15%. The tax rate withheld on the interest of all other corporate bonds is 20% for private investors and 40% for legal entities.

Foreign investors are exempted from the tax imposed on government bonds and Treasury bills. Furthermore, Greece has certified conventions with many countries for the avoidance of double taxation. Under these agreements direct tax is applied in accordance with the tax system of the country in which the investment is generated.

15.3.3 Rating Agencies

Greek bonds are rated by one or more of the following agencies, which rate both long term local and foreign currency debt:

* Fitch IBCA
* Moody's Investor Service
* Standard & Poor's
* Thomson-Bankwatch.

15.3.4 Public Trading

15.3.4.1 Exchange Information

The Athens Stock Exchange (ASE) was founded in 1876. It is governed by Law 2324/95, and operates according to all the relevant European Commission (EC) Directives regarding the capital market, adopted either by Laws or by Presidential Decrees. The ASE has 90 members, which are all brokerage firms licensed by the HCMC. They are entitled to provide all the core and noncore investment services described in EC Directive 93/22 on investment services.

Trades are conducted electronically through the automated exchange trading system (SHDO). Government bonds, bonds of supranational organizations, and corporate bonds are also listed for trading through the SHDO. Trading hours are from 9:30 a.m. to 1:15 p.m., with a 30-minute preopening period. All orders entered in the system before 9:30 a.m. are part of the formation of the opening prices. Closing prices are formulated by the weighted average of the last 10 minutes of trading. During trading, orders are matched by price. Bonds are traded clean, or at prices free of any accrued interest. Accrued interest on bonds linked to foreign currencies is expressed in their respective currency and is calculated on the basis of the average prices for the respective foreign currency during the 2 days prior to the ex-coupon date. International Securities Identification Number (ISIN) identifiers are available for all securities listed on the ASE.

The clearing and settlement of all transactions are performed by the Central Securities Depository SA (CSD). The CSD was established in 1991 as a joint-stock company, and has developed rapidly with the gradual dematerialization of all securities since 1999.

15.3.4.2 Electronic Trading Platform

The HDAT, operated by the Bank of Greece, is the electronic trading system of the organized market for Greek government securities. It was among the very first such platforms in Europe, established by Law 2515/97 and started operations in May 1998. The trading platform supports both secondary and primary market operations. Furthermore, all securities in book-entry form issued by other public entities and deposited in the securities settlement system of the Bank of Greece (BOGS) can also be traded in HDAT.

By the joint decision No. 2/75166/0023A/20.12.2002 of the Minister of National Economy and the Governor of the Bank of Greece, the following financial institutions are appointed as primary dealers in the market (ranked by activity in the first quarter of 2003):

1. National Bank of Greece SA
2. EFG Eurobank-Ergasias SA
3. Piraeus Bank SA
4. San Paolo-IMI Bank
5. HSBC Bank plc
6. Credit Suisse First Boston (Europe)
7. Alpha Bank SA
8. Deutsche Bank AG
9. ING Bank NV
10. Lehman Brothers International Europe
11. Citigroup Global Markets Ltd
12. Commercial Bank

13. BNP Paribas
14. Goldman Sachs International Ltd
15. JP Morgan Securities Ltd
16. UBS Ltd
17. Morgan Stanley & Co. International Ltd
18. Merrill Lynch International

The market is quote-driven in which all dealers, depending on their rights and obligations, can enter quotes. All quotes and orders are anonymous. During trading hours (9:15 a.m. to 4:00 p.m.) primary dealers are obliged to quote continuously binding bid and offer prices as well as amounts for a specified list of securities through their terminals. The spread between bid and offer prices may not exceed a certain cap (currently 15 price basis points). The minimum quantity of a quote is currently 20 lots (1 lot = €293 470 = GRD 100 million). The electronic system guarantees transparency because all the transaction details binding the parties (price, amount, and bid/offer prices) are available in real time to all interested parties. HDAT provides online information to the international electronic information providers, Reuters, Bloomberg, and Telerate. In October 1999 the electronic trading of repos was introduced in HDAT. The market is based on the "buy/sell-back" type of contract.

In January 2003 the Bank of Greece, in its capacity as manager of HDAT, implemented the New Central System of HDAT (HDAT-NCS). The new system architecture is fully compatible with the use of auto-quoting systems, accommodates an unlimited number of quotes, and allows convergence with the services of other systems such as EuroMTS. New functionalities have also been added for further market growth as well as for the development of new markets (e.g. corporate bonds).

BOGS settles transactions involving all Greek government debt instruments. Operated by the Bank of Greece, the system started operations in May 1998 and is subject to the control of the Bank of Greece's Internal Audit Department. In November 2000 the Bank of Greece introduced a new settlement platform in BOGS, which provides for real-time gross settlement through a delivery versus payment mechanism. The system follows the operating regime of TARGET (Trans-European Automated Real-Time Gross Settlement Express Transfer) and receives instructions between 9 a.m. and 4 p.m. These operating hours can be extended, when such a need arises, to help participants close their positions in TARGET.

15.4 THE GREEK GOVERNMENT BOND MARKET

15.4.1 Background

The concerted efforts undertaken by the Ministry of Economy and Finance to develop the Greek government bond market have resulted in a number of qualitative reforms in recent years. In the primary market, the Primary Dealer's Regulation has been revised and the number of primary dealers has increased to 18, of which 13 are international credit institutions (11 of them having no establishment in Greece). In addition, increased powers have been vested in the Committee of Primary Dealers' Supervision and Control, ensuring the effective control of the operation of the market and transparency of the system.

The immense competitive pressure in the Euro area to provide highly liquid government securities has fostered the establishment of benchmark instruments (see Table 15.3). This objective has been pursued with reopenings of selected old issues to increase their liquidity. The borrowing in 2003 continued to focus on the 3-, 5-, 10- and, 20-year issues, thus creating more

Table 15.3   Central government debt securities as in March 2003

	2000	2001	2002 (estimate)	2003 (forecast)
Treasury bills	4 666	2 261	1 630	1 480
Held by public sector	2 688	1 473	690	540
Held by private sector	1 978	788	940	940
Government bonds	87 568	100 363	112 774	124 356
Bonds	84 663	98 293	110 878	123 007
Consolidated loans	2 905	2 070	1 896	1 349

Source: Ministry of Economy and Finance.

Table 15.4   Average yields in June 2003

3 years	2.38
5 years	2.88
7 years	3.33
10 years	3.81
15 years	3.86
20 years	4.57

Source: Bank of Greece.

liquidity in the basic segments of the yield curve. These issues will account for 90% of the total borrowing, while the remaining 10% will include issues of Treasury bills and strategic issues that will cover existing investment needs. Moreover, reverse auctions for specific preannounced older issues, as well as buybacks and exchanges of issues, are being organized at regular intervals, aiming at the retirement of such issues, which are then refinanced through the issuance of lower coupon selected benchmark securities. For example, during the first 9 months of 2002, the Ministry of Economy and Finance bought back bonds of nominal value €1.5 billion by over-the-counter (OTC) operations. This strategy has paid off: the Greek benchmark issues are already tradable in the pan-European EuroMTS platform, which has now captured the bulk of government bond trading in Europe and guarantees liquidity by listing only those government bonds whose volume exceeds €5 billion. The average yields on benchmark instruments in June 2003 are shown in Table 15.4.

The Ministry (2001) has also implemented a number of modern management techniques to restructure the outstanding government debt in terms of currency and interest rates, the lengthening of its maturity and the smoothing of the maturities in the coming years. Notably, it has generally reduced outstanding Treasury bill and noneuro debt borrowing, and discontinued the issuance of floating-rate notes (FRN). As a result, the weighted average residual maturity of government securities increased from 5.8 years in March 2002 to 6.3 years by March 2003, although some restructuring in favor of securities with shorter maturities (3 and 5 years) has slowed the lengthening of the market's maturity profile.

As has been mentioned, significant measures have been undertaken in the secondary market since 2001 for the modernization of HDAT, which has shifted liquidity to a new level. During 2002, the average monthly volume of transactions on HDAT was €46.8 billion, which corresponds to a year-on-year increase of 80%. This increase is mainly due a shift of investors toward low-risk placements, because of uncertainty in the stock market. These positive market developments were also helped by the decision of the Ministry of Economy and Finance to grant foreign financial institutions, which participate in HDAT as remote members, the primary dealer status. The average monthly turnover of Greek government securities in the secondary market (including the OTC market) during the first 9 months of 2002 was €574 billion, a nearly twofold increase.

15.4.2 Types of Government Securities

(A) *Treasury bills*: These are discount instruments and are renewable at the holders' option at the end of the term. They are issued with maturities of 13, 26, and 52 weeks.

(B) *Treasury bonds*: The Greek government issues fixed-rate bonds with 2- to 20-year maturities and index-linked bonds with 5- and 10-year maturities. The issuance of index-linked bonds has been discontinued, although in March 2003 a 22-year bond linked to euro inflation was issued. The issuance of FRN has also been suspended, with the main volume expected to mature by the end of 2004 (although some outstanding debt has been converted into floating, partly replacing the maturing FRN). 20-year bonds were first offered in January 2000.

(C) *Foreign currency bonds*: These are fixed-rate or indexed bonds issued with 1–5 year maturities, and are largely denominated in US dollars. Their issuance has now been discontinued.

(D) *Privatization securities*: In August 2001 €800 million of Hellenic Tourist Properties Certificates, and in October 2001 another €1.7 billion of Prometocha Privatization Certificates were issued in the international market. The zero-coupon certificates, listed on the ASE, were issued at discount in bearer form and will be redeemed after 3 years at their nominal amount. The Hellenic Tourist Properties Certificates are exchangeable, at the option of the holders, for shares in Hellenic Tourist Properties SA or in any of its subsidiaries offered for sale by way of privatization, from the issue date to the redemption date. The Prometocha Privatization Certificates are exchangeable for shares in all companies offered for sale by way of privatization, excluding shares in the Agricultural Bank of Greece or in the Hellenic Tourist Properties SA. The certificates will be exchanged with shares at a 5% discount on the offered price of the share.

(E) *Asset-backed securities (ABS)*: The Greek government has launched seven securitization programs since 1999 to shift debt off its books and show a nominal reduction in public debt in line with the Stability and Growth Pact requirement. These programs are backed by assets such as receipts from the state lottery, dividends from a state bank, and also future revenues due from Eurocontrol to the Greek civil aviation authority for air traffic control services. The €2 billion program launched in October 2001 is a true novelty in the European market, since it is backed by payments from the EC under the third Community Support Framework. As with the previous deals the program is guaranteed by the state; the bullet repayments, of €1 billion each, are due in January 2005 and January 2007. Since then, Greece has frozen plans to launch new ABS programs because of concern over whether the EC Commission will continue to accept securitization as a way to reduce public debt (Hope, 2002).

15.4.3 Sale of Government Securities

In 1995 the Ministry of Economy and Finance (then Ministry of Finance) introduced an auction system for the issuance of government securities. Under the old system, prices were fixed but the supply was theoretically unlimited. The new auction system attempts to lower the costs associated with financing the country's budget deficit and improve market liquidity in government securities. When bonds are issued, the Ministry of Economy and Finance generally uses a Dutch auction, whereby the most competitive bids are accepted until the issue amount is fully subscribed. Recently, the number of auctions was reduced significantly with a simultaneous increase of the auctioned volume, inducing intense interest and increased competitiveness among market participants. The auction calendar is announced on a quarterly basis, but as of 2001 the total yearly volume to be auctioned is also preannounced.

More recently, the Ministry of Economy and Finance also adopted the syndication method for the uploading of long term government bonds to promote these to a broader basis of end-investors in the Euro area market. According to the new issuing policy adopted in 2002, all new benchmark bonds having maturity above 3 years are initially issued through syndication and then further tapped by auctions.

15.4.4 Market Conventions

On January 1, 2001, all dematerialized government debt issued in Greek drachma were rede-nominated into euro (the euro/drachma locking rate was 340.75). At the same time, the market conventions for all types of bonds issued after January 1, 2001, were harmonized to the rules applying to the Euro area. However, since the legislation does not allow any changes to the original terms and conditions of the issues, the day count applying to any instrument issued prior to December 31, 2000, and any reopening of these issues remains the same. Specifically, the day count basis for fixed-rate bonds issued in 2001 or later changed to Actual/Actual, but for those issued beforehand remained 30/360. Similarly, the holiday calendar of the EMU gross settlement system TARGET applies to all new issues but the old Greek holiday calendar applies to all old ones. The yield on bonds is calculated on the ISMA yield to maturity method. The value date is the same as the settlement date.

15.4.5 Repo Market

The repo market in Greece is quite active, especially after the abolition of taxation on repo agreements for domestic investors. Apart from the classic repo market, an electronic buy/sell back repo market was also introduced in HDAT in September 1999.

15.4.6 Futures Market

The bond futures market was organized by the Athens Derivatives Exchange and started op-erating in January 2000. However, the relatively low liquidity of the market combined with the vast portfolios of institutional investors and the small number of market makers in the domestic market resulted in a gradual transition of futures transactions to the German bond futures market. The lack of interest in the Greek bond futures market eventually forced the Athens Derivatives Exchange to suspend the operation of this specific market as of June 2001.

15.5 THE NONGOVERNMENT BOND MARKET

Table 15.2 showed that the Greek nongovernment bond market is diminutive: the amount of bank bonds in circulation is very small (around €100 million) as is the amount of bonds issued by nonfinancial corporations (roughly €200 million). This is partly due to the tax system (see

Section 15.3.2), which has contributed to discouraging the issue of bonds by sectors other than the central government. Although tax reforms were introduced in 1999 to encourage the establishment of a nongovernment bond market, development so far has been slow. At present only nine private borrowers have their bonds traded on the ASE, while the remaining issues are all privately placed, which obstructs the emergence of a secondary market for trading.

Overall, the funds raised through the issuance of nongovernment bonds amounted to only €85.3 million in 2002, which is still an improvement over the corresponding figure of €58.1 million for 2001. The Passenger Shipping Sector absorbed the largest portion, followed by the Holding & Consulting Companies Sector, the Construction Sector, and the Metal Products Sector. The introduction of the euro is expected to further boost issuance in the medium to long term, although it is unlikely that the market will flourish anytime soon, because the larger issuers will presumably tap the EU's more developed markets, such as London, instead.

REFERENCES

Bank of Greece (2002, January 9). Annual Review of the Greek Government Bond Market 2001. http://www.bankofgreece.gr/en/bank.

Hellenic Capital Market Commission (2002). Annual Report 2002. http://www.hcmc.gr.

Hope, K. (2002, April 30). Securitization Plans on Hold in Greece. *Financial Times*.

Ministry of Economy and Finance (2001, November 2). Recent Developments in Public Debt Management. Public Debt Division. http://www.mof-glk.gr.

Ministry of Economy and Finance (2002, December). Budget Report 2003 – Executive Summary. http://www.mof-glk.gr.

Ministry of Economy and Finance (2003, March). *Hellenic Republic Public Debt Bulletin* 29. http://www.mof-glk.gr.

16

Hungary

NÓRA NÉMETH AND LÁSZLÓ SZILÁGYI

16.1 INTRODUCTION

Hungary has been regarded as one of the leading Central Eastern European countries in implementing the reforms necessary for establishing a market economy. Having accomplished a smooth political transition to democracy after the fall of communism, the idea of joining the European Union (EU) has been uniformly supported by the society and the country's main political forces. Hungary's economic performance, in light of the country's already high degree of integration with the EU, makes it a top performer and one of the strongest candidates for accession to the EU. No wonder that the coming (on May 1, 2004) first-round accession, together with a timely adoption of the euro, is regarded as a major policy challenge.

The partial renouncement of the country's (e.g. legislative) sovereignty and the further need for policy measures to ensure good performance on an integrated market demands continuous effort. The central-left government, formed by the Hungarian Socialist Party and the Alliance of Free Democrats in 2002, must now maintain wide support for the idea of European integration, finish the adoption and appropriate application of the *acquis communitaire*, begin the needed structural reforms (especially in the health care system), and ensure that economic indicators gradually meet Maastricht criteria, while making certain that Hungary's real convergence continues with the EU Member States in terms of income and employment.

The above multiple goals must be met in a recently unfavorable external environment. Hungarian exports of goods reached the equivalent of about 60% of gross domestic product (GDP) in 2001 (up from 30.6% in 1991), which means that any global slowdown is a real threat to one of the region's most open economy. The fact that the EU accounts for around 75%[1] of exports (up from about 30% in 1990), and economic growth from the mid-1990s (until recently) had been fueled mainly by a revival in manufacturing industry as Hungary became part of the EU-based supply chains, shows how integrated (and vulnerable) the country is to the European market.

The effects of the global slowdown have been worsened by a significant real appreciation of the Hungarian forint (HUF) (the rate of appreciation of real effective exchange was 7.9% in 2001). Although a new monetary policy framework was successfully introduced in 2001[2] by widening the exchange rate band to ±15% against the euro (in May, this measure led to a higher exchange rate volatility), adopting inflation targeting (in June), and abandoning the crawling peg (in October), the government expressed its discontent with the interest rate policy

---

[1] Germany alone took 34.9% of exports in 2001.

[2] The former regime was introduced in 1995 as an important measure of fiscal restriction (the so-called "Bokros package," named after the Minister of Finance).

European Fixed Income Markets: Money, Bond and Interest Rate Derivatives. Edited by J.A. Batten,
T.A. Fetherston and P.G. Szilagyi. © 2004 John Wiley & Sons, Ltd. ISBN 0-470-85053-1

Table 16.1 Key economic indicators in hungary

	1997	1998	1999	2000	2001	2002
GDP per capita (€)	3987	4139	4477	5045	5690	6876
GDP real growth rate (%)	4.6	4.9	4.2	5.2	3.8	3.3
Budget balance/GDP (%, ESA95)	–	–	–	−3.0	−4.7	−9.5
Current-account balance/GDP (%)	−1.4	−4.7	−5.1	−6.2	−3.4	−4.1
FDI (€ million)	1653	1302	15.92	1519	1098	1281
Foreign-exchange reserves (€ million)	7640	8002	10874	12068	12195	9920
Consumer price index (%)	18.3	14.3	10.0	9.8	9.2	5.3
Public debt/GDP (%)	62.9	61.1	59.9	55.3	51.9	54.9
Unemployment (%)	8.7	7.8	7.0	6.4	5.7	5.8
Average annual currency/€	210.9	241.0	252.8	260.0	256.7	243.0

Source: European Commission. © European Communities, 1995–2003. Reproduced with permission.

of the National Bank of Hungary (NBH), which led to a tightening of monetary conditions. In the beginning of 2003, the collision between the government and the NBH, led by the former (central-right) Minister of Finance, Járai Zsigmond, resulted in a more resilient inflation target and a less hasty plan to adopt the euro (possibly in 2008).

The effects of external factors and exchange rate appreciation have been aggravated by an expansionary fiscal policy. The fiscal stimulus was estimated at about 2% of GDP in 2001 (and even more in 2002) at a time when private investment was being scaled back. The budget deficit was as high as 9.5%,[3] forcing the government to accept gradual spending restraints for the coming years, but at the same time hindering the execution of the remaining structural (health care) reforms. Another result of fiscal expansion was the distorted structure of growth (3.3% in 2002): while construction's production grew by 14.8%, manufacturing practically stagnated (1.1%) and gross fixed capital formation grew only by 5.8% (after 3.5% in 2001). Since the domestic use of GDP increased by 5.1% in 2002, no wonder that the growing demand of households can only be met by a worsening trade balance (even if it was somewhat offset by the drop in private investment), which in turn (together with the weak tourism receipts) increased the current account deficit.[4] What is more, the 2001 and 2002 increase of the minimum wage and the high real wage growth of the 2002 election year, together with the forint's appreciation, resulted in stagnating foreign direct investment to the country.

Inflation has come down gradually after the 1995 stabilization (starting from 31% in June), with a marked decrease between May 2001 and July 2002 (from 10.8% to 4.6%), mainly as a consequence of the strengthening of the exchange rate combined with other external developments (energy prices and declining external demand). Further disinflation has not been possible given the current expansionary fiscal policy and the end of appreciation (it has reached the border of the peg). Luckily, a somewhat higher than European Money Union (EMU) average inflation is now generally accepted as necessary to allow a higher growth rate and needed structural adjustment to the single market.

Apart from the somewhat alarming recent economic developments, Hungary's long term economic performance has been sound (see Table 16.1): between 1997 and 2001, the economy

---

[3] The Ministry of Finance claims that the budget deficit was "only" 6.5%, disregarding some single sections, not properly accounted for in previous years.

[4] The NBH implemented methodological changes to the balance of payments statistics in February 2003 (see http://english.mnb.hu/dokumentumok/fm_modszertan_2003_en.pdf).

recorded an average annual growth of 4.5%, compared to an average 2.6% in the Euro area. And, since the country is believed to preserve its extra impetus relative to EU Member States, Hungary should continue to outperform (by 2% points in GDP growth) the EU average in the long run. Accordingly, Hungary is on the way to catching up with the EU Member Countries: per capita income as a percentage of the EU average rose from 46.5% in 1996 to 52.8% in 2001.

Despite the good unemployment rate figures, the overall impression of the Hungarian labor market is not so bright: economic activity stagnated around 53% during the 1999–2002 period. Although the number of people in employment rose by some 250 000 and unemployment declined by 100 000 in 1997–2002, the pace of job creation and unemployment reduction has been slow (owing to rapid productivity growth, responsible for most of the good economic performance), and the adverse impact of the minimum wage rises of 2001–2002 are obvious. The latter policy measures meant a 57% and another 25% increase in the minimum wage introduced in January 2001 and 2002, causing the sudden distortion of the economy-wide wage hierarchy, which can only be adjusted to gradually. Year-average brut nominal wage growth thus reached only 18% and 18.3% in 2001–2002 (which is still high compared to the inflation of 9.2% and 5.3%). These conditions explain why one of the government's top priorities is job creation, and thus promoting economic activity even if the unemployment rate is rather low (especially in European comparison).

The Hungarian economy's near future and the possible policy routes are mainly determined by the coming EU and EMU accession. Having fulfilled the requirements for the former, the Maastricht convergence criteria must be met for the adoption of the euro in 2007 or 2008.[5] Public debt is already well under the required level, but inflation, interest rate,[6] and budget deficit continues to exceed the limits and the exchange rate of the forint seems to be highly volatile[7] so far. This is why to reach the desired goal of EMU accession, Hungary needs disciplined fiscal (and of course reconciled monetary) policy and smooth integration into the single market.

16.2   HISTORY AND STRUCTURE OF THE HUNGARIAN FINANCIAL MARKET

Creating liberalized markets and effective institutions in the financial sector has been a significant challenge in transition economies, and Hungary has been no exception. Nevertheless, although market-based banking systems and capital markets have been created from scratch, the practice in more developed countries, and recently the ongoing process of EU integration has served as a good guideline for legislation.

The development of a market-based Hungarian financial sector began in the socialist era, with reform occurring simultaneously in a number of areas. Corporate bonds were the first type of securities introduced in 1983, followed by Treasury bills in 1988 and government bonds in 1991 (the formerly existing government bonds marketability was limited). The two-tier banking system was launched on January 1, 1987. Households were allowed to buy shares

---

[5] Theoretically, the earliest possible date of EMU accession is 2006 (regarding the 2-year compulsory membership in the ERM II), but economists and even officials admit that a slower accession is more realistic and desirable.

[6] To meet this criterion, the establishment of a benchmark 10-year bond for comparison with the Euroland benchmark was necessary (of course, this was not the only reason to establish a bond market). It is generally accepted that in case of meeting inflation and budget deficit criteria, yield convergence would not threaten Hungary's EMU accession.

[7] In addition, if disinflation continues, steady appreciation will threaten the forint's exchange rate band according to the Balassa – Samuelson doctorine.

without restrictions in 1989. The Budapest Stock Exchange (BSE, *Budapesti Értéktőzsde, BÉT*) opened in June 1990; and its derivatives section, first with futures products, in 1995. Options products have been offered on the BSE since 2000. The independent clearing house and national depository was established in 1993.

Special laws on the financial sector were passed during the transition, with the first Securities Act passed in February 1990. New foreign exchange legislation in 1996 permitted the current account convertibility and liberalized international financial transactions. A new Securities Act, promulgated on January 1, 1997, made possible the issuing of dematerialized securities, and prescribed the formerly separate Banking Supervision and the Securities and Stock Exchange Supervision to merge into a new institution called the Hungarian Banking and Capital Market Supervision (HBCMS, *Állami Pénzés Tőkepiaci Felügyelet, ÁPTF*). The 1998 amendment of the law opened the possibility for universal banking. Following market trends, the Law on Single Supervision, which became effective on April 1, 2000, merged the HBCMS, State Insurance Supervision and State Pension Fund Supervision, into a single Hungarian Financial Supervisory Authority (HFSA, *Pénzügyi Szervezetek Állami Felügyelete, PSZÁF*) in an effort to improve the supervision of financial groups that emerged during the previous years. The legal framework for mortgage loan was created in 1997 to encourage the granting of long-term credits. The 2001 Act on the NBH granted the independence of the NBH in the EU compatible manner. Finally, the 2001 Capital Markets Act removed restrictions for companies (except credit institutions) on the issue limits regarding the amount of their shareholder's equity (Szalkai, 2001).

As a result of the above legislative changes, Hungary achieved a significant level of harmonization in its financial sector legislation with the EU, and practically full compliance with the EU's bond market regulation (Szalkai, 2001).

Despite the establishment of sound institutional background and legislation (and the continuous efforts of the BSE) to improve the performance of the Hungarian securities markets, many factors hinder their development, the most important being the size of the economy, aggravated by low per capita income. The domestic government bond market has expanded rapidly as a result of the resource needs of the budget and the establishment of a national institutional investor base through the 1997 pension reform, but the biggest international institutional investors are kept away by small quantities issued and low liquidity.

Another trouble is "the painful nonexistence" of a corporate bond market (see Figure 16.1). The reasons for this are high and variable inflation throughout the last decade was not favorable

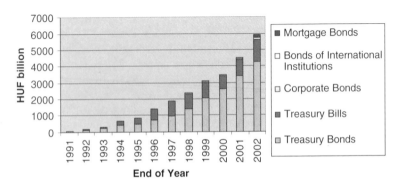

Figure 16.1   Capitalization of bonds on the Budapest Stock Exchange.
Source: Budapest Stock Exchange.

for developing fixed income markets; the privatized banking system was very successful in competing for corporate clients; transnational companies[8] have access to foreign resources; and remaining structural problems[9] owing to the size of the market. These points are so convincing that some experts even argue "it is not obvious that there is a need for a domestic-currency-denominated corporate bond market as the country marches into the EMU," and believe that Hungarian corporate finance will remain essentially bank-based (György, 2002; Köke, 2002).

16.3 PARTICIPANTS AND STRUCTURE OF THE HUNGARIAN BOND MARKET

16.3.1 Regulators

There are two main participants in the regulation and management of the financial markets in Hungary. The NBH is responsible for the formulation and conduct of monetary policy, while the HFSA is the single statutory body for financial services industry and ensures the stability and efficient operation of the markets.

16.3.1.1 National Bank of Hungary

The NBH (*Magyar Nemzeti Bank, MNB*) is Hungary's central bank. The 2001 Act on the NBH made its objectives, basic tasks, institutional, and organizational set-up fully compatible with EU requirements. Besides, the 2002 International Monetary Fund (IMF) Financial System Stability Assessment (FSSA) found that the NBH meets all criteria in terms of accountability and assurances of integrity, and thus complies completely with the IMF's Code of Good Practices on Transparency in Monetary and Financial Policies (MPC Code) (IMF, 2002, June).

The NBH Act establishes the governing bodies of the NBH. The President and three to five Vice Presidents govern the central bank. The President and Vice Presidents are appointed by the President of the Republic on the proposal of the Prime Minister. The organs of the NBH are the General Meeting, the Monetary Council (MC), and the Board of Directors. The MC is the highest monetary policy organ, in charge of formulating the NBH's monetary policy, while the Board of Directors is responsible for the implementation of the monetary policy decisions and for the operation of the NBH.

The primary objective of the NBH is to achieve and maintain price stability, and its autonomy in managing monetary policy is guaranteed by law. The NBH Act also stipulates that the main basic tasks of the NBH, which must be fulfilled without prejudice to its primary objective, are

- to maintain the stability of the national currency (the forint);
- to issue banknotes and coins by its exclusive right;
- to form and manage official reserves in foreign exchange and gold;
- to conduct foreign exchange operations in relation to the management of foreign exchange reserves and the implementation of exchange rate policy[10];

---

[8] Either through privatization or direct investment, transnational corporations now make up an enormous share of Hungarian GDP, and most of the relatively big companies belong to them.

[9] For example, lack of rating agencies and appropriate hedging instruments.

[10] Exchange rate regime decisions, however, are not the sole responsibilities of the NBH. The NBH Act states that the exchange rate regime is determined by the government, in agreement with the NBH, considering the NBH's primary objective of price stability.

- to develop and regulate the domestic payment and settlement systems, and support their efficient and sound operation;
- to collect and publish the necessary statistical information on the financial system;
- to promote the stability of the financial system and to develop and conduct policies related to the prudential supervision of the financial system.

The framework, instruments, and targets of monetary policy are disclosed and explained in a number of legal documents and NBH publications, of which the most important is the quarterly Report on Inflation. Further to this activity, the central bank is also engaged in theoretical research and publication.

A new monetary policy framework was introduced in the course of 2001 by adopting inflation targeting (and aborting the explicit target of exchange rate stability), widening the exchange rate band to ±15% against the euro, and abandoning the crawling peg.

The NBH conducts monetary policy through a variety of instruments, listed by the Act: accepting deposits from credit institutions; collateralized lending[11]; open market operations and repurchase agreements; issuing its own securities; influencing and determining exchange rates and interest rates; refinancing; and regulating minimum reserves. The instruments currently applied by the NBH are 2-week deposit, secured loan, and reserve requirements. The instruments directly influencing the bond market (open market operations, active and passive repo, and issuing NBH bonds) are included among the so-called business instruments of the central bank, i.e., the NBH has written business terms and conditions or regulations in force, but does not apply these instruments at the moment (NBH, 2002).

16.3.1.2 Hungarian Financial Supervisory Authority

The mission of the enlarged Supervisory Authority, established on April 1, 2000, is to promote the smooth operation of financial markets, to protect the interests of clients of financial institutions, enhance transparency of markets, and promote fair and lawful competition. A Chairman and two Deputy Chairmen govern the HFSA. The Chairman is appointed by the Parliament upon the Prime Minister's proposal. The HFSA is constituted of directorates, departments, and divisions as a uniform organization, with the lower part of the hierarchy reflecting the division of sectors of financial markets (money and capital markets, funds, and insurance companies).

In 2001, amendments to the Act for the establishment of the HFSA (through the Capital Markets Act) significantly strengthened the enforcement powers of the agency, especially by introducing supervision on a consolidated basis (because the financial system is dominated by financial conglomerates). With respect to the 2001 Capital Markets Act, the HFSA has supervisory authority over the BSE, the Budapest Commodities Exchange (BCE), the securities settlement system (KELER), securities intermediaries, issuance of securities to the public, and investment fund managers. The agency also has full responsibility – alongside the BSE and BCE – with regard to market conduct and sanctioning powers over market participants.

Since the adoption of the 2001 Act on Capital Markets, the Hungarian securities regulatory regime complies in most material respects with the implementation of the International Organization of Securities Commissions' (IOSCO) principles. The 2002 IMF FSSA found that the Authority's operation and the relevant regulation comply almost completely with IMF's

---

[11] There are two restrictions on the application of this instrument: the NBH may not extend loans to any agencies of the State; and cannot accept the debtor's securities as collateral.

MPC Code. According to the report, the only way by which the HFSA's autonomy could be further enhanced is by empowering it to issue legally binding regulations (the agency issues guidelines instead, to circumvent this handicap) (IMF, 2002, June).

The HFSA manages the following activities:

- Authorizes all financial businesses, firms, and individuals operating in the financial sectors.
- Keeps the records required by law, and controls the information systems of the financial market participants.
- Regularly monitors and evaluates compliance with the financial laws and regulations.
- Examines, analyses and evaluates the prudent operation of financial institutions, investment service providers, insurance brokers and pension funds.
- Investigates suspected business malpractice in its sphere of competence and takes enforcement actions.
- Proposes the adoption of statutory instruments and comments on those under preparation concerning the supervised sectors.
- Assists the operation of the National Deposit Insurance Fund (NDIF), the Investor Protection Fund.
- Publishes annual and quarterly reports on the agency's supervisory role and on developments in the supervised sectors.
- Maintains a public information service to disseminate policy decisions and announcements.
- Issues guidelines to the supervised institutions to communicate good market practices.

The Law sets out a few circumstances in which the HFSA must cooperate with other financial agencies. One is the granting of license to perform financial services in foreign currency and foreign exchange (consultation with the NBH); another when measures and exceptional measures are taken and fines are imposed on a financial institution (must inform the NBH); or when a credit institution's license is revoked (needs approval of the Ministry of Finance and the President of NBH).

16.3.1.3   *The Two Budapest Exchanges (BSE and BCE)*

There are two exchanges present in the Hungary, namely the BSE and the BCE (*Budapesti Árutőzsde, BÁT*). Under the 2001 Capital Markets Act, the HFSA can authorize either of the exchanges to list and trade all types of financial instruments, which implies that BSE and BCE competes in a rather narrow and not very liquid market.

Besides functioning as exchange markets, the Act on Capital Markets imposes (limited) regulatory functions on BSE and BCE as self-regulatory organizations (SROs). For example, the rules applicable to the BSE trading system are adopted by the BSE itself. On the whole, however, the regulating power of SROs is limited to tracing and sanctioning smaller cases of misconduct; the important infringements are exclusively treated by the HFSA. No wonder that the BSE and BCE cannot play a meaningful role in regulating and supervising important aspects of their respective markets and have limited impact on market activities. Although not a serious problem, the provisions of the Capital Markets Act prescribe the application of separate sanctioning by the HFSA and the SROs; therefore, double sanctioning at different levels for the same act of misbehavior might occur, which necessitates more coordination between HFSA and SROs.

16.3.1.4   Other Regulators

The Ministry of Finance (MoF, *Pénzügyminisztérium, PM*; under the oversight of the government) is solely responsible for the legal framework governing the financial sector, since the HFSA cannot issue binding rules and regulations according to Hungary's legal system. The relevant legislation includes the 2001 Act on the NBH, the 1999 Act on the HFSA, and the 2001 Capital Markets Act, the latter being an Act that amended regulation on the HFSA and replaced most provisions of the previous legislation (the 1996 Act on the Floating of Securities, Investment Services; the 1994 Act on the Commodities Exchange and transactions effected on the Commodities Exchange; and the 1991 Act on Investment Funds). By formulating the government's economic policy, forecasts, budget plan, and the issuing strategy of the debt management agency (GDMA; see Section 16.3.4), the MoF also has a serious influence on the marketing of government securities.

16.3.2   Categories of Investors

The main investors on the Hungarian fixed income market are credit institutions, investment funds, pension funds, and insurance companies, besides foreign investors (institutional investors mainly).

Institutional assets are smaller (relative to GDP) in Hungary than in the EU Member Countries, though institutional ownership is steadily growing. For Hungary, institutional investors appear to be risk-averse, investing 79% (1998) of financial assets in government bills or bonds and only 7% in stocks. Thus, the role of institutional investors in corporate finance remains small when compared to Western economies. Factors behind this include still young insurance and pension fund sector, prudential rules, and lack of appropriate rating services. On the other hand, growth has undoubtedly been stimulated by social security reform (pension reform introduced private pension funds in 1997, their funds amounted to 13% of GDP in 2001).

Investment funds became popular with household savers after the transition. Credit institutions manage most funds and the securities are primarily sold through the retail networks of banks, this is why the presence and turnover of investment notes on the BSE is very limited. According to February 2003 data published by the Association of Investment Fund Management Companies (AIFMC), there are 20 domestic and 8 international bond funds, with total net assets of HUF 702.8 and 7.7 billions respectively, comprising 66.9% of all Hungarian investment fund assets.[12] Currently, public open-ended funds dominate the market, although for reasons of taxation closed-ended funds were characteristic during the first half of the 1990s. The vast majority (60.6%) of public open-ended fund assets were invested in domestic government securities in the third quarter of 2002, while only 8.5% goes to other kinds of domestic bonds (5.3% to corporate and 1.3% to mortgage bonds). However, the high ratio of cash and deposit assets (18.6%), together with a growing proportion of foreign securities in their portfolios, suggests that investment funds could contribute to market growth should more bonds be available in the market.

Similar to other segments of the Hungarian financial markets, insurance shows considerable growth (and a long term potential): by the end of 2002, the portfolio of insurance companies' consolidated technical reserves and security capital reached HUF 786 billion (a 21.2% annual

---

[12] The dominance of bond investment trusts is largely due to the OTP Optima Fund, whose net assets comprised 51.2% of the investment fund sector's total net assets at the end of 2001.

growth). In 2001, 84% of the technical reserves' invested portfolio was in government securities (83.1% of which with a maturity over 1 year), compared to 4.5% in corporate and municipal bonds.

Private pension fund assets also grew steadily after the 1997 pension reform: by the end of 2001, the market value of the assets amounted to HUF 285 billion (a 61% increase), which represented 1.9% of the GDP. The share of government securities in the private pension funds' portfolio was 80% and corporate and municipal bonds represented 3%. Private pension funds were first allowed to make foreign investments in 2000, within the statutory limits, and at the end of 2001 such investments had a 2.5% share of the assets. Normally, there were stocks and bonds in the foreign investment portfolio.

The voluntary pension funds' assets (started to build up in 1994) now exceed HUF 293.6 billion in market value, having grown by more than 30% compared with the previous year. Government securities were the predominant (77%) investment instrument in the sector's consolidated portfolio. In addition to the above, corporate and municipal bonds comprised 5.5% of the assets.

Nonresident investors are also important participants in the forint-denominated Hungarian bond market; their investments in government securities have been constantly growing both in relative and absolute terms. Nonresidents are looking first of all for longer term government bonds, since they can profit from the exchange rate movements of the forint outside the bond market (exchange rate speculation can be an important motive to come to accession countries, though). In addition, risk averse pension funds and insurance companies are expected to partici-pate in the market as the accession process develops further,[13] thus strengthening the demand side, especially for longer maturities. The market share of foreign investments is constantly growing (foreign investors provided for more than half of the net financing need of the budget in 2002), thus their value reached 27% of the total stock (HUF 1873.6 billion) at the end of 2002 (compared to 8% and HUF 299.3 billion in 1998), with the average term to maturity reached 3.41 year in October 2002 (in contrast to 1.99 year in March 2001). The increase in volume was further helped by the ÁKK, which has raised funds since 1999 directly from the international capital markets by issuing foreign-currency-denominated bonds for the purpose of renewing the maturing foreign exchange debt. Nonresident investors were only allowed to acquire government bills after the complete liberalization of foreign exchange transactions in June 2001. This is another reason why they hold Treasury bonds in their portfolios to a much greater extent than short term government securities, keeping only HUF 86.4 billion (4.2% of the overall stock) in Treasury bills by the end of 2002, compared to 1 787.2 billion (36.9%) in Treasury bonds.

Domestic households' savings do not play a major role in the Hungarian bond market, with the exception of short term government bills, sold through retail facilities of investment service providers (ISPs) and the Hungarian State Treasury Branch Network. At the end of 2002, households owned HUF 819.8 billion of Treasury bills (39.9% of the total stock, which is the relatively stable proportion of their share in time), and only HUF 115.3 billion (2.4%) of longer term securities; together these two categories comprised 7.7% of the total assets of households.

In the future, the role of (domestic or nonresident) institutional investors will likely dominate the Hungarian bond market. With Hungary's accession to the EU (and integration into the

---

[13] So far, foreign investors regard the Hungarian securities market more as an emerging one. This notion will change with the EMU accession.

European financial markets) foreign capital remains mostly in the country's sovereign debt market, although small volume and liquidity will remain a major obstacle for the biggest institutional investors to enter the Hungarian market (or buy Hungarian securities). Domestic institutional investors, however, backed by their steadily growing assets and market experience, may become further involved (and make better use of) the corporate and municipal bond markets as they grow over time.

16.3.3 Market Makers

The primary dealer system of government securities was established in January 1996 for the purpose of providing a more secure basis for financing the budget deficit, reducing financing costs through market mechanisms, and facilitating the expansion and transparency of the secondary market for government securities. The basic responsibility of primary dealers is to trade large volumes of government securities with large investors, but they may also participate in the retail of government securities (interest-bearing Treasury bill and Treasury savings bond) if they own the required branch network. The most important obligation of primary dealers is to quote prices for a determined group of government securities, thereby ensuring liquidity and transparency of the market.

The following is a list of primary dealers in the Hungarian government bond market:

- CAIB Értékpapír Rt.
- CIB Bank Rt.
- Citibank Rt.
- Deutsche Bank Rt.
- ERSTE Bank Befektetési Rt.
- ING Bank Rt.
- Kereskedelmi és Hitelbank Rt.
- Magyar Külkereskedelmi Bank Rt.
- Magyar Takarékszövetkezeti Bank Rt.
- Országos Takarékpénztár és Kereskedelmi Bank Rt.
- Postabank és Takarékpénztár Rt.
- Raiffeisen Értékpapír és Befektetési Rt.

Primary dealers for retail government securities:

- CIB Bank Rt.
- Kereskedelmi és Hitelbank Rt.
- Magyar Takarékszövetkezeti Bank Rt.
- Országos Takarékpénztár és Kereskedelmi Bank Rt.
- Hungarian State Treasury Branch Network.[14]

Interdealer brokers for Hungarian government securities:

- Bondtrade Értékpapír Rt., Budapest
- Continental Capital Market, Geneva (Switzerland)

---

[14] The HST Branch Network is present as network dealer in 18 (out of 19) county towns and Budapest. The key responsibility of the branch network concerning government securities is to trade them with households and retail investors, complementing the activities of retail primary dealers. The primary objective of the network is to make government securities available throughout the country.

- Prebon Marshall Yamane, London (UK)
- Garban Intercapital plc, London (UK)

16.3.4   Other Market Participants

16.3.4.1   Hungarian Government Debt Management Agency (GDMA, ÁKK)

The ÁKK (*Államadósság Kezelő Központ*) is a single agency responsible for debt management and was established in 1995 under the supervision of the MoF. In 1996 the ÁKK took over all activities concerning domestic debt management, under the supervision of the Chairman of the State Treasury. The ÁKK has been responsible for foreign affairs since 1997, and has been entitled to collect resources from abroad since 1999. In 2001, in line with the international development of the debt management institutional framework, the ÁKK became an independent organization (as a joint-stock company).

The primary function of the ÁKK is to help to maintain the solvency of the central budget in line with the annual Budget Act (moved by the MoF); to arrange for financing public debt and budget deficit; and to keep a record of and to renew public debt. Thus ÁKK manages all tasks about sovereign debt with market compatible means; collects and publishes information on the government securities market; and analyses and helps to develop market processes and institutions.

16.3.4.2   Central Clearing House and Depository (Budapest) Ltd. (KELER)

The Central Clearing House and Depository (Budapest) Ltd. (*Központi Elszámolóház és Értéktár*) was incorporated by the NBH (50%), the BSE (25%) and the BCE (25%) on October 12, 1993. The functions of physical delivery of securities and the financial settlement of securities transactions were transferred to KELER on its establishment. Settlement cycle is $T + 2$ for the BSE government securities section and $T + 3$ in the equities section. From May 2002, KELER also provides central counterparty (CCP) function, i.e. provides full guarantee for securities transactions concluded on the BSE spot market.

16.3.4.3   Investment Service Providers

There are two groups of ISPs in Hungary: banks and investment enterprises. In the Hungarian financial markets the role of banks has always been dominant, all the more so since the legal admittance of universal banks in January 1, 1999. No wonder that recent consolidations of the financial sector, in line with international trends, has resulted in the integration of the existing subsidiary investment enterprises into their parent banks. (Not all the remaining ISPs are independent, however, banks control most of them.)

According to the BSE list of members, there are 38 ISPs present on the cash market: 19 of them are engaged in government securities trading; 16 of the latter category are occupied with other debt securities (corporate and mortgage bonds) as well; and only 10 companies trade on the OTC market. The total trading volume equaled HUF 3688.4 billion in 2002, of which 82.1% comprises the trading of equities, 13.1% government bonds, and 4.6% other debt securities.

The role of investment enterprises was dominant both on the stock market and in the OTC spot trade; however, their weight (90% in 2001) was bigger in the stock market turnover, than in the OTC transactions (70%). Both groups of ISPs had the overwhelming part of their turnover in the OTC market: 96% of the banks' total trading and 88% of the enterprises spot turnover took place on the OTC markets. The main explanation for that lay in regulation up to the end of 2001, only the commission transactions were subject to forced stock exchange participation, but most of trade is done for own account.

16.3.4.4 Ratings Agencies

The Hungarian sovereign debt is rated by all the major international rating agencies (Co-face, Fitch IBCA, Japan Credit Rating Agency, Moody's, Rating and Investment, and Standard and Poor's). All agencies gave investment grade ratings for Hungarian debt during the fall of 2000. Current grades are collected on the NBH's homepage (http://english.mnb.hu/dokumentumok/hitelmin_en.xls).

The 2001 Capital Market Act prescribes that (nonbank and nonstate) issuers of publicly placed bonds must attain bank guarantee or rating, if their total outstanding debt exceeds the value of their equity, or the bond is issued to finance the acquisition of particular assets. Rating agencies must be registered at HFSA, but the international agencies have not applied so far and there are virtually no domestic rating agencies[15] in the Hungarian market.

16.3.5 Secondary Market Trading

The secondary market trading of government securities may take place on the stock exchange or on the over-the-counter (OTC) market, the latter mostly through primary dealers or the branch offices of the Treasury. In fact, one of the most important objectives of establishing the primary dealer system, and the obligation to active market participation and price quotation, was to ensure the functioning of a liquid and transparent secondary market for investors. Accordingly, the primary dealers' basic obligation is to quote continuous two-way (bid and offer) prices for government securities included in the system, i.e., for Hungarian government bonds and discount Treasury bills with maturity longer than 90 days, both on the BSE and on the OTC market (ECB, 2002).

Secondary market liquidity of government securities is further enhanced by interdealer brokers' activity. Their job is to concentrate bids and offers for government securities and other publicly issued instruments, and provide market participants with reliable information on the movement of yields and prices. Other measures to promote liquidity are the calculation and publication of benchmark yields by the ÁKK, and reducing the number of outstanding bonds while increasing the issued amount of each individual security (e.g., increasing the number of trenches).

The ÁKK doesn't set procedures and rules for off-exchange price quotation. Primary dealers while calculating two-way prices for each government securities series decide freely the bid and offer spread in yield terms. However, because of the liquid secondary market, the usual spread at off-exchange price quotation is also less than 0.5% points.

Primary dealers quote off-exchange prices to each other on electronic trading systems (Reuters, Bloomberg), but phone dealing is quite common. The OTC government securities transactions are settled through KELER, from the issue date until the third working day preceding the redemption date, usually for $T + 2$ settlement cycle, but participants can agree on a different settlement date. The turnover of government securities transactions settled through

---

[15] Focus Investment Inc. was established in 1998 (one of the shareholders was Thomson BankWatch), but the company currently does not function for lack of order.

the KELER OTC system totaled HUF 10 994 billion in 2001, of which Treasury bonds represented 82%. Thirty three percent of the secondary market transactions of primary dealers were concluded with credit institutions and 23% with institutional investors, while the share of deals concluded with foreign investors accounted for 14%.

After a few years of stagnation, the total turnover hosted by ISPs on the spot market reached HUF 45 720 billion in 2002 (a 15.3% growth over the previous year) owing to growing speculation on government bond prices (first quarter of 2002) and the forint's appreciation (fourth quarter). Ninety percent of the secondary market trading volume of government securities was conducted by primary dealers (own account trading of universal banks remained its usual form), of which 19% was done for nonresidents.

16.3.6   Exchange Information

The BSE reopened in June 1990, and has gradually improved its services. The Budapest Stock Index (BUX) was introduced in 1991; an independent clearing house and national depository (KELER[16]) was established in 1993; and the derivatives section was started in March 1995. The MultiMarket Trading System (MMTS) electronic platform of the remote trading system was introduced in the cash market in 1998. The BSE was converted from a *sui generis* self-regulatory organization of broker companies into a joint-stock company in 2002.

At present, there are three sections operating on the BSE, comprising equities, debt securities (together they form the cash market), and derivatives. Corporate bonds and investment notes are traded in the equities section, while government securities, mortgage bonds, and bonds issued by international financial institutions are present in the debt securities section. The latter section accounted for 14.3% of the total turnover (HUF 1844 billion) of the cash market in 2002.

Derivatives products can be traded in three transaction categories (namely the equity- and index-based, the foreign exchange, and the interest-based transaction classes), with futures products from start-up, and options products introduced in 2000. Futures on 3- and 12-month discount Treasury bills and 3- and 5-year Treasury bonds are traded in the interest-based transaction category; along with 1 and 3 month BUBOR (interbank rate) contracts; however, market turnover in this section has decreased practically to zero (after HUF 127 billion in 1998). Only members of the BSE and banks may conduct trading activities on the BSE, where the cash market is order driven.

The BSE owes much to the onset of privatization in Hungary, which occurred simultaneously with its foundation. However, the 1998 Russian crises impeded its rapid development (in terms of both market capitalization and turnover), and started a long, forced consolidation process among market participants. Only the market capitalization of government securities (and mortgage bonds, introduced in 2001) has increased considerably since then, but market turnover decreased considerably in the debt securities section as well. It is not surprising that the BSE is trying to identify strategic cooperation opportunities with more developed and larger exchanges. The main competitor of the BSE is the London exchange SEAQ: 55% of the total turnover of Hungarian securities took place in London, where the government bonds are also listed.

The BCE was opened in 1990, and its financial section is a competitor of the BSE in futures products (foreign exchange and BUBOR contracts).

---

[16] KELER also conducts the clearing of OTC transactions.

16.4   THE HUNGARIAN GOVERNMENT BOND MARKET

16.4.1   Background

The Hungarian government securities market became a developed and mature market during the second half of the 1990s. The ratio of central government gross debt to GDP was steadily decreasing (see Table 16.1), while the form of outstanding debt was more converted to (mainly fixed rate) government securities, reaching 81.1% of the total HUF 9224 billion by the end of 2002 (50.4% in 1997).

In the early 1990s private placements of government securities were common, usually serving special purposes. Examples of such bonds include bank, loan, or debtor consolidation bonds intended to improve the solvency ratio and financial strength of banks. Nowadays, however, the share of privately placed government bonds is insignificant and all securities are sold through public offerings.

Different types of government securities have been introduced gradually, as market conditions evolved. In line with the main objective of debt management strategy, i.e., to provide low-cost funding in the long run for the borrowing requirement of the budget (taking into consideration the possible risks involved and adopting an integrated approach), the ÁKK repeatedly tried to increase the proportion of fixed rate bonds and to lengthen maturities. This process can be tracked by looking at the history of auctions: Treasury bills with maturity less than 1 year were introduced and sold on auctions as early as 1988. Treasury bonds were auctioned later to meet two goals: to finance the central budget deficit each year and to renew maturing public debt. The first auctions of the 2-, 3-, and 5-year fixed rate bonds were held in 1996 and 1997, respectively, while the 10-year bond was first auctioned in 1999. The large-scale demand and the macroeconomic events allowed the extension of the yield curve by introducing the 15-year maturity, in conjunction with terminating the issuance of 2-year bonds in 2001. The first auction of the floating rate bond, with a maturity of 5 years, was held in 1998.

The outstanding amount of (forint-denominated) Treasury bonds was HUF 4606.6 billion, or 49.9% of total public debt by 2002 (32.5% in 1997), of which 16.9% (42.8%) was privately placed. Government bonds constitute the main financing medium, while Treasury bills are important in liquidity management. The ratio of 5-year or longer maturity bonds in the bond portfolio was 45% (resulting in an average term to maturity of 2.33 years) in 2002, but was planned to increase to 79% (2.81 years) in 2003. The constant increase in the supply of government securities has been due to the gradual substitution of nonmarketable forms of debt to securities, and the usually big financing needs of the budget (see Figure 16.2).

The debt management strategy of the ÁKK has been modified from time to time because of the changing market circumstances and financing needs of the budget. Recent changes altered the foreign currency denomination ratio of newly issued government securities. In 2002, the ÁKK refinanced even the maturing foreign-currency-denominated debt (€1.2 billion) on the domestic market, but the excess amount was too great. Thus, in 2003 the ÁKK returned to the former strategy of funding maturing foreign-currency-denominated debt on the international capital markets and financing the budget deficit, all interest payments, and the maturing forint debt through the domestic channel. The rationale behind these strategy shifts can be explained on policy grounds: in 2002 the foreign exchange necessary for redemption was bought from the NBH, thus contributing to the reduction of reserves; in 2003 the new euro issues helped to stop further appreciation of the forint and to develop the nondomestic investor base on the Euromarket (vital after the conclusion of EMU accession). As a consequence of

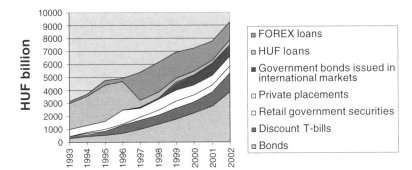

Figure 16.2   The central government gross debt.
Source: Hungarian Government Debt Management Agency Ltd. Reproduced by permission of Hungarian Government Debt Management Agency.

these strategies, the proportion of debt denominated in foreign currency has gradually declined, reaching 24.6% of total public debt in 2002 (41.3% in 1997) (IMF, 2002, September).

The foreign exchange portfolio of Hungarian sovereign debt consists traditionally of fixed-rate elements. However, to allow a more flexible approach to interest rate management, the ÁKK created an interest rate benchmark, which gives a fix/floating mix for the foreign exchange debt portfolio for each consecutive year. The actual portfolio is allowed to deviate by 5% from this proportion. In 2001 the interest rate benchmark consisted of approximately 80% fixed and 20% floating rate elements. To eliminate the cross-currency rates risk inherent in foreign-currency-denominated debt, while reflecting the actual foreign exchange basket of the forint, this debt is currency denominated only in euro.

Another, constant element of debt financing strategy has been the effort to increase the amount outstanding in single bonds. Thus the previous usual volume of HUF 120–200 billion was increased to 340–400 billion or €1 billion, depending on the maturity. Market turnover is highest for the 5-year bonds, but the volume and turnover of longer maturities is also steadily growing.

The maturity profile of the forint-denominated government securities portfolio is uneven, with large repayments concentrated in the period 2002–2006. The average maturity of this portfolio was 2.33 years at the end of 2002 (duration 1.96). In contrast to the domestic debt market, no short term debt has been issued in the international markets, thus contributing to a relatively even spread of issues by maturity (this phenomenon is partly because many of the more expensive foreign currency portfolio elements were prepaid and replaced by cheaper issues). The maturity and duration of the forint-denominated portfolio also increased because floating rate and 2-year bonds were not issued in 2002, and the 15-year bonds were introduced instead.

The Hungarian sovereign debt market is under speculative and restructuring pressure. The speculative pressure is related to the development of the forint's exchange rate; since the broadening of the fluctuation band in 2001 there has been a considerable appreciation (together with increasing volatility) helping disinflation processes, which in turn resulted in increasing bond prices. The demand for the government securities was further boosted by the fact that the central bank ceased to issue NBH bonds, shifting demand to the government market. Of course, unfavorable external conditions (low interest rates, collapsing stock exchanges) also

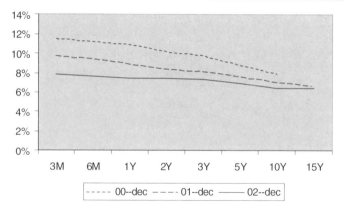

Figure 16.3   Hungarian government benchmark yield curve.
Source: Hungrian Government Debt Management Agency Ltd. Reproduced by permission of Hungarian Government Debt Management Agency.

contributed to the increasing attention given to the Hungarian market. Foreigners were looking first of all for longer term government securities because of the expectation that yields would converge to yields on European markets.[17] A big part of the currently remaining premium owes to higher than European inflation and to exchange rate uncertainties, since euro-dominated Hungarian government bonds had a premium of only about 50bp at the end of 2002 (27bp in January 2003) compared with benchmark Eurobond yields. It is generally believed that long term Hungarian maturities can already be regarded as Eurobonds, considering their redemption probably will take place in euro (their redenomination can be expected to take place in 2008) (DBR, 2001).

However, this process also challenges the debt management strategy of ÁKK, because instead of being the sovereign issuer on a small market, it has to be prepared to act as a minor participant in the single market. The agency tries to fulfill this task by issuing euro-denominated bonds as well as by converging the characteristics of forint-denominated bonds to their European counterparts.

The above market developments regarding the decreasing yields can also be seen from the continued flattening (combined with general decreasing) of the yield curve of forint-denominated bonds since disinflation gained momentum in mid-2001 (see Figure 16.3). The drop in yields has been more marked on the short side, naturally, but interest rate elasticity is greater on the long side, this is why investors anticipating further disinflation are more active on the long side of the market.

16.4.2   Types of Instruments

16.4.2.1   Discount Treasury Bills (Diszkont Kincstárjegy)

This category refers to discounted or zero-coupon bills with maturities shorter than 1 year, issued to finance the central budget deficit through the Hungarian State Treasury. Discount Treasury bills are issued for three benchmark maturities, with 3, 6, or 12 months. Discount

---

[17] Regarding the long term maturities, the convergence toward Euro-yields has been evident since 2001. The 10-year benchmark yield first exceeded the premium-limit stipulated by the Maastricht criteria, which is a maximum of 200bp, in early 2002.

Treasury bills were first auctioned in 1988. Currently, 3-month discount Treasury bills are issued every Tuesday, while 6- and 12-month bills are issued twice a month (every odd-numbered-week Wednesday and Thursday, respectively). Bills are issued by discriminatory price auctions.

16.4.2.2   Interest-Bearing Treasury Bills (Kamatozó Kincstárjegy)

Interest-Bearing Treasury bills are issued monthly, but are offered for sale continuously during a 2-week subscription period. These bills are issued with a maturity of 1 year, and pay a fix interest at maturity. The Government Debt Management Agency opens the series to subscription on the second week of each month. This type of security is targeted mainly at the small investors, and can be purchased through the Hungarian State Treasury Branch Network and three big banks' and some savings banks' ramifications.

16.4.2.3   Treasury Saving Bills (Kincstári Takarékjegy)

Treasury saving bills are 1- and 2-year interest-bearing government securities that pay interest together with the principal at redemption. Treasury savings bills are registered, materialized securities, which can be bought and transferred only by individual residents, in any of the 3200 offices of the Hungarian Post.

16.4.2.4   NBH Bills (MNB kötvény)

NBH bills are potential monetary policy instruments of the NBH, even if their issuance has been currently suspended[18] (since April 2002) because of the decreasing sterilization needs. NBH bills correspond to 3-month or 1-year discount Treasury bills sold through auctions organized by the ÁKK. Bill auctions were unscheduled, announced 1 week in advance; domestic and foreign investors and institutions could participate in the auction.

16.4.2.5   Treasury Bonds (Államkötvény)

This category currently includes 3-, 5-, 10-, and 15-year bonds bearing fixed interest rates and annual or semiannual (all bonds issued after January 2002 pay interest annually) interest payments. Treasury bonds are sold through auctions held on the Thursdays of every even-numbered week. At each auction, two types of bonds are offered for sale: the 3-year and the 5-year fixed rate bond at one auction and the 3-year fixed rate bond goes with the 10- or the 15-year fixed rate security at the next. All Treasury bonds are listed on the BSE on the issue date.

16.4.3   Auction Process

Hungarian government securities (except for interest-bearing Treasury bills and Treasury saving bills) are sold at discriminatory price auctions. Investors may purchase bonds by entrusting a primary dealer to submit their bids. The minimal nominal value of a bid is HUF 1 million. Each bidder may also submit noncompetitive bids without stating price or yield rate, thus

---

[18] The total portfolio of NBH Bills totaled HUF 557 billion in October 2001, after which it has gradually diminished (184 billion in March 2002) and diverted to central government securities.

indicating its will to purchase securities at the average yield rate or price of awards to competitive bidders. Auction bids must be delivered via the auction function of the automated trading system (MMTS) operated by BSE before 11 a.m.

The auction technique has been used for selling discount Treasury bills since early 1988, but has become the regular issuing technique for government securities since March 1996, when the first government bonds were sold using this technique. However, until 1998 government bonds could have been bought twice a month through subscriptions as well. All marketable bonds issued since April 1, 1999 have been dematerialized (paperless). Hungarian government bond and discount Treasury bill auctions are announced by GDMA 5 days before the auction in "Magyar Tökepiac." The issuing calendar for Hungarian government securities can be downloaded from http://www.akk.hu/kibocs/46e.htm.

16.4.4   Market Conventions

The market convention is for trade plus 2 (T+2) settlement for all government securities with the value date the same as the settlement date. In the case of both OTC and stock exchange trading, the ex-coupon date for T+2 delivery is the fifth working day preceding the coupon and principal payment date. Principal and coupon payments are made on the basis of positions registered on third working day preceding the payment date.

The Hungarian holiday calendar is employed; from March 2002, the day-count convention and calculation method for fixed interest Treasury bonds, and from January 2003, for all other government securities has been changed, and now follows the recommendations of the International Securities Market Association (ISMA), to be in line with the EMU Member States' practice.[19] The day count basis is thus Actual/360 for Treasury bills and interest-bearing Treasury bills, and Actual/Actual for Treasury bonds (see http://www.akk.hu/forg/allasfoglalas2e.doc). The new method is effective in relation to both outstanding series and new issuances. Government bonds are quoted clean for exchange transactions and dirty (with accrued interest) on the OTC market.

16.4.5   Benchmarks

The GDMA has regularly published secondary market benchmark yields of government securities since February 17, 1997. The basis for calculating benchmark yields are prices of government securities included in the primary dealer system with residual maturity being the same or close to benchmark maturities.

The Hungarian government bond indices, which cover the whole market for government securities, are calculated and released daily. The Short Term Hungarian Government Security Index (RMAX) reflects price changes in government securities with residual maturity shorter than 1 year (3–12 months), while the Hungarian Government Bond Index (MAX) illustrates market performance of longer than 1-year residual maturity papers. The MAX Composite Hungarian Government Bond Index (MAX Composite) contains all government securities, and thus characterizes the whole government security market. The government security indices are total return indices that reflect the effect of price movements as well as the impact of accrued or paid interest. The indices are officially released on the HUBONDINDEX Reuters page at 2:30 p.m. every day. The index basket contains the most liquid government securities, for

---

[19] Thus granting easy comparability to European bonds, as part of ÁKK's preparations to participate in the single market.

which primary dealers quote prices with narrow spread. The basis of government security indices was 100 points on December 31, 1996.

Besides (and fully compatible with) the MAX index family, the BMX3Y, BMX5Y, BMX10Y, and BMX15Y benchmark government bond indices are used for measuring the performance of benchmark government bonds belonging to the key maturities (3, 5, 10, and 15 years) that are considered as the core of the MAX portfolio. The indices are based on the total return concept and calculated by using gross prices. The prices required for calculating the indices are based on the appropriate benchmark yields published by the Government Debt Management Agency.

The DWIX, the first yield index published in Hungary, was published in November 1992 (its calculation was started after the first primary auction of 6-month Treasury bills was held on April 30, 1992) by Daiwa-MKB Investment and Securities Ltd; all rights and obligations associated to the index were transferred to the BSE in 1997. It is an index of the yield of government bills based on the average yields developing at the primary auctions by the GDMA of 3-, 6-, and 12-month discount Treasury bills. The DWIX basket includes turnover and elapsed time weighted average yields achieved at primary auctions by Treasury bills included in the DWIX basket in a period of 3 months before the day the index is published (BSE, 2002).

16.5   SEMIGOVERNMENT AND CORPORATE BOND MARKETS

16.5.1   Introduction

The Hungarian domestic debt market is less developed and liquid than the government securities market. Nongovernment domestic bond issues closely resemble their government counterparts (except that private placements are quite popular), but given the large denominations of most nongovernment bonds, they lack widespread appeal among individuals. Thus the nongovernment market tends to be dominated by domestic institutional investors, mainly investment and pension funds, and insurance companies. Investors tend to hold these securities until maturity, and OTC trades dominate the market. Prices are quoted in percentages, clean on exchange trades and dirty on the OTC market.

16.5.2   Semigovernment Bonds

The Hungarian Development Bank's (*Magyar Fejlesztési Bank, MFB*) position relative to the government and the budget, together with its need for additional sources, varies according to changes in the political sphere. In 2001, the bank decided to issue bonds instead of the usual borrowing techniques and, given the small domestic market, placed €450 million (5-year fixed rate) Eurobonds on the market. Under the current government, the MFB is integrated into the central budget (to meet the ESA 95 statistical criteria) and the amount of debt raised by the bank is likely to be reduced relative to the previous 4 years; but the bank remains active on the securities market, with acquiring HFSA permission to its 2-year issuing program of HUF 100 billion on the domestic market.

16.5.3   Local Government (Municipal) Bonds

The amount of debt that municipalities can raise annually is limited by the Act on Municipalities, to the extent of 70% of own current revenues minus redemption payments. Another factor hindering the development of the market is the essentially bank-based financial system, with the leading company (OTP Bank) trying to preserve its leading role in the municipal market by providing credit easily to local governments. Costs associated with bond issuance are also considered to be high (especially for public placement), even if the banks behind the organizing brokerage firms usually guarantee bonds.[20]

The first forint-denominated municipal bonds were introduced in 1998, but only 12 (out of 3158) local governments decided to apply this borrowing technique. The only attempt for public placement was that of Újpest (a district of Budapest), but it did not succeed to get on the BSE for lack of investors (to be admitted to the stock exchange, at least 25 investors must buy the issued bonds). The usual maturity of municipal bonds is 5 years, and the amount issued was only a few hundred thousand forints, mostly bought by investment companies and pension funds. Because of the small quantities, the municipal bond market is very illiquid – experts agree that a very minimum of HUF 1 billion should be issued to provide enough liquidity on the secondary market. However, local governments of major cities have a stable presence among issuers and some intend to make new placements.

16.5.4 Corporate Bonds

The corporate bond market on the stock exchange is very small, despite the forced stock-exchange participation for public placements above HUF 200 million, introduced by the 1997 Securities Act. Leasing companies were dominant on the market in the preceding years, but the Act imposed equity limit and compulsory auditing on issuers, because of the numerous bankruptcy scandals (WVM Lízing Rt., Első Hazai Faktorház Rt., Real Group, and Globex, between 1995 and 1998) hindering market growth. During the next few years, private placements became popular, and issue volumes increased,[21] as a result of the elimination of small companies from the market. Hungarian subsidiaries of transnational companies (e.g., Lehel Electrolux, Phillip Morris Hungary, Samsung Hungary, Novartis Hungária) enjoyed guarantee of the parent company (and thus were able to exceed the limit of Hungary's rating, resulting in cheaper financing possibilities than domestic companies)[22] and usually also issue their debt privately.

The 2001–2002 developments in the corporate bond market include a somewhat increasing, but still very small capitalization on the BSE, not reflected in the stock exchange turnover (most trading takes place on the OTC market, only the biggest companies' securities – banks, MOL, and Matáv – are present on the stock exchange). The increase was enabled by the fact that in case bank guarantee or rating by a recognized credit rating agency[23] was provided the own capital limit on issues made by nonbank issuers was removed. The "boom" was supported by the issue data: compared to 2000,[24] the nominal value of issued bonds was 130% higher in 2001 (HFSA, 2002). However, the number of market participants was still limited, and therefore, certain big issues heavily distort the picture. It was unfavorable that some corporate

---

[20] For example, Budapest decided to draw a syndicated loan to cancel its 3-year bond issued in 1999, even if it had an investment category rating.

[21] Even the biggest issue volumes could not compete with government issues, just look at the HUF 10 billion placement of MOL, or 24 billion of Pannon in 1997, or the 15 billion issue of Matáv and 28 billion of CIB in 1998.

[22] The MKB issued its forint-denominated bond abroad in March 2002, making use of the high rating of its mother bank (Bayerische Landesbank Girozentrale) and thus reaching interest conditions 1% point more favorable than MOL at the same time (just 0.3% point above government bonds).

[23] However, currently there are no recognized rating agencies on the Hungarian financial markets (see Section 16.3.2).

[24] The total amount of corporate bonds was HUF 77 billion in 2000, consisting of 36 issues of 29 companies.

issuers that did appear on the market presumably sought funding on the capital market because they reached the banks' large exposure limit.

In 2001, there were eight banks among the issuers, while the number of corporate issuers was only 19. The primary dealers of corporate bonds are the ISPs organizing the placement, while banks distribute their own bonds through their networks as well. Most of the issuers present on the BSE are banks (e.g., CIB, Erste, MKB, Raiffeisen), with only the MOL and Matáv present as regular corporate issuers. Other potential issuers prefer bank loan to bond financing because banking competition renders that market cheaper. Moreover, limited issue volume results in low liquidity on the secondary market, hindering the formation of an investor base[25] sufficient to develop the market. Thus, the MOL is the only independent participant on the BSE bond market, which, in order to diversify its financing sources, could issue its bonds (in its scope of a HUF 100 billion issue program) with a 0.46% point premium over the relevant government securities in September 2002, while smaller issuer companies (e.g., Axon, Freesoft, Univer) avoid the stock market.

16.5.5   Mortgage Bonds (*jelzáloglevél*)

The 1997 Act on mortgage credit institutions and mortgage bonds created this financial market segment following the German Pfandbrief model of specialized banking and covered mortgage bonds (Lassen, 2002). Currently, there are three mortgage banks present on the Hungarian market, the first one (FHB Ltd.) established in 1998. Two of the mortgage banks are subsidiaries of universal banks, while the (formerly state-owned privatized at the end of 2003) FHB cooperates with the rest of the market.

Mortgage bonds (*jelzáloglevél*) are typically 6-, 8-, or 10-year securities with annual (fixed or floating) interest payments, and were first introduced in the open market in 2001. Public issues of mortgage bonds are admitted to the BSE; at the end of 2002, 14 securities were present on the spot market (3 in 2001), with an overall capitalization of HUF 126.9 (15.7) billion. Market turnover was low, but growing steadily with HUF 2.8 billion in 2001, 20.2 billion in 2002, and 9.67 billion in the first 2 months of 2003. This type of securities is becoming increasingly popular among investors because of their security[26] (equal to that of Hungarian sovereign debt) and high yields (their premium is currently 96–120bp to the corresponding government bonds), and there has been abundant supply since the government began to subsidize housing heavily in 2000. Therefore, it is not surprising that the total growth in this market has been exponential: public issuance has reached HUF 102.5 billion in 2002 (after 8.3 billion in 2001), and FHB alone planned to issue HUF 120 billion in 2003 on the Hungarian market.[27] The main target group has been domestic institutional investors so far, but mortgage banks have tried to develop retail markets, and the FHB also tried to introduce its paper abroad (they planned to raise €1 billion in 2003).

The dynamic growth of the mortgage bond market is expected to continue in the future as well, which should be beneficial for all nongovernment issues. However, the Hungarian capital

---

[25] For example, domestic households have kept only about HUF 3.8 billion corporate bonds in their (in total 5711.9 billion in 2000) portfolio since the beginning of 2000, although they already had 16.9 billion in 1998, out of a 3870.9 billion portfolio.

[26] Currently only the FHB acquired rating so far, A1 at Moody's.

[27] The OTP Mortgage Bank has a HUF 300 billion issue program accepted in spring 2003 by the HFSA; however, members of the OTP group have an advantage even in "public" issues (HUF 135.9 billion was held within the group out of the total outstanding amount of 177 billion in 2002).

market is not sufficiently developed to fund the needs of mortgage banks, so they will have to move to the European market soon (FHB, 2001, p.17).

16.5.6 Foreign Bonds

The June 2001 foreign exchange liberalization allowed foreign issuers to appear with euroforint issues. In spite of the small number of issuers (12 in 2001 and 9 until September 2002) the scale of the issues was substantial amounting to HUF 143 billion in 2001 and HUF 82.5 billion in 2002, which was substantially above the volume of domestic bond issues. Most issuers were financing companies with very high (typically 'A' or 'AAA') credit rating, or international financial organizations (EIB and EBRD). The bonds had a fixed interest rate (roughly the same as government papers), with maturities between 1 and 10 (typically between 1 and 3) years. One reason to issue euroforint bonds was to finance investments in Hungary (the strong forint made import relatively cheap), while others often swapped the amount issued to euro right after registration. The forint bonds issued by EIB and EBRD are traded on the BSE, but they represent a very small volume in relation to the entire turnover of the stock exchange.

16.6 CONCLUSIONS

The Hungarian financial system is essentially bank-based, even if the legal and regulatory environment is now practically EU-compatible and suitable for the development of debt markets. The government bond market can be regarded as mature and ready for the EMU accession expected in 2007 or 2008. The GMDA is already prepared for the role of a minor issuer in the single market with euro-denominated issues. Also, the redenomination of the long term forint bonds should not be problematic, as market participants have already anticipated a smooth transition. However, the nongovernment segment of the market is significantly less developed, with Hungarian companies (and municipalities) practically excluded from the market for volume (thus liquidity) reasons; only subsidiaries of transnational corporations and the biggest Hungarian companies and cities are able to overcome this problem, and the situation is unlikely to change with EMU accession. In contrast to the corporate bond market, Pfandbrief-style mortgage bonds have been rapidly gaining ground and are likely to remain a competitive investment and financing vehicle with the internationalization of the Hungarian market over the next few years.

REFERENCES

Budapest Stock Exchange (2002). Annual Report 2001 (http://www.fornax.hu/cgi-bin/bet_file_en.cgi?file=kiad1_95) and various issues of monthly reports.

Deutsche Bank Research (2001, August). EU Enlargement Monitor No 5. http://www.dbresearch.de/PROD/999/PROD0000000000034085.pdf.

European Central Bank (2002, June). Bond Markets and Long-Term Interest Rates in European Union Accession Countries. http://www.ecb.int/pub/pdf/bondmarketacc2002.pdf.

György, Sándor (2002, June–July). Developments in the Hungarian Debt Markets. In: *The Development of Bond Markets in Emerging Economies, BIS Paper No. 11*. Basel: BIS, pp. 115–116. http://www.bis.org/publ/bispap11.htm.

FHB Land and Mortgage Bank (2001). Hungary: Start-Up Mortgage Banking – Covered Mortgage Bank Issuance. Presentation held at the *5th Central European Mortgage Bond Conference*, Riga. http://www.hypverband.de/hypverband/attachments/eur_vortr_mepfk_riga_meszaros.pdf.

Hungarian Financial Supervisory Authority (2002). 2001 Annual Report. http://www.pszaf.hu/english/reports/2001/2001annual.pdf.

Hungarian Government Debt Management Agency (2002). Government Securities Market Annual Report 2001. http://www.akk.hu/kiad/2001evese/2001reporte.pdf.

International Monetary Fund (2002, June). Hungary: *Financial System Stability Assessment Follow-Up*. Washington DC: IMF. http://www.imf.org/external/pubs/ft/scr/2002/cr02112.pdf.

International Monetary Fund (2002, September). Emerging Local Bond Markets. In: *Global Financial Stability Report*. Washington, DC: IMF, Ch. 4. http://www.imf.org/external/pubs/ft/GFSR/2002/03/pdf/chp4.pdf.

Köke, J. and M. Schröder (2002): The Future of Eastern European Capital Markets. EIB Papers Vol. 7, No 1. http://www.eib.org/efs/eibpapers/y02n1v7/y02n1a07.pdf.

Lassen, T. (2002, November). Mortgage Banks and Mortgage Bonds in Central Europe – An Overview. In: *6th Central European Mortgage Bond Conference*, Warsaw. http://www.hypverband.de/hypverband/attachments/eur_vortr_mepfk_warschau_lassen.pdf.

National Bank of Hungary (2002). Monetary Policy in Hungary. http://english.mnb.hu/dokumentumok/monet_en_2002.pdf.

Szalkai, I. (2001). Financial Markets in Hungary: Achievements and Prospective Challenges. In: L. Bokros, A. Fleming, and C. Votava eds., *Financial Transition in Europe and Central Asia. Challenges of the New Decade*. Washington DC: IBRD.

17

Italy

WALTER VECCHIATO

17.1 INTRODUCTION

Italy is one of the six original founder members of the European Union (EU). Now also an integral part of the Euro area, the economy shares many characteristics common to the single currency zone, constituting almost one fifth of the area's aggregate population and gross domestic product (GDP).

In the year 2000 the Italian GDP increased by a respectable 2.9%, almost double the increase in 1999; however, by 2002 growth slowed to just 0.4%. The grim economic situation in the United States, together with ongoing signals of uncertainty in the expectations of European enterprises, indicates an uncertain though somewhat improved outlook for the forthcoming years. Nonetheless, the growth differential compared to the EU and the Euro area has now decreased to less than half a percentage point per year, which compares with as high as one percentage point in the late 1990s.

The slowing of the economy has been caused by a slump in both domestic and overseas demand, and has been aggravated by worsening competitiveness stemming from exchange rate appreciation. The reduction of foreign demand is in sharp contrast with the dynamic export growth of 11.7% in 2000, which then surpassed aggregate growth in the Euro area, underpinned by significant development in the industrial sector and in services exports (up 12.4% against an imports growth of 6.7% in 2000), the latter also as a consequence of tourists' affluence in the jubilee year. This volatility of services exports is partly due to the fact that aside from tourism and design, Italy is not really competitive in most services sectors (Gabrielli and De Brung, 1999).

Declines in both investments and expenditures have contributed to the slump in domestic demand in 2002. The main role has been carried out by the transport and machinery and equipment sectors; also noticeable is the slowing of investments for high technology after three consecutive years of high growth. These tendencies have greatly affected the economy's key strength in manufacturing, especially small- and medium-sized firms specializing in products that require high-quality design and engineering.

The negative trend in demand has disrupted a previous recovery of production in all sectors of the economy, except agriculture, which has been struggling on an ongoing basis. The increase in employment previously boosted by growth, then emphasizing a trend that had emerged back in 1998, has also been broken. The prior positive trend in the job market did not reduce the gap in employment rate between the South, North, and Central Italy. In the South, more or less one person in five is looking for work. Currently this is one of the main concerns for Italian politicians and policy makers. Another concern is that most workers can retire on pensions in their 50s (early withdrawal from active working life permitted by current Italian labor and pension laws). Spending on pensions swallows up to 14% of Italy's GDP.

European Fixed Income Markets: Money, Bond and Interest Rate Derivatives. Edited by J.A. Batten,
T.A. Fetherston and P.G. Szilagyi. © 2004 John Wiley & Sons, Ltd. ISBN 0-470-85053-1

More recently, inflationary pressures have become more evident, outlining contingent factors, the gradual transfer onto final prices of input cost tensions, and the new impulses coming from abroad (the volatility of oil prices) despite the new strengthening of the euro. Therefore, the trend growth rate of consumer prices temporarily went beyond the 3% threshold, but has now settled to 2.7% in March 2003 on a year-on-year basis. Based on the provisional estimate of the national index for the entire community the acquired inflation rate for the year 2002 was about 2.2%. In Italy, many institutional and independent agencies forecast a GDP growth around 1% or slightly below for 2003 and 2.1% in 2004, with an inflation rate of about 2.4% in the current year.

The government's budget deficit is forecast to widen from 2.3% of GDP in 2002 to 2.7% in 2003. This will probably narrow somewhat in 2004 provided that the government introduces substantial corrective measures to comply with the budgetary constraints set forth by the EU's Stability and Growth Pact. In 2000, the public administrations' net debt, calculated on the basis of the Community rules and regulations, decreased by 4% points to 111% of GDP, chiefly because of revenues resulting from granting the UMTS mobile network licenses. To some extent this trend continued into 2001, but the level of public debt again reached 111% in 2002.

Regarding international and domestic debt securities issues, Italy showed a decreasing trend in domestic issuance until recently, with the outstanding amount of domestic issues declining by 16.5%, and the total of domestic and international issues falling by 8.1% between 1995 and 2000. This was largely due to the moderate funding needs of government, and so with the widening of the public deficit issuance has picked up again since 2001. Meanwhile, non-government issuance has been growing on a continuous basis, but these instruments constitute only about one third of the market. Today, the Italian bond market remains the second largest in the Euro area after the German market, with the total outstanding amount reaching €1.6 trillion in February 2003.

17.2   THE ITALIAN GOVERNMENT BOND MARKET

The Italian financial system has grown significantly in the last few years because the ratio of total outstanding amounts of financial assets to GDP has increased from less than 4 times in 1980 to 7 in 2000 (European Central Bank, 2002). The Italian government bond market includes Italian government bonds and other bonds issued by some government enterprises (for example, Italian Railways).

All banks and investment companies registered at the Bank of Italy are authorized dealers (see the decree of the Minister of Treasury of November 16, 2000). The market for Italian government bonds involves several participants: the Department of the Treasury, as the issuer, also responsible for the set up of the legal framework; Bank of Italy and Consob as supervisory bodies; the MTS Company as the secondary market manager; the specialists in Italian government bonds, as the main market makers. The introduction in 1994 of a category of intermediary called specialists in government securities has substantially improved the liquidity of the primary market.

17.2.1   Types of Instruments

17.2.1.1   *Treasury Bills (BOTs)*

BOTs are short term securities with maturities up to 365 days. The remuneration, determined entirely by the difference between the nominal value and the issued price, is considered anticipated, because tax for individual investors is applied at the moment of the subscription. BOT auctions are reserved to institutional brokers authorized in accordance with the decree of the Minister of Treasury of November 16, 2000.

17.2.1.2   Zero Coupon Bonds (CTZs)

CTZs are bonds with maturities between 18 and 24 months and are subject to reopening which can reduce their original duration. The remuneration is entirely determined by the difference between the nominal value and the issued price. CTZ auction is reserved for institutional brokers authorized in accordance with the legislative decree of February 24, 1998, No 58.

17.2.1.3   Treasury Certificates (CCTs)

CCTs are floating rate securities with a 7-year maturity. Interest is paid with deferred semi-annual coupons to the yield of 6-month BOTs. Also the difference between the nominal value and the issue price accounts for the yield. The auction is reserved to institutional brokers in accordance with the legislative decree of February 24, 1988, No 58.

17.2.1.4   Treasury Bonds (BTPs)

BTPs are medium and long term securities, with a fixed coupon paid every 6 months. Financial brokers who meet the conditions set by the Italian legislation can participate directly in the auctions and are, therefore, called "authorized dealers" (i.e. banks, investment companies, and financial institutions registered at the Bank of Italy; see the decree of the Minister of Treasury of November 16, 2000). In order to buy BTPs, investors who cannot participate in the auctions can turn to the previously mentioned brokers or to the secondary market. In addition, the Treasury has also increasingly resorted to new financial instruments, such as global bonds, interest rate swaps, and currency swaps.

17.2.2   List of Specialists

Here is the list of specialists in 2002:

- Abax Bank (CREDEM Group)
- Banca IMI (IMI – San Paolo Group)
- Deutsche Bank AG
- BNL (Banca Nazionale del Lavoro)
- BNP Paribas
- Caboto SpA (IntesaBci Group)
- Capitalia SpA
- Crédit Agricole Indosuez
- Crédit Suisse First Boston
- Goldman Sachs International
- ING Bank
- JP Morgan Securities Ltd.
- Morgan Stanley Int.
- MPS Finance (MPS Group)
- Salomon Brothers Int.
- UBM SpA (Unicredito Group)

17.2.3   Description of a Government Bond Auction

The auction takes place at Bank of Italy, Monetary and Exchange Policy Department, Public Debt Division, in the presence of an officer from the Ministry of Treasury (proposal making officer), who represents the Ministry of Treasury and is responsible for supervising the auction, and an officer of the bank itself. Authorized dealer bids are sent electronically, using a National Interbanking Network.

The issuance annual calendar released by the Ministry of Treasury fixes the days in which announcements, auctions, and settlement operation take place. At the moment of the announcement of the quantities to be auctioned, the security under consideration is specified. For BOTs, the settlement takes place 3 days after the auction and fall on the maturity date of the corresponding securities, to facilitate their reinvestment. For medium and long term securities the settlement takes place two business days after the auction. When the settlement date does not fall on the day in which security interest begins to accrue (the so-called ex-date) subscribers pay the Treasury the relative accrued interest. For all securities, the settlement takes place using the Bank of Italy Centralized System of Payments, through which the subscriber cash balance and position in securities is determined. The treasury uses two kinds of auction:

1. Competitive bidding without base price for BOTs
2. Marginal auction without base price for medium and long term securities (BTPs, CCTs, CTZs)

The competitive bidding allows a bid to be satisfied at the price offered. Every dealer can submit a maximum of three bids. Bid prices can differ from each other by 0.01%. The minimum bid is €1.5 million, whereas the maximum amount requested is equal to the quantity offered during the auction. The first bids to be accepted are those with the highest price and then all the others are allocated in descending order until the amount of accepted bids reaches the amount tendered by the Treasury. To avoid speculative bids a cutoff price is calculated, under which subscription applications are not taken into consideration.

The marginal auction ensures all the requests are auctioned at the same price, the so-called marginal price. Every dealer can submit a maximum of three bids differing from each other by at least 0.01%.[1] The minimum request is €500 000, while the maximum amount to be requested is equal to the quantity offered by the Treasury during the auction. The marginal price is determined by satisfying bids starting from the highest price until the total amount of bids accepted equals the amount offered. The price of the last successful bid is the marginal price. To avoid speculative behavior a cutoff price is calculated, under which the subscription applications are not taken into consideration.

The composition of the government bond market at December 2001 and June 2002, the weighted average yield of bond issues, and the notional amount of bond issues on the foreign markets and their respective interest rates are provided in Tables 17.1–17.4.

As can be seen from these tables the percentage of medium and long term bonds is about 90% and the average life of government securities, which was below 36 months at the beginning of the 1990s, rapidly increased to approximately 70 months at the end of the decade.

---

[1] For 30-year BTPs, the difference is 0.05%.

Table 17.1   Government bond composition at different recent dates

Bonds	Composition*			
	December 31, 2001		June 30, 2002	
BOTs	113 809	(9.94%)	135 650	(11.84%)
CCTs	218 348	(19.06%)	228 087	(19.91%)
BTPs	630 935	(55.08%)	638 492	(55.74%)
CTZs	48 577	(4.24%)	67 686	(5.91%)
Other (govt guarantees)	51 934	(4.53%)	41 013	(5.58%)
Foreign EMU	25 309	(2.21%)	45 101	(3.94%)
Foreign non-EMU	56 514	(4.93%)	36 718	(3.21%)
Total	1 145 426		1 192 747	
Average life	5.87		5.94	

Source: Ministry of Economy and Finance.
*Nominal amount in million euros.

Table 17.2   Weighted average yield of 2001 bond issues

Type of security	Amount allocated*	Weighted average yield (%)
CCTs	27 767	4.35
BTPs		
30-year BPTPs	11 682	5.80
10-year BPTPs	33 115	5.13
5-year BPTPs	26 478	4.59
3-year BPTPs	48 654	4.13
Total	119 929	4.67
24-month CTZs	35 528	4.12
BOTs		
Flexible BOTs	3 500	4.01
3-month BOTs	35 250	4.12
6-month BOTs	79 427	4.18
12-month BOTs	70 500	4.05
Total	188 677	4.11
Total 2001	371 901	4.31

Source: Ministry of Economy and Finance.
*Nominal amount in million euros.

Table 17.3   Issues on the foreign markets as at December 31, 2001

Currency	Total amount issued
USD	10 685 930 000
JPY	100 000 000 000
CHF	1 000 000 000
Euro	5 150 000 000
GBP	1 200 000 000

Source: Ministry of Economy and Finance.

Table 17.4   Key interest rates for the year 2001

Treasury securities	
Average interest rate	4.33%
of Treasury securities	
10-year BTPs	
Average interest rate	5.13%
of Treasury securities	
12-month BOTs	
Minimum interest rate	2.98%
Maximum interest rate	4.49%

Source: Ministry of Economy and Finance.

17.3   ITALIAN STOCK EXCHANGE (BORSA ITALIANA)

The gradual globalization and establishment of the European market has caused important changes in the market structure and in the issue and placement of financial instruments in Italy. Since 1988, Italy has had an electronic wholesale market for trading government securities, called MTS. This market has rapidly expanded in terms of daily trading volume. The average daily trading volume in MTS rose from initial €150 million to a peak of €21 billion and has now stabilized around €8 billion. The impressive growth in turnover in the middle of the 1990s reflected the exceptionally strong demand for Italian government securities, fueled by expectations of a rapid convergence of the interest rates on lira-denominated assets to the levels prevailing in Germany and France.

Borsa Italiana is the joint-stock company responsible for organizing and managing the Italian Stock Exchange, and was created in 1997 by the privatization of the stock exchange and operative since January 2, 1998. Borsa Italiana has aimed at developing the bond and government securities market (MOT). It has therefore introduced a new market sector, known as EuroMOT, for trading Eurobonds, bonds issued by foreign entities, and asset-backed securities (ABS). To facilitate this process Borsa Italiana introduced a new trading platform encompassing the entire MOT market in spring 2000. The advantages arise in terms of successfully integrating the government wholesale market (MTS) as well as in terms of the efficiency of trading activity (Borsa Italiana, 2001, 2002).

As for derivatives, the need to provide market participants with appropriate risk-hedging tools gave rise in 1992 to a market for government bond futures (MIF) and options (MTO). Despite a fast start, both these markets were outpaced by other more important markets especially LIFFE (London International Financial Futures Exchange; for short term instruments) and, more recently, EUREX (for long term instruments).

17.3.1   MOT Market

The MOT was founded as a retail market in July 1994, joining together the 10 existing Italian stock exchanges into 1 electronic market. Banks, investment agencies, and authorized market makers in accordance with the Ministry of Finance's Consolidated Law, carry out all transactions. The MOT market was created to facilitate the private investor's access to the bond markets by providing an easily understandable and transparent operating procedure even for nonexperts. It also enables professional investors to deal real time, with the certainty of being able to match buy and sell orders at the best price available on the regulated market.

The MOT is the part of the Exchange where Italian government securities and nonconvertible bonds are traded. Borsa Italiana sets the minimum tradable lots reconciling the need for the market to operate efficiently, for institutional investors to have easy access to it, and for the execution of orders to be cost-efficient. The financial instruments are divided into some different market segments, depending on the products traded:

1. BOT (short term up to 1-year government zero coupon note), BTP (fixed rate government bonds), and CTZ (long term government zero coupon bonds);
2. CCT (floating rate government bonds) and CTO (government bonds with embedded options);
3. Bonds in euro;
4. Foreign currency bonds.

Now new bonds of banks and firms represent a large share of the total amount of new issues (around 23% of the value of outstanding bonds issued by Italian residents). Contracts for traded securities are settled on the third trading day following their stipulation date except for those contracts relating to ordinary Treasury bonds that are settled on the second trading day.

The crossover of bid/ask orders drives trading. These are the expression of traders' willingness to trade through orders. Bid/ask orders are automatically ranked according to the price of each product, in decreasing order for bids and in increasing order for ask orders, and according to the time priority for equally priced orders. Trading times are different for each segment. Borsa Italiana sets the price variation cap as well as the other trading conditions necessary to ensure that market trading goes ahead in an orderly fashion.

Trading takes place in two successive stages. The opening auction aims to select the tradable financial instruments and determine a clear starting price, known as the opening price. It allows as many bids and offers as possible to be matched at a single price. Continuous trading serves to make trading fast and more efficient. In this way contracts are struck by matching or hitting opposing bids and offers available on the market. Borsa Italiana provides the public with real-time information of developments in trading. On a daily basis, at the end of trading, Borsa Italiana posts the official listings via electronic devices.

17.3.2   Listing Process

To list securities on MOT and EuroMOT, the issuer must apply to Borsa Italiana for admission. Borsa Italiana will inform the issuer if the application has been accepted or declined within 2 months from receiving it. They will also inform Consob (Consob is the public authority responsible for regulating the Italian securities market) of the decision and make a public announcement. The right to list expires after 6 months from the Borsa Italiana approval and depends on a quotation prospectus being submitted to Consob. Admission procedures are completed when Borsa Italiana has verified that the prospectus has been made available for public consultation and subsequently decides when trading will commence, informing the public of this through an announcement in at least two press agencies. Listing of government bonds placed at auction occurs after Borsa Italiana releases its certificate of issue (Borsa Italiana, 2002).

17.3.3   Participants

There are three participants in the MOT and EuroMOT trading.

1. Italian, EU, and non-EU banks authorized to trade their own accounts or on behalf of third parties in accordance with the Ministry of Finance's Consolidated Law.

2. Italian, EU, and non-EU investment institutions authorized to trade their own accounts or on behalf of third parties in accordance with the Ministry of Finance's Consolidated Law.
3. Market makers authorized to trade on behalf of third parties in accordance with the Ministry of Finance's Consolidated Law.

Members will be granted permission to trade following an audit by Borsa Italiana aimed at ensuring the regularity of market practices and to verify that they adequately meet organizational and technological requirements and that personnel in charge of trading are qualified. Final permission to trade will be granted when the direct or indirect member subscribes to the compensation, liquidation, and centralized bond deposit services. To trade Euroclear/Clearstream regulated financial instruments on EuroMOT, operators must join directly or through another company in their group dealing in compensation and liquidation services and the centralized deposit of financial instruments.

The presence of specialists is compulsory in order to ensure market liquidity, meaning continuity of trading and the presence of precise reference prices for each security. These specialists are authorized intermediaries admitted to trade on the EuroMOT, whose ongoing task is to ensure that there are bid and offer prices in the securities they are responsible for, with a maximum spread and a quantity established by Borsa Italiana.

17.3.4 Bonds Requirements

The issue must exceed at least 30 billion liras (ITL) or equivalent thereof in euros (approximately €15 million), and the payment of the capital may not take place at a lower than face value price. The issuer must have previously published and filed annual financial statements for the last three financial years, of which at least the latest must have been audited. In exceptional circumstances, Borsa Italiana may accept a smaller number of annual financial statements.

If a third party, for admission purposes, guarantees the issue, Borsa Italiana will base its decision on the guarantor's characteristics. In relation to structured bonds (index-linked to financial assets such as shares listed on a stock exchange in Italy or another country, or rather, share or currency indexes), the issuer must provide an indication of the risk-hedging strategy and demonstrate the availability in Italy of information on the prices recorded for the assets chosen for the linkage mechanism.

17.3.5 EuroMOT Market

EuroMOT is the electronic market for trading Eurobonds, foreign bonds, and ABS. Through EuroMOT, Borsa Italiana aims to widen its offering of tradable instruments, providing investors with an easy-to-reach product and the chance of diversifying their portfolios, while it offers professional traders the possibility of dealing in a new market segment and enhancing the services they can, in turn, offer their clients.

Eurobonds refer to bonds and other securities issued by companies and entities, domestic or foreign, as well as State and supranational bodies, which are subject to different regulations governing the issuer and which are placed in two or more countries. ABS are financial instruments in respect of securitized receivables, both present and future, or of other assets exclusively designated to satisfy the rights incorporated in the financial instruments issued and possibly to cover the costs of the securitization operation.

Borsa Italiana sets the minimum tradable lots reconciling the need for the market to operate efficiently, for institutional investors to have easy access to it, and for the execution of orders to be cost-efficient. It has opted for a new trading platform for EuroMOT that, in addition to offering a highly reliable and efficient operating environment, allows synergies to be created between wholesale and retail markets, with subsequent potential increase in liquidity and trading volumes as well as in the number of market-makers operating.

Trading takes place in accordance with continuous trading conditions from 9 a.m. to 5:30 p.m. Traders already authorized to trade on one or more of the markets managed by Borsa Italiana will only have to submit a simplified application. Banks, investment agencies, and authorized market makers in accordance with the Ministry of Finance's Consolidated Law, carry out all transactions.

Uploaded orders are executed by means of an automatic matching procedure and ranked according to price, or by entry time, where the prices are the same. Only limit price bid/ask orders may be placed. Orders may be specified with the following trading methods:

1. Good till canceled: any unfilled quantity remains on the book until the end of the session when it is automatically canceled.
2. Good till date: the order remains on the book with the unfilled quantity maintaining the original time priority until the specified expiry date.

To ensure market liquidity – continuous trading and the existence of firm price references for each financial instrument – specialist operators are envisaged, namely approved intermediaries admitted to trade in EuroMOT who undertake to display continuous bids and offers for the financial instruments they intend to trade in, with a maximum percentage spread and quantity established by the Borsa Italiana.

In the admission decision, the Borsa Italiana shall determine the minimum duration of the undertaking taking into account the duration of the financial instruments, their features, and their distribution. In return for their assistance in maintaining market liquidity, specialists are granted special conditions as established by the Borsa Italiana. Borsa Italiana has also installed completely automated settlement procedures by means of a daily trade-checking service.

Contracts stipulated for the varying financial instruments can be settled either through the clearing and settlement service referred to at Article 69 of the Ministry of Finance's Consolidated Law (Securities Centralized Administration – Clearing House) or by other means (Euroclear).

While dealing is underway, information on trends in trading is made publicly available for real-time consultation. More specifically, information on the prices and quantities of the best bid/ask orders, quantities selling and quantities to be bought at the best price levels, the price of the last contract concluded, indicating the time and relative quantity traded, are made available.

17.3.6   Eurobonds Requirements

Many requirements for Eurobonds are similar to the ones for bonds. The loan must exceed at least 30 billion liras (ITL) or equivalent thereof in euros, and the retribution of the capital may not take place at a lower than face value price. As for bonds, the issuer must have previously published and filed annual financial statements for the last three financial years, of which at least the latest must have been audited. In exceptional circumstances, Borsa Italiana may accept a smaller number of annual financial statements. If a third party, for admission purposes, guarantees the issue, Borsa Italiana will base its decision on the guarantor's characteristics.

Table 17.5 Borsa Italiana
government bonds volume

Year	Amount*
1998	160 707
1999	152 047
2000	141 886
2001	126 015

Source: Borsa Italiana.
*Nominal amount in million euros.

Table 17.6 Borsa Italiana
EuroMOT volume

Year	Amount*
2000	245
2001	969

Source: Borsa Italiana.
*Nominal amount in million euros.

In relation to structured bonds (index-linked to financial assets such as shares listed on a stock exchange in Italy or another country, or rather, share or currency indexes), the issuer must provide an indication of the risk-hedging strategy and demonstrate the availability in Italy of information on the prices recorded for the assets chosen for the linkage mechanism.

Furthermore, at least one specialist must undertake to support the liquidity of the financial instruments for which application for listing has been made. Finally, Tables 17.5 and 17.6 report volume activity in the market for government bonds and Eurobonds securities.

17.3.7 ABS Requirements

Single issues of ABS (tranche) related to a securitization operation may be admitted to listing. They must have a minimum value of 100 billion liras (ITL) or equivalent thereof in euros. The ABS tranches must have been rated at least equal to investment grade. The issuer must provide the Borsa Italiana with the following information for dissemination to the public: any changes in the rating, along with relative report; the full, qualitative, and quantitative report on the periodic monitoring of the collateral; changes in the amortization schedule of the tranche, in the seniority of tranches, and the pool factor of the tranche, if any. Furthermore, at least one specialist must undertake to support the liquidity of the financial instruments for which application for listing has been made. Since January 17, 2000, both Italian and foreign Asset/Mortgage-Backed Securities can be listed on the EuroMOT market of the Italian Exchange.

17.4 CONCLUSION

The Italian economy is now part of the Euro zone economy, not only for the common currency but also for a lot of economic and institutional characteristics. The Italian bond market is currently one of the most important bond markets in the Euro area both in volume and for types of securities traded. Overall, bond trading in Italy has risen from US$11.7 billion in 2001 to about US$16 billion in 2003. Italy is expected to perform structural reforms especially in the labor market since rigid labor and product markets curb the country's potential growth rate. These reforms shall be the main and the most difficult task for the charismatic new Prime Minister Silvio Berlusconi. Clearly, the current economic situation will not mitigate the painful adjustments that the proposed reforms should generate. The danger is that rising unemployment and depressing consumer confidence will make it even trickier to persuade voters to accept structural reforms. Moreover policies aimed at further stimulating domestic demand should be seen in the near future.

REFERENCES

Borsa Italiana (2001, December 21). Rules of the Markets Organized and Managed by the Italian Exchange.

Borsa Italiana (2002, April 8). Instructions accompanying the Rules for the Markets Organized and Managed by the Italian Exchange.

European Central Bank (2002). *Report on Financial Structures*.

Gabrielli, M. and S. De Bruno (1999). *Capire la Finanza*. Il Sole 24 Ore.

Websites
Borsa Italiana: www.borsaitaliana.it
Consob: www.consob.it
Italian Statistical Institute: www.istat.it
Eurostat: http://europa.eu.int/comm/eurostat/
Italian Ministry of the Economy and Finance: http://www.tesoro.it/web/ML.asp
European Central Bank: http://www.ecb.int/
Banca d'Italia: http://www.bancaditalia.it/

18

The Netherlands[1]

ALBERT MENTINK

18.1 INTRODUCTION

The introduction of the euro on January 1, 1999, changed the shape of the small market for Dutch bonds. The guilder bond market disappeared and was absorbed by the large euro-denominated bond market, with the guilder becoming 1 of the 11 legacy currencies. Before the introduction of the euro, the government yields of the future Euro Member States had already converged; the 10-year government yield spread between Germany and the Netherlands, for example, was only 9 basis points at December 31, 1998 (Bloomberg L.P.). So, for medium-sized government bond issuers, such as the Dutch government, the euro introduction meant that they had to find a way to improve the liquidity of their bonds. The euro also influenced the Dutch corporate bond issuers, which have become part of the growing euro-denominated credit bond market. In this newly established bond market, a company's home country has become less important than its rating and sector.

The investor base of both Dutch government bonds and corporate bonds has also become more international. Large institutional investors, both European and non-European, are also now investing in euro credit bonds that are issued by Dutch companies. So, it is clear that both issuers and investors have been affected by the introduction of the euro. One area of common ground for issuers and investors is the Amsterdam Stock Exchange (AEX), which has now merged with exchanges in Brussels, Lisbon, and Paris into Euronext, where Dutch government bonds, corporate bonds, issued by both domestic and foreign companies, and other types of bonds are all listed. Small and irregular bond trades dominate Euronext Amsterdam, suggesting that retail investors are the main participants in this part of the bond market. In contrast, large institutional investors mainly trade over the counter (OTC) with large investment banks. These same institutions are increasingly involved in web trading, without involving intermediaries.

There have also been changes to the Dutch financial supervision regime. As Jonk *et al.* (2001) explain, supervision has moved from a largely sector-oriented regime to one that is more cross-sectional based. The driving force behind this reform is the continuing financial market integration, with banks and insurance companies increasingly involved in selling each other's products. The Dutch supervisors want their structure to reflect these market developments although there is still some debate between the different European supervisors over the best way to implement a Europe-wide regime. In addition to this changing national supervision,

---

[1] Views expressed in this chapter are the author's own and do not necessarily reflect those of AEGON Asset Management, Netherlands.

European Fixed Income Markets: Money, Bond and Interest Rate Derivatives. Edited by J.A. Batten,
T.A. Fetherston and P.G. Szilagyi © 2004 John Wiley & Sons, Ltd. ISBN 0-470-85053-1

rating agencies also have an impact through their assessment of Dutch government debt and corporate bonds.

The content of this chapter consists of the following. First, in Section 18.2, the economic background of the Netherlands is given by analyzing its main economic indicators. Next, the tasks of De Nederlandsche Bank (Dutch Central Bank) and the Ministry of Finance are reviewed. Section 18.3 discusses details of the Dutch government bonds. Both guilder credit bonds and euro credit bonds that are issued by Dutch companies are analyzed in Section 18.4. The investors in these Dutch government bonds and euro credit bonds are discussed in Section 18.5. Euronext Amsterdam and OTC trading bring issuers and investors together as explained in Section 18.6. Dutch government regulators and private rating agencies that are active in the Dutch bond market are described in Section 18.7. Finally, Section 18.8 concludes.

18.2 THE NETHERLANDS

18.2.1 Economic Background

During the period 1996–2000, the Dutch economy performed very well as the real gross domestic product (GDP) growth averaged 3.7% per year. The breakdown of Dutch GDP is presented in Table 18.1. This shows the national accounts of the Netherlands in the year 2000 both in billions of euros and in percentage of GDP. The table demonstrates that the Netherlands is an open economy, as imports and exports as a percentage of GDP equal 62.4 and 67.2 respectively. Therefore, the downturn in the global economy that started in 2001 also slowed economic growth in the Netherlands. Moreover, rising oil prices, falling stock prices, stabilizing house prices, and animal diseases that led to a fall in exports all had a negative effect on economic growth (International Monetary Fund [IMF], 2002). In 2003, economic growth did not return and became negative.

Table 18.2 shows the percentage changes in national accounts, prices, wages and employment, personal sector, external trade, and public sector accounts of the Netherlands for the years 1997–2001, 2002 (estimation), and 2003 (projection) (IMF, 2003). All elements of GDP increased during the period 1997–2000, although imports often grew faster than exports, except in 2000, and gross fixed investments grew faster than both private and public consumption. In addition, employment rose and unemployment fell from 5.5% in 1997 to

Table 18.1 The national accounts of the Netherlands in 2000 at current prices in both billions of euro and in percentage of GDP

National accounts	Euro	Percentage of GDP
Private consumption	199.9	49.8
Public consumption	91.2	22.7
Gross fixed investment	90.9	22.7
Stock building	−0.4	−0.1
Exports	269.6	67.2
Imports	250.1	62.4
GDP	401.1	

Source: OECD.

Table 18.2 The percentage changes (unless otherwise noted) in the national accounts (constant prices), prices, wages and employment, personal sector, external trade and public sector accounts of the Netherlands for the years 1997, 1998, 1999, 2000, 2001, 2002 (estimation), and 2003 (projection)

	1997	1998	1999	2000	2001	2002	2003
National accounts							
Private consumption	3.0	4.8	4.7	3.6	1.2	0.9	1.2
Public consumption	3.2	3.6	2.5	1.9	3.1	3.7	1.1
Gross fixed investment	6.6	4.2	7.8	3.5	−0.8	−3.7	−4.0
Exports	8.8	7.4	5.1	10.9	1.7	−1.4	1.1
Imports	9.5	8.5	5.8	10.6	1.9	−2.1	3.1
GDP	3.9	4.3	4.0	3.4	1.2	0.2	−0.2
Prices, wages and employment							
Consumer price index (year average)	1.9	1.8	2.0	2.3	5.1	3.9	2.6
GDP deflator	2.0	1.7	1.5	4.1	5.3	3.2	3.0
Hourly compensation (manufacturing)	3.0	3.2	2.9	3.7	4.2	3.8	3.3
Unit labor costs (manufacturing)	−0.7	1.3	0.9	0.1	5.0	2.8	2.1
Employment	3.4	3.3	3.0	1.6	2.4	1.1	−0.4
Unemployment rate (in percent)	5.5	4.2	3.2	2.6	2.0	2.3	3.8
Personal sector							
Real disposable income	3.4	4.5	1.0	2.1	4.0	1.5	0.3
Household savings ratio (percent of real disposable income)	13.4	12.9	9.7	6.9	9.8	10.8	10.2
External trade							
Exports of goods, volume	9.2	7.4	5.3	10.3	1.7	−0.7	0.8
Imports of goods, volume	10.5	8.3	6.4	9.8	1.0	−2.6	2.8
Terms of trade	0.5	0.1	−1.5	0.0	1.0	0.2	0.4
Current account balance (percent of GDP)	6.6	3.3	3.2	1.2	2.1	2.2	3.5
Public sector accounts (percent of GDP)							
Revenue	47.1	46.4	47.6	47.4	46.5	46.1	45.6
Expenditure	48.2	47.2	46.9	45.3	46.4	47.3	47.8
General government balance	−1.1	−0.8	0.7	2.2	0.1	−1.2	−2.1
General government gross debt	70.0	66.8	63.1	55.8	52.8	52.6	52.5

Source: IMF

2.6% in 2000. Both the growth of real disposable income and the savings ratio were lower in 1999 and 2000 compared to 1997 and 1998. The current account balance showed a surplus during the whole period, despite the fact that imports increased faster than exports. The general government gross debt fell dramatically owing to surpluses starting in 1999 and GDP growth.

On the other hand, this strong economic growth caused the consumer price index and GDP deflator to rise. Both were higher than those in other Euro zone countries, and hourly labor compensation and unit labor costs also rose in 2001, 2002 and 2003. Consequently, in 2001 and 2002, GDP growth lowered compared to the preceding years with negative growth in 2003. Government consumption growth remained high compared to the other GDP elements; the employment rate lowered, the unemployment rate rose, and the general government surplus became smaller and again negative.

The prospects of the revival of economic growth in the short term remain gloomy as industrial and consumer confidence are still at low levels. Important risk factors for the Dutch economy (IMF, 2002) are the appreciation of the euro against other main currencies (damaging exports), rising oil prices producing inflation, and falling house prices causing lower consumption and distress in the financial sector. Nationally, the political situation was uncertain as the newly elected Dutch government resigned after only 3 months in office, while usually elections are held every 4 years. New elections were held in January 2003.[2]

18.2.2   Financial Sector

The Dutch financial sector can be typified by the following five main characteristics (European Central Bank [ECB], 2002). Compared to other Euro zone countries, this sector is large as a percentage of GDP. The sector's intermediary functions, such as bank lending, are important. Much of the dealing in this area occurs between financial institutions. The banking sector is very concentrated, with only four banks controlling 80% of the Dutch lending market, and the sector has an international focus with, for example, large operations in the United States. Within the sector there is much cross-sector consolidation such as banks selling insurance products and vice versa.

Institutional investors, both pension funds and the investment portfolios of insurance companies, constitute a considerable segment of the Dutch financial sector. For most employees, it is compulsory, not optional, to participate in a funded pension scheme. Therefore, Dutch pension funds manage huge investment portfolios compared to other countries in the Euro zone, with ABP, the government employees' pension fund, controlling an investment portfolio of €150 billion in 2000 (ECB, 2002).

18.2.3   De Nederlandsche Bank (DNB, Dutch Central Bank)

On January 1, 1999, the independent monetary policy of De Nederlandsche Bank disappeared. Seven months earlier, on June 1, 1998, DNB officially became part of the European System of Central Banks (ESCB), where the Governor of DNB took a seat in the Governing Council. Two of the tasks undertaken by DNB, numbered 1 and 2 below, are also known as the ESCB tasks. Under the 1998 Bank Act, the full list of DNB tasks reads as follows:

1. Within the framework of the ESCB, the Bank shall contribute to the definition and implementation of monetary policy within the European Union (EU). The Bank's objective is to maintain price stability. Without prejudice to this objective, the Bank shall support the general economic policy in the EU.
2. The Bank shall hold and manage the official foreign reserves, and shall conduct foreign-exchange operations.
3. The Bank shall collect statistical data and produce statistics.
4. The Bank shall promote the smooth operation of payment systems and take care of the banknote circulation.
5. The Bank shall supervise banks, investment institutions, and exchange offices.[3]

The Bank may, subject to permission by Royal Decree, perform other tasks in the public interest. The ECB may also ask the Bank to perform extra tasks (see Appendix, DNB).

---

[2] For a further explanation of the performance of the Dutch economy in an international perspective, see Ministry of Economic Affairs (2002).

[3] See also Section 18.7 below.

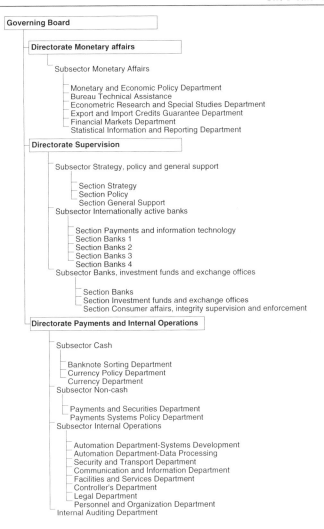

Figure 18.1   The organizational structure of DNB as at November 1, 2001.
Source: DNB.

Figure 18.1 shows the organizational structure of DNB: three main directorates – Monetary Affairs, Supervision, Payments, and Internal Operations – each directorate subdivided in sections and departments.

The Monetary and Economic Policy department plans the monetary policy to be pursued by DNB. Planning the positions to be taken with regard to monetary and macro-economic matters in the (inter)national fora in which DNB takes part. The Research department carries out pure research, model building and maintenance, historical research and consultative activities. The Export and Import Credit Guarantees department is involved in the reinsurance by the Dutch government of foreign payment risks in respect of exports, imports and investment transactions and any attending foreign exchange risks. The Financial Markets department plans and implements the market-oriented policy conducted by DNB in respect of the money, foreign exchange and capital markets. Investing DNB's gold and foreign exchange holdings, the general reserve, DNB's pension fund and the balances on staff accounts. The Statistical Information and Reporting department compiles, processes and provides (standard) data for monetary supervision, socio-economic policy and prudential supervision.

The directorate Supervision consists of eleven sections. The Policy section draws up rules and regulations (including the reporting framework) relating to banking supervision, prepares (inter)national policy consultations. The Strategy section makes long term analyses of supervisory issues. Internationally active banks section exercises supervision on large banking institutions, which operate internationally. Payment systems and information technology section exercises supervision on payment systems, payment products and providers of payment services. The Banks section exercises supervision on credit institutions subject to supervision. The Investment funds and exchange offices section performs DNB's tasks ensuing from the Act on the supervision of investment institutions and the exchange offices Act, and planning the policy to be pursued in these areas (see Appendix, DNB).

18.2.4   Ministry of Finance (MoF)

The Dutch Minister of Finance is primarily responsible for financial policy, although the Dutch Council of Ministers also has an input. This relationship also applies between the different ministries since the Dutch Ministry of Finance shapes financial and economic policies in conjunction with other government ministries. Thus, MoF is responsible for fiscal policy, i.e. overall financial policy and the management of government funds. Therefore, MoF is involved in both government income and expenditure, and looks at how government spending can best be financed, i.e. via taxes or from issuing government bonds. MoF is also responsible for both drafting and executing tax legislation. Three quarters of government income is raised via taxation. The Tax and Customs Administration, also part of this ministry, is responsible for the actual collection of taxes and duties (see Appendix, MoF).

The organizational structure of MoF appears in Figure 18.2, which shows the four Directorates-General: Treasury, Budget, Tax and Customs Policy and Legislation, and Tax and Customs Administration, together with the Central Directorates and Departments (see Appendix, MoF).

The financial and economic policy fall within the sphere of activity of the Treasury. The Treasury is comprised of six policy Directorates. The responsibilities of the Directorate-General are concerned with the coordination of fiscal policy. The Directorate-General is comprised of four Directorates. The Directorate-General for Tax and Customs Policy and Legislation is responsible for drafting national and international tax policy and for the incorporation of these in legislation and international agreements. Once legislation has been published in the Bulletin of Acts, Orders and Decrees it enters the realm of the Directorate-General for the Tax and Customs Administration. This Directorate is responsible for the implementation of tax legislation and non-tax legislation charged to the Administration. The Directorate-General draws up implementing regulations, which are laid down in instructions and resolutions (see Appendix, MoF).

18.3   DUTCH GOVERNMENT BONDS

18.3.1   Dutch Government Bond Market

In the run up to the introduction of the euro, the yield spread between government bonds of the future EMU Member States gradually narrowed. In other words, these government yields converged, because currency risk premiums faded and national monetary polices merged into one (Galati and Tsatsaronis, 2001).

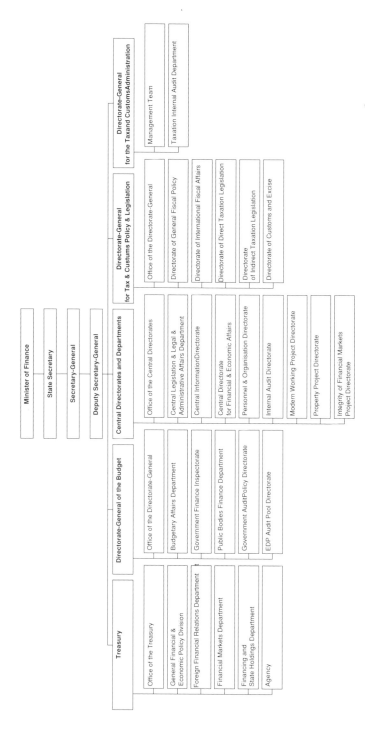

Figure 18.2 The organizational structure of MoF.
Source: MoF.

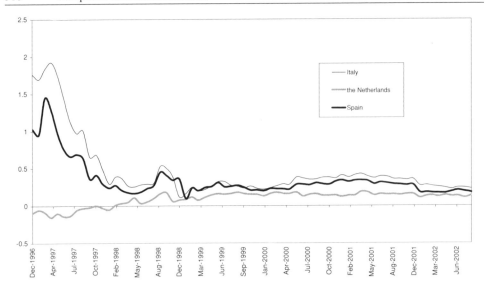

Figure 18.3   The 10-year yield spread of Italy, the Netherlands, and Spain, over the 10-year German yield during the period December 31, 1996 to August 31, 2002, on a monthly basis.
Source: Bloomberg L.P.

Figure 18.3 provides the calculated spreads of three EMU members, Italy, the Netherlands, and Spain, for the period December 31, 1996 to August 31, 2002, on a monthly basis.[4] This figure demonstrates the yield convergence as the spread between Italy and Spain versus Germany decreased. Of particular note is the very small yield spread between the Netherlands and Germany.

Although government yields have converged, small spreads still exist. In general, these spreads can be explained by differences in fiscal policy, ratings, and liquidity. Typically, the Dutch government yields are only a few basis points higher than those in Germany: for example, the 10-year spread was only 13 basis points as of the end of August 2002. Rating differences are not a factor as their Moody's and Standard & Poor's ratings are the same, i.e. Aaa/AAA. Moreover, the fiscal policy of each country is formally constrained by the "Stability Pact," which leaves both countries little room to maneuvre. So, yield differences between these two government curves can best be explained by liquidity differences.

From a Euro zone perspective, the Dutch central government is a medium-sized issuer of debt in terms of total amount of debt outstanding. Table 18.3 presents the percentage distribution of total nominal euro-denominated debt, both short and long term, of each Euro zone member state at the end of June 2002. As this figure demonstrates, the Dutch central government is not a very large debt issuer compared to France, Germany, and Italy. As a result, it is important for the Dutch government to make its debt securities as liquid as the debt of these larger countries. Section 18.3.2.5 below describes how this goal of increasing liquidity is implemented by the Dutch central government. Like the Dutch government, many governments attach high importance to the maintenance of liquid markets for their bonds (Bank for International Settlements, 2001).

---

[4] Subtracting the 10-year yield of German government bonds from the 10-year yield of government bonds from Italy, the Netherlands, and Spain gives the yield spread against Germany. As the German yield curve is the benchmark curve in the Euro zone, this yield is used here as the reference yield.

Table 18.3 Percentage distribution of nominal euro-denominated government debt securities by country in the Euro zone (end of June 2002)

Country	Percentage
Austria	2.9
Belgium	6.5
Finland	1.3
France	19.2
Germany	22.0
Greece	3.0
Ireland	0.6
Italy	30.0
Luxembourg	0.0
The Netherlands	4.9
Portugal	1.5
Spain	8.1

Source: ECB. Copyright © European Central Bank. Frankfurt am Main, Germany. Reproduced with permission.

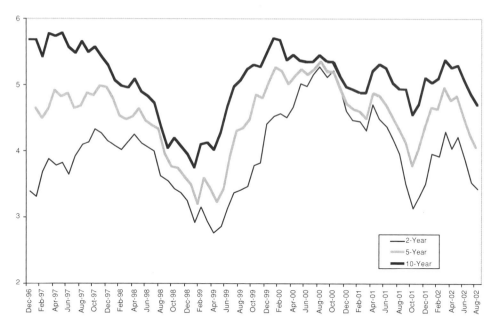

Figure 18.4 The Dutch government 2-, 5-, and 10-year yields for the period December 31, 1996 to August 31, 2002, on a monthly basis.
Source: Bloomberg L.P.

Dutch government 2-, 5-, and 10-year yields are displayed in Figure 18.4 for the same period December 31, 1996 to August 31, 2002, again on a monthly basis. During this period, the slope of the Dutch government yield curve has always been positive. During the months June–October 2000, the yield curve was very flat as the 2-, 5-, and 10-year yields were very close to each other. From June 1997 to February 1999, the 10-year yields decreased to around 3.75%, and then rose again to a peak of approximately 5.7% in January 2000 before falling once more to 4.7% in August 2002.

18.3.2   Dutch State Treasury Agency (DSTA, Agentschap van het Ministerie van Financiën)

The DSTA, part of the Dutch Ministry of Finance, is the debt manager of the central government of the Netherlands. It conducts the sale of both Dutch Treasury certificates (DTCs) and Dutch state loans (DSLs) to fund the central government borrowing requirement and accounts for public debt principal and interest payment (see Appendix, DSTA). The following sections outline DTCs and DSLs, their auction process, primary dealers, market conventions, debt restructuring program, and other government bond types.

18.3.2.1   Dutch Treasury Certificates and Dutch State Loans

DSTA manages the Dutch central government liquid funds. In the event of needing to raise funds, DSTA can issue DTCs, which are discount or zero coupon bills with initial maturity of 3, 6, or 12 months. DSTA started issuing DTCs in January 1997. During 2002, DTCs have been issued twice a month, on the first and third Monday. Typically, two maturities are auctioned during each issue.

DSLs are issued with three target maturities of 3, 10, and 30 years, and therefore do not cover the whole range of maturities. These new issues are in bullet form. Typically, issuance of DSLs takes place on a regular basis, on the second Tuesday of the month. Each quarter, the maturity and targeted volume of the issues are announced. The issuance calendar includes all issue and settlement dates and is available on their website (see Appendix, DSTA). At the end of October 2002, the benchmark DSLs for the three maturity segments were as follows (DSTA):

- 3-year segment: 4% July 15, 2005,
- 10-year segment: 5% July 15, 2012,
- 30-year segment: 5.5% January 15, 2028.

18.3.2.2   Auction Process

Since January 17, 2000, DTCs have been auctioned on a uniform price basis, the so-called Dutch auction. Primary dealers (for a full list see below) as well as seven single-market specialists can subscribe between 11:00 a.m. and 12:00 a.m., Amsterdam time. After this subscription has closed, DSTA will determine the uniform issuance yield. Subscriptions lower than this issuance yield will get a full allocation, subscriptions tendered equal to the issuance yield may get allocated in full or only in part. The issuance yield and total assigned volume will be published by DSTA.

DSTA with regard to DSLs issuance, works with the following procedure:

> in general, on Friday preceding the issuance of the first tranche of a new bond, the coupon rate, which is relevant for the determination of the yield to maturity, is announced. In addition, the terms and conditions of DSLs apply to the issue, as well as the various ways of settlement. On the day of issue at 10 a.m. Amsterdam time, the initial issue price will be announced. It may be revised at any time. Primary dealers and other parties admitted by the DSTA can put buying orders. Individuals are advised to contact a primary dealer, another bank or a commissioner (see Appendix, DSTA).

18.3.2.3   Primary Dealers

The Dutch state contracted the services of 13 financial institutions to constitute its group of primary dealers for the year 2002. Each primary dealer was committed to take, distribute, and promote DSLs (see Appendix, DSTA). The list of those primary dealers is:

- ABN AMRO Bank
- BBVA
- Credit Suisse First Boston
- Deutsche Bank
- Fortis Bank
- ING Barings/BBL
- J.P. Morgan
- Merrill Lynch
- Morgan Stanley
- NIB Capital
- Rabobank International
- Schroder Salomon Smith Barney
- Société Générale

18.3.2.4   Market Conventions

The market conventions of both DTCs (DSTA) and DSLs (Bennett *et al.*, 2001) regarding market characteristics, accrued interest characteristics, settlement characteristics, and trading basis are listed in Table 18.4. In this table, TARGET, t, bp, and ISMA stand for the payment

Table 18.4   Market conventions of both DTCs and DSLs

	DTCs	DSLs
Market characteristics		
Longest maturity issued (years)	1	30
Typical denomination (local)	1	1
Typical outstanding per issue (local, millions)	3000–5000	10 000–20 000
Accrued interest characteristics		
Coupon (date)	Discount	Annual
Accrual basis	Actual	Actual
Year basis	360	Actual
Holidays	TARGET	TARGET
Settlement characteristics		
Timeframe		
Domestic investors	t+2	t+3
International investors	t+2	t+3
Trading basis		
Quotation	Yield	Price (clean)
Tick	Decimal	Decimal
Bid/offer spread	1–3 bp	0.03–0.20 cent
Commission (%)	0	0
Tax (nonresident, %)	0	0
Typical transaction size (local, millions)	10–100	10–50
Price/yield method	ISMA discount basis	ISMA

Sources: Bennett *et al.* (2001), DSTA, and Reuters.

system consisting of the interlinked real-time gross settlement systems of the EU Member States (Trans-European Automated Real-Time Gross Settlement Express Transfer), trading day, basis points, and International Securities Market Association respectively. In terms of trading basis, the figures associated with the bid/offer spread, commission, and transaction size apply to the OTC market in Amsterdam and London. As for the typical transaction size, it must be noted that in the OTC market often smaller transactions are also executed. Tax in this table refers to withholding tax on interest payments.

There are three methods for clearing and settlement of DSLs and DTCs (see Appendix, DSTA):

1. Fully domestic, through Necigef, the Dutch clearing institute. The paying agent is DNB.
2. Directly through Euroclear, or via Necigef with ABN AMRO Bank as cash correspondent and depository.
3. Directly through Cedel, or via Necigef with Rabobank as cash correspondent, and Kas Bank as depository for DLSs, and ABN AMRO Bank as depository for DTCs.

18.3.2.5   Debt Restructuring Program

As indicated above, the Dutch central government wants to improve the liquidity of its bonds by concentrating on large liquid issues.

In order to accelerate the process of concentration of government debt into a smaller number of large volume benchmark issues and to increase market liquidity, DSTA developed a debt restructuring programme. The concentration process had already started by limiting the issuance of DSLs to mainly two maturity segments, i.e. three- and ten-year, and by reducing the number of new issues to two per year. In addition, an exchange offer was set up to enable conversion of smaller size issues. Hence, investors could benefit from the resulting liquidity increase, thereby avoiding the transaction costs of illiquidity. The restructuring programme made it possible to withdraw smaller bonds from the market and to replace them for liquid ones. As a result a total amount of over 30 billion euros has been added to liquid bonds and the Dutch government debt has been concentrated in some 15 large liquid bonds, with an average outstanding size of 10 billion euros (see Appendix, DSTA[5]).

18.3.2.6   Other Government Bond Types

Apart from DTCs and DSLs, the Dutch state has also issued other types of bonds, although these only represent a tiny portion of the total Dutch government debt. An example is STRIPS, Separate Trading of Registered Interest and Principal of Securities. This is a zero coupon bond. From February, 15, 1993, onwards, MoF allowed trading in STRIPS and DTSA makes a market in them by issuing STRIPS and buying back DSLs or vice versa. This should ensure STRIPS (and DSLs) are priced efficiently. STRIPS are also traded at Euronext Amsterdam. Table 18.5 shows three DSLs that are partly stripped. The liquidity of STRIPS remains low as can be inferred from the small amounts outstanding. DSTA has also issued perpetual bonds, i.e. bonds without a maturity date. As with STRIPS, the liquidity of perpetuals is low. As Wouters (2002) states, inflation indexed bonds, such as issued recently by the French state, have not been issued by the Dutch state.

---

[5] The results of these operations are also described at the DSTA website

Table 18.5 Three DSLs that are partly stripped

Maturity year of DSLs	Nominal amount of DSLs (billions, euro)	Nominal amount of STRIPS (billions, euro)	Stripped percentage of nominal amount
2028	8.89	0.40	4.5
2023	8.24	1.75	21.2
2004	9.27	1.06	11.4

Sources: Toorman (1997).

18.3.3 Futures

The most liquid standardized bond futures in the Euro zone are the Bund (10-year), Bobl (5-year), and Schatz (2-year) future, traded at the exchange EUREX. These futures have German government bonds as their underlying asset, not Dutch government bonds. Because the German and Dutch government yields have converged and now move in tandem, interest rate risk of Dutch government bonds can be hedged with Bund, Bobl, and/or Schatz futures; in other words the basis risk is small.

18.4   CREDIT BONDS

18.4.1 Guilder Credit Bond Market

After the introduction of the euro, the small Dutch guilder corporate bond market was absorbed by the large euro-denominated bond market. Investors now usually judge credit bonds on sector and credit rating, and the issuer's country has been become less important. For example J.P. Morgan's Telecom sector report by Levene *et al.* (2002) is a clear example of this new approach. One exception to this sector-based approach is the banking and insurance sector in the Euro zone. Here the country of residence is still important because of the persistent differences in national regulatory environments and the dependency on home markets.

There has been little published research about the Dutch guilder credit bond market, one exception being Oorschot and Stork (1995). They analyzed the relationship between credit spreads of Dutch corporate bonds and long term interest rates, economic growth, and bond market volatility. They found that these credit spreads are negatively related to long term interest rates and positively related to both economic growth and bond market volatility. However, this research was based on pre-euro introduction data.

Analysis of the composition of the investment grade Dutch guilder credit bond market is available for December 31, 1998, i.e. one day before the introduction of the euro. This bond market is proxied by the Lehman Brothers Euro-Aggregate Bond Index Netherlands Guilder.[6] The structure of the umbrella index, the Euro-Aggregate Bond Index, consists of investment grade, plain vanilla euro-denominated and legacy bonds with a minimum amount outstanding of €100 million (Munves and Flores, 1998).[7]

As of the end of December 1998, the market capitalization of the guilder bond market was €28.9 billion. Table 18.6 displays the four main characteristics of this bond market, i.e. ratings, maturities, sectors, and local versus foreign bonds respectively. This table shows that bonds

---

[6] We thank Lehman Brothers Inc. for providing this data.
[7] This minimum amount has been increased two times, first to €150 million and later to €300 million.

Table 18.6   The rating maturity, and sector distribution and the division between domestic versus nondomestic bonds of the Dutch guilder credit bond market as of December 31, 1998

Rating	AAA	AA1	AA2	AA3	A1	A2	A3
	(58%)	(11%)	(15%)	(13%)	(1%)	(1%)	(1%)
Maturity	1–3 year	3–5 year	5–7 year	7–10 year	10+ year		
	(86%)	(12%)	(1%)	(1%)	(0%)		
Sector	Financial	Industrial	Utility	Supra-national	Asset-backed		
	(86%)	(5%)	(0%)	(6%)	(3%)		
Country	Domestic	Nondomestic					
	(82%)	(18%)					

Source: Lehman Brothers Inc.

with a high rating, with a short (remaining) maturity from the financial sector and from local issuers dominated the Dutch guilder corporate bond market.

18.4.2   Dutch Euro Credit Bond Market

18.4.2.1   Investment Grade Bond Market

As mentioned above, investors in euro-denominated credit bonds typically analyze the rating and sector of these bonds; whether companies are located, in one of the Euro area countries or elsewhere, is of less importance. This also applies for credit bonds of the Dutch credit issuers that dominated the guilder bond market, as described in Section 18.4.1 above. These guilder bonds are now merged in the euro-denominated credit bond market. Again, the Lehman Brothers Euro-Aggregate Bond Index represents the investment grade euro credit bond market. This index is often used as a benchmark for investors who invest in this market. A subindex of this index contains the bonds that are issued by Dutch companies only. Analyzing this subindex provides an understanding of the development of this part of the investment grade euro-denominated market since its inception, January 1, 1999 to August 31, 2002.

The development in the composition of two subindices, the Netherlands Credit and Securitized subindex, of the Euro-Aggregate Bond Index is displayed in Table 18.7. The percentages of the comparable subindices for the total euro-denominated bonds appear in brackets to allow a comparison between Dutch euro issuers and all issuers in euro. All percentages in this table are market weighted. Analyzing this table, the following observations can be made: during the sample period, the average maturity of the Dutch issuers index lowers as maturity block 5–7 grows in importance at the expense of maturity block 7–10. Second, the average rating decreases, most notably the percentage of AAA-issues goes down and the percentage of A- and BAA-bonds goes up as a consequence of rating downgrades and issuance. Finally, the industrial sector grows in importance at the expense of the financial sector.

Compared to all euro-denominated bonds, the bonds that are issued by Dutch companies have a lower percentage in the 1–3-year and 3–5-year maturity buckets and a higher percentage in the longer maturity buckets, 7–10-year and 10+-year. There is also a difference in average rating, with Euro zone bonds having more AAA-rated, fewer AA-rated, and A-rated bonds, except for the year 1999, and more BAA-rated bonds than their Dutch counterpart, except for the year 2001. Finally, the distribution of sectors – financial, industrial, utility, or other – is different. The presence of (Jumbo) Pfandbriefe in the combined Euro-Aggregate Credit and Securitized Index explains the large differences in the financial sector and the other sectors.

Table 18.7 Maturity, rating, and sector distribution of the Lehman Brothers Euro-Aggregate Bond, the Netherlands Credit plus Securitized index versus their euro-counterpart between brackets for the period December 31, 1999 to August 31, 2002

	December 31, 1999	December 31, 2000	December 31, 2001	August 31, 2002
Maturity				
1–3 year	22.2% (28.3%)	21.4% (27.1%)	22.9% (26.1%)	23.4% (28.3%)
3–5 year	25.9% (29.3%)	26.7% (27.8%)	26.9% (28.4%)	25.4% (28.1%)
5–7 year	15.5% (16.6%)	17.4% (16.8%)	22.7% (18.1%)	27.2% (20.8%)
7–10 year	32.7% (22.5%)	30.4% (25.0%)	24.6% (23.9%)	21.1% (19.2%)
10+ year	3.8% (3.3%)	4.1% (3.2%)	2.9% (3.4%)	3.0% (3.7%)
Rating				
AAA	53.6% (58.2%)	41.9% (56.6%)	33.7% (48.1%)	32.3% (44.2%)
AA	38.7% (26.9%)	37.1% (24.9%)	33.7% (23.6%)	36.7% (24.5%)
A	7.4% (12.6%)	18.6% (14.4%)	17.9% (16.9%)	19.5% (18.3%)
BAA	0.2% (2.3%)	2.5% (4.2%)	14.7% (11.3%)	11.4% (13.0%)
Sector				
Financial	88.9% (28.5%)	81.9% (24.8%)	69.2% (22.6%)	64.4% (22.9%)
Industrial	9.8% (8.2%)	15.5% (11.9%)	27.4% (20.9%)	23.8% (21.1%)
Utility	0.0% (2.2%)	0.0% (2.4%)	0.0% (3.2%)	7.8% (4.3%)
Other	1.3% (61.1%)	2.6% (60.9%)	3.4% (53.3%)	4.0% (51.7%)

Source: Lehman Brothers Inc.

(Jumbo) Pfandbriefe alone constitutes about 48% of the two combined sectors above. The other two sectors show that more Dutch issuers are present in the industrial sector and there are fewer in the utility sector, except for the end of August 2002.

The amount of corporate bonds issued by Dutch companies increased after the euro introduction. Figure 18.5 shows the growth of the amount outstanding in Dutch corporate nonfinancial issuers and financial institutions (in billions of US dollars) for the period December 1996 to September 2002. Over the period, the amount outstanding has grown in both sectors. The growth of nonfinancial debt shows a more volatile pattern than debt issued by the financial sector as can be explained by, for example, funding mergers and acquisitions and finance third generation mobile phone licenses.

In the Netherlands, special financial institutions issue a large amount of bonds. These institutions are "Netherlands-based companies which specialize in group financing and whose shares are directly or indirectly held by nonresidents" (DNB, 2000). For that reason, they are not part of the analysis above. So, they fund themselves in a foreign country and invest almost entirely outside the Netherlands. The Netherlands is attractive to these financial institutions mainly for tax reasons. At the end of 1999, the total number of special financial institutions was over 9000. During 1999, their combined issue size was about €70 billion, of which 42 billion in euro-denominated issues (DNB, 2000).

18.4.2.2 *Bank Nederlandse Gemeenten (BNG, Bank for the Dutch Municipalities) and Nederlandse Waterschapsbank (NWB, Bank for the Dutch Water Control Boards)*

The BNG is a public sector bank that was founded in 1914 on the initiative of the Association of Dutch Municipalities. BNG is the principal banker for the Dutch public sector and the largest public sector lender in the Netherlands, with an overall market share of 35% (Thomson

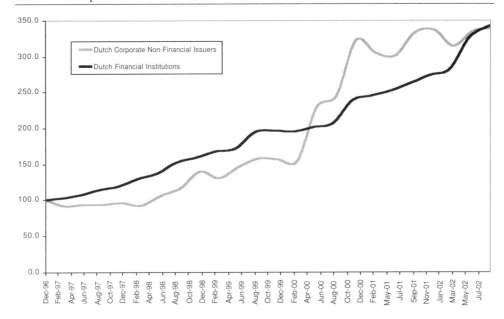

Figure 18.5   Amount outstanding of Dutch corporate nonfinancial issuers and financial institutions (in billions of US dollars) for the period December 1996 to September 2002.
Source: BIS. Copyright © Bank of International Settlements, Basle, Switzerland. Reproduced with permission.

et al., 2001). At present, BNG is ranked the fifth largest bank in the Netherlands in terms of total assets. Moody's, Standard & Poor's, and Fitch IBCA have assigned their highest credit rating to BNG, i.e. Aaa/AAA/AAA. Most of BNG's long term funding comes from bond issuance.

The Dutch central government owns 50% of BNG's shares, while Dutch municipalities, provinces, and one water board institution own the other 50%. In spite of these owners, BNG has no formal guarantee from the Dutch state; i.e., the principle behind all lending continues to be the solvency of the borrower. BNG is supervised by DNB. The bank can only lend to: local governments, entities guaranteed – either directly or indirectly – by local governments, or central government and entities controlled by local government or central government (Thomson *et al.*, 2001).

The NWB is also a public sector bank. NWB was formed in 1954 in response to the severe floods in the Netherlands during the previous year. Now, it is the seventh largest bank in the Netherlands by assets and holds AAA ratings from both Moody's and Standard & Poor's. NWB issues debentures, MTNs, and commercial paper.

The bank's shareholders are the central government (17%), water control boards (Waterschappen) (81%), and provinces (2%) (Greenwood and Dutton, 2000). Since 1989, NWB has no longer a state guarantee and is currently supervised by DNB. According to the NWB's articles of association, NWB can only lend to the public sector, including central and local government authorities (including water control boards), entities under state control, and all business transacted under state guarantee (including social housing). Most lending is long term. In addition, NWB also acts as the treasurer of the water control boards.

18.4.2.3   High Yield Bond Market

The number of Dutch companies that issue subinvestment grade or high yield bonds has been very limited; only 13 euro-denominated high yield bonds are present in the euro-denominated high yield market as represented by Lehman Brothers Pan-European High Yield the Netherlands Index in 1999 (22, 25, and 10 in 2000, 2001, and August 30, 2002, respectively). Most of these are linked to the industrial sector, with ratings that cover the whole sub investment grade spectrum. The 7–10-year maturity bucket dominates this market.

18.4.2.4   Convertible Bond Market

Dutch companies have also issued convertible bonds, but this type of bond is rare in the Dutch credit bond market. As Grubben and van Summeren (1999) show, Dutch convertibles make up only 3.6% of the global convertible bond market as represented by the Merrill Lynch Global Convertible Bond Index.

18.5   CATEGORIES OF INVESTORS

18.5.1   Investors in Dutch Government Bonds

DTSA provides an overview of the investors in Dutch government bonds as displayed in Table 18.8. This table presents the breakdown of the total Dutch government debt into two categories: public debt and private placements. Investors in public debt are divided in resident investors and nonresident investors. Resident investors in public debt are broken down into investment funds, private investors, banks, insurance companies, and pension funds. This type of debt and type of investor is given in billions of euro and spans the years 1996–2000 (as of year-end).

Investment funds, private investors, and pension funds invested less in Dutch public debt in the period 1996–2000. In contrast, insurance companies and banks invested more and an equal amount respectively in the same period. Investments by nonresidents increased and this group held more than 40% of public debt in the year 2000. During this period, there was a significant fall in private placements outstanding, because of the central government's debt restructuring program combined with no new issuance of this type of government debt. For a description of the Dutch private placement market, see de Haan (1991).

18.5.2   Investors in Euro Credit Bonds

The distribution of type of investors in large euro-denominated credit bonds, with an issued amount of €300 million or more, is shown here using a sample of large, recently issued credit bonds. On average, each credit bond transaction in this sample involved 192 investors.[8] Tables 18.9 and 18.10 display the distribution by investor type and by geographical distribution of investors respectively. These tables show that banks and investment funds are the dominant type of investors in this sample and investors from the countries in the Euro zone, most notably Germany and France, put their money in these euro-denominated credits. However, in general, banks do not invest in bonds, but it is possible they have a temporary exposure to bonds they bring as new issues to the market.

---

[8] We thank J.P. Morgan for providing their estimates.

Table 18.8 The breakdown of type of debt instrument and type of investors in Dutch government bonds during the period 1996–2000 in billions of euro

	1996		1997		1998		1999		2000	
Public debt										
Residents:										
Investment funds*	5	(3%)	6	(4%)	7	(4%)	5	(3%)	2	(1%)
Private investors†	16	(11%)	10	(6%)	13	(8%)	10	(6%)	2	(1%)
Banks	23	(15%)	27	(17%)	29	(18%)	28	(16%)	23	(14%)
Insurance companies	20	(13%)	24	(15%)	25	(15%)	38	(22%)	37	(22%)
Pension funds	50	(33%)	50	(32%)	46	(28%)	35	(20%)	34	(20%)
Nonresidents	37	(25%)	39	(25%)	45	(27%)	58	(33%)	71	(42%)
Sum of public debt	151	(100%)	156	(100%)	164	(100%)	174	(100%)	169	(100%)
Private placements	33		22		18		11		5	
Total debt	184		178		182		185		174	

Source: DSTA.

*Up to 1996, this category included social security funds. Since 1997, social security funds hold their assets in account at the Dutch state.

†It should be noted that the "private investors" category is not restricted exclusively to natural persons, but also include legal entities (for example, companies, foundations and cooperatives), which do not count financial services among their principal activities (see Appendix, DSTA).

Table 18.9   The distribution by type of investor in euro-denominated credit bonds

Banks	31%
Insurance companies	13%
Investment funds	50%
Retail customers	6%

Source: J.P. Morgan estimates.

Table 18.10   The geographical distribution of investors in euro-denominated credit bonds

France	20%
Germany	21%
Iberia	4%
Italy	9%
Scandinavia	5%
United Kingdom	20%
Other	21%

Source: J.P. Morgan estimates.

18.6   EURONEXT AMSTERDAM AND OTC MARKET

18.6.1   Euronext Amsterdam

All DSLs, credit bonds from Dutch issuers, both investment grade and high yield, and other bond types, such as convertible bonds, are listed at Euronext Amsterdam, where irregular trading in small amounts of Dutch government bonds takes place. Both traded amounts and their frequency suggest that mainly retail investors use this exchange to trade bonds. Most Dutch government bond trading occurs in the OTC market in Amsterdam or London, or via web-based trading platforms, as described below.

Different types of credit bonds are also traded at Euronext Amsterdam from time to time. Again, their trading pattern is irregular and only small amounts are bought and sold. Most trading of credit bonds occurs in the OTC market.

18.6.2   OTC Market

In general, large Dutch institutional investors trade DSLs with investment banks and brokers in the OTC market. Both banks and brokers make markets in these types of bonds. Nowadays, this way of trading is disappearing as more and more sovereign debt trading occurs via web-based trading systems, such as Bloomberg, TradeWeb, and MTS SpA.

Dutch government securities are traded via an electronic trading platform that is managed by MTS Amsterdam. The shareholders of MTS Amsterdam are the Dutch state (5%), MTS SpA (30%) and the 13 primary dealers (5% each) designated by DSTA (see Section 18.3.2.3). Three types of eligible financial institutions participate in this market and must satisfy the following requirements (see Appendix, MTS Amsterdam):

- Market makers are primary dealers in the Dutch primary market designated by DSTA that commit themselves to market-making obligations for both DSLs and DTCs.

Table 18.11   Traded volumes in both DTCs and DSLs at MTS Amsterdam in 2001 and 2002 as of November 2002 (in millions of euro)

	2001 (214 days)		2002 (214 days)		
	Volume	Daily average	Volume	Daily average	Year-to-date change in volume
DTCs	30 686.0	143.39	43 800.0	204.7	42.74%
DSLs	76 586.0	357.88	77 410.0	361.7	1.08%
Total	107 272.0	501.27	121 210.0	566.4	12.99%

Source: MTS Amsterdam.

- Single market specialists are financial institutions in the Dutch primary market of DTCs, designated by DSTA, that commit themselves to market-making obligations for DTCs only.
- Market takers, financial institutions that traded at least €300 million in Dutch secondary government bond market in the previous year.

The obligations of the market makers are defined by MTS Amsterdam, which insists that two-way quotes are available for no less than 5 hours each day on all Dutch government bond benchmark issues and an assigned subset of nonbenchmark bonds.

MTS Amsterdam reports the traded volumes of DTCs and DSLs in millions of euro in 2001 and 2002, as shown in Table 18.11. During this period, the traded amount in DTCs (DSLs) rose 42.74% (1.08%), but the total volume of DSLs remained higher than that of DTCs.

However, these web-based trading systems that are used in the euro sovereign bond market are not common practice for the euro corporate bond market yet. This is due to the fact that the secondary market in euro-denominated corporate bonds is not as liquid as expected when it was opened.

Trading hours of DSLs at the various markets, with Amsterdam time equaling GMT + 1 hour, are the following (Bennett *et al.*, 2001):

- Euronext Amsterdam: 08:00 a.m. to 06:00 p.m.,
- MTS Amsterdam: 08:15 a.m. to 05:30 p.m.,
- London (GMT):   08:00 a.m. to 05:00 p.m.

18.7   REGULATORS

The landscape of the Dutch supervision regime of financial companies is changing. Jonk *et al.* (2001) explain,

> from being predominantly sector-oriented, the Dutch supervisory regime is becoming more cross-sectional in nature. The driving force behind this reform is the continuing financial market integration, for example banks selling insurance products and services and vice versa. The Dutch supervisors want their structure to reflect these market developments. This restructuring from sector to cross-sector supervision has been implemented during 2002 and it will be followed by formal legislation (Tweede Kamer der Staten-Generaal [House of Representatives of the States General in the Netherlands], 2001–2002a, 2001–2002b).

Table 18.12 presents this new cross-sector oriented supervisory regime (Jonk *et al.*, 2001). This new regime is built on the following two pillars. First, systemic stability supervision is combined with prudential supervision. Systematic stability supervision falls within the

Table 18.12 The new financial supervision structure in the Netherlands

	Systemic stability	Prudential		Conduct of business		
				Nonsecurities		
		Sectoral	Cross-sector	Sectoral	Cross-sector	Securities
Banking/ investment	DNB	DNB	DNB/PVK	AFM	AFM	AFM
Securities	DNB	DNB	DNB/PVK	AFM	AFM	AFM
Insurance	DNB	PVK	DNB/PVK	AFM	AFM	AFM

Source: MoF.

jurisdiction of DNB, as described earlier in Section 18.2. Prudential supervision of the banking, investment funds, and security firms sectors is also carried out by DNB. "Prudential supervision addresses the question of whether participants in the financial markets can rely on their contracting parties to meet their financial obligations" (see Appendix, AFM). The insurance supervisor, the Pensions and Insurance Supervisory Authority of the Netherlands (Pensioen- & Verzekeringskamer, PVK), performs the prudential supervision of the insurance sector and pension funds. DNB and PVK join forces through cross-board appointments and combined teams for prudential supervision of financial conglomerates, and have plans for a merger.

Second, the conduct of business supervision is placed under separate supervision of the Netherlands Authority for the Financial Markets (Autoriteit Financiële Markten, AFM), the legal successor of the Securities Board of the Netherlands (Stichting Toezicht Effectenverkeer, STE). "The supervision of market conduct focuses on the question of whether the participants in the financial markets are treated properly and whether they have accurate information" (see Appendix, AFM).

Kremers *et al.* (2001) state that there is still disagreement among supervisors throughout Europe of the preferred regime. Policy recommendations regarding the organizational structure of financial supervision range from enhanced cooperation to a centralized structure at a European level.

18.7.1 De Nederlandsche Bank

As shown in Section 18.2, one of the main tasks of DNB is to supervise the banking system, collective investment schemes, and exchange offices. DNB (2002) describes that its main two objectives within banking supervision are "to protect the interests of the public who have entrusted their money to banks" and "to protect the stability of the financial system. What this means in practice is that the financial system must be 'sound' enough to absorb the failure of an individual institution without a knock-on effect that brings the whole system down."

Before entering the Dutch market, banks must first obtain authorization from the DNB. After obtaining this authorization, DNB continues to monitor these banks. In order to carry out its tasks, DNB collects detailed information from banks. "DNB has also issued guidelines for assessing the solvency and liquidity of banks" and further banks are required to "keep their administrative affairs in good order and to maintain adequate internal control" and "DNB supervises the structure of cooperative links between banks and other businesses."

As mentioned above, DNB also supervises "companies whose business it is to invest money on behalf of third parties" with the goal of "the smooth operation of financial markets and to protect investors in these markets." Further exchange offices must be registered with DNB in order to counter money laundering via these offices and in this way protecting the integrity of the Dutch financial system. Finally, DNB contributes to the supervision of institutions that provide loans to consumers.

18.7.2 Pensions and Insurance Supervisory Authority of the Netherlands (Pensioen- & Verzekeringskamer, PVK)

The Pensions and Insurance Board supervises the insurance companies and pension funds that operate in the Netherlands with the aim of ensuring that these institutions are and remain financially sound and that they are also able to meet their obligations in the future. A further important task is the testing of the fitness and properness of new and existing executive directors of insurance companies and pension funds (see Appendix, AFM).

The responsibilities and activities of PVK are carried out in accordance with a number of acts of Parliament.

PVK describes its policy as having a dual character: on the one hand, the PVK applies existing supervision legislation, and on the other hand, PVK can exercise its own authority by means of regulations, policy rules, and recommendations, each described below (see Appendix, PVK).

Regulations are the PVK's most compelling powers. Institutions are obliged to comply with the regulations, which are always directly related to statutory or ministerial provisions. If an institution fails to do so, sanctions may be imposed. In issuing a policy rule, the PVK gives its own interpretation of statutory provisions. This is an indication of how the PVK itself will approach the matters in question. In the first instance, these policy rules are binding on the PVK. If, however, an institution deviates from an interpretation, the PVK may impose a sanction or withhold a requested facility or service. The PVK can also make recommendations. These are not obligatory and the PVK cannot enforce compliance with its recommendations by imposing sanctions.

PVK also works alongside other European bodies such as the insurance committee set up by the EU Council, the conference of EU/EEA Insurance Supervisory Authorities, and the EU Council working papers to support MoF and pension supervision. This has involved the Conference of Pension Supervisory Authorities, working with British, Irish, and German pension supervisory authorities, and work with the EU Council working party in support of the Dutch Ministry of Social Affairs and Employment.

18.7.3 Netherlands Authority for the Financial Markets (Autoriteit Financiële Markten, AFM)

The Netherlands Authority for the Financial Markets has been responsible for supervising the operation of the financial markets since 1 March 2002. This means that AFM supervises the conduct of the entire financial market sector: savings, investment, insurance and loans. By supervising the conduct of the financial markets, AFM aims to make a contribution to the efficient operation of these markets. AFM is an autonomous administrative authority (zelfstandig bestuursorgaan) that comes under the political responsibility of the Minister of Finance. The minister appoints the board members of AFM and also approves its budget and any amendments to its statutes.

The three objectives of the supervision by AFM are the following:

1. To ensure that the financial markets operate in an efficient, fair and orderly manner,
2. To promote transparency between all of the participants in the financial markets and in this connection,
3. To protect the consumer.

AFM supervises:

1. All Dutch securities exchanges and institutions that offer securities services in or from the Netherlands,
2. All Dutch credit institutions that offer consumer credit (as from 3 March 2002),
3. The provision of Financial Information Leaflets by banks, investment institutions, credit providers, insurance companies and securities institutions (as from 8 March 2002).

AFM carries out its supervisory role by checking, enforcing and transferring standards and acts specifically on tip-offs from the market and the findings of its own control organisation. If AFM ascertains that there has been a breach, it may impose penalties. It may issue a reprimand or give a public warning, appoint a secret receiver, withdraw a licence, cancel or refuse a registration, or report an offence to the Public Prosecutions Department. It can also impose penalties and fines (see Appendix, AFM).

One of the areas that are subject to supervision by AFM is the operation of Euronext Amsterdam. Because this securities exchange is a merger of the Amsterdam, Brussels, Paris, and Lisbon stock exchanges, AFM cooperates closely with the Belgian, French, and Portuguese securities supervisory authorities in relation to regulations and supervision of Euronext. AFM also participates in the Committee of European Securities Regulators.

18.7.4   Rating Agencies

In addition to the impact of the Dutch national regulators, foreign rating agencies, such as Moody's Investor Services, Standard & Poor's, and Fitch IBCA, also affect bond markets. These organizations often rate large euro-denominated corporate bonds and/or their Dutch issuers. Most Dutch issuers from the Lehman Brothers the Netherlands Index at August 31, 2002, have a high credit rating as is displayed in Section 18.4. DSLs receive the highest possible credit rating of Aaa/AAA/AAA from these three rating agencies.

18.8   CONCLUSIONS

The introduction of the euro on January 1, 1999, changed the shape of the small market for Dutch bonds. The Dutch government had to find ways to improve the liquidity of their bonds as national monetary policy and currency differences between countries disappeared. The euro also influenced the Dutch corporate bond issuers, which have become part of the growing euro-denominated credit bond market. In this newly established bond market, a company's home country has become less important than its rating and sector. The investor base of both Dutch government bonds and corporate bonds has also become more international. So, it is clear that both issuers and investors have been affected by the introduction of the euro. One area of common ground for issuers and investors is Euronext Amsterdam, which has now merged with other exchanges in Europe, and the OTC bond markets. There have also been changes to the Dutch financial supervision regime since Dutch supervision has moved from a largely sector-oriented regime to one that is more cross-sectional based. Finally, rating agencies also have an impact through their assessment of Dutch government debt and corporate bonds.

APPENDIX: USEFUL WEBSITES[9]

Section	Website
The Netherlands	
Bank for International Settlements	http://www.bis.org/
De Nederlandsche Bank	http://www.dnb.nl/
European Central Bank	http://www.ecb.int/
Eurostat	http://www.eurostat.com/
International Monetary Fund	http://www.imf.org/
Ministry of Economic Affairs	http://www.ez.nl/
Ministry of Finance	http://www.minfin.nl/
Organization of Economic Cooperation and Development	http://www.oecd.org/
Dutch Government Bonds	
Dutch State Treasury Agency	http://www.dutchstate.nl/
Credit Bonds	
Bank Nederlandse Gemeenten NV	http://www.bng.com/
Nederlandse Waterschapsbank NV	http://www.nwb.nl/
Euronext Amsterdam and OTC Markets	
Bloomberg LP	http://www.bloomberg.com/
MTS Amsterdam NV	http://www.mtsamsterdam.com/
Euronext NV	http://www.euronext.com/
TradeWeb Ltd.	http://www.tradeweb.com/
Regulators	
Fitch IBCA Inc.	http://www.fitchibca.com/
Moody's Investors Service	http://www.moodys.com/
Netherlands Authority for the Financial Markets	http://www.autoriteit-fm.nl/
Pensions and Insurance Supervisory Authority of the Netherlands	http://www.pvk.nl/
Tweede kamer (House of Representatives of the States General in the Netherlands)	http://www.tweede-kamer.nl/
Standard & Poor's Rating Group	http://www.standardandpoors.com/

ACKNOWLEDGMENTS

The author thanks Patrick Houweling, Colin Renton, and Ton Vorst for their constructive comments.

---

[9] English language versions of Dutch websites can usually be reached by clicking on one of the following words: "Engels" or "English (version)," or on a picture of the Union Jack.

REFERENCES

Bank for International Settlements (2001, September). The Changing Shape of Fixed Income Markets (Study Group on Fixed Income Markets). BIS Working Paper, No. 104.

Bennett, R., L. Brusadelli, and J.D. Simons (2001, October 31). *Government Bond Outlines*, 14th edn. New York: J.P. Morgan.

de Haan, J. (ed.) (1991). *De onderhandse kapitaalmarkt in Nederland*. Amsterdam: NIBE.

De Nederlandsche Bank (2000, March). Special Financial Institutions in the Netherlands. *Statistical Bulletin*, pp. 19–29.

De Nederlandsche Bank (2002). *De Nederlandsche Bank: Its Role in the Netherlands and Europe*. Amsterdam: DNB.

European Central Bank (2002). *Report on Financial Structures*. Frankfurt am Main: ECB, pp. 205–224.

Galati, G. and K. Tsatsaronis (2001, July). The Impact of the Euro on Europe's Financial Markets. BIS Working Paper, No. 100.

Greenwood, N. and P. Dutton (2000, October). Analysis Nederlandse Waterschapsbank N.V. *Standard & Poor's Financial Institutions*.

Grubben, J.H. and J.D.M. van Summeren (1999). Convertible Indices. In: C.J.G.M. Hendriks, (ed.) (2002). *Obligatiebeleggingen*. Deventer: Kluwer.

International Monetary Fund (2002, May 16). Kingdom of the Netherlands. *Staff Report for the 2002 Article IV Consultation*. Washington: IMF.

International Monetary Fund (2003, July 7), Kingdom of the Netherlands. *Staff report for the 2003 Article IV Consultation*. Washington: IMF.

Jonk, A., J. Kremers, and D. Schoenmaker (2001, December). A New Dutch Model. *The Financial Regulator* **6**(3), pp. 35–38.

Kremers, J., D. Schoenmaker, and P. Wierts (2001, December). Does Europe Need a Euro-wide Supervisor? *The Financial Regulator* **6**(3), pp. 50–56.

Levene, P., S. Marchakitus, and M. Soderberg (2002, July). European Telecoms, Survival of the Fittest. *J.P. Morgan Credit Research*. London: J.P. Morgan.

Ministry of Economic Affairs (2002, March 1). *Benchmarking the Netherlands 2002, Benchmarking for Growth* (02AEP02). The Hague: Ministry of Economic Affairs.

Munves, D. and A. Flores (1998, August). The Lehman Brothers Euro-Aggregate Index: A New Index for a New Market. *Lehman Brothers Fixed-Income Research*. London: Lehman Brothers Inc.

Oorschot, M.M.H.P. and P.A. Stork (1995, December). The Dutch Credit Bond Market. *The Journal of Fixed Income*, pp. 89–94.

Thomson, J., A. Cunnigham, and S.S. Theodore (2001, June). Bank Nederlandse Gemeenten N.V. *Moody's Investor Service Global Credit Research*.

Toorman, R. (1997). De markt voor Nederlandse strips. In: C.J.G.M. Hendriks (ed.) (2002). *Obligatiebeleggingen*. Deventer: Kluwer.

Tweede Kamer der Staten-Generaal (2001–2002a). *Hervorming van het toezicht op de financiële marktsector*. Tweede Kamer, vergaderjaar 2001–2002a, 28 122, nr. 2.

Tweede Kamer der Staten-Generaal (2001–2002b). *Hervorming van het toezicht op de financiële marktsector*. Tweede Kamer, vergaderjaar 2001–2002b, 28 122, nr. 5.

Wouters, T.I.M. (2002). Inflatiegeïndexeerde obligaties. In: C.J.G.M. Hendriks (ed.) (2002). *Obligatiebeleggingen*. Deventer: Kluwer.

19

Poland

PETER G. SZILAGYI

19.1 INTRODUCTION

Poland has been one of the most successful transition economies in Central and Eastern Europe. It was the first of the region's economies to end its recession in the early 1990s, and for the rest of the decade Polish economic growth remained among the highest in the former Soviet bloc, and indeed across the Organisation for Economic Co-operation and Development (OECD). The economy's vigour was supported by sweeping reforms as well as a reduction of its foreign debt burden, the provision of economic aid, and the lowering of trade barriers by developed countries (see Table 19.1). The country became a full member of OECD in 1996 and NATO in 1999, and graduated from USAID assistance in 2000. It completed European Union (EU) accession negotiations at the Copenhagen summit in December 2002, and is to become a member of the EU in May 2004.

Notwithstanding these achievements, however, the Polish economy has weathered a tough last 3 years. Following exogenous shocks – the Russian crisis and oil prices, an aggressive policy response to expanding domestic consumption, and a slowdown in the EU, practically every economic trend turned unfavorable. By 2001, gross domestic product (GDP) growth dipped below 1%, the lowest among the 10 prospective EU members. At the heart of the economic slowdown was a collapse in investment, owing to decelerating internal and external demand, low profitability, and the burdening effects of high interest rates (IMF, 2003). The downturn has taken its toll: from below 10%, the unemployment rate has risen back to the high teens; the government's fiscal deficit has widened sharply; and the stock of nonperforming loans in the banking sector has grown. The accompanying progress in lowering inflation and the current account deficit has done little to improve public sentiment. In the autumn 2001 elections the Solidarity Electoral Action, previously the majority coalition partner, was wiped out; and social dissatisfaction also appears to be on the rise with the new coalition government, headed by the Democratic Left Alliance (SLD, successor to the communist party) and Prime Minister Leszek Miller.

Despite the recent economic difficulties Poland has nonetheless proved to be a safe place to invest thus far. Slow growth and tight monetary policy have helped temper inflation, which was down to just 1.9% in 2002. Interest rates have been cut substantially, from 11.5% in January 2002 to 6.5% in January 2003, and are set to further decrease. The decline in the current account deficit has also reduced vulnerability to foreign creditors. The budget deficit remains a source of concern, however. The slowing economy drove up the deficit to an estimated 4.3% of GDP in 2001, which increased further, to 5.1% in 2002. As a result, although Standard & Poor's has maintained Poland's BBB+ rating for foreign currency liabilities, it recently lowered the

European Fixed Income Markets: Money, Bond and Interest Rate Derivatives. Edited by J.A. Batten, T.A. Fetherston and P.G. Szilagyi. © 2004 John Wiley & Sons, Ltd. ISBN 0-470-85053-1

Table 19.1 Key economic indicators in Poland

	1998	1999	2000	2001
GDP per head ($ at PPP)	7970	8450	8990	9280
GDP (% real change pa)	4.8	4.1	4	1
Government consumption (% of GDP)	16.37	16.5	16.53	16.59
Budget balance (% of GDP)	−1.01	−0.93	−0.1	−4.6
Consumer prices (% change pa; av)	11.73	7.31	10.14	5.5
Public debt (% of GDP)	42.89	42.98	39.3	39.9
Labor costs per hour (US$)	2.01	2.39	2.46	2.8
Recorded unemployment (%)	9.98	11.98	14.01	16.22
Current-account balance/GDP	−4.31	−7.45	−6.31	−4.05
Foreign-exchange reserves (million $)	27 325	26 354	26 562	25 648

Source: Economist Intelligence Unit. © European Communities, 1995–2003. Reproduced with permission.

Figure 19.1 Zloty/euro and zloty/US dollar exchange rate (in 2002, daily).
Source: National Bank of Poland.

rating for liabilities denominated in the local currency, the Polish zloty, from A+ to A−. It is also noteworthy that the zloty has been one of the most volatile Eastern European currencies since its full floating in April 2000, and therefore the currency risk remains relatively high. Since the end of 1999, the currency has appreciated by some 25% against the US dollar, a process that consecutive interest rate cuts have thus far failed to stem (see Figure 19.1).

Economy-wise, recent indicators suggest that Poland is poised for a recovery. Lagged effects of fiscal and monetary stimuli and the slow pickup in the EU cemented economic recuperation in 2003. Beyond 2004, the economy's growth prospects are strong; however, much depends on the forceful implementation of reforms. In a bid to define well-designed policy action guidelines, the generally promarket Leszek government announced the comprehensive medium term program "Entrepreneurship-Development-Employment" in early 2002. This three-pillar policy framework for 2002–2006 aims at promoting growth, stabilizing public finances, and preparing for EU membership. Immediate aims include improving the business environment, increasing infrastructure spending, and mobilizing domestic savings, including through strengthening and developing the banking system and the capital market.

19.2   HISTORY AND STRUCTURE OF THE POLISH BOND MARKET

The establishment of the legal framework for Polish capital markets was initiated in 1991 through the parliament's passing of the Act on Public Trading in Securities and the reopening of the Warsaw Stock Exchange (WSE), closed in 1939. The development of the bond market did not accelerate until the second half of the 1990s, however. In December 2001, the outstanding amount of Polish domestic debt securities was PLN 193.4 billion or 28% of GDP, which makes it the second largest emerging European market behind Turkey and by far the largest in the former Eastern bloc. The market now comprises Treasury bills and bonds, short term nongovernment-issued commercial paper (CP), corporate and bank bonds as well as municipal bonds. Nonetheless, while development has been impressive, the market is far from European levels in terms of product variety, soundness, and cost, and remains small in both relative and absolute terms.

Figure 19.2 illustrates the percentage of total Polish debt outstanding by security type. The largest segments of the market are the Treasury bond (72.8%) and Treasury bill (18.2%) markets, which add up to more than nine tenths of the total outstanding amount. Such disproportions largely owe to the fact that the reestablishment of the bond market itself was initially related to facilitating the management of public debt and macroeconomic stabilization in the early 1990s. The emergence of the Treasury market was linked to the securitization of loans denominated in local currency to the central government, which went in parallel to the declining importance of the central bank as a creditor to the public sector (Polish Ministry of Finance, 2001).

In comparison, the nongovernment segment of the market remains limited in scale and scope despite its dynamic growth since 1997. Development in the segment was for a long time hindered by high inflation and real interest rates as well as infrastructural deficiencies and prohibitive related costs. The more recent impetus behind the market has been the deceleration of inflation, which has allowed corporations to limit the issuance of floating-rate instruments and increase that of fixed-rate bonds. The growth of the municipal bond market has also been linked to the increasingly widespread acceptance of bond financing among municipalities, hastened by the gradual decentralization of responsibilities from the central government, and increased funding needs due to the central government's budgetary problems. It is regrettable, however, that the recent market growth has not been underpinned by adequate qualitative changes. This continues to impede market expansion, because potential borrowers continue to seek funds in the Eurobond market despite the significant currency risk involved: Bank for International Settlements (BIS) data reveal that Polish nongovernment borrowers have more than US$6.5 billion of outstanding debt in international securities. The main defects of the market remain infrastructural and cost-related. Chief among these is the absence of a

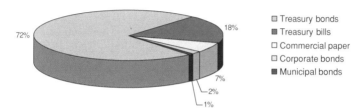

Figure 19.2   Polish domestic debt by type of security (December 2001).
Source: Polish Ministry of Finance, Fitch Polska S.A.

liquid secondary market, whose establishment is hindered by most domestic debt issues being privately placed because of cost efficiency and less stringent regulatory requirements. The consequent lack of market transparency is demonstrated by the continuingly weak correlation between issuer creditworthiness and risk premia.

A further impediment that hinders the universal development of the Polish bond market, with respect to both the government and the nongovernment segments, is the continuingly low level of issuance at longer maturities. At short maturities, the market is relatively well developed, which is reflected in the strong issuing activity in Treasury bills and CP. At longer maturities, however, the market is totally dominated by medium term Treasury bonds, while nongovernment issues are of much lesser importance. This pattern results not only from the situation on the debt market – high real interest rates acting as a disincentive to raising long term loans – but also from the approach of domestic investors, who have a particularly prudent approach toward long term investments because of the lack of a liquid secondary market. The overall maturity structure of the Polish bond market therefore remains very short in international comparison. The average maturity of Treasury securities was 2.61 years in June 2002, with long term 10- and 20-year bonds making up only 14% of total government debt. The average maturity is even shorter in the nongovernment segment, where CP with maturities of 6 months or less constitutes 73.1% of the market.

Recognizing the need to establish a developed market that is liquid at all maturities, the government has now developed a medium term strategy to lengthen and standardize the maturity of public debt (see Polish Ministry of Finance, 2002). As part of this strategy, 20-year Treasury bonds were issued for the first time in April 2002. Bond switching auctions have also been introduced, whereby illiquid bonds are traded in for benchmark issues. The Ministry of Finance (MoF) has also launched a system of primary dealers, the Treasury Securities Dealer System, which is aimed at increasing market transparency and liquidity, and lowering the government's debt servicing costs. It is hoped that these actions will lead to the establishment of a more reliable benchmark yield curve, thus also working toward the creation of a liquid secondary market for nongovernment issues.

Corporate issuers are now also contemplating the lengthening of the maturity spectrum, because of the burden of short term service, and the shifting of issuance from privately to publicly placed instruments. They are aided by the changes made to the Bond Act of 1995, enacted in 2000, which liberalized the procedures of bond issuance and of secondary trade. The amendments, which are all in compliance with EU regulations, include the following (see Stosio and Rose, 2001):

- It is no longer obligatory to appoint a representative bank to represent the interests of bondholders in public offerings, which substantially reduces issuance costs.
- Nonpublic bonds may now be issued in dematerialized form, which reduces related costs and introduces the possibility of creating a balance in the legal status of bonds in private and public trading. The National Depository may maintain registers of dematerialized bonds for securities (NDS, National Depository for Securities), brokerage houses, or banks. Public bonds must always be dematerialized.
- The regulatory distinction between secured and unsecured bonds has been abolished. Loss-making companies are now allowed to issue unsecured bonds, as are entities that have been in existence for less than 3 years.
- Issuers, except municipalities or other local government bodies and public utility corporations, are no longer obliged to specify the purpose for which the bonds are to be issued.

- The offering of bonds in large denominations (€40 000) to institutional investors such as Qualified Institutional Buyers (QIBs) has been exempted from the public offering requirements, including the prospectus regime imposed on most publicly traded securities under the Act on Public Trading in Securities.
- Municipalities or other local government bodies and public utility corporations are now allowed to issue revenue bonds.
- Financial institutions of which Poland, the National Bank of Poland (NBP), or at least one OECD country or its central bank is a member are now allowed to issue bonds.

The more recent changes in the market infrastructure should also provide impetus to the development of the market. The NDS has now implemented multibatch settlements and a real-time gross settlement (RTGS) system, which allows for the settlement of transactions and transfers of bonds in real time, and has lowered its safekeeping and settlement fees. The preparation and the implementation by the NDS of the repo and sell-buy-back transactions settlement procedures should also become an important factor in the development of the market. It is also hoped that the pension system reform of 1999 and the rapid expansion of other institutional investors such as insurance companies and investment trusts will dramatically increase demand for longer term securities. The gradual growth of the market, with regard to both the number and complexity of instruments, should increase demand for credit ratings, which will encourage further consolidation.

Notwithstanding these actions, however, further incentives are necessary to increase the depth and liquidity of the market. In particular, more concerted efforts are required to increase market transparency through the firmer establishment of a liquid benchmark and the promotion of secondary market making. This is all the more pivotal, because Poland, with its population of 39 million and substantial potential for growth, is widely regarded as a lucrative long term market, where foreign strategic investors, mostly banks and insurance companies, must be facilitated in exploring business opportunities. With Poland now having graduated from the emerging markets class, the country's domestic debt is of particularly great interest to convergence funds. To facilitate these long term structural allocations to Polish debt, JP Morgan was the first to launch its Polish Government Bond Index in July 2000, and others have promptly followed suit.

19.3   MARKET PARTICIPANTS AND STRUCTURE

19.3.1   Legal Regulations

The basic legal act regulating capital market activities is the Act on Public Trading in Securities and Trust Funds of August 21, 1997, as amended. It determines the principles and scope of operations of such capital market institutions as the Securities and Exchange Commission, stock exchanges, the NDS, and brokerage houses. The issue, sale, and purchase of bonds are regulated by the Bond Act, which was enacted on June 29, 1995, and substantially amended in 2000. Additional laws, including the Investment Funds Act of August 28, 1997, as amended, regulate other aspects of market activities.

19.3.2   Regulators

The main participants in the regulation and management of the financial markets are the following.

19.3.2.1   National Bank of Poland (Narodowy Bank Polski)

The mission of the NBP is to maintain price stability and to ensure the stability of the financial system. The NBP is organized around a series of departments and offices that are overseen by the President of the NBP, the Monetary Policy Council, and the NBP Management Board. The NBP manages the following activities:

(i) *Issuance and management of banknotes.* The NBP has the sole right of issuing currency, which is a legal tender in Poland, and it is responsible for maintaining the currency's liquidity through organizing money circulation.

(ii) *implementation of monetary policy.* Since 1999, the NBP has been pursuing the strategy of the so-called direct inflation target, maintaining interest rates at a level consistent with the accomplishment of the assumed target.

(iii) *Passive exchange rate policy.* Since April 12, 2000, the zloty exchange rate has been fully floating, although the NBP reserves the right to engage in interventions, if considered necessary, in achieving the inflation target.

(iv) *Providing payment and settlement services, and ensuring the stability of the financial system.* Financial transactions between financial institutions are settled by transferring funds across the current accounts held by each institution at the NBP, which is also a participant in payment systems. In order to facilitate such fund transfers, the NBP operates an electronic RGTS system, the so-called SORBNET, and systems of securities settlements (SKARBNET for Treasury bills and SEBOP for NBP bills). The NBP also plays the role of settlement agent for clearing systems of the National Clearing House and of the securities settlement system operated by the NDS.

(v) *Monitoring and examination of the financial and management conditions of financial institutions.* The NBP supervises the activity of commercial banks, and in particular compliance with the provisions of banking law trends. The NBP also performs regulatory functions in order to ensure the safety of banks and to maintain liquidity in the banking system.

(vi) *Function as the lender of last resort.* In the case of temporary liquidity problems a commercial bank may obtain financial assistance from the NBP in the form of either a rediscounting loan or a lombard loan.

(vii) *Treasury and government securities-related operations.* The NBP provides banking services to the state budget, operates bank accounts of the government and central state institutions, targets state funds and state budget entities, and executes their payment orders. In addition, the NBP is the issue agent of the Treasury securities offered on the domestic wholesale market.

(viii) *Statistical, analytical, and research activities.* The NBP compiles data adjusted to standards binding at the European Central Bank, and reviews Poland's financial and economic conditions.

(ix) *Further to the above activities, the NBP also engages in educational projects aimed at propagating growth of economic awareness and improving the economic knowledge of state authorities and the financial sector.*

19.3.2.2   Ministry of Finance (Ministerstwo Finansów)

While the NBP is responsible for the management of the nation's assets, the responsibility of debt management belongs to the MoF (see Figure 19.3). The MoF's Bureau of Public Debt handles the issuance of Treasury securities. The legal framework is laid down in the Budget

Figure 19.3 Organization chart of the Polish Ministry of Finance.
Source: Polish Ministry of Finance.

Act, the Act on the Minister of Finance's Office, Tax Offices and Chambers, the annual Budget Acts, and Regulation No. 23 of the Minister of Finance on the Issuance of Treasury Bills of April 24, 1995, as well as resolutions of the Minister of Finance on the issuance of Treasury bonds. The Budget Act obliges the MoF to develop a 3-year strategy for public finance sector debt management. The latest such strategy, for 2003–2005, was announced in September 2002, and contains the following objectives:

- Increasing the liquidity, efficiency, and transparency of the Treasury securities market;
- Starting the program of refinancing repayments of foreign debt falling in the years 2004–2009 in the best way from the point of view of risk and cost incurred;
- Improving the primary dealer system;
- Developing a system of state budget liquidity management;
- Developing a system of retail instruments sale;
- Continuing the conversion of nonmarketable debt to marketable instruments.

19.3.2.3   Securities and Exchange Commission (PSEC, Komisja Papierów Wartościowych I Giełd)

The PSEC regulates and supervises the Polish securities market. In order to guarantee the institution's political independence, the Chairman of the PSEC is appointed by the Prime Minister upon the joint request of the NBP and the MoF, with consideration given to opinions expressed by appropriate parliamentary commissions. Commission members include representatives of the Ministy of Finance, the Ministry of Treasury, the Ministry of Economy, the Ministry of Agriculture and Food Economy, as well as the President of the NBP and the President of Competition and Consumer Protection Office. The scope of responsibilities includes the following:

• Licensing and monitoring the activity of market participants;
• Admitting securities to public trading upon the fulfillment of appropriate requirements with regard to the issue prospectus;
• Supervising compliance with the rules of fair trading and competition, and providing public access to reliable information;
• Inspiring, organizing, and taking appropriate measures in order to ensure the smooth operation of the securities market and the protection of investors;
• Cooperating with the government, the NBP, and other institutions in order to create such a national economic policy that would foster the development of the securities market;
• Promoting a knowledge of rules regulating the operation of the capital market;
• Taking other measures provided for in the Securities Act.

19.3.2.4   Other Regulators

Two supervisory authorities set rules and guidelines for actual trading. The Warsaw Stock Exchange (WSE, Giełda Papierów Wartościowych w Warszawie), which was established under the Act on Public Trading in Securities in 1991, regulates exchange trading of securities. The Central Table of Offers (CeTO, Centralna Tabela Ofert), a self-regulatory body that was established in 1996 and is owned by the WSE and 48 banks and brokerage houses, is responsible for the organization and operation of public trading in securities on the regulated over-the-counter (OTC) market.

All debt instruments admitted to public trading must be registered as book-entries with the NDS (Krajowy Depozyt Papierów Wartościowych), an independent joint stock company whose shares are held by the State Treasury, the NBP, brokerage firms, investment funds, and banks. Transactions are settled at the NDS, and the settlement of related funds is made via Bank Śląski SA. The delivery versus payment principle is fulfilled; securities are settled in real time on a gross basis, and funds on a net basis. The counterparties need to have securities accounts at brokerage houses or banks on which their securities are registered.

19.3.3   Categories of Investors

Until the late 1990s, the main investors in Polish debt instruments were domestic commercial banks. In more recent years, however, the share of domestic nonfinancial entities and nonresidents in debt purchases has grown substantially, with local nonbanks now being the single largest class of investors (see Table 19.2). This trend owes as much to the expansion of nonbank institutional investors such as insurance companies, pension funds, and investment funds, as to a strong interest by foreign investors in the market, which is currently the largest and most liquid debt market in Central and Eastern Europe (see Figure 19.4). It is noteworthy, however,

Table 19.2   Structure of buyers of wholesale bonds in 1998–2001 (as of end of period)

Year	Nonresidents (%)	Nonbank entities (%)	Domestic banks (%)	Total (million PLN)
1998	16	27	57	31 193
1999	15	38	46	42 615
2000	22	42	36	70 921
2001	21	47	32	92 815

Source: Reports of dealer banks and applicants for the function. In: National Bank of Poland (2002), Financial Market in Poland 1998–2001.

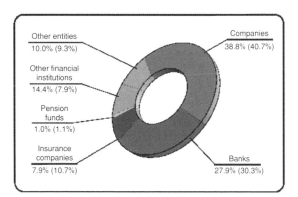

Figure 19.4   The nongovernment debt market breakdown by investors (by nominal debt value in December 2002 and December 2001).
Source: Fitch Polska's calculation on the basis of NBP data from 16 banks (2001 share calculations based on NBP data from 20 banks).

that in the nongovernment segment of the market, because of its short maturity profile, the holdings of institutional and nonresidents remain limited. The Foreign Exchange Act expressly restricts nonresident purchases of private debt with maturities of less than 1 year.

Nonresidents invest primarily in the most liquid 2-year zero coupon and 5-year fixed-rate Treasury issues (see Table 19.3). These instruments appeal mainly to mainstream Euro area investors, since Poland has now graduated from the emerging markets class, and yields have been rapidly converging toward those in the Euro area. This shift in the investor base has been assisted by economic progression as well as the government's active debt management, whereby the MoF bought back outstanding Brady bonds from emerging market investors and issued new debt for convergence investors. As a result, Poland's bonds now trade at tighter spreads than those of Italy or Portugal before the introduction of the euro.

Foreign investors are subject to basically the same regulations as domestic investors. For individual domestic investors, income from interest on Treasury bonds is subject to 20% tax, while domestic legal entities pay a 28% income tax. Tax obligations of foreign investors deriving income in Poland are regulated by intergovernmental agreements on the avoidance of double taxation, as well as by relevant reciprocity agreements.

19.3.4   Rating Agencies

Polish bonds are rated by one or more of the following agencies, which rate both long term local and foreign currency debt:

- Fitch Polska

Table 19.3   T-bonds in nonresidents' portfolios (in nominal value)

Year	T-bonds (million PLN)	Fixed-rate bonds (million PLN)	Varlable-rate bonds (million PLN)
1998	1280	4 645	228
1999	566	6 500	101
2000	656	15 664	7
2001	898	19 218	19

Source: Reports of dealer banks and applicants for the function. In: National Bank of Poland (2002), Financial Market in Poland 1998–2001.

- Moody's Investor Service
- Standard & Poor's

Fitch Polska was formed in 2001 through the merger of Fitch IBCA and Poland's first local agency, the Central European Agency (CERA), originally established in 1996. Fitch Polska and Standard & Poor's also rate short term debt.

19.3.5   Platforms of Public Trading

Trading in publicly issued bonds may take place on the WSE, the wholesale platform Electronic Treasury Securities Market, and the Polish Financial Exchange. Nonetheless, well over 95% of trading in bonds, including exchange-listed bonds, takes place in the nonregulated OTC market, where the main participants are both domestic and foreign banks (see KDPW, 2002b). The NBP (2002) notes that this concentration of trading is dictated by higher transaction costs in the regulated markets, associated with the compulsory use of intermediaries, and the possibility in the nonregulated market to conclude transactions using the 1-day transaction settlement procedure, the so-called uncleared transactions, which are partially cleared by the NDS (securities), and partially by the transaction participants (liquid funds).

19.3.5.1   Warsaw Stock Exchange (Gielda Papierów Wartościowych w Warszawie)

Capital market traditions in Poland go back to 1817, when the Warsaw Mercantile Exchange was established. The market could not be recreated after World War II, and the WSE joint stock company was not established in its present form until April 16, 1991. Today, the WSE operates based on the Act on Public Trading in Securities of August 21, 1997, as amended, under the supervision of the PSEC, and it has 48 shareholders, including banks, brokerage houses, and the State Treasury (see Warsaw Stock Exchange, 2002).

The task of the WSE is to organize regulated public securities trading. The following securities are traded: equities, bonds, subscription rights, allotment certificates and investment certificates, as well as derivative instruments. The trading system is order-driven, whereby prices of securities are determined based on buy and sell orders. Trading sessions are held Monday–Friday from 10:00 a.m. to 4:10 p.m., while futures contracts are quoted from 9:00 a.m. to 4:10 p.m.

Bonds are traded in the continuous trading system Warset. The majority of instruments listed are Treasuries. Trading of corporate bonds, for which the same rules apply as for Treasury bonds, was first executed in 2000. The first corporate bonds issued by a foreign entity, the European Investment Bank, were introduced a year later. The settlement cycle is T+2.

The WSE launched its derivatives market in 1998. It trades a number of financial futures contracts, including stock index futures and US dollar and euro exchange rate futures contracts. Interest rate futures have not yet been introduced. The liquidity of WIG20 stock index futures places the WSE among the leading of medium-size European markets in terms of the value of futures trading; the liquidity of currency futures, however, is very low.

19.3.5.2   Polish Financial Exchange (PFE, Polska Giełda Finansowa)

The PFE was founded on April 3, 1996, by a group of the largest Polish banks and the Polish Bank Association. It offers electronic brokerage services for futures transactions as well as executing spot market trading operations on Treasury bills and bonds, and repo and reverse repo transactions. The exchange has three types of members: (i) clearing members, which guarantee clearing operations; (ii) direct members, which are entitled to trade and settle only their own transactions; and (iii) nonclearing members, which are entitled to trade transactions, but settle them exclusively through clearing members. Futures products include US dollar and euro exchange rate futures, and contracts on the 1-month and 3-month WIBOR (Warsaw Interbank Offered Rate). In the spot market, the trading unit for Treasury bills is 10 bills, with a total value of PLN 100 000, while the trading unit for Treasury bonds is 100 bonds, with a total value of PLN 100 000. Trading sessions take place on business days between 9:30 a.m. and 3:00 p.m. Treasury futures and options have yet to be introduced.

19.3.5.3   Electronic Treasury Securities Market (ETSM)

The ETSM is a wholesale electronic trading platform for bulk transactions of PLN 5 million in Treasury securities. It was launched by the CeTO in April 2002 as part of the Treasury Securities Dealer System (DSPW) introduced by the MoF. The market is managed by the CeTO in close partnership with the dealer community and institutions directly involved in Treasury securities trading. The CeTO Management Board hopes that within 2–3 years the platform will capture a daily trading turnover of 50–60% of current trading on the interbank market. The Board is also planning to introduce new instruments to trading such as futures-type futures and repo transactions (see KDPW, 2002a).

Only those banks designated as Treasury Securities Dealers, i.e., primary dealers, can use the platform. As of 2003, the following banks have primary dealer status:

- ABN AMRO Bank (Polska) SA
- Bank Handlowy w Warszawie SA
- Bank Pekao SA
- Bank Zachodni WBK SA
- BIG Bank Gdański SA
- BPH PBK SA
- BRE Bank SA
- Deutsche Bank Polska SA
- ING Bank Śląski SA
- Kredyt Bank SA
- PKO Bank Polski SA
- Societe Generale SA Oddział w Polsce.

The following candidates are to be granted primary dealer status in 2004:

- Bank Amerykański w Polsce SA
- Bank Gospodarki Żywnościowej SA
- BNP Paribas Bank Polska SA
- Invest-Bank SA
- Raiffeisen Bank Polska SA
- Westdeutsche Landesbank Polska SA.

On the platform, listing takes place in continuous trading. The NDS carries out settlement for securities. For the settlement of each transaction, a fixed fee of PLN 50 has been set, which compares favorably with the PLN 65 fee for settlements in the nonregulated interbank market. For fixed-rate securities, informational prices are generated by way of fixing (calculating the average bid and ask offers with the lowest spread), which allows institutional investors to calculate the price of their Treasury portfolios. The CeTO publishes daily fixing of prices and yields of benchmark bonds at around 3:30 p.m. local time following a several-minute fixing session. The trading session lasts between 9:00 a.m. and 4:00 p.m. Data is posted on the CeTO website and on the Reuters service.

19.4   THE POLISH TREASURY MARKET

19.4.1   Background

The size of the Polish Treasury market relative to GDP remains small compared to most developed markets. This owes to a relatively low public debt burden, to some extent due to the partial write-off of external debt by the London Club and the Paris Club in 1994, and to the high (inherited) share of foreign currency denominated debt in total public debt. By one crucial measure, the market is still not a mature one (see Table 19.4). At 6%, returns on 5-year Treasury bonds far surpass those of the EU or the United States. With the country joining the EU in 2004 and the EMU (Economic and Monetary Union) before the end of the decade, Polish Treasuries have now become a classic convergence play, however, a market opportunity that hasn't happened since the second half of the 1990s, when the countries of Southern Europe were preparing for the euro.

In the market, instruments are distinguished as to whether they are privately or publicly placed. Private placements, where the maximum number of investors does not exceed 300, were made in the first half of the 1990s and were linked to (i) the recapitalization of commercial

Table 19.4   Polish government bond yields (Wednesday, February 12, 2003)

Yield on government securities	Coupon (%)	Average yield	Date of last tender
13 weeks	0.00	6.053	13/01/2003
26 weeks	0.00	6.012	10/02/2003
52 weeks	0.00	5.917	10/02/2003
2 years	0.00	5.764	12/12/2002
5 years	5.75	5.559	24/06/2003
10 years	5.00	5.614	24/10/2003
20 years	5.75	6.219	23/09/2002

Source: National Bank of Poland.

banks; (ii) the securitization of zloty-denominated NBP loans to the central government; and (iii) the conversion of foreign currency denominated government bonds held by the central bank into zloty-denominated ones. Initially, privately placed bonds were mostly nonmarketable; however most of them have now been transformed into marketable bonds.

Publicly issued bonds may be both marketable and nonmarketable. Non marketable retail bonds are savings bonds directly aimed at households, which were first issued in 1999. Marketable securities include Treasury bills and bonds, and are chiefly issued to finance budget deficits. Trading structure and liquidity in the secondary market varies with the type of security traded. The volume of bonds has been increasingly outstripping that of Treasury bills, which reflects the success of financial stabilization and disinflation. Another sign of development is the growing share of fixed-rate bonds. The NBP also issues bills, limited to domestic institutional investors in open-market operations, as part of its monetary policy.

19.4.2   Types of Instruments

(A) *Treasury bills*: This category refers to discounted or zero-coupon bills with maturities less than 1 year. At present, bills are issued with maturities of 13, 26, and 52 weeks. They are denominated in zloty and issued as registered securities. Auctions are held on the first business day of each week, usually Monday. They are actively traded over the counter, although market liquidity is declining as the size of the market shrinks, and more and more bills are held by the domestic nonbanking sector that treats them as an investment rather than a trading instrument. Transactions register and their settlement are handled by the NBP Central Registry of Treasury bills (CRTB).

(B) *Two-year zero-coupon bonds (OK)*: These bonds carry zero coupons, and were first issued in October 1999 as a replacement for the just-finished 12% two-year Treasury bond series (AS). They are sold at competitive auctions held monthly.

(C) *Three-year floating-rate bonds (TZ and TP)*: This category includes 3-year floating-rate bonds, which are split into TZ and TP bonds depending on the method of issuance. TZs are sold through subscription and public sale through a retail network of customer service outlets operated by the issue agent, the Central Brokerage House (CDM) Pekao. TPs, sold at competitive auctions, were discontinued in 2000 because of low demand and high service costs. Interest, which is paid quarterly, is set on the basis of the arithmetic mean of the weighted average yield on the last four 13-week Treasury bills auctioned prior to the start of the interest accrual period, times a ratio.

(D) *Five-year fixed-coupon bonds (PS/OS)*: The MoF began issuing fixed-coupon bonds in January 1994. The first PS series was issued in October 1999 as a replacement for the 5-year OS series, with identical terms and conditions except for the lower coupon. They are auctioned once a month. The interest, paid annually except the first interest period, is 8.5%. Orders are executed in round lots through continuous trading on the WSE. If the bonds are not sold immediately, they are reoffered in subsequent years, therefore with maturities of 4–2 years. The bonds can be replaced when requested by the MoF.

(E) *Ten-year fixed-coupon bonds (DS)*: These bonds carry fixed coupons, and were first issued in May 1999. The issuance of the 10-year DS series reflected a more stable economic situation and lower inflation in Poland. The bonds are auctioned each second month and pay an annual coupon of 6%.

(F) *Ten-year floating-rate bonds (DZ)*: These floating-rate bonds were first issued in December 1995 to lengthen the term structure of Polish debt and allow institutional investors such as insurance companies and pension funds to diversify their portfolios. The bonds are auctioned each second month and pay an annual coupon. The coupon rate, reset annually, is the weighted average yield of 52-week Treasury bills in the 2 months prior to the first month of a particular interest period plus 100 basis points.

(G) *Twenty-year fixed-coupon bonds (WS)*: These fixed-coupon bonds – the longest in Eastern Europe – were first issued in April 2002. It is yet unknown how often auctions will be held in the future, but it has been confirmed that the offered amount will rise. The bonds pay an annual coupon of 5.75%. Secondary market trading has been scarce because of low liquidity and the majority of the primary offer being sold to long term institutional investors.

(H) *Savings bonds*: These interest-bearing bonds, first issued in 1999, are aimed directly at Polish households, and are therefore nonmarketable. They are sold through retail points of sale; the issue agent is CDM Pekao. Available instruments include 2-year fixed-rate (DOS) and 4-year indexed (COI) bonds. All bonds feature a put option.

(I) *NBP bills*: These discounted short term instruments are issued by the NBP and used in the implementation of monetary policy. The regular maturity is 28 days, with the minimum yield being the official NBP reference rate. They are available only to domestic banks through auctions held each Friday. Large denominations limit them to large institutional investors; foreign investors are not allowed to purchase them. Issuance volumes depend on the forecast of excess liquidity of the commercial banking sector in Poland. Market liquidity is increasing, contrary to Treasury bills.

(J) *Nonmarketable Treasury bonds*: In the 1990s, several special or dedicated Treasury bonds were issued to achieve some specific goals of the government such as (i) securitization of part of government debt; (ii) conversion of foreign debt into domestic debt; and (iii) undertaking new liabilities outside the financial market. Most of the issues, typically characterized by the virtual nonexistence of the primary and secondary markets, were absorbed by the NBP and domestic commercial banks. A large share of these instruments has now been converted into marketable fixed-rate Treasuries.

(K) *Nonmarketable NBP bonds*: These instruments were issued in September 1999 to absorb liquidity from banks that was released after the NBP lowered the mandatory reserve requirement. The bonds had initial maturities between 6 and 10 years and are indexed to the inflation rate.

19.4.3 Auction Process

All Treasury securities are issued in dematerialized form. Auctions are organized by the NBP, the issue agent of the MoF, although the Ministry may organize additional auctions depending on the needs of the government. The auctions are conducted in the American system, whereby buyers pay the price they offered if it is above the accepted minimum price. The settlement agent is the NDS. The MoF reserves the right to buy back the securities through an auction at any time after issue.

According to the Act on Public Finance, the Finance Minister determines the general conditions of the issues in an ordinance, while detailed conditions are presented in the issue letters, published in the nationwide press and on the website of the Ministry. The timetables of issues cover 12 months; however, only the dates of the auctions and types of securities offered for sale are published. The announcement of a forthcoming auction, with the size of the issue, is published in the daily newspaper Rzeczpospolita 2 days before the auction date, and in the Reuters service (page PLMINFIN).

(i) Treasury bills: The eligible direct participants of auctions are the entities that purchased at least 0.2% of all bills sold in the primary market in the last quarter. Bids are submitted to the NBP by 11 a.m. local time on the auction day. The official announcement is made on the auction day. Payment for bills purchased and redemption of maturing bills are usually effected on the second day after the auction through banks' current accounts maintained by the NBP Payment System Department.

(ii) Treasury bonds: Only direct participants of the NDS are eligible for participation at auctions. The characteristics and offer details, including the auction dates, are provided in issuing letters issued by the MoF and published in national newspapers, the MoF website, and in the Reuters bulletins. The official announcement is made on the next day after the auction, at the latest. Settlements in cash and in securities occurs directly through the NDS.

In 2001, the MoF introduced a new debt management tool, the bond switching auctions. The switching operation is conducted through repurchasing of the bonds of a given series before maturity. In return for bonds, which are being repurchased, investors receive bonds of benchmark issues, which increase the liquidity of the market.

19.4.4   Market Conventions

The market convention is for trade plus 2 (T+2) settlement for all government securities, with the value date the same as the settlement date. The Polish holiday calendar is employed and yield is calculated on the Polish simple yield method. The yield on Treasury and NBP bills as well as 3-year floating-rate bonds is calculated on a 360-day basis; 2-year zero-coupon bonds employ a 365-day basis; and 10-year floating-rate and all fixed-rate bonds employ an actual basis. There is an intention to move to T+1 settlement.

19.4.5   Repo/Reverse Repo and Sell-Buy-Backs/Buy-Sell-Backs (SBB/BSB)

Banks chiefly use Treasury bills and NBP bills for these types of operations; Treasury bonds are rarely used for this purpose owing to the high costs associated with depository system commissions. Transactions employing NBP bills are used for liquidity management by banks, while operations with nonbanking entities aim at attracting collateralized deposits. The use of SBB is a way of avoiding the obligatory reserve system. Some 80–90% of operations have 10 days or less to maturity. There is no information on the number of participants and the share of nonresident participants. Interest rates on these types of operations are generally 100 basis points below WIBOR (see Bednarski and Osinski, 2002).

19.4.6   Benchmarks

The MoF is committed to creating large, standardized benchmark issues at key maturities along the yield curve, and has therefore decided that the benchmark issues must exceed PLN 2.5 billion in nominal value. Those issues that do not meet these criteria may also obtain the benchmark status but market participants attribute particular importance to them (e.g., because of the high probability that they will have large issues in the future).

The first issue, which could be considered as benchmark, was an issue of 10-year fixed-rate bonds, in 1999. Since then, the average value of individual issues has increased from PLN 1.2 billion to more than PLN 5 billion in 2003. The most liquid issues are the 2-year

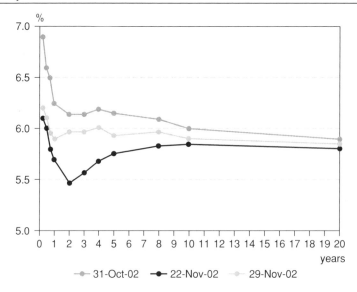

Figure 19.5   Benchmark yield curve.
Source: Bank Zachodni WBK.

zero-coupon and 5-year fixed-rate bonds. The issuance of 10- and 20-year bonds, essential to extend and consolidate the benchmark, has been insufficient, however, with further improvement depending on market development, interest rates, and investor demand.

Bank Zachodni WBK (2002) provides an example of the construction of the Polish benchmark yield curve in Figure 19.5. The bonds included in the yield curve are made up of 13-, 26-, and 52-week Treasury bills and 2-, 5-, 10-, and 20-year Treasury bonds, selected on the basis of maturity. The instruments for periods less than 3 months are the respective deposit rates.

19.5   THE NONGOVERNMENT BOND MARKET

19.5.1   Introduction

The Polish nongovernment debt market (see Table 19.5) is still at an early stage of development despite displaying dynamic growth since the mid-1990s. The market remains chiefly used for short term funding by both banks and nonfinancial corporations by way of CP issues, which now amount to almost a quarter of short term banking loans to the corporate sector. Corporate bonds, municipal bonds, mortgage bonds, and asset-backed securities (ABSs) are of much lesser importance, which partly owes to falling interest rates and higher investor demand for shorter term instruments, the latter attributable to the lack of a liquid secondary market and the limited role of the domestic institutional investor base.

19.5.2   Commercial Paper

Commercial paper, which constitutes a competitive instrument to short term bank loans, has been issued since 1992. As of March 2002, some 300 corporations and 10 banks were tapping

Table 19.5   Nongovernment debt market in 1997–2002 (end of period)

	1997	1998	1999	2000	2001	2002
Commercial paper						
Debt value (million PLN)	2 544.2	5 610.7	6 657.8	10 931.0	12 719.8	11 543.5
Dynamics (annual)		120.5%	18.7%	64.2%	16.4%	−9.2%
Number of issuers	113	176	229	328	309	272
Corporate bonds including banks (over 365 days maturity)						
Debt value (million PLN)	563.5	1 378.8	1 830.9	2 492.8	3 052.4	6 074.3
Dynamics (annual)		144.7%	32.8%	36.2%	22.4%	99.0%
Number of issuers	19	47	46	52	56	59
Municipal bonds (over 365 days maturity)						
Debt value (million PLN)	296.9	526.1	653.6	859.6	1 628.6	2 218.8
Dynamics (annual)		77.2%	24.2%	31.5%	89.5%	36.2%
Number of issuers	28	40	53	89	149	192
Total						
Debt value (million PLN)	3 404.6	7 515.6	9 142.3	14 283.4	17 400.8	19 836.6
Dynamics (annual)		120.7%	21.6%	56.2%	21.8%	14.0%

Source: Fitch Polska S.A.

the market. In terms of value, the single largest issuer is the banking sector, although nonbank financial institutions such as leasing companies are also present. The main nonfinancial corporate issuers operate in the IT and telecommunications, construction, and energy sectors. The instruments may be issued both as bearer and registered securities, and may carry coupons. Maturities range from 7 to 364 days, although they tend to be 3 months or less. Yields are calculated on a 360-day basis.

A peculiarity of the market is that issues are distributed on a private placement basis, whereby they are offered to less than 300 investors, because of the high costs of public issuance and the long procedures of public trading. Individual issue sizes are consequently limited: only three issues reached an upper limit of PLN 1 billion in 2002, and another two reached PLN 500 million. The issues are carried out through lead manager banks that also play the role of depositories, settlement agents, and underwriters. Regrettably, they tend to squeeze out relatively high margins, which lowers the achievable yield for investors (National Bank of Poland, 2002).

Typically, the rationale behind lead managers handling the register of investors is attributable to a major deficiency of the market: the absence of a centralized depository and settlement system. Although the Act on Public Trading in Securities allows the NDS to manage nongovernment securities, no CP has been registered with it so far because of high-related costs and complex registration procedures. The fragmentation of the market is also strengthened by the fact that there is no uniform legal basis for the issuance of CP as yet: instruments may be issued under the Bond Act, the Civil Code as well as the Act on Bills of Exchange. Coincidentally, the majority of new issues are now executed under the Bond Act because of the substantial amendments made to the Act in 2000, as well as legal limits of some institutional investors in purchasing CP issued under other laws.

The dominant groups among investors are nonfinancial corporations and banks, the latter often being the lead managers. An increasing share is now accommodated by investment funds and domestic insurance companies. The participation of foreign investors is negligible, reflecting both restrictions contained in the Foreign Exchange Act on nonresident holdings and the illiquidity of the secondary market. The secondary market is very fragmented, and liquidity is indeed scarce, although the NBP does not have exact statistical data on the market turnover. The current scope of trading is limited in practice to transactions executed between lead managers and their clients.

19.5.3   Corporate Bonds

Corporate bonds are issued under the Bond Act. They may be fixed or floating rate; floating interest is typically defined as WIBOR or Treasury yield plus margin. Maturities vary from 2 to 10 years. The organization of the market, with respect to both primary and secondary trading, is the same as that of the CP market.

There are varying estimates as to the outstanding amount of bonds. (Data obtained by Fitch Polska and the NBP differ.) It is certain, however, that the size of the market remains small compared to the Treasury and CP markets, owing to various factors including high issuance costs, the absence of a well-developed institutional investor base as well as some legal provisions. The amendment of the Bond Act in 2000 nonetheless appears to have brought a major breakthrough in the market: according to Fitch (2002), the value of debt outstanding increased from PLN 2.5 billion in 2000 to PLN 6.1 billion in 2002.

As in the case of CP, most corporate bonds are privately placed. The first public issue was launched in February 2000, but met negligible interest. The only public issues of 2001–2002 were the 10- and 15-year zero-coupon bond issues launched by the European Investment Bank (EIB), a supranational organization with triple-A ratings. The EIB, which issues under a debt program worth PLN 3 billlion, is also the first nonresident issuer in the market.

Nonfinancial corporations and banks again hold the majority of issues, although the share of insurance companies has been increasing rapidly in recent years. Foreign investors have historically been fairly active in the market, although their share has now declined substantially to around 15%. Turnover in the secondary market is relatively small, which forces investors to treat their holdings as long term investment. Lead manager banks have now taken over the obligation to quote bid and ask prices for certain issue series; however, in practice such quotations are conducted only for information purposes. The development of the secondary market is also limited by a tax imposed on retail investors.

19.5.4   Municipal Bonds

Municipal bonds are issued under the provisions of the Bond Act by nearly 200 municipalities and counties (poviats) as well as 2 voivodships. The majority of bonds are issued in the third and fourth quarters of the year because of the budgetary planning process. They usually carry floating-rate coupons with the interest rate indexed to the yield on 52-week Treasury bills. Interest is payable annually. Maturities vary from 1 to 5 years.

Municipal bonds comprise a relatively small segment of the debt market. Growth has been nonetheless dynamic, with the outstanding amount increasing, according to data obtained from Fitch Polska, from PLN 860 million in 2000 to PLN 2.2 billion in 2002. The strong interest owes as much to the aggravation of the central government's recent budgetary problems as to the low debt servicing costs (up to 2 percentage points less than on bank loans) and the flexibility of the various conditions. The introduction of revenue bonds in the amended Bond Act has also encouraged issuance, since these instruments are not included in the regulatory debt limit for municipalities as defined in the Public Finances Act.

Because of the small issue sizes and the high costs of public placement, all issues, with the exception of the town of Ostrow Wielkopolski, are privately placed, and the lead managers organize the market. Around 20 banks currently service the market. In practice, there is no secondary market for these instruments. The quotations are therefore mostly published for informative purposes only, without conducting actual transactions. The breakdown of investors is similar to that in the corporate bond market.

19.5.5 Pfandbrief-Style Mortgage Bonds

The legal basis for the issue of mortgage bonds is the Act on Mortgage Bonds and Mortgage Banks of August 29, 1997. They are registered or bearer securities backed by receivables of a mortgage bank, and may be denominated in Polish zloty as well as foreign currencies. The bonds may be issued only by mortgage banks, established and operated under the provisions of the above Act. Those banks that own mortgage banks organize the issues; the lead manager bank performs the multiple functions of dealer, payment agent, and custodian. The bonds are usually held until maturity by domestic banks, and consequently have no secondary market.

As in mid-2003, three banks have been licensed to conduct mortgage-banking operations: HypoVereinsbank Mortgage Bank SA, Rheinhyp-BRE Mortgage Bank SA, and Slaski Mortgage Bank SA. Of these, Rheinhyp-BRE was the first to issue mortgage bonds in the total amount of PLN 30 million, with 3- and 4-year maturities, although HypoVereinsbank has also launched an issue. These bonds are denominated in zloty, US dollar, and euro, and rated by Fitch Polska.

Despite the recent activity, there remain notable obstacles to market development. Issuance is discouraged by various statutory limitations, including the following: (i) the amount of a single mortgage credit cannot exceed 80% of the value of the underlying real estate; (ii) additional liabilities of mortgage banks cannot exceed 200% of the value of their own funds; and (iii) mortgage bonds cannot be backed by municipal receivables. A further impediment is the time-consuming nature of related procedures. For example, the funds that are to be raised cannot be put at the disposal of the borrower before the mortgage is established.

19.5.6 Asset-Backed Securities and Mortgage-Backed Securities

By spring 2003, only two asset-backed issues have been completed in Poland, both by exporter Coface in 1998. The market is expected to grow sharply in the near future, however, with consecutive finance ministers considering the securitization of lottery revenues, commercial mortgages, and fees from telecommunications licenses. A notable attempt will be that of the state-owned Bank Gospodarstwa Krajowego (BGK), which, as part of a broader plan by the government to replace run-down housing, is considering the issuance of PLN 2 billion of mortgage-backed securities. Even more important, Polskie Sieci Elektroenergetyczne, the state-owned company that operates Poland's power grid, is planning to sell up to PLN $8 billion of securities backed by special fees on electricity bills. Fitch Polska also anticipates the development of bank asset securitization. International Finance Corp., the commercial lending arm of the World Bank, has already indicated to market players that it would contemplate investing in, or guaranteeing, transactions by Polish issuers.

To help facilitate the planned deals, the Polish Bank Association recently formed a committee to prepare those legislative changes, to be passed in 2003, that would specifically allow securitizations by public and private issuers. Securitization is not expressly permitted under existing law, and strict disclosure requirements further complicate the process for would-be issuers. Aside from legal problems, the preparation of securitization transactions remains time consuming.

19.6 CONCLUSION

Poland's debt market, which has now graduated from the emerging markets class, is the largest and most liquid in Central and Eastern Europe. However, while development has been impressive, the market is far from European levels in terms of product variety, soundness, and cost, and remains small in both relative and absolute terms. The nongovernment segment of the market remains especially limited in scale and scope despite its dynamic growth since 1997, and continues to be used mainly for the issuance of short term CP.

The main defects of the market remain infrastructural and cost-related. Chief among these is the absence of a liquid secondary market, whose establishment is hindered by most domestic debt issues being privately placed. In light of this, the government has now adopted a medium term strategy for market development, and it is hoped that the rapid expansion of institutional investors as well as recent changes in the market infrastructure will only assist their efforts. Further incentives are nonetheless necessary to increase the depth and liquidity of the market, particularly as regards the firmer establishment of a benchmark yield curve and the promotion of secondary market making. This is all the more pivotal, because Poland, with its population of 39 million and substantial potential for growth, is widely regarded as a lucrative long term market, where foreign strategic investors, mostly banks and insurance companies, must be facilitated in exploring business opportunities.

REFERENCES

Bank Zachodni WBK (2002, December). MACROscope: Polish Economy and Financial Markets.

Bednarski, P. and J. Osiński (2002). Financial Sector Issues in Poland. In: Thimann, C., ed., *Financial Sectors in EU Accession Countries*. Frankfurt: European Central Bank, pp. 171–88.

Fitch Ratings (2002). Polish Non-Government Debt Market. Quarterly Summary (various issues).

IMF (2003, June). Republic of Poland: Staff Report for the 2002 Article IV Consultation. IMF Country Report No. 03/137.

KDPW (2002a). Settlement by KDPW of the CeTO Electronic Treasury Securities Market: Hoping for a Growth in Trading. *KDPW Newsletter* **2**(7): 6.

KDPW (2002b). The Polish Debt Securities Market. *KDPW Newsletter* **1**(6): 7–8.

National Bank of Poland (2002). Financial Market in Poland 1998–2001. Report.

Polish Ministry of Finance (2001). Annual Report 2001. Public Debt.

Polish Ministry of Finance (2002, September 28). The Public Finance Sector Debt Management Strategy in the Years 2003–05. Warsaw.

Stosio, A. and N. Rose (2001, October 30). Changes to the Polish Bond Act. Will the Market Benefit? *GT News*.

Warsaw Stock Exchange (2002). Fact Book 2001.

20

Portugal

PETER G. SZILAGYI

20.1 INTRODUCTION

Portugal is a European Union (EU) success story of the 1990s, with a politically and economically isolated nation transformed into a ful-fledged member of the European and world community. The country was admitted to the EU in 1986, together with Spain, in recognition of its successful transition from authoritarian rule to parliamentary democracy in 1974–1976 and its subsequent macroeconomic transformation. EU membership has produced robust economic growth for the best part of the past decade and a half through increased trade ties with other Member States and an inflow of structural adjustment funds. As a result, the country's gross domestic product (GDP) per capita on a purchasing power parity basis rose from 51% of the EU average in 1985 to 78% in early 2002.

The gradual closing of Portugal's income gap relative to more mainstream European states has been a result of the ambitious privatization and modernization policies of successive governments, which have continuingly pursued greater integration with the EU. With economic policy in the 1990s focused on meeting the criteria for entry into the Economic and Monetary Union (EMU), the country did a credible job of correcting many economic imbalances and undertaking structural reforms, and adopted the euro at its launch in 1999. These efforts were aided by a unanimously strong commitment to European integration by all of the country's major political forces.

Regrettably, the fulfillment of the Maastricht criteria created a sense of contentment among policymakers, and once the single currency was introduced, the Socialist (PS) government of the time failed to exercise fiscal constraint. In March 2002, the new center-right cabinet led by Prime Minister Durao Barroso and his Social Democrats (PSD) inherited a budget that was in breach of the 3% deficit ceiling set out by Stability and Growth Pact, adopted by the EU Council of Ministers to safeguard the stability of the euro. This could theoretically have led to EU sanctions against Portugal including fines of up to 0.5% of GDP and/or a denial of access to the EU's "cohesion" funds.

The high budget deficit has all but eased the recent consumption-led overheating of the economy, a result of entry-related declines in interest rates. Excess demand caused the country's inflation rate to grow from an average 2.7% during 1998–2000 to 4.4% in 2001 and a further 3.6% in 2002. Meanwhile, in the 11 years to 2001 the level of debt held by Portuguese households increased from less than 20% of disposable income to more than 100%. The country has also been running a chronically large current account deficit at 7–10% per annum for 4 years in a row now.

Altogether, the main objective of government policy relates to restoring order in the public finances while reducing the external deficit. The need for fiscal constraint is all the more acute,

European Fixed Income Markets: Money, Bond and Interest Rate Derivatives. Edited by J.A. Batten,
T.A. Fetherston and P.G. Szilagyi. © 2004 John Wiley & Sons, Ltd. ISBN 0-470-85053-1

Table 20.1   Key economic indicators in Portugal

	1998	1999	2000	2001
GDP per head (US$ at purchasing power parity)	16 145	16 997	17 983	18 580
GDP (% real change per annum)	4.55	3.46	3.54	1.66
Government consumption (% of GDP)	18.95	19.68	20.33	20.5
Budget balance (% of GDP)	−2.3	−2.27	−1.61	−4.1
Consumer prices (% change per annum; average)	2.76	2.34	2.87	4.35
Public debt (% of GDP)	54.76	54.21	53.49	54.9
Labor costs per hour (US$)	5.48	5.35	4.75	5.22
Recorded unemployment (%)	4.98	4.38	4	4.05
Current-account balance (% of GDP)	−6.97	−8.5	−10.34	−9.17
Trade balance (% of GDP)	−10.8	−11.9	−13.1	−12.0
Foreign-exchange reserves (billion US$)	15	8	8	9

Source: Economist Intelligence Unit. © European Communities, 1995–2003. Reproduced with permission.

because the Bank of Portugal's GDP growth estimate is negative for 2003 and has now been lowered to between 0.5% and 2.5% for 2004, a level that is still thought to be unrealistically optimistic by the Economist Intelligence Unit (EIU). This calls for the urgent undertaking of structural reforms in several areas, which affect the central budget, including health care services, education, and social security.

In the meantime, the government must also accelerate productivity growth in the economy to underpin the closing of Portugal's income gap against the rest of the EU. Notably, the agricultural sector has been losing its competitive advantage to more efficient producers in countries such as Spain and France, while it continues to constitute 12.1% of employment but only 3.3% of GDP. And, despite the markedly low labor costs, foreign industrial investment has also slowed in recent years because of the emergence of alternative low-cost manufacturing locations in Central and Eastern Europe. Other key economic data is provided in Table 20.1.

20.2   RECENT HISTORY AND STRUCTURE OF THE PORTUGUESE BOND MARKET

As at August 2002, the total outstanding amount in Portugal's bond market was €99.6 billion, equal to 80% of the country's GDP (see Table 20.2). This is relatively low compared with other markets within the Euro area where the aggregate amount of outstanding euro-denominated instruments issued by residents reach about 110%. The Portuguese market has nonetheless come a long way in the past two decades. At the beginning of the 1980s, the country's financial system was still being affected by the consequences of the 1974 revolution and by the direct controls that had been introduced to deal with the two payment crises of the 1970s and early 1980s. The foundations of an institutional investor base were not laid until 1983 when the banking and insurance sectors were finally reopened to private initiative. The bond market began to gain real depth only in the early 1990s on the back of the privatization process of 1989, which greatly enhanced competition and stimulated investors' portfolio diversification. The wave of reforms accelerated further because of the prospect of participating in the European Single Market in 1992. New issuance reached a critical mass of nearly €5 billion in 1995. In the remainder of the decade, the main structural changes were directed toward the harmonization of procedures and regulations within the EU and, more specifically, the future Euro area.

Table 20.2 Euro-denominated debt securities by country of residence (in billion euro)

August 2002	Total	General government		Monetary financial institutions		Nonmonetary financial corporations		Nonfinancial corporations	
		Short term	Long term	Short term	Long term	Short term	Long term	Short term	Long term
Euro area	7368.6	332.2	3495.7	266	2395.7	4.4	420.1	86.4	368.2
Portugal (% of Euro area)	99.6 (1.4%)	1 (0.3%)	56.3 (1.6%)	0.1 (0.0%)	25.4 (1.1%)	0.3 (6.8%)	2 (0.5%)	8.3 (9.6%)	6.4 (1.7%)
Austria	207.5	1	109.8	2.1	86.8	0	3.5	0	4.3
Spain	415.1	36.1	269.3	11.4	47.6	1.1	33.1	3.5	12.8
Greece	116.7	1.9	114.3	0.2	0.1	0	0	0	0.1

Source: European Central Bank Securities Statistics. Copyright © European Central Bank, Frankfurt am Main, Germany. Reproduced with permission.

For the market, like other smaller European markets, the euro has proved to be a double-sided coin. The convergence of interest rates to the Euro area level and the elimination of currency risk enhanced its international integration, in particular with the European markets. Government debt issued in the single currency has pulled in welcome nonresident investors attracted by the rapidly narrowing but still favorably high spreads of Portuguese paper over comparable German or French issues. Meanwhile, the Public Debt Management Institute (IGCP, Instituto de Gestão Crédito Público) has completely revamped its debt management operations in line with EU requirements, which has helped Portugal face up to increased competition as a government bond player on a pan-European level. The market has enjoyed additional recognition with the inclusion of Portuguese public debt in all major world bond indices including the JP Morgan Index and the World Government Bond Index (WGBI) of Solomon Brothers.

Regrettably, the market's nongovernment segment has failed to go through such transformation. The domestic funds that once sustained the market have now diversified into other Euro area markets, which offer better trade-off between risk, liquidity, and pricing and, as opposed to Portuguese private debt, are not subject to Portugal's 20% withholding tax. Bond issuance by domestic corporations has promptly eclipsed with only one public offering since August 1999, with corporate treasuries resorting to the more liquid mainstream markets in Europe, or issuing commercial paper (CP) and rolling them over. In a very similar fashion, activity in the Caravela market intended for nonresidents has also collapsed, because the introduction of the euro has eliminated the only major attraction of the market: the Portuguese escudo. As a result, the nongovernment bond market is now primarily used by the large local financial groups, which regularly issue debt as a means of financing their current activities. In particular, there has been considerable growth in the structured finance market, which owes to the fact that the balance sheets of banks are growing very fast, creating strong demand for securitization.

In light of the above developments in the nongovernment market, the Securities Market Commission (CMVM, Comissão do Mercado de Valores Mobiliários, 2001) has undertaken concerted efforts to identify the factors that detract from the market's competitiveness. Naturally, the Commission recognizes that the creation of incentives for issuance by corporate borrowers is indispensable. Nonetheless, unless the government moves on the withholding tax issue, the market will inevitably fail to realize its full potential. This is however unlikely before a resolution of the complex issue of a pan-European withholding tax, to which the United Kingdom has been strongly opposing.

20.3   MARKET PARTICIPANTS AND STRUCTURE

20.3.1   Regulators

The legal framework of the Portuguese securities market was created by the Securities Market Code (Cód do Mercado de Valores Mobiliários), which was approved by Decree-Law No. 142-A/91 of 10th of April and amended by Decree-Law No. 473/99 of 8th of November. Today, the supervision of the market and the coordination of the activities of its agents is the duty of the Minister of Finance, in accordance with the economic and social policy of the government. The various agents are, however, also subject to the prudential supervision, according to the situation at hand, of the Bank of Portugal, which has a special supervisory power over money market and currency instruments, and the CMVM.

20.3.1.1   Ministry of Finance

The role of the Ministry of Finance is to engage in Portugal's fiscal and economic management in accordance with the economic and social policy defined by the Parliament and the government as well as the competent bodies of the European Community. The Ministry manages the budget and state finances, monetary funds, and national debts, and has a regulatory role in the domain of the financial system. It is charged with tasks in the following areas:

- Monetary, banking, and foreign exchange systems; financial relationships with foreign countries;
- System of taxes, contributions, duties, customs-duties, and other types of public income;
- Systems of insurance, securities, funds, and other financial organizations;
- System of gaming activities;
- Public expenditure system and the budget, including public procurement and the system of accountancy, auditing, and financial operation, as well as joint tasks of the country's administrative bodies and governmental services in conducting financial and accountancy services.

Created by two departments of the Ministry in 1996, the IGCP is now responsible for the management of the government debt and the execution of the government borrowing program, in accordance with the Public Debt Law and the guidelines defined by the Ministry. The Minister of Finance is empowered to define specific guidelines to be followed by the IGCP in the execution of the financing policy and in the completion of other transactions concerning the buyback of securities and the active management of the debt portfolio.

The responsibilities of the Ministry with respect to the securities market are set out in the Securities Market Code and include:

- establishing policies relating to the securities markets and, generally, to matters regulated by the Code and complementary law;
- exercising, in relation to the CMVM, the administrative supervision conferred by the legal framework;
- coordinating supervision and regulation of securities, when the competence belongs to more than one public entity.

The Ministry also sets up the general framework regarding securities and derivatives contracts upon commodities, services, currency, money market instruments, or any other transactions not yet comprised in the Securities Code.

The National Securities Market Council is an advisory body of the Ministry, integrated in the Supreme Finance Council. The Council is convened by the Minister of Finance and advises on (i) general governmental policies regarding the securities market or significant securities market matters; (ii) legal provisions related to the securities market; and (iii) the situation and evolution of the securities market.

20.3.1.2   Bank of Portugal (Banco de Portugal)

The Bank of Portugal is an integral part of European System of Central Banks (ESCB), which is composed of the European Central Bank (ECB) and the national central banks of all 15 EU Member States. The Bank is also a member of the Eurosystem, which comprises the ECB and the central banks of the 12 EU Member States, which have joined the EMU.

As a member of the Eurosystem, the Bank's sovereignty has been transferred to the ECB in a number of fields. Within the scope of its participation in the ESCB, the Bank now manages the following activities:

- Definition and implementation of the monetary policy of the Euro area;
- Conduction of foreign exchange operations consistent with the provisions of Article 109 of the Treaty on European Union;
- Holding and management of official reserves of the Member States;
- Promotion of the smooth operation of payment systems in the Euro area.

In addition, the Bank's Organic Law stipulates the performance of the following functions:

- *Issuance and management of banknotes upon authorization by the ECB.*
- *Regulation, supervision, and promotion of the smooth operation of payment systems, and provision of payment and settlement services.* Interbank and securities transactions are settled by transferring funds across the deposit accounts held by each financial institution at the Bank. Large interbank payments are facilitated by a real-time gross settlement (RTGS) system named SPGT (Large-Value Payment System). The SPGT is part of the EMU gross settlement system TARGET (Trans-European Real-Time Gross Settlement Express Transfer), mainly intended to carry out the operations associated with the single monetary policy.
- *Supervision of credit institutions and financial companies.* This occurs by controlling compliance with the rules set forth, issuing recommendations for the correction of any deviations, sanctioning any breaches should they occur, and taking extraordinary measures of reorganization.
- *Function as the lender of last resort.* When a financial institution becomes insolvent and this is likely to pose a threat to the financial system, the Bank may provide emergency liquidity to prevent financial disorder.
- *International activities.* The Bank participates in several international organizations and acts as intermediary in Portugal's international monetary relations. The Bank has developed intensive cooperation with other central banks, mainly of the Portuguese-Speaking African Countries (PALOP), and is a depository in the relationship between the government and the Inter-American Development Bank (IDB), the African Development Bank (ADB), and the African Development Fund (ADF).
- *Collection and compilation of statistics within the scope of the Bank's cooperation with the ECB.*
- *Further to the above activities, the Bank is also engaged in advising the government in the economic and financial matters.*

20.3.1.3 Securities Market Commission (CMVM)

The CMVM, subject to the supervision of the Ministry of Finance, is a public agency independent at both administrative and financial levels owning its own assets. It is guided by three strategic goals: (i) investor protection; (ii) the guarantee of market integrity and transparency; and (iii) the promotion of securities markets development. To that extent, the Commission manages the following tasks:

- *Supervision of the securities markets.* The Commission monitors the activity of those operating within the securities markets, be it from a prudential standpoint or a behavioral stance.

- *Market regulation.* The Commission regulates the public offers of securities and the activity of all market operators, and in general all matters pertaining to the securities markets and the activity of the respective operators. It may issue recommendations as well as general opinions over relevant issues.
- *Cooperation.* The Commission cooperates with other national authorities with supervision and regulatory responsibilities within the financial system, including the Bank of Portugal and the Portuguese Insurance Institute (Instituto de Seguros de Portugal). It also cooperates with the authorities of other states and participates in international organizations including the International Organization of Securities Commissions (IOSCO) and the Committee of European Securities Regulators (CESR).
- *Support on policy decisions.* The Commission supports the government and the Ministry of Finance, on request or on its own initiative, in policy decisions governing securities, markets, and respective operators.

20.3.2   Categories of Investors

As a result of the IGCP's market-oriented financing strategy, a widening and greater geographical diversification of investors has been observed in the Portuguese government bond market. Since the start of EMU in 1999, 75–80% of new OT (Obrigacoes de Tesouro) issues have been placed through foreign primary dealers each year. It is estimated that more than two thirds of tradable Portuguese government debt is now held by nonresidents, chiefly EMU-based investors, which is one of the highest percentages in the EU. In the secondary market, according to data reported by primary dealers, more than 70% of the turnover involves nonresidents.

In the nongovernment market nonresident holdings are considerably lower, reflecting the effect of more liquid euro markets for big institutional investors as well as the deterring effect of the 20% withholding tax. It is estimated that nonresidents hold about one third of outstanding bank-issued instruments and one fourth of corporate papers. Resident banks and other financial institutions hold the bulk of these instruments, while insurance, pension funds, and mutual funds remain comparatively minor holders. Households hold about 10% of Portuguese debt securities overall, which is broadly consistent with the Euro area average.

20.3.3   Withholding Tax

Interest payments on Portuguese bonds are subject to 20% withholding tax. In practice, however, this applies only to corporate bonds, because nonresidents and financial institutions have been granted special exemption from the tax on public debt instruments. Nonresident investors in bonds issued by securitization vehicles (Sociedades de Titularizacao de Creditos) and in securitization funds (Fundos de Titularizacao de Creditos) are also exempted. There are also tax reductions on interest paid to investors based in countries with which Portugal has double-taxation treaties.

20.3.4   Market Makers

The following is a list of the market makers in the Portuguese market. All except those marked with an asterisk are also specialized primary dealers of public debt (OEVT, Operadores Especializados de Valores do Tesouro) recognized by the IGCP.

- ABN Amro Bank
- Banco Espírito Santo
- Banco Português de Investimento
- Banco Santander Central Hispano
- Barclays Bank PLC*
- BCP de Investimento*
- BNP Paribas
- Caixa Geral de Depósitos
- Commerzbank
- Crédit Agricole Indosuez
- Deutsche Bank
- Fortis Bank*
- Goldman Sachs International
- HSBC CCF*
- Merrill Lynch International
- Schroder Salomon Smith Barney
- Société Générale

20.3.5   Rating Agencies

Portuguese government bonds are rated by the following rating agencies:

- Fitch IBCA
- Standard & Poor's
- Moody's Investor Services

20.3.6   Trading and Exchange Information

Regulated trading of debt securities takes place in four regulated cash markets recognized in Directive No. 93/22/CEE approved by Ministerial Decree No. 505/2002. Trades are by and large concentrated to the wholesale Special Public Debt Market or MEDIP (Mercado Especial de Dívida Pública), which accounted for a trading volume of €106.5 billion in 2001 or 85% of total trades. Trading in the other regulated markets, operated by the exchange Euronext Lisbon, is negligible. Over-the-counter trading (OTC) is also modest in international comparison with only 14% of total trades or a volume of €17.6 billion in 2001. Trading of nongovernment issues is very limited with the average monthly trading reaching only about 5% of total capitalization. A growing number of government bonds (OTs) are available for transaction and are actively traded in the pan-European platform EuroMTS, where most benchmarks of eight EU members are traded, attracting large European investors into the market. In EuroMTS, only those instruments with a minimum outstanding volume of €3 billion are eligible for listing.

20.3.6.1   Euronext Lisbon

For the effects of the Directive, the exchange Euronext Lisbon is responsible for the management of three of the regulated cash markets as well as the derivatives market. The exchange is also the owner of Interbolsa, the Portuguese Central Securities Depository (CSD).

The predecessor of Euronext was the Lisbon and Oporto Exchange (BVLP, Bolsa de Valores de Lisboa e Porto), which was created in 2000 with the merger of the Lisbon Stock Exchange and the Oporto Derivatives Exchange. In 2002, the BVLP merged with Euronext, the first pan-European exchange created by the merger of the Amsterdam, Brussels, and Paris exchanges, and changed its name to Euronext Lisbon.

All three cash markets operated by Euronext Lisbon trade both shares and bonds. Listing requirements are most demanding on the main market, which has official quotations. The second market has less demanding requirements and also lists securities suspended or excluded from the main market. A third regulated cash market called the new market is also available. In addition, Euronext has a nonregulated market known as the unlisted market, which has minimal listing requirements and also lists securities excluded from the main market and the second market. Trading takes place by either continuous trading or by multi-fixing/auction trading. The trading system in use is called LIST (Lisbon Trading), which is a Portuguese version of the NSC trading platform of France. Trading takes place between 9:30 a.m. and 4:30 p.m. GMT (10:30 a.m. to 5:30 p.m. CET). Trading of nongovernment securities is negligible.

In the derivatives market, also managed by Euronext, the development of new products is still ongoing. In 2001, a total of 4.7 million futures and options contracts were traded. All trades are executed on SEND (Electronic Derivatives Trading System), the Portuguese version of the Spanish MEFF platform. In relation to government bond benchmarks, 134 operations, mostly interest rate swaps, were carried out during 2001 in a total nominal amount equivalent to €13.4 billion. Currency forwards and swaps were mostly associated to the hedging of the exchange rate risk resulting from the issuance of US dollar-denominated commercial paper.

In addition to these regulated markets, Euronext Lisbon also provides OTC services. These include a newly designed repo registration system, which was widened to include securities lending 1999 with the launch of the Automatic Securities Lending System (SEA). Through the use of these markets, Euronext offers the possibility of combining strategies between standardized futures and customized OTC operations.

20.3.6.2 Special Public Debt Market (MEDIP)

The fourth regulated cash market contained in the Directive is the electronic wholesale market for public debt called MEDIP, operated by MTS Portugal. The market was adopted in 2000 from the MTS system, also implemented in other European bond markets. The MEDIP finally created the necessary conditions for a higher participation in the government bond market by nonresident investors and financial intermediaries, and brought a dramatic increase of liquidity. With the launch of the market, trading in the Special Block Trading Market (MEOG), previously used for wholesale trading of public debt, collapsed from €154 billion in 1999 to just €70 million in 2001.

All fixed Treasury bonds (OTs) may be traded on the MEDIP. New bonds are admitted to trade immediately after the first issuing transaction and as soon as the pricing is defined. In an initial stage, OTs can be traded on a when-issued basis in the grey market. Trading is supported by the MTS-Telematico electronic platform. Settlement follows the T+3 standard through Euroclear and Clearstream, with straight-through-processing (STP). Quotes and prices at which trading occurs are disseminated in real-time through Reuters, and a market bulletin is published at the end of each day on www.mtsportugal.com. Trading takes place between 7:15 a.m. and 4:30 p.m. (8:15 a.m. to 5:30 p.m. CET), with the premarket open 7:30 a.m. to 8:00 a.m. and the preliminary market 8:00 a.m. to 8:15 a.m.

Liquidity in the market is supported by designated market makers (see Section 20.3.4), obliged to quote bid and offer prices for a group of liquid bonds according to minimum quantities and maximum bid/offer spreads. All public debt primary dealers automatically become market makers. Designated market dealers (so-called market takers) also operate, which are not subject to quoting obligations but may only accept prices from market makers.

In a bid to support the market making obligations of primary dealers, the IGCP created a repo window of last resort, which was extended to all market makers in January 2002. All OTs under market-making obligations are available through this window against cash (repurchase transaction). Since May 2001, OTs are also included in the Repo Trading Facility of EuroMTS, which is based on the same technological infrastructure as MEDIP. All MEDIP and EuroMTS participants have access to this facility and there are no market-making obligations imposed. As from July 2002, Portuguese Treasuries have also been included in the repo trading facility of BrokerTec.

20.4   THE PORTUGUESE GOVERNMENT BOND MARKET

20.4.1   Background

The final stage of preparations for Monetary Union brought a steady convergence of yields on bonds issued by EU sovereigns including Portugal. Spreads shrank even further when the single currency eliminated foreign exchange risk within the Euro area. Nevertheless, Portuguese government bonds continue to trade at a substantial premium of more than 20 basis points to comparable German or French issues, which is attractive for investors but a challenge to the country's public liability managers (Banco de Portugal, 2001).

This spread premium has persisted because Portugal, rated AA by Standard and Poor's and Fitch and Aa2 by Moody's, remains somewhat less creditworthy than most of its European peers, and because the local market remains predictably modest in size and liquidity. This latter fact is not surprising given that the Portuguese economy contributes just 1.8% of the Euro area's GDP, but it is of ever-growing concern because investors' initial appetite for the attractive Portuguese yields is now beginning to tail off. Figure 20.1 provides an indication of current yields on the 10-year benchmark.

In preparation for these foreseen challenges, the IGCP (2001) has completely revamped its debt management operations in recent years, which has significantly enhanced the market's

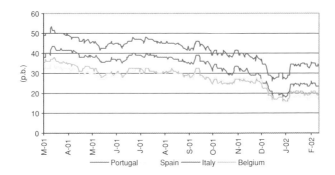

Figure 20.1   10-year spreads versus Germany – interpolated.
Source: IGCP (2002). Reproduced by permission of IGCP.

technical stance and international integration. First, in a bid to increase liquidity and make Portuguese debt eligible for trading in the pan-European EuroMTS, the IGCP pinpointed a target size of €5 billion for selected debt lines. In a context of the government's reduced borrowing requirements to be met via the issuance of bonds (around €10 billion per year), issuance was concentrated on the benchmark 5- and 10-year fixed-rate Treasury bonds for which there are derivatives markets, while Treasury bills and floating-rate Treasury bonds were discontinued. A debt exchange program was also introduced, promoting the repurchase of the government's Eurobonds and illiquid Treasury bonds with short term residual maturities.

The IGCP has been equally quick to respond to technological challenges. In 2000, an electronic auction platform run through Bloomberg was launched. This has resulted in a significant improvement in efficiency, with the full results of the allocation being communicated to primary dealers about 3 minutes after the cut-off time for bids. The average auction size also increased from €161 million in 1998 to €664 million in 2001. And, the IGCP boosted secondary market liquidity in a spectacular fashion by the creation of MEDIP (see Section 20.3.6).

20.4.2   Types of Instruments

(A) Treasury Bills (BTs, Bilhetes de Tesouro): This category refers to discount or zero coupon bills with maturities shorter than 1 year. Although the option of issuing BTs still exists, no new Treasury bills have been issued since March 1999. Maturities ranged between 91, 182, and 364 days. They are issued through a syndicate, by auction, or on tapping in registered form with a minimum denomination of €250. They are listed and traded in the interbank secondary market.

(B) Treasury Bonds (OTs, Obrigacoes de Tesouro): This category includes registered medium to long term bonds with either fixed-rate or no coupons. They constitute approximately 60% of total direct government debt, designed to cover the budget deficit and regular previous debt. The maturity range includes 3, 5, 7, 10, and 15 years. They are issued through a syndicate, by auction, or on tapping, as a single issue or as a line of fungible issues, with the possibility of stripping. They are listed on Euronext Lisbon with trading in MEDIP. Prior to 1994, they paid semiannual coupons but new issues pay on an annual basis. Redemption is only at maturity. They are issued at a discount if issued before the dated date.

(C) Floating Rate Treasury Bonds (OTRVs, Obrigacoes de Tesouro com Rendimento Variavel): This category includes floating rate 6- and 7-year bonds, first introduced in 1994. In 1997, the IGCP stopped issuing them because of lack of investor interest. OTRVs are registered, listed on Euronext Lisbon, and traded in MEDIP. They pay coupons on a semiannual basis with redemption at maturity. The coupon is indexed to the 6-month EURIBOR. Issues in 1996 and 1997 have call options attached, which can be exercised upon a 3-month or 6-month notice from the Ministry of Finance.

(D) Multicurrency Instruments: The IGCP has two main multicurrency programs running:
   - *Euro-Commercial Paper (ECP) Program:* Tradable instruments issued at discount with maturities up to 1 year, denominated in US dollar and euro. The maximum outstanding amount is restricted to €4 billion. The group of dealers include Caixa Geral de Depósitos, Citibank, Deutsche Bank, Goldman Sachs, Lehman Brothers, and UBS.
   - *Medium Term Notes (MTN or CEDIC) Program:* Tradable instruments issued at discount with minimum maturity from 1 month to more than 1 year, depending on the currency. The maximum maturity of 5 years is applicable only to issues denominated in British pound sterling. MTNs are exchanged in nonregulated markets. The program allows the

issue of a maximum amount of US$4 billion or equivalent). The interest computation can use fixed rates, floating rates, index-linked, or dual currency notes. Distribution is made through the following dealers: Caixa Geral de Depósitos, Daiwa, Goldman Sachs, Lehman Brothers, Merrill Lynch, Morgan Stanley, BNP Paribas, and UBS.

(E) Nontradable Saving Certificates: These instruments, which comprise around 20% of total direct government debt, are retail distributed and can only be subscribed by households. They are nontradable and may only be transferred because of the death of the owner. The issue and redemption is done directly through IGCP's customer counter or through the customer counters of other institutions hired by IGCP: the post office (CTT) and retail banks.

(F) Other Nontradable Instruments: There are other issues that still exist in the market but do not have any liquidity. These instruments were launched in the late 1970s, and include Consolidados (perpetual bonds), Fundo de Investimento Publico (FIP, Public Investment Fund Bonds), Tesouro Nacional e Expropriacoes (TNE, National Treasury Expropriation Bonds), and Tesouro Fundo de Investimento para Desenvolvimento Economico e Social e Fundo de Investimento Atlantico (Fides e Fia). TNEs were introduced to compensate for the nationalization of property, while Fides e Fia were created to compensate for the nationalization of funds.

20.4.3   Auction Process

The auction calendar for Portuguese government securities is managed by the IGCP and communicated to the market via the Bank of Portugal. Only those institutions with the status of Specialized Primary Dealer (OEVT) or Other Auction Participant (OMP) are permitted to participate.

There are three methods of selling government securities: through syndication, by auction, or on tapping, as a single issue or as a line of fungible issues with the possibility of stripping. Banking syndicates composed of primary dealers have been used increasingly heavily since 1998, because they offer better distribution, more competitive pricing, and size. The size of such offerings also means they can be traded on EuroMTS.

The auction method used is the modified Dutch system. The system is supported by an electronic platform – the Bloomberg Auction System (BAS) – through which market players can now place bids directly and have immediate feedback about yields and allocation.

(A) Treasury Bills (BTs): No new BTs have been auctioned since 1999. They were sold through competitive auctions based on a monthly schedule, which was usually announced 2 weeks prior to the beginning of each month. Ninety-one-day BTs were auctioned on Wednesdays/Fridays, 182-day BTs on Mondays, and 365-day BTs on Wednesdays.

(B) Treasury Bonds (OTs and OTRVs): Treasury bond auction schedules are announced at the beginning of the year or quarter by the IGCP. The specific characteristics of each auction are announced directly to the authorized dealers until 3 days before the auction takes place. Usually, auctions take place on the second Wednesday of each month. Prior to the cessation of their issuance in 1997, OTRVs were auctioned on every third Tuesday of the month. Auctions are developed in two stages:

  (i) Competitive stage: All authorized dealers are permitted to participate. Each participant can present a maximum of five proposals in multiples of €1 million with a total amount that should not overcome the indicative amount for the auctions. OTs are distributed, in a growing order of yields proposed, until the yield for which the amount of proposals equals or exceeds the total amount that the IGCP decides to issue is hit (cut rate). For OTRVs, bids were arranged on the basis of price, beginning with the highest price. The proposals must be submitted until 10:30 a.m. (11:30 a.m. CET) on the day of the auction. The results are announced within the following 15 minutes (usually after 3 minutes). The IGCP may decide to issue an amount until one third above the announced amount, and may also decide not to issue part or the entire announced amount.

(ii) Noncompetitive stage: Any unallotted amount in the competitive auction, provided it does not exceed one third of the total issue amount, is offered to the primary dealers at a higher yield accepted in that stage. Each dealer may subscribe bonds until the amount that results from applying its global share in the competitive stage of the last three auctions. The proposals must be presented until 12:00 p.m. (1:00 p.m. CET).

20.4.4   Market Conventions

Since the market has not applied the calendar convention of the EMU gross settlement system TARGET, the Portuguese national holiday calendar remains employed. The market convention is for trade plus 3 (T+3) settlement for all Treasury bonds with the value date the same as the settlement date. The settlement date on Treasury bills was T+2. Treasury bonds employ an Actual/Actual day count basis, while Treasury bills employed an Actual/360 day basis.

20.4.5   Benchmarks

The IGCP's management strategy is founded on a market-oriented funding strategy aimed at building a yield curve with liquid instruments at different maturities and based on a transparent *modus operandi*. Accordingly, the IGCP has shown great commitment to creating benchmark issues at key maturities along the yield curve, with priority given to the 5- and 10-year maturities. In 2001, a new 10-year benchmark OT was opened with a total issuance, via syndicate, of nearly €5.3 billion. In 2002, the bulk of issuance was again heavily concentrated on the 5- and 10-year maturities.

The benchmark yield curve is constructed from a pool of outstanding 5-, 10-, and 15-year OTs based on maturity, liquidity, coupon, and amounts outstanding. The newly auctioned 10-year OT is always treated as the 10-year point on the yield curve. The graph below (Figure 20.2) provides an example of the yield curve's construction compared with some other Euro area yield curves.

20.5   NONGOVERNMENT BOND MARKET

20.5.1   Introduction

With the introduction of the euro, the foreign exchange risk that prevented Portuguese investors from fully diversifying their portfolios into other Euro area markets suddenly disappeared. It is hardly surprising therefore that since 1999, the domestic funds that once sustained Portugal's nongovernment bond market have shifted to other mainstream European markets, which has reduced demand for domestic bonds.

This has been particularly true for the corporate bond market, where the volume of outstanding issues declined by €1 billion in 2000 and a further €0.2 billion in 2001. Since 1999,

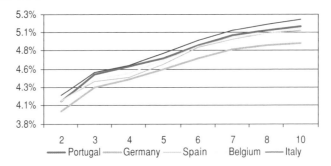

Figure 20.2   Government yield curves – interpolated (February 18, 2002).
Source: IGCP (2002). Reproduced by permission of IGCP.

only one publicly subscribed offer has been registered at the CMVM, an issue of subordinated perpetuities by Caixa Económica do Montepio Geral. The country's big companies and financial groups are engaged in a wave of acquisitions, mergers, and overseas investments, and so demand for funds is strong. But, the 20% withholding tax that deters nonresident investors has combined with the allure of more liquid euro markets, diverting local investors (Euromoney, 2002). Left with insufficient demand in the domestic marketplace, the largest and better-rated corporations have started to access foreign bond markets instead by setting up MTN programs. And, those smaller companies that would previously have raised money in the domestic market are increasingly turning back to bank credit because, as pointed out by Wise (2000), in the unified euro market investors expect an issue size of at least €100 million.

Other corporations have turned to the CP market. Institutional investors and banks have successfully used these instruments as an important liquidity management tool, and the stability of demand has allowed issuers to use CP for medium term financing through rollovers. The outstanding volume of CP issued by nonfinancial corporations grew from €2.2 billion in 1999 to €5.4 billion in 2001, with the bulk of issuance accounted for by real estate, rental, and other service companies as well as, to a lesser extent, manufacturers.

The relative apathy seen in the corporate bond market has also been apparent in the Caravela market for nonresident issuers. Despite issuance in the region of €2 billion each year in 1995–1998, the volume of new issues collapsed with the introduction of the euro and has stayed around €200 million per year since then. Supranational and sovereign entities have shown particularly thin interest in the conditions prevailing in the market, with only Mexico launching a modest €9 million issue in 2001.

Because of the lackluster performance of the corporate and Calavera markets, the large domestic financial groups now primarily use Portugal's nongovernment bond market. Net issuance by banks (Monetary Financial Institutions, MFIs) reached €4.3 billion in 2000, although activity fell somewhat to €3.9 billion in 2001. Such commotion in the market owes to banks increasingly financing their current activities through the placement of structured products among retail customers, a direct result of the recent rapid growth of their balance sheets. The CMVM (2001) notes that these securities have been a great success with investors, because they combine a potentially attractive performance with the guarantee of the full refund of the initial investment. As opposed to some major European markets, Pfandbrief-style mortgage bonds have not really taken root in Portugal as yet.

Table 20.3   Issues of nongovernment bonds (in million euro)

	1996	1997	1998	1999	2000	2001
Ordinary	3.891	3.558	3.187	1.172	303	115
Bearer	1.608	1.619	1.791	2.404	2.067	2.802
Subordinated cash	494	337	172	434	184	455
Zero coupon	267	1.164	1.683	1.342	1.589	744
Others	469	849	354	140	299	808
Total	6.728	7.527	7.187	5.492	4.442	4.924

Source: CMVM Annual Report 2001.

20.5.2   Types of Bonds

The types of bonds outstanding in the corporate market include the following (see Table 20.3):

(A) Straight Bonds (Obrigacoes Classicas): This category includes bonds with or without (zero) coupons. Coupons can be fixed or variable. Redemption is bullet with the possibility of attaching call or put options. For floating-rate notes, the most commonly used indexer is the 3- and 6-month EURIBOR.

(B) Cash or Bearer Bonds (Obrigacoes de Caixa): Cash bonds are restricted to issuance by financial institutions. Otherwise, they are no different from other bonds. The Bank of Portugal supervises issuance. The maturity range is between 2 and 5 years. They can be issued in series or continuously.

(C) Subordinated Bonds (Obrigacoes Subordinadas): Investors in subordinated bonds are ranked inferior to holders of issues in defaults.

(D) Convertible Bonds (Obrigacoes Convertiveis) and Bonds with Warrants (Obrigacao com warrants): Convertible bonds permit the investor to convert the bonds into equity. More commonly in Portugal, however, bonds are issued with warrants, detachable rights to subscribe to the issuer's shares at a predetermined price.

(E) Mortgage Bonds (Obrigacoes Hipotecarias): Mortgage bonds are secured by real estate. The maturity range is between 3 and 30 years.

20.5.3   Market Conventions

All issues must be registered with the CMVM. Bonds issued by public placements have to be first underwritten by financial institutions, unless the issuer is a financial institution. Corporate issues can be listed in the Second Market of Euronext Lisboa. Since the market has not applied the TARGET calendar convention, the Portuguese national holiday calendar is employed. Settlement is three business days before coupon. All bonds employ an Actual/Actual day count basis.

20.5.4   Asset-Backed Securities

The structured finance market is still in its relative infancy in Portugal, with the first securitization transaction being executed in 1998. Securitization activity is nevertheless set to significantly deepen following on the success of recent years. Year-end volumes for 2001 came in at around €4.5 billion, 3% of total securitization activity in Europe and a significant leap from the €740 million seen a year earlier. Standard and Poor's (2002) notes that this increase is chiefly a result of the transactions being executed on a much larger scale rather than an increase in the number of issues: the number of transactions being brought to market rose from four in 2000 to just seven in 2001.

The surge in Portuguese volumes has been primarily supported by growth in collateralized debt obligations (CDO), which accounted for about half of total volumes in 2001. CDOs are expected to remain the principal asset class over the short term, buoyed by banks and financial institutions in search of improved liquidity ratios after the significant loan growth of recent years. The residential mortgage-backed securities (RMBS) sector, in comparison, has been slower to take off, in sharp contrast to most other European jurisdictions where it has been the barometer of growth. The first RMBS deal was concluded only toward the end of 2001, a €1 billion transaction originated by Portugal's largest bank, Banco Comercial Portugues (A-/Stable/A-2).

The primary impediment to market development remains the lack of a cohesive legal framework. This is despite the fact that the Decree Law 453/99 and its recent refinement through decree laws enacted in August 2001 and April 2002 have attempted to pave the way for securitization through for example the exemption of bonds issued by securitization vehicles (Sociedades de Titularizacao de Creditos) and in securitization funds (Fundos de Titularizacao de Creditos) from withholding tax. In spite of these efforts, there remains a general consensus in the marketplace that further changes are needed to make local special purpose vehicles cost-effective. Several investment banks are waiting for critical legal amendments before starting their mortgages securitization deals.

REFERENCES

Banco de Portugal (2001). Annual Report.
Comissão do Mercado de Valores Mobiliários (2001). Annual Report.
European Central Bank (2002). *Report on Financial Structures*, pp. 249–271 (Country Chapter on Portugal).
Euromoney (2002, February). The Portuguese Bond Market, pp. 6–7.
Instituto de Gestão do Crédito Público (IGCP) (2001, 2002). Annual Report.
IGCP (2002, February). Portuguese Treasury Bonds – An Efficient Debt Market. Investors' Presentation.
Standard & Poor's (2002, March 12). Strong Growth in Iberian Securitization Predicted for 2002.
Wise, P. (2000, March). The Quest for Domestic Investors. pp. 92–96.

21

Russia

LEONID V. PHILOSOPHOV AND VLADIMIR L. PHILOSOPHOV

21.1 HISTORY OF THE RUSSIAN BOND MARKET

In the planned economy of the Soviet Union there was originally no place for financial markets in general and a bond market in particular, though bonds were sometimes issued. The most intensive period of issuance occurred during World War II and the subsequent postwar years of restoration of the national economy of the USSR.

At this time bonds were issued each year (once a year) and were distributed via state-owned enterprises and organizations, which employed the vast majority of USSR citizens. Formally a subscription was voluntary but in fact each employee was urged to buy bonds for an amount equivalent to approximately 1 month's salary. These bonds were sold at par value and were redeemed by the state for the same value 10–15 years later, in parts determined by lotteries. The Soviet leader Nikita Khrushtshov stopped this practice in 1957 when he revealed that the redemption of previous issues required more money than was received from new bond issues. Simultaneously, the state postponed for 20 years redemption of all earlier issues. In fact they were redeemed only in 1980th at par value. After this period and up to the disintegration of the Soviet Union, bonds were issued by the state in minor quantities. These bonds were sold to the USSR public and redeemed by the state-owned Savings Bank of the USSR at prices assigned by the bank.

Investment programs of the Soviet enterprises were financed from the state budget via corresponding ministries. Major investment projects were launched by joint decrees of the Central Committee of the Communist Party of USSR and the Counsel of Ministers. These decrees provided the financing of investment projects and their supply with deficient raw materials and equipment. There was no necessity for Soviet enterprises to issue bonds, and a Western analyst would be probably astonished to discover that there was little long term debt at all.

Radical economic reforms were started in Russia after the disintegration of the USSR in January 1992. The main aim was to free the prices of consumer goods and industrial products. Russian firms were allowed to produce what they wanted and find their own suppliers and customers. Foreign trade (previously a state monopoly) was also liberalized and the ruble exchange rate was allowed to fluctuate on the basis of supply and demand for foreign currency. State regulation (limitation) of workers' salaries was also abolished.

These radical economic changes affected companies whose production was determined by State Plan rather than by demand and whose prices did not reflect the true cost of production. The vast majority of these firms manufactured industrial or military equipment. The first consequence of liberalization was hyperinflation, which reached 1650% in 1992. This devalued the cash assets of companies and made it difficult for them to attract investment so that they

European Fixed Income Markets: Money, Bond and Interest Rate Derivatives. Edited by J.A. Batten,
T.A. Fetherston and P.G. Szilagyi. © 2004 John Wiley & Sons, Ltd. ISBN 0-470-85053-1

could switch to the production of more saleable consumer goods. Since no market research had been undertaken and the new managers, born in the Soviet era, had no experience of such research, no one had any idea of what to produce.

Finding it impossible to adapt to the rapid changes in the demand structure, Russian enterprises continued to produce the same goods as before, but were unable to find customers. Their goods remained in the warehouse or else were delivered on credit with no hope of receiving quick payment. A total insolvency ("no payment") crisis developed and total production started to fall. All these events caused a significant decrease in industrial production, which, in combination with the new system of tax legislation and tax collection, resulted in a sharp reduction of tax inflow to the state budget. This in turn caused a decrease in state social programs, as well as in healthcare, education, science, and defense expenses.

By 1993, in order to attract sources of funding to cover the deficit in the state budget, the government of the Russian Federation promulgated a decree for the issuance of short-term discounted Treasury bills GKO (Gosudarstvennye Kratkosrochnye Obligatsii). 1993 was characterized by further high inflation (about 860%) and the appearance of many commercial banks and finance companies that collected deposits from households and enterprises promising very high rates of interest. To remain competitive and to preserve the principal from inflation GKO had to offer similar rates of return to bank deposits. As a result, the market yields of GKO and middle term Treasury coupon notes OFZ (Obligatsii Federalnogo Zaima), which appeared later, were about 150% in 1993 and up to 300% in 1994. As industrial production in the Russian Federation continued to deteriorate, the state in the following years also continued the practice of issuing GKO and OFZ with high coupons and selling them with high discounts.

In 1996 foreign investors were admitted into the Russian domestic bond market. Investments in GKO–OFZ were very profitable because of the support provided to the ruble by the Bank of Russia. Specifically, since 1995 the ruble–dollar exchange rate traded in a narrow band near 6000 rubles per dollar. (From the beginning of 1998, the ruble was denominated at the rate of 1000 old rubles = 1 new ruble.) Thus the yield of GKO (annual in rubles) in 1997 was about 30% while inflation remained at 11%.

At the end of 1997 and the first half-year of 1998 conditions in the Russian financial market deteriorated because of several reasons simultaneously:

- After the crisis of 1997 in South East Asia, investors from developed countries began to withdraw their money from emerging markets generally, and also from the Russian market. This caused a decrease in the market prices of GKO–OFZ (increase in yield) and increased the cost of new bond issues for the state.
- The crisis caused a fall in oil prices and a reduction in the income of Russian oil companies, which were the major contributors to the state revenues.
- Because of continuing inflation, the ruble–dollar exchange rate stepped behind the official boundaries. Thus to maintain the official rate within the band, the Bank of Russia spent a significant part of its currency reserves. Thus the foreign reserves decreased to a critical value of $12 billion.

In the spring and summer of 1998, the Russian government tried to apply various measures to resolve the situation, but no positive effect was achieved. Consequently, on August 17, 1998, the government of the Russian Federation and the Bank of Russia issued a joint statement abolishing new issues of GKO–OFZ and postponed the redemption of outstanding government bonds. This statement had catastrophic consequences for the Russian economy.

This financial shock greatly increased demand for hard currency (US dollars) within Russia. The Bank of Russia was unable to keep the exchange rate within the stated boundaries and announced the transfer to a floating mechanism determined on the basis of market demand and supply. Consequently, the price of the US dollar increased from 6 to 16 rubles within a few days and to 20 rubles at the very beginning of 1999. The prices of imported goods also increased significantly, and then prices of domestic goods also rose. By 1998 inflation had increased to 84.4%, although it was just 11% in 1997.

All the large Russian commercial banks by that time kept their assets mainly in GKO–OFZ. After August 17, 1998, many ceased operating and many became bankrupt. These institutions held significant household deposits; Russian citizens, for the second time since the beginning of the economic reforms, lost their savings.

The only corporate bonds traded at that time were state-guaranteed bonds of "RAO Vysokoskorostnye magistrali" – the firm founded for the construction of the high-speed railway between Moscow and Sankt-Petersburg (Saint Petersburg). These bonds shared the same destiny as GKO–OFZ and the Russian bond market ceased to exist.

21.2   THE RUSSIAN ECONOMY IN THE POSTCRISIS PERIOD

In the long run the 1998 crisis had positive consequences for the Russian economy. The depreciation of the ruble by nearly 3.5 times to the beginning of 1999 caused a sharp increase in the prices of imported goods, which became inaccessible to the majority of the Russian people, while the competitive power of Russian exports increased. Russian manufacturers received a chance to increase production to replace imported goods and they succeeded at least in some areas, primarily in food production. This in turn increased employment and household income.

Since 1999 Russia enjoyed strong gross domestic product (GDP) growth. According to the official data of the Bank of Russia, while in 1998 GDP decreased 4.9%, it increased in 1999 by 4.6%, in 2000 it grew 10.2%, and in 2001 there was an additional growth of 5.7%. The most intensive increase was observed in oil and gas production, nonferrous metallurgy, food production, construction, and production of construction materials. Some increase was also observed in machine building.

The world prices of oil and gas, which are the main Russian exports, started to increase from the beginning of 1999 and from that time have remained at historic highs. This has ensured a high inflow of hard currency, and in all these years Russian exports noticeably exceeded imports. The excess in 1999 was $36.2 billion, in 2000 was $60.7 billion, and in 2001 was $47.8 billion.

By law, Russian exporters must sell 75% of their hard currency revenues on domestic markets. The excess of currency enabled the Bank of Russia to increase currency reserves from $12 billion in 1998 to $45 billion by the middle of 2002. These developments enabled the government to attract new foreign loans and announce its intention to repay all existing loans (in 2003 Russia must return about $17 billion of foreign debt).

According to the Russian Ministry of Finance, the state foreign debt of the Russian Federation (as of January 1, 2002) equaled $130.1 billion, including those debts of the USSR accepted by the Russian Federation. This sum includes the following:

- Debt to foreign countries: US$57.1 billion.
- Debt to international finance organizations: $15.2 billion.
- Commercial debt of Soviet foreign trade organizations: $6.1 billion.
- Eurobond loans: $35.3 billion.
- Internal hard currency loans: $10 billion.

To buy foreign currency the Bank of Russia issues additional ruble notes. The bank states that these are restricted and controlled, but in fact they have contributed to domestic inflation. In 2001 inflation was as high as 18.5% and in 2002 the level was 14%. Another component of inflation is increases in domestic oil prices and prices for utility services (gas, electricity, water, heat, communal transport). These prices are controlled in Russia, and federal and regional governments increase them from time to time, attempting to bring revenues in line with the costs of services. Bringing these prices to market level is considered to be a key element of communal reform.

The Bank of Russia establishes the official US dollar (and euro) exchange rate every day, following the results of dollar trades at the Moscow Interbank Currency Exchange. The Bank of Russia actively participates in these trades to minimize exchange rate volatility. Generally the exchange rate increases (falls in 2003) but the rate of its increase falls behind the rate of inflation. In 2001, for example, the increase of dollar exchange rate was about 7% while inflation was 18.5%. This occurred because after the 1998 crisis, the dollar was severely overvalued. The parity value of the dollar (determined on the basis of payment balances) at the end of 1998 was estimated at 7.3 rubles per dollar, while the market value increased to 20 rubles per dollar. The difference is a measure of the risk associated with instability in the political and economic situation in Russia, and a lack of confidence in the ruble after the 1998 crisis. Last year the decrease in the buying power of the dollar suggested a gradual return of confidence in the ruble. The Bank of Russia now prefers to refer to these developments as the strengthening of the real value of the ruble. By the end of 2002 the official dollar exchange rate was about 31.80 rubles per dollar.

Bonds (GKO–OFZ) that were outstanding before the 1998 crisis were restructured at the end of 1998 to new bonds (OFZ) with a circulation period of 3–5 years with a partial return of the principal (10%). At the beginning of 1999 the total face value and coupon of new bond issues was much less than that in the precrisis years.

The current annual return on GKO–OFZ is about 12–15% – less than the level of inflation, which is 14–18%. Nevertheless there is strong demand for these bonds since there is no suitable alternative investment in the Russian market. Bank deposits, for example, have lower returns. Investments in dollar (and recently in euro) are also popular, but the dollar is still overvalued and such investments are often less profitable than are investments in GKO–OFZ.

All this can be considered as an encouragement for banks and other investors to consider investing in the real sector, but such investments in Russia are still very risky because of imperfections in Russian legislation and the legal system. For firms in turn the cost of investment is too high because of continuing inflation; they prefer to use internal sources for the financing of investment projects or, when possible, to attract on favorable terms credits from federal and local governments.

In 2001–2002 Russia carried out tax reforms. A new Tax Code was adopted and corporate profit tax was reduced to 24% while personal income tax was reduced to 13%.

21.3   REGULATION OF THE RUSSIAN BOND MARKET AND ITS PARTICIPANTS

21.3.1   Background

The principal legislative act regulating securities markets in the Russian Federation and bond market as its part, is the Federal Law "On the Securities Markets" (April 22, 1996, #39). This law regulates relations between issuers and investors, the issuance and circulation of securities, as well as the rules of the foundation and activities of professional participants in the securities market.

The law describes the main types of activities at the securities market – dealer and broker activities, portfolio management, clearing, and deposit and registration activities. The stock exchange can be acknowledged as an organizer of trades that does not carry out any other activities (except deposit and clearing activities). A stock exchange must be established as a noncommercial partnership. The law describes procedures for the issuing of securities and procedures for the disclosure of information on securities and their issuers. Article 30 of the law introduces civilized norms of disclosure of information, but in fact access by investors to corporate information is still very difficult.

State regulation of securities market includes

- establishing the obligatory requirements for issuers and professional participants in securities markets, and standards of those activities;
- registering securities issues and prospectuses, and control over issuers' compliance with the terms of issue; and
- licensing professional participants in the security market.

The Russian Federation established the Federal Commission on the Securities Market whose goal is to conduct state policy in this area. The commission has the status of a Ministry of the Russian government.

The issuance and circulation of federal and municipal securities is additionally regulated by Federal Law #136 (June 29, 1998) "On the Peculiarities of Distribution and Circulation of Federal and Municipal Securities". The law prescribes a three-stage procedure for the issuance of federal and municipal securities:

1. The government of the Russian Federation or subject of the Russian Federation or municipal government asserts General Terms of Issuance and circulation of federal, subfederal, and municipal securities. The terms must include type of securities, form of issue (registered, bearer), time of circulation (short, middle, or long term), and the currency of denomination.
2. Issuer (a financial body of a government) in compliance with General Terms asserts the Terms of Issuance indicating type of securities, maximum and minimum circulation period, face value, income (coupon) value or rule of its calculation, and procedure of offering.
3. In compliance with General Terms and Terms of Issuance, the issuer makes a decision on a particular issue of securities. The decision must contain the date of the beginning and time interval of offering, volume of the issue, and the name of the registrar.

21.3.2 Regulating Organizations and Their Functions

21.3.2.1 Federal Commission on the Securities Market (FCSM)

The FCSM was established in accordance with law to regulate the Russian securities market. According to law the Commission must act in the following areas:

- Coordination of activities of federal executive bodies in decisions related to problems associated with the securities market.
- Development of rules for issuing securities by domestic and foreign issuers, which issue securities on the territory of the Russian Federation, and determination of registration procedures for issuers and their prospectus.

- Elaborating unified rules of professional activities for securities markets.
- Establishing obligatory requirements for operations on the securities markets, norms of public offering, circulation, quotation and listing, and clearing activities.
- Establishing obligatory requirements and rules of maintaining registers of securities and their owners.
- Licensing professional participants of the security market and interruption and cessation of licenses of those violating law.
- Establishing rules, licensing, and keeping a registry of self-regulating organizations of professional participants in the security market; cancelation of licenses if an organization violates law or those rules established by the Commission.
- Establishing rules of activities of investment and private pension and insurance funds and their managing firms as well as insurance companies on the security market.
- Ensuring disclosure of information on registered securities issuances, market participants, and market regulations.
- Elaborating requirements for the professional qualifications of market participants.

21.3.2.2   Central Bank of the Russian Federation (Bank of Russia)

The Bank of Russia holds a number of regulatory functions of the Russian securities market. Bank activities are subject to a special law. According to law, the Bank of Russia is responsible for the following:

- Elaborate and conduct a unified money policy aimed at the defense and stabilization of the national currency (ruble) in collaboration with the Russian government.
- Issue cash currency and organize its circulation.
- Establish rules for settling accounts in the Russian Federation.
- Provide the state registration and licensing of commercial banks, cancel licenses of credit and audit organizations, and supervise the activities of credit organizations.
- Regulate the circulation of foreign currencies in Russia, including buying and selling of foreign currencies, and establish the rules of settling accounts with foreign states.

The regulating activities of the Bank of Russia on the securities market are aimed at the realization of a unified credit and monetary policy in Russia. In its activities the Bank employs the following instruments:

- Establishes rate of refinancing (discount rate) for commercial banks.
- Establishes norms of the obligatory reserves of commercial banks held in the Bank of Russia.
- Buys and sells state securities on the open market.
- Buys and sells nonstate bonds and other securities. (According to law the Bank of Russia can buy and sell nonstate securities whose time to maturity is less than 1 year.)
- Issues its own bonds. (The right to issue bonds was given to the Bank of Russia temporarily until the end of 1999. Later it was prolonged and was valid until January 1, 2003.)

The Bank of Russia accomplishes the registration of bond issues carried out by credit organizations. The Bank functions as a general agent to serve issues of government bonds GKO–OFZ. Via authorized organizations it organizes public offering (auctions), registration, and the redemption of state bonds; the bonds are redeemed from the state budget. By law, the Bank of Russia generally provides services for state internal debt of the Russian Federation – organizes distribution of debt obligations, pays interest, and redeems other obligations.

21.3.2.3 *Ministry of Finance of the Russian Federation*

The Ministry of Finance is a body of federal executive power responsible for developing a unified finance, budget, and tax and currency policy in the Russian Federation and coordinates activities in this area for other federal executive bodies. Activities of the Ministry of Finance are subject to regulations established by Government Decree #273 (March 6, 1998). The main tasks of the Ministry according to the regulations are as follows:

- Development of the budget system of the Russian Federation and of budget federalism.
- Development and realization of a unified finance, budget, and tax policy in the Russian Federation.
- Concentration of financial resources in the priority directions of social and economic development of the Russian Federation.
- Elaboration of a draft of federal budget and ensure the execution of the budget; elaboration of accounting information on the execution of federal budget.
- Elaboration of programs of state borrowings and their realization in the name of the Russian Federation. Control over the state internal and external debts of the Russian Federation.
- Elaboration and realization of a unified policy in the area of financial markets in the Russian Federation.
- Elaboration of a unified methodology of composition of budget on all levels and accounts on their execution.
- Execution of the state financial control.
- Elaboration of principles and methodology of accounting and audit in the Russian Federation (except accounting in the Bank of Russia and the bank system).

In accordance with law the Ministry of Finance acts as the issuer of state securities, provides the already mentioned Terms of Issuance of state securities, makes decisions on the issuance of specific issues of securities, and establishes parameters of these issues. The Ministry of Finance registers Terms of Issuance of securities issued by subjects of the Russian Federation (by autonomous republics and regions) and municipal formations.

21.3.3 Russian Stock Exchanges

21.3.3.1 *Moscow Interbank Currency Exchange (MICEX)*

MICEX was initially set as an exchange for trades by foreign currencies. The Bank of Russia is the principal currency trader at the exchange and since 1992 it establishes the daily official US dollar–ruble exchange rate taking in account the results of trading at MICEX. By now MICEX is the largest currency exchange in Russia; its total volume of trades in 2001 was about $73 billion. MICEX organizes interregional currency trades by means of an electronic trading system as well as usual trades. The main currencies traded are the US dollar and euro. Micex is the principal place where the Bank of Russia organizes initial offerings (auctions) and secondary trades of Treasury bonds.

MICEX also organizes the initial offerings and secondary trades by subfederal and municipal bonds and bonds of leading Russian corporations. In the stock section of the exchange are traded stocks of about 100 Russian firms. For the first time in Russia MICEX ensured secure trades with preliminary deposits of shares (bonds) and money.

MICEX also acts as a nationwide trading system, which links eight principal industrial and financial centers of Russia. More than 1400 distant working places in banks and other financial institutions in Moscow, Sankt-Peterburg, Novosibirsk, Rostov on Don, Ekaterinburg, and Vladivostok are connected with the exchange by means of satellite, optic, and other telecommunication lines. MICEX in collaboration with Clearing Center and National Depository Center also serves more than 1500 participants of stock market.

21.3.3.2 Stock Exchange RTS

The abbreviation RTS means the Russian Trading System. The exchange was founded in 1995 as a NASDAQ-like system for trades by Russian corporate stocks for US dollars. Until 1998 RTS used software presented by NASDAQ. Today RTS is the biggest stock exchange in Russia and quotes about 400 stocks of Russian enterprises. For another 550, low-liquid stock indicative quotations are available. RTS calculates "Index RTS" – the most popular and worldwide acknowledged index of the Russian stock market. RTS carries out stock trades using both national currency and US dollars in two regimes:

- Secured regime, with post deposits of stocks and money.
- Conventional regime, with conclusion of agreements via telephone.

A section for trades by corporate, subfederal, and Treasury bonds was organized in RTS in 2002. The section ensures trades in secured regime, with preliminary deposits of bonds and money, as well as in unsecured regime. For corporate bonds RTS also organizes initial offerings.

21.3.3.3 Other Trading Centers

There are several regional stock exchanges in Russia. The main ones are situated in Sankt-Peterburg (Sankt-Peterburg Currency Exchange [SPCEX] and Exchange "Sankt Peterburg"), Ekaterinburg, and Novosibursk but their trading volumes are incomparable with those of MICEX or RTS. Usually they organize initial public offerings (IPOs) and trades by bonds of regional governments and enterprises of nearby regions. For example, SPCEX serves regions of the North Western area of Russia. There is some evidence of integration of the regional exchanges with the above-mentioned main exchanges of Russia.

21.3.3.4 Analysis, Consultations & Marketing

AK&M (Analysis, Consultations & Marketing) mainly acts as an information agency. AK&M also acts as an organizer of the over-the-counter securities market in Russia. Since 1993 AK&M maintains a daily updated database, AK&M-LIST. The database contains proposals to buy or sell shares of stocks and other securities by various investment companies and banks that act in Russia. By now it contains information on 2800 issuers and 1100 investment companies. The database is distributed daily to subscribers via e-mail.

21.3.3.5 Self-Regulating Organizations of Professional Participants in the Securities Market

In Russia several self-regulating organizations of professional participants in securities market exist, which are noncommercial organizations that act in compliance with Federal Law "On the securities market." A self-regulating organization is established by professional participants in the securities market to ensure due conditions of professional activities of market participants, maintenance of standards of professional ethics, and defense of interests of securities owners and other clients, and to establish rules and standards of operations. These organizations are

(a) National Association of Professional Participants of Stock Market. The Association was founded in November 1995 by companies-professional participants in the stock markets, from various regions of Russia. The main goals of the Association consist of monitoring the professional activities of the securities market, maintaining ethical standards, defending the interests of investors, and developing training programs for professional participants in the securities market.
(b) Professional Association of Registers, Transfer agents and Depositories. The Association was founded in 1994. Since 1997 it has acted as a self-regulating organization. Since 2002 the Association also includes clearing organizations. It unites about 200 registers and depositories.
(c) National Stock Association. The National Stock Association was founded in 1996 as an association for participants in the Treasury bond market. The Association includes nearly 200 credit organizations from 20 regions of Russia. The Association takes part in the licensing of professional participants and helps FCSM control their activities.

21.3.4 Leading Dealers in the Russian Bond Market

21.3.4.1 Dealers at MICEX

Treasury bonds are traded in a special section of MICEX. Probably because of the high liquidity of bonds and the restricted number of types traded, there are no official market makers in this section. The Bank of Russia regularly publishes a list of leading dealers of Treasury bonds market. There are nearly 300 organizations in the list. Eighty-five percent of dealers are commercial banks; the rest are financial and investment companies. Among banks are those with foreign participation and the subsidiaries of foreign banks, including Credit Suisse First Boston, Chase Manhattan Bank, Raiffeisen Bank Austria, ING Bank, and Credit Lyonnais.

There are 50 organizations that are leading dealers of municipal and corporate bonds. Only 40% of dealers are commercial banks; the rest are again financial companies. These are not the familiar foreign banks, seemingly because of the underdeveloped state of this market. In contrast with MICEX, Stock Exchange RTS has official market makers, which are not divided between stock and bond sections. The list of market makers includes one foreign company (a subsidiary of Bransweeck UBS Wartburg), two or three commercial banks, and five finance companies.

21.3.5 Rating Agencies and Ratings

The determination of the rating of a firm or a specific bond issue is not necessary for offering the bond on the domestic market. Russian investors have not yet acquired the culture of relying upon ratings. Ratings are mainly determined for Russian Eurobonds.

According to law, the Russian Federation, subjects of the Russian Federation (republics, regions), and municipal formations can issue state securities and increase state external debt only if they receive a credit rating in accordance with international standards. The rating must be determined by at least two leading international rating agencies. In fact, Standard & Poor's, Moody's Investor Service, and Fitch IBCA usually determine the credit ratings of Russian issuers.

The rating of Russia assigned by Standard & Poor's (other agencies assign approximately the same) is noninvestment grade and comparable with that of Vietnam, Peru, Paraguay, or Grenada. The long term rating is BB−, with the prognosis "stable." During the financial crisis of 1996–1998 Russia's credit rating was lowered to CCC−. Russian regions also issue Eurobonds and have ratings. At present, Standard & Poor's maintains a foreign currency rating for eight "subjects" of the Russian Federation (the total number of subjects in the Russian Federation is 89 and includes the various republics, regions, and the cities of Moscow and Sankt-Peterburg).

Standard & Poor's has also assigned ratings to about 20 Russian firms. These are mainly oil, metallurgy, and telecommunication companies, representing the most intensively developing sectors of the Russian economy. These ratings vary from CCC for some telecommunication companies to B+ for leading oil companies and the gas giant Gasprom. One can observe some attempts at launching rating activities in Russia. The information agency Interfax and economic journal *Expert* established subsidiary rating agencies but they have not yet gained popularity and confidence among investors and issuers.

21.3.6   Agencies of Financial Information

In Russia there are several agencies that distribute economic and financial information to the press and electronic mass media as well as via the Internet. All of them have Internet sites. Some are listed below:

- RIA NOVOSTI: http://www.rian.ru/
- ITAR-TASS: http://www.itar-tass.com/russ/
- PRIME-TASS: http://www.prime-tass.ru
- INTERFAX: http://www.interfax.ru/
- FINMARKET: http://www.finmarket.ru/
- SKATE-PRESS: http://rus.skate.ru/
- AK&M: http://www.akm.ru/
- ROSBUSINESSCONSULTING: http://www.rbc.ru/
- OREANDA: http://www.oreanda.ru/

Usually in addition to Russian, these sites present information in English.

21.4   MARKET FOR RUSSIAN STATE BONDS

The main instruments issued in the Russian state bond market are as follows:

- State short term discount bills (GKO).[1]
- Coupon notes of federal loan (OFZ).

---

[1] Abbreviations in bond names are English substitutes of first letters of their names in Russian.

- Coupon bonds of state savings loan (OGSZ).
- Bonds of Bank of Russia (OBR).

The history of the Russian state bond market is tightly connected with the recent history of economic reforms in Russia, which was briefly described at the beginning of this chapter. Its main landmarks were

1993 – launch of GKO–OFZ market at MICEX;

1995 – launch of interregional trades at GKO–OFZ market at MICEX;

1996 – admission of foreign institutional investors to the market;

1998 – stoppage of all operations at the GKO–OFZ market; and

1999 – resumption of operations at the GKO–OFZ market; restructuring of defaulted bonds in the main into new obligations.

The initial offering and the bulk of secondary trades by GKO–OFZ are carried out at MICEX. At the present time there are nearly 35 issues of GKO–OFZ whose maturity years range from 2002 through 2017. The bulk of bonds mature in 2002–2003.

The initial offering of GKO–OFZ is carried out in the form of an auction, at which participants enter "competitive" applications containing the desired number and the proposed price of the bonds. Additionally, each dealer can enter "noncompetitive" applications to buy bonds at the weighted average price. The total sum of noncompetitive applications of a dealer must not exceed 30% of his/her competitive applications.

In the auction process, the Bank of Russia considers all applications and establishes cutoff prices. All applications with prices exceeding the cutoff are accepted; bonds that stay unsold in the auction, the Bank of Russia sells in the secondary market. Information concerning the forthcoming auctions is published in the official publications of the Bank of Russia, Ministry of Finance, and MICEX and placed on their Internet sites.

21.4.1   Types of Treasury Bonds and Their Characteristics

21.4.1.1   *State Short Term Bills (Treasury Bills) (GKO)*

State short term bills are registered discount bonds with a par value of 1000 rubles and circulation period up to 1 year. Decisions concerning dates and parameters (volume, maturity date, etc.) of specific issues are made by the issuer – The Ministry of Finance. In fact circulation periods vary widely from one issue to another but do not exceed 365 days. The usual value of each issue is from 3 to 6 billion rubles. Outstanding issues in circulation are normally up to seven to eight issues of GKO.

21.4.1.2   *Notes Federal Loan (Treasury Notes or OFZ)*

This common name describes several types of middle and long term coupon bonds denominated in rubles and differing by the way of assigning coupon value.

- OFZ–VC: bonds with varying coupon. Value of each coupon is established by the issuer before the beginning of coupon period depending on current yield of circulating issues of GKO–OFZ and the level of inflation.
- OFZ–CC: bonds with constant coupon. Value of all coupons is constant and is announced beforehand.

Table 21.1   General information on Russian bonds

Name of bond	Type of bond	Par value (rubles)	Circulation period (years)	Coupon payments per year
Short term discount bills (GKO)	Registered, discount	1000	<1	
Long term notes with varying coupon (OFZ–VC)	Registered, coupon	1000	1–5	2 or 4
Long term notes with constant coupon (OFZ–CC)	Registered, coupon	1000	1–30	1
Long term notes with fixed income coupon (OFZ–FI)	Registered, coupon	1000 or 10	>4	4
Long term notes with amortization of debt (OFZ–AD)	Registered, coupon	1000	1–30	4

Source: Based on data of Bank of Russia, Ministry of Finance, MICEX.

- OFZ–FI: bonds with fixed income. Value of all coupons is announced beforehand but can vary from one coupon to another.
- OFZ–AD: bonds with "amortization of debt." Principal value of debt is returned by parts.

All OFZ are registered bonds with a par value of 1000 rubles. Some issues of OFZ–FI have a par value of 10 rubles. Depending on the type and issue of OFZ their circulation period varies from 1 to 30 years (maximum period permitted by law). The coupon is paid from one to four times per year. Some generalized data concerning GKO–OFZ is presented in Table 21.1.

21.4.1.3   Bonds of the Bank of Russia

Bonds of the Bank of Russia are bearer discount bonds with a circulation period less than 1 year. The Bank of Russia issues bonds from time to time to control the liquidity of the banking system of Russia and distributes them among commercial banks only.

21.4.1.4   Federal Savings Notes (OGSZ)

Federal savings notes are bearer coupon bonds issued in documentary form. The notes are issued by the Ministry of Finance and destined for distribution among the local population and are often bought by small investors. The initial offering of the bonds is carried out at MICEX among authorized dealers (mainly banks), which in turn sell them to retail investors. Accounting for a bank's commission, the return on OGSZ for an end purchaser appears to be less than the return on GKO–OFZ though greater than the return on deposits in those banks. At the present time OGSZ are not issued and the redemption of earlier bonds issued is nearly complete.

21.4.1.5   Subfederal and Municipal Bonds

Each of the 89 subjects of the Russian Federation has the right to issue its own bonds. These bonds are generally referred to as subfederal bonds. Cities and other municipal formations also have the right to issue their own (municipal) bonds.

According to the Budget Code of the Russian Federation, subfederal and municipal internal borrowings can be used to cover the deficit of the corresponding budget and also to pay off subfederal or municipal debts. The budget deficit, according to law, cannot exceed 15% of the income (excluding donations from above budgets) of the subfederal budget and 10% of own income of municipal budget. The total volume of state debt of a subject of the Russian Federation and municipal formation in all its forms cannot exceed the yearly income of the budget.

According to estimations by the Ministry of Finance, total state internal debt for all subjects of the Russian Federation, in the middle of 2002, was about 120 billion rubles ($4 billion), of which 21 billion rubles was in the form of subfederal bonds. About 80% of these distributed bonds are bonds issued by Moscow and Sankt-Peterburg.

According to federal law, Terms of Issuance of securities of a subject of the Russian Federation and municipal securities must be registered in the Ministry of Finance. From 1997 through 2002 there were 83 registrations including those by 30 municipalities (mainly big cities). These were for the issuance of middle term registered coupon bonds in a nondocumentary form with a circulation period from 1 through 5 years. Some issues were for short term bills like GKO. The law does not demand that the terms must contain information on dates and volumes of issuance.

After the terms are registered, issues of subfederal and municipal bonds can be realized by separate issues whose times and volumes are determined by the responsible government financial body of government or municipality. These issues are not registered, and so obtaining a generalized picture of these issues is difficult. The Ministry of Finance believes that this is the drawback of the law, and issuance must be controlled; otherwise some newly elected governors of a region can inherit heavy debts from their predecessors, whose administrations have issued bonds uncontrollably.

Only a small part of the subfederal and municipal bonds passed listing procedures and are traded at the exchanges, mainly at MICEX, SPCEX, and RTS. At MICEX and RTS are traded mainly bonds of Moscow city loans; at SPCEX are traded bonds of the city of Sankt-Peterburg.

Starting from 1997, the city of Moscow issued 23 bonds for internal financing with a total value of 21.36 billion rubles. At the present time, there are 12 issues with a total value of 11.06 billion rubles in circulation. Mainly these are coupon notes with short (1–2 year) maturities and have a current annual yield of 15–18%. The return on Sankt-Peterburg bonds also lie in this range.

One of the principal obstacles in the development of the market of subfederal and municipal bonds includes the difficulties in obtaining objective information on the financial state of a subject of the Russian Federation. Specialists note that accounts for regional budgets, published by the Ministry of Finance, are practically the single source of information though this information is sometimes contradictory and not in compliance with law.

21.5   CORPORATE BONDS

During the period of the USSR all large and middle enterprises and the vast majority of small enterprises were the property of the state and were financed from the state budget. There was no necessity for them to attract commercial credits by issuing bonds and such activities would have been at odds with the main dogma of the planned economy of the USSR.

The first years of economic reforms in Russia were characterized by very high inflation and by the appearance of many commercial banks and "investment" companies that attracted money from the public and from enterprises. These banks and companies promised very high interest rates and acted as a financial pyramid. A typical case is the commercial bank of the watch industry ("Chasprombank"), which even in 1995 attracted ruble deposits for interest payments of 0.32% per day that corresponded to 315% annual interest and was equal to the inflation in 1994. For deposits in US dollars the bank paid 22% annual interest. Not surprisingly the bank became bankrupt in 1995.

Industrial enterprises had no likelihood of competing with banks and the first chance for them to attract investments appeared only in 1997 when inflation was reduced to 11%.

The high level of inflation still complicates the problem of attracting investment funds for corporations. Managers prefer to use internal sources of financing, issue equity, or use reduced credits from central or regional governments. Moscow, for example, subsidizes socially and economically important Moscow enterprises.

From the commencement of the registration process in 1996 to October 2002, FCSM registered a total of 594 issues of corporate bonds of which 19.2% were bearer bonds and the rest were registered bonds. To assess this amount note that within the same time interval FCSM registered 112 533 issues of common shares. This is further evidence of the fact that issuance of equity is the preferred way of corporate financing in today's Russia.

The biggest trading place for corporate bonds is MICEX. From 1999 to 2002 the exchange organized IPOs of about 100 issues of (mainly bearer) bonds of nearly 50 issuers with a total volume of 65 billion rubles (more than $2 billion). These bonds were offered as short term bills with a circulation period of about 6 months, while middle and long term bonds have a circulation period up to 4 years.

At present time the exchange quotes 28 issues of bonds of 12 issuers – industrial firms. The volume of an issue depends on the size of a firm and varies between 100 million and 3 billion rubles. RTS also organizes trades by corporate bonds. Currently listed at the exchange are nearly 27 issues of bonds of 16 industrial firms, partially the same as at MICEX. According to some estimates the total value of the corporate bond market in Russia is nearly 75 billion rubles.

21.6   THE MARKET FOR RUSSIAN EUROBONDS

Russian Eurobonds is the common name for bonds issued by the government of the Russian Federation, by subjects of the Russian Federation and municipal formations, and by Russian firms and denominated in hard currencies. One can identify two causes of issuance for such bonds:

- Restructuring of external and in part internal debt of the former USSR. According to the agreement between former republics of the USSR, the Russian Federation accepted all foreign debts and simultaneously all foreign assets of the former USSR.
- Attracting foreign financing, which in many cases appeared and still appears to be less expensive than internal financing.

Russian Eurobonds were first issued by the federal government in 1993 to restructure the hard currency debts of "Vnesheconombank" – the Soviet bank for foreign trade. In Soviet times, citizens of the USSR who worked abroad or received money from abroad, or foreign trade organizations, kept their currency in the state-owned Vnesheconombank. In 1993 the bank appeared to be insolvent and its debts totaling about 8 billion dollars were restructured into dollar-denominated bonds of an internal currency loan OVVZ (Obligatsii Vnutrennego Valutnogo Zaima). The bonds were issued in five tranches with maturities up to 2008 and annual coupon payments of 3%.

Table 21.2 Existing and recently expired tranches of Russian government bonds

Tranches	Maturity date	Coupon (annual)	Total volume (US$ million)	Market yield as of Aug 2002 (%)
3	14.05.99	3	121	
4	15.05.03	3	3462	6.20
5	14.05.08	3	2837	11.20
6	14.05.06	3	1750	10.35
7	14.05.11	3	1750	11.20

Source: Ministry of Finance.

In the following years the government issued the sixth and the seventh tranches of the bonds and was unable to redeem the third tranch, which is now in the process of being restructured (see Table 21.2). The bonds are actively traded at domestic and foreign markets and have a credit rating of BB−.

In 2000, the government of the Russian Federation reached an agreement with commercial banks and credit organizations – members of the London Club of Creditors. According to the agreement, the principal debt of the Russian Federation to the club members was restructured (with a discount of 37.5%) into newly issued dollar-nominated bonds with a total value of $18.2 billion and a maturity of 2030. The bonds bear a stepped coupon whose value varies in range from 2.25 to 7.5%. The coupon is paid semiannually.

Accumulated interest was also restructured (with a discount of 33%) into another issue of state bonds with a maturity of 2010 and a total value of $2.8 billion. The bonds pay a constant annual interest of 8.25%. The interest also is paid semiannually.

The federal government has now confirmed the General Terms of Issuance of Eurobonds for restructuring the commercial debts of the foreign trade organizations of the former USSR to their partners abroad. The debts will be exchanged partly for Eurobonds with maturity from 2006 to 2010, partly for Eurobonds with maturity from 2007 to 2030, and partly returned for cash. The total amount of issues will be up to $2 billion. The amount of debt is now conformed to each creditor.

In addition to the restructuring of debts of the former USSR, the federal government issues hard-currency-denominated bonds to borrow money abroad. So do the regional governments and some Russian corporations. This is because foreign borrowings appear to be cheaper than borrowings in the domestic market. There are many objective causes for this phenomenon:

- High inflation urges issuers to pay high interest on ruble-denominated domestic bonds.
- Russian legislative and court systems (court proceedings and execution of court decisions) are quite imperfect. Receiving back money in the event of default is very problematic. Each of the numerous court proceedings in the second half of 1990 against commercial banks and financial companies and even against the state continued for 2, 3, and more years. Within this period, the owners and managers of a firm in default usually succeeded in withdrawing and hiding all remaining assets so that investors received back only a small part of their money (in addition to losses on account of the devaluation effects of inflation). Russian Eurobonds sold at foreign markets do not bear such risks.
- The dollar is overvalued in Russia and the exchange rate lags behind the inflation rate. This requires an increase of interest on dollar-denominated bonds sold in the domestic market.

Table 21.3   Foreign bond issues issued by the Russian Federal Ministry of Finance

No. of issue	Date of issue	Volume of the issue (in billion)	Maturity date	Annualized coupon	Coupon period	Market yield as of Aug 2002 (%)
2	25.03.97	€1.02	25.03.04	9	Annual	7.1
3	26.06.97	$2.4	26.06.07	10	Semiannual	8.7
4	31.03.98	€0.64	31.03.05	9.375	Annual	7.35
5	30.04.98	€0.39	30.04.03	9	Annual	6.10
6	10.06.98	$1.25	10.06.03	11.75	Semiannual	5.1
7	24.06.98	$2.5	24.06.28	12.75	Semiannual	10.63
8	24.07.98	$2.97	24.07.05	8.75	Semiannual	7.35
9	24.07.98	$3.47	24.07.18	11	Semiannual	10.1
10	25.08.00	$2.82	31.03.10	8.25	Semiannual	8.51
11	25.08.00	$18.34	31.03.30	2.25–7.5	Semiannual	10.58

Source: Ministry of Finance.

- According to widespread opinion, the Russian public has savings in dollars whose total value is estimated at something like $40 billion. Those savings are kept mainly at homes in "banka" – sounds like "bank" but in translation from Russian means jar or can. The public does not readily invest this money because of a deep distrust of Russian commercial institutes and the state as well.

From 1996 through 2000, the Federal Ministry of Finance placed at foreign markets 11 Eurobond issues, 10 of which are in circulation at the present time. Originally the bonds were denominated in US dollars (7 issues), Deutsche Mark (2 issues), and Italian Lira (1 issue). General information on these issues is presented in Table 21.3.

Some Russian regional governments also issue Eurobonds. Remember that according to law these bonds must have ratings assigned by international rating agencies. By the end of 2002 there were only two issues of Eurobonds by Moscow (total 750 million euro) and issues by Sankt-Peterburg (US$300 million), the Yamal-Nenets Autonomous region (US$100 million), and the Kaliningrad region (US$10 million). The major Russian corporate Eurobonds include those of Vympelcom (US$250 million), Gasprom (US$500 million), Gasprombank (200 million euro), MMK (100 million euro), Mosenergo (US$200 million), MTS (US$300 million), Rosneft (US$150 million), Sibneft (US$400 million), and Tatneft (US$300 million). The longest maturity of these bonds is for the Gasprom issue, which matures on April 25, 2007.

21.7   CONCLUSION

After reading this chapter one can conclude that the bond market in Russia is quite undeveloped with the exception of the Treasury bond market. In fact the Russian bond market must undertake considerable reform before it can be the preferred financing vehicle for real sector development.

- Managers of Russian firms must accept and strictly follow norms of honest corporate behavior, and finance procedures must become absolutely transparent.
- The legal system of Russia inherited from the USSR must be reformed. Now many more people are involved in the economic processes, their economic relations are much more

complex and diverse, and Russia must have a better legal system and judiciary to resolve their conflicts. It is critical that the judiciary be independent of central and local administrations.

- Inflation in Russia must be suppressed.

After the above changes occur, investors in Russia must recognize that change has occurred and that investing is now safe and profitable. The public must have its faith restored in Russian institutional investors – private investment, insurance, and pension funds – many of which in the past were fraudulent.

22

Spain

PETRA PÉNZES

22.1 INTRODUCTION

The idea of Spain playing an active role within the European Community, now European Union (EU), has been uniformly supported by the country's main political forces ever since it embarked on a political transition to democracy after the death of General Franco in 1975. It is only natural, therefore, that Spain's securing participation in the introduction of the euro in 1999 was generally regarded as the accomplishment of a major economic policy challenge.

The renouncement of the country's monetary sovereignty has imposed a new challenge for policymakers, however. The central-right Popular Party government must now maintain an appropriate balance between national fiscal policy and monetary policy in the Euro area, while ensuring that Spain's real convergence continues with the more developed EU Member States in terms of income and employment. And, as with other Euro area governments, the very means of fiscal policy have also been largely restricted by the Stability and Growth Pact, which is intended to prevent the respective national governments from overspending by penalizing budget deficits in excess of 3% of GDP.

The chances of Spain exceeding the 3% threshold have been particularly slim because of Prime Minister Jose Maria Aznar's self-confessed obsession for balanced accounts, which is now enshrined in the Budgetary Equilibrium Act. This is in sharp contrast with other major Euro area countries such as Germany and France, which have been accused by the European Commission of deliberately allowing their public finances to deteriorate. Standard and Poor's (2002), however, point out that Aznar's extreme focus on balanced accounts has nonetheless proved costly in economic and inflationary terms. The government's inflation target of 2% was missed by close to 1% in 2002 as the direct result of a series of indirect tax rises. Similarly, gross domestic product (GDP) growth hit barely 2.1% against the official 2.4% projections, and the risks surrounding the outlook continue to be skewed to the downside. The Economist Intelligence Unit (EIU) projects 2.1% GDP growth for 2003 which will be the highest rate among the large EU economies.

Aside from the economy, the stance of the Basque Country continues to dominate Spain's political agenda. The regional Basque government has proposed a radical redefinition of the country's political status, which, if implemented, would lead to de facto independence from Madrid. Although the proposal has no legal basis, the regional government has now committed itself to holding an unofficial referendum during the current legislative period, which will cause a further deterioration of relations with Madrid.

European Fixed Income Markets: Money, Bond and Interest Rate Derivatives. Edited by J.A. Batten,
T.A. Fetherston and P.G. Szilagyi. © 2004 John Wiley & Sons, Ltd. ISBN 0-470-85053-1

Table 22.1 Key economic indicators in Spain

	1998	1999	2000	2001	2002
GDP per head ($ at PPP)	18 010	19 043	20 080	20 935	21 450
GDP (% real change pa)	4.34	4.20	4.18	2.67	2.01
Government consumption (% of GDP)	17.45	17.44	17,60	17.50	17,58
Budget balance (% of GDP)	−2.56	−1.15	−0.60	−0.13	−0.24
Consumer prices (% change pa; average)	1.84	2.29	3.43	3.60	3.53
Public debt (% of GDP)	81.33	75.58	72.37	68.38	64.45
Labour cost per hour (US$)	12.14	12.03	10.78	10.88	11.98
Recorded unemployment (%)	18.83	15.75	13.95	10.53	11.35
Current-account balance/GDP	−0.53	−2.28	−3.42	−2.58	−2.60
Foreign-exchange reserves (billion US$)	55	33	30	29	34

Source: Economist Intelligence Unit. © European Communities, 1995–2003. Reproduced with permission.

Spain has nonetheless been successful in catching up with some of its more developed European counterparts (see Table 22.1). Between 1997 and 2001, the economy recorded an average annual growth of 3.9%, which compared with an average of 2.6% in the Euro area. Accordingly, Spanish per capita income as a percentage of the Euro area average rose from 78.9% in 1996 to 82.6% in 2001. And, despite the economy having losing some of its impetus, Spain should altogether continue to outperform the other major EU Member States over the coming years.

Despite the slowing of the economy, employment figures have held up well and sustained robust growth. In 2000–2001, the number of people in employment rose by some 750 000, while unemployment declined by 350 000. The pace of job creation and unemployment reduction has nonetheless been tapering off, perhaps because of the adverse impact of wage rises in the past two years and the deterioration of business expectations. Job creation in 2002 reached 1.1% in terms of full-time equivalent jobs per year, while unemployment is projected to decline to 11% by the end of 2003.

Spain's trade account indicates that the more recent improvement in employment conditions has not yet translated into a substantial increase in imports. Overall, merchandise exports rose from US$106.9 billion in 1997 to US$117.6 billion in 2001, while imports, which had risen from US$120.3 billion in 1997 to US$151 billion in 2000, fell slightly to US$149.1 billion in 2001. As a result, the trade deficit, which had increased steadily since 1997, eased to US$31.5 billion in 2001. This, combined with a record surplus on the services account, caused the current-account deficit to fall to US$15.1 billion, equivalent to 2.6% of GDP. The economic slowdown of Spain's main trading partners has more recently reduced external demand for Spanish goods and services, however. Accordingly, the EIU has made a downward revision to its forecast for Spanish export growth in 2003, from 6.6% to 4.6%.

22.2 HISTORY AND STRUCTURE OF THE SPANISH BOND MARKET

In recent years, the national financial systems of EU Member States have undergone an intense transformational process of integration, technological innovation, and competition, and Spain is no exception to this rule. Nonetheless, there remain numerous differences between the individual systems, most notably as to whether corporations raise funds by borrowing from banks or directly through capital markets.

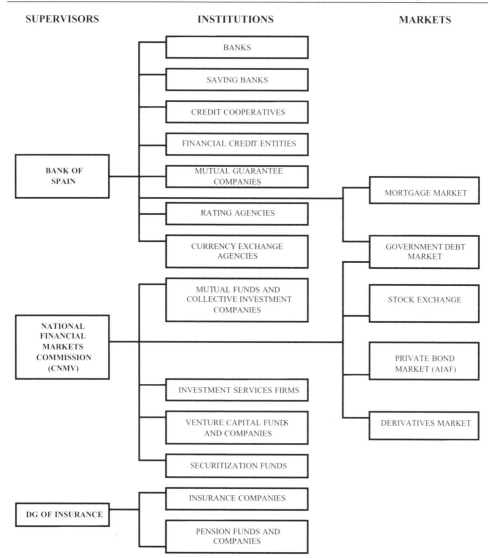

SUPERVISORS   INSTITUTIONS   MARKETS

BANKS

SAVING BANKS

CREDIT COOPERATIVES

FINANCIAL CREDIT ENTITIES

BANK OF SPAIN

MUTUAL GUARANTEE COMPANIES

MORTGAGE MARKET

RATING AGENCIES

CURRENCY EXCHANGE AGENCIES

GOVERNMENT DEBT MARKET

MUTUAL FUNDS AND COLLECTIVE INVESTMENT COMPANIES

STOCK EXCHANGE

NATIONAL FINANCIAL MARKETS COMMISSION (CNMV)

PRIVATE BOND MARKET (AIAF)

INVESTMENT SERVICES FIRMS

VENTURE CAPITAL FUNDS AND COMPANIES

DERIVATIVES MARKET

SECURITIZATION FUNDS

INSURANCE COMPANIES

DG OF INSURANCE

PENSION FUNDS AND COMPANIES

Figure 22.1 Structure of the Spanish financial system.
Source: Bank of Spain. In: Carbó (2002), Financial Sector, Regulation and Corporate Performance: The Case of Spain.

The Spanish financial system is essentially bank-based, which implies that most corporations are largely dependent on bank financing. This is in sharp contrast with some other Member States, most notably the United Kingdom, where the financial system is market-based and corporations have ready access to capital markets. In Figure 22.1 Carbó (2002) gives an overview of Spain's financial system.

Because banks have historically conducted the bulk of financial business, Spanish capital markets have been relatively slow to develop until recently. In order to provide some impetus for development, various regulatory changes were implemented, the first major one of which was the Reform of Capital Markets undertaken in 1998. Changes contained in the Reform

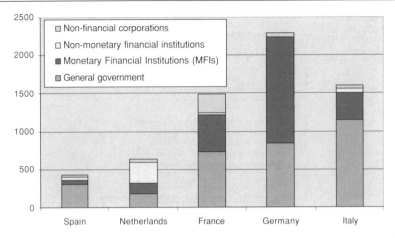

Figure 22.2   The Spanish bond market and other European bond markets by issuer type (in billion euro). *Source*: European Central Bank. Copyright © European Central Bank, Frankfurt am Main, Germany. Reproduced with permission.

included (i) the recognition of the market for private bonds (termed Association of Financial Assets Intermediaries [AIAF] market); (ii) the introduction of the necessary procedures to improve transparency and efficiency in the clearing and settlement systems; (iii) the promotion of interaction between markets and financial institutions; and (iv) the undertaking of various measures to foster the development of Spain's institutional investor base, particularly mutual funds.

The recent regulatory changes have greatly encouraged competition in Spain's financial system and fostered market evolution. However, while stock exchange and derivatives markets have experienced considerable growth, the development of debt markets, and the nongovernment segment of these in particular, continues to lag behind. As a result, small- and medium-sized enterprises (SMEs) continue to depend on bank credit and have very limited access to disintermediated forms of financing (Carbó, 2002). Given that SMEs comprise 90% of Spain's corporate sector, it is not surprising the Spanish bond market remains small relative to its European peers, representing barely 0.5% of the aggregate European market in 2000 (Figure 22.2).

In light of these developments, it is clear that future progress in the bond market continues to hinge upon further stimulatory initiatives on the part of policymakers, whereby market access must be facilitated and promoted among borrowers and investors alike. According to Carbó (2002) such an initiative implemented in November 2002 is the New Financial Reform Act, which aims to undertake a multitude of measures including (i) the provision of easier access to factoring and securitization techniques by corporations; and (ii) the integration of all clearing and settlement systems into a single system for public and private debt as well as equity. The Act conforms to the objectives of the Financial Services Action Plan (FSAP), an initiative by the European Commission approved in 1999, directly aimed at the development of integrated and open wholesale and retail capital markets across Europe, where corporations may access finance easily. The most relevant measures of the FSAP relating to securities markets should be fully implemented by 2003–2005, as recommended by the European Council, although at present there is general concern about whether Spain will meet the deadline.

22.3   PARTICIPANTS AND STRUCTURE OF THE SPANISH BOND MARKET

22.3.1   Regulators

22.3.1.1   Bank of Spain (Banco de España)

The Bank of Spain is an integral part of European System of Central Banks (ESCB), which comprises the European Central Bank (ECB) and the national central banks of all 15 EU Member States. In addition, the Bank is also a member of the Eurosystem, which comprises the ECB and the central banks of the 12 member states of the Economic and Monetary Union (EMU). The Bank is organized around a series of departments, which are overseen by the Governor, the Deputy Governor, the Governing Council, and the Executive Commission.

As a fully-fledged member of the Eurosystem, the Bank is no longer entitled to conduct an autonomous monetary and exchange policy. Within the scope of its participation in the ESCB, it now manages the following activities:

- Defining and implementing the Eurosystem's monetary policy, with the principal aim of maintaining price stability across the Euro area.
- Conducting currency exchange operations consistent with the provisions of Article 109 of the Treaty on European Union, and holding and managing the States' official currency reserves.
- Promoting the sound working of payment systems in the Euro area.
- Issuing legal tender banknotes.

In addition, the Law of Autonomy stipulates the performance of the following functions by the Bank:

- The supervision of all credit institutions including banks as well as the monitoring of the interbank, foreign exchange, mortgage, and government debt markets, the latter jointly with the National Financial Market Commission (CNMW).
- Acting as financial agent for government debt and the provision of management services to the Spanish Treasury in relation to the debt market.
- The promotion of the sound working and stability of the financial system and of national payment systems. To that end, the Bank is in charge of the oversight of the three settlement systems: (i) the SLBE (Bank of Spain Settlement Service, a real-time gross settlement or RTGS system set up as part of the EU trans-European payment transfer system or TARGET); (ii) the SNCE (National Electronic Clearing System); and (iii) the SPI (Spanish Interbank Payment Service).
- The placement in circulation of coins.
- The holding and management of currency and precious metal reserves not transferred to the ECB.
- Preparation and publication of statistics relating to its functions.
- Advising the government as regards the preparation of the appropriate reports and studies.

22.3.1.2   Spanish Treasury

The Spanish Treasury, a department of the Spanish Ministry of Finance, is the issuer of government debt. Its function relates to covering the central government's borrowing requirements at the lowest possible cost, while maintaining risk within acceptable bounds. To that end, the

Treasury's main objectives are as follows:

- To achieve stable financing flows by

  (i)   the establishment of a regular, well-publicized issues schedule with announcement of placement targets;
  (ii) controlling refinancing risk by increasing medium and long term issues;
  (iii) ensuring information transparency by drawing up issue schedules and notifying the financing strategies; and
  (iv) smoothing out the maturities profile of the yield curve through bond exchange programs and buyback policies.

- To reduce the cost of finance through managing debt issuance by means of (i) yield curve management; (ii) buyback policies; and (iii) interest rate swaps.
- To ensure an adequate degree of market liquidity by (i) increasing the amount of issues to over €10 billion; and (ii) by exchanging illiquid issues in order to streamline debt references.
- To offer investors an attractive financial instrument by tailoring the assets issued to investor demand.

22.3.1.3   National Financial Markets Commission (Comisión Nacional del Mercado de Valores, CNMV)

The CNMW is Spain's securities regulatory agency created by the Law 24/1988. The CNMV oversees Spain's entire financial market including the stock exchanges as well as the debt and derivatives markets. Its competence extends to investment services companies, mutual, securitization, and venture capital funds, as well as any individuals and entities involved in the investment business, as far as their activities on their markets are concerned. The CNMV also drafts regulations on a continuing basis and provides advisory assistance to the government and the Minister of Economy.

22.3.1.4   Other Regulators

The legal framework for the regulation of Spanish securities market is set up in the Law 24/1988 of July 28, 1988. The Law was amended 10 years later by Law 37/1998, which was designed to prepare the Spanish securities legislation to be part of the European unified financial market, with the ultimate target of accomplishing the unified securities market. In November 2002 Law 44/2002 was passed in order to make financial markets more effective, improving new technologies and increasing the competition. The stock exchange company Sociedad de Bolsas, which comprises the four regional stock exchanges of Spain, regulates exchange trading of securities. The regulated secondary market for the trading of corporate debt securities is supervised by the Association of Financial Assets Intermediaries (AIAF, Asociación de Intermediarios de Activos Financieros). Derivatives trading is overseen by the Spanish Futures and Options Market (MEFFSA, Mercado Español de Futuros Financieros, Sociedad Anónima).

22.3.2   Categories of Investors

The single largest group of investors in Spanish bonds are nonresident entities (see Figure 22.3). In the government bond market, 37% of outstanding instruments were held by nonresidents as at the end of July 2002, chiefly French, German, Japanese, and UK investors. It is notable that in the first 7 months of 2002, nonresident holdings of medium and long term bonds grew

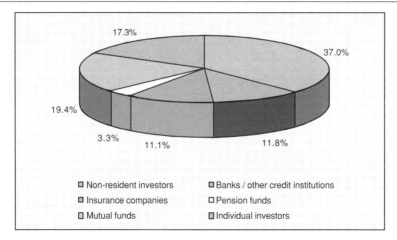

Figure 22.3 Central government debt holdings at the end of July 2002 (in percent).
Source: TesoroPúblico Kingdom of Spain Government Debt Markets, Monthly Bulletin No 96 – September 2002.

by €8.7 billion or 13% over the same period of the previous year. At the same time they were the main investors on the AIAF market too. According to MEFF Annual Report (2002) their investments focused mainly on asset-backed products in 2002. Domestic investors holding significant amounts of government debt include mutual funds (19% as of July 2002), individual investors (17%), banks (12%), and insurance companies (11%).

22.3.3 Market Makers

The following is a list of primary market makers for government securities and strips:

- ABN Amro Bank NV London Branch
- Banco Popular Español
- Banesto
- Bank of America Intl. Ltd.
- Bankinter
- Barclays Bank Plc.
- B Bilbao Vizcaya Argentaria, SA
- Caja A y Monte de Piedad de Madrid
- Confederación Española de Cajas de Ahorros (CECA)
- Crédit Agricole Indosuez, Suc. España
- Crédit Suisse First Boston (Europe) Ltd.
- Deutsche Bank AG
- Dresdner Bank AG
- Goldman Sachs International
- JP Morgan Securities Ltd.
- Caja A y Monte de Piedad Barcelona (La Caixa)
- Merrill Lynch International
- Morgan Stanley and Co. International Ltd.
- Salomon Smith Barney Ltd.
- Santander Central Hispano, SA
- Société Générale, SA

22.3.4 Other Market Participants

Four interdealer brokers operate in the market, which serve as brokers among market makers:

- Gesmosa SA
- CIMD SA
- Capital Market Interdealer Broker SA
- ALL Trading SA

Most bonds are rated by one or more of the following three agencies:

- Fitch IBCA
- Standard and Poor's
- Moody's

22.3.5 Secondary Market Trading

The single largest secondary market for Spanish bonds is the unregulated over-the-counter (OTC) market, whereby trading takes place over the telephone. Trading also occurs in three regulated markets, however. Futures on 10-year government bonds are traded on Spain's futures exchange. Note that the ECB (2001) Blue Book gives a detailed overview of trading, clearing and settlement in the market.

22.3.5.1 Stock Exchanges

Spain has four local stock exchanges: Madrid, Barcelona, Bilbao, and Valencia. The exchanges are run by nonprofit stock exchange governing companies, which together comprise the stock exchange company Sociedad de Bolsas.

The trading volume of debt securities in these exchanges reached €56 billion in 2001; however the bulk of this is attributable to local government securities issued by Catalonia, Euskadi, and Valencia, while trading in other instruments is practically negligible. Like equities, bonds are traded via two systems: the traditional public outcry and the electronic trading platform termed SIBE (Sistema de Interconexión Bursátil Español, or Spanish Stock Market Interlinking System). Open outcry accounts for less than 1% of combined trading, and takes place between 10:00 a.m. and 12:00 noon.

The SIBE has a separate electronic market for fixed income securities, where trading takes place between 9 a.m. and 4 p.m. Trading can be either multilateral or bilateral. Multilateral trading is screen-based and anonymous, and is used in (i) the market of orders and (ii) the market of block trades (for blocks of public debt over €300 506.05 and for blocks of corporate bonds over €150 253.03). For bilateral trading, the minimum volume is €150 000 for corporate debt, and there is no limit for public debt.

It is notable that Spain's exchanges are mainly used by residents, therefore trading volume is low compared with exchanges in other major member states of the EU.

22.3.5.2 Book-Entry Market for Public Debt

The Mercado de Anotaciones en Cuenta del Banco de España is an electronic book-entry market for public debt as well as securities issued by some regional governments and state organizations. Although the market is primarily decentralized, therefore OTC operations prevail, there are also two electronic trading platforms through which transactions are settled:

INFOMEDAS and the pan-European EuroMTS. The market is managed by the Bank of Spain, which publishes a daily fixed income bulletin quoting the average trading price for each instrument traded. Trading in public debt takes place between 9 a.m. and 1 p.m., and other securities between 9 a.m. and 2 p.m.

The trading platform INFOMEDAS, which caters mainly for interdealer brokers, is managed by SENAF (Electronic Trading System of Financial Assets, or Sistema Electrónico de Negociación de Activos Financieros). In 2001, 43% of total trading in public debt, or €321 billion, took place here, more than two thirds of which was in benchmarks. Liquidity in the market is extraordinary, with a minimum transaction amount of €1 million and an average daily brokerage volume of €3 billion. Management plans to operate other financial assets as well in the future, including nongovernment bonds, sovereign debt of other countries, and repos.

22.3.5.3   AIAF Market for Private Debt

The AIAF market is the regulated secondary market for the trading of corporate debt securities, organized by the AIAF. It is a price market (i.e. not blind) without participation from the public. The market trades private and semigovernment bonds, matador bonds, and commercial paper, but is not engaged in the trade of Treasury debt. In 2001, trading exceeded €141 billion, increasing by 42% over 2000, with commercial paper and securitized bonds comprising 69% and 18% of the total, respectively (AIAF, 2002). Most of the traded instruments are dematerialized,[1] although there is a small percentage of physical securities.

Trading is mainly conducted through the OTC market, and the information on offers and prices is available on-screen. Since 2001, securities in the market have been cleared on the Bank of Spain's CADE clearing and settlement platform along with government instruments, which has led to a significant simplification of back-office processes. Also in 2001, repos on AIAF securities were introduced.

In 2002 AIAF strengthened its activity particularly in innovative assets and securities (AIAF, 2002), trading volume in these grew by more than 40%.

22.3.5.4   Spanish Futures and Options Market

The Spanish Futures and Options Market (MEFF SA, Mercado Español de Futuros Financieros, Sociedad Anónima) runs two separate derivatives markets on financial underlying assets:

- MEFF RF (Mercado Español de Futuros Financieros, renta fija) is the market for futures on fixed income securities; while
- MEFF RV (Mercado Español de Futuros Financieros, renta variable) is the market for futures and options on equities.

The only future contracts available on Spanish public debt are written on a notional 10-year government bond with an annual coupon of 4%. The number of contracts reached 250 595 in 2001, having shown a severe decline in previous years. The securities deliverable on expiry are those bonds appearing on the list drawn up by MEFF RF. The standard contract size is €100 000. The contract months are March, June, September, and December, with expiration date on the third Wednesday of the contract month. The last trading date is 2 days before expiration date, settlement occurs upon delivery.

---

[1] Paper instruments are dematerialized and kept in the central securities depository, the SCLV (Securities Clearing and Settlement Service, or Servicio de Compensación y Liquidación de Valores).

Option contracts are only available on the 10-year futures. Expiry is monthly: January, February, April, May, July, August, October, and November. The option is American.

The MEFF RF also trades futures on a synthetic basket of European 10-year sovereign bonds (DEBS). The basket comprises 30% German debt, 30% French debt, 20% Italian, and 20% Spanish. The references selected are the most liquid and the maturities the nearest existing to 10 years within each country's interest rate curve.

In 2002 MEFF was the global leader by volume of single stock futures contracts, since its total trading volume increased by nearly 8% (MF, 2002).

22.4   THE SPANISH GOVERNMENT BOND MARKET

22.4.1   Background

The Spanish government bond market is the fourth largest in the Euro area, representing 8.1% of the total euro-denominated sovereign debt portfolio with an outstanding of €310.3 in June 2002. The outstanding amount has been consistently on a rising trend, growing by more than 50% since 1994. However, the breakdown of debt by type of security has changed substantially in recent years, reflecting continuing efforts on the part of policymakers (i) to extend the maturity composition of government debt in response to declining interest rates; and (ii) to replace nonmarketable securities with marketable ones.

In accordance with the first objective, the average maturity of Spanish government debt increased from 3.8 to 5.5 years between 1995 and 2002. This was in large part achieved by a gradual reduction in the volume of short term Treasury bills in circulation. Figure 22.4 shows that the weight of these instruments in total outstanding government debt declined from 31% to 12% between 1995 and 2002, while the weight of longer term government bonds increased from 51% to 78% over the same period. The increase in the average life of debt has proved compatible with the reduction of the average cost of debt, which declined from 9.6% to 5.6%. The average yield at issuance is currently in the region of 4%, less than half of that in 1995.

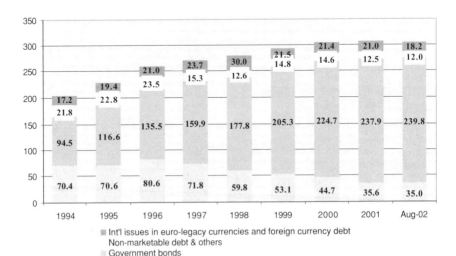

Figure 22.4   Central government outstanding debt (in billion euro).
Source: TesoroPúblico Kingdom of Spain Government Debt Markets, Monthly Bulletin No 96 – September 2002.

Since the mid-1990s, significant advances have also been made in the field of retiring the government's nonmarketable debt. Notably, the share of nonmarketable debt fell from 11% to 4% between 1994 and 2002. Further developments include Spain's declining reliance on fund-raising in overseas markets: between 1998 and 2002, the weight of international issues decreased from 11% to 6%.

It is worth noting that the policy of reopening lines in tranches targeting an outstanding balance of around €12 billion and the Treasury exchange operations have also delivered a public debt structure that is broadly concentrated in a small number of issues of relatively large size, thus ensuring the existence of very liquid benchmark references along the yield curve. In fact, the average size of the outstanding strippable medium and long term bonds now stands upwards of €11 billion per reference.

The efficient management of the Spanish public debt in the framework of the substantial improvement in the macroeconomic situation has altogether resulted in an impressive reduction of the yields demanded by investors. For example, the spread of the 10-year Bono versus its German Bund equivalent has declined from around 700 basis points (bp) in 1995 to 16–17 bp today. These considerable achievements have also been honored by rating agencies, most notably Moody's, which upgraded Spain to its highest rating status of Aaa in June 2002.

22.4.2   Types of Instruments

(A) *Treasury bills (Letras del Tesoro)* are discounted or zero coupon bills with maturities of 6, 12, or 18 months (Table 22.2). They were first issued in June 1987 and became a main funding vehicle for the government. Since 1991, nonresident holders have been exempt from withholding taxes on interest income from the bills.

(B) *Medium term notes (Bonos del Estado) and long term bonds (Obligaciones del Estado)* are interest-bearing instruments with fixed annual coupons issued through competitive auctions. They only differ in terms of maturity: medium term notes have maturities of 3 or 5 years, and long term bonds 10, 15, or 30 years. They are issued in consecutive tranches in order to reach a global issue size, which may grant high secondary market liquidity.

All bonds are registered in the book-entry system for government securities termed Central de Anotaciones en Cuenta del Banco de España. Average prices are published in the Bank of Spain's daily bulletin. Taxes on annual coupon payments to nonresidents and corporate holders are not withheld at source. When-issued trading is permitted, whereby new issues are traded prior to issuance in the so-called grey market.

When Spain redenominated its government debt from pesetas to euros in January 1999, the only ECU bond issued in June 1998 with a 5.15% coupon and maturity in July 2009, consolidated with the 5.15% government bond also maturing on 30 July 2009. Post-EMU new issues are strippable; i.e., the principal and coupon payments may be sold separately.

(C) *Strips (Deuda Segregable)* are zero coupon bonds created by coupon-stripping, whereby the coupons of medium and long term notes and bonds are stripped and sold separately from the principal amount. Actual stripping and trading of the resulting strips began in 1998, and has various benefits in that (i) investors subject to corporate taxation are exempt from withholding tax on the coupons or the return on strips; and (ii) strips facilitate the construction of benchmark yield curves, thereby fostering price discovery for nongovernment issues. The minimum principal value is €1 million, and the minimum unit of strips

Table 22.2 Main features of central government debt

Type	Treasury bills 12- and 18-month Letras	Government bonds 3- and 5-year Bonos*; 10-, 15-, and 30-year Obligaciones*
Face value	€1000	€1000
Coupon type	Discount/zero coupon	Fixed
Interest	At a discount	Annual coupon
Method of issuance	Auction	
Minimum bid	€1000	€5000†
Final date for bids		
Market members	Auction date	Auction date
Nonmembers	Two trading days before auction	One or two‡ trading days before the auction
Settlement date	Two trading days after the auction	Three trading days after the auctions
Payment date		
Market members	Settlement date	Settlement date
Nonmembers	One trading day before settlement	One trading day before settlement
Taxation		
Residents (corporations)	No withholding tax on accrued interest	Strippable bonds: exempt from withholding tax on coupon payments. Nonstrippable bonds: withholding tax (18%) on coupon payments. No withholding tax on coupon payments. Income and capital gains are tax exempt.
Nonresidents§	Income accruing from Treasury bills is tax exempt and not withheld at source	

* Bonos and Obligaciones only differ in terms of maturity.
† Noncompetitive bids, 1000.
‡ One day before the auction for 3- and 5-year Bonos and 15- and 30-year Obligaciones; two days before the auction for 10-year Obligaciones.
§ Taxation for nonresidents does not apply if nonresidents operate through a "permanent establishment" in Spain or the residence country is considered a tax haven by Spanish tax regulations.
Source: TesoroPúblico Kingdom of Spain Government Debt Markets, Monthly Bulletins (various issues to September 2002).

that can be held is €100 000. As of September 2002 there were 19 principal strips in the market, with maturity dates ranging between 1 and 30 years.

The Bank of Spain is the only institution authorized to strip or reconstitute the bonds. Banks and financial companies listed below have been appointed as bond-stripping managers, and must maintain quotes on the most active strips:

- Deutsche Bank
- Banco Español de Crédito
- Banco Central Hispanoamericano
- Barclays Bank
- Banco Santander
- Bank of America
- Banco Exterior de España

Table 22.3   Auction schedule in the Spanish government bond market

Name of instrument	Auction schedule
Letra del Tesoro (Treasury bill): 12- and 18-month	Biweekly (Wednesday)
Bono del Estado (Treasury bond): 3-year	Monthly (first Wednesday)
Bono del Estado (Treasury bond): 5-year	Monthly (first Thursday)
Obligación del Estado (Treasury bond): 10-year	Monthly (first Wednesday)
Obligación del Estado (Treasury bond): 15-year	Bimonthly (first Thursday)
Obligación del Estado (Treasury bond): 30-year	Bimonthly (first Wednesday)

Source: TesoroPúblico Kingdom of Spain Government Debt Markets, Monthly Bulletins (various issues to September 2002).

- Societe Generale, Spanish branch
- Bankinter
- Credit Agricole Indosuez, Spanish branch
- ABN Amro Bank NV, Spanish branch
- Banco Bilbao Vizcaya
- Confederación Española de Cajas de Ahorro
- Caja de Ahorros y Monte de Piedad de Madrid
- Caja de Ahorros y Pensiones de Barcelona
- Merrill Lynch Capital Markets, SVB

22.4.3   Auction Process

Government bonds are typically issued by way of competitive auctions. The Treasury launched its first ever syndicated issue in March 2002. The Treasury publishes the auction schedule at the beginning of each year (see Table 22.3).

22.4.3.1   Auction Method

The auction method employed is a modified Dutch system. Bids by market members must be submitted on the auction day before 10:30 a.m., while those by nonmembers two trading days before the auction for Treasury bills and 10-year Obligaciones; one trading day before the auction for 3- and 5-year Bonos and 15- and 30-year Obligaciones. There are no limits as to the size or number of bids submitted.

The stop-out interest rate and the amount to be allotted is decided by the General Director of the Treasury upon advice by a committee comprised by representatives of the Bank of Spain and the Treasury. Bids at or above the minimum price are accepted and the weighted average price is calculated for the auction. Bids at the stop-out rate are awarded at that price. If the bid price is between the minimum and the weighted average, the price chosen is the bid price. Bids at prices higher than the weighted average price and noncompetitive bids are allotted at the weighted average prices. The second round of the auction results is published at noon two business days after the auction date. Treasury bills settle and are available two business days after the auction, and bonds settle three business days after the auction. The auction schedule is shown in Table 22.3.

The Treasury began Treasury exchange auctions in 1997. These exchange auctions are intended to enhance the liquidity of on-the-run, strippable debt lines, while offering the holders of older debt the opportunity to exchange their holdings for more attractive, strippable securities.

Table 22.4   Conventions in the Spanish government bond market

Convention	Treasury bills	Treasury bills (18-month)	Government bonds
Settlement	T+2	T+2	T+3
Value date	Same as settlement	Same as settlement	Same as settlement
Day count	Actual/360	Actual/360	Actual/Actual
Ex-dividend	Same as coupon	Same as coupon	Same as coupon
Holidays	TARGET	TARGET	TARGET
Calculation type	Money market yield	ISMA yield to maturity	ISMA yield to maturity

Source: Bank of Spain.

22.4.3.2   *Syndicate Method*

The Treasury launched its first syndicated 15-year bond issues in March 2002, following Italy, Greece, Belgium, Austria, and Portugal in their bid to develop their international investor base. The underwriting syndicate included JP Morgan, Deutsche Bank, Credit Agricole Indosuez, Santander Central Hispano, and BBVA, which the Treasury named as the most dynamic primary dealers in the Spanish debt market.

22.4.4   Market Conventions

Table 22.4 contains the most important market conventions.

22.4.5   Redenomination

Instruments originally denominated in Spanish peseta were redenominated based on the following conventions:

- Tradable bonds were redenominated by the investor-holding (bottom-up) method, so each investor-holding was redenominated separately to new euro units.
- Figures were initially rounded to the nearest euro cent, applying the commercial rounding rules.
- The minimum trading unit for redenominated bonds is 1 euro cent.
- Minimum nominal amount is €1000 for Treasury bills and government bonds and €100 000 for strips.
- Odd lots in euro cents were repackaged.
- No cash compensation was granted.
- ISIN or local clearing codes remained the same.

22.4.6   Benchmarks

The Spanish Treasury has developed a full benchmark yield curve, with regular issuances in seven maturities, from 12- and 18-month Treasury bills to 3-, 5-, 10-, 15-, and 30-year bonds. The benchmark bonds, which are the most liquid for a particular maturity at any one time, are strippable issues in the 3-, 5-, and 10-year maturities and on-the-run issues in the 15- and 30-year maturities. Figure 22.5 shows the benchmark yield curve on July 31, 2002, and August 30, 2002.

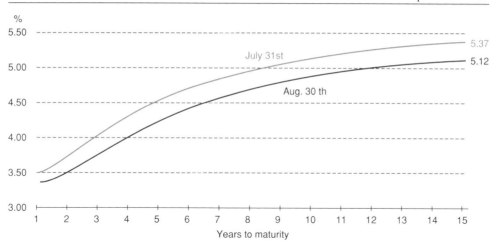

Figure 22.5 Spanish benchmark yield curve.
Source: TesoroPúblico Kingdom of Spain Government Debt Markets, Monthly Bulletin No 96 – September 2002.

22.5   SEMIGOVERNMENT AND CORPORATE BOND MARKETS

22.5.1   Introduction

Activity in the nongovernment segment of Spain's bond market is significantly lower than in the government segment. This largely owes to the bank-based profile of Spain's financial system, whereby corporations are highly dependent on bank financing. Contrary to the corporate borrowers, semi- and local governments have been increasingly keen to raise funding through debt issues, however. And, as in much of Europe, Pfandbrief-style mortgage bonds have been rapidly gaining ground. Table 22.5 enumerates the different types of instruments with their coupon type.

22.5.2   Semi- and Local Government Bonds

Semi- and local government bonds are either fixed or floating rate bonds and have maturities up to 30 years. They are typically rated AA– and above by Standard and Poor's, as indicated in Table 22.6. The bulk of these instruments are usually bought by Spanish and German investors.

The market for these securities has been growing into an important segment of the corporate bond market. This owes as much to the introduction of the euro, which allows issuers to tap a wider range of investors, as to the deregulation of European banking. Development in the market has been gradually freeing local authorities from their traditional house banks, as they come under mounting pressure to tap more competitive sources of funding while struggling to cut budgets. Issuance has been also greatly encouraged by the fact that in 1998, the Bank of Spain decreed that bond issues from autonomous communities should command a zero risk weighting.

In terms of issuance, the pathfinder has been Catalonia, which is understandable given that the region accounts for 20% of Spanish GDP. In addition, Valencia, Madrid, and Andalucia have also shown remarkable activity in the market. The four Spanish issues launched throughout 2001 totaled €750 million, accounting for 9.5% of total euro-denominated issuance by local

Table 22.5   Types of instruments in Spain's nongovernment bond market

Name of instrument	Maturity range	Coupon type
Semi- and local government bonds	Up to 30 years	Fixed/FRN
Fixed bonds	Up to 30 years	Fixed
Floating rate notes	Up to 30 years	FRN
Cédulas Hipotecarias (mortgage bonds)	10 years	Fixed/FRN
Bonos de Titulización (mortgage-backed securities)	10 years	Fixed/FRN

Source: TesoroPúblico Kingdom of Spain Government Debt Markets, Monthly Bulletins (various issues to September 2002).

Table 22.6   Semi- and local government Eurobond issues in Spain in 2001–2002

Issuer	Euro	Annual date	Coupon	Moody's rating	S&P rating	Maturity date
		Eurobond issues in Spain in 2001				
Generalitat Valenciana	300 000	19/02/2001	Fixed 4.75	Aa3	AA−	29/07/2005
Generalitat de Catalunya	200 000	27/06/2001	Floating 6-month EURIBOR + 0.01%	A1	AA	13/07/2016
Institut Catala de Finances	100 000	09/07/2001	Fixed 5.50		AA−	12/07/2011
City of Madrid	150 000	17/12/2001	Fixed 5.10	A1	AA+	21/12/2011
Total	750 000					
		Eurobond issues in Spain in the first quarter of 2002				
Generalitat Valenciana	100 000	27/03/2002	3-month EURIBOR + 0.03%		AA−	12/04/2005
Total	100 000					

Source: Dexia Capital Markets Credit Research, January 2002.

authorities in the Eurobond market. This compares with issuance of just €278 million in the previous year, demonstrating the enormous impetus behind the market. According to the Dexia report Spain accounted for as much as 18% of local government Eurobond issuance (€3.8 billion) in 2002, a massive increase over 2001.

22.5.3   Corporate Bonds

The corporate bond market remains relatively modest in size. Data obtained from the ECB show that as of June 2002, the outstanding volume of debt issued by Spanish nonfinancial corporations amounted to €16.5 billion or 3.7% of total debt issued by Euro area nonfinancial corporations. This comes as no surprise, however, since 90% of Spain's corporate sector is comprised by SMEs with very limited access to debt markets. In contrast, the outstanding volume was €249.9 billion in France, €61 billion in Germany, and €33.5 billion in Italy. The biggest issue thus far comes from the oil group Repsol, which issued €3.25 billion in May 1999, while the first ever high-yield junk bond issue was in the same year by telecommunications company Jazztel.

   The bulk of corporate bonds outstanding in the market are fixed rate bullet or straight bonds, while the issuance of floating rate notes (FRNs) is less frequent. FRNs are typically priced over 3-month EURIBOR. The majority of issues are placed by way of competitive auctions through

Table 22.7   Market conventions in the semi- and local government and corporate bond markets

Convention	
Settlement	T + 3
Value date	Same as settlement
Day count	Actual/Actual
Ex-dividend	Same as coupon
Holiday	TARGET
Calculation type	ISMA yield to maturity

Source: TesoroPúblico Kingdom of Spain Government Debt Markets, Monthly Bulletins (various issues to September 2002).

monthly tenders. Up to 90% is placed to institutional investors in a main auction termed "tramo mayorista," while the remaining 10% is offered through a general public auction termed "tramo minorista." The market conventions are the same as those for semi- and local government bonds, as shown in Table 22.7.

Commercial paper (pagarés de empresa or pagarés financieros) comprise 20% of the market or €3.3 billion. Commercial paper is generally issued with a maturity of minimum 7 days and maximum 21 months, although 18 months is the preferred maximum maturity, as it determines the liquidity classification of the title. It is mostly traded in the AIAF and, to a lesser extent, the stock exchanges.

22.5.4   Pfandbrief-Style Mortgage Bonds (Cédulas Hipotecarias)

Regulated by the Mortgage Market Law of 1981, Cédulas Hipotecarias are mortgage-collateralized bonds similar to the German Pfandbriefe. They are standard bullet bonds issued by banks and savings institutions with 5- or 10-year maturities. Their immense popularity owes to their extremely high credit quality: rating agencies rate Cédulas up to two (ratings) notches higher than the senior debt of the issuing banks.

Although Cédulas were first introduced in the retail market as early as 1861, open market issuance did not begin until 1999, when the introduction of the euro finally allowed issuers to tap the entire euro market rather than just the narrow peseta market. That year, the government also gave a boost to demand for these securities by exempting institutional investors in corporate fixed income bonds listed on a Spanish exchange from withholding tax.

These factors have ensured that since the launch of the first Jumbo issue with designated market-making commitments in March 1999, growth in the Cédulas market has been explosive. Market growth has been further underpinned by the phenomenal success of similar products in Germany and France. By the end of 2002, the outstanding volume reached €26 billion, compared with €5.6 billion at the end of 2000.

Although market makers provide a degree of liquidity similar to that of French or German Jumbos, the overall turnover in Cédulas was rather limited until very recently. This in large part owed to the fact that none of the bonds became eligible to EuroCredit MTS trading, which requires a minimum outstanding volume of €3 billion. This has now changed because more and more issuers are increasing not only their volume in outstanding issues but in every single issue amount. The third deal launched by AyT Cédulas Cajas in October 2002 is the largest in the market so far at €3.5 billion. The 10-year Cédulas issue was rated AAA by all three agencies and priced at around 16 bp over mid-swaps. Earlier in September, BBVA launched a €3 billion 5-year issue, led by ABN Amro, BBVA, Barclays Capital, Dresdner Kleinwort Wasserstein, and SG.

Because of the huge success of Cédulas in recent years, legislation allowing the issuance of a public sector version of the product termed Cédulas Territoriales is now being prepared, which will sit alongside Germany's Offentliche Pfandbriefe and Europe's other public sector covered bond products. Day (2002) notes that the most often mentioned institution in discussions about the new product is Banco de Crédito Local de Espana (BCL), which is 100% owned by BBVA and specializes in public sector lending.

22.5.5   Asset-Backed Securities

The Spanish asset-backed securities market has been growing rapidly in recent years. In 2001, issuance in the market exceeded €10.4 billion, increasing by 46% over the previous year. Since banks have remained the core issuers, the market is today polarized into two distinct bank-driven asset classes: (i) the growing residential mortgage-backed securities sector and (ii) the government-sponsored FTPYME collateralized loan obligations. The synthetic market has been limited to a handful of discreet issuers (Unmack, 2002).

22.5.5.1   Residential Mortgage-Backed Securities (RMBS, Bonos de Titulización)

Bonos de Titulización are pooled mortgage obligations that pass through to investors the interest and principal paid by debtors. These bonds continue to comprise almost half of securitization activity, accounting for 48% of new issuance in 2001 or €5 billion.

The underlying rationale behind the viability of the RMBS market is the inability of smaller or lower rated banks to tap the Cédulas market owing to its restrictive nature. These banks have been able to pool their own mortgage-backed securities into a single special-purpose vehicle, which then becomes bankrupt, remote from the originator, and can also carry a 10% risk weighting, similar to the Cédulas issues, as well as an AAA rating. The first Cédulas club funding securitization was launched by Ahorro Corporacion Financiera in April 2001 for 15 Spanish savings banks. The model has been repeated several times since then, including a record €3.5 billion deal for 17 banks in June 2002 this year. Unmack (2002) noted that syndicate officials continue to report strong and increasing demand for these instruments from international investors.

The use of RMBS technique has also been greatly encouraged by the government decree of May 1998. The decree allows banks to use RMBS as collateral for repurchase transactions with the Bank of Spain. As a result, a number of institutions including La Caixa, one of the largest savings banks in Europe, have chosen to structure RMBS transactions, only to buy them back at launch at tight spreads and use the securities as a liquidity tool. Other banks to have build an established securitization brand name include Santander Central Hispano (SCH) through its Hipotebansa program and Union de Creditos Inmobiliarios (UCI), jointly owned by BNP Paribas and SCH.

22.5.5.2   FTPYME Collateralized Loan Obligations

Funded collateralized loan obligations have grown sharply since the launch of the government-sponsored FTPYME program, which derives from the line of credit extended by the state funding agency Instituto de Credito Official for SMEs. A certain portion of tranches for securitizations of SME loans are government-guaranteed, provided that 50% of the deal proceeds are reinvested in the sector.

The first issue, a club deal for six banks worth €474 million, was launched in September 1999 by Credit Agricole Indosuez and EBN Banco with management company Titulizacion de Activos. Since then, the sector has grown rapidly and is now a dominant feature of the Spanish market. Unmack (2002) finds this hardly surprising, because the guarantee structure provides banks the twin benefits of funding at near EURIBOR levels as well as capital relief to originate further loans. Banks are now having to deploy new structures and tap fresh investors, as a result of which JP Morgan structured a €500 million deal for Banesto in June 2002, using bullet maturities as well as passthrough notes across nine different tranches. The program's size is nonetheless limited by the total guarantee granted by the government at each annual budget. The allotted guarantee for 2002 was exhausted in just 7 months, creating a log jam for many originators hoping to bring deals to market.

22.5.5.3   Synthetic Securitization

So far, only a handful of Spanish banks have launched synthetic securitizations. Unmack (2002) notes that this may in large part owe to the fact that some Spanish investors including money market funds are restricted from buying credit-linked notes. In June 2002, Caja de Madrid bucked this trend by launching the first synthetic securitization of consumer and SME loans worth €3 billion via Credit Suisse First Boston, and a second €4 billion deal is set to follow.

22.6   CONCLUSIONS

Spain's financial system is essentially bank-based, which has delayed the development of the country's capital markets. The recent regulatory changes have greatly encouraged competition in the system and fostered market evolution; however, the development of debt markets, and the nongovernment segment of these in particular, continues to lag behind.

The Spanish government bond market is the fourth largest in the Euro area. The efficient public debt management in the framework of a substantial improvement in the macroeconomic situation has altogether resulted in an impressive reduction of the yields demanded by investors, which has also been acknowledged in the country's AAA credit ratings.

Activity in the nongovernment segment of the market is significantly lower. In the corporate sector, SMEs continue to depend on bank credit and have very limited access to disintermediated forms of financing. This has been somewhat contrasted by increasing activity in the semi- and local government segment of the market, owing as much to the introduction of the euro as to the deregulation of European banking. And, as in much of Europe, Pfandbrief-style mortgage bonds termed Cédulas Hipotecarias have been rapidly gaining ground and now constitute an essential ingredient of not only the local Spanish but the entire pan-European debt market.

REFERENCES

Association of Financial Assets Intermediaries (2002). Monthly Report (various issues).

Carbó, S. (2002). Financial Sector, Regulation and Corporate Performance: The Case of Spain. Presented at the *International Conference on European Financial Systems and the Corporate Sector*, October 4–5, 2002, Maastricht.

Day, N. (2002, October). Cédulas Issuers Flying as Rivals Suffer. Euroweek (Supplement – Spain in the Capital Markets 2002), pp. 16–17.

European Central Bank (2001, June). *Blue Book Spain*. Frankfurt: ECB.

The Economist Intelligence Unit (2003). *Country Briefings: Spain*. London: EIU. www.economist.com.

MEFF Mercados Financieros (2002). Annual Report. MF Publication.

Spanish National Financial Markets Commission (2001). *Annual Report on Activities*.

Spanish Treasury (2002b). Strategy. Annual Publication.

Standard and Poor's (2002, March). Strong Growth in Iberian Securitization Predicted for 2002. *GT News* Article No. 6/4375.

Standard and Poor's MMS (2002, December). EMU Sovereign Supply Outlook.

Unmack, N. (2002, October). Spain Moves Beyond RMBS Market. *Euroweek* (Supplement – Spain in the Capital Markets 2002), pp. 16–17.

23

Switzerland

HEINZ R. KUBLI

23.1 INTRODUCTION

Swiss investors are important to the international securities markets, and particularly to the Eurobond market. The two Swiss big banks, UBS AG and CS Group AG, rank among the world's largest fund management houses according to several international surveys. The country's unique standing in terms of political, economic, and financial stability gives Switzerland a strong competitive edge as a distribution channel for capital market products (Euromoney, 1998). The risk-averse investment style, still a characteristic of Swiss investors, makes it a good place for bond markets. Also mutual funds in Switzerland invest from half up to two thirds of the money received in bond markets.

Following the bad economy in 2003, and a brighter outlook for 2004, investors in search of higher returns have started to invest anew in financial products being of credit-grade single A and lower but only in conjunction with a good investment story and a brand recognition.

With the introduction of Basle II over the coming years, banks need higher equity capital for credits to small and mid-sized companies. These higher boundaries are not as much of a problem for Swiss banks as they are for German or Austrian banks, since privately owned companies in Switzerland have a larger equity base than their peers in the neighboring countries.

Switzerland is a prosperous and stable modern market economy with a gross domestic product (GDP) per capita higher than that of the big Western European economies. The Swiss in recent years have brought their economic practices largely into conformity with the European Union's (EU's) to enhance their international competitiveness. Although Switzerland is not pursuing full EU membership in the near term, Berne and Brussels signed agreements to further liberalize trade ties in 1999. They continue to discuss further areas for cooperation. Switzerland remains a safe haven for investors, because it has maintained a degree of bank secrecy and has kept up the franc's long term external value.[1]

The Swiss National Bank (SNB) can build a large degree of political autonomy because its prime target is to maintain price stability. As a result of its long-standing stability-oriented monetary policy, Switzerland has one of the world's hardest currencies and the lowest nominal and real interest rates in Europe (Euromoney, 1998).

The GDP growth rate dipped to 0.0% in 2002. GDP growth year-on-year was mainly positive since the second quarter of 1997 with peaks of about 3% in the first quarter of 1998 and 2000, but lately being at negative numbers (see Table 23.1). GDP growth would have been weaker if it had not been for private and largely increasing public consumption.[2] GDP growth

---

[1] http://www.cia.gov/cia/publications/factbook/geos/sz.html#Econ, as of December 23, 2002.
[2] See SNB, 2003, Section P1: Bruttoinlandprodukt nach Verwendungsart – nominal, p. 102.

European Fixed Income Markets: Money, Bond and Interest Rate Derivatives. Edited by J.A. Batten, T.A. Fetherston and P.G. Szilagyi © 2004 John Wiley & Sons, Ltd. ISBN 0-470-85053-1

Table 23.1 Key economic indicators in Switzerland

Economic indicators	1998	1999	2000	2001	2002
GDP (US$ billions)	191.81	197	207	226	231
GDP growth rate (%)	2.4	1.6	3	1.3	0
Per capita GDP (USD), estimated*	26 400	27 100	28 600	31 100	31 700
Imports (CHF billions)	95.5	99.0	91.6	91.4	94.4
Exports (CHF billions)	94.4	98.5	91.3	91.4	100.3
Annual inflation rate (%)	-0.1	1.6	1.5	0.3	0.5
Unemployment rate (%)	3.4	2.5	1.9	2.4	1.9
Average annual currency/(US$)	1.45	1.50	1.69	1.69	1.56

Source: EC. © European Communities, 1995–2003. Reproduced with permission.
* CIA – The World Fact Book 1999 to 2003.

projections for 2003 and 2004 are at around −0.4% and 1.4%, respectively.[3] The GDP per capita increased continuously from 1998 to 2002. In 2002, Switzerland was ranked number four among European countries in terms of GDP per capita, outranking the large European economies.[4] The Swiss economy is largely service-based and services represent 69.1% of the labor force and 64% of the GDP. Industry represents 26.3% and 34%, respectively, and agriculture the remainder.[5] Switzerland usually runs a balanced trade account, though in 2002, imports decreased much faster than exports, lifting the trade balance surplus within a year by CHF 4.2 billion to CHF 12.2 billion by end of the second quarter of 2003.[6]

Consumer price inflation has been very low for the last several years in Switzerland. Deflation was 0.1% in 1998, down from 0.3% inflation in the previous year. It increased up to 1.6% in 1999, only to drop back to 0.3% by 2001. There is only a slight probability of a deflationary scenario; rather it is expected that consumer prices increase at a low rate around 0.6% in 2003 and in 2004. Unemployment rose to 4.0% by end of September 2003, after a low of 1.9% in 2000, with a large number of people from the financial service industry being unemployed. Over the next few months, it is expected that unemployment rate may decrease slightly.[7]

23.2   SIZE AND RATINGS OF THE SWISS BOND MARKET

The Swiss bond market includes Swiss federal bonds ("Eidgenossen"), "other bonds," which are usually corporate bonds and local government bonds, floating rate notes Swiss and foreign convertible and "cum warrants" bonds, the Swiss Exchange (SWX) Eurobonds, foreign currency bonds and delisted bonds. The Swiss repo market, bank debentures, and interest rate futures on federal bonds traded at EUREX are further instruments that are highly interrelated to the bond market.

Over the six years from 1997 to 2002, a decreasing number of domestic bonds have been issued while the foreign bond section did not change much in number of issues except a drop in 2002 (see Table 23.2). Because of the ongoing mergers among the large issuers worldwide the number of issuers has also decreased lately. Another reason for the lower number of issuers is that Swiss municipalities stopped to issue their own bonds. They fund themselves commonly

[3] See http://www.moneycab.com/de/home/business/konjunktur/konjunktur/daten_prognosen.html, as of November 4, 2003.
[4] See http://www.hhs.se/personal/suzuki/o-English/ne04.html, as of December 24, 2002.
[5] See Footnote 1.
[6] See SNB, 2003, Section Q1, Ertragsbilanz p. 107.
[7] See Footnote 3.

Table 23.2 Overview of listed bonds and issuers, end-1998 till end-2002

| | December 31, 1998 | | December 31, 1999 | | December 31, 2000 | | December 31, 2001 | | December 31, 2002 | |
	Securities	Issuers	Securities	Issuers	Securities	Issuers	Securities	Issuers	Securities	Issuers
Swiss	1092	189	1020	179	961	187	887	174	775	162
Foreign	738	296	737	291	782	275	733	253	573	246
Total	1830	485	1757	470	1743	462	1620	427	1348	408

Source: SWX (http://www.swx.com/market/reports/2002/j02_1_0e.xls, as of November 4, 2003). Reproduced by permission of SWX Swiss Exchange.

Table 23.3 Market capitalization (in million CHF) of listed bonds, end-1997 till end-2001

	1998	1999	2000	2001	2002
Swiss	225 789.7	227 084.4	221 998.0	220 948.3	245 149.4
Foreign	162 071.9	172 744.2	181 168.6	181 002.6	189 940.0
Total	387 861.6	399 828.6	403 166.6	401 950.9	435 089.4

Source: SWX (http://www.swx.com/market/reports/2002/j02_2_le.xls, as of November 4, 2003). Reproduced by permission of SWX Swiss Exchange.

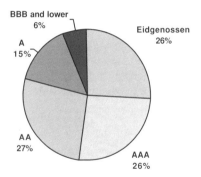

Figure 23.1 Outstanding Swiss bonds by credit rating (2002).
Source: ZKB, Swiss Rating Guide July 2002, p. 6. Reproduced by permission of ZKB.

through the issuing center of Swiss communities or the issuing center of Swiss regional banks. A similar trend has taken place within the EU and Scandinavia, where former municipal and sovereign bonds are now issued via institutions like Kommunekredit, Kommunalbanken, and Kommuninvest.

Market capitalization of the Swiss bond market (see Table 23.3), not including the SWX Eurobond market, reached more than CHF 400 billion by 2000. Partially, this increase has been supported by the decreasing interest rates. Recently, there has been growth in the market for foreign bonds (bonds issued by non-Swiss corporations).

In July 2002, excluding the SWX Eurobond segment, the Cantonalbank of Zurich counted that 26% of the bonds listed at the SWX were Eidgenossen or Swiss federal bonds. They rated another 26% of the bonds as AAA, 27% with a rating of AA, and 15% with a rating of A. Issues with a rating of BBB and lower made up only 6% of the Swiss bond market. This rating distribution mirrors the Swiss investors' preference for safe investments (see Figure 23.1).

23.3   MARKET PARTICIPANTS AND STRUCTURE

23.3.1   Regulators and Covering Law

A definition of bonds does not exist under Swiss law, but there are several rules covering bond trading in Switzerland. These are

- the Federal Act on Stock Exchanges and Securities Trading (Stock Exchange Act) of March 24, 1995,
- the Ordinance on Stock Exchanges and Securities Trading (Stock Exchange Ordinance) December 2, 1996, and
- the Stock Exchange Ordinance.

The SWX is organized with its own rules and regulations. Namely, the listing rules are important for bonds being traded at the SWX. The Swiss exchange has to ensure that it has an organizational structure in respect of its operations, administration, and supervision that is appropriate to its activities. The operation of the stock exchange is subject to authorization by the supervisory authority,[8] which is the Swiss Federal Banking Commission (SFBC). The organization of the SFBC is a constitutional framework for its supervisory activities, based on Art. 98 of the Federal Constitution of April 18, 1999, which entered into force on January 1, 2000. Additionally, there is the ordinance of December 2, 1996, on the charge of taxes and fees by the SFBC.

The Swiss central mortgage bond institutions are based on the federal law of June 25, 1930, and the corresponding ordinance of January 23, 1931. Other laws covering the Swiss financial markets are the Takeover Ordinance and the Regulations of the Takeover Board, though they only apply for the equity markets. Because of the increasing integration of the banking and the insurance sectors, there is an effort to integrate the SFBC and the Federal Office of Private Insurance into a new supervisory authority.[9]

23.3.2   Other Regulators

The Swiss Takeover Board is a Federal Commission established under the Federal Act on Stock Exchanges and Securities Trading of March 24, 1995. It has jurisdiction to issue general rules and ensure compliance with the provisions applicable to public takeover offers.

23.3.3   Federal Institutions

23.3.3.1   Swiss National Bank (SNB)

The SNB conducts the country's monetary policy as an independent central bank governed by special provisions of federal law. In conjunction with fiscal and competition policy, this serves to create an appropriate environment for economic growth. The National Bank is obliged by the Constitution and statute to act in accordance with the interests of the country as a whole. It considers price stability to be a primary goal.[10] Price stability is considered to be equivalent to an inflation rate of less than 2% per annum, measured by the national consumer price

---

[8] See the Federal Act on Stock Exchanges and Securities Trading, October 1, 1999, Art. 3.1.
[9] http://www.efd.admin.ch/d/dok/medien/medienmitteilungen/2000/11/finanzmarkt.htm, as of December 22, 2002.
[10] http://www.snb.ch/e/snb/index.html, as of December 18, 2002.

index. Currently, the SNB applies an expansionary monetary policy with a target range for the 3-month LIBOR at 0.00–0.75%.[11]

Important to the bond market is the SNB's role as banker to the Confederation and its advisory to the federal authorities on issues of monetary policy. Further activities of the SNB are to promote the efficiency of the payment system, ensuring the supply of money, provision of cashless payment transactions for payments between banks, the investment of currency reserves, the support of the stability of the financial system primarily with its stability-oriented monetary policy, and the compilation of statistical data, notably regarding banking activities and Switzerland's balance of payments.[12]

The supervisory bodies of the SNB are the Bank Council with 40 members and the Bank Committee with 10 members of the Bank Council including its President and its Vice President. Local committees consist of 3 members each at the head offices and the six branches. Also an auditing committee is in place.[13]

23.3.3.2   *Federal Finance Administration (FFA)*

The Federal Council of Switzerland has established a financial mission statement for its financial policy with two main objectives[14]: First, the intention to provide for stability and economic growth, and therewith to lift employment, welfare, and social coherence; and second, the goal to obtain healthy public finances, therewith to carry out the duty of permanently meeting socio-political and economic goals.

The duties of the FFA include to estimate the cost of the federal financial budget, to keep the accounts of the Confederation, and to judge the affecting expenses of all federal departments. The FFA further deals with national and international financial and monetary topics, maintains the relationship between the Confederation and the SNB and the International Monetary Fund (IMF), and is leading the legislative process for laws in banking and finance.[15]

In order to fulfill the mission statement resulting from the obligations in the monetary policy, the FFA was established as the interface between the Confederation and the SNB and is leading the business with respect to the Confederation.[16] Thus, it is the FFA who decides about the need for capital by the Confederation and how much money has to be raised by the issue of federal bonds and the money market debt register claims. During the nineties the Confederation's debts more than doubled. While back in 1991 the Confederation's debts amounted to CHF 43.9 billion, they reached CHF 105.7 billion in 2001. Although the financial years had positive net results in 1998, 2000 and 2002, for 2003 a loss of CHF 246 million is estimated.[17]

23.3.4   Categories of Investors

The main investors in Swiss bonds are private investors followed by institutional investors like Swiss pension funds and insurance companies, investment funds, and some foreign institutions, especially from the European Community.

---

[11] http://www.snb.ch/e/aktuelles, Geldpolitische Lagebeurteilung, as of September 18, 2003.

[12] http://www.snb.ch/e/snb/, as of December 18, 2002.

[13] http://www.snb.ch/e/snb/aufsicht/aufsicht.html, as of July 31, 2002.

[14] See: http://www.efd.admin.ch/d/dok/faktenblaetter/efd-schwerpunkte/104_finanzleitbild.htm, as of December 24, 2002.

[15] See: http://www.efd.admin.ch/d/dasefd/aemter/efv/, as of December 24, 2002.

[16] http://www.efv.admin.ch/d/wirtsch/rechtsgr/index.htm, as of December 22, 2002.

[17] SNB, 2003, Section H1, "Rechnungsabschlüsse und Schulden von Bund, Kantonen und Gemeinden," p. 61.

Switzerland has a three-pillar pension system comprising the state pay-as-you-go system (AHV/AVS or 1st Pillar), a funded occupational scheme (2nd Pillar), and a personal scheme (3rd Pillar) (CSFB, 2000, p. 42). The AHV/AVS invested approximately CHF 3.8 billion in the CHF-denominated bonds and about CHF 2.3 billion in foreign-currency-denominated bonds as of end of August 2003.[18] Swiss pension funds, the 2nd Pillar, have traditionally held a significant proportion of their assets in domestic bonds. In general, investment rules limit in-house funds invested in bonds at a maximum of 75% of assets under management (AuM). All of them are required to be of investment grade. Swiss pension funds have approximately CHF 500 billion AuM.[19] Thereof, approximately 50–60% are invested in interest-rate-bearing instruments. For example, the pressure group KGAST, an association of 12 endowment funds, which manages funds for smaller pension funds, invests CHF 25 billion of their CHF 47 billion AuM in bonds.[20] The other 25–50% of the AuM can invest in higher yielding asset classes such as equities and alternative investments, though the last asset class is only now introduced slowly by some pension funds. The reason for not allocating more to alternative investments immediately is that the investment rules stated in the funds' regulation have to be adjusted first, which is a tedious process.

The largest group of investors is private investors with Swiss bank accounts. In August 2003, Swiss private investors held approximately CHF 502 billion in bonds, while foreign investors with Swiss bank accounts held CHF 653 billion in bonds.[21] Foreign investors who directly invest in the Swiss capital markets held CHF 150 billion in assets from Switzerland as of end of 2001.[22] This figure accounts for both equity and bond holdings.

23.3.5 Market Makers

The following is a list of the major issuers and market makers in the Swiss franc bond market[23]:

- CS First Boston
- UBS Warburg
- Cantonalbanks[24]
- Bank von Ernst & Cie AG
- ABN Amro
- Deutsche Bank
- Cantonalbank of Zurich
- BNP Paribas
- Swiss Association of Raiffeisen Banks
- Commerzbank
- Coop Bank
- Dresdner Bank
- Swiss National Bank

The latest issues of the lead tables with their details and the acceptance of the new issues in the Swiss market are well described in the weekly IFR publications.

---

[18] SNB, 2003, Section D7, p. 38.
[19] Finanz und Wirtschaft, 2002b, p. 17, "Pensionskassen zwischen Furcht und Zuversicht".
[20] Finanz und Wirtschaft, 2002b, p.17, "PK-Anlagestiftungen: Aus Aktien umgeschichtet."
[21] SNB, 2003, Section D5, p. 35.
[22] SNB, 2003, Section S2, 2a, p. 1.
[23] Finanz und Wirtschaft, 2002a, Nr. 69, p. 5, quoted from a study by CSFB.
[24] Without Cantonalbank of Zurich.

23.3.6   Other Market Participants

23.3.6.1   Interdealer Brokers

Since the secondary market in Swiss bonds is fully automated at the SWX, there are hardly any interdealer brokers present. Since all market makers are present, only PKB (Privat-Kreditbank) Lugano is acting on Reuters as an interdealer broker for smaller company debts. In the grey market, ahead of the SWX listing, Aurel Leven and Yaron SA are active. The SWX, however, plans to include the primary market on its platform. The need for interdealer brokers will then also be negligible in the primary market.

23.3.6.2   Rating Agencies

There are no official rating agencies headquartered in Switzerland. In the SFBC Circular 98/3 however, the following agencies are recognized[25]:

- Dominion Bond Rating Service, Limited, London
- Fitch Inc., New York/Fitch Limited, London
- Mikuni & Co., Limited, Tokyo
- Moody's Investors Service, Inc., New York
- Standard & Poor's Services, New York
- Thomson Bank Watch, Inc., New York

Of the CHF 400 billion in debentures listed at the SWX, either Moody's or Standard & Poor's rate about 45% of the foreign debtors. Of about 170 national debtors only about 30 are rated by either Moody's or Standard & Poor's.[26,27]

Additionally, banks like UBS, CS Group, Cantonalbank of Zurich and Vontobel produce credit research reports, providing investors with credit ratings for different CHF issuers.

23.3.7   Exchange Information

There is one official domestic stock exchange in Switzerland, the Swiss Exchange (SWX) in Zurich. The fully electronic trading within the SWX replaced the traditional floor trading system at the stock exchanges of Geneva, Basle, and Zurich in 1996. The SWX divides its segments in the CHF section into Swiss federal bonds, other bonds (usually corporates and financials) floating rate notes, Swiss and foreign convertible and "cum-warrants" bonds, derivatives on federal bonds, and other interest rate derivatives. Foreign currency bonds denominated in USD, €, GBP, or JPY are either in the SWX Eurobonds or the foreign currency bonds section. Foreign convertibles in € and USD are traded in the Eurobond segment.

The SWX Interest Products Guide provides information on the current trading organization and product specifications of Swiss franc bonds, Swiss and foreign Swiss franc convertibles and warrant bond issues, warrants on federal bonds as well other interest rate options. The specific

---

[25] SFBC Circular 98/3: Recognized Rating Agencies, as of June 1, 2001.

[26] Rated national debtors are Cantonalbank of Argovia, ABB, Adecco, Cantonalbank of the County of Basle, City of Basle, Cantonalbank of Basle, Ciba Specialty Chemicals, CSFB, CS Group, Swiss Government, issuing center of Swiss municipalities, issuing center of Swiss Regional Banks, Eurofima, Canton of Geneva, Holcim, City of Lausanne, Migrosbank, Migros-Genossenschaftsbund, Nestlé, Novartis, Pfandbriefbank, Swiss Re, Cantonalbank of Schwyz, Sika, Cantonalbank of St. Gall, Syngenta UBS, Cantonalbank of Zurich, Canton of Zurich, and Zurich FS.

[27] See "Swiss Rating Guide 2002/03 – Schuldnerübersicht über den Schweizer Kapitalmarkt", July 2002, Credit Research provided by the Cantonalbank of Zurich.

list of reference price/round-lot correlations is also available in the SWX Equity Products Guide, or, as applicable, the SWX Interest Products Guide.[28]

23.3.8 Trading Rules[29]

Most of the bonds trading in Switzerland occur at the SWX. All listed securities are permanently traded, with the option of voluntary market making, during official trading hours. The minimum trading lot at the SWX is equivalent to the smallest tradeable denomination, which is usually one unit. The SWX reviews the classification of securities according to specific round-lot categories on a monthly basis.

For most of the bond sections, trades with a ticket size of lower than CHF 100 000 must be executed within official trading hours through the SWX trading system, whereas orders above these size limits may be traded off-exchange. Only SWX Eurobonds are exempted from this rule. Over-the-counter (OTC) transactions on the national market have to be reported within 30 minutes of their conclusion (reporting-obligation). OTC transactions in Eurobonds do not have to be reported to the SWX.

Fixed interest bearing securities are in general quoted in percentages of their nominal value. These prices are quoted without accrued interest. The buyer of the bond, however, has to pay accrued interests on to the seller for the time between the last coupon payment and the third day after the trade, the value date, also if the delivery follows later than that (Albisetti *et al.*, 1990, p. 235). For foreign currency bonds, which are not quoted in either USD or €, a fixed currency cross-rate is used for the calculation of their prices. Only double currency bonds and distressed bonds are traded on a flat rate, without the calculation of accrued interest. The traded prices of all securities are constantly monitored during the SWX Swiss Exchange's opening phase and main trading session. As soon as the difference between two successive traded prices is greater than a specific predefined value, a brief trading suspension, called "stop trading," is automatically triggered.[30]

The SWX publishes daily price quotes on most corporate bonds, Swiss government bonds, foreign currency bonds, SWX Eurobonds, and their benchmark electronically via its website. The SWX platform for bond trading is a fully integrated electronic trading platform for the secondary bond market, which has the benefit of full transparency and benefits from low transaction costs.

23.4 MARKET CONVENTIONS

The market convention is for trade plus 3 days (T+3) settlement for all government securities with the value date the same as the settlement date. The Swiss holiday calendar is employed and accrued interest is calculated with the simple yield method. In general, the 30/360-day basis is employed, but there are a lot of exceptions in the Eurobond market: Floaters are usually employing the actual/actual-day basis; US domestic and sterling bonds employ actual/365-day basis; and Eurocurrencies usually use the actual/360-day basis. On the Bloomberg pricing system, day-basis is given in the description of the individual issues.

---

[28] See http://www.swx.com/market/trading_organization_en.html, as of December 19, 2002.
[29] See http://www.swx.com/market/trading_organization_en.html, as of December 19, 2002.
[30] See Appendix for the predefined trigger value for these stops.

23.5 BENCHMARKS

In Switzerland about 63 bond indices and subindices are published on a regular basis. There are three main providers for these indices:

- The SWX with the Swiss Bond Indices family consisting of 18 indices and subindices,
- Pictet & Cie with the Pictet Bond Indices consisting of 15 indices and subindices, and
- Cantonalbank of Zurich with the ZKB Bond Indices consisting of 30 indices and subindices.

Other indices are also used in Switzerland, especially for foreign and international bond markets. Among them, Salomon Smith Barney's, Lehman Brothers', and Datastream benchmark bond indices are often mentioned. Instead of an index, UBS presents an overview of benchmark bonds on www.ubs.com/quotes. However, instead of looking at bond indices, Swiss investors often benchmark yields of the bonds to buy against the CHF swap rate or the yield curve derived from Confederation bonds.

23.5.1 Swiss Bond Index (SBI®)[31]

The SBI® measures the performance of CHF bonds with a minimum maturity of 1 year. It consists of a domestic segment (Swiss Domestic Bond Index) and a segment for bonds issued by foreign borrowers (Swiss Foreign Bond Index). All bonds included in the Swiss Foreign Bond Index must be AAA-rated.

The domestic segment includes the government index (Swiss government bonds); a nongovernment index comprising bonds issued by the cantonal and municipal authorities, the cantonal banks, the mortgage bank institutions, and selected issuing agencies; as well as bonds of companies with a minimum rating of AA or Aa3. The foreign segment is divided into three subindices covering government, corporate, and supranational bonds, respectively. Further, the domestic and the foreign segment are broken down into further subsegments by maturities (1–3, 3–5, 5–7, 7–10, 10+ years). The nongovernment index as well as the maturity subindices was introduced on October 1, 1998.

In addition to total return, a price index as well as the average yield and duration are calculated for all the SBI® indices. Since August 3, 1992, they have been published in real time with a baseline of 100 on December 31, 1991. This baseline was reset back to 100 on January 1, 1996.

23.5.2 Pictet Bond Indices[32]

The Pictet Bond Index family consists of two main indices: the "Pictet General Index" and the "New Issue Index." The two Pictet Bond Indices measure the performance of the market as a whole (General Index) and the performance of the market segment in which trading is most active (New Issues Index). The Pictet General Index contains domestic and international bonds denominated in CHF, with consideration given to debtor quality, coupon rate, and probable residual duration in accordance with stock market capitalization. Its subindices are segmented into Swiss, foreign, and maturity subindices. The Swiss subindex is further segmented into "Confederation and local Government bonds," power supplies, "banks and financials," and "industries and others." The foreign subindex is further segmented into "foreign government

---

[31] http://www.swx.com/products/products_indexfamily_en.html, as of December 19, 2002.
[32] Compare http://www.pictet.com/en/services/research/pictet.html, under Pictet Bond Indices, as of December 21, 2002.

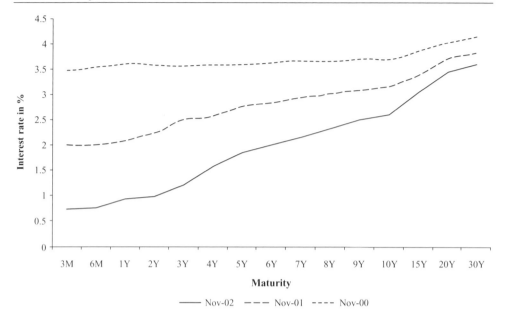

Figure 23.2   Swiss government benchmark yield curve (November 2000, November 2001, and November 2002).
Source: Open Bloomberg LP.

and foreign local government bonds", and others. And the maturity indices are segmented into maturities below 3 years, maturities of 3–7 years, and maturities above 7 years.

The New Issues Index measures the performance of the market segment in which trading is most active. The average term of new issues is longer than that of the general index because the bonds have just been launched. This index measures the performance of the most volatile segment of the bond market. The New Issues Index is further segmented into Swiss bonds and foreign bonds. As of January 1, 2004 the Pictet Bond Indices will be replaced by the SBI® Index family.

23.5.3   ZKB Bond Indices[33]

The ZKB Bond Index family consists of six main indices representing the SWX segments of Confederation bonds, and bond portfolios of Swiss bonds and foreign bonds, with credit ratings of AAA, AA, and A, respectively. Their subindices are segmented into maturity subindices, representing maturities of 1–3 years, 3–5 years, 5–7 years, and 7–10 years; only for Confederation bonds there is an additional subindex with maturities above 10 years. The indices are constructed as price and performance indices of synthetic zero-coupon debts, and have, therefore, constant duration.

23.5.4   Federal Benchmark Bonds

The FFA is committed to creating benchmark issues at key maturities along the yield curve. The issued size federal bonds are reported monthly on the SNB homepage on

---

[33] Compare "ZKB Bond Index Reglement" issued by the Cantonalbank of Zurich, on: http://www.zkb.ch/boerse/bondindex_files/pdf/ZKB_Bondindex.pdf.

http://www.snb.ch/e/aktuelles/index.html?file=pressemit/content_mit.html (as of December 21, 2002). The graph in Figure 23.2 shows the Swiss benchmark bonds yield curve on November 30, 2000, November 30, 2001, and November 29, 2002. The benchmark yield curve has decreased in the short rates over the period because of increased money flow into the federal bonds.

23.6   THE SWISS FEDERAL BOND MARKET

23.6.1   Background

Although the deficits in Switzerland have decreased recently, and even turned slightly positive in some of the recent years, the Confederation's debt level had reached new highs in 2001. To meet its monetary objectives, the Swiss government traditionally issues fixed rate bonds from 2 to 30 years. Recently, most of the bonds issued (97.3% in the period from 2000 to January 2003) in the domestic bond market had maturities between 11 and 15 years. These bonds represent 21.7% of total issues of the Swiss Confederation, excluding the money market debt register claims.

The flight into safe harbors due to the market turmoil in 2002 has increased the demand for federal bonds. But since the Confederation had more or less balanced accounts, interest rates have fallen, mostly on short end interest rates. The investor preference for shorter maturities is due to the fear of market participants of an interest rate pick up, which would hurt longer termed duration portfolios. The effects of the low-interest rate policy resulted in a 3-month LIBOR dropping below 0.7% by end of 2002. Average annual inflation is expected to lie between 0.6% and 1.6% in the next 3 years.

With about 66% of the turnover at SWX in 2002, Government issues dominated Swiss domestic bond market, whereas private sector issues dominated the Swiss Eurobond market. Foreign government issues comprised only about 11% of that turnover in 2002. The largest stake in the Eurobond markets is traded in financials. Many nonSwiss borrowers, first and foremost German financials and industrials, have been attracted by the lower yields demanded on Swiss franc denominated securities in both domestic and Eurobond markets compared to the Euro zone, although economic data are highly correlated with each other.

23.6.2   Types of Instruments

The Swiss federal bond market is split in two segments: the money market debt register claims and the Swiss Confederation or federal bond market.

23.6.2.1   *Money Market Debt Register Claims of the Swiss Confederation*

Money market debt register claims are discounted or zero-coupon bills with maturities shorter than 1 year. They are issued by the SNB for the FFA. Typically bills are issued either with a 1-, 6-, or 12-month maturity.

Money market debt register claims are issued on a weekly basis. Maturities issued are 3-month issues about three out of four times. Twice a year, 12-month claims are issued and another six times 6-month claims are being issued. The series to be issued including their ISIN code, closing date for subscription, date of payment, date of redemption, and days to maturity are published on the SNB's homepage.[34]

---

[34] See http://www.snb.ch/e/aktuelles/index.html?file=bundes/content_bund.html, as of December 20, 2002.

23.6.2.2 Federal Bonds

The first federal bond in Switzerland was issued in 1848. The newly founded Confederation raised money from the public in order to pay for its debt from the Swiss religious civil war of 1847 (Sonderbundkrieg) (Schmid and Meier, 1977, p. 58).

Outstanding Swiss federal bonds have maturities between April 2004 and April 2033. All of these instruments carry fixed-rate coupons and are straight bonds. The issue expiring in November 2006, issued in 1992, is callable. To raise money on capital markets the FFA and the SNB are issuing Confederation bonds on a monthly basis. In 2002, the Swiss government sold CHF 9.38 billion in bonds. Compared to other Western industrial countries, a benchmark bond in Switzerland is much smaller in its issue size and accounts for only CHF 1 billion to CHF 8 billion.[35]

23.6.3 Auction Process

The SNB and the FFA announced on December 16, 2002, that the FFA decided to continue issuing Confederation bonds on a monthly basis. The closing date for subscription is the fourth Wednesday of the month, except December, when no issue is planned. The date of payment will be announced together with the respective issue. For 2003, it was planned to issue bonds with a total volume of approximately CHF 8 billion net, i.e. CHF 11 billion gross, on the Swiss market (debt issuance in 2002 included the Confederation's own tranches: CHF 7.8 billion net, CHF 12.7 billion gross).

As previously discussed, the auctions will be conducted via the electronic platform operated by EUREX, which is also used for the repo market. The auction calendar for Swiss Confederation Bonds is managed by the FFA and is published on the webpage of the SNB.[36]

There is only one method of selling bonds, a uniform-price, sealed-bid auction (Rhee, 2000, p. 13). The FFA decides which bond it wants to increase or issue in terms of coupon and expiration, as well as the amount of money it wants to raise one day ahead of the final subscription. Market participants are requested to enter their bids for the number of bonds they would take over for different prices. From the highest to the lowest bid, the FFA chooses the highest bids to fill the credit amount to raise. Thus, bidders pay only the price of the lowest accepted bid (highest yield), rather than the actual price they bid.

Heller and Lengwiler (1998) showed that moving to a price discriminating auction would not have made much difference in terms of the cost of financing the government debt. "If anything, it would have made it a little more expensive for the treasury" (Heller and Lengwiler, 1998, p. 10).

23.7 OTHER BONDS

23.7.1 Introduction

The SWX segment "other bonds" includes a wide range of different issuers and structures. Their common attributes are the CHF denomination, not being issued by the Swiss Government, not being floating rate notes and not being a convertible or "cum warrants" bond. Foremost, there is a wide range of corporate bonds. Other bonds include issues by cantonal authorities and by municipalities, mortgage bonds, foreign interest payment securities (FIPS), and guaranteed

---

[35] Compare: http://www1.worldbank.org/finance/assets/images/Filipsson-bldg_supply_slides.pdf, as of December 22, 2002.
[36] See http://www.snb.ch/e/aktuelles/index.html?file=bundes/content_bund.html, as of December 18, 2002.

investment contracts (GICs). At their issue, these bonds usually have a time to maturity between 3 and 10 years. The preferred maturities however are 5 and 10 years.

For all these bonds, there is no official pipeline directory. However, the daily newspaper *Neue Zürcher Zeitung* lists bonds for subscription on Wednesdays. Also Credit Suisse First Boston publishes its pipeline on http://www.primedebt.csfb.ch/primedebt/franc-launched.asp.

23.7.2   Corporate Bonds

Banks issue the largest stake of corporate bonds in Switzerland. Since about 70% of the GDP in Switzerland is produced by smaller and mid-sized companies without any access to capital markets, private equity and bank financing remain the primary sources of funds for Swiss corporations. Banks issues account for about 24.8% of the total amount outstanding in Swiss bonds denominated in CHF. Corporations usually issue bonds sized from CHF 100 million to CHF 500 million, with preferred sizes of CHF 200 million and CHF 250 million, although sometimes the size is as large as CHF 1 billion. The preferred nominal value of a corporate bond is CHF 5 000, CHF 10 000 ranking second.

23.7.3   Mortgage Bonds (Pfandbriefe)

The federal law of 1930 about the issue of mortgage bonds preconditioned the founding of the two Swiss central mortgage bond institutions, the "Pfandbriefzentrale der schweizerischen Kantonalbanken" and the "Pfandbriefbank schweizerischer Hypothekarinstitute." Both are incorporated as public limited companies, issue mortgage bonds, and grant with that money favorable credits to their affiliated banks for their funding of prime mortgage debentures.

The Pfandbriefzentrale der schweizerischen Kantonalbanken has exclusively 24 Swiss cantonal banks as its members whereas the Pfandbriefbank schweizerischer Hypothekarinstitute comprises almost exclusively mortgage credit institutions in the sense of the federal law of 1930.[37] Mortgage bonds make up about 21.2% of the total amount outstanding in Swiss bonds denominated in CHF.

23.7.4   Cantonal Authorities and Municipal Bonds

By 1905 already 16 cantonal authorities had bonds issued and quoted at the Zurich exchange (Schmid and Meier, 1977, p. 179). At that time, they issued the bonds individually. Today, there are 7 cantonal authorities left at the board. The other cantonal authorities and municipalities issue straight bonds in Swiss francs either themselves as needed or through the issuing center of Swiss municipalities. This category accounts for about 12% of the total amount outstanding in Swiss bonds denominated in CHF.

23.8   SWISS AND FOREIGN CONVERTIBLE AND "CUM WARRANTS" BONDS

Back in the late 1980s and early 1990s, the convertible market in Switzerland was one of the largest worldwide. End of 2002, there were 35 CHF-denominated issues left, representing

---

[37] BankingToday.ch, June 2002, p. 7, as of December 20, 2002, on: http://www.bankingtoday.ch/de/lehrmittel/lektionen/12bws/pdf/12_bankwesen_d_6_2002.pdf.

about CHF 9.8 billion in nominal value. The demand for these products denominated in CHF has almost disappeared because of the unfavorable interest rate and volatility situation, as well as the sluggish outlook for stock markets in the coming years. Since May 4, 2001, convertibles (including exchangeable bonds) denominated in € and USD have been admitted to trading at the SWX. As of December 23, 2002, 48 issues in € and 22 issues in USD were listed at the SWX Eurobond segment.

A "cum warrants" bond can be traded as the entire vehicle "cum warrants," or as separate bond "ex warrants" and separate warrants. Each of these instruments has their own security code. End of 2002, bonds "ex warrants" represented a nominal value of CHF 9.0 billion and bonds "cum warrants" one of CHF 190 million at the SWX.

23.9 FOREIGN CURRENCY BONDS

Bonds issued by foreign borrowers in Switzerland are denominated in CHF, USD, €, GBP, or JPY and are quoted in the foreign bond section at the SWX. Foreign currency bonds (currently in USD and €), which are issued in Switzerland by foreign issuers and whose original certificates Sega Intersettle AG holds in safekeeping, are called "Alpine bonds." End of 2002, there were three Alpine bonds listed on SWX Swiss Exchange.

Foreign bonds denominated in Swiss francs have six types according to their structure. The simplest structure is straight bonds, when bonds pay both principal and interest in Swiss francs. With about 91% of the foreign bond turnovers in 2002, straight bonds are by far the largest segment among the foreign bonds. Other bond segments are convertible bonds, floating rate bonds, dual currency bonds, FIPS, and others. Dual currency bonds, where the principals were paid in Swiss francs and interests in a foreign currency (or vice versa), ceased to exist in April 2002, though the segment at the SWX still exists.

23.9.1 Foreign Interest Payment Securities (FIPS)

Foreign interest payment bonds are usually perpetual obligation debts, with the exception being the bond issued by Svensk Exportkredit AB. These securities are denominated in CHF and interest coupon payments are in a foreign currency, usually in USD. The bonds include a callable and a puttable construction and have a fixed foreign currency exchange rate for CHF/USD somewhere between 1.80 and 1.95 CHF/USD. This is also the reason that all of these structures are traded below par with the lower current exchange rate. Calling the bonds would not be of benefit to the issuers at the moment, given the current exchange rate. Only about seven of these issues are still quoted at SWX. There has not been any new issue of such structures since 1986. The liquidity of these issues is poor and most of the time there is not even a tradeable price quoted, because of the difficult bond pricing formula.

23.9.2 Guaranteed Investment Contracts (GICs)

The GICs are policy level insurance obligations and obligations of the general account of an insurance company. Instruments are ranked "pari passu" to other insurance obligations and ranked senior-to-senior unsecured debt. They are structured like bonds with a guaranteed rate of return and a predetermined payment stream. Among the Swiss issues, there is only one GIC structured as a floater. GICs often differ from other insurance policies in that they are not covered by state guaranty funds in the event of insolvency. There are about 20 issues of five names[38] listed at the SWX, with a nominal amount of approximately CHF 7.25 billion. When GICs were launched in the early 1990s, there was good demand for them, because of their AAA-ratings. Nowadays, the demand for them has diminished, since most of the institutional investors stopped buying them because of GICs being structured financial products.

23.9.3 Asset-Backed Securities (ABS)

The ABS market started in 1998. Before 1998, the Swiss market regulations and listing rules at SWX were not flexible enough for their listing. Nowadays, ABS in Switzerland are traded at the SWX. A prerequisite to their listing is it being rated by at least one of the recognized rating agencies. A minimum debt rating, however, is not required.[39] Recently, the largest ABS entering the Swiss market were the Citibank Credit Card Master Trust I, the MBNA Master Credit Card Trust II, the GMAC Swift Trust 1999–1, Beta Finance Corporation, Holmes Financing (No. 4 and 5) PLC, and the HAT Helvetic Asset Trust AG. While the first two issues are backed with credit card credits, the last one is backed with loans for small and mid-sized nonlisted companies. While credit card credits are the dominant underlying assets, only loans to privately owned companies and estate-related securitizations are other relevant underlying assets for the ABS market. Auto-, student loans-, and equipment-related securitizations are not popular yet in Switzerland. In total, ABS have been issued for a size of CHF 4.5 billion.

One reason that ABS are not very popular for Swiss issuers is that ABS are treated very restrictively by the Swiss regulators, such that the usual advantage for, e.g., a commercial bank securitizing its credit portfolio is not given. In general, by pooling lower rated credits, setting them off into a special-purpose vehicle (SPV), and simultaneously taking these credits off the bank's balance sheet, a lower equity-funding requirement for the smaller balance sheet should result. But in Switzerland, the equity-funding requirements for the remaining equity stake in the SPV held by the bank are about as high as for the entire credit portfolio. Consequently, there is no advantage for the bank in terms of equity funding. Depending on the structure of the SPV, the bank may reach to set off some credit risks off its balance sheet.

23.10   SWX EUROBONDS

Eurobonds denominated in USD were introduced at the SWX on July 31, 1998 (SWX Swiss Exchange, 1998, p. 12), with a nominal value of CHF 162 240 million. Since then nominal value of the USD issues have increased threefold in size to CHF 594 124 million by end of 2002. €-denominated Eurobonds were introduced in February 1999, and GBP- and JPY-denominated bonds in June 2000. However, it was only in March 2001 that JPY-denominated bonds appeared on the board, while JPY-denominated Eurobonds were negligible in size. At the moment there is no such bond listed on SWX. AUD-, CAD-, NOK- and NZD-denominated bonds were introduced September 1, 2003.

€-denominated Eurobonds have reached a nominal issue size of € 520 692 million and GBP-denominated Eurobonds one of GBP 35 253 million. Data released by the SWX are provided in Table 23.4. For Eurobonds, there is no official pipeline directory. However, the daily newspaper *Neue Zürcher Zeitung* lists bonds for subscription on Mondays.

Recent issuers with nominal values of € 5.0 billion include the European Investment Bank, Kreditanstalt für Wiederaufbau, Freddie Mac, the Republic of Austria, Ford Motor Credit

---

[38] The names include Monumental Global Funding Ltd., Jackson National Life Funding, Nationwide Financial Funding LLC, Allstate Life Funding LLC, and Pacific Life Funding LLC.

[39] SWX Publications: Asset-Backed Securities December 1998, p. 27.

Table 23.4 SWX Eurobonds: year-end values, 1998–2001

	Total nominal value (millions)		
	USD	€	GBP
1998	175 190	–	–
1999	371 410	119 166	–
2000	432 512	287 577	22 500
2001	529 371	520 692	35 253
2002	594 124	659 645	48 738

Source: SWX (http://www.swx.com/market/downloads_monthly_02_en.html).
Reproduced by permission of SWX Swiss Exchange.

Company, and KFW International Fin. Inc. Large USD-denominated Eurobonds have been issued by the European Investment Bank, the International Bank for Reconstruction and Development, the Kreditanstalt für Wiederaufbau, KFW International Fin. Inc., and Italy. In 2002, more than 100 issues were launched in the € and the USD segment, while only two GBP Eurobonds were introduced at the board and none in JPY.

23.11   THE SWISS REPO MARKET

The Swiss repurchase agreement (repo) market developed only recently after the Federal Tax Administration revised the stamp tax law in 1997 to exempt repurchase agreements from stamp duties. Since the introduction of the electronic clearing and settlement system in June 1999, the EUREX Repo has become a highly cost efficient, liquid, and transparent market (CSFB, 2000, p. 19). Today, the SNB carries out its open market operations exclusively via repo transactions executed via the EUREX Repo electronic platform. It has become the most important instrument for the SNB's monetary policy (Hirszowicz, 2001, p. 6). The SNB regularly selects securities accepted as collateral for the repurchase agreements.[40] The updated list of securities accepted are published on the SNB website under "SNB basket for repos."[41] Further specifications on this market can be found on the EUREX Repo homepage: www.EUREXrepo.com (as of November 20, 2002).

23.12   BANK DEBENTURES (CASH BONDS OR KASSENOBLIGATIONEN)

Bank debentures are a typical funding instrument for Swiss banks and all banks are authorized issuers of these instruments. They usually have fix maturities between 2 and 8 years and have a nominal value of normally CHF 1000 or CHF 5000. Bank debentures are "issued" at the counter (German = "Kasse") of a bank on a continuous basis as a bearer debt security. Depending on a bank's needs for funding, the issuing bank can influence the demand for their cash bonds by slightly adjusting the coupon payments off the actual interest rate level.

The volume of cash bonds issued in 2002 was CHF 38.8 billion.[42] Thereof, the big banks issued CHF 5.8 billion. The previous compares to CHF 58.6 billion back in 1997 and CHF 112.7 billion in 1990 (Emch *et al.*, 1998, p. 215). The investments decreased gradually from

---

[40] http://www.eurexchange.com/index2.html?eh&1&1&errors/request_pw_form_en.html, Additional Markets, as of November 20, 2002.

[41] See http://www.snb.ch/e/aktuelles/index.html?file=pressemit/content_mit.html, as of December 25, 2002.

[42] SNB, 2002, p. A60.

1990 to 1999 because of more investment vehicles available with higher yield pick ups and similar credit ratings and more money that flowed into the equity markets during the 1990s. With the equity market crash in installments starting in 2000 until first quarter 2003, some of that money has found its way back to bank debentures.

23.13   INTEREST RATE FUTURES ON THE EUROPEAN EXCHANGE (EUREX)

EUREX is a public company and is owned in equal parts by Deutsche Börse AG and the Swiss Exchange. Aside from operating an electronic trading platform, EUREX provides an automated and integrated joint clearinghouse for products and participants, thereby achieving centralized, cross-border risk management. Through its structure, EUREX offers participants a high-quality, cost-efficient, and comprehensive range of services covering the entire spectrum from trading to final settlement via a single electronic system. Synergy effects are created for all participating exchanges through the operation and maintenance of only one trading and clearing platform.[43]

The Exchange has three types of members: general clearing members, who must perform a number of tasks and meet several requirements[44] and guarantee clearing operations; direct clearing members, who can clear their own transactions and those of their clients and affiliated nonclearing members; and nonclearing members.

EUREX is the Swiss platform for exchange-traded derivatives. Of possible interest rate derivatives, EUREX products include only the CONF Futures. The contract standard is a notional long term debt instrument issued by the Swiss federal government with a term of 8–13 years and an interest rate coupon of 6%. The contract size of the futures is CHF 100 000 and their delivery months are the three successive months within the cycle March, June, September, and December.

For settlement, a delivery obligation arising out of a short position in a CONF Futures contract may only be satisfied by the delivery of specific debt securities. Namely, long term Swiss federal government bonds with a minimum issue amount of CHF 500 million and a remaining term upon delivery of 8–13 years are to be delivered. In the case of callable bonds, the first and last call dates must be between 8 and 13 years. Further details of the specification of the CONF Futures are published on http://www.eurexchange.com/index2.html?mp&1&5& marketplace/products_specification_conf_en.html.

23.14   CONCLUSIONS

Swiss-based accounts are important to international securities markets. Although the Swiss federal bond market is rather small compared to larger European countries, the entire bond market including the Eurobonds is one of the largest in Europe. With the ongoing innovation at the SWX Swiss Exchange for the inclusion of bonds denominated in currencies other than the CHF, more foreign issuers find their way to one of the most efficient exchanges. Also for investors, the fully integrated transactions at SWX lower transaction costs and are preferable to them. Thus, the infrastructure for a prospering bond market in the future is given in Switzerland.

---

[43] http://www.eurexchange.com/index2.html?eh&1&entrancehall/about_goals_en.html, Corporate Profile, as of November 20, 2002.

[44] Requirements are listed under clearing membership/General Clearing Membership on http://www.eurexchange.com/index2.html?cl&1&clearing/overview_intro_en.html.

APPENDIX: SWX GUIDE INTEREST RATE PRODUCTS

	Swiss federal bonds	Other bonds	Floating Rate Notes	Swiss and foreign convertible and "cum warrants" bonds	SWX Eurobonds	Foreign currency bonds	Delisted bonds
Type of trading	Continuous	Continuous	Continuous	Continuous	Continuous	Continuous	Continuous
Trading hours	8:30 a.m to 5:00 p.m	9:30 a.m to 5:00 p.m	9:30 a.m to 5:00 p.m	9:30 a.m to 5:00 p.m	9:30 a.m to 5:00 p.m	9:30 a.m to 5:00 p.m	9:30 a.m to 5:00 p.m
Limit for Exchange duty to trade	<CHF 100 000	<CHF 100 000	<CHF 100 000	<CHF 100 000	None	<Equivalent of CHF 100 000	<CHF 100 000
Round lots	A standard round lot is equivalent to the smallest tradeable denomination	A standard round lot is equivalent to the smallest tradeable denomination	A standard round lot is equivalent to the smallest tradeable denomination	A standard round lot is equivalent to the smallest tradeable denomination	A standard round lot is equivalent to the smallest tradeable denomination	A standard round lot is equivalent to the smallest tradeable denomination	A standard round lot is equivalent to the smallest tradeable denomination
Price increments	0.01%	0.05% (<18 months: 0.01%)	0.01%	0.05% (<18 months: 0.01%)	0.01%	0.01%	0.01%
Stop trading during opening	Delay of 15 min if potential opening price (quoted as percent) deviates by 1% or more from reference price	Delay of 15 min if potential opening price (quoted as percent) deviates by 2% or more from reference price. Exception: interest markdown on securities traded "flat". Delay of 5 min if potential opening price deviates by 25% or more from reference price in securities priced less than CHF 10	Delay of 15 min if potential opening price (quoted as percent) deviates by 2% or more from reference price. Exception: interest mark-down on securities traded "flat". Delay of 5 min if potential opening price deviates by 25% or more from reference price in securities priced less than CHF 10	No stop trading	Delay of 15 min if potential opening price (quoted as percent) deviates by 5% or more from reference price	Delay of 15 min if potential opening price (quoted as percent) deviates by 2% or more from reference price	Delay of 5 min if potential opening price (quoted as percent) deviates by 25% or more from reference price

Stop trading during continuous trading	Interruption of 15 min if potential follow up price (quoted as percent) deviates by 1% or more from reference price	Interruption of 15 min if potential follow up price (quoted as percent) deviates by 2% or more from reference price. Exception: interest markdown on securities traded "flat". Interruption of 5 min if potential follow up price deviates 25% or more from reference price in securities priced less than CHF 10	Interruption of 15 min if the potential follow up price (quoted as percent) deviates by 2% or more from reference price. Exception: interest mark-down on securities traded "flat". Interruption of 5 min if the potential follow up price deviates by 25% or more from reference price in securities priced less than CHF 10	No stop trading	Interruption of 15 min if potential follow up price (quoted as percent) deviates by 5% or more from reference price	Interruption of 15 min if potential follow up price (quoted as percent) deviates by 2% or more from reference price	Interruption of 5 min if the potential follow up price (quoted as percent) deviates by 25% or more from reference price
Dependency on other securities for stop trading	None	None	None	Stop trading if underlying instrument in stop trading mode	None	None	None
Appendix	*	*	*	*	*	*	

* Substantial price movements in a security will possibly cause a change in the stop trading range. The SWX will alert all participants of changes via an SWX message.

Source: SWX Guide Interest Products, valid as of October 21, 2003.

REFERENCES

Albisetti, E., M. Gsell, and P. Nyffeler (1990). *Bankgeschäfte*. 4. Auflage, Zurich.

CSFB (2000, June). The Swiss Fixed Income Market. CSFB Swiss Fixed Income Research.

Emch, U., H. Renz, and F. Bösch (1998). Das Schweizerische Bankgeschäft – Das praktische Lehrbuch und Nachschlagewerk. Ott Verlag Thun, 5.Auflage, Thun.

Euromoney (1998, March). The Unique Swiss Asset Base.

Finanz und Wirtschaft (2000a, August 31). Nr. 69/2002.

Finanz und Wirtschaft (2002b, December 11). Nr. 98/2002.

Heller, D. and Y. Lengwiler (1998). The Auctions of Swiss Government Bonds: Should the Treasury Price Discriminate or Not? The Federal Reserve Board, Finance and Economic Discussion Series, 1998 FEDS Paper, 11, as of December 20, 2002. http://www.federalreserve.gov/pubs/feds/1998/199811/199811pap.pdf.

Hirszowicz, C. (2001). Die Geldpolitik der SNB. Überarbeitung des Kapitels 3 des Buches Schweizerische Bankpolitik (1996). Working Paper at the University of Zurich, Swiss Banking Institute.

Rhee, S.G. (2000). Further Reforms after the "BIG BANG": The Japanese Government Bond Market. Working Paper. http://cei.ier.hit-u.ac.jp/wp/wp2000–3.pdf, as of December 20, 2002.

Schmid, H.R. and R.T. Meier (1977). Die Geschichte der Zürcher Börse. Effektenbörsenverein Zürich.

SNB (2002). Die Banken in der Schweiz 2002.

SNB (2003). Statistisches Monatsheft October 2003.

SWX Publications. Asset-Backed Securities December 1998.

SWX Swiss Exchange (1998). Annual Report.

Websites

www.bankingtoday.ch

www.efd.admin.ch (Swiss Federal Finance Administration)

www.efv.admin.ch (Swiss Federal)

www.eurexchange.ch

www.eurexrepo.com

www.swx.com (SWX Swiss Exchange)

www.snb.ch (Swiss National Bank)

www1.worldbank.org

http://www.cia.gov/cia/publications/factbook/geos/sz.html#Econ

http://www.moneycab.com/de/home/business/konjunktur/konjunktur/daten_prognosen.html

http://www.pictet.com/en/services/research/pictet.html

24

Turkey

CANER BAKIR AND KYM BROWN

24.1 INTRODUCTION

Turkey is the only secular democracy in the Moslem world. It has always attached great importance to developing its relations with European countries. Not surprisingly, full membership of the European Union (EU) is one of the top items in the political agenda and will be so over the next few years. In the words of two senior World Bank officers, Turkey's "level of economic development is in line with the average EU accession candidate, and not too far behind levels of development in Greece, Portugal, and Spain when they entered" (Chhibber and Linn, 2002, p. 19). The Copenhagen European Council of December 12–13, 2002, decided that "if the European Council in December 2004, on the basis of a report and a recommendation from the Commission, decides that Turkey fulfils the Copenhagen political criteria, the EU will open negotiations without delay" (Anatolian Agency, 2002).[1] The government's impressive work on the harmonization of Turkish legislation with the EU updated legal system and laws, eliminates the biggest obstacles in the way of Turkey's half-hearted quest to become a member of the EU (Commission of the European Communities, 2002).

In the absence of macroeconomic stability, Turkey started the liberalization of its financial market in 1980. Major reforms included the removal of interest rate controls and all restrictions on foreign direct investment, the establishment of full currency convertibility, and capital account convertibility. However, the high fiscal deficits and inflation in Turkey, along with the economy's vulnerability to external shocks, have overshadowed the gains that could have been attained through this broad-based liberalization of the economy in the 1980s. In particular, financial and economic crises of 1994, November 2000, and February 2001 devastated the Turkish economy:

> While external factors played a role, the main reasons for these crises were: (i) the development of an unsustainable domestic debt dynamic and (ii) the unhealthy structure of the financial sector, with particular problems caused by the state banks and by the failure to address structural problems. (Turkish Treasury, 2001, p. 1)

The share of public sector net debt stock in gross national product (GNP) rose to 61% from 29% between 1990 and 1999 (Turkish Treasury, 2001). The ratio of net domestic debt to GNP increased to 42% from 6% during the same period (Turkish Treasury, 2001). Total domestic

---

[1] Turkey's relations with the EU are basically governed by the stipulations of the Association Agreement of 1964 (Ankara Agreement), which has been supplemented and specified by an Additional Protocol in 1973. Its basic goal was the establishment of a Customs Union between Turkey and the EU. The European Parliament ratified the Customs Union on December 13, 1995. Turkey was recognized as a candidate for accession at the Helsinki European Council in December 1999. This marked a new era in relations between Turkey and the EU.

European Fixed Income Markets: Money, Bond and Interest Rate Derivatives. Edited by J.A. Batten, T.A. Fetherston and P.G. Szilagyi. © 2004 John Wiley & Sons, Ltd. ISBN 0-470-85053-1

Table 24.1   Key economic indicators in Turkey

	1998	1999	2000	2001	2002*
GDP (% real change per annum)	3.09	−4.71	7.36	−7.50	6.20
Government consumption (% of GDP)	7.85	6.48	7.15	−8.54	6.00
Gross national savings rate (%)	25.17	22.62	19.58	18.80	18.50
Budget balance (% of GDP)	−8.40	−13.02	−10.64	−16.10	−12.90
Consumer prices (% change per annum; average)	84.64	64.87	54.92	54.40	44.96
Budget balance (% of GDP)	−8.40	−13.02	−10.64	−16.10	−12.90
Public debt (% of GDP)	41.42	53.55	60.45	100.00	92.10
Money market interest rate (%)	74.60	73.53	56.72	91.95	50.50
Labour costs per hour (US$)	1.51	1.51	1.55	1.22	1.44
Population (millions)	63.95	64.82	65.67	66.49	67.31
Recorded unemployment (%)	6.80	7.65	6.60	8.53	10.80
Current account balance/GDP	0.99	−0.74	−4.93	2.29	−0.30
Current account balance (million US$)	1 984	−1 360	−9 819	3 396	−520
IMF credit (million US$)	0	797	3 458	11 324	12 861
Foreign exchange reserves (million US$)	19 489	23 346	22 488	18 879	23 803
CPI (% change from previous period)	84.6	64.9	54.9	54.4	45.3

Source: Economist Intelligence Unit.
* Estimated figures for 2002.

debt stock increased to US$122.1 billion (or 69.2% of GNP) in 2001 from US$36.4 billion (or 29% of GNP) in 2000 (Turkish Treasury, 2003a, Table 7). This was chiefly a result of a rapid government expenditure growth and a steady worsening of the performance of the state-owned enterprise sector. These difficulties were mirrored in high real interest rates and subdued private investment demand. For example, annual real interest rate for government securities averaged at 32% while the average GNP growth was below 4% between 1992 and 1999.[2] (There has been considerable annual variation in real GNP figures, reflecting the uncertain course of macroeconomic policies.) From 1992 to 2001, Turkey's weighted average annual rate of inflation was 65.85%, compared to about 30% in the mid-1980s. The high and chronic inflation rate presented a persistent threat to the economy and created a high-risk environment.

Turkey's GDP contracted by 9% – the largest economic depression in its history – in 2001 following the financial crises of November 2000 and February 2001 (see also Table 24.1). However, the Turkish economy rebounded quickly in 2002. The GDP grew by 7.9% in the year to the third quarter while industrial production rose by 8.6% in the year to December (*Economist*, 2003, p. 94). Annual increases in consumer prices dropped to 26.4% in January 2003 from 73.2% in January 2002, respectively (Central Bank of Republic of Turkey [CBRT], 2003, Table 1).

In the field of financial services, substantial progress has been made to reform the financial industry following these crises.[3] In particular, the Turkish Parliament passed the

---

[2] Huge budget deficits necessitate an extensive reliance on domestic and foreign borrowing in Turkey. The short term and so-called hot money policy of high interest rates for Treasury bills and low devaluation has been used by the Turkish governments to compensate for an increasing growth of government expenditure since 1990. Thus, the government offers high real interest rates for Treasury bills auctions in order to find sources for its expenditures. The result has been a rapid increase in the share of interest expenditures in the budget. For example, out of every 100 Turkish liras of tax revenue, 31 Turkish liras were spent on interest payments in 1990 whereas the same figure reached TRL 72 in 1999 (Turkish Treasury, 2001, pp. 4–5).

[3] Because of sharp increases in interest and foreign exchange rates during the financial crises of November 2000 and February 2001, nine private sector banks became insolvent and were taken over by the Savings Deposit Insurance Fund (these banks are also

IMF-sponsored radical laws related to banking reform legislation to incorporate market risk into capital adequacy requirements; to clarify definitions for reporting and accounting purposes; to include repurchase agreements on the balance sheet; to improve monitoring and supervision of the banking system; and to adopt international accounting standards between 2001 and 2002 (Aksac and Gokce, 2002).[4] These reform efforts were partly motivated by an incentive to receive the IMF's rescue package of US$8 billion to reform the corruption-addled banking sector in 2002.[5]

A number of legislative and administrative initiatives to foster more transparency in Turkey's public life were taken in 2001. However, in practice, corruption remains a serious problem. Turkey was ranked the 64th corrupt country among 102 countries in the world according to the Transparency International Corruption Perceptions Index 2002, which measures misuse of public office for private gain. Enhancing transparency and accountability to achieve good governance in the public sector must be translated into practice. Turkey needs to reduce its public debt, lower interest rates and inflation, and strengthen transparency and accountability in its public administration in order to stabilize its economy.

24.2 RECENT HISTORY AND STRUCTURE OF THE TURKISH BOND MARKET

The first attempt to sell the government debt securities through periodic auctions started in 1985. The Istanbul Stock Exchange (ISE) and Interbank Money Market were established in 1986. Government bonds and Treasury bills began trading on the ISE in 1991 and repo/reverse repo transactions began in 1993. The 1990s was a period of rapid development for the bond and bill markets. In August 2001, the first futures contract on TRL/US$ rate was launched, with a maturity date of September 2001.

As Table 24.2 shows, total debt securities issued in Turkey reached TRL 91 183 trillion as of October 2002. The public sector owns 95.8% of the total where Treasury bills and government bonds, with 75.1% and 8.8% share, respectively, the dominant debt instruments. FX-indexed government securities have 11.8% share in the total (see also Figure 24.1). The domestic debt market for private sector securities, on the other hand, is underdeveloped as evidenced by its 4.2% share in total debt securities issued. This is mainly due to the high public sector borrowing requirement, financial and economic crises, and loss of investor confidence.

---

known as "SDIF banks"). By the end of 2002, there were 19 private deposit-taking banks and 17 foreign banks operating in Turkey. The banking sector is still in the process of consolidation. And, the banks do not yet channel sufficient savings toward productive investment. To illustrate, government domestic securities increased from 10% of total assets of deposit-taking banks in 1990 to 23% in 1999 (Turkish Treasury, 2001, p. 6). During the same period, the share of loans to the private sector in the total assets of the banks declined from 36% to 24%. Using data on 32 commercial banks in Turkey for end-2001 via the Bankscope database, we find that 64.6% of normal lending is short term. Total assets for the banking sector amount to US$179.8 billion and loans accounted for only 25.4% of these total assets at US$45.7 billion. These commercial banks have on average 29.7% of their total assets as government securities or US$53.2 billion, which is higher than their total loan portfolio.

[4] The considerable progress in the structural reforms (e.g., amendments in the Banking Law, the founding of the Banking Regulatory and Supervisory Board, improvements in the agricultural subsidy system, introduction of the new Central Bank Act, and the introduction of the international dispute settlement system) had a very positive impact on the bonds and bills markets.

[5] Holding companies control the ownership and management of some of the banks as well as that of industrial corporations. Cross-ownerships and interlocking directorates have been used by some of the bank owners to defraud their own banks by transferring vast sums out of their banks into their nonfinancial companies. *Euromoney* (2002, p. 74) notes that "dozens of former bankers are on trial in Turkey for allegedly stealing US$17 billion from the 20 banks that have been seized by the Government since the end of 1990s." Furthermore, as the *Economist* (2001) notes, a sustained political will is needed in "stopping the country's many crooked and mediocre politicians from buying votes and influence through jobs and handouts from state banks and institutions. This vicious cycle of patronage and corruption lies at the root of Turkey's financial ills."

Table 24.2 Securities by issuing sectors (in billions of TRL)

	1999	Share (%)	2000	Share (%)	2001	Share (%)	October 2002	Share (%)
Public sector	30 258 147.0	97.3	47 234 310.0	89.1	41 045 143.0	88.0	87 330 201.0	95.8
Government bonds	21 377 744.0	68.7	40 635 405.0	76.6	449 127.0	1.0	8 030 368.0	8.8
Treasury bills	8 880 403.0	28.5	6 598 905.0	12.4	40 596 016.0	87.0	68 514 410.0	75.1
Revenue sharing certificates	0.0	0.0	0.0	0.0	0.0	0.0	0.0	0.0
Foreign currency indexed bonds	0.0	0.0	0.0	0.0	0.0	0.0	10 785 423.0	11.8
Private sector	855 541.7	2.7	5 792 295.6	10.9	5 622 103.7	12.0	3 853 630.8	4.2
Shares	678 870.7	2.2	3 007 974.1	5.7	1 576 207.8	3.4	1 493 408.3	1.6
Bonds	0.0	0.0	0.0	0.0	0.0	0.0	0.0	0.0
Bank bills	0.0	0.0	12 471.0	0.0	147 696.7	0.3	0.0	0.0
Corporate papers	0.0	0.0	0.0	0.0	0.0	0.0	0.0	0.0
Profit & loss sharing certificates	0.0	0.0	0.0	0.0	0.0	0.0	0.0	0.0
Participation certificates	176 671.0	0.6	2 767 908.0	5.2	3 830 878.7	8.2	2 253 181.7	2.5
Foreign mutual fund participation certificates	0.0	0.0	3 942.6	0.0	67 320.6	0.1	107 040.7	0.0
Asset-backed securities	0.0	0.0	0.0	0.0	0.0	0.0	0.0	0.0
Real estate certificates	0.0	0.0	0.0	0.0	0.0	0.0	0.0	0.0
Total	31 113 688.7	100.0	53 026 605.6	100.0	46 667 246.7	100.0	91 183 831.8	100.0

Sources: Various reports of Capital Markets Board, Undersecretariat of Treasury, State Planning Organization. Reproduced by permission of Capital Markets Board and State Planning Organization. www.dtp.gov.tr.

Note: TRL per US$ – 1 642 500 (October 2002); 1 223 140 (2001); 625 219 (2000); 418 783 (1999).

Table 24.3   Turkey's credit ratings (as of February 2003)

Rating agency	Local currency			Foreign currency		
	Long term	Outlook	Short term	Long term	Outlook	Short term
S&P	B−	Stable	C	B−	Stable	C
Moody's	B3	Stable	n.a.	B1	Negative	n.a.
Fitch	B	Stable	B	B	Stable	C

	Long term bonds	Outlook
JCR	B+	Negative

Sources: F, Moody's, Standard & Poor's, Japan Credit Rating Agency (JCR). © Standard & Poor's, A Division of the McGraw-Hill Companies, Inc. Reproduced with permission of Standard and Poor's, Moody's, and Japan Credit Rating Agency.

According to JP Morgan's Emerging Market Bond Global Index, average return was 12% in 2002 (Ostrovsky and van Duyn, 2002). Turkey's bonds were the second best performing asset class[6] with 21% return due largely to optimism triggered by the general election results[7] and expectation of progress toward full EU membership.

International credit rating agencies (see Table 24.3) did not change Turkey's credit rating following the general elections. However, in the short term, the present Justice and Development Party (AKP) government's inexperience, doubts on political will for the implementation of the so-called EU reforms and IMF-imposed banking sector reforms, the lack of progress over resolution of the Cyprus issue, and the uncertainty generated by the US-led military campaign against Iraq pose risks for Turkey's economy.

24.3   MARKET PARTICIPANTS AND STRUCTURE

24.3.1   Regulators

Turkish debt markets operate under the auspices of two legislations, specifically the Capital Market Law (CML) and the Decree of Law No. 91 regarding security exchanges. The CML is implemented by the Capital Markets Board (CMB), which also regulates the securities markets. Supervision of government securities in the primary and secondary markets is undertaken by the Undersecretariat of Treasury, while the CMB also plays a role in the government debt secondary market and in all transactions in relation to corporate bonds. The ISE, under the Futures and Options Market Operations and Membership Regulation, and the Futures and Market Clearing Centre Regulation, regulates derivatives. Article 22 of CML, dated July 28, 1981, provides the relevant legislation.

24.3.1.1   *Undersecretariat of Treasury (Hazine Mustesarligi)*[8]

The role of the Undersecretariat of Treasury (hereafter the Treasury) is to undertake the considerable task of equalizing revenues and expenses of the state.[9] The Central Bank of the

---

[6] Russia's bonds were the best performing assets delivering returns of 35%.

[7] Parliamentary stability came with the Justice and Development Party (AKP) winning control of nearly two-thirds of parliamentary seats in the November 2002 elections.

[8] This section relies on information provided on the Turkish Treasury website available at http://www.treasury.gov.tr.

[9] The Undersecretariat was separated from Foreign Trade with the name of Undersecretariat of Treasury by legislation dated December 9, 1994, with Decree No. 4059.

Republic of Turkey and the Treasury jointly undertake debt management for Turkey. Under Article 2 of Law No. 4059, enacted on December 9, 1994, the Treasury has a number of General Directorates. These include Public Finance, State Economic Enterprises, Foreign Economic Relations, Banking and Exchange, Insurance, Foreign Capital, Incentives and Implementation, and finally Economic Research. Specifically, the General Directorate of Public Finance and the General Directorate of Foreign Economic Relations are responsible for domestic and foreign borrowing respectively.

Latest amendments include the harmonization of economic and banking legislation with the EU. Treasury is responsible for a number of vital areas, via Law dated December 9, 1994, and Numbered 4059, including the following:

- playing an active role with government and other associated institutions in selecting adequate economic policies and their implementation;
- performing public finance operations;
- monitoring the activities of SEEs (state economic enterprises) and other noncommercial state institutions;
- carrying on bilateral and international economic and financial relations with other countries and international and regional organizations;
- enacting regulations on borrowing/lending policies of the country and employing adequate procedures for grants and for other capital flows;
- enacting and monitoring regulations on banking, insurance, and the financial sector; and
- enacting regulations on investment incentives for domestic and foreign capital.

The competences of the Treasury with respect to the securities market are set out in Article 2(a) under the duties of the General Directorate of Public Finance. These include the following:

- carrying out the domestic borrowing operations of the state;
- issuing government bonds, Treasury bills, and other domestic borrowing instruments;
- selling and causing to be sold the above instruments by the method of competitive bidding, the method of regular sale, and other methods; and
- determining the quantities to be sold of such government bonds, Treasury bills, and other domestic borrowing instruments and their values and interest rates.

24.3.1.2 Capital Markets Board (Sermaye Piyasasi Kurulu, SPK)[10]

As previously mentioned, the Capital Markets Board (CMB) is the body responsible for enacting the CML. The CMB was established in 1982 and operates under a chairman appointed by the Prime Minister. The main focus of the CMB is to promote, regulate, and supervise Turkish securities in a transparent, fair manner and to provide essential protection to investors. At the promotion level the CMB has ensured that developments are in line with international standards for both government and corporate bonds. This is illustrated by the fact that the CMB has membership of the International Organization of Securities Commission (IOSCO) and Memorandums of Understanding exchanges with some developed countries.

More specifically the CMB is charged with tasks in the following areas:

- enhancing investor protection;
- adopting the norms of the international capital markets and fully integrating them into regulations;

---

[10] This section relies on information provided by the CMB (2002).

- promoting and enhancing the effectiveness of both the supply and the demand side of the markets;
- promoting transparency and fairness in the capital markets;
- facilitating modernization of the market structure;
- enhancing the infrastructure of the capital markets; and
- enhancing the quality of the work products and staff members of the board.

Nonresidents are permitted to invest in Turkish securities via Decree No. 32 called "Protection of the Value of the Turkish Currency." The Decree also enabled the removal of capital flow controls for foreign investors and for investment in foreign bonds.

Current projects of the CMB include introducing hedging products with interest rate futures contracts (based on government bonds, Treasury bills, TRLIBOR) and index futures based on equities.

24.3.1.3   Central Bank of the Republic of Turkey (CBRT) (Turkiye Cumhuriyet Merkez Bankasi, TCMB)[11]

The Central Bank, along with the Treasury, is involved in Turkish debt management. Using instruments considered appropriate in open market operations, including the outright purchase and sale of securities, repurchase and reverse repurchase agreements, lending and borrowing securities, and lending and borrowing of Turkish lira deposits, it is able to regulate the supply and liquidity of Turkish lira. At the domestic level, the Central Bank is an intermediary for Treasury.

Under Chapter III, Article 52 (as amended by Law No. 4651 of April 25, 2001), the Central Bank has some scope under open market operations. Liquidity bills (not exceeding 91 days maturity) may be issued and traded in secondary markets. However, a limitation applies that prevents the bills from being used as a continuous financing tool.

Functions of the Central Bank include:

- carrying out money and credit policy in accordance with the needs of the economy so as to maintain price stability;
- protecting the domestic and international value of the national currency including regulating its volume and circulation;
- extending credit to banks and conduct open market operations in order to regulate money supply and liquidity in the economy;
- managing gold and foreign exchange reserves and trades in foreign exchange and precious metals on the stock exchange;
- being a financial and economic adviser, fiscal agent, and treasurer to the government;
- issuing bank notes as required; and
- taking decisions on money and credit issues and submiting proposals to the government.

24.3.2   Categories of Investors

Banks predominantly purchase government debt. During 2002, banks purchased 84% of Treasury bills and 75% of government bonds issued. Other investors included the public sector (8% of bills and 23% of bonds), the private sector (7.5% of bills issued and 0.7% of

---

[11] Information for this section was obtained from the Central Bank's website available at http://www.tcmb.gov.tr/

bonds issued), with the little remaining taken up by householders (Turkish Treasury, 2002, Table 12).

The major investors of corporate bonds are investment management funds and individuals. The issuer bases of corporate bonds are generally banks, leasing companies, and manufacturing companies. In a government bond issued on November 7, 2002, for US$250 million, European investors bought 48%, Turkish investors bought 28%, and US investors bought 24%. By investor type, asset managers bought 38%, banks 32%, hedge funds 11%, insurance companies 9%, retail 7%, and others 3% (Euroweek, 2002b).

24.3.3 Withholding Tax

There is no withholding tax on primary market security issues. Secondary market transactions attract a Banking and Insurance Transaction tax. It is levied on the commissions (5%) received by all intermediaries and this is passed on to investors. The commission rate is 0.015% of trade value (IOSCO, 2002, p. 99). International securities operate in a tax-free environment. Additionally foreign investors are not restricted in investing in Turkey, including the repatriation of funds.

24.3.4 Market Makers[12]

A primary dealership mechanism has operated in Turkey since May 2000 with the aim of increasing market liquidity. This is achieved by having market maker banks make bids and offers on securities issued. Selection criteria for banks include their size, position in currency transactions, currency exposures, capital adequacy, and bad loans. Market maker banks are obliged to buy at least 2% of total bonds offered each quarter in return for certain privileges. These include the ability to participate in auctions without collateral, to issue uncompetitive bids before an auction, and to attend any buyback auctions.

Screen-based trading is used with an electronic trading system. The following is a list of commercial bank names as authorized dealers in international bonds and bills:

- ABN Amro Bank
- Adabank
- Akbank
- Alternatifbank
- Arap TurkBankasi
- BNP-Ak Dresdner Bank
- Citibank
- Denizbank
- Disbank
- Finansbank
- HSBC Bank
- JPMorgan Chase Bank
- Kocbank
- MNG Bank

---

[12] This section relies on information from the ISE website available at http://www.ise.org/.

- Societe Generale Paris
- T.C. Ziraat Bankasi
- Tekfenbank
- Tekstil Bankasi
- Turk Garanti Bankasi
- Turkiye Halk Bankasi
- Turkiye IS Bankasi
- Turk Ekonomi Bankasi
- Turkiye Vakiflar Bankasi
- Yapi ve Kredi Bankasi

24.3.5 Rating Agencies

Banks and holding companies can provide credit guarantees. Turkish government bonds are rated by the following ratings agencies:

- Duff & Phelps
- Fitch IBCA
- Japan Credit Rating Agency
- Moody's Investment Services
- Standard and Poor's
- Thomson Bank Watch

24.3.6 Trading and Exchange Information

24.3.6.1   Istanbul Stock Exchange (ISE) (İstanbul Menkul Kıymetler Borsasi, IMKB)[13]

The Istanbul Stock Exchange (ISE) began operations in 1985. From 1929 the Istanbul Securities and Foreign Exchange Bourse had been where securities had changed ownership. In fact the first organized market in Turkey was established in 1866 and called "Dersaadet Securities Exchange" where even then investors could obtain higher returns in these markets. The ISE aims to supply an efficient and transparent secondary market for equities, bonds, and bills. Specifically bonds and bills began trading in 1991, while repo/reverse repos began in 1993 and real estate certificates in 1996. The US Securities and Exchange Commission recognized the ISE as a suitable investment market in 1993, alongside the Japanese Securities Dealers Association that followed in 1995. As of February 2003, 145 institutions were authorized by the ISE to operate in the domestic bond market while 53 members could operate in international bond markets. These include brokerage houses and investment and commercial banks.

In 2002 about one-fourth of bond market transactions took place through the ISE; however, this is expected to increase. Therefore most trades occur OTC (over the counter), which implies an exchange occurring outside a formal exchange. OTC trades need to be registered with the ISE weekly. The ISE is moving to implement a fully computerized trading system, which should also increase trading volumes. Clearing and settlement services are provided through Takasbank. Table 24.4 illustrates the level of government bond turnover

---

[13] Information for this section was taken from the ISE website available at http://www.ise.org.

Table 24.4 Turnover on the ISE

Year	Stock exchange trading volume	Government securities direct transactions trading volume
1999	82 931	83 843
2000	180 182	262 943
2001	79 944	37 297
2002	69 990	67 255

Source: State Planning Organization (Table VII.17); http://ekutup.dpt.gov.tr/teg/ 2002/12/mei.html.

as comparable to equities. Trading in government securities grew faster than in the equity markets.

On an international level, the ISE is a member of several international institutions. These include the Federation of EURO-Asian Stock Exchanges (founding member), the Federation International des Bourses de Valuers, the International Society of Securities Administrators, the International Securities Market Association, the European Capital Market Institute, and the World Economic Forum.

Some indices are reported by the ISE for securities with up to 6 months maturity. The Price Index is an indicator reflecting price fluctuations of Treasury bills or government bonds. A general index is also computed to reflect the overall tendency of the market. The Performance Index' shows price changes of the bonds/bills due to current interest rate fluctuations but also as time to maturity diminishes. The Performance Index is an indicator of the yield gained by an investor within a certain period (see: http://www.ise.org/indices/bondindx.htm).

24.3.6.2   *Takasbank (Takas ve Saklama Bankasi A.S)*[14]

Takasbank was originally set up as a department of the ISE in 1998. In 1991, the operations of that department were reorganized under a separate company named the ISE Settlement and Custody Company, Inc. This company was transformed into a sector bank and renamed Takasbank (ISE Settlement and Custody Bank, Inc.) in 1996. It has 103 owners including the ISE, which are limited to a 5% stake except for the ISE. Ownership includes the ISE (22.6%), 24 banks (41.4%), and 78 brokerage houses (36%) as of June 2003.

Takasbank carries out the clearing and settlement of securities trading on all markets of the ISE. Takasbank acts as a central counter party (CCP) for securities trading on the ISE. Settlement is based on delivery versus payment (DVP). Receivables of the members are pledged against their obligation. Thus, members do not get their receivables unless they fulfill their obligations.

Settlement is conducted in book entry form at Takasbank. The Takasbank computer system is on-line connected to all ISE members, the ISE, the CMB, and the Central Bank. ISE members can transfer securities from their main accounts to the subaccounts of their clients and to other ISE members' accounts with Takasbank through their office terminals.

Takasbank is the National Numbering Agency of Turkey, authorized by the CMB. Securities issued in Turkey are assigned International Securities Identification Numbers (ISIN) by Takasbank according to international standards (ISO 6166); government debt securities are also included.

---

[14] Dr. Osman Gunsel Topbas and Mrs Ozlem Ozturk from Takasbank kindly provided the information for this section.

Table 24.5   Government securities issues (trillion TRL)

	1997	1998	1999	2000	2001
Privatization Bonds	117.3	38.8	36.6	49.7	87.1
Treasury bills	3 074.4	9 546.3	6 858.6	5 782.7	45 492.9
Government bonds	3185.6	4708.1	20 027.8	26 685.9	164 225.2
Government securities outstanding/GNP	20.7%	22.2%	29.8%	29.2%	68.5%

Source: CMB, 2002, p. 29. Reproduced by permission of Capital Markets Board.

Takasbank is regulated by rules of the CMB and the Banking Regulation and Supervision Board.

24.4   THE TURKISH GOVERNMENT BOND MARKET

24.4.1   Background[15]

The government debt market has grown significantly in the past few years because of continuing fiscal deficits and debt. The deficit grew from TRL 9.3 quadrillion in 1999 to TRL 28.8 quadrillion in 2001 because of depreciation of the Turkish lira after the 2001 crisis. As Table 24.5 shows, government bonds rose from TRL 26.7 quadrillion in 2000 to TRL 164.2 quadrillion in 2001. Provisional figures released by the Turkish Treasury shows that Turkey's total debt stock reached TRL 145.3 quadrillion as of November 2002 (Turkish Treasury, 2003b, p. 12). Of this total, TRL 110 quadrillion was in bonds and TRL 35 quadrillion was in Treasury bills. As of September 2002, outstanding international bonds and notes for Turkey were US$23.3 billion while domestic debt was US$81.1 billion (BIS, 2002). From end 2001 to the third quarter of 2002, total external debt stock increased from US$115 186 million to US$127 477 million respectively (Turkish Treasury, 2003b, p. 15).

In January 2003, the Treasury has borrowed a total of US$1.6 billion from international markets (47% of the bond issuance target of US$3.5 billion for 2003 as a whole). The first and the second bonds were denominated in US dollars and euro with the total sale of US$750 million and €500 million respectively. The first bond will mature in January 14, 2013, and bears an annual interest rate of 11.25% while the second bond will mature on January 24, 2008, and the annual interest rate on this paper is 9.875%. Finally, Turkey has increased its 2008-dollar bond (first launched on November 7, 2002) by a further US$350 million (priced at 100.875% of face value).

The level of domestic securities outstanding increased in 2001 because of further requirements of the Savings Deposit Insurance Fund (SDIF) to take over and restructure the banking industry. Therefore government domestic debt increased by 235% in 2001, to TRL 122 quadrillion (see Table 24.6). In particular, noncash domestic stock rose to 81.2% in 2001 compared to 47.8% in 2000 (Central Bank 2002, p. 41). Noncash stock increased as a response to the duty losses of the state banks and to strengthen the financial structure of the SDIF banks.

The structure of government debt outstanding changed during 2001 for several reasons. These included FX and FX-linked securities given to SDIF banks, swap operations, credit from

---

[15] Information for this section relies on information provided by the Central Bank and the Treasury.

Table 24.6   Purchasers of domestic debt stock

	2000		2001	
	Amount (trillion TRL)	Share (%)	Amount (trillion TRL)	Share (%)
i. *Cash (A + B)*	29 591	100.0	58 354	100.0
A. Market	22 987	77.7	32 932	56.4
B. Public sector (1 + 2 + 3 + 4)	6 607	22.3	25 423	43.6
1. Central bank	0	0.0	13 768	23.6
2. State banks	2 731	9.2	4 253	7.3
3. SDIF	152	0.5	132	0.2
4. Other public	3 724	12.6	7 270	12.5
ii. *Noncash* (1 + 2 + 3 + 4)	6 829	100.0	63 837	100.0
1. Central bank	0	0.0	18 778	29.4
2. State banks	2 911	42.6	22 722	35.6
3. SDIF	3 850	56.4	19 514	30.6
4. Other public	68	1.0	2 823	4.4
Total Stock	36 420		122 191	

Source: Central Bank of Turkey, 2002, p. 42. Reproduced by permission of Central Bank of Turkey.

Table 24.7   Weighted interest rates of domestic Treasury securities

	1999	2000	2001	2002
3 months	0.0	33.0	64.5	48.8
6 months	86.0	0.0	68.8	57.1
9 months	0.0	0.0	0.0	0.0
1 year	0.0	32.6	n.a.	61.7
2 years*	0.0	40.2	0.0	0.0
3 years*	87.4	0.0	0.0	0.0
Irregular maturity	104.6	36.9	82.3	57.4

Source: State Planning Organization, Table VII.14, http://ekutup.dpt.gov.tr/teg/2002/12/mei.html.
*Variable return payments for each 3-month period.

the IMF used to finance the budget deficit, and FX-denominated borrowing from the domestic market. Domestically, FX-denominated and FX-indexed government securities increased some 27% in 2001 (CBRT, 2002, p. 15). Securities offering more safety such as the flexible-rate, CPI-indexed, FX, and FX-linked securities rose to 85.3% of the total domestic debt stock (see Figure 24.1; CBRT, 2002, pp. 15, 41).

The initiating level to pay income tax on government securities was increased to TRL 50 billion in July 2001, effectively reducing tax payable for many investors and increasing their appeal. The issuance of FX-linked papers through direct and public sales methods was an important factor that led to significant changes in the structure of the domestic debt stock. This method of borrowing extended the maturity of borrowing on the one hand, and raised the share of bonds in budget financing on the other hand.

Treasury bill maturities range from 1 month to 12 months (see Table 24.7). When the government has tried to reduce interest and inflation rates, investors have preferred short-dated zero coupon bonds. In 2000, the government managed to issue a US$1.5 billion equivalent, 30-year Japanese yen bond paying a coupon of 11.875% and issued at a spread of 525 basis

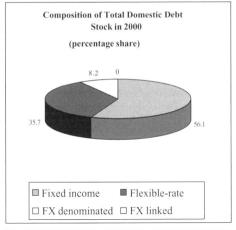

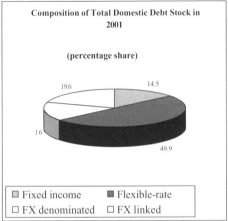

Figure 24.1 Composition of domestic debt stock.
Source: Central Bank, 2002, p. 42. Reproduced by permission of the Central Bank.

points over Treasuries. Investors including investment bankers were impressed with this trans-action; however, since then maturities have been more limited. Some 55% of Turkey's debt was floating-rate in March 2002, compared with 36% at the end of 2000. During the same period, foreign-exchange-denominated debt rose to 28% from 8% of total debt, leaving Turkey vulner-able to macroeconomic shocks. A swap option was provided on Turkish government securities in 2000 to lengthen the average maturity time from 5 months to 37 months. The increased time period was to effectively improve confidence in domestic government investments and to help stabilize government financing (ISE, 2002).

Analyzing a 15-year period from 1986, Dew (2001) found that excess returns on Treasury bills were independent of world market risk and Turkish real risk (opposite to results from the equity markets) but dependent on Turkish financial risks. Whenever a new financial crisis occurs in Turkey, the government has had difficulty in raising funds, and therefore has had to lift interest rates offered in return for higher risks to investors. In such instances investors have also preferred shorter-dated maturities. Nevertheless, Turkey has provided good fee income for emerging market bankers.

24.4.2 Types of Instruments

(A) *Turkish government Treasury bills*: Treasury bills refer to government instruments issued with maturity of 1 year or less. A variety of maturities are offered from 1 month to 12 months. Coupons are typically fixed or floating. Fewer securities are offered as zero-coupon as compared to floating-rate notes.

(B) *Public offering Treasury bills*: Given the high inflation in Turkey, the general public has been investing in government Treasury bills. Otherwise the characteristics are as above.

(C) *Treasury bonds:* The maturities of Treasury bonds are generally 1 to 10 years. High inflation rates and uncertain macroeconomic conditions have meant that investors have preferred shorter-dated debt.

(D) *Wholesale price index bonds (TEFE, Toptan Esya Fiyat Endeksi)*: The TEFE offers a bond that is linked with the wholesale price index. This type of bond is not as popular as TUFE (see below) but is available also because of the high inflation in the Turkish economy and uncertainty. The wholesale price index is published monthly with the yield of the bond related to the change in the wholesale price index. One-year and 9-month TEFE bonds pay interest at maturity while those with longer maturities are set annually in arrears and paid annually.

(E) *Consumer price index bonds (TUFE, Tuketici Fiyat Endeksi)*: The TUFE is similar to TEFE except that it is linked to the consumer price index (which is also published monthly). The coupon rate of the bond is determined by adding the percentage change of the TUFE index rate and an auction-determined risk premium. One-year TUFE bonds pay interest, plus the inflation differential on the principal, at maturity. The two-year TUFE bond pays interest quarterly.

(F) *Republic of Turkey Eurobond*: These are bonds issued in currencies other than the Turkish lira, usually with a fixed coupon. In 2001, Eurobonds issued by the Treasury were approximately US$20 billion denominated as follows: US$8.1 billion, Eurodollar 6.9 billion, German deutschmark US$2.4 billion, Japanese yen US$2.2 billion, Great Britain pound US$180 million, and Italian lira US$136 million (note US dollar amounts are equivalents except for US Eurobond) (ISE, 2002).

(G) *Real estate certificates market*: Real estate certificates were first issued in 1996 with the aim of providing finance to help develop the housing market and work residence projects. The unit of trading is the amount of real estate certificates with a nominal value of TRL 10 million. All settlement and custody activities are carried out by the Takasbank on a T + 2 basis (two work days following trade date). Physical delivery of real estate certificates is possible (ISE, 2002).

(H) *Privatization bonds – Administration of the Prime Ministry of the Republic of Turkey*: As part of the privatization program, which began in 1985, some bonds have been issued. Between 1985 and 1995 some 108 entities were privatized under the Privatization Administration. Privatization bonds outstanding for 2001 were TRL 730.9 trillion, growing from TRL 381.6 trillion in 2000 (Central Bank, 2002, p. 145).

24.4.3 Auction Process

(A) *Auction system*: The Treasury uses an auction process for primary issues of both Treasury bills and government bonds. The Treasury provides details of the securities to be auctioned to the Central Bank who then carry out the auction with market makers. Bidders need to place 1% of their collateral with the Central Bank.

(B) *Tap system*: The tap system is used for securities with maturities greater than 1 year. A tap sale occurs over a period where the issuer fixes the price or sets a minimum price. The Treasury places bonds with the Central Bank, and investors can purchase them within the tap limits set by the Treasury.

(C) *Direct selling*: Small parcels of securities are sold directly to the public or individual investors. Turkish Lira or Eurobond may be offered with rates of LIBOR + Spread.

(D) *Household selling*: Special types of government bonds may be issued such as for the Social Security and Fund Institution. Interest rates offered are generally below market rates.

24.4.4   Market Conventions

The market convention for government securities is settlement same day as trade employed on an actual/365 basis. The markets observe Turkish holidays.

24.4.5   Benchmarks

In Turkey, government securities are not formally used as benchmarks; nevertheless secondary market participants use them as benchmarks. Government securities used as a benchmark are issued on an open auction system with a preannounced calendar. The large dominance of government securities means that ratings are based on sovereign ratings. Benchmark securities include those traded by exchange and OTC (IOSCO, 2002).

24.5   NONGOVERNMENT BOND MARKET

24.5.1   Introduction

In recent years there have been no corporate bonds issued in Turkey. Overall the market has been very small compared to the government debt market issues and other developing economies (see Table 24.8 and Figure 24.2). The average level of corporate bonds outstanding between 1990 and 2000 was only 0.51% of the GDP (IOSCO, 2002, p. 16). Outstanding corporate issues at the end of 1999 were US$0.40 billion of international bonds and US$0.01 billion of domestic bonds (IOSCO, 2002, p. 78). A major impediment to a corporate bond market is the unstable macroeconomic environment characterized by high and volatile inflation rates. The high borrowing requirement of the Treasury has virtually crowded out the private sector although the government claims that this is not the major impediment for corporate debt market development. The domestic interest rates are so high that borrowers prefer to obtain funds in cheaper international funds although then exposing themselves to exchange rate risks.

Prior to 1994 there were 600 corporate issues. The main issuers of nongovernment domestic debt were corporations and banks. In terms of issuance there is no limitation on denominations provided that they are issued in round values. Coupons are mostly fixed and paid annually or semiannually. Major investors in corporate bonds include banks, leasing companies, investment management funds, and individuals.

Some of the last commercial bond issues in Turkey were by Halkbank in 2000 of a €150 million 3-year fixed-rate note and by Commerzbank. Also in 2000, Vakifbank issued a US$200 million 3-year floating-rate note. To attract investors, rates were up to 475 basis points over bonds, which has attracted further issues (Parsons, 2001). An electronics company withdrew a

Table 24.8   Size of financial sectors, 2000 (as percentage of GDP)

	GDP (US$ billion)	Domestic credit provided by banking sector	Stock market capitalization	Outstanding domestic bonds	Of which domestic corporate bonds as a % of total domestic bonds	Domestic bonds as percentage of total bonds
Argentina	285.2	23.1	58.5	29.9	n.a.	61.3
Brazil	557.4	31.4	27.5	52.5	0.7	58.2
Mexico	567.5	11.8	22.1	11.9	11.9	95.5
Turkey	189.2	22.4	36.8	28.9	0.0	60.4

Source: Hong Kong Monetary Authority, 2001, p. 3. Reproduced by permission of Hong Kong Monetary Authority.

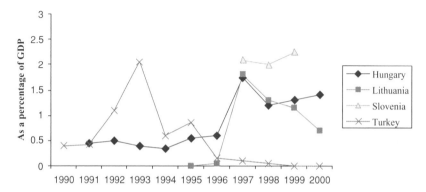

Figure 24.2   The growth of the corporate bond market.
Source: IOSCO, 2002, p. 15. Reproduced by permission of IOSCO.

5-year bond issue of US$200 million because of allegations of illegal trading actions in Europe (Euroweek, 2002c).

24.5.2   Types of Bonds

The type of bonds in the corporate market include

(A) *Asset-backed bonds*: This category has a maturity range of 1–10 years with a discounted, fixed, or floating coupon.
(B) *Commercial paper*: This is the corporate equivalent of Treasury bills. Maturities range from 1 month to 1 year with zero coupons.
(C) *Corporate bonds*: These generally are with a maturity of at least 2 years and a fixed- or floating-rate coupon. Coupon rates are mainly fixed. Both fixed and floating rates are used for corporate bonds, though fixed rates are more prevalent. Volatile inflation results in fixed coupon rates being limited to short-maturity bonds. The choice over fixed or floating rates is determined by expectations of interest rate direction.

Table 24.9 Corporate sector security issues registered with Capital Markets Board of Turkey (trillion TRL)

	1996	1997	1998	1999	2000
Real estate certificates	2.7	0	0	0	0
Foreign mutual funds	0	1.8	0	0	3.9
Mutual funds	0	0	131.4	176.7	2767.9
Bank bills	2.4	9.9	0	0	12.5
Asset-backed securities	41.6	23.0	11.0	0	0
Commercial paper	2.9	2.2	2.5	0	1.2
Bonds	1.2	1.5	2.5	0	1.2
Shares	102.2	305.7	696.8	678.9	3008.0

Source: CMB, 2002. Reproduced by permission of Central Markets Board.

(D) *Eurobonds*: These are issued in currencies outside of the Turkish lira, generally with a maturity of 2 to 5 years and a fixed- or floating-rate coupon.

24.5.3 Market Conventions

Corporate bonds follow Turkish holidays and settlement occurs on the same day as trade on an Actual/365 basis. Corporate bond trading occurs on the ISE and the OTC. The law allots 30 days for the regulator to review a registration application to issue corporate bonds, if the offer document is complete. No restrictions apply with regard to issuance size and frequency. But certain limits apply to different types of debt securities based on equity capital outstanding and profitability (IOSCO, 2002, p. 91).

24.5.4 Asset-Backed Securities (ABS)

A formal asset-backed securities (ABS) framework exists, although this instrument has not been used for some years (see Table 24.2). ABSs are regulated by the CMB (see Table 24.9) via a Communiqué on the "Registration of the Asset Backed Securities with the Board and the Principles of Establishment and Operation of General Finance Companies." Mortgage-backed securitization is not specifically regulated. Historically, banks have been the main participants although, after the Austerity Program in 1994, and amendments to the legislation, the use of ABS subsided (Paksoy, 2002).

REFERENCES

Aksac, A. and D.G. Gokce (2002, July). Turkey. *International Financial Law Review* 179–182.

Anatolian Agency (2002, December 13). EU Copenhagen Summit Ends.

Bank for International Settlements (2002, December). *BIS Quarterly Review*.

Capital Market Board of Turkey (2002). Annual Report 2001. Available at http://www.spk.gov.tr/english/news/annualreport/Annual_Report_2001.pdf.

Central Bank of the Republic of Turkey (2002). Annual Report 2001. Available at http://www.tcmb.gov.tr/yeni/eng/index.html.

Central Bank of the Republic of Turkey (2003). January Inflation and Outlook. Available at http://www.tcmb.gov.tr/yeni/eng/index.html.

Chhibber, A. and J. Linn (2002, November 27). Turkey's Chance to Become European. *Financial Times*, p. 19.

Commission of the European Communities (2002). *2002 Regular Report on Turkey's Progress Towards Accession*. Available at http://www.mfa.gov.tr/grupa/ad/adc/2002ProgressReport.doc.

Dew, K. (2001, September). How Robust Are the Profits from Assuming Risk Internal to Turkey's Securities Markets? *SSRN Working Paper*.

Economist, The (2001, May 19). Harsh Medicine.

Economist, The (2003, January 18). Emerging Market indicators, p. 94.

Euromoney (2002, November). The Law's Delays, the Insolence of Office, p. 74.

Euroweek (2002a, September 20). Republic of Turkey, p. 15.

Euroweek (2002b, November 29). Turkey Uses Rally to Tap 2008 Bond. Issue 781, p. 15.

Euroweek (2002c, May 3). Vestel Debut Delivers $200m for Investors, $4m for ABN. Issue 571, p. 21.

Hong Kong Monetary Authority (2001, November). *Quarterly Bulletin*.

International Organization of Securities Commissions (2002, May). *The Development of Corporate Bond Markets in Emerging Market Countries*. Available at <http://www.iosco.org/library/pubdocs/pdf/IOSCOPD127.pdf>.

Istanbul Stock Exchange (2002). ISE Annual Report 2001.

Ostrovsky, A. and A. van Duyn (2002, December 20). Bond Returns Outstrip Equities: Debt from World's Biggest Economies and Emerging Markets Have Led the Way. *Financial Times*, p. 32.

Paksoy & Co (2002). Securitization in Turkey. Available at http://www.info.martindale.com/paksoy-law/html/securitization.html.

Parsons, N. (2001, January). Emerging Markets, *Euroweek*, pp. 168–170.

Turkish Treasury (2001). *Strengthening The Turkish Economy: Turkey's Transition Program 2001*. Available at www.hazine.gov.tr/140401program_eng.doc.

Turkish Treasury (2002). *Statistical Tables*. Available at http://www.treasury.gov.tr.

Turkish Treasury (2003a). *Domestic Debt Statistics*. Available at http://www.hazine.gov.tr/stat/2003stok-gnp.htm.

Turkish Treasury (2003b). *Economic Program Report November–December 2002*. Available at http://www.hazine.gov.tr/Standby/monthlyreport_novdec2002.pdf.

25

United Kingdom

FRANK S. SKINNER

25.1 INTRODUCTION

The United Kingdom has one of the most developed economies in the world where almost 75% of gross domestic product (GDP) is provided by the services sector and the remaining 25% is mainly provided by industry. Within the financial services sector, the United Kingdom has particular strengths in banking, insurance, and business services. It is home to the city of London, one of three major worldwide capital markets. The city's position is due to location, being able to trade with Tokyo in the morning and New York in the afternoon, a flexible regulatory regime, and a supply of skilled labor.

The Blair labour government was reelected in June 2001 with a strong majority. Under the management of the Blair government since May 1997, a major theme has been reform in health, education, and transportation. Consistent with this trend, the financial regulatory regime has been altered in recent years. Monetary policy is now implemented by the monetary policy committee of the Bank of England (the Bank) rather than the central government (from June 1, 1998), government finances are raised by the Debt Management Office (DMO) rather than the Bank (from April 1, 1998), and regulatory control of the financial services industry has been centralized in a new agency, the Financial Services Authority ([FSA] from October 1997).

During the last two decades the country has greatly reduced public ownership so that government controlled expenditure as a percentage of GDP has fallen from 48.1% during fiscal year 1981–1982 to 38.4% during fiscal year 2000–2001.[1] In recent years the Blair government has also generated fairly large budgetary surpluses that reduced the need for debt financing. Consequently participants in the UK sovereign debt market faced a shrinking market size and fewer new bond issues. However the 2002–2003 budget announced a major long term increase in spending on health care to be funded by what many analysts believe is an optimistic economic growth forecast. If this growth is not realized then in all likelihood we can expect stronger growth in the UK government bond market.

The Blair government is generally favorable on UK membership in the European Monetary Union (EMU). However it has declined to enter the Euro claiming that five economic tests must be met first before a referendum on joining the Euro would be put before the British people. Specifically these five tests are as follows[2]:

1. Sustainable convergence between the United Kingdom and the economies using the euro.
2. Sufficient flexibility to cope with economic change.

---

[1] HM Treasury, Public Finances Databank, April 2002.
[2] HM Treasury, http://www.hm-treasury.gov.uk/documents/the_euro/euro_index_index.cfm.

European Fixed Income Markets: Money, Bond and Interest Rate Derivatives. Edited by J.A. Batten, T.A. Fetherston and P.G. Szilagyi. © 2004 John Wiley & Sons, Ltd. ISBN 0-470-85053-1

Table 25.1   Key economic indicators in the United Kingdom

Economic indicators	1997	1998	1999	2000	2001
GDP (billions US$)	1346	1436	1454	1382	1427
GDP growth rate (%)	3.4	3	2.1	3	2.2
Per capita GDP (US$)	22 809	24 246	24 435	23 090	23 886
Imports (billions US$)	384	397	407	412	418
Exports (billions US$)	384	382	382	388	387
Annual inflation (%)	3.1	3.4	1.5	3	1.8
Unemployment (%)	6.4	6.2	5.8	5.1	5.1
Average annual currency/$US	0.6025	0.5986	0.6199	0.68376	0.6931

Source: National Statistics, Datastream.

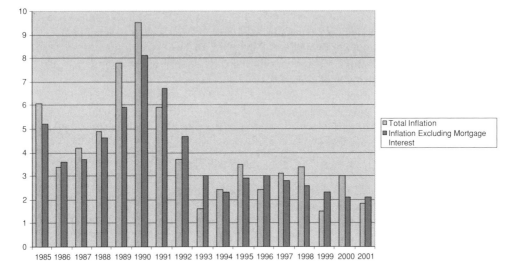

Figure 25.1   UK retail price inflation
Source: National Statistics.

3. The effect on investment.
4. The impact on the financial services industry.
5. The effect on employment.

The Blair government has instructed Her Majesty's Treasury (HM Treasury) to complete an analysis of the five economic tests within 2 years from the start of the 2001 Parliament.

As illustrated in Table 25.1, the economy of the United Kingdom has enjoyed uninterrupted growth since the second quarter of 1992 along with falling unemployment and a low rate of inflation. This performance seems to vindicate the Bank's monetary policy of explicitly targeting retail inflation, excluding home mortgage interest, at 2.5%, and setting the Bank's official interest rate in accordance with this policy. Figure 25.1 shows that since the UK government granted independence to the Bank to implement this policy in May 1997, the target rate of inflation averaged 2.4% compared to the previous 5-year average of 3.2%.

Measured in terms of US dollars however, GDP does not show much improvement. This can be explained in part by the strength of the US dollar, and in part by the UK's balance of

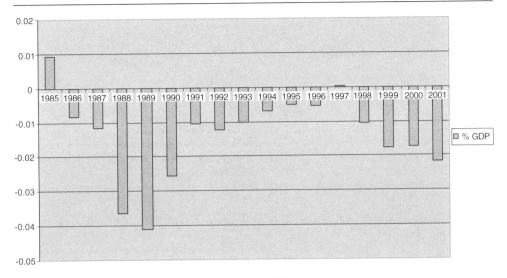

Figure 25.2   Balance of payments as a percentage of GDP
Source: National Statistics.

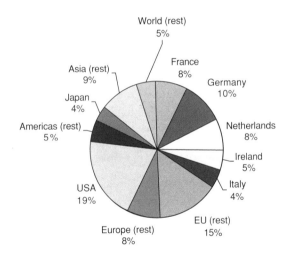

Figure 25.3   UK current account credits for 2000
Source: National Statistics.

payments situation, where the UK balance of payments has been negative almost every year since 1985 (see Figure 25.2). By the third quarter of 2001, the impact of these modest annual trade imbalances resulted in a cumulative £111.5 billion deficit with the rest of the world or about 11% of GDP.[3]

Figures 25.3 and 25.4 give a geographical breakdown of the UK current account credits and debits. No one country dominates the international trade scene, where only 15–20% of credits and debits are with the United States, UK's largest single trading partner. However, a

---

[3] Economic Update, Office for National Statistics, December 2001.

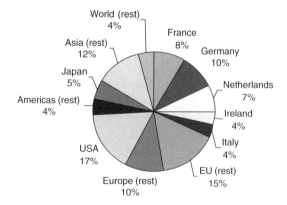

Figure 25.4 UK current account debits for 2000
Source: National Statistics.

quick glance at the current account statistics reveals that the United Kingdom is a European economy, where approximately 50% of the UK's exports and imports are with the European Union (EU) countries, underlining the importance of the UK's choice whether to join the EMU.

25.2   HISTORY AND STRUCTURE OF THE UK BOND MARKET

The UK bond market traces its origins to the £1.2 million loan of 1694 used to finance a war with France.[4] Over the centuries the bond market has grown in size and complexity as out of fashion securities, such as undated gilts, remain outstanding and more modern securities are issued. Today the UK bond market includes gilts or UK sovereign bonds, domestic corporate, foreign corporate, and Euro corporate bonds and ranks as the fourth largest debt market in the world. Some idea of the relative importance of these types of securities can be obtained by looking at the sample of UK bonds covered by Reuters, as reported in Figure 25.5. The largest segment is Euro corporate partly because London is the center of the Eurobond market and partly because the vast majority of domestic corporations prefer to issue Eurobonds rather than domestic bonds. The second largest is domestic government, which is virtually all central government debt because of the UK's unitary governmental structure and attractive central government financing that is made available to municipalities. The foreign corporate or bulldog and the domestic corporate bond markets are much smaller, representing approximately 10% of the overall sterling bond market.

The UK bond market has enjoyed strong growth in recent years. According to the BIS,[5] the UK bond market has increased by 77% over the last 5 years ending December 2000 to $1461.9 billion. Most of this increase is due to the increase in external debt where the UK bond market experienced 149% growth in international securities compared to 49% growth in domestic securities in the 5 years ending December 2000. However the gilt market has been shrinking as the government surplus of the last few years reduce the need for debt financing of government goods and services. To the end of December 2000, the total gilt and treasury

---

[4] Debt Management Office (1999, September). Gilts: An Investors Guide.
[5] BIS, *Quarterly Review: International Banking and Financial Market Developments.*

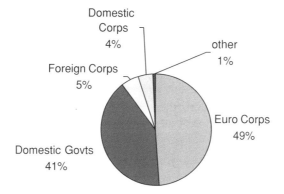

Figure 25.5   The sterling bond market (in US$)
Source: Reuters 3000 fixed income database.

borrowing stood at £287.7 billion, down almost £10 billion from its peak of £297 billion at the end of March 1998 (DMO, 2001).[6]

25.3   MARKET PARTICIPANTS AND STRUCTURE

25.3.1   Regulators

There are three main regulators concerned with the stability of the UK's financial system, HM Treasury, the Bank, and the FSA. The relationship among these institutions and their areas of responsibility are outlined in the *Memorandum of Understanding* published by HM Treasury. In general, the Bank is concerned with the stability of the financial system as a whole, while the FSA is concerned with the financial condition of individual financial institutions. Meanwhile HM Treasury is responsible for the overall institutional structure and legislation of the financial system. Coordination on matters of shared jurisdiction is accomplished by the Standing Committee, a committee consisting of representatives of the Bank, the FSA, and HM Treasury that regularly meets monthly or at the request, at short notice, of any of the three participating regulatory institutions.

25.3.1.1   *The Bank of England*

The Bank has three core purposes.

Maintaining the Integrity and Value of the Currency

This is the main purpose of the Monetary Policy Committee (MPC) of the Bank. The MPC sets the official repo rate that is used by financial institutions needing to borrow money from the Bank to meet liquidity requirements. In general the Bank lends some £2 billion daily in sale and repurchase agreements to financial institutions needing to meet the demand for sterling bank notes and to refinance maturing repo agreements with the Bank (Bank of England, 2002, p. 9). Changes in the repo rate influence other money market interest rates and financial institutions'

---

[6] http://www.dmo.gov.uk/gilts/data/stock/f3out.htm.

lending rates, thereby serving as the mechanism for the Bank to set the structure of interest rates for the UK economy. Changes in the repo rate have a direct fiscal impact as well, for approximately 50% of all UK home mortgages are variable rate. The official repo rate is set with the objective of maintaining core inflation, defined as retail price inflation less mortgage interest, at the target rate as set by the UK government. Currently this target is 2.5%. The MPC believes that its ability to maintain the integrity and value of the currency is enhanced by transparent dealings with the money market. Hence the timing of its decisions on the settings of the official repo rate is known well in advance, at 12:00 noon of the second day of the monthly MPC meetings, and the minutes of the meeting are published 2 weeks later.

Maintaining the Stability of the Financial System

The Bank's Financial Stability Committee meets every month to consider market developments and the impact these developments may have on the stability of the financial system. The focus of discussions is proactive, seeking to identify potential problems and possible responses. Information is shared with HM Treasury and the FSA, who are also concerned with financial stability under the terms of the *Memorandum of Understanding*, in regular meetings of the Standing Committee. Here common positions are established on how these three institutions may respond to problems. The Bank may, in exceptional circumstances, act as a lender of last resort. However the Bank would do so only if, in their judgement, the failure of the candidate financial institution would impose unacceptable risks to the financial system as a whole.

Maintaining Effectiveness of the UK Financial Services

The Bank is unapologetic in its aim to ensure the competitive position of the City of London as a major international financial center. It seeks to accomplish this by taking a lead role in fostering change when it believes there are structural barriers for the private sector from doing so. A concrete example of the Bank acting in this capacity was the development of the CREST settlement system in 1996. Another was the development of technical arrangements to ensure the successful launch of the euro.

25.3.1.2   The Financial Services Authority

The FSA began life in October 1997. Under the Financial Services and Markets Act 2002 (FSMA) the FSA is the sole regulator for deposit taking, insurance, and investment organizations. The FSA has nine main purposes.

(A) *Maintaining confidence in the UK financial system*: The focus here is the financial viability of specific financial institutions rather than the financial heath of the entire financial system. In this role the FSA supervises market infrastructure providers such as settlement houses and exchanges, and monitors the market.
(B) *Promoting public understanding of the financial system*: The FSA is concerned with helping educate consumers so that they can manage their financial affairs effectively. This is necessary in the United Kingdom since astonishingly complex financial products are sold at the retail level.

(C) *Securing the right degree of protection for consumers*: The FSA ensures that individuals and firms who provide financial products and advice to consumers meet minimum criteria. The FSA monitors such individuals and firms, and if they fail to maintain standards, the FSA may prosecute.

(D) *Helping to reduce financial crime*: The FSA is responsible for investigating market abuses such as insider dealing, fraud, and money laundering.

(E) *Registering mutual societies*: The FSA is responsible for registration and public records of mutual companies such as credit unions, building societies, and provident societies.

(F) *Enforcing Unfair terms in consumer contracts*: The FSA can take action to enforce the Unfair Terms in Consumer Contract Regulations 1999.

(G) *Regulating Lloyd's insurance market*: The FSA is responsible for regulating the Society of Lloyd's and the underwriting agents that deal in the Lloyd's insurance market.

(H) *Enforcing Code of market conduct*: The FSA can exercise power under civil law to deal with market abuse.

(I) *Supervising overseas investment exchanges*: The FSA is responsible for follow-up on applications from overseas investment exchanges and clearing houses that are subject to the requirements of the FSMA. The requirements under the FSMA are designed to ensure that UK investors obtain the same level of protection they would receive from equivalent UK institutions. The FSA relies on the financial institution's home regulators for effective supervision.

25.3.1.3 HM Treasury

HM Treasury is a UK government institution under direct political control by the Chancellor of the Exchequer, arguably the number 2 UK politician after the prime minister. In regard to financial regulation, the primary responsibility of HM Treasury is to set the framework of legislation and regulation within which the financial system is to operate. According to the *Memorandum of Understanding*, HM Treasury has no operational responsibility for either the Bank or the FSA and thus these organizations are not under direct political control. Nevertheless HM Treasury expects to be kept up to date on market developments by the FSA and the Bank, as HM Treasury may need to support these institutions through international diplomacy. HM Treasury may also need this information to reform existing laws or to answer ministers' questions in Parliament. Much of this information sharing occurs in the monthly meeting of the Standing Committee.

25.3.1.4 Other Regulators

The London Stock Exchange (LSE) still plays a role in regulating the fixed income market through its role in listing debt instruments. Firms wishing to issue debt securities on the exchange are subject to the LSE's listing and trading rules and may be subject to investigation by the LSE in the case of suspected market abuse.

25.3.2 Categories of Investors

Insurance companies and pension funds are by far the largest investors in gilts. These institutions at the end of March 2000 held 65.3% of all gilts. Other significant investors in gilts, with the percentage held of the total gilts outstanding as of end of March 2000, are overseas investors

(18%), households (7.5%), bank and building societies[7] (2.9%), local authorities and public corporations (1.2%), and other financial institutions (5%) (DMO, 2001). Sectoral holdings by investor categories have been fairly stable in recent years. Holdings for Eurosterling bonds are difficult to assess by the very nature of the Eurobond market. Eurobonds are in bearer rather than registered form and so there is a lack of publicly available information.

25.3.3   Market Makers

The following is a list of the Treasury bill market makers:

- Barclays Bank plc
- Cater Allen International Ltd
- Credit Lyonnais
- Deutsche Bank
- Halifax Group Treasury & Wholesale Banking
- JP Morgan Securities Ltd
- The Royal Bank of Scotland plc
- Salomon Brothers International Ltd
- USB Warburg

The following is a list of the gilt-edged market makers (Gemm). Those tagged with an asterisk are also index-linked gilt-edged market makers.

- ABN Amro Bank NV
- Barclays Capital*
- CS First Boston Ltd
- Deutsche Morgan AG
- Dresdner Bank AG*
- Goldman Sachs International Ltd
- HSBC Bank plc*
- JP Morgan Securities Ltd
- Lehman Brothers International*
- Merrill Lynch International*
- Morgan Stanley & Co International Ltd*
- Salomon Brothers International Ltd
- Royal Bank of Canada
- Royal Bank of Scotland
- Warburg Dillon Reed
- Winterflood Gilts Ltd*

25.3.4   Other Market Participants

Following is a list of interdealer brokers, which serve as brokers among market makers:

(a) *Interdealer brokers*
  - Cantor Fitzgerald
  - ICAP WCLK

---

[7] Building societies are similar to savings and loan companies.

(b) *Ratings agencies:* UK government is rated at issue by Standard & Poors, Moody's Investment Services, and by IBCA. Currently UK gilts enjoy triple A status by all three rating agencies. Unsecured corporate debt is rated by these agencies but secured corporate debt is not.

25.3.5 Exchange Information

The LSE is the only domestic exchange for stocks and bonds in the United Kingdom while the London International Financial Futures and Options Exchange (LIFFE) specializes in derivative contracts, including a wide range of bond futures and options contracts. The LSE has recently reformed itself as a limited liability company. The LSE lists over 12 000 quoted debt and equity securities and provides an active market for the secondary trading of these securities. Measured in terms of nominal value, annual turnover by both customer and interdealer market traders in the listed gilt securities totaled more than £1.3 trillion in 2000. For all other debt securities the corresponding turnover was slightly more than £400 million.[8] The LSE also operates the Alternative Investment Market (AIM) that provides a stepping stone for small and medium sized companies to eventually become listed on the main exchange. Primarily an equity market, some 850 companies have been listed on AIM since inception in 1995.

LIFFE offers a futures and a futures option contract on 3-month sterling interest rates and a futures and a futures option contract on a 7% fixed coupon £100 000 face value gilt. In addition, a midcurve option on a 3-month sterling futures contract is available. LIFFE also offers a variety of options and futures options based on the Euroswiss, Euroyen, LIBOR (London Interbank Offer Rate), and EURIBOR interest rates and on German Bunts and Japanese bonds.

25.3.6 Trading Rules

Even though many UK bonds, including all coupon bearing gilts and all gilt strips, are listed on the LSE, most trades occur over the counter. However, the LSE publishes an official closing price on the Daily Official List for all bonds listed on the LSE. Yields and prices (in decimals) are quoted without accrued interest. Electronic trading is widely used and there are a number of electronic settlement systems, most notably CRESTco (recently merged with Euroclear).

25.4 THE UNITED KINGDOM GOVERNMENT BOND MARKET

25.4.1 Background

In recent years the UK government bond market has experienced a number of important innovations that promise to enhance the liquidity and transparency of the market. These innovations include the introduction of a strip facility for benchmark gilt bonds, the use of the repo market to set the official repo rate used to conduct monetary policy, and a greater reliance on issuing gilts and Treasury bills via competitive auction rather than on reissuing existing bonds on a more or less *ad hoc* basis (tap). The DMO has also conducted a number of "reverse auctions," essentially a buyback transaction typically targeted at old illiquid gilt issues, and "switch auctions," essentially an offer to replace an old illiquid gilt with a newer, more marketable gilt, in an attempt to maintain market liquidity in the face of a declining number of new issues.

---

[8] *Source*: LSE, web page http://www.londonstockexchange.com/cmsattach/305.xls. One should note that most of these trades occur over the counter. The LSE requires that trades in all listed securities even if over the counter be reported to the exchange.

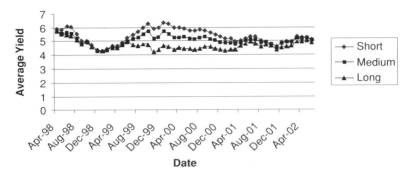

Figure 25.6 Moving average gilt yields, April 1998–April 2002.
Source: Debt Management Office. © Crown copyright. Reproduced with permission.

Evidently these measures are at least modestly successful. During the period April 2001 to March 2002, turnover by value was approximately £1.9 trillion or £7.6 billion per day. Of this amount the average value traded per day among wholesale counterparties was £3 billion (DMO, 1998–2000).

The maturity structure of domestic government debt, averaging 11.05 years by the end of December 2000, is among the longest of the Organization for Economic Cooperation and Development (OECD) countries.[9] This continues the trend of lengthening maturities in recent years that appears set to continue. In fact, of the seven gilts issued from April 2000 to March 2001, only one was for a term of less than 15 years to maturity, and that exceptional bond had a scheduled maturity of 13 years. The DMO explains that this is due to strong demand by pension funds and life insurance companies for long term gilts and does not signal a change in the government's long term optimal issuance strategy.

Figure 25.6 gives an indication of the UK government yield curve and reinforces the rationale for issuing long term debt. Evidently the yield curve for conventional gilts is downward sloping, reflecting in part the demand for long term debt that the DMO seeks to satisfy.

25.4.2   Types of Instruments

There are a wide variety of UK government bonds outstanding including conventional gilts and Treasury bills and also exotics that include index-linked gilts, strips, Euro Treasury bills, and Euro Treasury notes. Also, conventional gilts encompass double dated (callable), convertible (extendible), undated (perpetual) as well as the traditional straight fixed-coupon or "bullet" bonds. Gilts with less than 7 years maturity are considered short term while gilts between 7 and 15 years to maturity are considered medium term and those over 15 years are considered to be long term.

25.4.2.1   Short Term Bills

The UK government issues 91-day Treasury bills. These are zero-coupon instruments and are issued by the DMO every Friday by competitive auction. The DMO, in its cash management role for the UK government, expects that a wider range of maturities of Treasury bills will be

---

[9] Debt and Reserves Management Report, Her Majesty's Treasury, 2001.

issued in the future. Specifically it suggests that 1-, 3-, 6-, and 12-month Treasury bills will be issued, with the majority of issues being concentrated in the 1- and 3-month maturities.

25.4.2.2   Conventional Gilts

Conventional gilts are sold mostly by competitive auction on the third Tuesday of most months. Some conventional gilts are named according to the purpose for which they were issued, for example, the 12% Exchequer Stock of December 12, 2017. However this has no practical meaning since all gilts are direct obligations of the UK government. The preferred gilt instrument of the DMO is the straight, semiannual pay fixed-coupon bonds of bullet maturity. However there are some callable and convertible (into a longer term gilt) gilts still outstanding. Undated gilts are no longer issued.

25.4.2.3   Index-Linked Bonds

Index-linked bonds pay coupon and principal that is adjusted in accordance to changes in the UK retail price index (RPI), an inflation index similar to the consumer price index (CPI) in the United States. Typically an 8-month lag is used where a "base RPI" is set as the RPI 8 months prior to the date the issue was first sold. Then any subsequent coupon or principal payment would be the stated amount multiplied by the ratio of the RPI 8 months prior to the coupon date divided by the base RPI.

There were about £70 billion index-linked bonds outstanding by the end of December 2000, representing slightly less than one quarter of the UK government's marketable sterling debt.[10] The DMO appears favorably disposed toward continued issuance of index-linked bonds in spite of its belief that there is no significant inflation risk premium included in the prices of conventional gilts compared to index-linked gilts. The DMO suggests that index-linked gilts may play a useful hedging role for the UK government. If tax receipts are positively correlated with inflation then decreases in inflation would reduce revenue receipts but the cost of servicing index-linked debt will decrease as well, thereby reducing the variance of government budget balances. Index-linked gilts are sold by auction on the fourth Wednesday of most months.

25.4.2.4   Strips

A recent innovation in the UK government debt market is the introduction of a strip facility for benchmark gilts. As of the end of December 2000, Table 25.2 shows the list of strippable gilts, the nominal amount outstanding, and the amount held in stripped form. Only Gemms, the Bank, and the DMO can strip gilts or reconstitute them into the underlying gilt. By the end of 1999, £2.8 billion of strips were then outstanding but weekly turnover averaged only £70 million (Deacon, 2000, p. 26). To enhance liquidity in the strips market, the DMO's current policy is to make all new conventional gilts strippable.

25.4.2.5   Euro Securities

The UK government issues Euro Treasury bills and notes. The former are zero coupon with a 6-month maturity and are denominated in euros. The Euro Treasury bills are sold by competitive

---

[10] Debt and Reserves Management Report 2001–2002, Her Majesty's Treasury, March 2001.

Table 25.2   Strippable gilts outstanding

Gilt	Nominal amount, end December 2000 (million £)	Nominal amount held in stripped form (million £)
7% Treasury 2002	9 000	176
6.5% Treasury 2003	7 987	41
5% Treasury 2004	7 408	119
8.5% Treasury 2005	10 373	277
7.5% Treasury 2006	11 700	206
7.25% Treasury 2007	11 000	267
5.75% Treasury 2009	8 827	237
8% Treasury 2015	7 288	491
8% Treasury 2021	16 500	372
6% Treasury 2028	11 512	249
4.25% Treasury 2032	11 580	0
Total	101 595	2435

Source: Debt and Reserves Management Report 2001–2002, HM Treasury. © Crown copyright. Reproduced with permission.

auction the second Tuesday of every month, but issues with 1- or 3-month maturity may also be sold by tap at the same time. Like Euro Treasury Bills Euro Treasury notes are denominated in euros and are direct obligations of the UK government. Maturities range from 3 to 10 years. They are issued by auction on the third Tuesday of every quarter.

25.4.3   Auction Process

The DMO publishes a tentative auction calendar in the Debt Management Report during March for the next fiscal year commencing on April 6. Just before each quarter the DMO confirms the dates of auctions and 8 days prior to auction announces the amounts to be auctioned. Typical issues sizes are £500 million to £3.5 billion for gilts and £100 million to £1 billion for Treasury bills. In recent years the DMO has relied almost exclusively on the competitive auction method for conventional gilts and the Dutch auction method for index-linked gilts but it reserves the right, rarely exercised since 1997, to use a tap auction should market conditions warrant. The DMO chose Dutch auctions for index-linked gilts because a lack of liquidity in the secondary market and a lack of suitable hedging instruments for indexed gilts means that bidders find it too difficult to price and hedge their bids. Additionally, because of the surplus in government revenues in recent years, the DMO occasionally makes conversion offers and conducts switch auctions and reverse auctions typically targeted at old illiquid issues.

25.4.3.1   Competitive Auction Method

Anyone can bid for conventional gilts either through a Gemm, who in turn bids by telephone, or by mailing in an application form. All bidders may choose to bid competitively or noncompetitively. If they choose to bid competitively they must specify the desired amount and price they are willing to pay. They can bid for any amount but the minimum amount is £500 000 nominal and the DMO can, at its discretion, restrict allocations. For example, if the discount is thought to be too high or if the successful bidder is bidding for more than 25% of the amount on offer the DMO may exercise its right to restrict allocations. If the bidders choose to bid noncompetitively they bid for the amount they are willing to buy and receive allocations at a price based on the average accepted competitive bid. Non competitive bidders can bid for a minimum of £1000 nominal up to a maximum of 0.5% of the amount on offer.

25.4.3.2 Dutch Auction

Index-linked gilts are offered exclusively via Dutch auction where all successful bidders pay the same price. Only Gemms can bid competitively for any amount, in multiples of £1 million subject to a £1 million minimum. As with the competitive auction method, the DMO may restrict allocations to successful bidders particularly if the successful bidder is bidding for more than 40% of the amount on offer. Anyone can bid noncompetitively either through a Gemm, who in turn bids by telephone, or by mailing in an application form. Noncompetitive bids are in multiples of £100 000 nominal. The total allocation of noncompetitive bids to Gemms is 10% of the amount on offer. Allocations of noncompetitive bid amounts to individual Gemms is based on successful bid performance in the prior three auctions and the precise amount a particular Gemm can bid for is announced 8 days prior to the auction.

25.4.3.3 Tap

Rarely used in recent years, taps are *ad hoc* reissues of existing conventional and index-linked gilts. The DMO intends to use taps only to smoothen excess demand if this excess demand is, in the opinion of the DMO, disrupting the gilt market. The DMO has made a commitment not to tap an issue sold via auction on either side of 3 weeks from the date of the auction. Tap issues are typically much smaller than auction issues, being in the range of £100 to £400 million.

25.4.3.4 Conversion Offers

Occasionally the DMO will offer investors the opportunity to convert holdings of one gilt into another gilt at rates related to market prices. The DMO intends to use conversion offers to build liquidity in new benchmarks in times of low issuance and to concentrate outstanding gilts into fewer, more liquid current coupon gilts. Typical conversion candidates would be unstrippable gilts with more than 5 years to maturity and less than £5 billion nominal outstanding. Also, the DMO has committed not to target issues that are, or may likely become, the cheapest to deliver for any futures contract listed on LIFFE. Acceptance of conversion offers is voluntary.

25.4.3.5 Switch Auctions

A switch auction is essentially a limited size conversion offer. In addition to the same objectives as with conversion offers, the DMO intends to use switch auctions to help index tracker funds switch to longer issues as the target issue approaches the limit of a benchmark maturity range. The switch auction will be made on a competitive basis on Wednesdays and will be a maximum of £500 million to £2 billion. Unlike a conversion offer, the DMO will preannounce the auction of the target security in accordance with the quarterly auction calendar. On the Tuesday prior to the auction week, the details of the auction, including the size and maximum allotments, will be announced. On the switch day the DMO will announce the clean price of the target bond and bidders will bid on the basis of the clean price of the destination bond. Switch auctions will not be used to issue entirely new bonds or to reduce the target debt to "rump" status. Therefore the DMO will not likely target issues such that post switch, the nominal amount of the target bond may fall below £4.5 billion. As with a conversion offer, the DMO will not target issues that are, or may likely become, the cheapest to deliver for any futures contract listed on LIFFE.

25.4.3.6 *Reverse Auctions*

Because of the surplus in government revenues in the recent past the DMO has conducted reverse auctions. These are buybacks of less liquid issues. These auctions are conducted via competitive auction where the most desirable bids are based on the price relative to the DMO's own yield curve model. The DMO aims to announce the target issues in the end of quarter announcement and on Tuesdays in the week prior to the auction they intend to announce the target amount.

25.4.4 Market Conventions

For gilts, interest is calculated on an Actual/Actual basis, but for Treasury bills and euro Treasury bills interest is calculated on an Actual/365 basis. Trades are settled on the next business day for gilts but trade plus two business days for euro Treasury bills. Treasury bills settle on the day of trade. The UK holiday calendar is used for all UK government securities and all gilt yields are calculated according to International Securities Market Association (ISMA) yield to maturity conventions.

25.4.5 Benchmarks

The DMO attempts to maintain liquid benchmarks in the face of the declining volume of new gilt issues in recent years. New issues are skewed in favor of conventional long term gilts with more than 15 years to maturity.

Reuters provides a good example of the UK Treasury benchmark yield curve. Bonds are included on the basis of maturity and liquidity. Currently Reuters includes 1-, 3-, and 6-month Treasury bills and conventional gilts annually from 1 to 10 years maturity plus a 15-, 20-, and 30-year gilt. This represents one additional point at 6 months maturity as the DMO began to issue more 6-month Treasury bills recently.

Figure 25.7 shows Reuters' benchmark yield curve in September 1999 and September 2000. There has been a noticeable flattening of the benchmark yield curve over the year. This is due to the decrease in yields as monetary policy was effective in reducing inflation.

Approximately one half of all overnight Sterling transactions occur in the repo market. This market is strongly supported by the Bank and the DMO as the Bank uses the repo market to implement monetary policy and the DMO uses the repo market to smoothen the net daily cash flows between the government and the private sector. There are two types of repo, general collateral and specific collateral. In the general collateral repo the gilt to be received as collateral is not specified whereas in the specific collateral repo the gilt to be used as collateral is identified. In general the specific collateral repo is used when the underlying gilt is relatively scarce. The specific repo rate is often 5–10 basis points or more below comparable repo rates on general collateral repo.

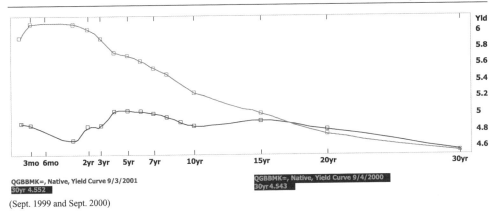

(Sept. 1999 and Sept. 2000)

Figure 25.7   UK government benchmark yield curve (September 1999 and September 2000)
Source: Reuters 3000 fixed income database.

25.5   CORPORATE AND SEMIGOVERNMENT BOND MARKETS

25.5.1   Introduction

There is a relatively small domestic corporate and semigovernment sterling bond market in the United Kingdom. There were 378 bonds in this category (349 corporate, 29 semigovernment), with an average issue size of approximately $140 million, in Reuters fixed income database as of July 2002. As already mentioned, there are very few municipal bonds since they have access to central government financing on attractive terms. There are 219 bulldog issues with an average issue size of $265 million.

By far the largest segment is the Eurosterling bond market, as most organizations prefer to issue sterling-denominated Eurobonds. Eurobonds are popular with investors as the bonds are issued in bearer form and no withholding tax is applied. As London is the home of most trading in Eurobonds, the UK government is firm in resisting calls from Brussels to apply withholding tax to Eurobonds. Reuters' coverage of the Eurosterling bond markets includes 5840 bonds with an average issue size of nearly $100 million as of July 2002. In recent years the UK international bond market has enjoyed strong growth, increasing by almost 150% in the 5-year period ending in December 2000. During this period sterling-denominated international bonds grew from 44% of the domestic bond market to 63% and looked set to rival the domestic bond market by size.[11]

25.5.2   Eurosterling Bonds

Sterling-denominated Eurobonds now comprise more than 8% of the Eurobond market and rank fourth behind the euro, the US dollar, and the Japanese yen. It appears that sterling-denominated bonds will maintain their share of the Eurobond market, for during the period from January 1999 to October 2000, the latest period for which this information is available, sterling-denominated bond issues accounted for slightly more than 8% of new issues. Settlement takes 3 days for both straight bonds and floating-rate notes. The 30E/360 day count convention is used for

---

[11] All figures are compiled from the Reuters 3000 Fixed Income Database.

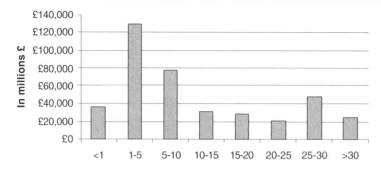

Figure 25.8   Eurosterling by maturity as of September 2002
Source: Reuters 3000 fixed income database.

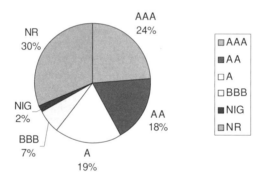

Figure 25.9   Eurosterling bonds by rating
Source: Reuters 3000 fixed income database.

straight bonds but the Actual/365 is used for floating-rate notes. Prices and yields are quoted flat in decimals using the ISMA yield to maturity conventions.

It used to be said that the typical Eurobond was a fixed-coupon 5-year investment grade bond targeted at a Belgian dentist. However the picture is changing. Today there are many larger and longer term issues targeted at pension funds and life insurance companies. While it is true that the most common issue is around 5 years, Figure 25.8 shows that there are many longer term bonds outstanding in the Eurosterling bond market. In addition nearly half of all bonds are either variable or floating rate or zero coupon. Indexed linked and convertible bonds are also available.

Figure 25.9 shows that most Eurosterling bonds are rated and 68% of all Eurosterling bonds have an investment grade rating. Only 2% have less than investment grade. There has been a sharp rise in the number of large size issues in recent years. As of September 2002 there were more than 42 issues of £1 billion or more outstanding. The European Investment Bank is a particularly active issuer in the larger sized end of the Eurosterling market, with 14 issues of more than £1 billion in size based on nominal amounts. The largest issue is £7 billion from the Hamburgische Landesbank-Girozentrale. As a result it is possible to think of certain straight, large issue size Eurosterling bonds as candidates for benchmark status. For example, Table 25.3 shows that there are a number of straight European Investment Bank bonds, currently

Table 25.3   Candidate bonds for forming a benchmark Eurosterling yield curve

Bond	Coupon	Maturity	Amount (in billions £)
European Investment Bank	7	08/12/2003	2.100
European Investment Bank	6	26/11/2004	2.950
European Investment Bank	6.125	07/12/2005	1.350
European Investment Bank	7.625	07/12/2006	1.550
European Investment Bank	6.25	07/12/2008	1.200
European Investment Bank	5.5	07/12/2009	2.300
European Investment Bank	5.5	07/12/2011	1.200
European Investment Bank	6.25	15/04/2014	1.500
European Investment Bank	8.75	25/08/2017	1.000
European Investment Bank	5.375	07/06/2021	1.875
European Investment Bank	6	07/12/2028	3.495

Source: Reuters 3000 fixed income data base.

rated AAA by S&P, of sufficient size that may well form a basis for constructing a benchmark yield curve for the Eurosterling bond market.

25.5.3 Domestic Corporate Bonds

The long history of the UK bond market has contributed to the wide variety of types of bonds on offer. There are a few perpetual bonds that date from the 1880s for example. Consequently UK corporate bonds employ a wide variety of coupon payment types, fixed-, variable-, and zero-coupon bonds are all well represented, and maturity ranges from the ultra short to the ultra long, 50 years or more, and so there is no typical UK corporate bond. Convertible and retail price indexed bonds are also available. In recent years there has been a trend to issue bonds with 15 years or more to maturity and so at present the average maturity of UK domestic corporate bonds is more than 15 years. New issues are typically noncallable and do not include sinking funds. The largest issue in recent years, with £286 million still outstanding, was BAE systems PLC. However most large issues are floated in the Eurobond market.

Debentures are secured bonds whereas ordinary bonds (often called loan stocks) are not, just the opposite of American terminology. Many of these bonds trade on the LSE. Corporate bonds may take as long as five business days to settle and use the Actual/365 day count convention and the UK holiday schedule.

25.5.4 Bulldogs

Bulldogs are sterling-denominated bonds issued in the UK domestic corporate bond market by unities domiciled outside the United Kingdom. Most are investment grade and are foreign government and semigovernment bonds. Most are of the bullet maturity type and there are no callable or puttable bonds outstanding and only very few zero-coupon bonds. Most of these bonds were issued in the 1980s and few have been issued since.

25.5.5   Asset-Backed Securities

Most UK asset-backed securities (ABSs) are issued in the Eurobond market rather than the domestic sterling bond market. The underlying collateral for most ABSs is mortgages but credit card receivable and auto loan backed securities have also been issued. Most ABSs are rated AAA and AA at issuance. As with all ABSs, maturity is uncertain as pass throughs of early repayments on the underlying loan are used to redeem ABSs tranches. Like their US counterparts the structures of ABSs can be quite complex. With only a few exceptions ABSs are floating rate reset every 3 months based on LIBOR.

25.6   CONCLUSIONS

The domestic UK bond market is dominated by central government debt whereas corporate debt is primarily issued in the Eurobond market. The domestic bond market has been challenged by reductions in liquidity brought on by fewer new issues and a shrinking overall market size as the UK government generated budgetary surpluses in recent years. However there is a question mark concerning whether this will continue. The UK government has recently committed itself to a major spending increase to be financed by what most observers believe is an optimistic projection of future economic growth. The UK government has been innovative in maintaining liquidity and improving transparency in the domestic bond market and is strongly supportive of the city of London as one of the three premier capital markets in the world. For example, the current labour government is firmly supportive of no withholding tax on Eurobonds. The biggest financial issue facing the United Kingdom is the decision whether to join the Euro. The potential benefit is underlined by the fact that more than 50% of external trade is with Euro zone countries. With expansion of the Euro zone due to new entrants, the importance of Euro-based external trade will grow. The potential risk is underlined by the growing Eurosterling bond market as a source of cheap financing for domestic institutions. It appears that the Euro sterling bond market is now of sufficient size with enough large issues to construct Euro sterling benchmark yield curves.

REFERENCES

The Bank of England (2002, May). *The Bank of England's Operations in the Sterling Money Markets.*
Deacon, M. (2000, August). Stripping Facilities. *The Actuary* 26–27.
Debt Management Office (2001, March). Debt & Reserves Management Report.
Debt Management Office (1998–2000). Gilt Review.
Debt Management Office (1999, September). Gilts: An Investor's Guide.
National Statistics. Economic Update (2001).
National Statistics (2001). The United Kingdom Balance of Payments.

Websites
Bank of England: http://www.bankofengland.co.uk/.
Debt Management Office: http://www.dmo.gov.uk/.
Financial Services Authority: http://www.fsa.gov.uk/.
HM Treasury: http://www.hm-treasury.gov.uk/.
London International Financial Futures and Options Exchange: http://www.liffe.com/.
London Stock Exchange: http://www.londonstockexchange.com/.
Office of National Statistics: http://www.statistics.gov.uk/.
UK Government and Agency link site: http://www.tagish.co.uk/links/centgov.htm.

Index

Index compiled by Terry Halliday